Microsoft 365 Security Administration: MS-500 Exam Guide

Plan and implement security and compliance strategies for Microsoft 365 and hybrid environments

Peter Rising

BIRMINGHAM—MUMBAI

Microsoft 365 Security Administration: MS-500 Exam Guide

Copyright © 2020 Packt Publishing

All rights reserved. No part of this book may be reproduced, stored in a retrieval system, or transmitted in any form or by any means, without the prior written permission of the publisher, except in the case of brief quotations embedded in critical articles or reviews.

Every effort has been made in the preparation of this book to ensure the accuracy of the information presented. However, the information contained in this book is sold without warranty, either express or implied. Neither the author, nor Packt Publishing or its dealers and distributors, will be held liable for any damages caused or alleged to have been caused directly or indirectly by this book.

Packt Publishing has endeavored to provide trademark information about all of the companies and products mentioned in this book by the appropriate use of capitals. However, Packt Publishing cannot guarantee the accuracy of this information.

Commissioning Editor: Ravit Jain
Acquisition Editor: Shrilekha Inani
Senior Editor: Arun Nadar
Content Development Editor: Pratik Andrade
Technical Editor: Sarvesh Jaywant
Copy Editor: Safis Editing
Project Coordinator: Neil Dmello
Proofreader: Safis Editing
Indexer: Manju Arasan
Production Designer: Aparna Bhagat

First published: June 2020

Production reference: 2280121

Published by Packt Publishing Ltd.
Livery Place
35 Livery Street
Birmingham
B3 2PB, UK.

ISBN 978-1-83898-312-3

`www.packt.com`

To my very patient wife, Louise, I would not have been able to do this without your unwavering love and support, and to my two amazing boys, George and Oliver. I do it all for the three of you! – Peter Rising

Packt.com

Subscribe to our online digital library for full access to over 7,000 books and videos, as well as industry leading tools to help you plan your personal development and advance your career. For more information, please visit our website.

Why subscribe?

- Spend less time learning and more time coding with practical eBooks and videos from over 4,000 industry professionals
- Improve your learning with Skill Plans built especially for you
- Get a free eBook or video every month
- Fully searchable for easy access to vital information
- Copy and paste, print, and bookmark content

Did you know that Packt offers eBook versions of every book published, with PDF and ePub files available? You can upgrade to the eBook version at packt.com and, as a print book customer, you are entitled to a discount on the eBook copy. Get in touch with us at customercare@packtpub.com for more details.

At www.packt.com, you can also read a collection of free technical articles, sign up for a range of free newsletters, and receive exclusive discounts and offers on Packt books and eBooks.

Contributors

About the author

Peter Rising has over 25 years' experience in IT. He has worked for several IT solutions providers and private organizations in a variety of technical roles focusing on Microsoft technologies. Since 2014, Peter has specialized in the Microsoft Office 365 platform, initially carrying out mail migrations from on-premises platforms and tenant-to-tenant migrations. Since joining Softcat PLC in 2016, Peter has shifted his focus to Microsoft 365 Security and Compliance and is now a senior consultant in Softcat's public cloud technical practice. He holds a number of Microsoft certifications, including MCSE: Productivity; MCSA: Office 365; Microsoft 365 Certified: Enterprise Administrator Expert; and Microsoft 365: Security Administrator Associate.

About the reviewers

Will Moore has over 20 years' experience working in IT, and started his professional life working on Windows NT 4 and Novell NetWare. He has passed over 25 Microsoft exams, from Windows 95 to the current MS, AZ, and MD series of exams. Messaging has been a passion for Will over the years. More recently, this passion has migrated to the Office 365 suite, with a growing focus on security. Will works as a principal consultant on the public cloud at a UK-based company, working across the public and private sectors.

Ronni Pedersen works as a cloud architect at APENTO in Denmark. His primary focus is Enterprise Client Management solutions, based on technologies such as Azure Active Directory, Microsoft Endpoint Manager, and System Center Configuration Manager. Ronni is also a Microsoft Certified Trainer and Microsoft MVP in Enterprise Mobility. APENTO is a dedicated Microsoft Partner, focusing on providing highly specialized and highly skilled consultants with competencies in the Microsoft 365 and Microsoft Azure area. Ronni has also reviewed *Microsoft System Center Endpoint Protection Cookbook*, also published by Packt.

Thank you, Vaidehi Sawant for always being understanding when I was late with my review during the COVID-19 outbreak.

Packt is searching for authors like you

If you're interested in becoming an author for Packt, please visit `authors.packtpub.com` and apply today. We have worked with thousands of developers and tech professionals, just like you, to help them share their insight with the global tech community. You can make a general application, apply for a specific hot topic that we are recruiting an author for, or submit your own idea.

Table of Contents

3
Implementing Conditional Access Policies

4
Role Assignment and Privileged Identities in Microsoft 365

5
Azure AD Identity Protection

Section 2: Implementing and Managing Threat Protection

6
Configuring an Advanced Threat Protection Solution

7
Configuring Microsoft Defender ATP to Protect Devices

8
Message Protection in Office 365

9
Threat Intelligence and Tracking

10

Using Azure Sentinel to Monitor Microsoft 365 Security

Section 3: Information Protection in Microsoft 365

11

Controlling Secure Access to Information Stored in Office 365

12

Azure Information Protection

13

Data Loss Prevention

14

Cloud App Discovery and Security

Section 4: Data Governance and Compliance in Microsoft 365

15

Security Analytics and Auditing Capabilities

16

Personal Data Protection in Microsoft 365

17

Data Governance and Retention

18

Search and Investigation

19
Data Privacy Compliance

Section 5: Mock Exam and Assessment

20
Mock Exam

21
Mock Exam Answers

22
Assessments

Other Books You May Enjoy

Index

Preface

In this book, you are going to learn how to manage security and compliance principles within your Microsoft 365 environments.

By the end of this guide, you will understand how to securely implement and manage hybrid identity, implement advanced security features in order to protect your users and devices, and deploy compliance and information protection features in order to ensure that business and regulatory requirements for your organization are being fulfilled.

Who this book is for

This book is for IT professionals who are already well versed in the implementation and administration of an Office 365 tenancy, and who wish to learn how to apply modern security and compliance principles to Microsoft 365 hybrid environments in line with Microsoft best practices, whilst providing a user environment that is accessible and easy to use.

What this book covers

Chapter 1, Planning for Hybrid Identity, teaches you how to plan your hybrid environment with Azure AD Connect and introduces you to additional authentication security methods.

Chapter 2, Authentication and Security, covers the implementation of Azure AD dynamic groups, Azure AD **self-service password reset** (**SSPR**), **multi-factor authentication** (**MFA**), and how to perform Azure AD access reviews.

Chapter 3, Implementing Conditional Access Policies, explains the principles of Azure AD Conditional Access, how it integrates with Microsoft Intune, and how Conditional Access may be used with device- and app-based policies.

Chapter 4, Role Assignment and Privileged Identities in Microsoft 365, shows you how **Role-Based Access Control** (**RBAC**) is used to assign access to built-in Microsoft 365 roles, and how, with the help of **Privileged Identity Management** (**PIM**), you can reduce your permanently assigned admin roles and implement eligibility with just-in-time access.

Chapter 5, Azure AD Identity Protection, introduces the principles of Identity Protection, how to configure user- and sign-in-based risk policies, and how to manage and respond to alerts.

Chapter 6, Configuring an Advanced Threat Protection Solution, explains how to set up and manage an Azure ATP instance.

Chapter 7, Configuring Microsoft Defender ATP to Protect Devices, helps you to understand how to reduce your attack surface by configuring policies for Windows Defender Application Guard, Application Control, Exploit Guard, and Secure Boot. In addition, you will learn how BitLocker device encryption can protect Windows 10 devices.

Chapter 8, Message Protection in Office 365, covers how to protect users and domains with anti-phishing and anti-spam protection, and the application of safe attachments and safe links policies.

Chapter 9, Threat Intelligence and Tracking, shows you how to understand the threat management dashboard and how to use Threat Explorer and Threat Trackers. It also examines how to manage quarantined messages and files and perform controlled, simulated attacks.

Chapter 10, Using Azure Sentinel to monitor Microsoft 365 Security, explains how to understand Azure Sentinel, and how to set it up from the Azure portal, then connect to workspaces, configure playbooks, and connect to both Microsoft native and third-party data sources.

Chapter 11, Controlling Secure Access to Information Stored in Office 365, explains the principles of privileged access management, Customer Lockbox, Azure B2B sharing for guest user access, and how to protect access to the collaboration components of Office 365.

Chapter 12, Azure Information Protection, explains how to plan, set up, and implement AIP labels to classify and protect content in Office 365, how to track and revoke protected content, and how the AIP scanner can autoclassify and protect on-premises SharePoint and file storage content.

Chapter 13, Data Loss Prevention, covers the planning and creation of DLP policies, the use of built-in sensitive information types, the creation of custom sensitive information types, and how to review DLP alerts.

Chapter 14, *Cloud App Discovery and Security*, demonstrates how Cloud App Security enables you to track your SaaS application usage, configure Cloud App Security with policies, integrate with Conditional Access, and navigate dashboards and logs.

Chapter 15, *Security Analytics and Auditing Capabilities*, provides an understanding of Desktop Analytics, Windows diagnostics, and Office Telemetry, and shows how to configure Office 365 auditing and complete an audit log search, and how you can configure alerting policies.

Chapter 16, *Personal Data Protection in Microsoft 365*, explains the process of conducting searches for personal data within Microsoft 365, how to use retention labels to protect personal data, and how to access logs to search for and monitor personal data leaks.

Chapter 17, *Data Governance and Retention*, teaches you how to understand data governance and retention requirements for your organization, how to configure retention tags and retention policies, supervision policies, and litigation holds to preserve data, how to import data into Office 365 from the Security and Compliance Center, and how to configure online archiving.

Chapter 18, *Search and Investigation*, teaches you the principles of eDiscovery and how to create and manage eDiscovery cases and content searches in Microsoft 365.

Chapter 19, *Data Privacy Compliance*, explains the process of planning for regulatory compliance in Microsoft 365, how to access GDPR dashboards and reports, and how to complete data subject requests.

Chapter 20, *Mock Exam*, includes 25 exam questions that will help to prepare you for the actual test.

Chapter 21, *Mock Exam Answers*, includes answers and explanations to the exam questions from the previous chapter.

Chapter 22, *Assessments*, includes answers to all of the practice questions that are provided at the end of each chapter.

To get the most out of this book

In order to get the most from this book, it is highly recommended to create a test Office 365 environment where you can follow along and recreate the steps that are covered in each chapter. You may sign up for an Office 365 E5 trial at `https://www.microsoft.com/en-gb/microsoft-365/business/office-365-enterprise-e5-business-software?activetab=pivot:overviewtab` and an EM+S E5 trial at `https://www.microsoft.com/en-gb/microsoft-365/enterprise-mobility-security?rtc=1`.

The preceding trial subscriptions will allow you to recreate the steps covered in the chapters contained in this book. Should you wish to test the process of establishing a hybrid identity, it is recommended that you acquire a trial Azure subscription, which will allow you to create a Windows 2016 VM that you may use to install Azure AD Connect and synchronize to your test Microsoft 365 tenant.

This book also has some example PowerShell commands that can be used instead of, or in preference to, the Microsoft 365 admin centers. Therefore, it is recommended to have a Windows 10 device available to you where you can run PowerShell and practice some of the commands included in the chapters.

A Windows 10 device will also be useful for the purposes of testing how to set up Office 365 test profiles to fully test and deploy features such as Microsoft Intune, Azure AD Conditional Access, multi-factor authentication, Azure Information Protection, and many more of the features described in the book.

A mobile device, such as an iOS or Android device, will also be useful for testing Microsoft Intune in particular.

Download the color images

We also provide a PDF file that has color images of the screenshots/diagrams used in this book. You can download it here: `http://www.packtpub.com/sites/default/files/downloads/9781838983123_ColorImages.pdf`

Conventions used

There are a number of text conventions used throughout this book.

`Code in text`: Indicates code words in text, database table names, folder names, filenames, file extensions, pathnames, dummy URLs, user input, and Twitter handles. Here is an example: "The `Start-ADSyncSyncCycle -PolicyType Initial` command will run a full synchronization."

Any command-line input or output is written as follows:

```
New-RetentionPolicyTag -Name "Personal-2-year-move-
to-archive" -Type All -AgeLimitForRetention 730
-RetentionActionMoveToArchive
```

Bold: Indicates a new term, an important word, or words that you see on screen. For example, words in menus or dialog boxes appear in the text like this. Here is an example: "Click **Save** to complete the setup of your retention tag."

Tips or important notes
Appear like this.

Get in touch

Feedback from our readers is always welcome.

General feedback: If you have questions about any aspect of this book, mention the book title in the subject of your message and email us at `customercare@packtpub.com`.

Errata: Although we have taken every care to ensure the accuracy of our content, mistakes do happen. If you have found a mistake in this book, we would be grateful if you would report this to us. Please visit `www.packtpub.com/support/errata`, selecting your book, clicking on the Errata Submission Form link, and entering the details.

Piracy: If you come across any illegal copies of our works in any form on the internet, we would be grateful if you would provide us with the location address or website name. Please contact us at `copyright@packt.com` with a link to the material.

If you are interested in becoming an author: If there is a topic that you have expertise in, and you are interested in either writing or contributing to a book, please visit `authors.packtpub.com`.

Reviews

Please leave a review. Once you have read and used this book, why not leave a review on the site that you purchased it from? Potential readers can then see and use your unbiased opinion to make purchase decisions, we at Packt can understand what you think about our products, and our authors can see your feedback on their book. Thank you!

For more information about Packt, please visit `packt.com`.

Section 1: Configuring and Administering Identity and Access in Microsoft 365

In this first section, we will be examining the principles of identity and access in Microsoft 365.

This part of the book comprises the following chapters:

- *Chapter 1, Planning for Hybrid Identity*
- *Chapter 2, Authentication and Security*
- *Chapter 3, Implementing Conditional Access Policies*
- *Chapter 4, Role Assignment and Privileged identities in Microsoft 365*
- *Chapter 5, Azure AD Identity Protection*

1
Planning for Hybrid Identity

Configuring a Microsoft 365 hybrid environment requires an understanding of your organization's identity needs, which will enable you to plan and deploy the correct **Azure Active Directory** (**AD**) authentication and synchronization method within your environment. This chapter covers planning your identity methodology and describes the process of monitoring and understanding the events recorded by Azure AD Connect.

By the end of this chapter, you will be able to determine your business needs, analyze on-premises identity infrastructure, and develop a plan for hybrid identity. You will understand how to design and implement authentication and application management solutions, how to enhance data security through strong identity, and how to analyze events and configure alerts in Azure AD Connect.

In this chapter, we will cover the following topics:

- Planning your hybrid environment
- Synchronization methods with Azure AD Connect
- Additional authentication security
- Event monitoring and troubleshooting in Azure AD Connect

Planning your hybrid environment

Identity is key when planning and implementing a Microsoft 365 environment. While the default identity method within Microsoft 365 is cloud-only, most organizations will need to plan for deploying hybrid identities when introducing Microsoft 365 to their organization. So, what is hybrid identity? Well, in simple terms, it is the process of providing your users with an identity in the cloud that is based on their on-premises identity. There are several ways that this can be achieved, and the available methods will be explained in detail later in this chapter.

The basic principles of hybrid identity in Microsoft 365 are shown in the following diagram:

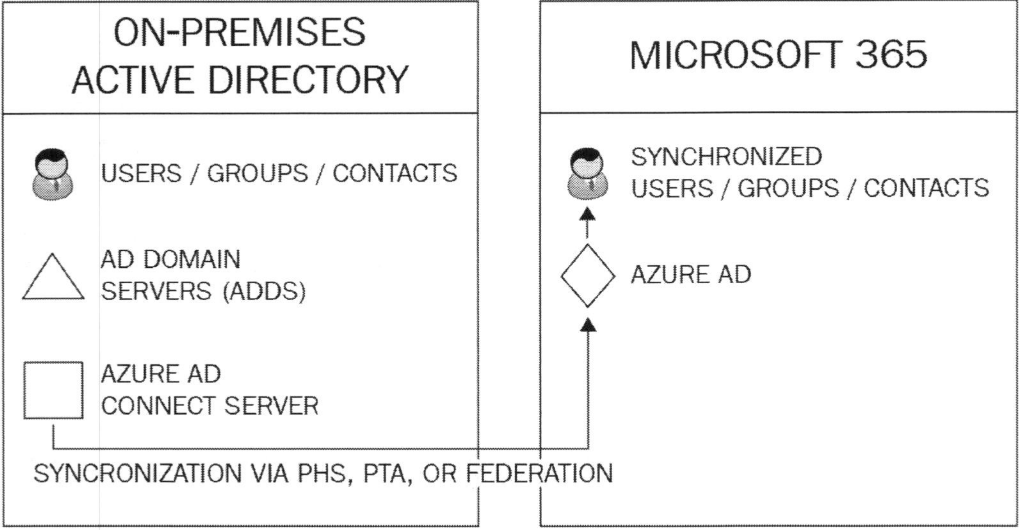

Figure 1.1 – Hybrid identity

Let's examine how to start planning for hybrid identity in Microsoft 365.

The first step to establishing the correct identity lies in determining the business needs of your organization. It is important, at this stage, to recognize who your stakeholders will be in this process, understand their current working tools and practices, and assess how a modern and agile platform such as Microsoft 365 could be used to enable them to work more efficiently and securely.

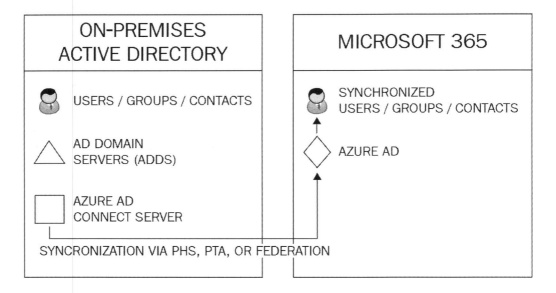

The following are some examples of your possible stakeholders:

- Users
- Power users
- IT team
- Compliance team
- Business owners

Each of the given stakeholders will have their own specific challenges that you will need to address. However, your users will obviously account for the highest percentage of your stakeholders and your primary focus will need to be ensuring that any transitions to new ways of working are as seamless as possible. Many users can be very wary of change and how you introduce them to new technologies and working practices is directly tied to the success or failure of your project. If your users buy in to the changes you are introducing and can realize the benefits, then the rest of your stakeholders are also more likely to follow suit.

While your main users will be focused on doing their job, the remaining stakeholders will have a deeper interest in how a Microsoft 365 hybrid environment meets the requirements of the business.

Some of the common business requirements are as follows:

- The modernization of existing IT software
- Providing and securing cloud (SaaS) applications
- Reducing risk by providing a secure identity solution

Let's examine some approaches for addressing these requirements. Examining how on-premises identities are currently provided is a logical starting point that will give you a better understanding of what you need to plan and implement for identity authentication in the cloud. You need to be aware of any current on-premises synchronization solutions that may be in place, including any third-party solutions.

You will also need to consider any existing use of cloud applications in the organization. These will need to be identified and plans made for their continued use, integration, or possible replacement.

> **Important note**
>
> Microsoft Cloud App Discovery can be used to analyze existing SaaS app usage within your organization. Cloud App Discovery and security will be covered in a later chapter in this book.

Understanding your on-premises identity infrastructure will help you to plan for modernization. So, what is modernization considered to be in the world of IT? Well, essentially, it is based on the principle that IT users now wish and expect to be more mobile. They want quick and easy access to their emails and documents anywhere, anytime, and on any device.

This requirement creates the challenge of how to effectively secure and protect the services within the Microsoft 365 platform while ensuring that these services are highly available and accessible to the users.

So, how do we achieve this? It is not possible to wrap a firewall around Microsoft 365 in the traditional sense. Instead, we need to look at the various modern authentication security methods that are available within the Azure AD Premium licensing plans. We will address these methods later on in this chapter, but before this, we will examine the process of establishing your hybrid identity by synchronizing your on-premises AD to Microsoft 365.

Synchronization methods with Azure AD Connect

Now that you understand the concept of hybrid identity and authentication, we will turn our attention to the process that makes hybrid identity possible—directory synchronization. The tool used to configure directory synchronization is called **Azure AD Connect** (previously known as Azure AD Sync Service and DirSync). Azure AD Connect consists of three essential components, as follows:

- Synchronization services
- **Active Directory Federation Services** (**AD FS**)—an optional component
- Health monitoring

Azure AD Connect supports multiple AD forests and multiple Exchange organizations to a single Microsoft 365 tenant. It leverages a one-way process, where the tool is used to synchronize users, groups, and contact objects from your on-premises active directory to Microsoft 365.

The principles of Azure AD Connect are shown in the following diagram:

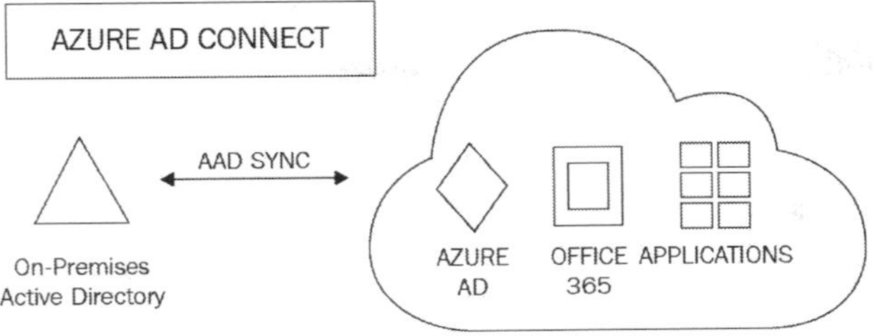

Figure 1.2 – Azure AD Connect

Once Azure AD Connect is configured and in place, the source of authority for these newly synchronized objects remains with on-premises AD and, therefore, these objects must be managed by on-premises tools, such as AD Users and Computers or Windows PowerShell. Microsoft 365 administrators will, therefore, not be able to make changes to cloud objects in the Microsoft 365 portal that are synchronized from on-premises AD.

When setting up Azure AD Connect for the first time, the installation wizard will guide you to select either an **Express Settings** installation or a custom settings installation. The **Express Settings** installation is the default setting for Azure AD Connect and is designed for use with password hash synchronization from a single AD forest. The **Express Settings** installation dialog is shown in the following screenshot:

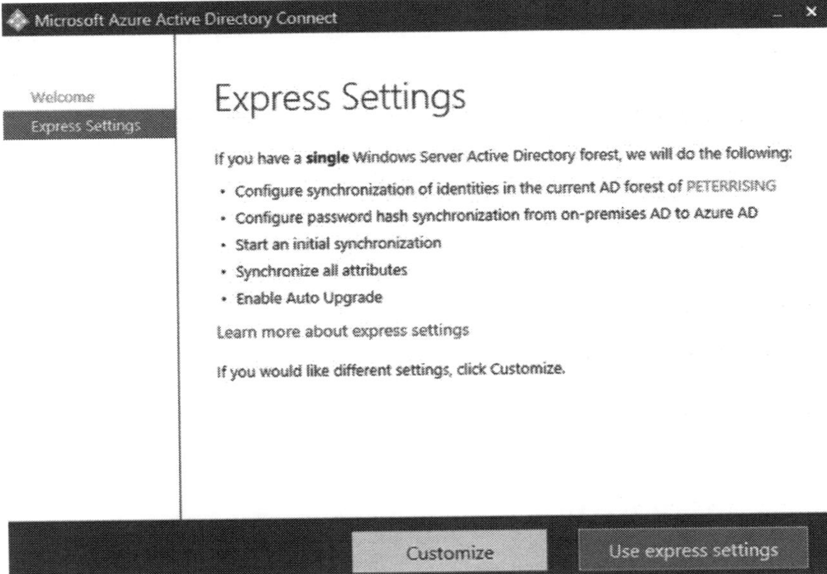

Figure 1.3 – Express Settings

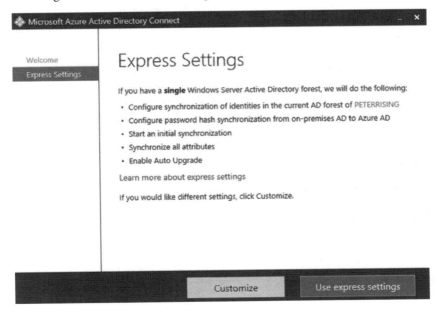

The custom settings installation provides a richer selection of optional features that can be configured to provide enhanced functionality if required. You can start a custom settings installation by clicking **Customize**:

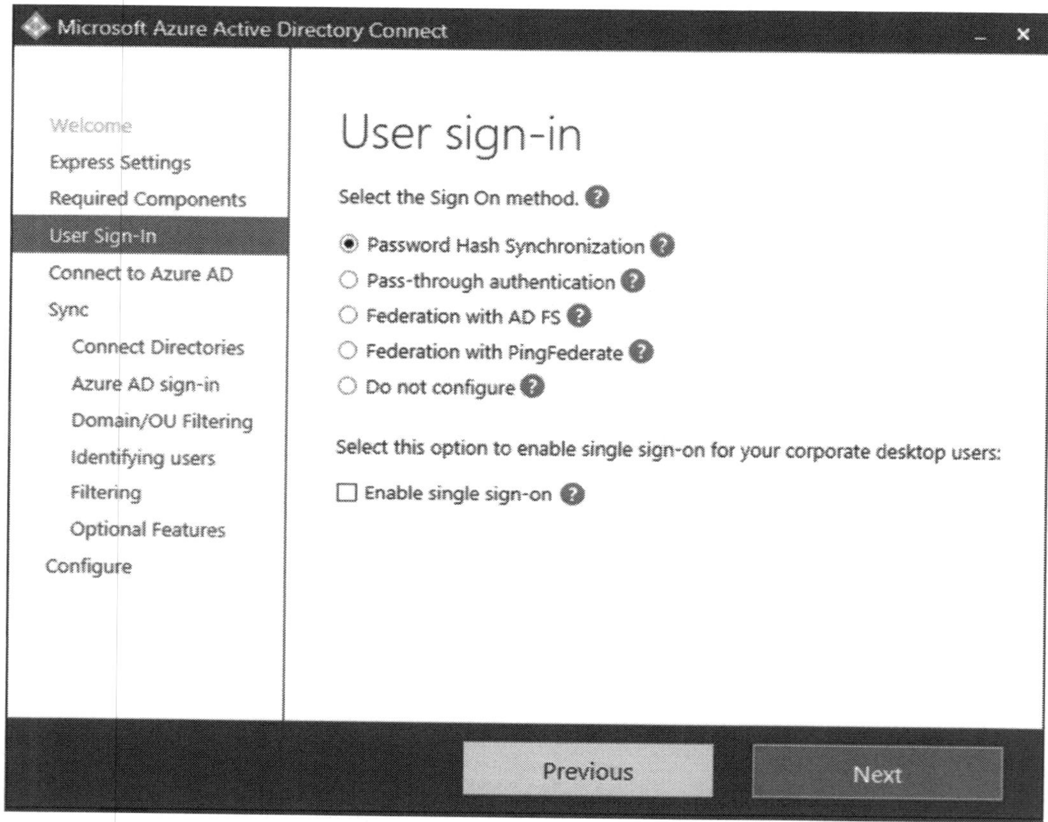

Figure 1.4 – Custom settings

With the custom settings installation, you are provided with the following options for extending your on-premises identities into the cloud using Azure AD Connect:

- Password hash synchronization
- Pass-through authentication
- Federation with AD FS
- Federation with PingFederate
- Enable single sign-on

We will now examine each of these methods in turn.

Password hash synchronization

Password hash synchronization is the simplest method to establish a hybrid identity with Azure AD. Also commonly known as **same sign-on**, password hash synchronization can be set up using Azure AD Connect to synchronize a hash, of the hash, of user passwords to Azure AD from your on-premises active directory.

With password hash synchronization, users logging onto their cloud accounts via the Microsoft 365 portal will authenticate directly to Microsoft 365 cloud services as opposed to leveraging on-premises authentication and security:

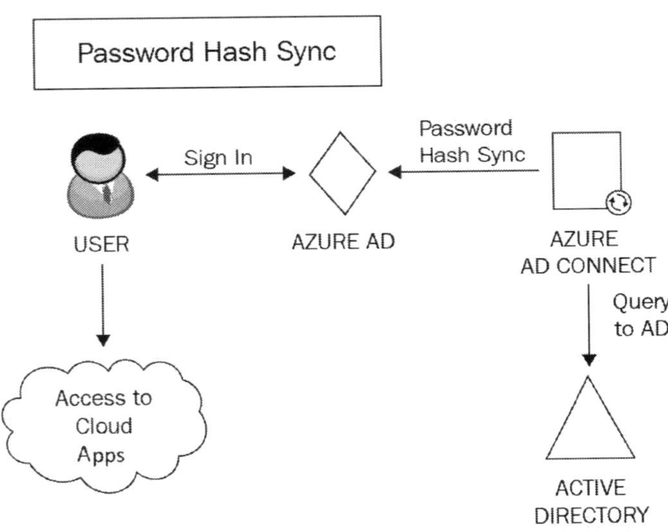

Figure 1.5 – Password hash synchronization

So, how does this work? Here is the process in a few simple steps:

1. The password synchronization agent within Azure AD Connect will request stored password hashes at 2-minute intervals from a domain controller. In response to this, the domain controller will encrypt the hash. This encryption is executed with a key that is acquired from the RPC session key and then salted.
2. The domain controller will then send the result, along with the salt, to the sync agent using RPC. The agent can now decrypt the envelope. It is important to point out that the sync agent never has any access to the password in cleartext.
3. Once decrypted, the sync agent performs a re-hash on the original password hash, changing it to a SHA256 hash by imputing this into the PKDF2 function.

4. The agent will then sync the resulting SHA256-hashed password hash from Azure AD Connect to Azure AD using SSL.
5. When Azure AD receives the hash, it will then be encrypted with an AES algorithm and then stored in the Azure AD database.

The result of all this is that when a user signs in to Azure AD with their on-premises AD username and password, the password is taken through the process we have just described, and if the hash result is a match for the hash stored in Azure AD, the user will be successfully authenticated.

Pass-through authentication

Pass-through authentication is an alternative to password hash synchronization. This method is commonly used when Microsoft 365 administrators require users to authenticate their Microsoft 365 logins on-premises as opposed to directly to Microsoft 365.

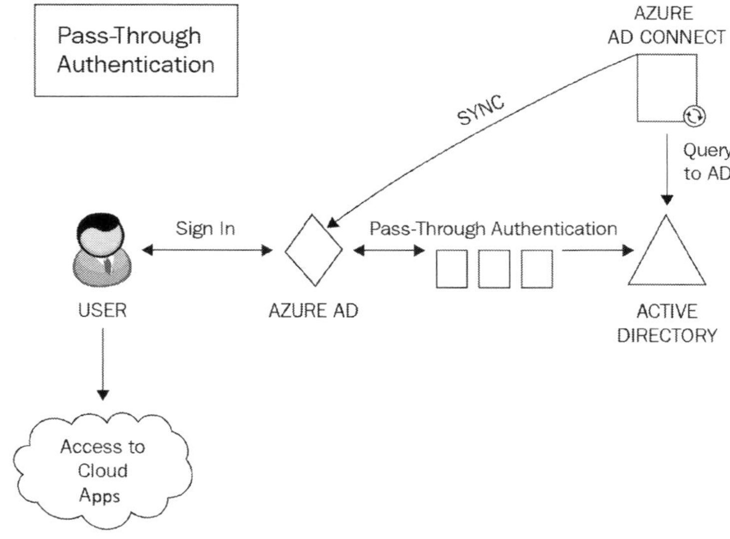

Figure 1.6 – Pass-through authentication

Unlike password hash synchronization, pass-through authentication does not synchronize passwords from on-premises active directories to Microsoft 365, but instead allows users to log on to both on-premises and cloud applications and services using the *same* password, which provides a far more cohesive experience to users, with the added benefit that on-premises passwords will never be stored on the cloud in any form.

A lightweight agent is all that is needed to set this up with Azure AD Connect and this agent is automatically installed on the Azure AD Connect server when you run the initial setup for pass-through authentication. In order to provide resiliency to your pass-through authentication solution, the agent can be installed onto additional domain controllers or servers in your on-premises AD sites.

> **Important note**
> It is recommended to configure a minimum of three authentication agents in your environment. The maximum number of agents that can be installed is 40. It is generally good practice to have at least one agent deployed to each of your AD sites to make pass-through authentication resilient and highly available.

The authentication agents must be able to make outbound requests to Azure AD over the following ports in order to function:

Port	Requirement
`80`	SSL certificate validation and certificate revocation list download.
`443`	Provides outbound communication for the service.
`8080`	While this port is optional and not required for user sign-ins, it is useful to configure this port as authentication agents will report their status through port `8080` at 10-minute intervals.

Federation

Federation, in simple terms, can be described as domains that trust each other in order to share access to resources across organizations, with authentication and authorization settings configured to control the trust.

It is possible to federate your on-premises AD environment with Azure AD to provide authentication and authorization. As is the case with pass-through authentication, a federated sign-in method will enforce all user authentication via on-premises methods as opposed to the cloud.

The main benefits of federation are that it provides enhanced access controls to administrators. However, the drawback of this method is that additional infrastructure will inevitably need to be provisioned and maintained.

In Azure AD Connect, there are two methods available to configure federation with Azure AD. These are AD FS and the more recently added PingFederate.

To explain the infrastructure requirements in more detail, we will use AD FS as an example. In order to configure AD FS in line with Microsoft's best practices, you will need to install and configure a minimum of two on-premises AD FS servers on your AD environment and two web application proxy servers on your perimeter network.

This configuration will provide the necessary security principles to ensure that both internal and (especially) remote users are authenticating to the services within your hybrid environment in a manner that provides appropriate authentication and authorization. The process of federation is shown in the following diagram:

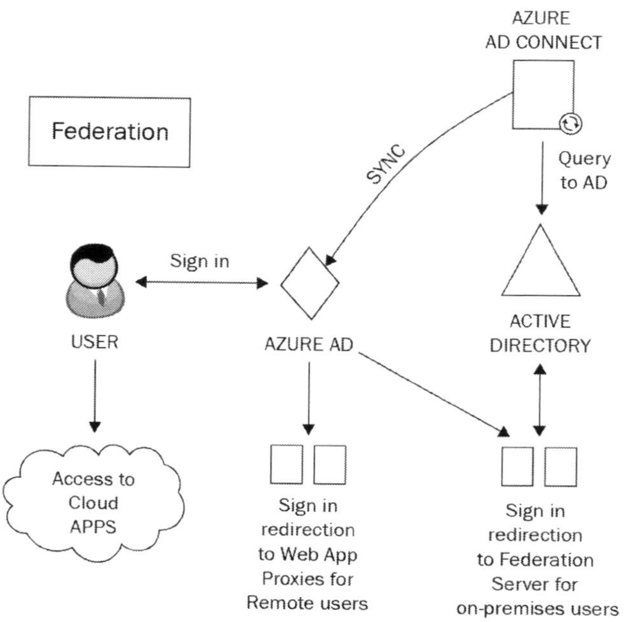

Figure 1.7 – Federation

So, how does federation actually work? Well, there are two main principles that you need to understand. These are claims-based authentication and federated trusts. We will examine each of these in detail now.

Claims-based authentication

Claims-based authentication works on the principle of users making statements about themselves in order to authenticate and gain access to applications by using industry-standard security protocols. User claims rely on the claims issuer, which is the **Security Token Service** (**STS**). The STS can be configured on your AD FS server. The statements provided by users can relate to name, identity, key, group, privilege, or capability.

A claim is issued by the user to the claims provider. It is then assigned values and packaged into a security token by the claims issuer (STS). This security token is essentially an envelope that contains the claims relating to the user. The token is sent back to the user and then passed to the application that the user wishes to access.

The claim relies on the explicit trust that is established with the issuer and the application that the user wishes to access will only trust the user's claim if it subsequently trusts the claims provider (the STS).

With claims-based authentication, you can configure a number of authentication methods. The more commonly used ones are as follows:

- Kerberos authentication
- Forms authentication
- X.509 certificates
- Smart cards

Although many older applications will not support claims-based authentication, the main use-case argument for those applications who can is that it simplifies the process of trust for those target applications. Instead of having to place their trust directly in the user making the claim, they can be secure in the knowledge that they can absolutely trust the claims issuer instead.

Federated trusts

Federated trusts expand on the capabilities of claims-based authentication by enabling your issuer to accept security tokens from other issuers as opposed to a user having to directly authenticate. In this scenario, the issuer can both issue and accept security tokens from other trusted issuers utilizing the federation trust.

This process essentially establishes a business relationship or partnership between two organizations.

Federated trusts enable trusted issuers to represent the users on their side of the trust. The benefit of this configuration is that should you need to revoke the trust, this can be achieved in a single action. Rather than revoking a trust with many individual external users, you can simply terminate the trust with the issuer.

So, what does this mean? Well, a good example would be if you need to authenticate remote users to your environment, a federated trust would remove the requirement to provide direct authentication for those users. Instead, you will have a trust relationship with the user from the remote user's organization. This enables these remote users to continue using their own single sign-on methodology and provides an efficient, decentralized way for the remote users to authenticate to your organization.

> **Important note**
>
> An alternative method of providing many of the features that federation offers is to use pass-through authentication in conjunction with the rich features of Azure AD Premium, such as Conditional Access and Identity Protection.
>
> Although additional licensing may be required within Azure AD to deploy these features, this method offers simplified setup and administration and also removes the requirement for any additional infrastructure.

Azure AD Seamless Single Sign-On

Azure AD Seamless Single Sign-On (**Azure AD Seamless SSO**) is a free-to-use feature of Azure AD that can provide a single set of credentials for your users to authenticate to applications within Azure AD while connecting to your organization's network using a business desktop device. This essentially means that once connected to your network on their Windows 10 domain-joined devices, they will not be asked to provide further credentials when opening any available Azure AD applications. The principles of Seamless SSO are shown in the following diagram:

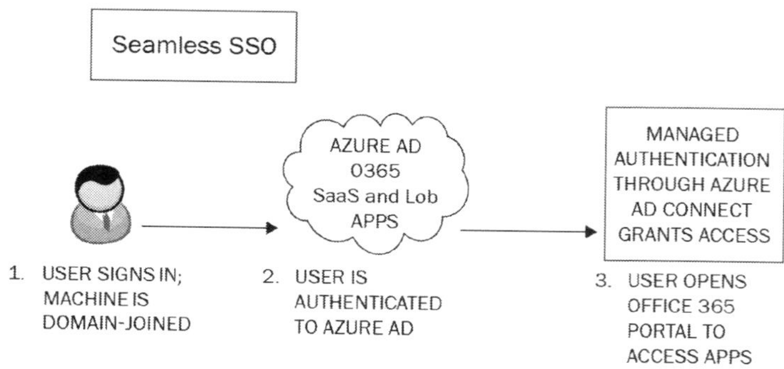

Figure 1.8 – Seamless SSO

Seamless SSO is configured via the Azure AD Connect wizard or Windows PowerShell and can be used in conjunction with password hash synchronization and pass-through authentication. It is not compatible with federations such as AD FS or PingFederate, however.

There are some prerequisites to be aware of when planning to implement Seamless SSO. These include the following:

- If you are using AD Connect with password hash sync, ensure that you are using AD Connect version 1.1.644.0 or later and, if possible, ensure your firewall or proxy is set to allow connections to the `*.msappproxy.net` URLs over port `443`. Alternatively, allow access to the Azure datacenter IP ranges.
- Be aware of the supported topologies that are shown at `https://docs.microsoft.com/en-us/azure/active-directory/hybrid/plan-connect-topologies`.
- Ensure that modern authentication is enabled on your tenant.
- Ensure that your users' Office desktop clients us a minimum of 16.0.8730.xxxx or above.

Once you have verified these prerequisites, you can go ahead and enable the feature. This is most commonly done when setting up AD Connect for the first time by performing a custom installation using the Azure AD Connect wizard and, from the **User sign-in** page, ensuring that the **Enable single sign-on** option is selected:

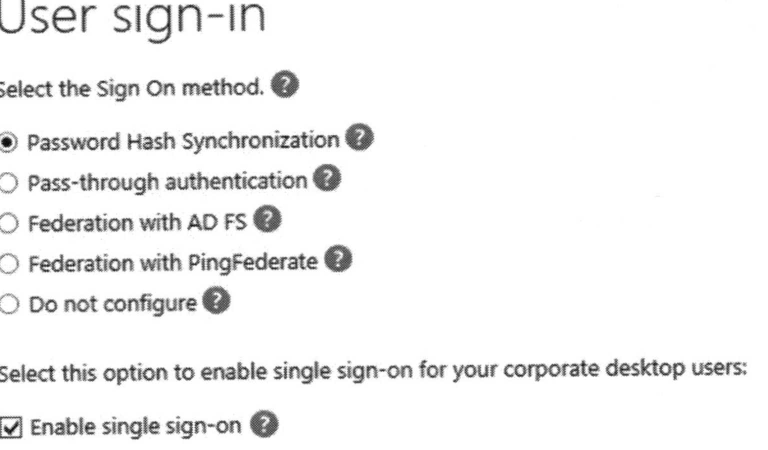

Figure 1.9 – User sign-in methods

It is also possible to use PowerShell to set up Seamless SSO. This is a particularly useful method if you need to specify a particular domain(s) in your AD forest to use the feature.

If you need to enable the feature when you already have Azure AD Connect deployed, then you can re-run the setup wizard and choose the **Change user sign-in** option under the **Additional tasks** section:

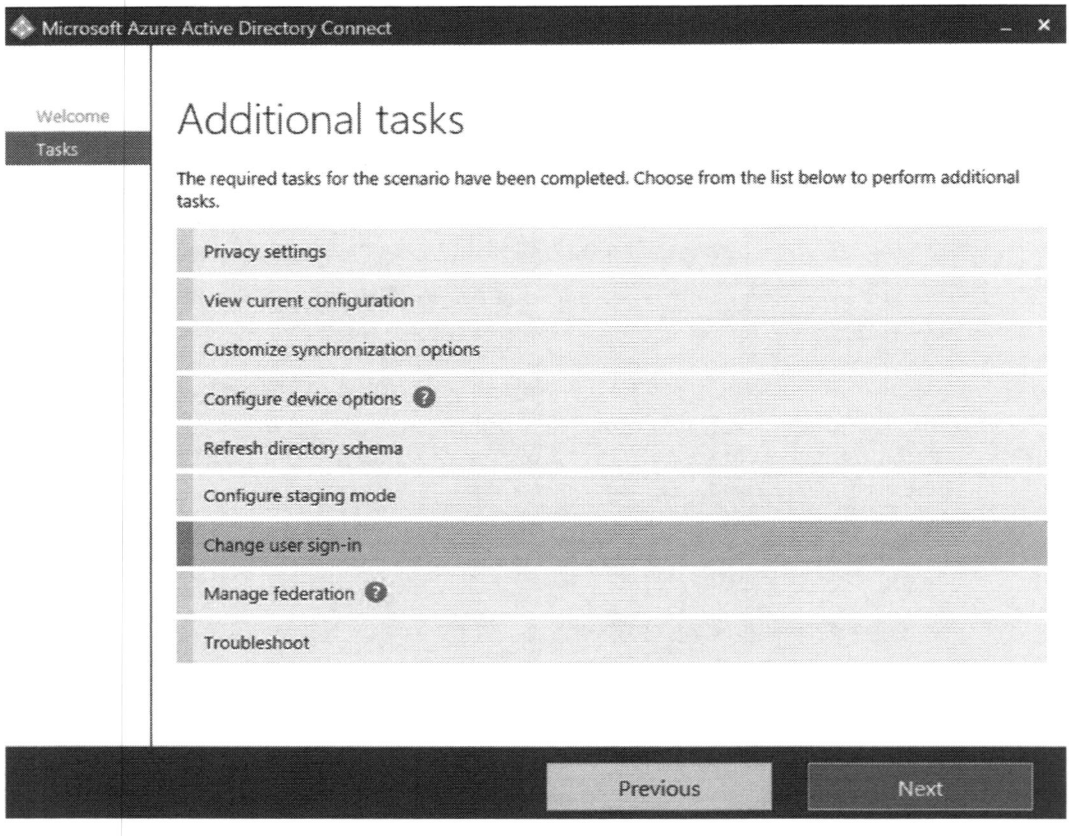

Figure 1.10 – Additional tasks

> **Important note**
>
> You will need domain administrator credentials in order to complete the process of setting up Seamless SSO. However, these credentials are only required to enable the feature and will not be further required after the setup is complete.

To verify that the setup of Seamless SSO has completed successfully, log on as a global administrator to `https://portal.azure.com` and navigate to **Azure Active Directory | Azure AD Connect**.

From this page, you will be able to verify that Seamless SSO has a status of **Enabled**:

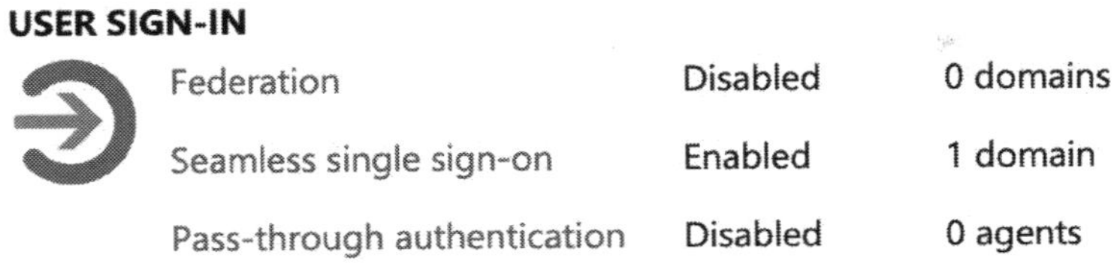

USER SIGN-IN		
Federation	Disabled	0 domains
Seamless single sign-on	Enabled	1 domain
Pass-through authentication	Disabled	0 agents

Figure 1.11 – User sign-in settings

Finally, when completing your custom settings installation of Azure AD Connect, you are presented with several additional optional features, as shown in the following screenshot:

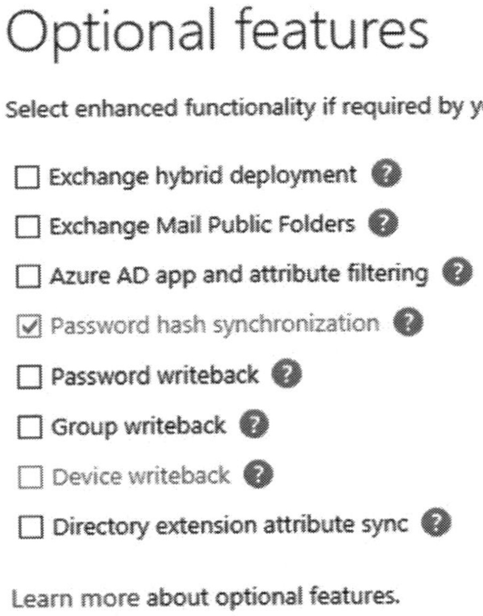

Figure 1.12 – Optional features

The most commonly used of these features are **Exchange hybrid deployment** and **Password writeback**. Further information on all of the available optional features can be viewed at `https://docs.microsoft.com/en-us/azure/active-directory/hybrid/how-to-connect-install-custom`.

To deploy the feature to your users, you need to ensure that the following URL is added to the required user's Intranet Zone settings by using Group Policy:

`https://autologon.microsoftazuread-sso.com`

One of the advantages of deploying this setting with Group Policy is that you can roll out Seamless SSO to groups of users at your own pace.

Now that we have our directory synchronization taken care of, we have established our hybrid identity. Let's now examine how we can help protect that identity for our users with some of the additional authentication security methods we briefly referred to earlier in this chapter.

Additional authentication security

The authentication security methods available in Microsoft 365 are as follows:

- **Multi-factor authentication** (MFA)
- **Self-service password reset** (SSPR)
- Conditional Access

We will briefly introduce the principles of these methods; however, each of these will be described and explored in greater detail in *Chapter 2*, *Authentication and Security*, and *Chapter 3*, *Implementing Conditional Access Policies*, of this book.

Multi-factor authentication

MFA in Azure AD provides two-step verification to Microsoft services via a combination of approved authentication methods that are determined by Microsoft 365 administrators. The available methods can be based on the following:

- Something you know, such as your password
- Something you own, such as your mobile phone or an OAuth token
- Something you are, such as biometric identification (fingerprint or facial recognition)

When setting up MFA for users in your Microsoft 365 environment, users must first complete a registration process to provide information about themselves to Azure AD and set their authentication method preferences.

Once set, users will be challenged with an MFA prompt when accessing Microsoft 365 services and applications using their Azure AD credentials, as shown in the following diagram:

Figure 1.13 – Azure MFA

MFA can also be configured to work in conjunction with Conditional Access, with trusted locations that you define by entering the IP ranges of your business operating units so that users will not be issued an MFA challenge while working in these locations. Conditional Access with MFA also enables you to apply a further layer of security by ensuring that any access requests to specific apps and resources can be secured and protected by requiring that the requesting user completes an MFA challenge before being granted the access they require.

> **Important note**
>
> It is recommended that you configure MFA for all privileged user accounts within your Microsoft 365 environment, except for your permanent break-glass account, which should be a cloud-only account with the domain suffix of the `.onmicrosoft.com` domain name.

Self-service password reset

SSPR is a feature designed to remove the requirement of IT staff having to respond to user requests to reset their passwords in Azure AD. An initial registration process is required for each user to set up SSPR, during which time they must provide authentication methods to verify their identity.

SSPR can be used for both cloud-only and hybrid identity users. If the user is cloud-only, then their password is always stored in Azure AD, whereas hybrid users who use the feature will have their password written back to on-premises AD. This is achieved using a feature that can be enabled in Azure AD Connect called password writeback.

The basic principles of SSPR are illustrated in the following diagram:

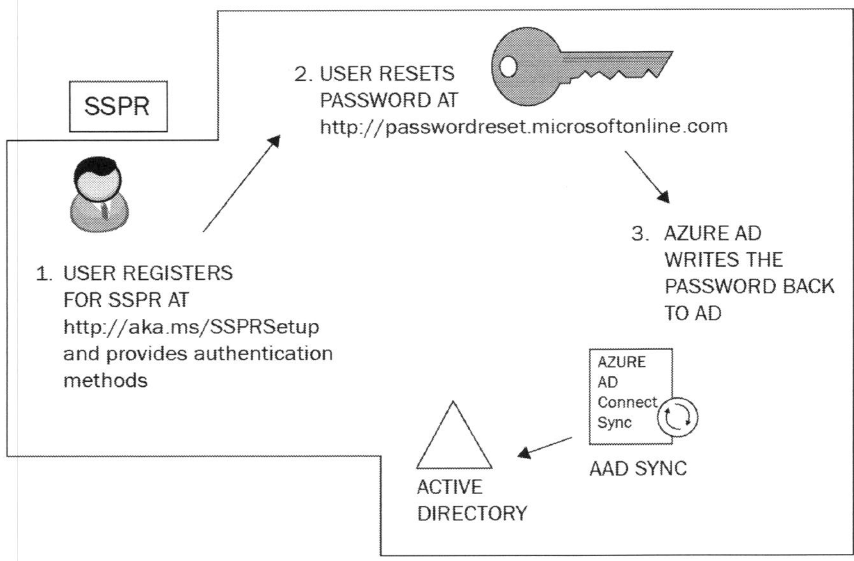

Figure 1.14 – Self-service password reset

The process of registering your users for SSPR is separate from that of MFA registration. This can lead to confusion and frustration for users who need to use both SSPR and MFA as they need to go through a similar registration process for both features.

> **Important note**
>
> There is now a Microsoft-combined security information registration process (which at the time of writing this book is in preview mode) that allows users to register for both SSPR and MFA at the same time.

When SSPR is enabled on your Azure AD environment, you can assist your users further by configuring helpful notifications so that they are aware when their passwords have been reset and also increase security by setting administrator notifications to monitor and alert whenever an administrator changes a password. It is also possible to customize a *helpdesk email or URL* to provide immediate guidance to users who experience problems when attempting to reset their passwords.

> **Important note**
>
> When using SSPR with password writeback for your hybrid identities, Azure AD Premium P1 licenses are required.

Conditional Access

Conditional Access is a powerful feature of Azure AD Premium P1 that allows Microsoft 365 administrators to control access to applications and resources within your organization. With Conditional Access, you can automate the process of controlling the level of access that users will have to these applications and resources by setting Conditional Access policies. Azure AD will then make decisions on whether to grant or deny access based upon the conditions that you set in these policies. The basic principles are shown in the following diagram:

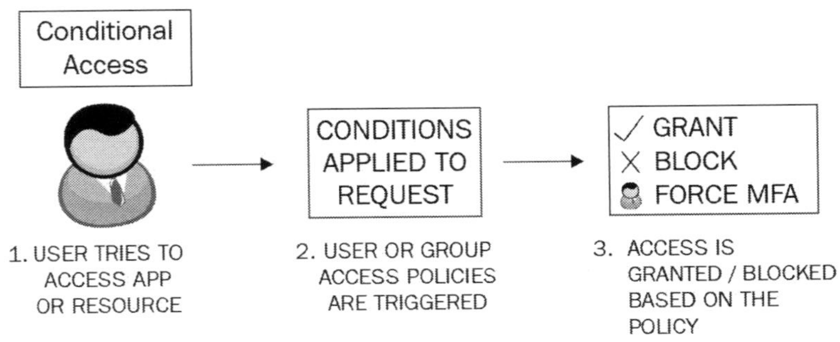

Figure 1.15 – Conditional Access

While it is possible to apply some default security settings to your Microsoft 365 environment with a selection of legacy baseline policies and the more recently introduced security defaults, there will undoubtedly be a requirement for you to plan and define some custom policies with specific conditions and exceptions. For example, you would not wish to force MFA on your permanent break-glass global administrator account. We will examine Conditional Access in greater detail in *Chapter 3, Implementing Conditional Access Policies*.

> **Important note**
>
> Conditional Access settings will frequently require some additional features of Azure AD to be configured, for example **Azure AD Identity Protection**. This will have an impact on your decision-making process as it relates to licensing since Conditional Access is a feature of **Azure AD Premium P1**. The use of Azure AD Identity Protection features would necessitate **Azure AD Premium P2** licenses.

Event monitoring and troubleshooting in Azure AD Connect

So, now that you have your hybrid identity method configured, hopefully it will all run smoothly for you. However, occasionally you may encounter some problems, and this is where the ability to assess and troubleshoot Azure AD Connect with tools and from the Microsoft 365 portal can assist administrators to quickly identify and resolve issues. Administrators will be able to perform the following tasks:

1. Review and interpret synchronization errors by accessing the Microsoft 365 admin center via `https://portal.office.com` and examine the Azure AD Connect directory sync status. Here, you will see an overview of any directory synchronization errors. A common example may be a duplicate *proxy address* or *UPNs* causing conflicts and preventing an object from syncing. The following screenshot shows the Azure AD Connect tile you will see in the admin center. Any issues with your synchronization will be shown here in red:

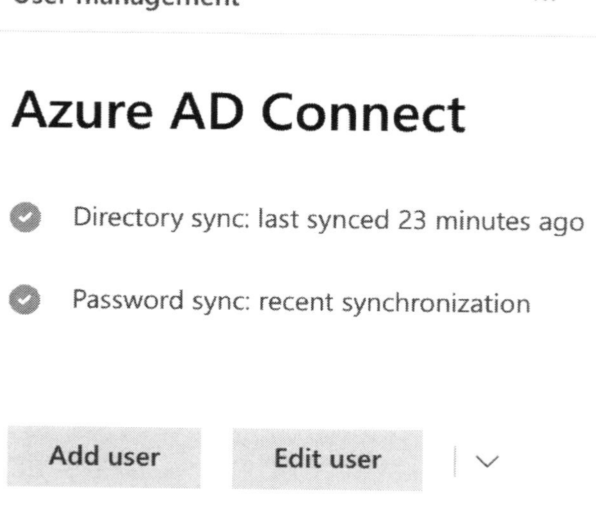

Figure 1.16 – The Azure AD Connect status

2. If you drill down further, you will see additional details about your directory sync status, as shown in the following screenshot. One of the tools you can download from here is `IdFix`, which you can run from any domain-joined workstation on your environment. It provides detailed information on synchronization issues and guidelines on how to resolve them:

Directory Sync Status

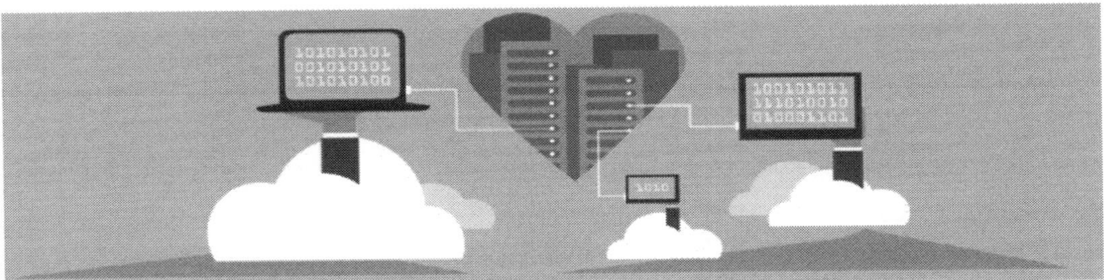

Integration with local Active Directory

Company Name	Chrysalis Technologies
Domains verified	5
Domains not verified	0
Directory sync enabled	True
Last directory sync	last synced 25 minutes ago
Password sync enabled	True
Password sync	recent synchronization
Directory sync client version	1.3.21.0
IdFix Tool	Download IdFix Tool
Directory sync service account	Sync_CHRYSALIS03_bacade3d32e4@chrysalistech.onmicrosoft.com

Figure 1.17 – Directory Sync Status

3. Receive and act on email notifications relating to an unhealthy identity synchronization. These email alerts are configured by default to alert *only* the technical contact who is defined in your Microsoft 365 tenant under **Organization profile**. These emails will continue to be sent to the technical contact until they are resolved.

4. Check **Synchronization Service Manager** on the Azure AD Connect server to confirm that the operations required for a successful synchronization have been completed. If any errors occur, they will be displayed here with explanations as to why the operation has failed:

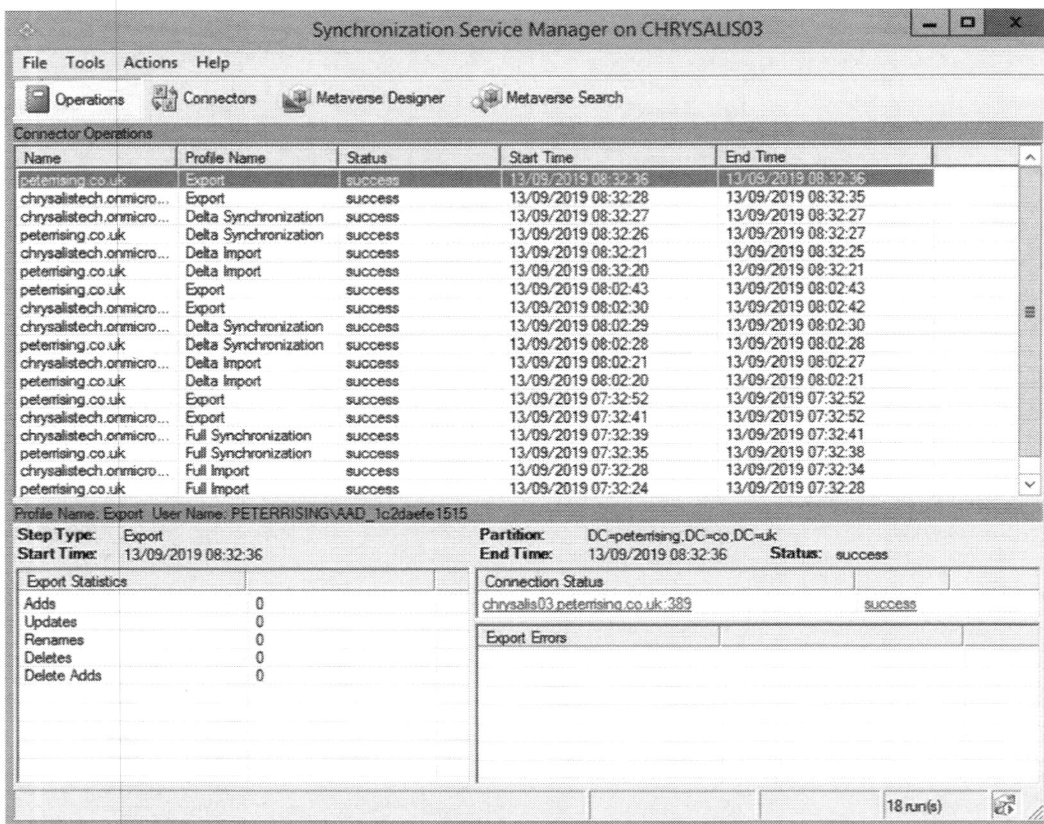

Figure 1.18 – Synchronization Service Manager

5. Directory synchronization occurs every 30 minutes by default. However, you can generate a synchronization on demand by opening the **Connectors** tab and manually starting the process, as in the following screenshot:

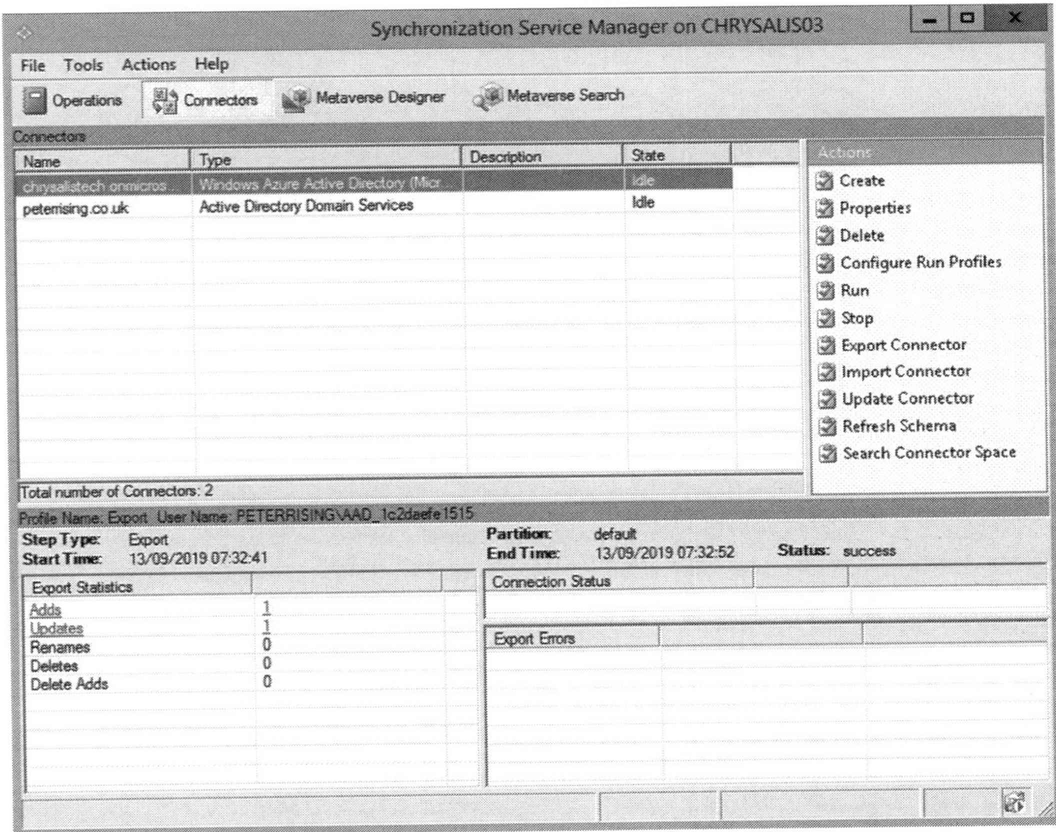

Figure 1.19 – Synchronization Service Manager

6. Click on **Actions** and select **Run**:

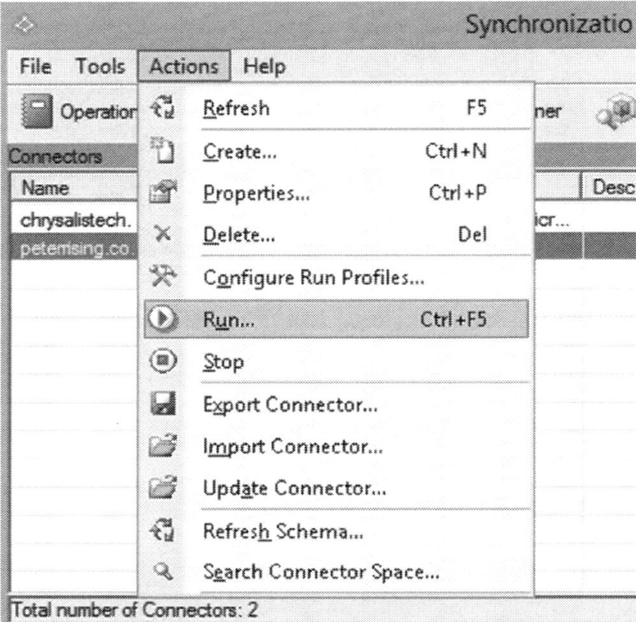

Figure 1.20 – Connector actions

7. You will be able to run the desired connectors from here, as shown:

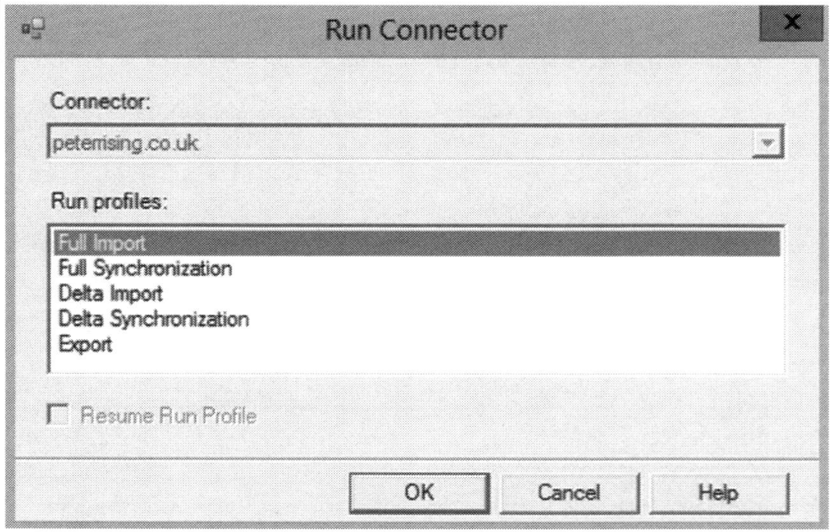

Figure 1.21 – Connector options

8. It is also possible and far simpler to run a manual synchronization process using PowerShell from your AD Connect server with the following commands:

   `Start-ADSyncSyncCycle -PolicyType Initial` (initiates a full synchronization)

   `Start-ADSyncSyncCycle -PolicyType Delta` (initiates a delta synchronization)

In this section, we examined event monitoring and troubleshooting techniques in Azure AD Connect. You learned how to review, interpret, and respond to synchronization errors in the Office 365 portal and by checking the Synchronization Service Manager tool. We also showed you how you can manually trigger the synchronization process from the Synchronization Service Manager tool and by using PowerShell.

Summary

In this chapter, we discussed the steps and considerations for planning and implementing hybrid identity in Microsoft 365. You should now have an understanding of the synchronization methods available to you and how to choose the correct one for your environment, along with the principles of additional security authentication and how to understand and troubleshoot events and alerts when required.

In the next chapter, we will dive deeper into those security and authentication features within Microsoft 365, including MFA and SSPR. We will also take a look at Azure AD dynamic groups and managing access reviews.

Questions

1. Which of the following is not one of the identity methods available with Azure AD?

   a. Pass-through authentication

   b. Federation

   c. MFA

   d. Password hash sync

2. Which of the following tools could you use to assess your organization's readiness to synchronize their active directory to Azure AD?

   a. The Remote Connectivity Analyzer tool

   b. The IdFix tool

c. The OffCAT tool

d. Synchronization Service Manager

3. True or false – with password hash synchronization, users will always authenticate to on-premises AD when logging onto Azure AD.

a. True

b. False

4. Which of the following Microsoft 365 licenses allow users to use SSPR (choose two)?

a. Azure AD Premium P2

b. Intune

c. Azure Information Protection P1

d. Azure AD Premium P1

5. Which of the following PowerShell commands could you use to run a full Azure AD Connect sync manually?

a. `Start-ADSyncSyncCycle -PolicyType Initial`

b. `Start-ADSyncSyncCycle -PolicyType Delta`

c. `Start-ADSyncSyncCycle -PolicyType Full`

d. `Start-ADSyncSyncCycle -PolicyType Immediate`

6. True or false – Conditional Access is a feature of Azure AD Premium designed to give Microsoft 365 administrators control over user and device access requests to services and applications within Azure AD and to apply actions based on certain conditions.

a. True

b. False

7. What is the maximum number of authentication agents that can be configured in Azure AD for pass-through authentication?

a. 5

b. 10

c. 30

d. 40

8. How frequently does Azure AD Connect automatically synchronize on-premises AD changes to Azure AD?

   a. Every 20 minutes

   b. Once an hour

   c. Every 30 minutes

   d. Every 15 minutes

9. Which two of the following methods can be used to authenticate users to Azure AD with MFA?

   a. Code with the Microsoft Authenticator app

   b. SMS messages to mobile device

   c. Security questions

   d. Email address

10. When deploying federation with AD FS, what is the minimum number of web application proxy servers you should configure on your perimeter network?

    a. 5

    b. 2

    c. 3

    d. 7

References

Please refer to the following links for more information:

- Refer to `https://docs.microsoft.com/en-us/azure/active-directory/hybrid/plan-hybrid-identity-design-considerations-business-needs?wt.mc_id=4039827` to help you to plan for hybrid identity.
- Information on how to select the most appropriate synchronization method for Azure AD Connect can be found at `https://docs.microsoft.com/en-us/azure/security/fundamentals/choose-ad-authn`.

- For help with additional authentication security, please refer to `https://docs.microsoft.com/en-us/azure/active-directory/authentication/concept-mfa-howitworks`, `https://docs.microsoft.com/en-us/azure/active-directory/authentication/concept-sspr-howitworks`, and `https://docs.microsoft.com/en-us/azure/active-directory/conditional-access/overview`.
- Further guidance on troubleshooting synchronization with Azure AD Connect can be found at `https://docs.microsoft.com/en-us/azure/active-directory/hybrid/tshoot-connect-objectsync`.

2
Authentication and Security

Now that you have implemented your hybrid identity model, it is equally important to be able to assign access to applications and resources within your Microsoft 365 environment in a manner that is safe and secure, but also user-friendly. Azure AD Premium allows you to do this.

By the end of this chapter, you will be able to create Azure AD groups with dynamic membership rules, configure self-service password reset capabilities for users, and set up **Multi-Factor Authentication** (**MFA**). In addition, we will show you how to carry out access reviews to ensure that users have appropriate access.

We will cover these topics in the following order:

- Implementing Azure AD dynamic group membership
- Implementing Azure AD **self-service password reset** (**SSPR**)
- Implementing and managing **Multi-Factor Authentication** (**MFA**)
- Managing Azure AD access reviews

Implementing Azure AD dynamic group membership

Before we dive into the principles of Azure AD dynamic groups, it is important to take a step back and ensure you have an overall appreciation of the available methods you can use to assign access rights to your users in Azure AD. These are as follows:

- **Direct assignment**: Permissions to Azure AD resources are granted by manually assigning access for the resource to an individual Azure AD user object.
- **Group assignment**: Permissions to Azure AD resources are granted by manually assigning access for the resource to an Azure AD group that contains a set of Azure AD user objects that are added or removed from the group manually.
- **Rule-based assignment**: Permissions to resources are granted by dynamically assigning users to a group by defining rules for membership based on specific user object attributes (such as the department field).
- **External authority assignment**: Permissions to resources are granted by creating groups in order to provide access to resources for sources external to Azure AD. In this situation, the external source is given permission to manage group membership.

This essentially means that the most basic way to provide access rights to resources in Azure AD is to grant access directly to individual users. However, this has obvious disadvantages compared to the use of groups. By using group assignment, permissions to resources can be assigned directly to that group and all its members in a single action, instead of us having to provide access to individual users. This can be a laborious and ongoing task for administrators, who will need to add and remove users from groups on a constant basis.

Rule-based assignment using Azure AD dynamic groups simplifies this process and provides a secure method for maintaining appropriate access to resources. Let's look at how this works.

Creating a dynamic group in Azure AD using the Azure portal

To create a dynamic group, we need to log in to the Azure portal at `https://portal.azure.com` as a Global Administrator, Intune Administrator, or User Administrator, and navigate to **Azure Active Directory | Groups | All groups**:

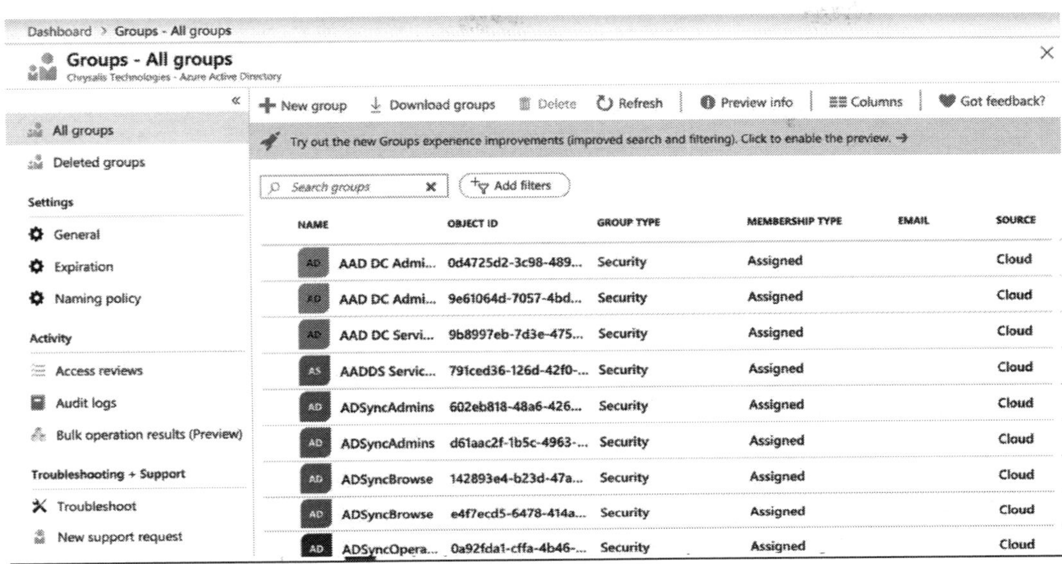

Figure 2.1 – Azure AD groups

The following steps will enable you to set up the group:

1. We will start by clicking on **New group**:

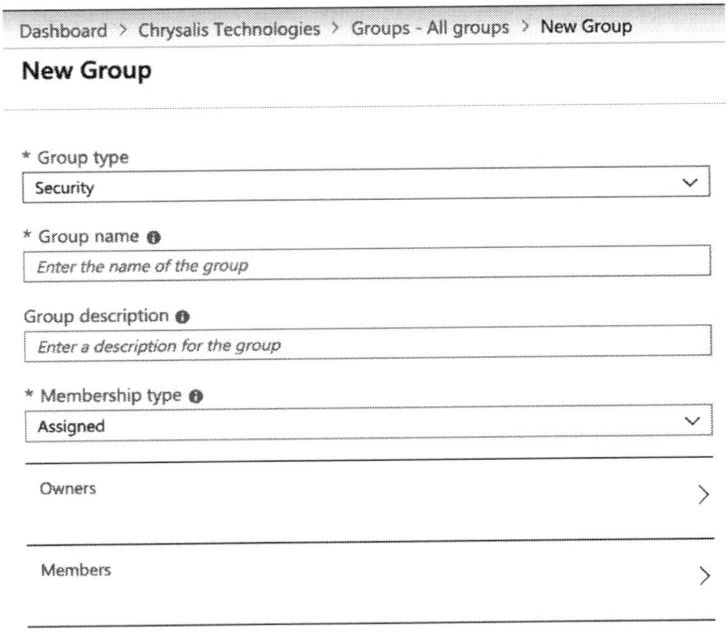

Dashboard > Chrysalis Technologies > Groups - All groups > New Group

New Group

* Group type

Security

* Group name

Enter the name of the group

Group description

Enter a description for the group

* Membership type

Assigned

Owners

Members

Figure 2.2 – New group settings

2. Choose between the available group types, that is, **Security**, which is used to grant access to users and devices, and **Office 365**, which is used to grant access only to users and can be assigned a group email address:

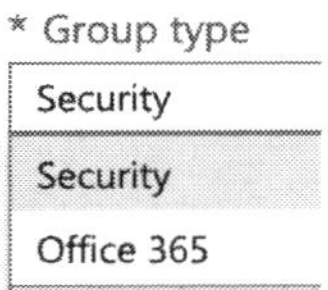

Figure 2.3 – Group type

3. Enter a name and description for the group. In this example, I have named my group `Marketing Users` and provided a description that states, `For access to the Marketing Dept SharePoint Team Site`. You can choose your own name and description here. Please always try and give logical names and descriptions that will be easy for your users to understand.
4. Choose the desired membership type: **Assigned**, **Dynamic User**, or **Dynamic Device** (only with Security Groups).

   For this example, I have chosen to create a Security Group for the Marketing Department. I have set the membership type to **Dynamic User** and selected an **Owner** for the group:

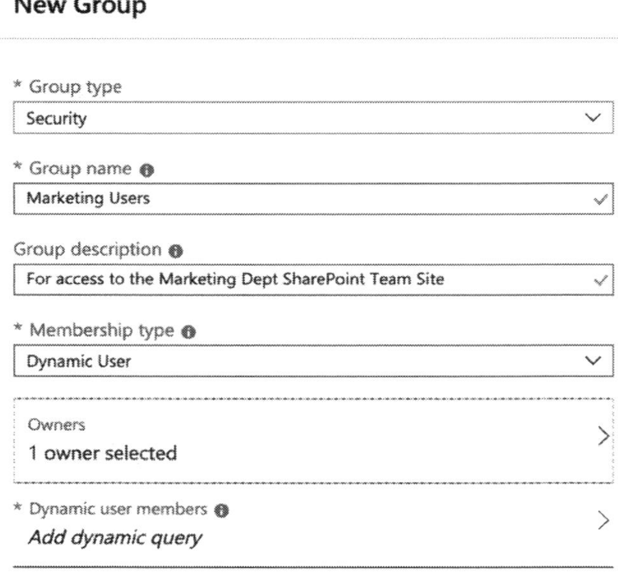

Figure 2.4 – New group settings

5. I can now go ahead and choose **Add dynamic query** so that I can begin creating my dynamic membership rules. The rule builder allows you to add up to five expressions. In the following example, I have configured a simple rule for adding members to this group where the user's **department** field equals **Marketing**:

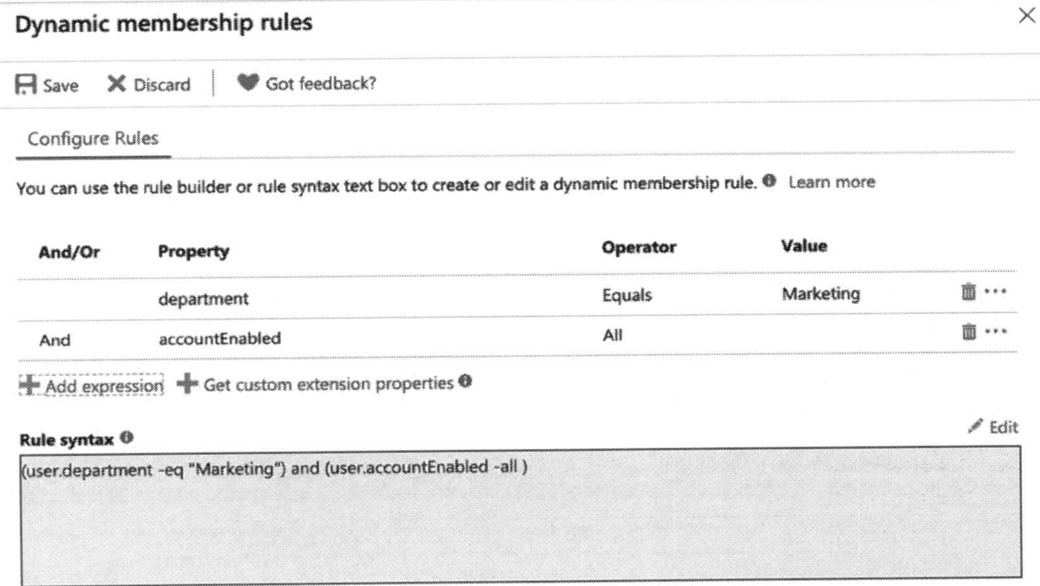

Figure 2.5 – Dynamic membership rules

6. The **Rule syntax** text box can be used if you need to add more than five expressions and create more advanced rules. In addition, you can use the **Get custom extension properties** option to add an Application ID (if applicable). This can be either synced from your on-premises AD or from a connected SaaS application:

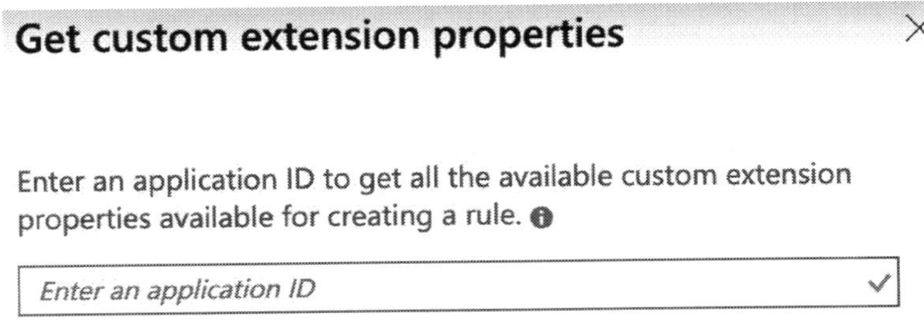

Figure 2.6 – Custom extension properties

7. When you are happy with your selections, click **Save** and then **Create**.

Creating dynamic groups with Azure AD PowerShell

It is also possible to create and manage Azure AD groups with PowerShell. Let's look at the Marketing Users group we created in the Azure portal using PowerShell.

First, we need to launch PowerShell. I always recommend running PowerShell as an Administrator. Once we have PowerShell open and ready, we need to perform the following steps:

1. Run `install-module azuread`.
2. Run `import-module azuread`.
3. Run `get-module azuread`.
4. Run `connect-azuread`:

Figure 2.7 – Connecting to Azure AD with PowerShell

   We will be prompted for our credentials, and will need to connect as a Global Administrator, Intune Administrator, or User Administrator. This will connect us to Azure AD in the PowerShell session. Now, we can retrieve a full list of all Azure AD groups by running `Get-AzureADGroup`.

5. However, we need to view our Marketing Users group. To do this, we will filter our command, as follows:

```
Get-AzureADGroup -Filter "DisplayName eq 'Marketing
Users'"
```

   The executed command is shown in the following screenshot:

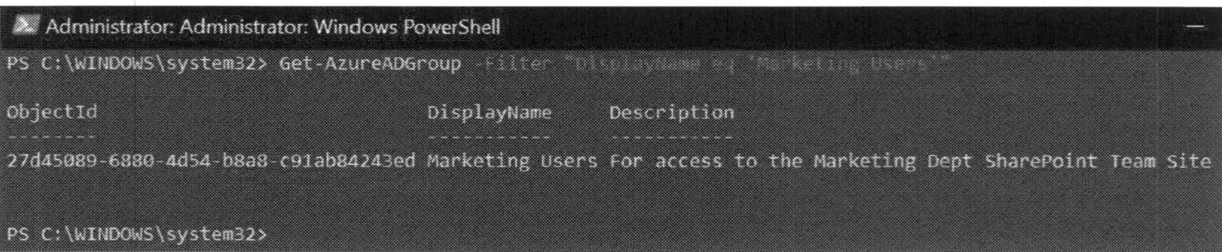

Figure 2.8 – Viewing groups with PowerShell

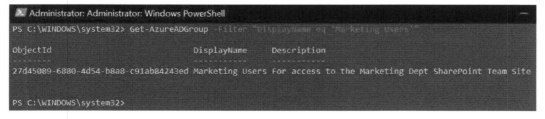

The output of this command will show you the `ObjectID`, `DisplayName`, and `Description` values of your group.

6. Creating a group in PowerShell is just as simple. Let's say we need to create another dynamic security group with the same settings for the Sales Department users, but this time, we want to do this in PowerShell. To do this, run the following code:

```
New-AzureADMSGroup -Description "For access to the Sales
Dept SharePoint Team Site" -DisplayName "Sales Users"
-MailEnabled $false -SecurityEnabled $true -MailNickname
"SalesDynamic" -GroupTypes "DynamicMembership"
-MembershipRule "(user.department -eq ""Sales"")"
-MembershipRuleProcessingState "On"
```

The executed command is shown in the following screenshot:

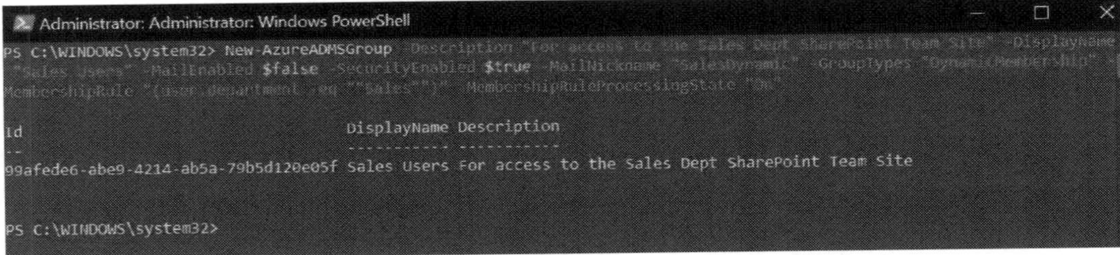

Figure 2.9 – Creating a group with PowerShell

7. With this, the group is created for you. We can search for and view it in the Azure portal as follows:

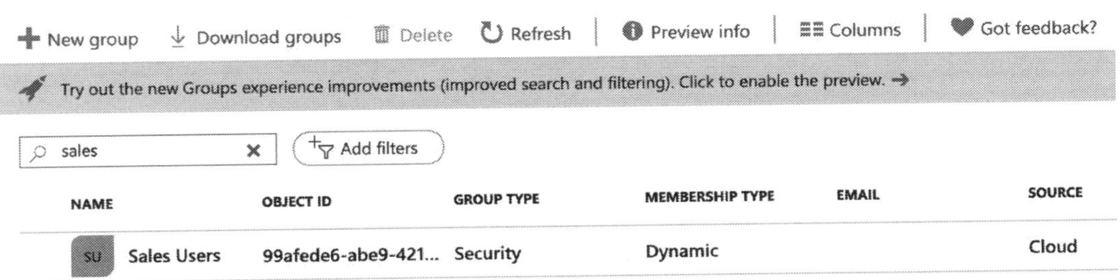

Figure 2.10 – Group details

8. You can click on the group name (in this case, **Sales Users**) to open and inspect the group settings. This will show you the **Group** overview:

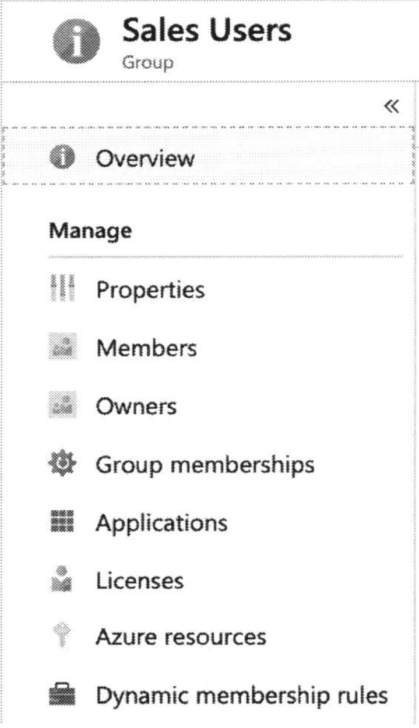

Figure 2.11 – Group settings

9. Select **Dynamic membership rules**. Here, you will see the rule syntax that we defined in the PowerShell command:

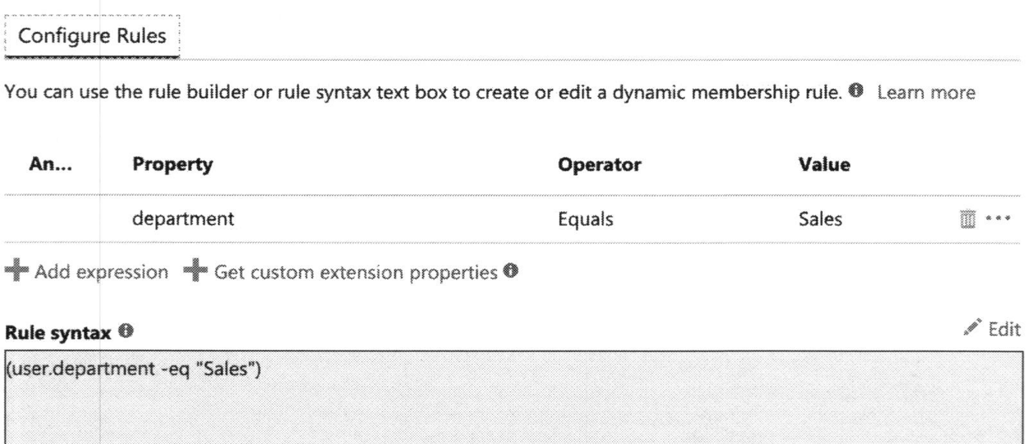

Figure 2.12 – Dynamic membership rules

The `New-AzureADMSGroup` command not only allows us to create Security Groups, but Office 365 Groups as well.

> **Important note**
>
> When creating an Office 365 Group, a welcome email is sent to all the members of the group. It is possible to change this behavior, if desired, by using the Exchange Online PowerShell with the `Set-UnifiedGroup` command and the `-UnifiedGroupWelcomeMessage` switch set to enabled.

Links to all the relevant PowerShell commands related to Azure AD groups can be found in the *References* section at the end of this chapter.

Using group-based licensing in Azure AD

It is also possible to use Azure AD groups to assign licenses to users within Microsoft 365. You can configure this from the Azure AD portal by navigating to **Azure Active Directory** and then selecting **Licenses** followed by **All products**:

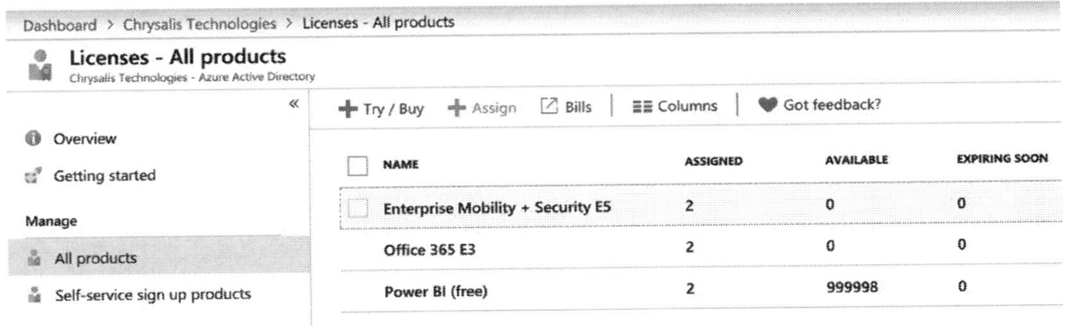

Figure 2.13 – Licenses – All products

Let's say we wish to assign an **Office 365 E3** license to everyone in the Marketing Users group we created earlier in this chapter. To do this, we need to follow these steps:

1. Click the **Office 365 E3** license selection.
2. Select **Licensed groups** and click **Assign**.

3. Click on **Users and groups**, search for **Marketing Users**, select the group, and click on **Select**:

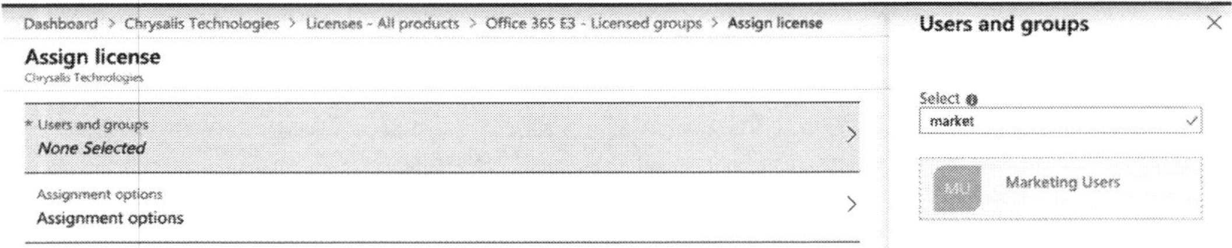

Figure 2.14 – Assign license

4. Now, click **Assignment options**. When assigning a license, we may not be ready to deploy and support all the features of the E3 license to users just yet, so we can turn off what we don't need to give them, as shown in the following screenshot:

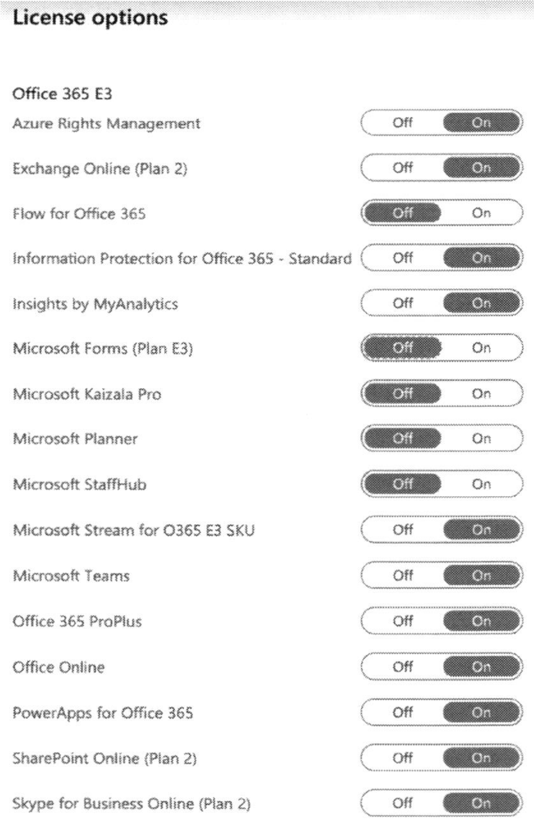

Figure 2.15 – License options

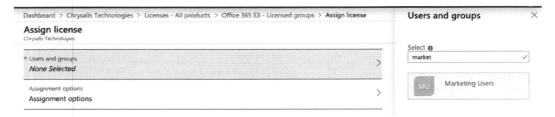

5. Once you are happy with your selections, click **OK** and then **Assign**. This will automatically assign all the members of the Marketing Users group an E3 license with only the features you wish to release at this time. The assignment option can be modified at any time when you are ready to add or remove more features.

> **Important note**
> Know your PowerShell. While a great deal of administration of Azure AD groups can be carried out in the Azure portal, you can expect PowerShell questions in the exam.

So, here, you can see how these features can enable you, as an administrator, to empower your users with some easy administration. Next, we will look at another feature of Azure AD Premium that promotes user convenience – Azure AD self-service password reset.

Implementing Azure AD self-service password reset (SSPR)

One of the common challenges faced by IT administrators is responding to user requests to reset forgotten passwords. This issue is addressed in Azure AD by **self-service password reset** (**SSPR**).

SSPR allows Azure AD users to reset their own passwords without the need to contact their IT department. In order to use this feature, users must complete a registration process, during which they will need to choose one or more authentication methods that have been set up by administrators in Azure AD.

When planning for SSPR, you need to consider the different types of user identities within your Microsoft 365 tenant and how SSPR will behave when users wish to reset their own passwords. These are as follows:

- In-cloud only users
- Hybrid identity users

Both user types can register for and use SSPR, but the experience and license requirements will differ. In-cloud user passwords are stored within Azure AD, whereas hybrid identity users will need to be enabled for **password writeback**, which is a feature of **Azure AD Premium P1 licensing**. With password writeback, users will use SSPR to reset their password, where it is then written back to on-premises Active Directory.

Setting up SSPR

So, how do we set this up? The first step, as an administrator, is to enable the feature in Azure AD and to set up the available user authentication methods. To do this, follow these steps:

1. From the Azure portal, select **Azure Active Directory**, then **Users**, and finally **Password reset**.
2. Here, we have the option to activate SSPR for selected users or groups, or for all users within the tenant:

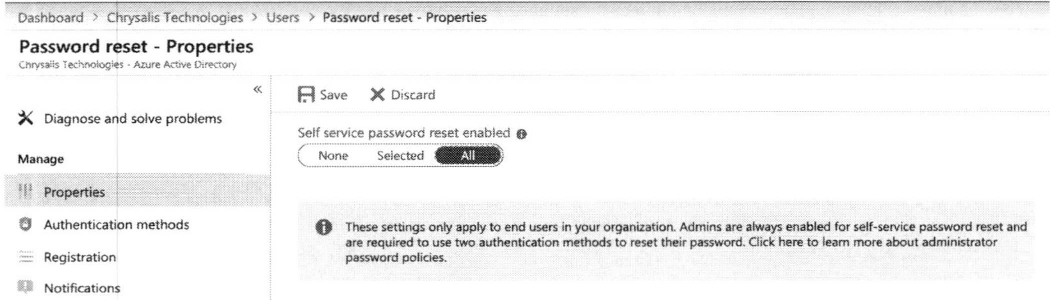

Figure 2.16 – Password reset-Properties

3. Next, we set up the **Authentication methods**. I recommend requiring two methods to perform the password reset. There are six methods available in total, as shown in the following screenshot:

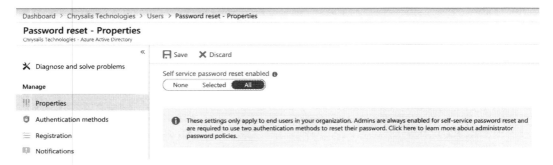

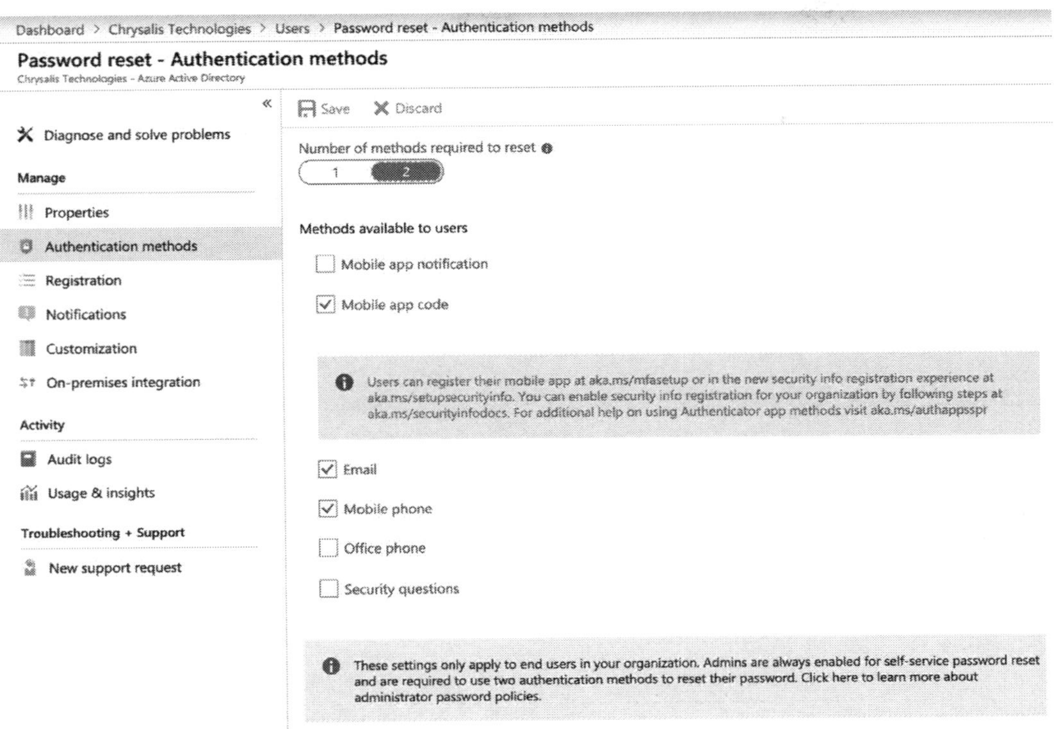

Figure 2.17 – Password reset-Authentication methods

4. Next, we can configure the user **Registration** options. This setting will determine whether users must register for SSPR the next time they sign in, as well as the number of days before the user must reconfirm their authentication information:

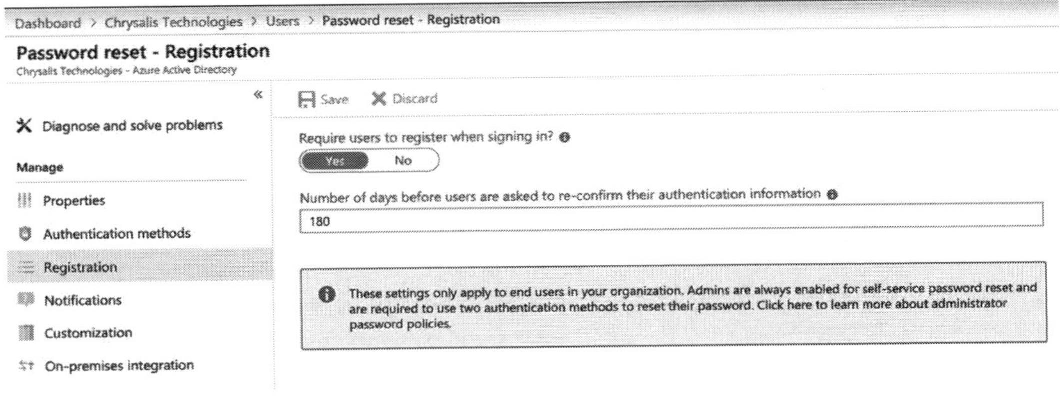

Figure 2.18 – Password reset-Registration

5. It is also possible to set notifications to alert users when their password is reset, and also alert admins when another admin resets their password:

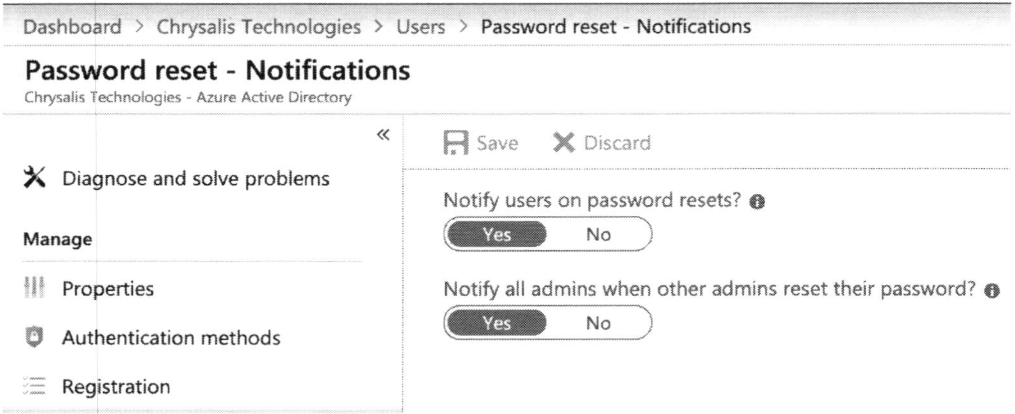

Figure 2.19 – Password reset-Notifications

6. There is also the option to enable a custom helpdesk link or email address for users who may be struggling with this feature:

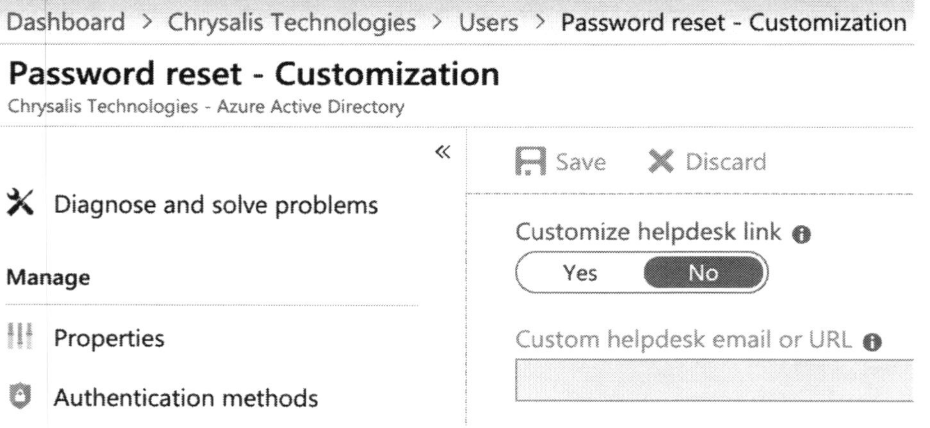

Figure 2.20 – Password reset-Customization

7. Finally, configure the on-premises integration. If the password writeback feature is not enabled in your Azure AD Connect configuration, you will need to rerun the AADC setup wizard with a custom installation and ensure that the setting is selected:

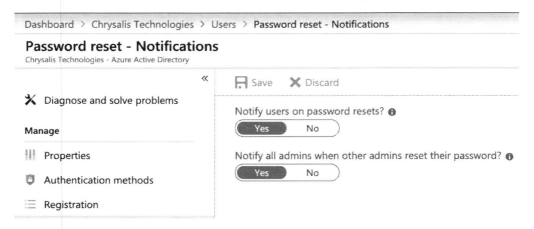

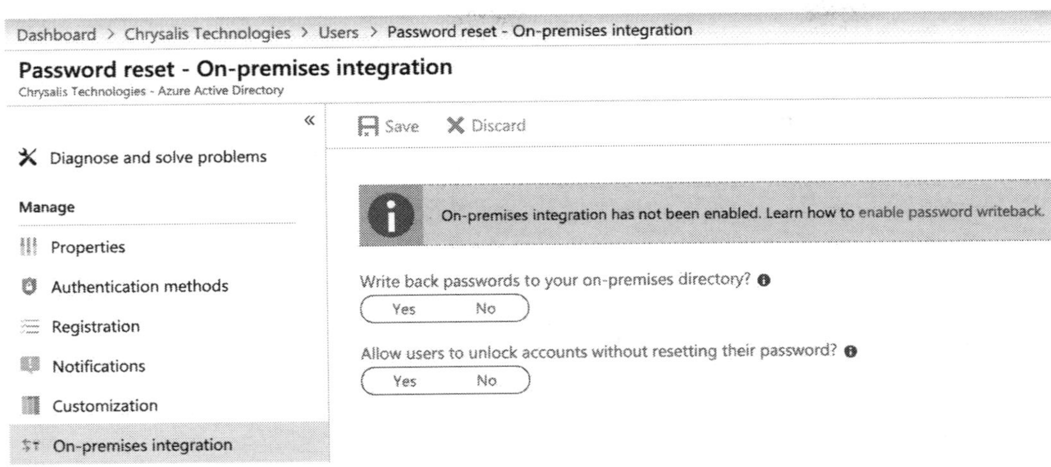

Figure 2.21 – Password reset-On-premises integration

8. The **Password writeback** option can be enabled from the **Optional features** section of the AADC setup wizard:

Optional features

Select enhanced functionality if required by your organization.

- [ ] Exchange hybrid deployment
- [ ] Exchange Mail Public Folders
- [ ] Azure AD app and attribute filtering
- [ ] Password hash synchronization
- [x] Password writeback
- [ ] Group writeback
- [ ] Device writeback
- [ ] Directory extension attribute sync

Learn more about optional features.

Figure 2.22 – Optional features

Now that we have finished setting up SSPR, let's take a look at how users can register for the feature.

Registering for SSPR

Users can complete the registration process for SSPR by accessing the following URL: `https://aka.ms/ssprsetup/`

The user will be prompted to provide their user ID and will be taken to the following page. Before continuing, they will be prompted to re-enter their current password:

confirm your current password
In order to keep your security information private, we need you to re-enter your current password on the next page.

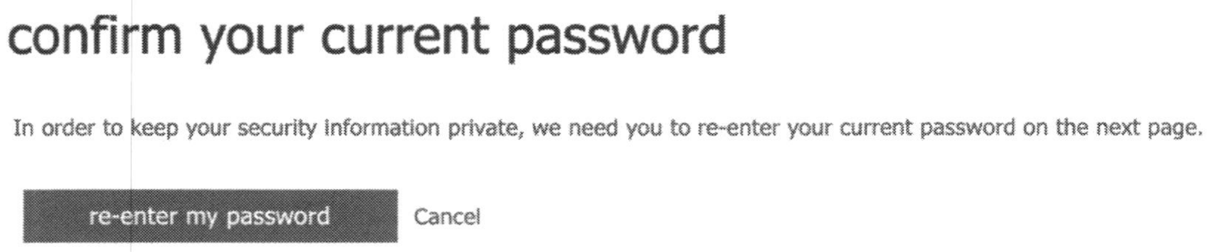

re-enter my password
Cancel

Figure 2.23 – Confirm your current password

Next, they will be prompted to enter authentication responses based on how their Microsoft 365 administrator has set up SSPR. In the following example, the user must register an authentication phone number, along with an authentication email address:

don't lose access to your account!
To make sure you can reset your password, we need to collect some info so we can verify who you are. We won't use this to spam you - just to keep your account more secure. You'll need to set up at least 2 of the options below.
Authentication Phone is not configured. Set it up now
Authentication Email is not configured. Set it up now
finish
cancel

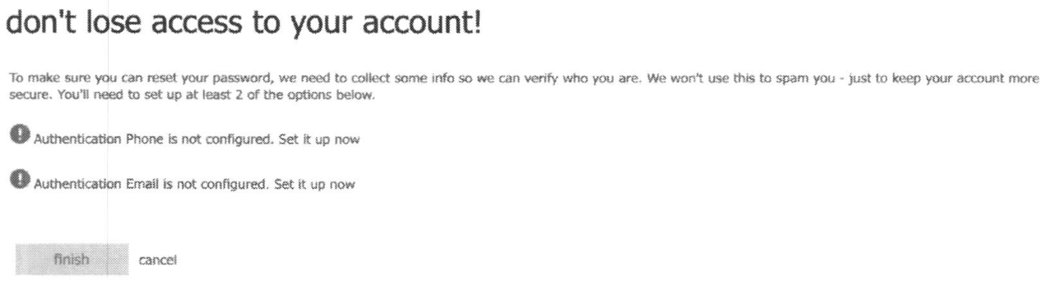

Figure 2.24 – Don't lose access to your account!

Finally, the user will click **finish** and the registration process will be complete.

Using SSPR to reset passwords

Now that the user has registered for SSPR, it is ready to be used when needed. If they need to reset their password, they can do so by going to `https://aka.ms/sspr/` and completing the following steps:

1. Enter your **User ID** and complete the CAPTCHA, and then click **Next**:

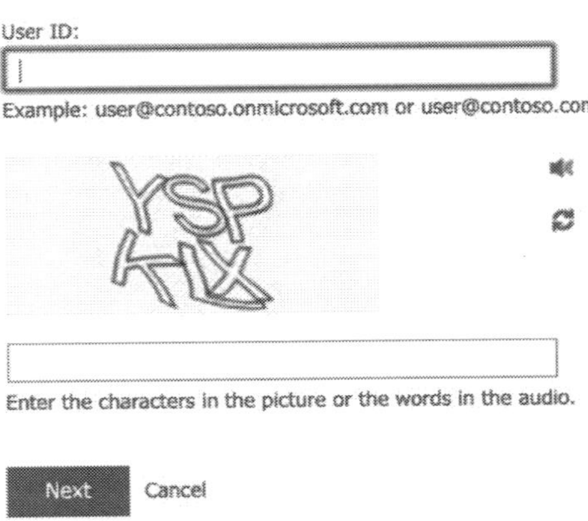

Figure 2.25 – Get back into your account

2. Based on the number of authentication challenges defined in the registration process, the user now needs to enter their authentication email and mobile phone details in turn:

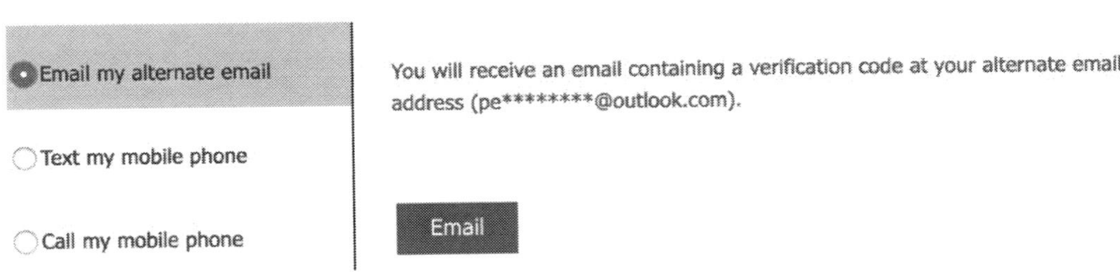

Figure 2.26 – Get back into your account

3. Once they have completed the two-step authentication, they are now able to enter a new password for their account:

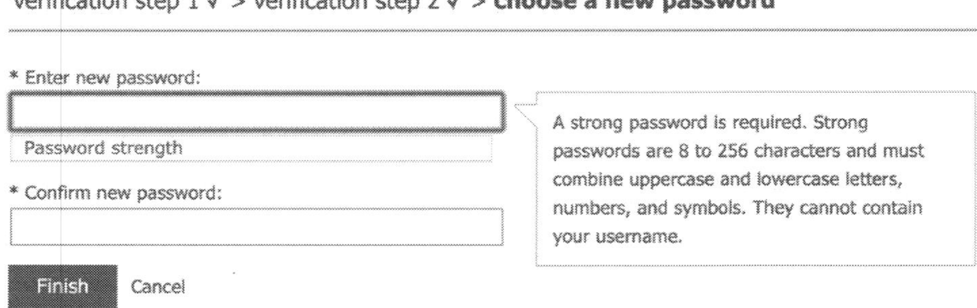

Figure 2.27 – Get back into your account

4. Once completed, they will see the following message:

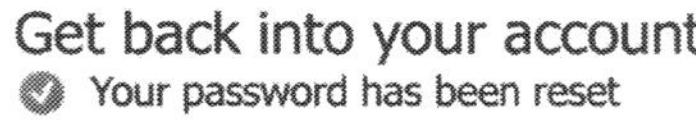

Figure 2.28 – Password reset message

5. The registration process is now complete.

Combined registration for SSPR and MFA

If you are planning to deploy both SSPR and MFA within your Microsoft 365 environment, it is worth considering configuring **User feature previews**, which can be found in the Azure portal under **Azure Active Directory** | **Users** | **User settings**:

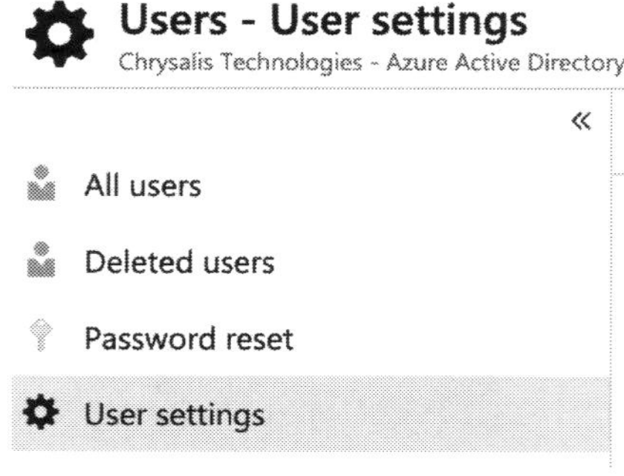

Figure 2.29 – User settings

Once you click on **User settings**, you will see the option for **User feature previews**:

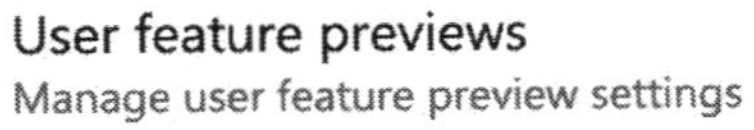

User feature previews
Manage user feature preview settings

Figure 2.30 – Manage user feature preview settings

When this feature is enabled, there is a single registration process for both SSPR and MFA for all users. This provides ease of administration and helps minimize user confusion. However, it is important to point out that, at the time of writing this book, the feature is still in preview.

> **Important note**
>
> When planning your SSPR rollout, ensure that you test it with a pilot group first. You can do this by activating SSPR for specific users, or preferably groups. Test thoroughly and diligently, and when you are ready to deploy SSPR to all your users, ensure that you communicate effectively with your users and inform them that the feature will soon be available to them.

Implementing and managing Multi-Factor Authentication (MFA)

In the modern workplace, users are increasingly accessing their data from almost anywhere in the world and from multiple devices. This increases the burden on Microsoft 365 administrators who need to support this modern and more agile way of working, while also ensuring that users, resources, and data within Microsoft 365 are secure and protected. By default, Microsoft 365 user accounts authenticate to Azure AD with only a user ID and password. In the modern security landscape, this simply does not provide enough protection from threats such as phishing attacks.

As we briefly highlighted in *Chapter 1*, *Planning for Hybrid Identity*, **Multi-Factor Authentication** (**MFA**) within Microsoft 365 can help protect your organization by providing two-step verification to Microsoft services via approved authentication methods. As a quick reminder, these authentication methods can be based upon the following aspects:

- Something you know, such as your password
- Something you own, such as your mobile phone or an Oauth token
- Something you are, such as biometric identification (fingerprint or facial recognition)

So, as an example of how this may work, when a user logs on with their user ID and password, before they can gain access to Microsoft 365, they may also need to enter a six-digit code that has been sent to their smart phone by text message or, alternatively, a code that has been provided to them from the Microsoft Authenticator app. If all the required authentication challenges are met, then the user is granted access.

Enabling MFA

MFA can be enabled from the Microsoft 365 admin center as follows:

1. Open **Services & add-ins** from the **Settings** menu:

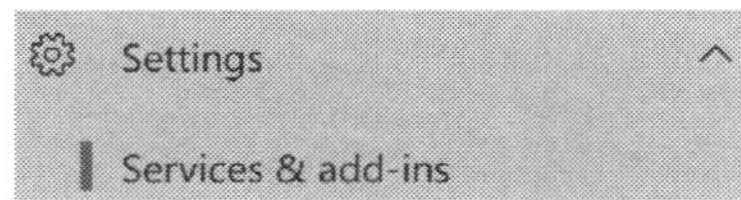

Figure 2.31 – Services & add-ins

2. Select **Azure multi-factor authentication**:

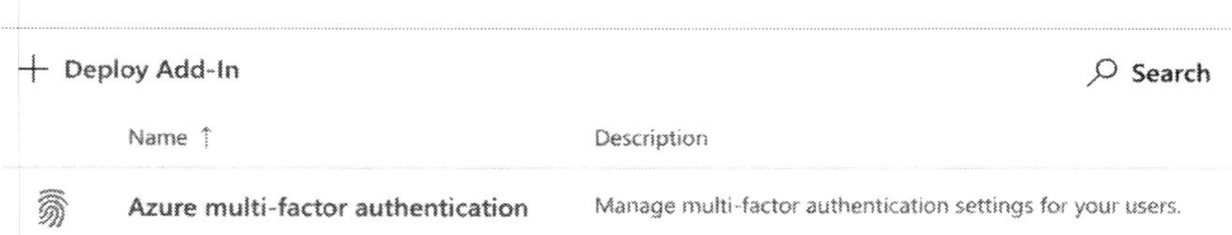

Figure 2.32 – Azure multi-factor authentication

3. Now, select **Manage multi-factor authentication**:

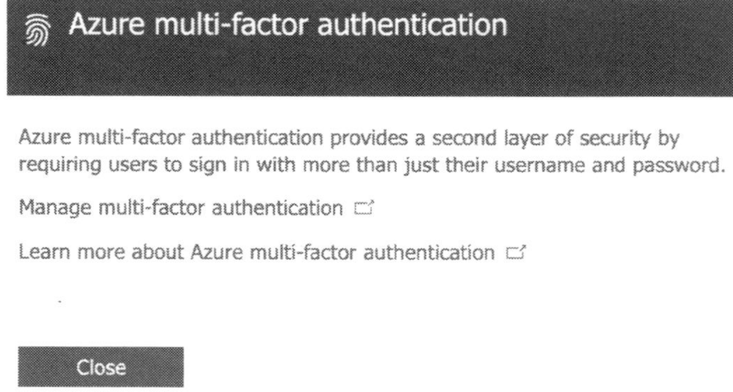

Figure 2.33 – Azure multi-factor authentication

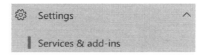

4. On the **multi-factor authentication** page, select the users you wish to use MFA and click **Enable**:

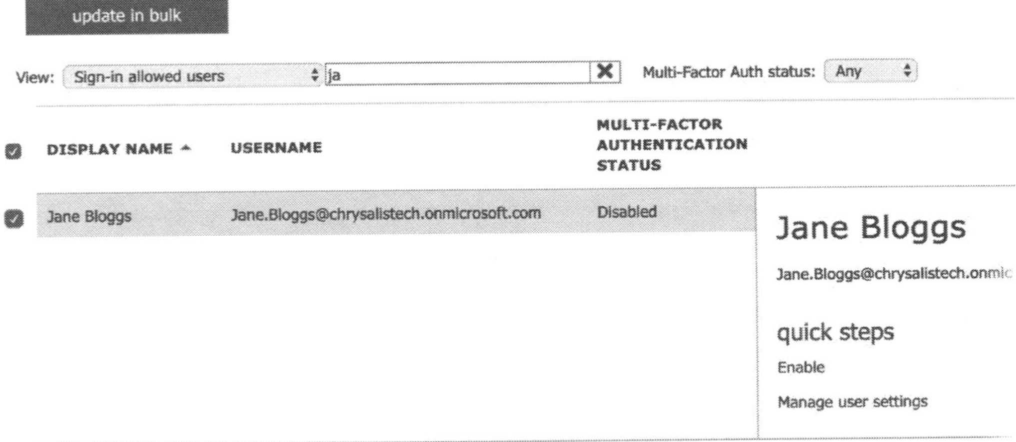

Figure 2.34 – Managing multi-factor authentication

You can also choose the **update in bulk** option if you wish to enable MFA for several users. You can download a sample CSV file from here, which you can then upload to enable multiple users.

5. You can also enable MFA for your users via PowerShell. The following example shows the process to enable a single user via PowerShell.

   First, connect to `MsolService` via PowerShell:

```
$UserCredential = Get-Credential
Import-Module MSOnline
Connect-MsolService -Credential $UserCredential
```

   Next, create a variable, as follows:

```
$mfa = New-Object -TypeName Microsoft.Online.
Administration.StrongAuthenticationRequirement
$mfa.RelyingParty = "*"
```

   Choose between Enabled or Enforced for your desired MFA state, as follows:

```
$mfa.State = "Enabled"
```

Then, to enable MFA for a single user, enter the following command:

```
Set-MsolUser -UserPrincipalName <UserPrincipalName>
-StrongAuthenticationRequirements $mfa
```

If you wish to enable MFA for all your users via PowerShell, you can use the following command:

```
Get-MsolUser -All | Foreach{ Set-MsolUser
-UserPrincipalName $_.UserPrincipalName
-StrongAuthenticationRequirements $mfa}
```

Service settings

Administrators can also configure some additional service settings, which include the following:

- Allow/disallow users to create App passwords
- Set a list of trusted IP addresses or IP ranges that may skip the MFA process
- Choose the available verification options, which include the following:

  a. Call to phone

  b. Text message to phone

  c. Notification through mobile app

  d. Verification code from mobile app

  e. OAuth hardware token

Next, let's look at secondary authentication methods.

Configuring the secondary authentication method

Once a user has been enabled for MFA, they will be prompted to configure their secondary authentication method the next time they log in with their Microsoft 365 user ID and password.

This is what the user will see when they log in with their credentials once MFA is enabled:

1. More information is required from the user:

jane.bloggs@chrysalistech.onmicrosoft.com

More information required

Your organization needs more information to keep your account secure

Use a different account

Learn more

Next

Figure 2.35 – More information required

2. The next stage of the process enables the user to select from the available methods that have been defined:

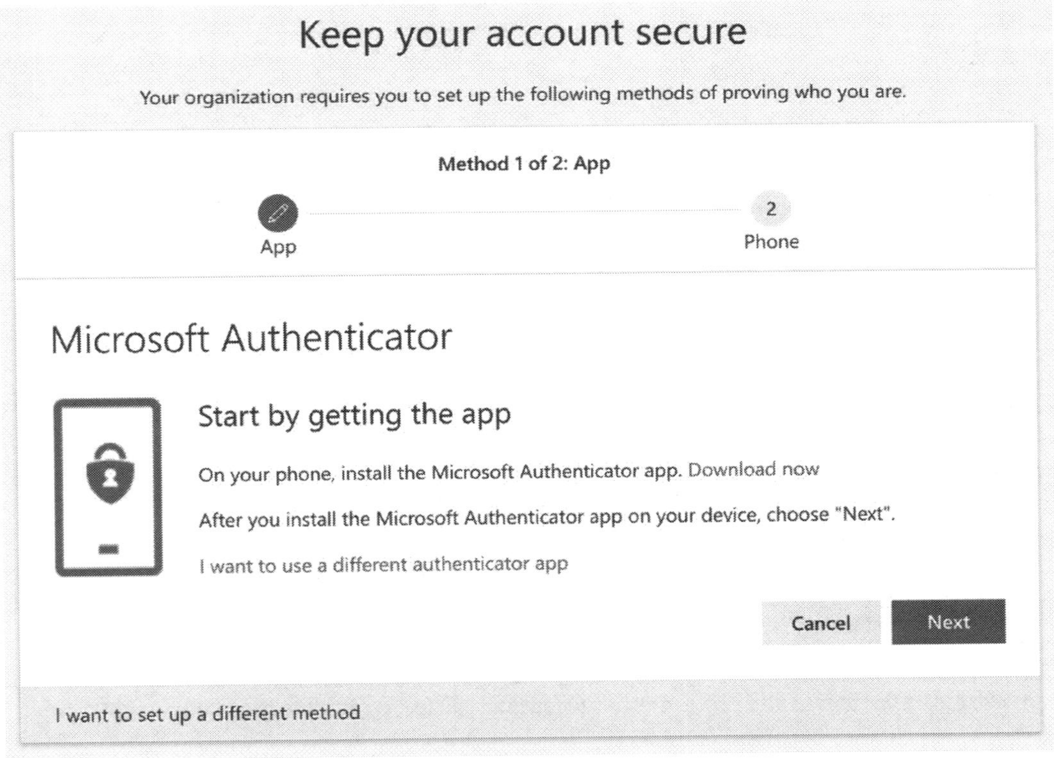

Keep your account secure
Your organization requires you to set up the following methods of proving who you are.
Method 1 of 2: App
App
2
Phone
Microsoft Authenticator
Start by getting the app
On your phone, install the Microsoft Authenticator app. Download now
After you install the Microsoft Authenticator app on your device, choose "Next".
I want to use a different authenticator app
Cancel
Next
I want to set up a different method

Figure 2.36 – Keep your account secure

3. The user may follow this process through until completion. When finished, they should see the following:

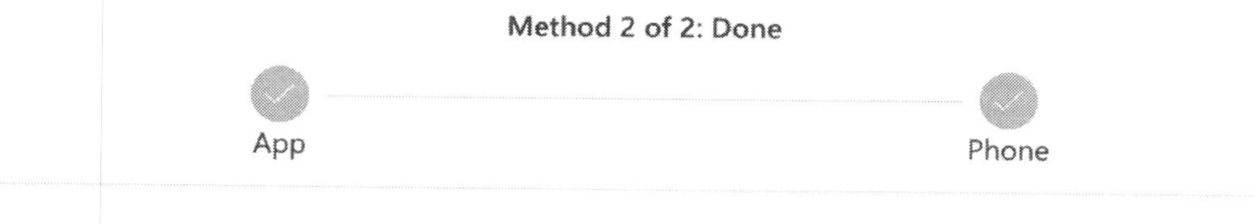

Success!

Great job! You have successfully set up your security info. Choose "Done" to continue signing in.

Default sign-in method: Microsoft Authenticator - notification

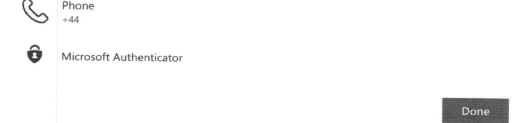

Figure 2.37 – Success!

MFA is now set up for their account, and they will be prompted for it when logging into apps on their Windows, Mac, and mobile devices.

> **Important note**
>
> If you have Azure AD Premium P1, you can configure MFA for Microsoft 365 via Conditional Access policies. This will be covered in the next chapter. In addition, with Azure AD Premium P2, you can configure Azure AD Identity Protection to trigger MFA verification based on user sign-in risk detections.

Please remember that if enabling both SSPR and MFA in your Microsoft 365 environment, you are also able to use the combined registration portal, which we described earlier in this chapter.

Managing Azure AD access reviews

Azure AD access reviews are a feature of Azure AD Premium P2. It enables Microsoft 365 administrators to ensure that users within the tenant have the appropriate level of access. Users are able to participate in this process themselves, or alternatively, their supervisor can review and access the users' current level of access. Once a review is completed, changes can be made and access can be revoked from users, as deemed appropriate.

Performing an access review

To create and execute an access review, you need to follow these steps:

1. Log in to the Azure portal as either a Global Administrator or a User Administrator.
2. Open the **Identity Governance** page and click **Access reviews**.
3. Choose the option to create a **New access review**:

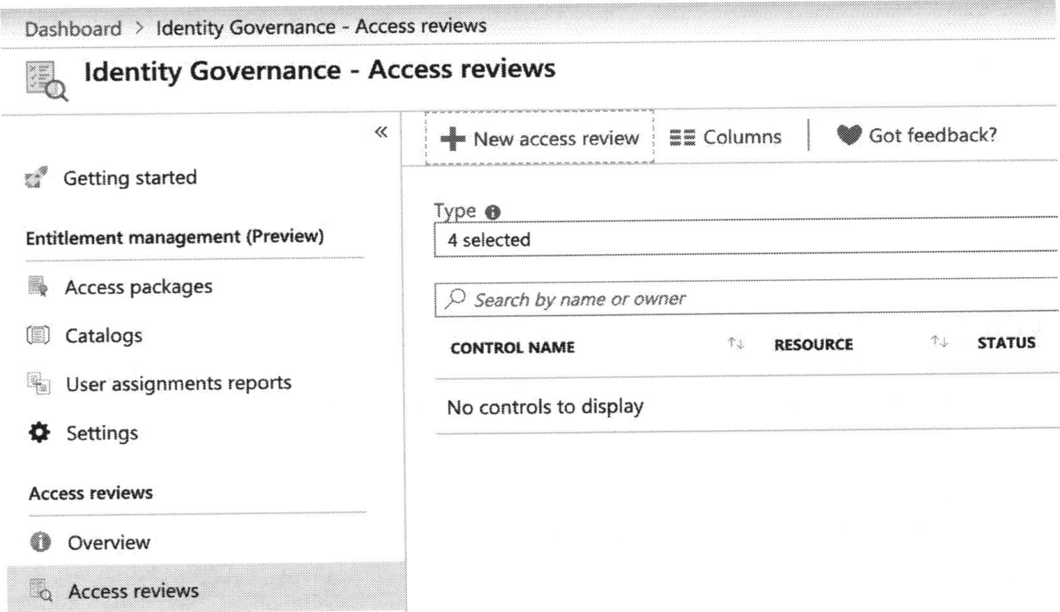

Figure 2.38 – Access reviews

4. In this example, we will create an access review that has been configured to run only once, and which targets the members of the **Sales Users** group (alternatively, you could configure a recurring schedule for the review):

> **Important note**
> If you assign more than one group, an additional and separate access review will be created for each group that you add.

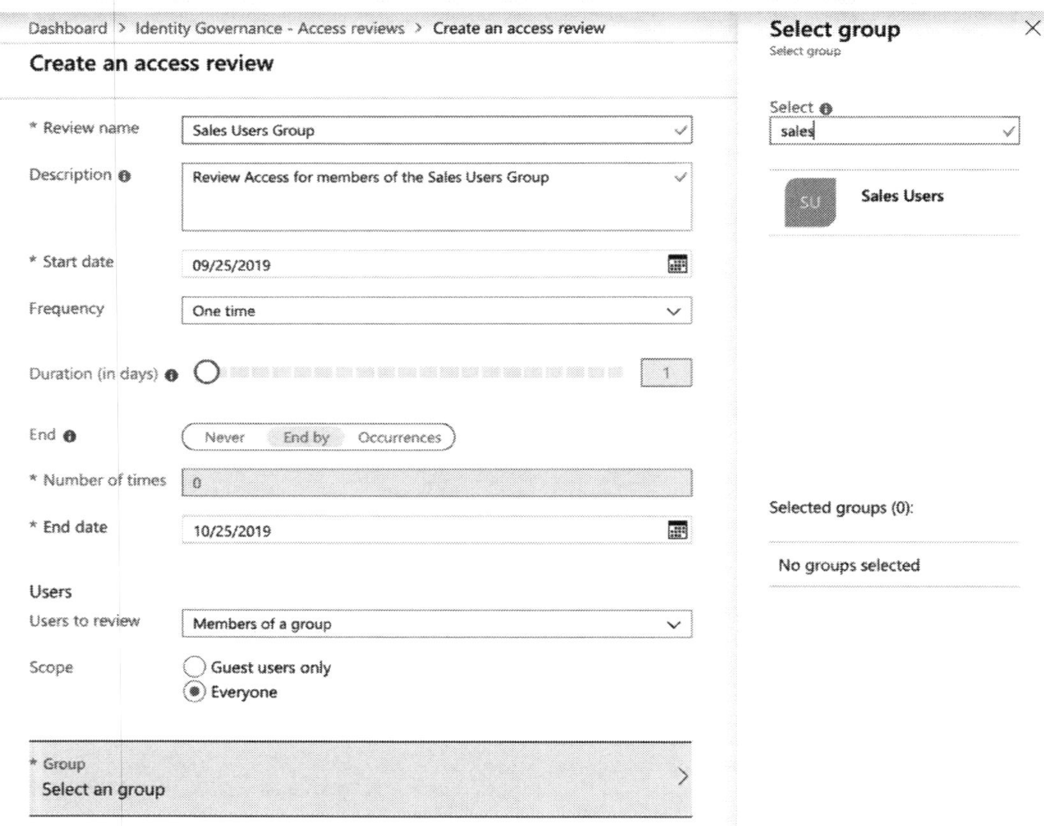

Figure 2.39 – Create an access review

5. Under **Reviewers**, you have the following choices:

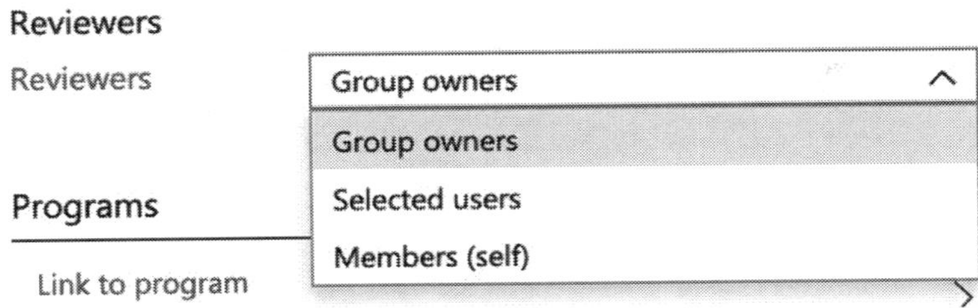

Figure 2.40 – Reviewer options

6. Once you've selected your reviewers, you can configure any program that you wish to check these users against for access:

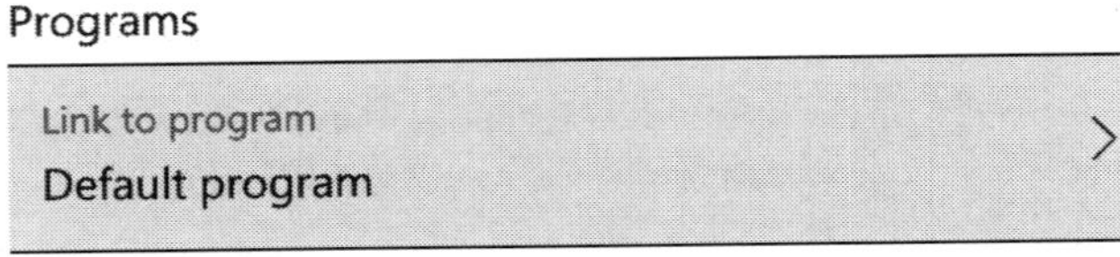

Figure 2.41 – Programs

7. You can also select what actions you wish to take once the review has been completed:

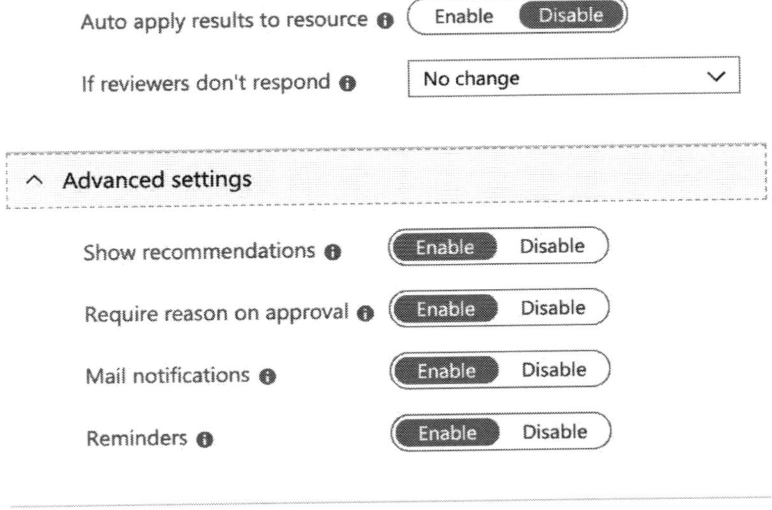

Figure 2.42 – Further settings

8. Once you are happy with your access review settings, click **Start** to trigger it. It will appear in the list shown in the following screenshot:

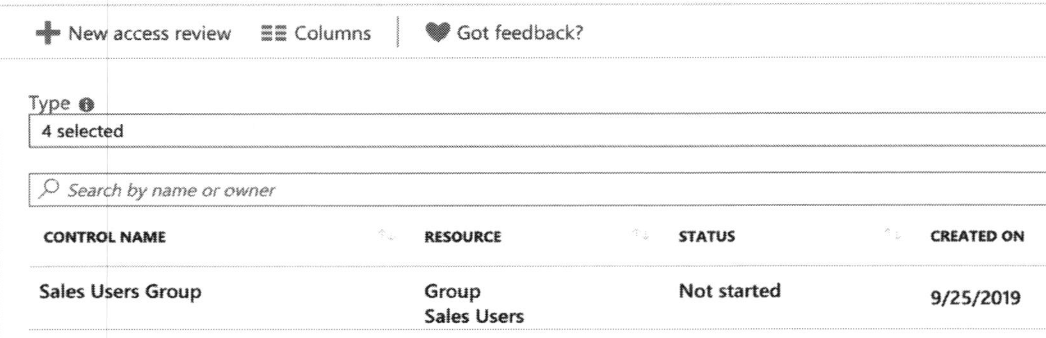

Figure 2.43 – New access review ready to be started

9. Once an access review is completed, the results can be viewed by Global Administrators, User Administrators, Security Administrators, or anyone who has been granted the Security Reader role.
10. An email will be sent to all reviewers after the review is started.

> **Important note**
> It is also possible to create access reviews by using APIs with Microsoft Graph. Please check the references section at the end of this chapter for further information.

Summary

In this chapter, we examined the process of assigning access rights to users and groups by using Azure AD dynamic groups. You will now be able to configure dynamic groups, membership rules, and rules syntax for more advanced rules. We also showed you how SSPR and MFA can provide authentication security within a Microsoft 365 environment, as well as how these services can be enabled independently or via the newer combined registration portal.

Finally, we demonstrated how group or user access reviews can be carried out to ensure that users' access can be regularly and diligently assessed and adjusted as deemed appropriate.

In the next chapter, we will focus on Azure AD Conditional Access policies and how they can be used in conjunction with features such as MFA to promote compliance.

Questions

1. True or False: Group-based licensing is a feature that can be configured with Azure AD dynamic groups.

   a. True

   b. False

2. Which of the following is not a self-service password reset authentication method?

   a. Security questions

   b. OAuth token

   c. Mobile app code

   d. Mobile app notification

3. Which of the following roles is needed to set up Azure AD access reviews?

   a. Service Administrator

   b. SharePoint Administrator

   c. Global Administrator

   d. Billing Administrator

4. With Azure AD dynamic groups, how many expressions can be set in a dynamic query before you will need to use the textbox?

   a. Three

   b. Ten

   c. Five

   d. Fifteen

5. True or False: Access reviews can be performed by users.

   a. True

   b. False

6. Which of the following PowerShell commands could you use to create an Azure AD Dynamic Security group?

    a. `New-AzureADMSGroup`

    b. `New-AzureADGroup`

    c. `New-UnifiedGroup`

    d. `Set-UnifiedGroup`

7. True or False: Azure AD access reviews can be set to run according to a schedule.

    a. True

    b. False

8. Once a user has had MFA enabled for their Microsoft 365 account, when will they be forced to set up their authentication methods?

    a. Immediately

    b. The next time they log in with their Microsoft 365 account

    c. After 14 days

    d. At a time of their choosing

9. Which of the following is a true statement in relation to self-service password reset?

    a. SSPR is enabled automatically for all users

    b. SSPR with password writeback is a feature of Azure AD Premium P1

    c. SSPR with password writeback will apply to In-cloud only users

    d. SSPR with password writeback is a feature of Azure AD Premium P2

10. True or False: Azure AD Dynamic group membership can be assigned to users based on the attributes of their Microsoft 365 account, such as the department field.

    a. True

    b. False

References

Please refer to the following links for more information regarding what was covered in this chapter:

- Creating a basic group and adding members via Azure Active Directory: `https://docs.microsoft.com/en-us/azure/active-directory/fundamentals/active-directory-groups-create-azure-portal?context=azure/active-directory/users-groups-roles/context/ugr-context`
- Creating or updating a dynamic group in Azure Active Directory: `https://docs.microsoft.com/en-us/azure/active-directory/users-groups-roles/groups-create-rule`
- Dynamic membership rules for groups in Azure Active Directory: `https://docs.microsoft.com/en-us/azure/active-directory/users-groups-roles/groups-dynamic-membership`
- Azure Active Directory version 2 cmdlets for group management: `https://docs.microsoft.com/en-us/azure/active-directory/users-groups-roles/groups-settings-v2-cmdlets`
- Using the `Set-UnifiedGroup` command in PowerShell: `https://docs.microsoft.com/en-gb/powershell/module/exchange/users-and-groups/Set-UnifiedGroup?view=exchange-ps`
- Planning for **Self-service password reset**: `https://docs.microsoft.com/en-us/azure/active-directory/authentication/howto-sspr-deployment`
- Deploying **Self-service password reset** without requiring user registration: `https://docs.microsoft.com/en-us/azure/active-directory/authentication/howto-sspr-authenticationdata`
- Tutorial for enabling **Self-service password reset**: `https://docs.microsoft.com/en-us/azure/active-directory/authentication/howto-sspr-writeback`
- How to enable **Self-service password reset** from the Windows login screen: `https://docs.microsoft.com/en-us/azure/active-directory/authentication/howto-sspr-windows`
- Combined security information registration overview: `https://docs.microsoft.com/en-us/azure/active-directory/authentication/concept-registration-mfa-sspr-combined`

- Setting up your security information from a sign-in prompt: `https://docs.microsoft.com/en-us/azure/active-directory/user-help/user-help-security-info-overview`
- How **Azure Multi-Factor Authentication** works: `https://docs.microsoft.com/en-us/azure/active-directory/authentication/concept-mfa-howitworks`
- Features and licenses for **Azure Multi-Factor Authentication**: `https://docs.microsoft.com/en-us/azure/active-directory/authentication/concept-mfa-licensing`
- When to use an **Azure Multi-Factor Authentication** provider: `https://docs.microsoft.com/en-us/azure/active-directory/authentication/concept-mfa-authprovider`
- Planning an **Azure Multi-Factor Authentication** deployment: `https://docs.microsoft.com/en-us/azure/active-directory/authentication/multi-factor-authentication-security-best-practices`
- Managing user access with **Azure AD access reviews**: `https://docs.microsoft.com/en-us/azure/active-directory/governance/manage-user-access-with-access-reviews`
- Using **Azure AD access reviews** to manage users excluded from **Conditional Access** policies: `https://docs.microsoft.com/en-us/azure/active-directory/governance/conditional-access-exclusion`
- Creating an **Azure AD access review**: `https://docs.microsoft.com/en-us/azure/active-directory/governance/create-access-review`

3
Implementing Conditional Access Policies

One of the common frustrations of IT administrators is finding a good balance between usability and security. This is especially relevant in a Microsoft 365 environment where your users only access cloud-based resources. It is not possible to wrap a firewall around Office 365 in the traditional sense. Conditional Access is an Azure **Active Directory** (**AD**) Premium feature that helps you address this challenge in a modern way.

In this chapter, we will discuss how you can configure compliance policies for Conditional Access within your Microsoft 365 environment. You will learn how you can allow or block access to the features in your tenant and how device compliance can be enforced with system security settings, such as a minimum password length and data encryption.

We will cover these topics in the following order:

- Explaining Conditional Access
- Enhancing Conditional Access with Intune
- Device-based Conditional Access
- App-based Conditional Access
- Monitoring Conditional Access events

Explaining Conditional Access

Conditional Access is a feature within Azure AD Premium P1 and P2 (and is also now part of Microsoft 365 Business) that is designed to provide a balance between security and productivity in modern workplace environments where there is an increasing demand from employees to work on company documents and data from anywhere and on any device. Conditional Access enables Microsoft 365 administrators to control requests from devices and apps when they attempt to access company resources.

This is achieved with granular access control policies that can be used to define and apply conditions to determine whether access is granted or denied. Some examples of how these conditions can be triggered are the following:

- Location
- Device type
- Device state
- User state
- Application sensitivity

So, how does this work? Well, the most basic description of a Conditional Access policy is *when this happens > then do this*. This is essentially an action and a consequence and is shown in the following table:

Condition statement	Access control result
When this happens	Then do this

This combination of the condition with the access control is what makes up the Conditional Access policy. The access control result is either a step that must be completed by the requesting party in order to gain access, or it can be a restriction that is applied after sign-in that determines what they can or cannot do.

Conditional Access policies can be configured by Microsoft 365 administrators from the Azure portal by going to `https://portal.azure.com`, selecting **Azure Active Directory**, and then navigating to the **Security** section and **Conditional Access**:

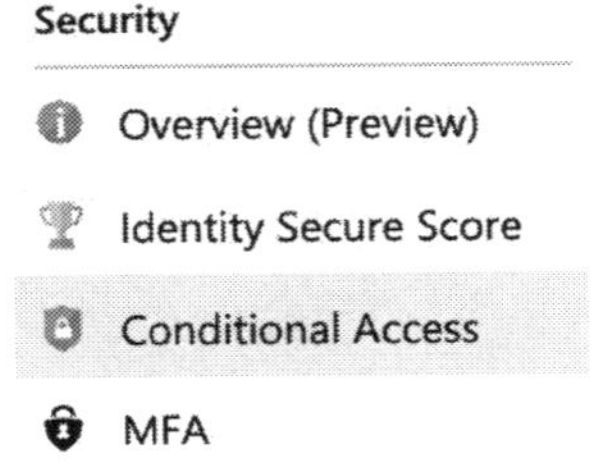

Figure 3.1 – Conditional Access

This takes you to the following page:

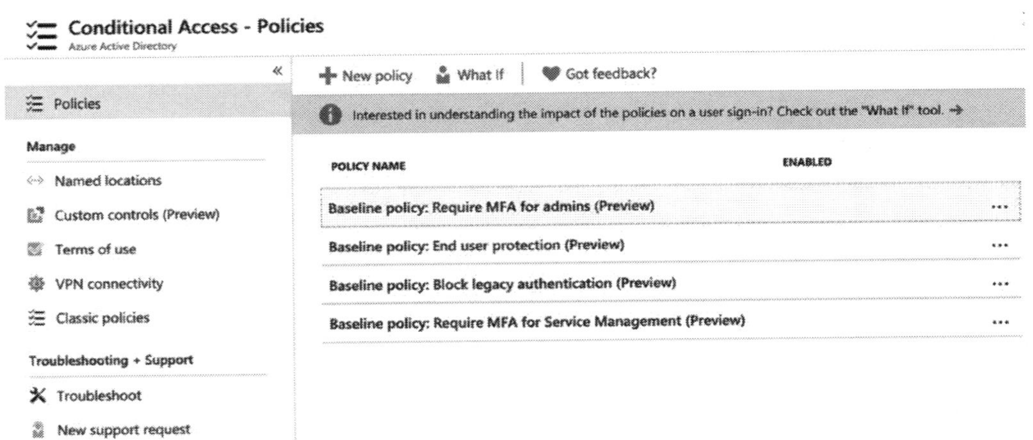

Figure 3.2 – Conditional Access-Policies

As we learned in *Chapter 1*, *Planning for Hybrid Identity*, some legacy baseline policies are still available. However, these policies will be deprecated by Microsoft in the near future and should not be used. The recommended practice is to define your own policies to meet your organizational needs. Let's look at configuring a simple Conditional Access policy and applying it to a user.

Creating a simple Conditional Access policy

In the following example, we will create a Conditional Access policy to trigger the following conditions and results:

Policy Name	`Enforce MFA for James Smith when accessing Exchange Online`
Applied to	Specified users (in this case, `James Smith`)
Cloud Apps or Actions	Exchange Online
Conditions	Location is set to Any Location
Access Control	Require Multi-Factor Authentication (MFA)

To create the policy, we need to go to the Azure portal and select **Conditional Access | Policies | New Policy**:

1. You will see the following screen. Enter a name for your policy. In this example, we will call it `Enforce MFA for James Smith when accessing Exchange Online`:

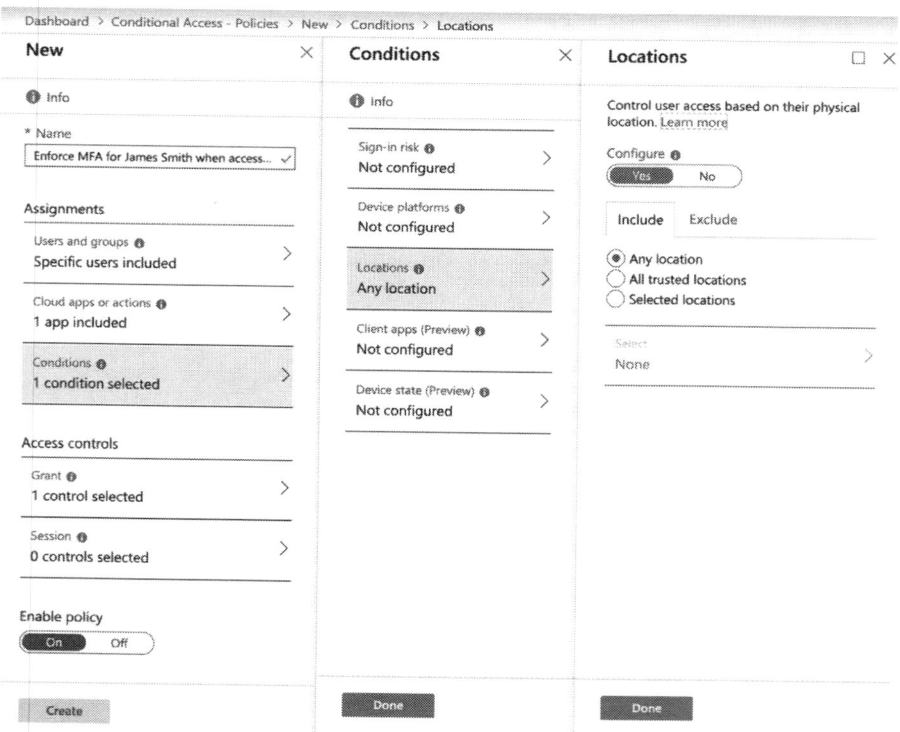

Figure 3.3 – New conditional access policy

2. Under **Users and Groups**, choose **Select users and groups** and we can select our targeted users or groups (in this case, **James Smith**):

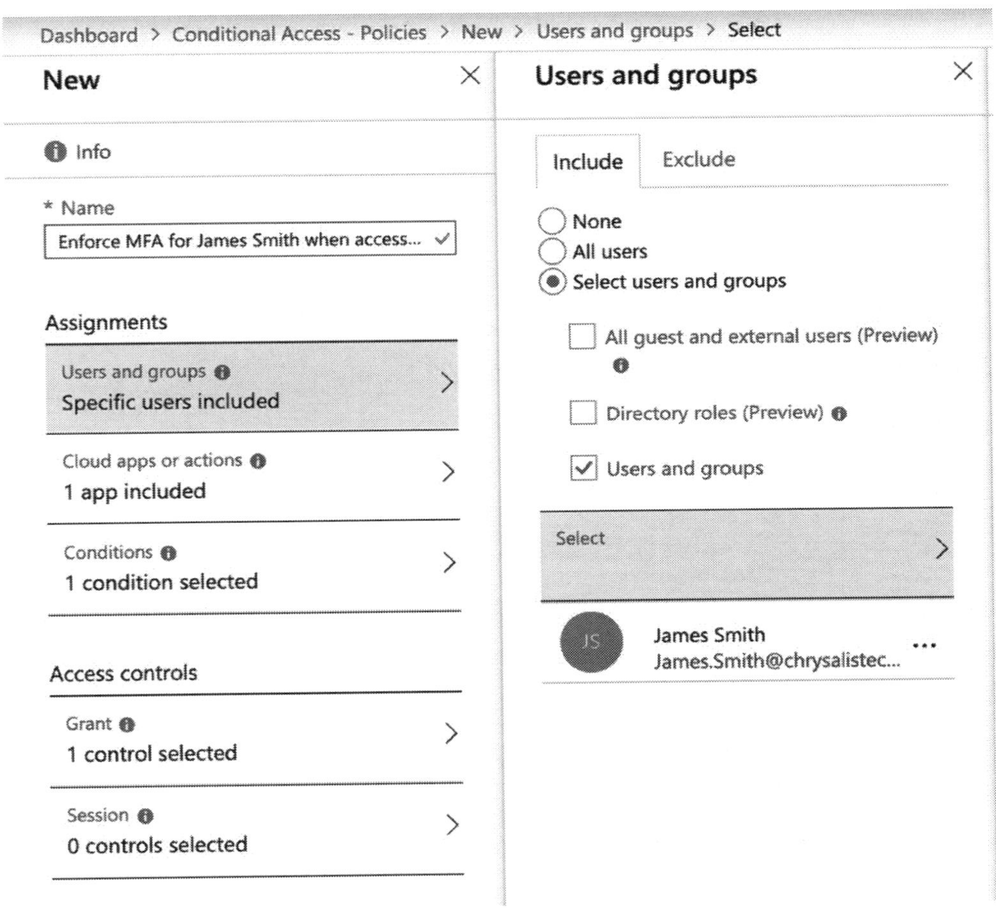

Figure 3.4 – Selecting users and groups

3. Next, under **Access Controls**, select **Grant Access** and choose **Require multi-factor authentication**.

4. Click **Select**, and then set **Enable policy** to **On** and click **Create**:

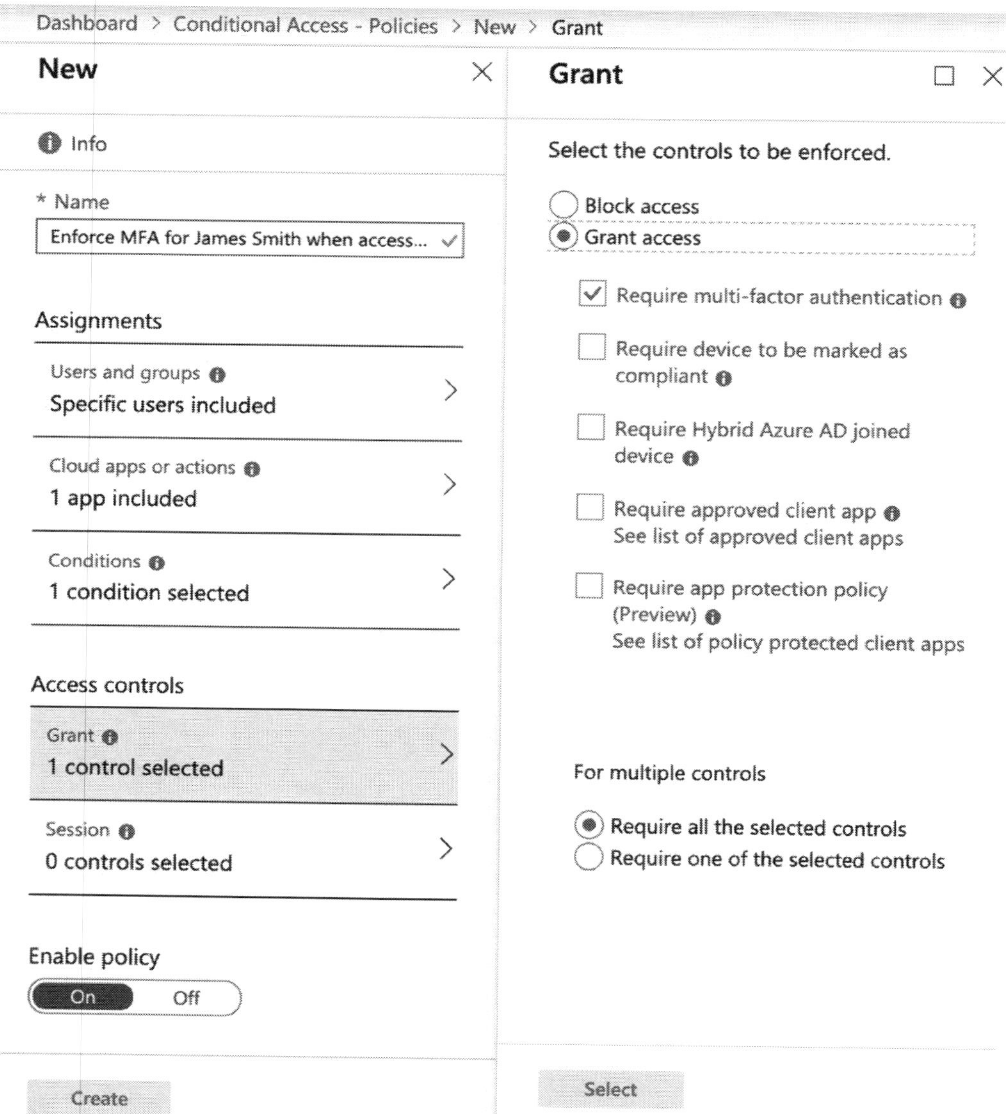

Figure 3.5 – Creating the policy

5. The policy is created, as shown in the following screenshot, and the result is that `James Smith` will be required to complete an MFA authentication whenever he logs in to Exchange Online (regardless of his location):

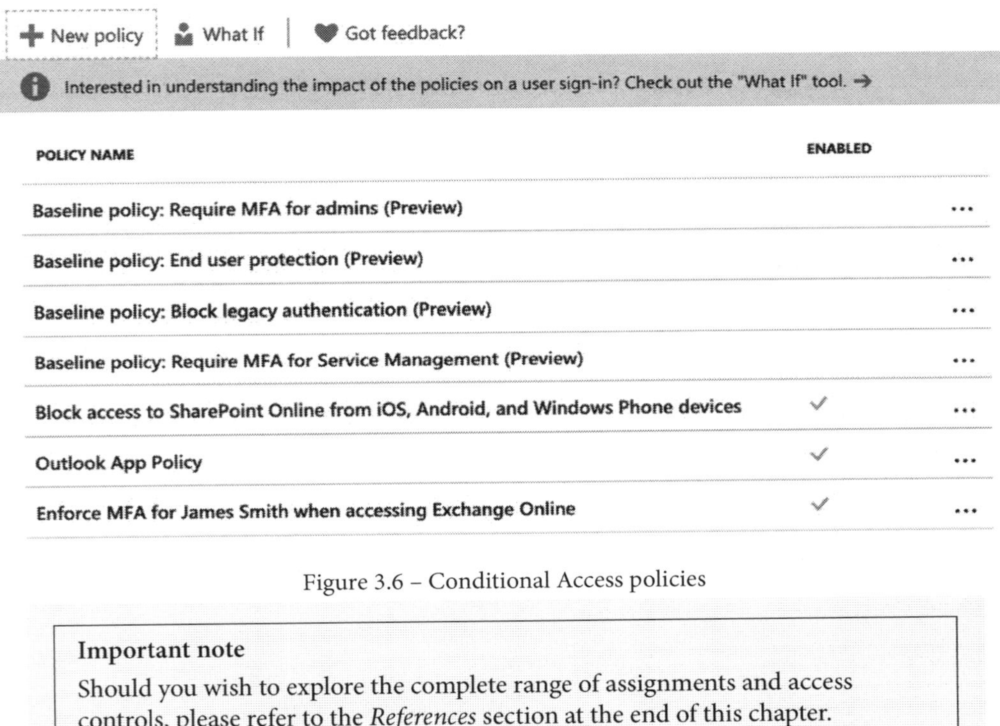

Figure 3.6 – Conditional Access policies

> **Important note**
>
> Should you wish to explore the complete range of assignments and access controls, please refer to the *References* section at the end of this chapter.

So, now you understand the basic principles of Conditional Access in Azure AD. Next, we will examine how Intune can take the capabilities of Conditional Access even further.

Enhancing Conditional Access with Intune

While conditional access is a feature of Azure AD Premium, Microsoft Intune further empowers it by adding mobile device compliance and mobile app management capabilities.

Conditional Access is available from the Intune node of Azure AD, as shown:

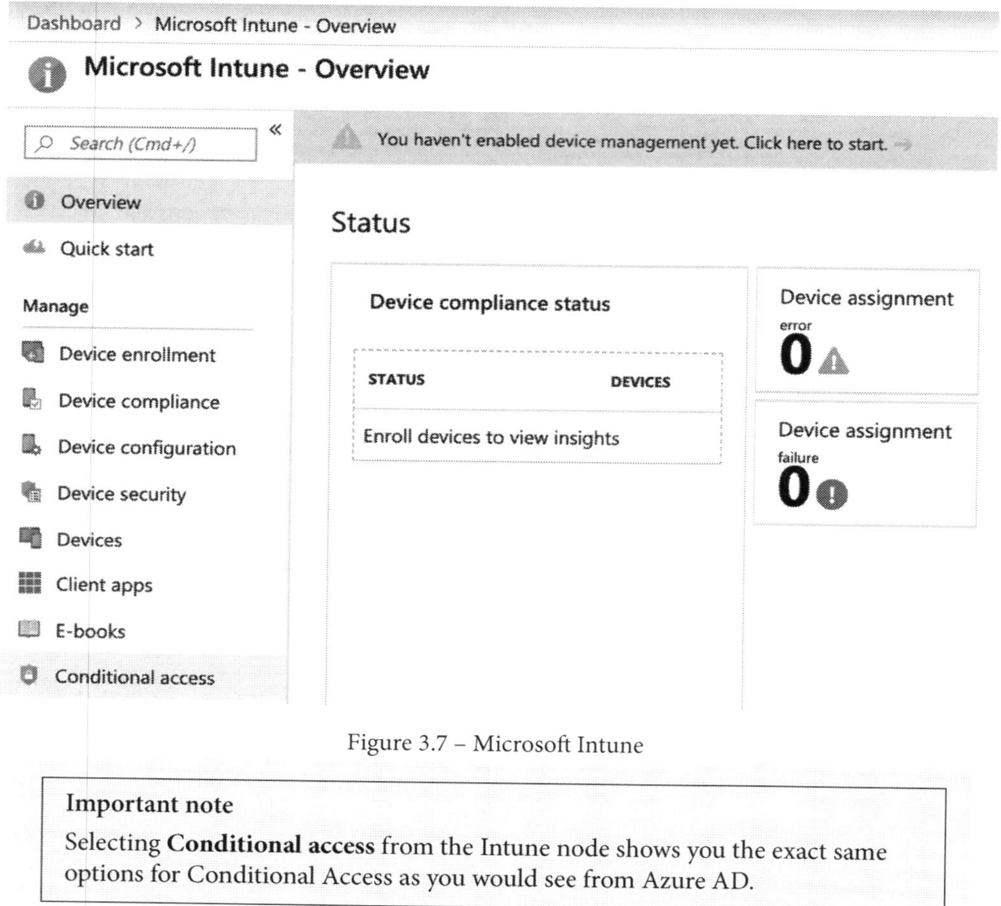

Figure 3.7 – Microsoft Intune

> **Important note**
>
> Selecting **Conditional access** from the Intune node shows you the exact same options for Conditional Access as you would see from Azure AD.

Intune provides two types of Conditional Access—device-based conditional access and app-based conditional access. Let's examine each of these.

Device-based Conditional Access

With Intune, you can ensure that only devices that are managed and compliant can access services provided by Microsoft 365, such as Exchange Online, **Software as a Service (SaaS)** apps, and even on-premises apps. It is also possible to set specific requirements, such as that computers must be hybrid Azure AD-joined or require an approved client app, as well as mobile devices, in order to be enrolled in Intune to access services.

Device policies can be configured to enforce device compliance and give administrators visibility on the compliance status of devices that have been enrolled in Intune. This compliance status is passed to Azure AD, which then triggers a Conditional Access policy when users attempt to access resources. The Conditional Access policy either allows or blocks access to resources based on the compliance status of the requesting device.

In the modern workplace, you will increasingly need to consider and plan for the following device types and Conditional Access scenarios:

- Corporate-owned devices, which can include the following:

  a. On-premises domain-joined Azure AD

  b. Domain-joined Azure AD

  c. Domain-joined Azure AD also registered with System Center Configuration Manager

- **Bring Your Own Device** (**BYOD**) devices, which can include the following:

  Workplace, joined and managed by Intune

Next, let's look at how you can use Conditional Access to create a device-based policy.

Creating a device-based Conditional Access policy

In the following example, we will create a device-based Conditional Access policy to trigger the following conditions and results:

Policy Name	`Block access to SharePoint Online from iOS, Android, and Windows Phone devices`
Applied to	Specified users (in this case, `Jane Bloggs` and `James Smith`)
Cloud Apps or Actions	Office 365 SharePoint Online
Conditions	Include the following device platforms: • Android • iOS • Windows Phone
Client Apps	To include the following: • Browser • Mobile apps and desktop clients
Access Control	`Block Access`

To create the policy, we need to go to the Intune dashboard and select **Conditional Access | Policies | New Policy** and follow the given steps:

1. You will see the following screen. Enter a name for your policy. In this example we will call it `Block access to SharePoint Online from iOS, Android, and Windows Phone devices`:

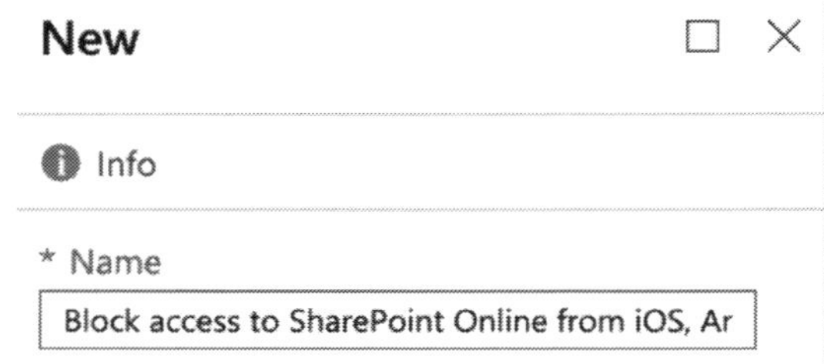

Figure 3.8 – New policy creation

2. Next, we need to target the users and groups we wish to apply the policy to. In this case, we wish to target two specific users—**Jane Bloggs** and **James Smith**. We can achieve this from the **Assignments | Users and groups** section of the new policy wizard, as shown:

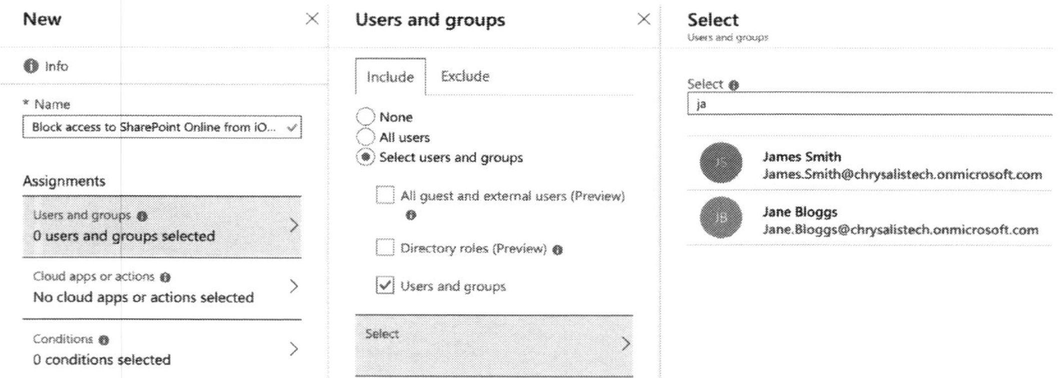

Figure 3.9 – New policy user and group settings

3. Once you are happy with your selections, click **Select**, and then click **Done**.

4. Next, we need to set **Cloud apps or actions** and choose **Office 365 SharePoint Online** as the targeted cloud app:

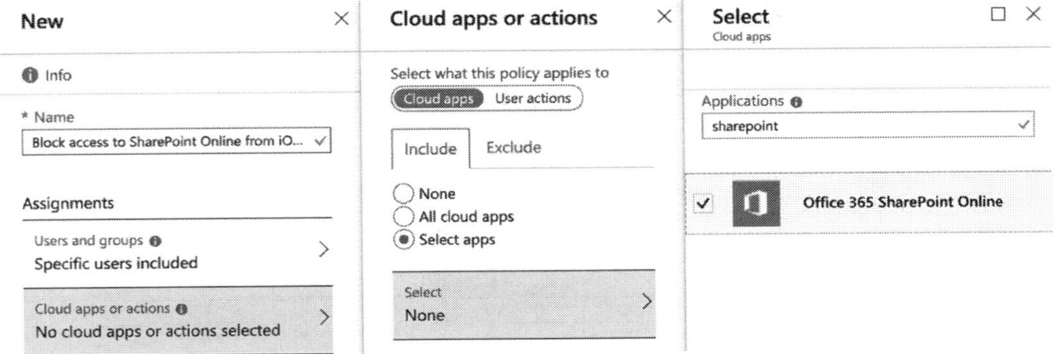

Figure 3.10 – New policy application settings

5. We are not going to select any user actions (at the time of writing, this is a preview feature), so let's go ahead and click on **Select**, and then **Done** once again.
6. Now, we need to choose the conditions that will trigger our policy. Under **Conditions**, we first need to select **Device Platforms**:

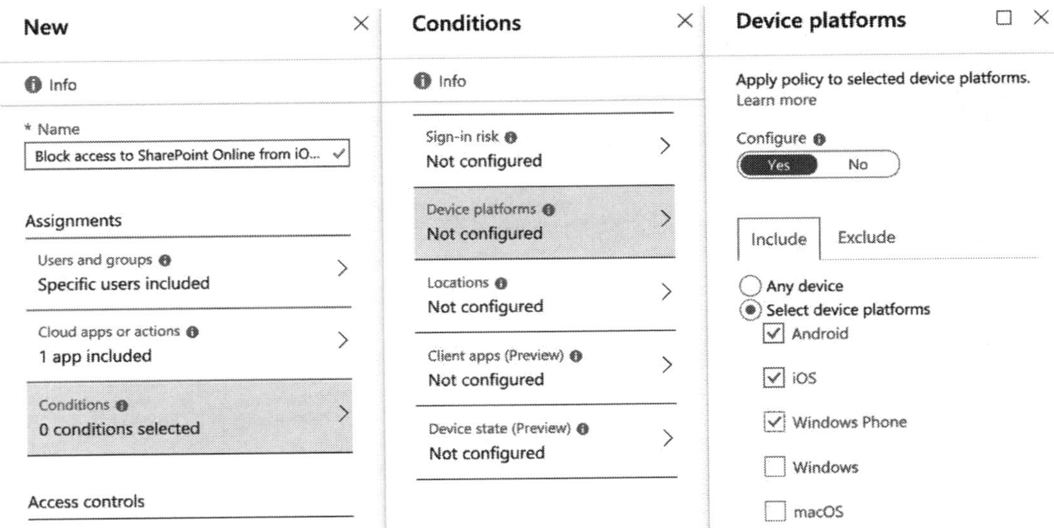

Figure 3.11 – New policy device platforms

7. We need to select **Configure**, then **Select device platforms**, and then choose **Android**, **iOS**, and **Windows Phone**. Click on **Done**, and then **Done** again.

8. Next, under **Access Controls**, we need to select **Grant**. In this example, we are going to choose **Block access**:

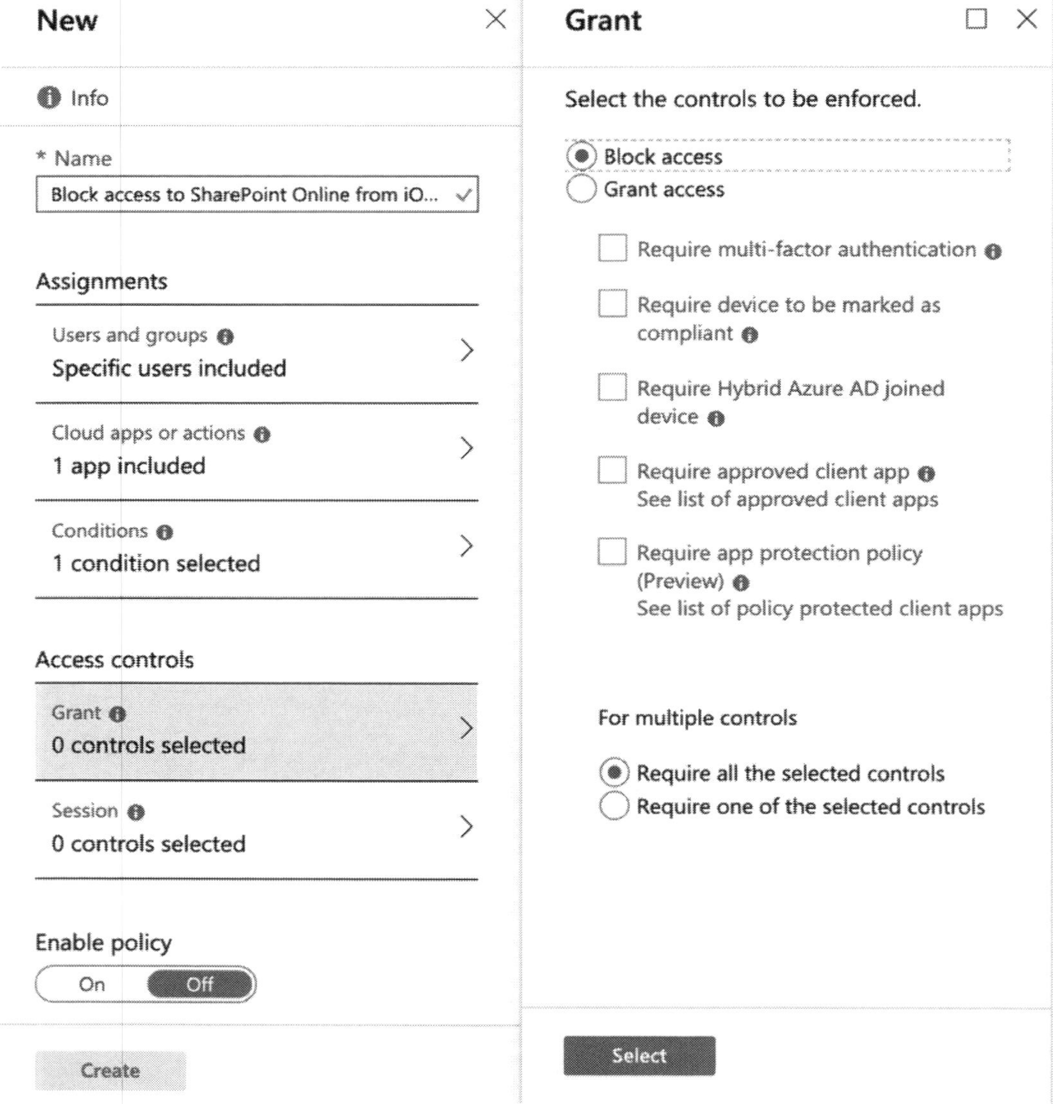

Figure 3.12 – Access controls

9. Click **Select**. This is the final selection for our policy, which should now look as follows:

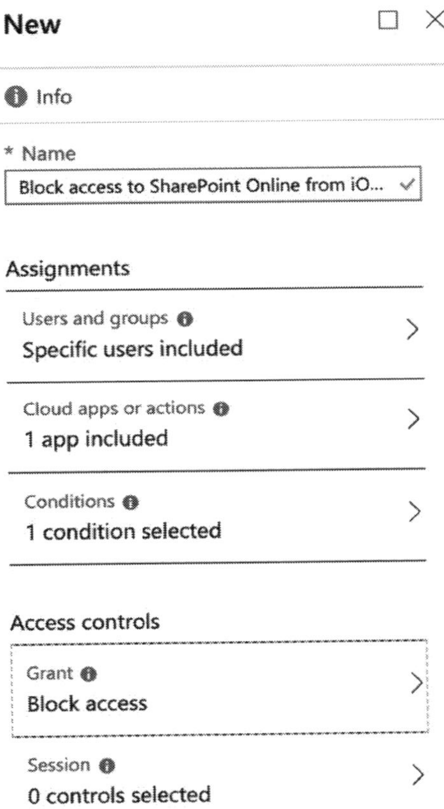

Figure 3.13 – Access controls

10. In order to enable and apply this policy, select **Enable policy** and click **Create**:

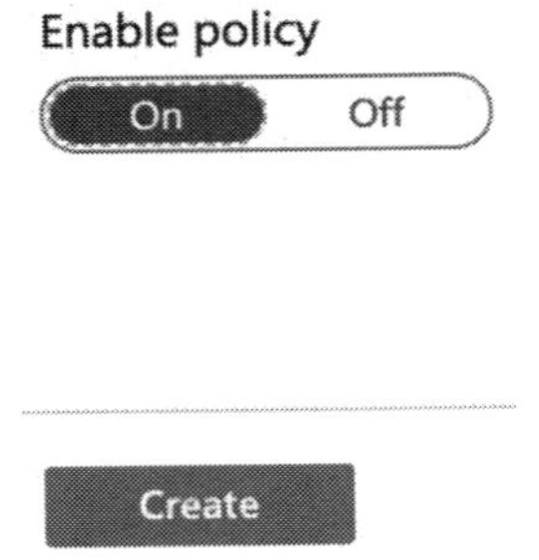

Figure 3.14 – Enabling the policy

11. The policy is successfully created and shown in the list of policies, as in the following screenshot:

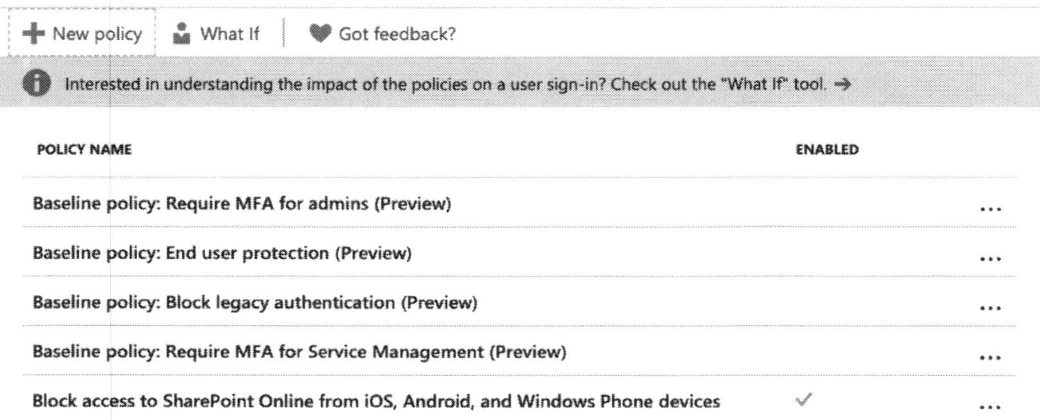

Figure 3.15 – List of policies

So, now we can test whether our policy works. To do this, let's see what happens when our user, **Jane Bloggs**, logs in with her Office 365 ID and tries to access SharePoint Online.

12. First, we will try this from an Apple Macintosh device via the web browser. The Conditional Access policy should not block this, which is confirmed when we log in to SharePoint:

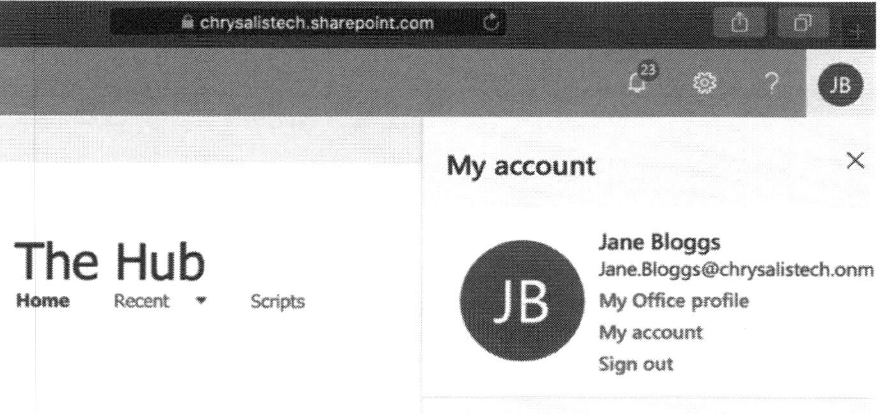

Figure 3.16 – Access to SharePoint via the macOS web browser

13. However, if we try the same thing from Jane's Apple iOS device, we get the following result:

jane.bloggs@chrysalistech.onmicrosoft.com
You cannot access this right now
Your sign-in was successful, but does not meet the criteria to access this resource. For example, you might be signing in from a browser, app or location that is restricted by your admin.
Sign out and sign in with a different account
More details

Figure 3.17 – Access to SharePoint blocked on the iOS device

So, the policy works exactly how we wish. As you will have noticed from the earlier screenshots, there are many ways that you can tailor assignments and access controls in your Conditional Access policies.

App-based Conditional Access

Intune allows you to create app protection policies that enforce app-based Conditional Access to ensure that only apps that support these policies can access Microsoft 365 services. This is particularly useful when dealing with BYOD devices and allows you to further protect your Microsoft 365 environment from requests from apps on non-corporate-owned devices.

Creating an app-based Conditional Access policy

In order to create an app-based Conditional Access policy, we need to take the following steps:

1. First, we need to ensure that we have an Intune app protection policy applied to any apps that we use. To do this, we need to log in to the Intune portal and select **Client Apps | App protection policies**:

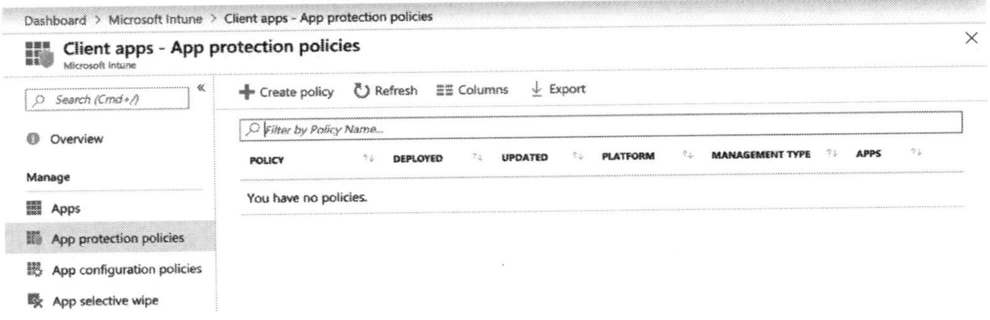

Figure 3.18 – App protection policies

2. Click on **Create policy**. In this example, we will create a policy for Microsoft Outlook on Apple devices, named and described as follows:

   Name: `Microsoft Outlook on iOS and iPadOS`

   Description: `Policy for settings and access requirements when using the Outlook App on Apple iOS or iPadOS devices`

3. Under the **Targeted apps** selection, we need to ensure that **Outlook** is selected, as in the following screenshot:

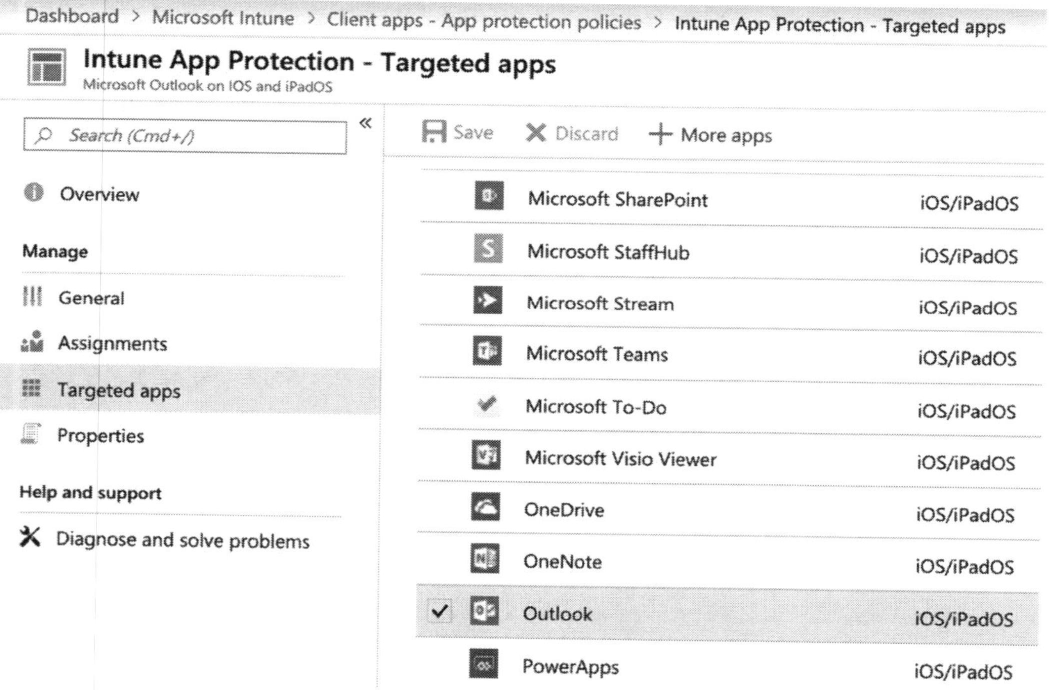

Figure 3.19 – Targeted apps

4. Next, we need to configure the available settings:

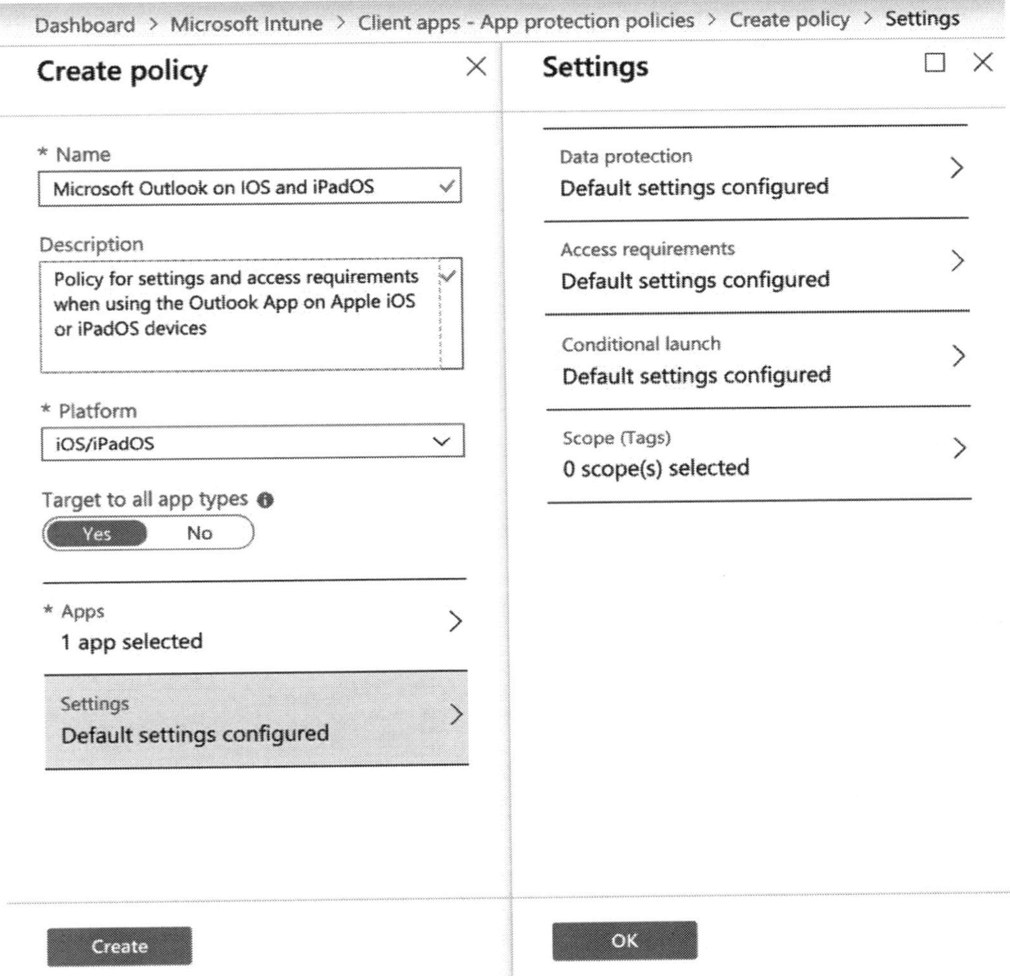

Figure 3.20 – Targeted apps settings

5. Review and complete the required settings options for your policy. These are **Data Protection**, **Access Requirements**, **Conditional Launch**, and **Scope (Tags)**.
6. Once you are happy with your selections, click **OK** and then click **Create**. Now that we have our app protection policy, we can proceed to create our app-based Conditional Access policy.
7. Go to the Intune dashboard and select **Conditional Access | Policies | New Policy**. We will name this policy `Outlook App Policy` in this example.

8. Under **Assignments**, we can configure the desired settings and apply them to the required users and groups. **Mobile Application Management** can only be applied to iOS or Android devices, so we must also choose the selected device platforms from the **Device platforms** section:

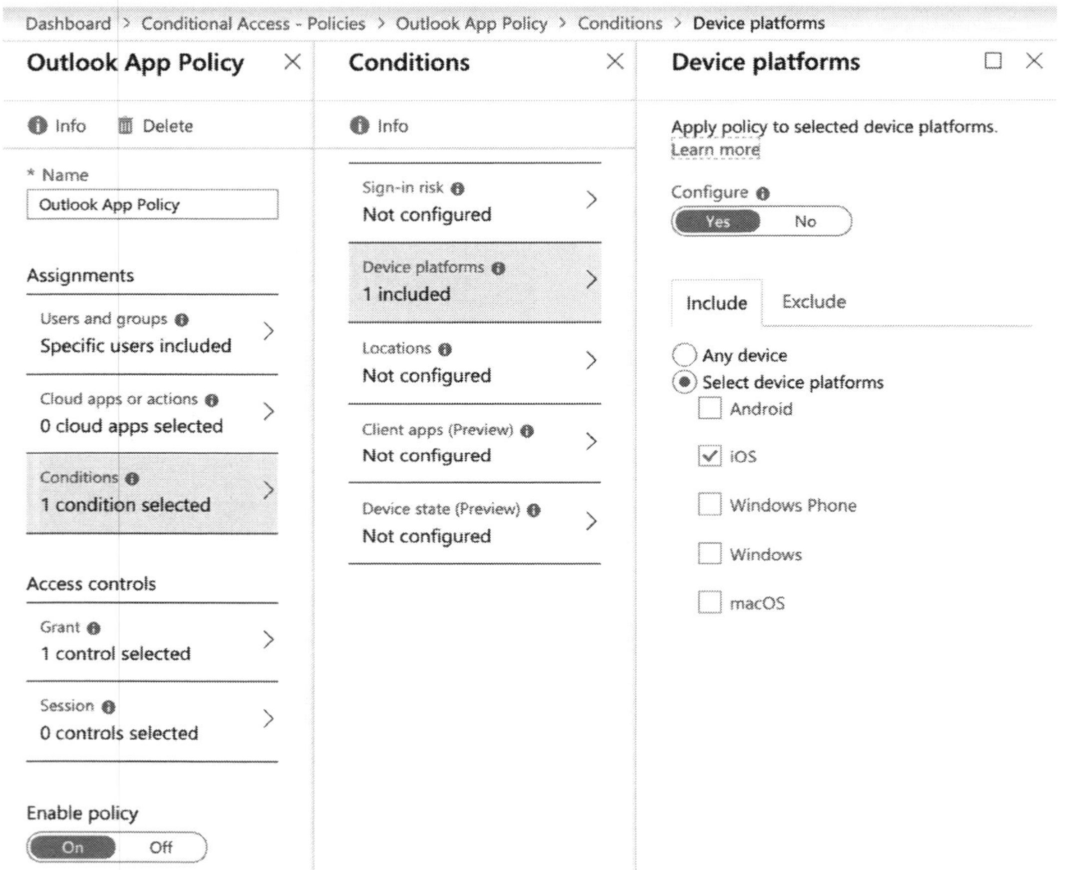

Figure 3.21 – Device settings

9. Next, under **Access controls** and **Grant**, we need to select **Require approved client app**:

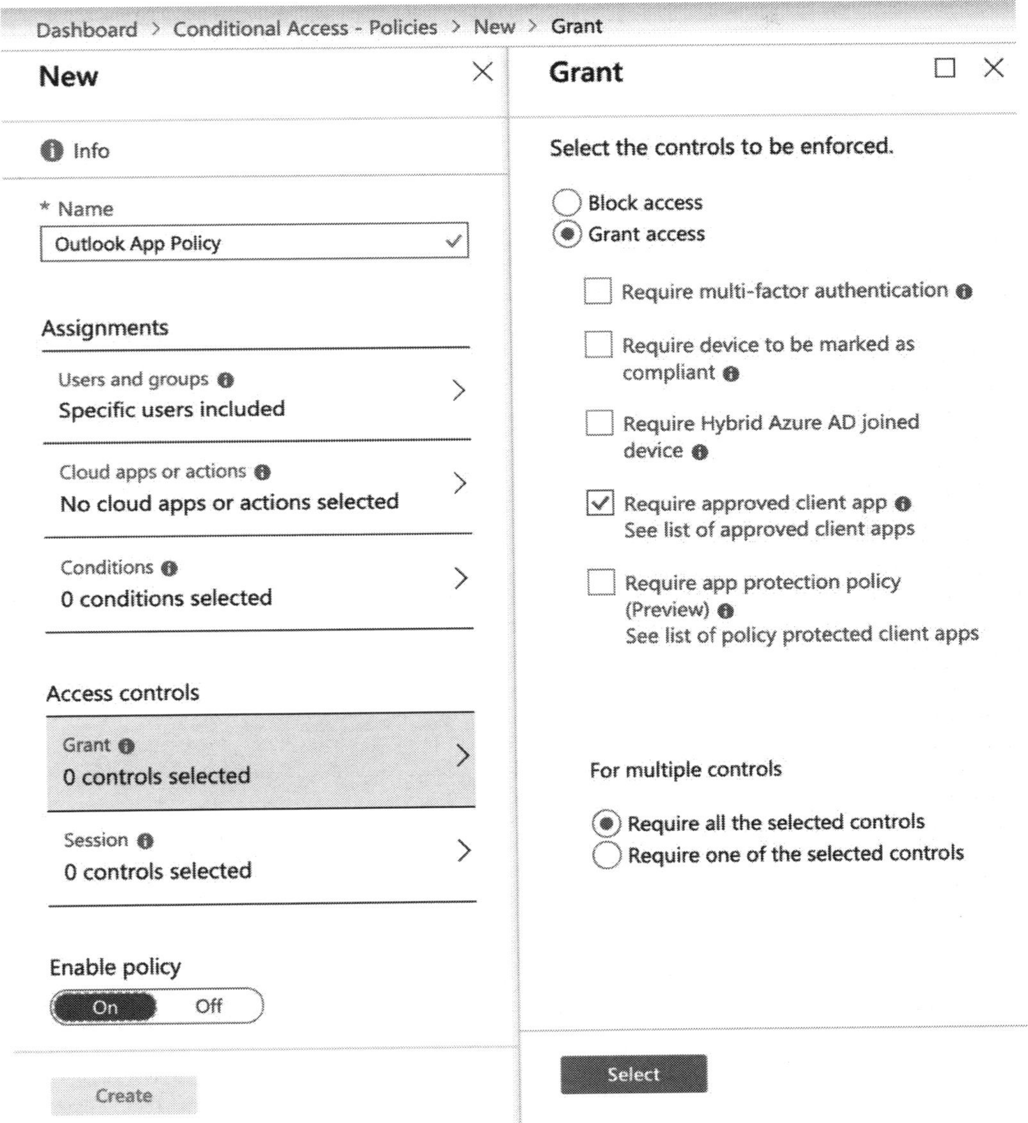

Figure 3.22 – Require approved client apps

10. Click **Select**, ensure that **Enable policy** is set to **On**, and click **Create**. We can now see that our new policy is added to our list of existing Conditional Access policies:

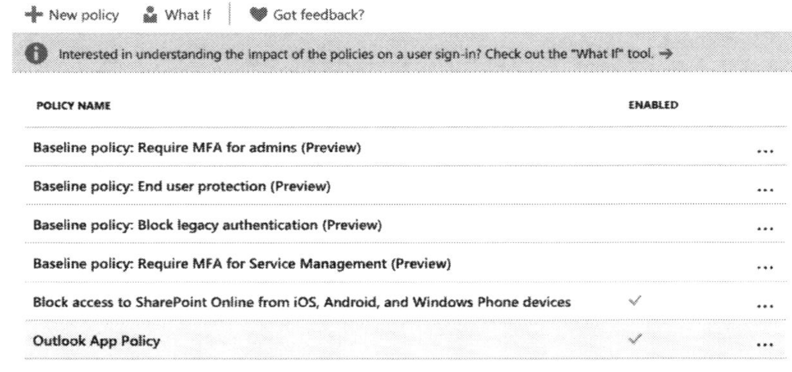

Figure 3.23 – Policy enabled

> **Important note**
> In order to create Conditional Access policies from the Intune portal, an Azure AD Premium license is required.

Next, we will look at how we can monitor device compliance with Conditional Access.

Monitoring Conditional Access events

In order to monitor and search for Conditional Access policy matches in Azure AD, we need to take the following steps:

1. From the Azure portal, select **Azure Active Directory** and choose **Sign-ins**:

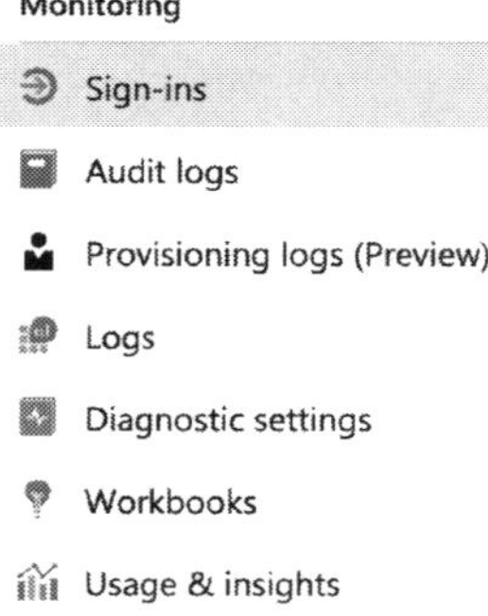

Figure 3.24 – Monitoring Conditional Access

2. From the results displayed, we can filter by **Conditional access**:

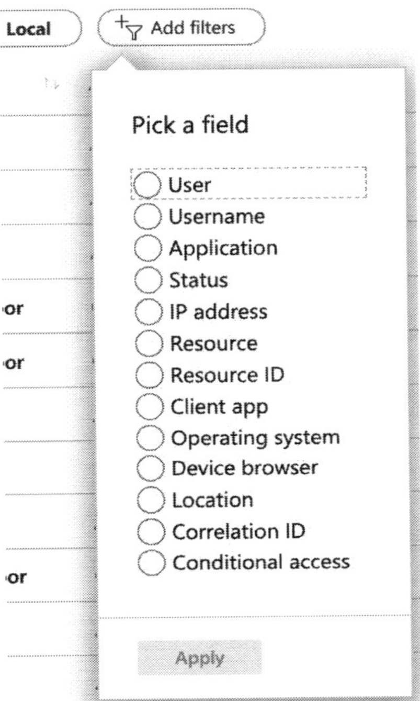

Figure 3.25 – Filtering by Conditional access

3. We can further filter the results by **Success** or **Failure**:

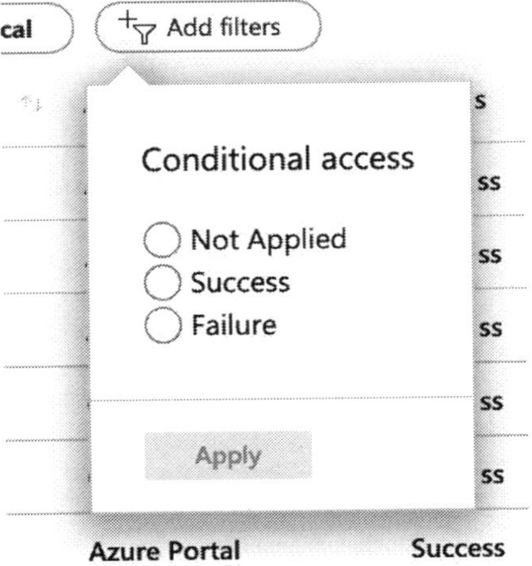

Figure 3.26 – Filtering results

> **Important note**
> You can also monitor the device compliance status from the Intune portal by selecting **Device compliance | Overview**. This will take you to the **Device compliance** dashboard.

Summary

In this chapter, we introduced you to Conditional Access policies in both Azure AD and Intune. We demonstrated how Conditional Access helps you address traditional security requirements with a modern approach, where instead of configuring a firewall (which is not possible in a Microsoft 365 environment), we can configure policies in Azure AD and Intune to provide additional protection for our users and resources. We learned how to create a simple Conditional Access policy, as well as more advanced app-based and device-based policies using Intune. In addition, we showed you how you can search the Azure AD **Sign-ins** page to track successful and failed Conditional Access policy events.

In the next chapter, we will show you how role assignment and privileged identities can be used in Azure AD to ensure that correct access is provided to your users.

Questions

1. Which of the following is not a possible response to a Conditional Access policy being triggered?

   a. Requiring Azure Advanced Threat Protection

   b. Requiring MFA

   c. Requiring an approved client app

   d. Requiring a device to be marked as compliant

2. True or false: Conditional Access is included with an Azure AD Premium P1 license.

   a. True

   b. False

3. Which of the following is not one of the baseline policies included with Azure AD Conditional Access?

   a. Requiring MFA for admins

   b. Blocking legacy authentication

   c. End user protection

   d. Blocking modern authentication

4. What are two possible methods of bypassing Conditional Access?

   a. Setting named locations in Azure AD

   b. Using **Role-Based Access Control** (**RBAC**)

   c. Setting up MFA-trusted IPs

   d. Enabling self-service password reset

   e. Enabling pass-through authentication

5. True or false: With Intune, you can use device-based compliance and app-based compliance in conjunction with Conditional Access.

   a. True

   b. False

6. Where would you look to monitor Conditional Access events?

   a. The Intune dashboard under **Client Apps** | **App protection policies**

   b. The Intune dashboard under **Device compliance** | **Policies**

   c. The Azure portal under **Azure Active Directory** | **Security** | **Conditional Access** | **Policies**

   d. The Azure portal under **Azure Active Directory** | **Monitoring** | **Sign-ins**

7. Which of the following assignments can you use to set the conditions of a Conditional Access policy (choose three)?

   a. Sign-in risks

   b. Locations

   c. MFA

   d. Directory roles

   e. Device platforms

8. True or false: With the **What if** feature, you can test the impact of Conditional Access on a user when signing in under certain conditions.

   a. True

   b. False

9. Which of the following is not an available device platform with Conditional Access?

   a. Android

   b. Windows Phone

   c. macOS

   d. Linux

   e. Windows

10. True or false: With Conditional Access, it is possible to both include and exclude users, groups, and cloud apps from policy assignments.

   a. True

   b. False

References

Please refer to the following links for more information:

- The following link is an example of a device compliance policy. Before configuring the device compliance policies, make sure that you are aware of all of the device types in your organization that you will need to protect: `https://docs.microsoft.com/en-gb/intune/protect/quickstart-set-password-length-android?wt.mc_id=4039827`
- The following link shows how to configure a device-based Conditional Access policy. When using these, always test them thoroughly with a small pilot group before targeting all users: `https://docs.microsoft.com/en-gb/intune/protect/create-conditional-access-intune`
- This policy helps you to set rules on your devices to allow access. The *Ways to deploy device compliance policies* section will give you a greater understanding of how to plan for device rules: `https://docs.microsoft.com/en-gb/intune/protect/device-compliance-get-started`
- This link will show you how to plan for app-based Conditional Access using Intune: `https://docs.microsoft.com/en-gb/intune/protect/app-based-conditional-access-intune`

- This link will show you how to set up app-based Conditional Access policies using Intune. Remember that you need an Azure AD Premium license to create Conditional Access policies from the Intune portal: `https://docs.microsoft.com/en-gb/intune/protect/app-based-conditional-access-intune-create`
- This link will show you how to create and assign app protection policies: `https://docs.microsoft.com/en-gb/intune/apps/app-protection-policies`
- This link will show you how you can monitor your Intune device compliance policies. Remember that devices must always be enrolled in Intune in order to take advantage of these policies: `https://docs.microsoft.com/en-us/intune/protect/compliance-policy-monitor`

4

Role Assignment and Privileged Identities in Microsoft 365

In this chapter, we will be looking at **role-based access control** (**RBAC**), which is a system that authorizes specific access management capabilities to Azure resources by creating role assignments. You will learn how to plan and configure RBAC, as well as how to view activity logs to monitor RBAC changes.

We will also be looking at Azure AD **Privileged Identity Management** (**PIM**) and how it enables you to manage, control, and monitor access to resources within Azure AD. PIM can help you identify and minimize the number of people who have access to sensitive or secure information and resources within your organization.

We will cover the following topics:

- Planning, configuring, and monitoring RBAC
- Planning, configuring, and monitoring PIM

Planning, configuring, and monitoring RBAC

RBAC is system that provides very specific access management capabilities to Azure resources. It enables Microsoft 365 administrators to manage access to these resources, the actions the users can take, and what resources are accessible to them.

You can configure RBAC from multiple locations within the Azure portal. RBAC is presented in the form of the **Access Control (IAM)** pane when accessed from an Azure Visual Studio subscription, as shown in the following screenshot:

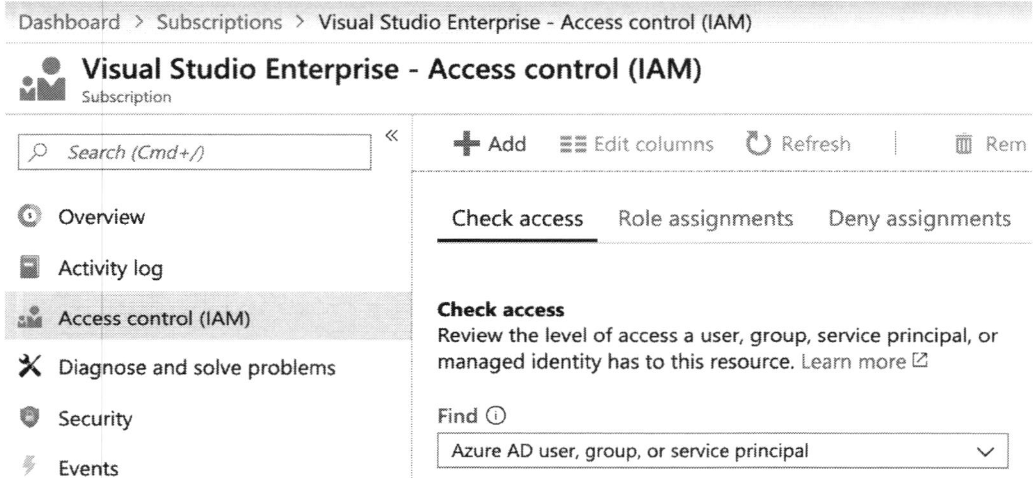

Figure 4.1 – Access Control (IAM)

Let's look at some key planning considerations when implementing RBAC.

Planning RBAC

When we are planning to assign RBAC permissions to users within Azure AD, you first need to understand **Role Assignments**. From the **Access Control (IAM)** pane, you have the choice of adding role assignments, viewing existing role assignments, and viewing deny assignments. The following screenshot shows these choices for role assignment:

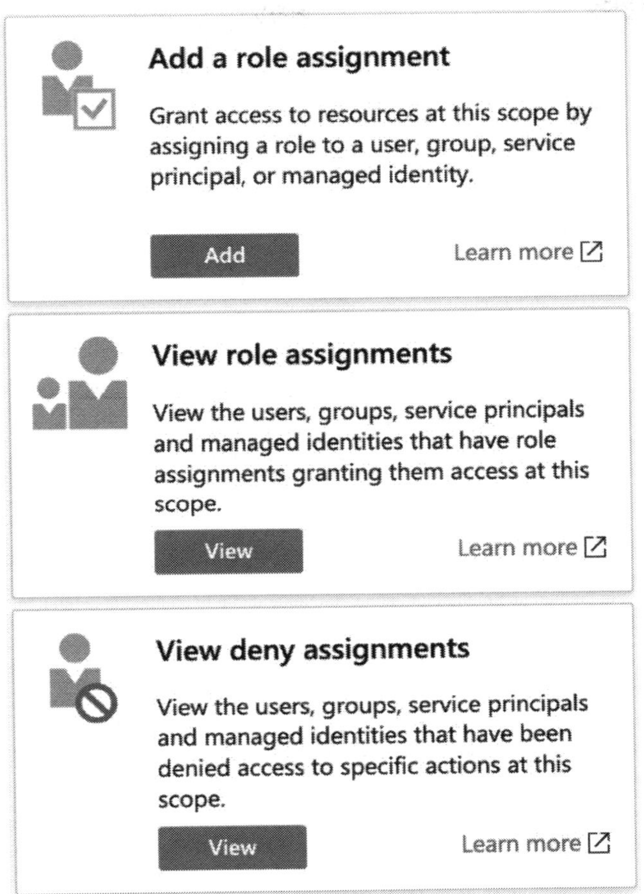

Figure 4.2 – Role assignments

We can choose to add a new role assignment by clicking **Add | Add role assignment**:

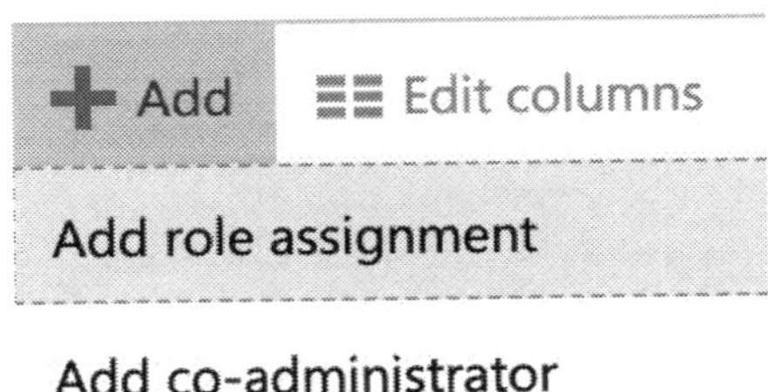

Figure 4.3 – Adding a role assignment

Click the **Role** drop-down box. You will see a list of roles that are available for assignment:

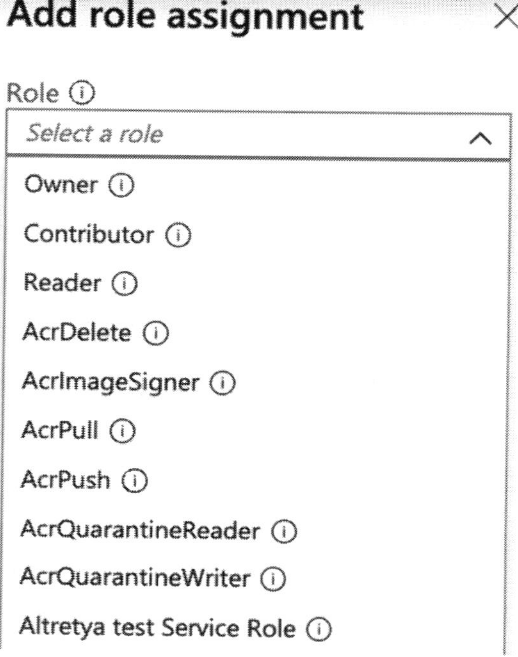

Figure 4.4 – Available role assignments

So, how does this help us with planning for RBAC? There are three key questions you need to answer when doing this:

- Who needs access?
- What do they need to access?
- What permissions do they need?

When you have the answers to these questions, you will be able to effectively plan the correct RBAC role assignment settings. In the example shown here, where we wish to grant access to a Visual Studio subscription, we can use RBAC to do things such as the following:

- Grant a user access to the **Billing Reader** role for the subscription.
- Grant a group access to the **SQL DB Contributor** role so they can manage SQL databases.
- Grant an application access to all resources within a resource group.

RBAC enables you to grant explicit access to your users with the principle of least privilege, which means they will have only the access required to do their jobs. This granular level of access removes the requirement to assign more established roles to users that include features they may not require, and for which they are not authorized.

How role assignments work

Role assignments consist of three components:

- **Security principal**: This is the requesting party, which can be a **user**, **group**, **service principal**, or **managed identity**, as illustrated in the following diagram:

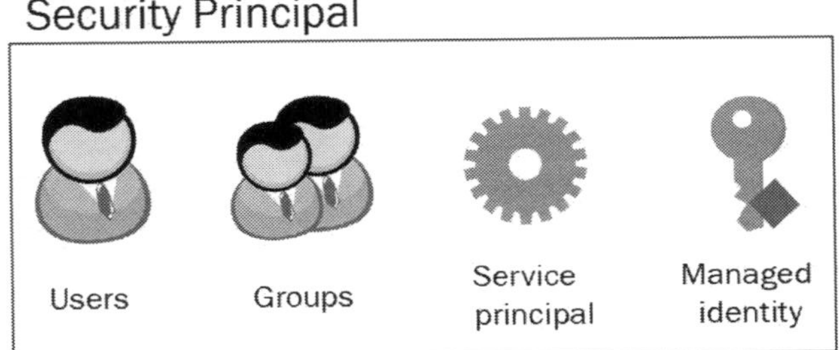

Figure 4.5 – Security principal

- **Role definition**: A set of permissions that defines the actions that can be performed by the security principal (such as read, write, or delete). Role definitions are also known as roles and there are many built-in roles that can be used, such as **Owner**, **Contributor**, and **Reader**. The following diagram illustrates the concept of **Role definition**:

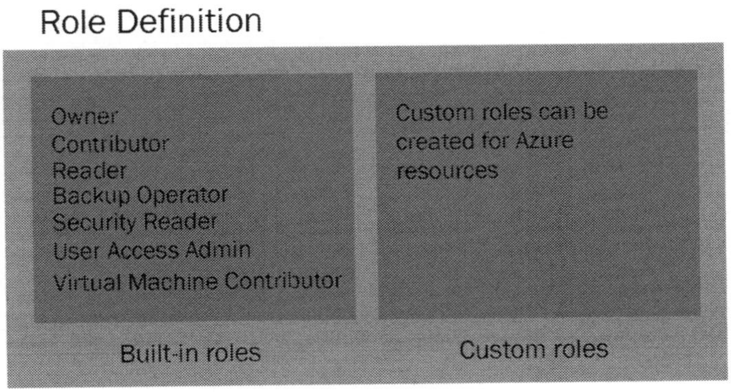

Figure 4.6 – Role definition

- **Scope**: The scope can be defined as the resources to which access will be granted. An example would be assigning contributor access to a user for a specific resource group. The following diagram shows how the scope process works:

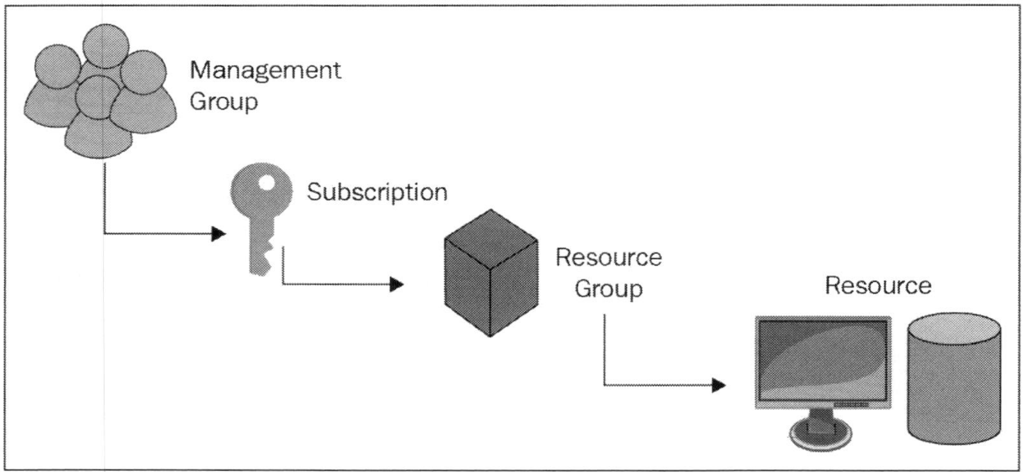

Figure 4.7 – Scope

Now that you understand the steps required to plan for RBAC, we can examine the process of configuring RBAC.

Configuring RBAC

Now that you understand what RBAC does and the principles of role assignments, you can start to configure role assignments with RBAC for your users. Role assignments can be added or removed in the Azure portal by using the **Access Control (IAM)** pane.

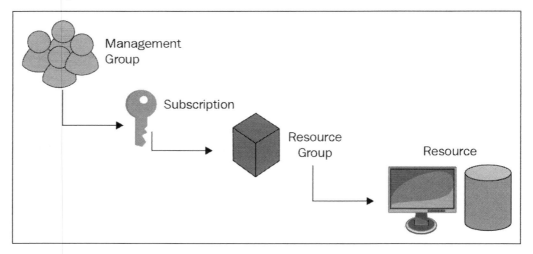

> **Important note**
>
> In order to configure role assignments, you will need to have User Access Administrator or Owner permissions.

In the following example, we will configure a user so that they can log in to a VM in Azure. Here are their details:

- User: `James Smith`
- Resource: A VM called `chrysalis03`

To provide our user with the access they require to the VM, we need to take the following steps:

1. Log in to the Azure portal and navigate to **All resources | chrysalis03**.
2. Now, we need to select **Access Control (IAM)**. The following screen will appear:

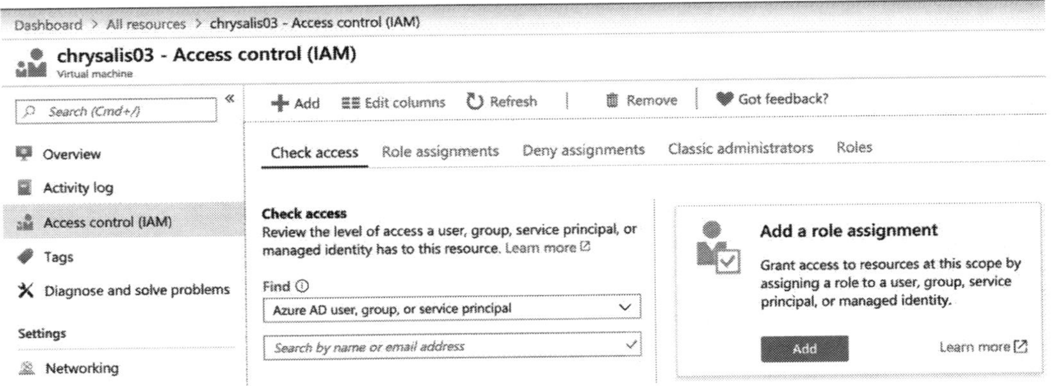

Figure 4.8 – Access control (IAM)

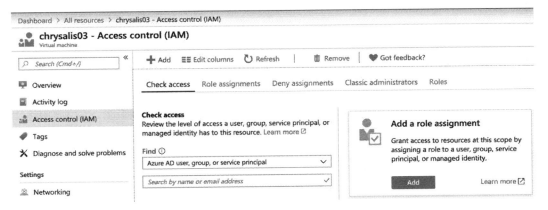

3. If you click on **Roles**, you will see all the roles available for this resource:

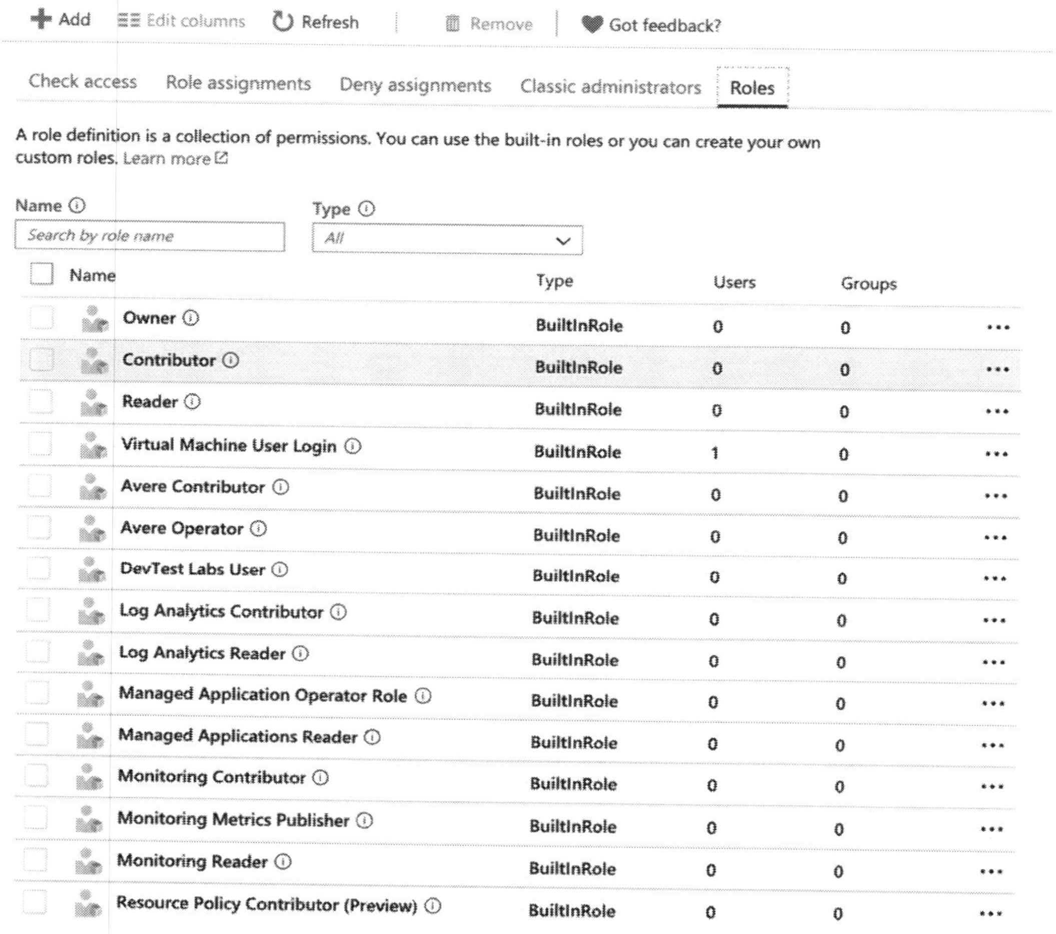

+ Add Edit columns Refresh Remove Got feedback?

Check access Role assignments Deny assignments Classic administrators Roles

A role definition is a collection of permissions. You can use the built-in roles or you can create your own custom roles. Learn more

Name ⓘ Search by role name Type ⓘ All

Name	Type	Users	Groups	
Owner ⓘ	BuiltInRole	0	0	...
Contributor ⓘ	BuiltInRole	0	0	...
Reader ⓘ	BuiltInRole	0	0	...
Virtual Machine User Login ⓘ	BuiltInRole	1	0	...
Avere Contributor ⓘ	BuiltInRole	0	0	...
Avere Operator ⓘ	BuiltInRole	0	0	...
DevTest Labs User ⓘ	BuiltInRole	0	0	...
Log Analytics Contributor ⓘ	BuiltInRole	0	0	...
Log Analytics Reader ⓘ	BuiltInRole	0	0	...
Managed Application Operator Role ⓘ	BuiltInRole	0	0	...
Managed Applications Reader ⓘ	BuiltInRole	0	0	...
Monitoring Contributor ⓘ	BuiltInRole	0	0	...
Monitoring Metrics Publisher ⓘ	BuiltInRole	0	0	...
Monitoring Reader ⓘ	BuiltInRole	0	0	...
Resource Policy Contributor (Preview) ⓘ	BuiltInRole	0	0	...

Figure 4.9 – Available roles

4. Next, click on **Add** and then **Add Role Assignment**.
5. Under **Role**, choose **Select a role**, scroll down, and choose **Virtual Machine User Login**.
6. Under the **Assign access to** option, we need to leave this set as **Azure AD user, group, or service principal** as we wish to assign this resource to a user.
7. Finally, in the **Select** box, we need to type in the person's username and select it. You should then see something like this:

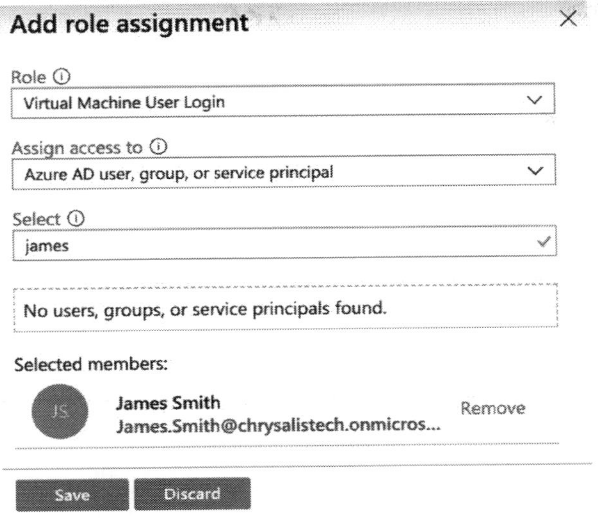

Figure 4.10 – Add role assignment page

8. Click **Save**.
9. Now that we have created our role assignment, we can view it by clicking **Role Assignments**, as shown here:

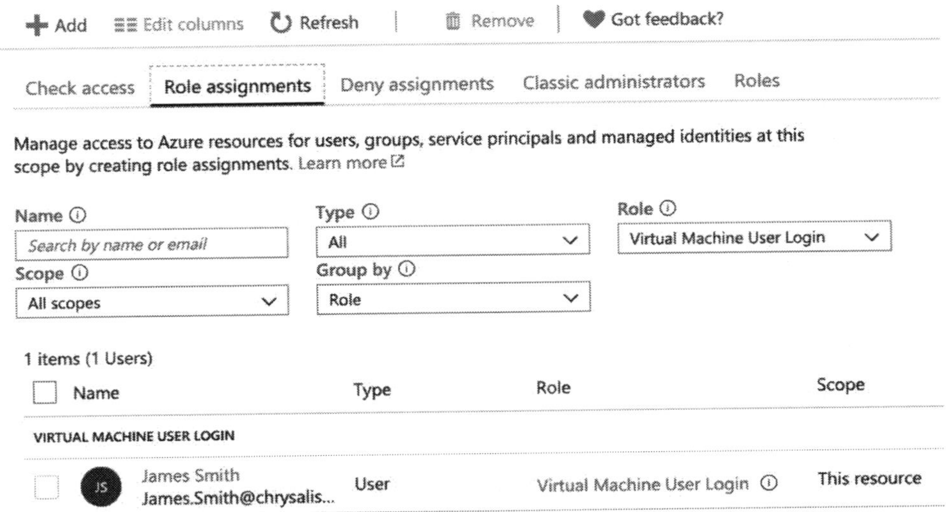

Figure 4.11 – Viewing the role assignment

10. We can easily remove the role assignment should we need to by selecting it and clicking on **Remove**.

11. From the **Access Control (IAM)** pane, we also have the options to **Check access** and configure **Deny Assignments**.
12. We have now successfully configured a role assignment for our user to enable them to access the resources they need using RBAC.

Managing RBAC using PowerShell

It is also possible to configure settings for RBAC using PowerShell. To do this, you will need one of the following:

- PowerShell in the Azure Cloud Shell
- Azure PowerShell

The easiest way to connect to Azure PowerShell is to launch it directly from the Azure portal from the **Cloud Shell** button on the top bar, as shown here:

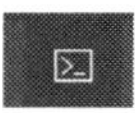

Figure 4.12 – Azure Cloud Shell

Selecting the **Cloud Shell** button will immediately open the shell at the bottom of the screen, as shown in the following screenshot:

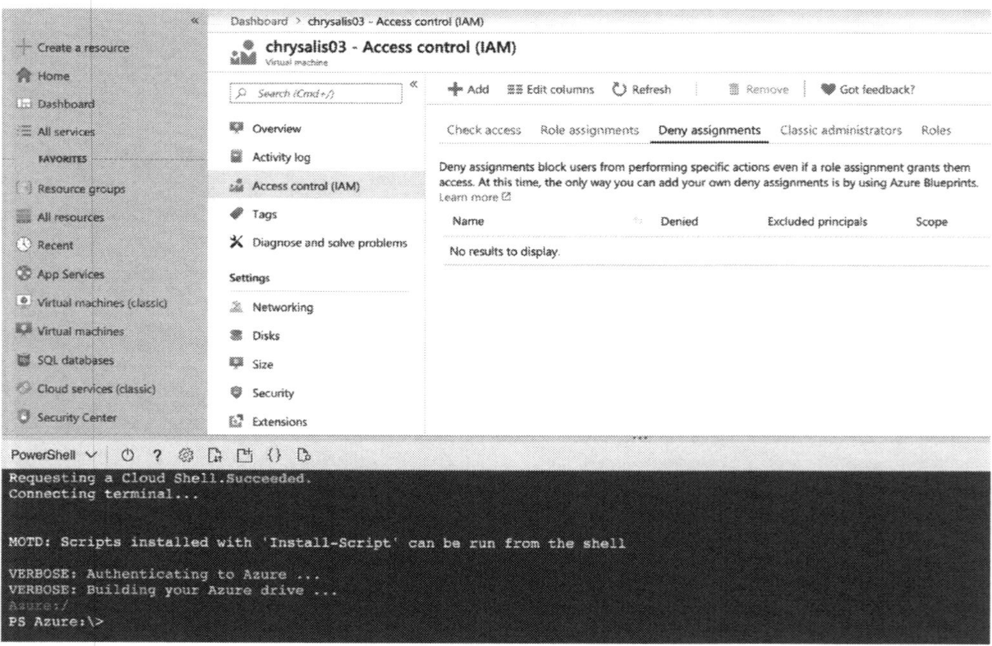

Figure 4.13 – Azure Cloud Shell

Once you are connected to Azure PowerShell, you can get a list of the available RBAC roles by typing the following:

```
Get-AzRoleDefinition
```

This returns a complete list of the available roles, as shown in the following screenshot:

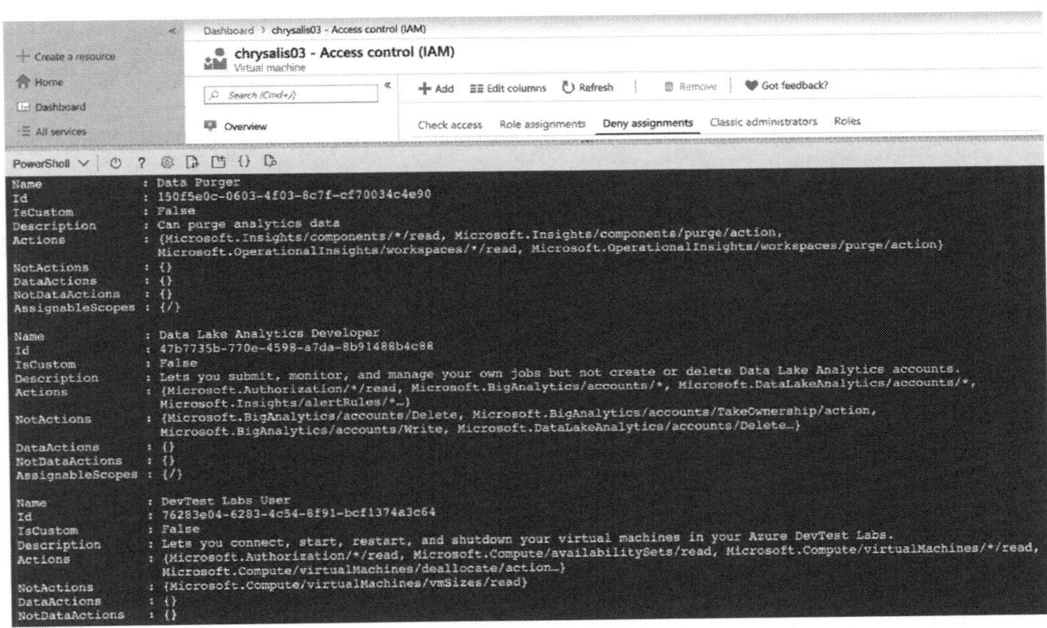

Figure 4.14 – Role definition results

In the previous section, we used the Azure portal to grant the user, James Smith, access to the Virtual Machine User Login role. Using the Azure Cloud Shell, we can enter the following command to verify that this role was assigned successfully:

```
Get-AzRoleAssignment -SignInName james.smith@chrysalishtech.
onmicrosoft.com
```

From the following screenshot, we can see that it was assigned successfully:

```
PS Azure:\> Get-AzRoleAssignment -SignInName james.smith@chrysalistech.onmicrosoft.com

RoleAssignmentId   : /subscriptions/e8612c2d-64a2-44dc-a059-c41cd9795e26/resourceGroups/Resource3/providers/Microsoft.Compute/virtualMachines/chrysa
                     lis03/providers/Microsoft.Authorization/roleAssignments/92046bb2-e075-4639-a59f-1cac77f86f33
Scope              : /subscriptions/e8612c2d-64a2-44dc-a059-c41cd9795e26/resourceGroups/Resource3/providers/Microsoft.Compute/virtualMachines/chrysa
                     lis03
DisplayName        : James Smith
SignInName         : James.Smith@chrysalistech.onmicrosoft.com
RoleDefinitionName : Virtual Machine User Login
RoleDefinitionId   : fb879df8-f326-4884-b1cf-06f3ad86be52
ObjectId           : d5bdb90e-29a6-487c-96ea-980a8d9d026c
ObjectType         : User
CanDelegate        : False
```

Figure 4.15 – Get-AzRoleAssignment result

Instead of using the Azure portal to set the role for our user, we could have done the same from the Azure Cloud Shell by entering the following command:

```
New-AzRoleAssignment -SignInName james.smith@chrysalistech.
onmicrosoft.com -RoleDefinitionName "Virtual Machine User
Login"
```

As we have already set this role via the Azure portal for James Smith, the following screenshot shows the command that's used to activate the same role for another of our tenant users, Jane Bloggs, using the Azure Cloud Shell:

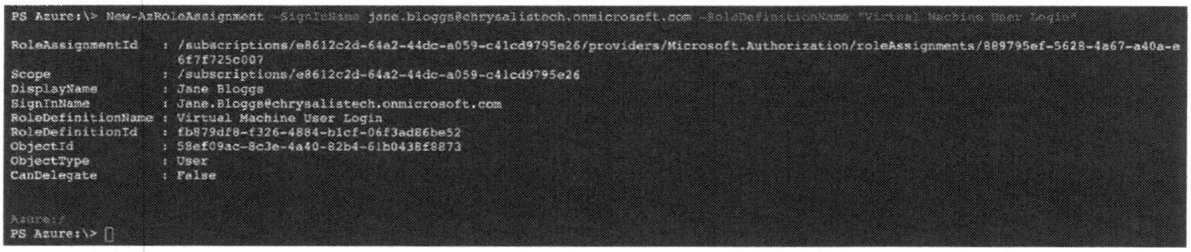

```
PS Azure:\> New-AzRoleAssignment -SignInName jane.bloggs@chrysalistech.onmicrosoft.com -RoleDefinitionName "Virtual Machine User Login"

RoleAssignmentId   : /subscriptions/e8612c2d-64a2-44dc-a059-c41cd9795e26/providers/Microsoft.Authorization/roleAssignments/889795ef-5628-4a67-a40a-e
                     6f7f725c007
Scope              : /subscriptions/e8612c2d-64a2-44dc-a059-c41cd9795e26
DisplayName        : Jane Bloggs
SignInName         : Jane.Bloggs@chrysalistech.onmicrosoft.com
RoleDefinitionName : Virtual Machine User Login
RoleDefinitionId   : fb879df8-f326-4884-b1cf-06f3ad86be52
ObjectId           : 58ef09ac-8c3e-4a40-82b4-61b0438f8873
ObjectType         : User
CanDelegate        : False

Azure:/
PS Azure:\>
```

Figure 4.16 – Adding a role assignment using Azure Cloud Shell

> **Important note**
>
> Further information about using PowerShell to configure RBAC can be found in the *References* section at the end of this chapter.

Monitoring RBAC

From a security standpoint, it is extremely important for Azure AD administrators to regularly monitor for any changes that have been made to RBAC role assignments in Azure AD subscriptions. Whenever such a change is made, it is recorded and logged in the **Azure Activity Log**. The changes that can be viewed in this log are only available for the previous 90 days.

The logs enable you to see when a role assignment (built-in or custom created) has been created or deleted.

The simplest way to view the Azure Activity Log is from within the Azure portal. As shown in the following screenshot, we can see the role assignment we created earlier in this chapter to grant our user, James Smith, the role of **Virtual Machine User Login**:

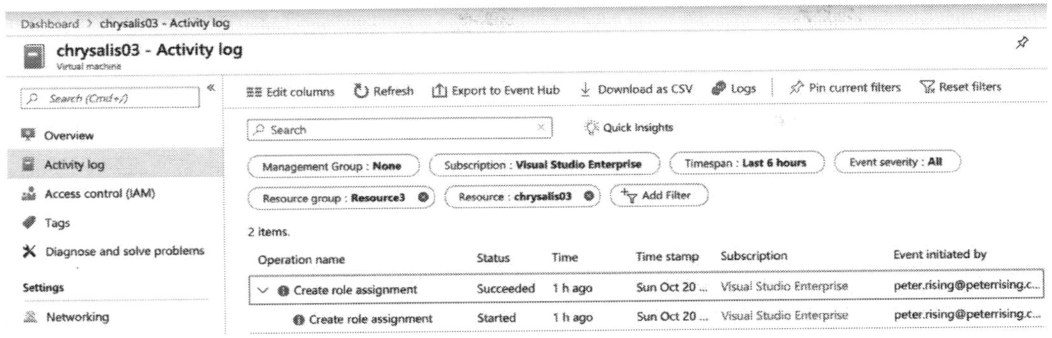

Figure 4.17 – User role assignment

If we drill down further, we will be able to see more details of this log event, which includes the following sections:

- **Summary**
- **JSON**
- **Change history (Preview)**

You will see these details displayed as follows:

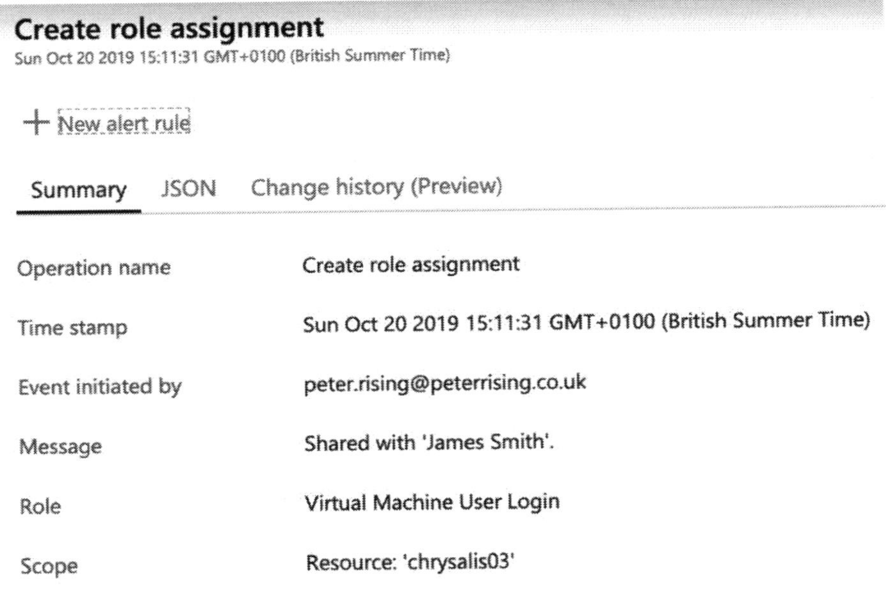

Figure 4.18 – Create role assignment

The activity log results may be filtered as required, and also downloaded to a `.csv` file.

> **Important note**
> Azure PowerShell and Azure CLI may also be used to monitor RBAC. Further information on this may be found in the *References* section at the end of this chapter.

Now that we have introduced you to the principles of RBAC, we will spend the rest of this chapter looking at Privileged Identity Management in Azure AD.

Planning, configuring, and monitoring PIM

Azure AD Privileged Identity Management (PIM) enables you to take greater control of your privileged accounts within Azure AD. So, what exactly is a privileged account? Essentially, this is any user account within your Microsoft 365 environment that grants elevated privileges above the scope of a standard user.

By default, Microsoft 365 standard user accounts are created without any sort of administrative privileges. However, it may be necessary to grant certain users elevated privileges to be able to carry out their jobs. There are a number of built-in administrator roles within Microsoft 365 for this, including the following:

- Billing Administrator
- Exchange Administrator
- Global Administrator
- Helpdesk Administrator
- Service Administrator
- SharePoint Administrator
- Teams Administrator
- User Administrator

> **Important note**
> The preceding roles are the core admin roles in Microsoft 365. There are others available, and a link to a document that includes information on all of these has been included in the *References* section at the end of this chapter.

Let's examine how you can plan for PIM in your organization.

Planning PIM

PIM provides you with the ability to control and monitor access to your resources in Azure AD by minimizing the number of users who have permanent administrative access with admin roles such as those described previously. Reducing the number of permanent administrative accounts has the obvious benefit of reducing your attack surface, and therefore reducing the risk of a malicious actor gaining access to your resources.

However, there will undoubtedly be a business requirement for certain users to perform administrative tasks within Azure AD from time to time, and this is where PIM comes into play. PIM can allow you to provide **just-in-time** (**JIT**) privileged access to your resources in Azure AD, which will help prevent the risk of access rights becoming compromised and misused in any way.

When thinking about your users, who may require occasional admin access to Azure resources, consider how the following features of PIM allow you to configure them:

- JIT privileged access to activate roles
- Time-bound access (using start and end dates)
- An approval process for privileged role activation requests
- The requirement for MFA when activating certain roles
- A justification process where users must explain why they require a privileged role
- Notifications to alert you when privileged roles are activated
- Access reviews to assess ongoing requirements for privileged roles

PIM must be explicitly activated in the Azure portal. The Azure administrator who sets up PIM is automatically granted the Security Administrator and Privileged Role Administrator roles in Azure AD. PIM rules can only be assigned by role, not by user. This means that it is currently not possible to have different rules for internal and external users.

To access the PIM feature, go to the Azure portal and search for **Azure AD Privileged Identity Management**, as follows:

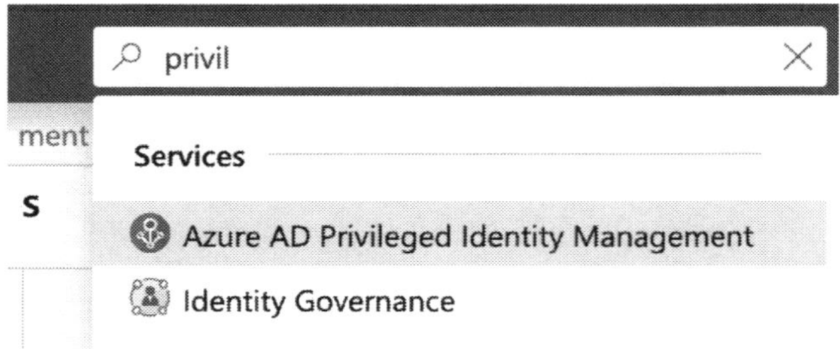

Figure 4.19 – Searching for Privileged Identity Management

Here, you will be directed to the PIM console:

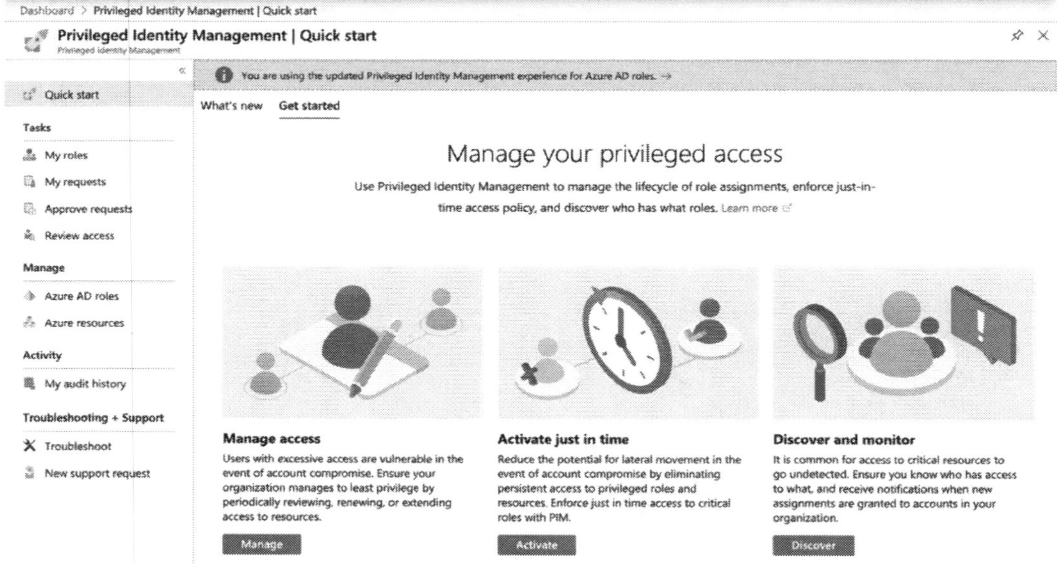

Figure 4.20 – Privileged Identity Management

In this example, which is from my own tenancy, you can see that in addition to being a Global Administrator, my Azure AD account has been granted two roles associated with PIM. We can verify this by choosing **My Roles | Active Roles**:

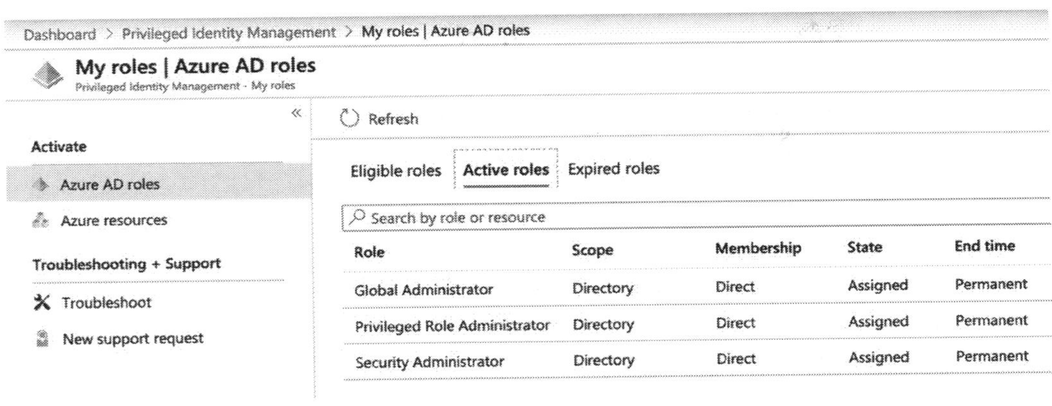

Figure 4.21 – Assigned Azure AD roles

As a PIM administrator, you can grant other administrators the ability to manage PIM, Azure AD Roles, and Azure Resources, as shown in the following screenshot:

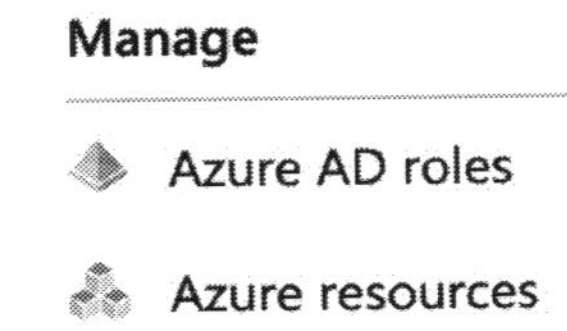

Figure 4.22 – Managing roles and resources

As a PIM administrator, you can also allow other users to be **Approvers**, who can then view and approve/reject requests from users to elevate their privileges. Additionally, it is possible to make specific users eligible for privileged roles so that they can request access to them on a just-in-time basis.

> **Important note**
>
> In order to use the features of Azure AD PIM in your Microsoft 365 environment, you must have an **Azure AD Premium P2**, **Enterprise Mobility + Security E5**, or **Microsoft 365 E5** license for all users who wish to leverage the feature. The **Microsoft 365 E5 Security** add-on may also be added to use Azure AD PIM, but this must be used in conjunction with a **Microsoft 365 E3** subscription

Now that you understand what PIM is and the considerations for planning its deployment, let's move on and start configuring PIM.

Configuring PIM

When running PIM for the first time, the first thing you may need to do is enable and consent to PIM. Since early 2020, this step has been removed from many Microsoft 365 tenants, but should you still encounter the requirement to consent to PIM, you can achieve this by completing the following steps:

1. Sign in to the Azure portal as a Global Administrator.
2. Search for **Privileged Identity Management** and click to open the PIM pane.
3. Click the option to **Consent to PIM**:

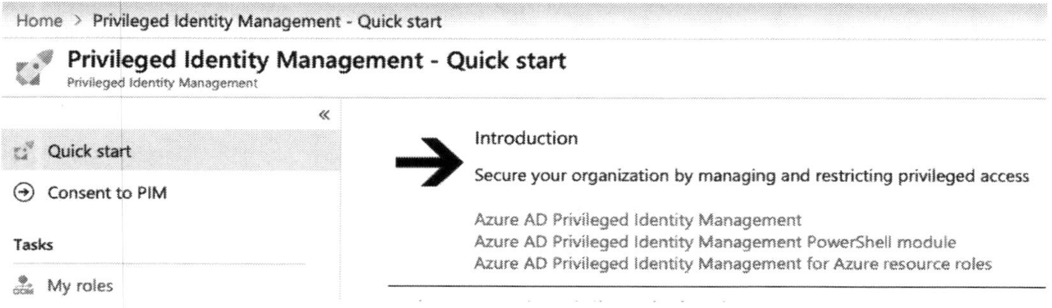

Figure 4.23 – Consenting to PIM

4. Next, you will need to select **Verify my identity** and confirm your account by using MFA. If you have not registered for MFA, this wizard will walk you through the steps regarding how to set it up:

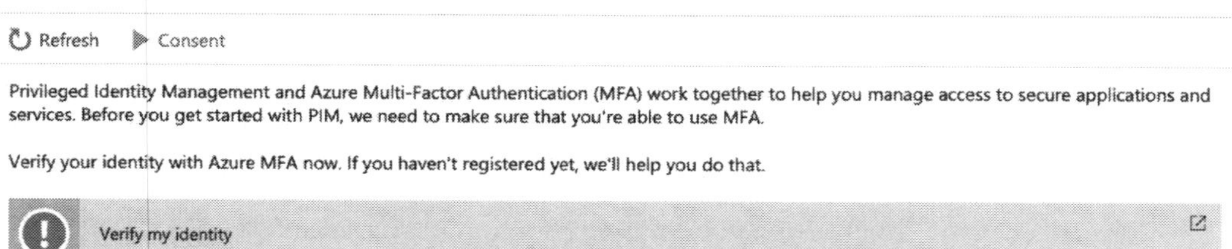

Figure 4.24 – Verifying your identity

5. When you've completed the MFA registration process, you will see the following screen:

More information required

Your organisation needs more information to keep your account secure

Use a different account

Learn more

Figure 4.25 – MFA registration process

6. Once you have done this, click the **Consent** button, and then click on **Yes**:

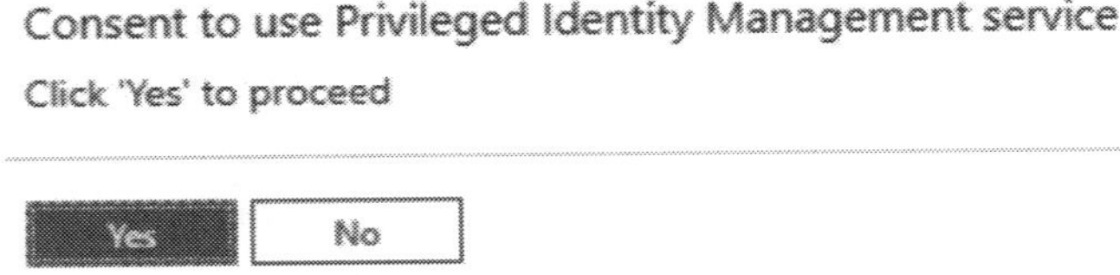

Figure 4.26 – Consenting to PIM

PIM is now enabled, with you as the first/primary administrator. You now need to sign up PIM for Azure AD roles. To do this, you need to follow these steps:

1. Open **Privileged Identity Management** in the Azure portal.
2. Select **Azure AD roles** and click **Sign up**:

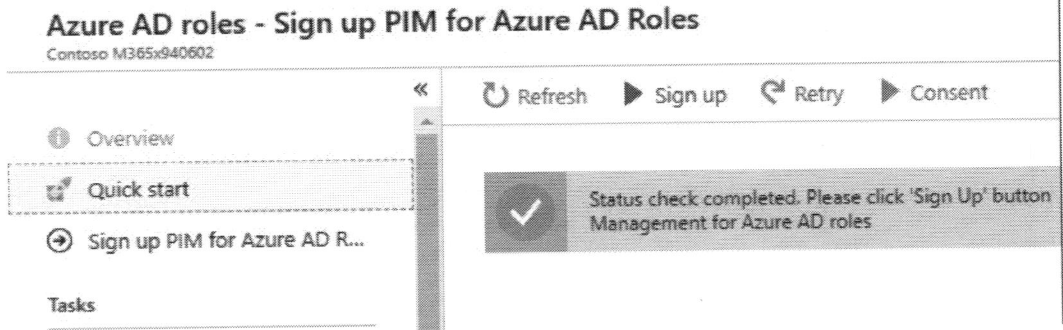

Figure 4.27 – Sign up PIM for Azure AD Roles

3. Click **Yes** if prompted:

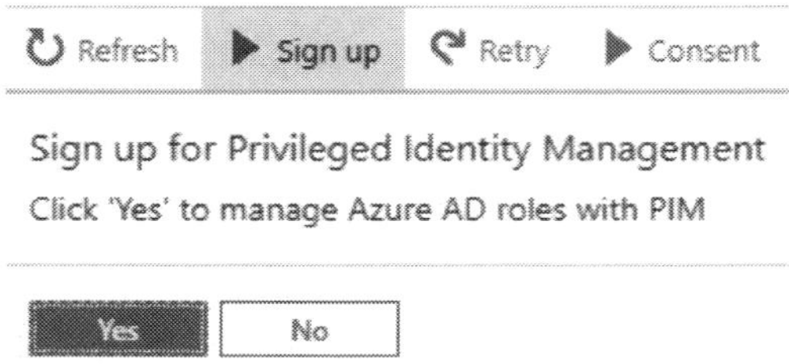

Figure 4.28 – Sign up for Privileged Identity Management

4. The sign-up process is now complete and everything should be enabled.

> **Important note**
> Remember that the preceding steps to consent to PIM and sign up PIM for Azure AD Roles may no longer appear in some tenants as Microsoft have changed this experience. The steps are included in this book in the event that you still encounter them in your testing.

Now, you will be able to perform tasks within PIM and manage roles and resources. The actions available to you as a PIM Administrator can be viewed under the **Tasks** and **Manage** sections of the PIM portal, as shown in the following screenshot:

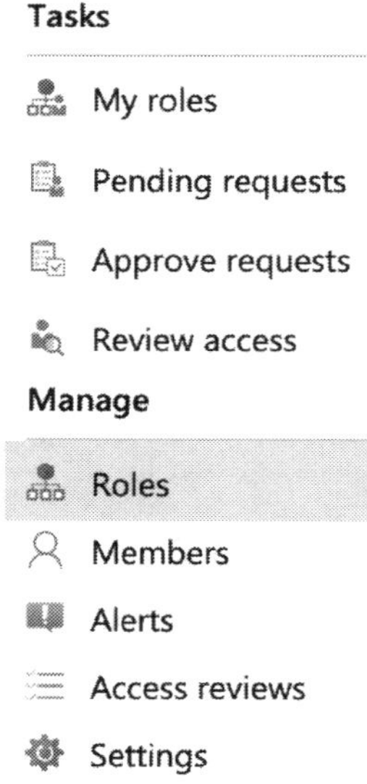

Figure 4.29 – Tasks and Manage settings

Let's examine the options in these sections in greater detail to understand what they can do.

Tasks:

- **My roles**: Shows the active roles that are assigned to you and any roles you are eligible for
- **Pending requests**: Shows your pending requests to activate eligible role assignments
- **Approve requests**: Shows a list of activation requests from other users that you will need to action, approve, or deny
- **Review access**: Shows any access reviews that are assigned to you. You will see access reviews here for yourself and for other users

> **Important note**
> Azure AD Access Reviews were covered in detail earlier in *Chapter 2, Authentication and Security*.

Manage:

- **Roles**: PIM administrators can use this dashboard to manage role assignments. Only PIM administrators can see this dashboard.
- **Members**: PIM administrators can use this section to search for Azure AD users and check which roles they are eligible for. They can also add new role assignments to members from here.
- **Alerts**: PIM administrators can use this dashboard to view any administrators who are not using their privileged roles, potential stale accounts in a privileged role, and warnings if there are too many Global Administrators.

So, now that we have PIM enabled and understand the Tasks and Manage options within the PIM pane in Azure, let's look at PIM in action and configure some of the common settings. These will include the following:

- Making a user eligible for a role
- Making the role assignment permanent
- Removing a role assignment
- Approving a role request

Making a user eligible for a role

In this example, we will assign the role of Billing Administrator to one of our users (Jane Bloggs) in Azure AD. In the first instance, we will make the user eligible for the role so that it can be activated as and when required. However, there may be occasions where the user requires the role permanently to do their job. In order to demonstrate this, we will also demonstrate how to change the role assignment so that it's permanent.

Here are the steps you need to follow in order to make a user eligible for a role:

1. Open the **PIM** pane in the Azure portal.
2. Select **Manage** | **Roles**. You will be able to see a list of all the available roles that can be assigned:

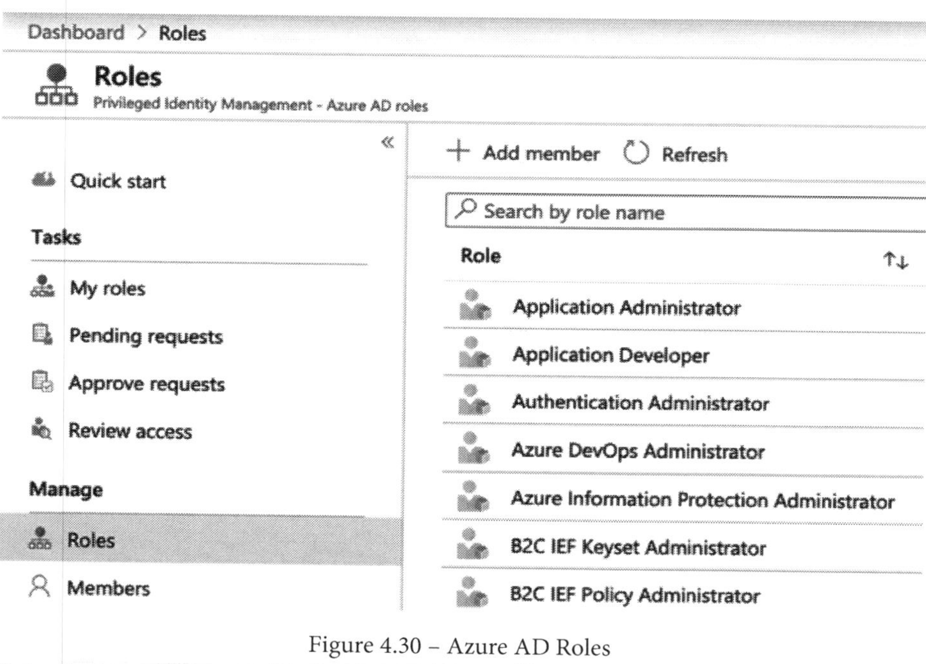

Figure 4.30 – Azure AD Roles

> **Important note**
>
> If you select **Members**, you will be able to see a list of which users are already assigned to the various roles and whether the assignments make the user eligible or are permanent.

3. Now that we have our list of roles available, we need to find and select the **Billing Administrator** role from the list:

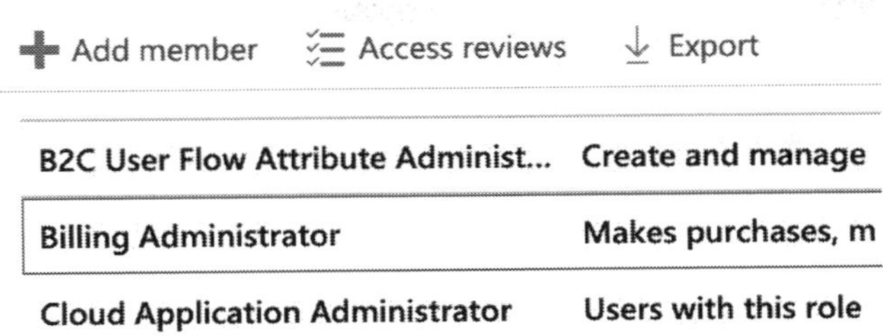

Figure 4.31 – Finding a role

4. Under **Assignments**, click on **Add member**. This will take you to the Member list for this role so that you can add the required user:

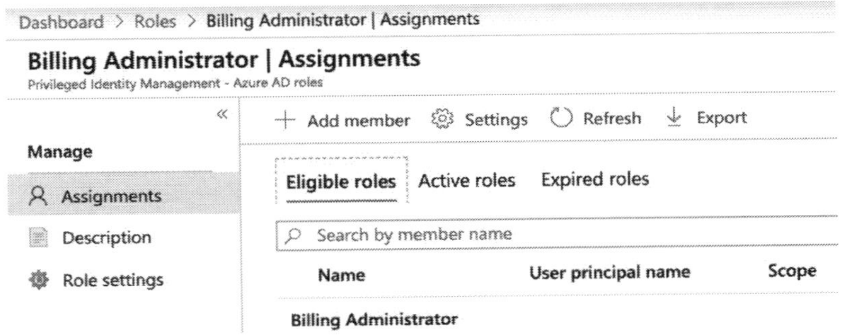

Figure 4.32 – Adding the required user to the role

5. Click on **Select a member** and search for the name of the required user (in this case, Jane Bloggs). Click **Select**; you will see the following options:

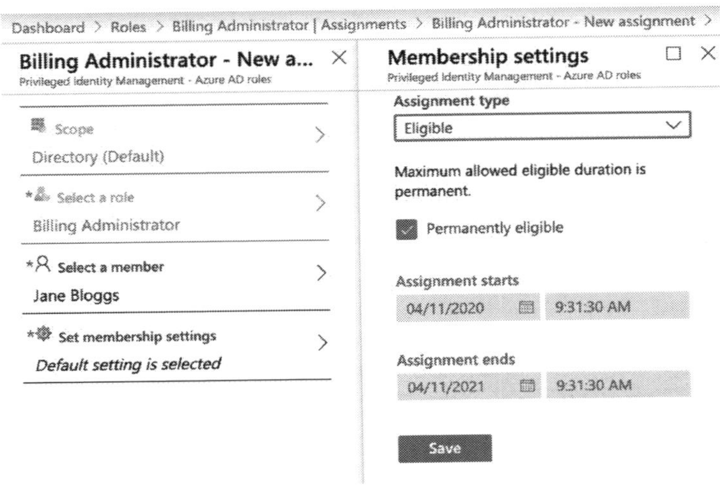

Figure 4.33 – Adding members to the role

6. You can choose to make the user permanently eligible for the role here or set a duration for eligibility. In this example, we will make the user permanently eligible. Click **Save**, and then click **Add**. You may need to refresh the page. Then you should see the user appear as eligible for the role, as shown in the following screenshot:

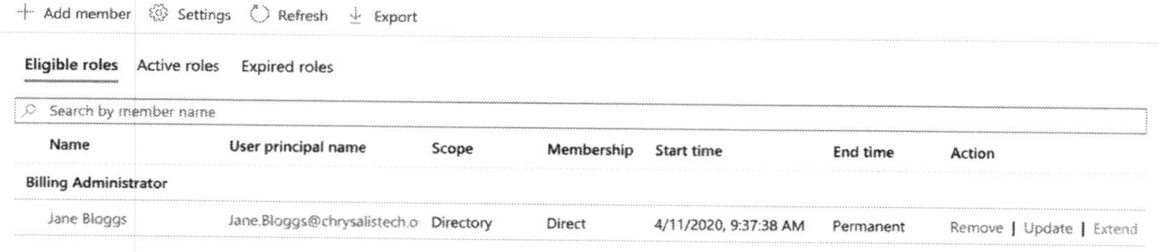

Figure 4.34 – Viewing user eligibility

7. Jane can now log in to the Azure portal herself and navigate to **Tasks | My Roles**. Then, under **Azure AD roles**, she can activate her eligible role by clicking **Activate**. This is illustrated in the following screenshot:

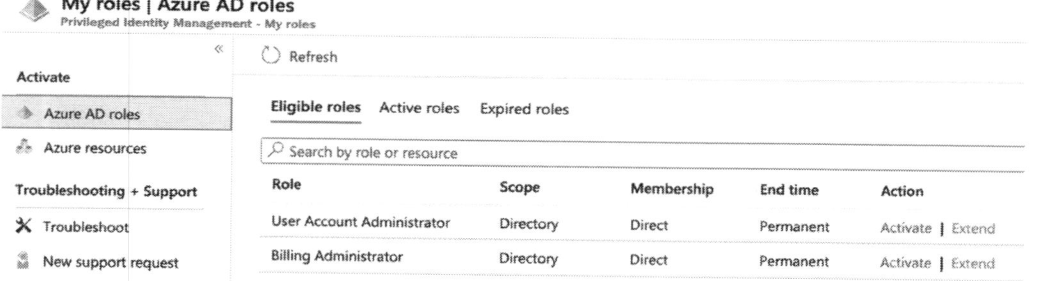

Figure 4.35 – Activating a role

8. Next, Jane needs to choose an activation duration. The duration is set to 1 hour initially; however, the user can set a shorter duration if less time is needed. She will also need to enter a reason for activating the role and then click on **Activate**, as shown in the following screenshot:

Activate - Billing Administrator
Privileged Identity Management - Azure AD roles

Assignment details

Scope
Chrysalis Technologies

Start time *
04/11/2020
9:43:29 AM

duration (hours)
1

*Reason (max 500 characters)
I need to check the monthly invoices for our Microsoft 365 subscriptions

Activate

Figure 4.36 – Selecting activation duration

9. The activation request will start processing:

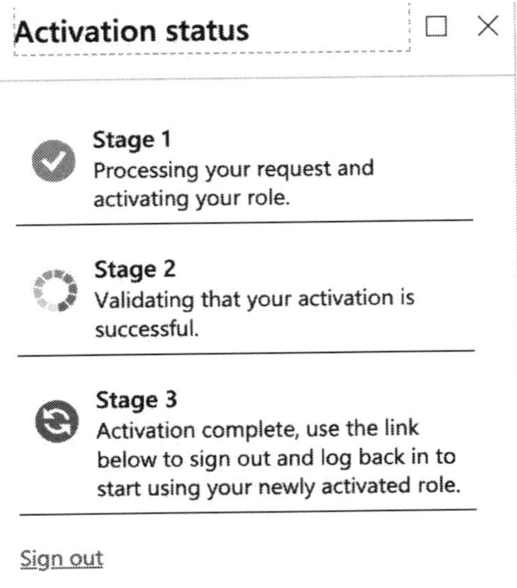

Activation status
Stage 1
Processing your request and activating your role.
Stage 2
Validating that your activation is successful.
Stage 3
Activation complete, use the link below to sign out and log back in to start using your newly activated role.
Sign out

Figure 4.37 – Activation process

10. If there are no issues, activation will be completed:

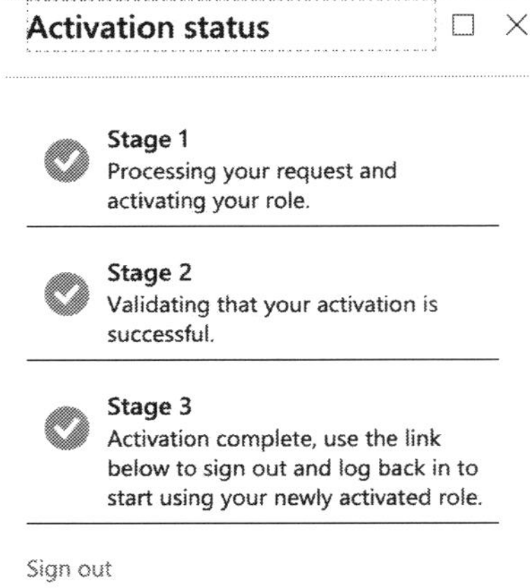

Figure 4.38 – Activation completion

11. Jane should now sign out and then log back in. By doing this, she will have access to the Billing Administrator role for the 1-hour duration and have permanent eligibility for the role.

> **Important note**
> Eligible users will be asked to set up MFA on their Azure AD account as part of this process if they are not already registered for MFA.

If the eligibility period had not been permanent, then it would expire, and access to the Billing Administrator role would be removed from Jane's account.

Additionally, the PIM administrator can track that Jane has activated the role and can check what time it's due to expire.

The settings we have configured are shown in the following screenshot:

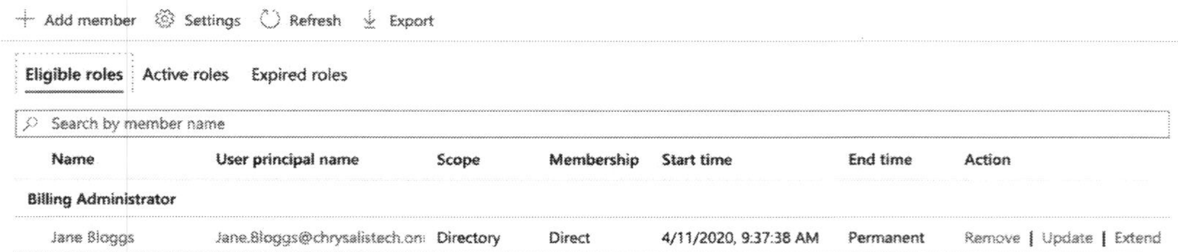

Figure 4.39 – User eligibility for a role

Removing a role assignment

Removing a role assignment is just as simple for the PIM administrator and can be achieved as follows:

1. Open the Billing Administrator assignments page once again, as shown in the previous screenshot, and select the user that you wish to remove the role assignment from. Click **Remove**. You will be asked to confirm the removal, as shown in the following screenshot:

Remove

Are you sure you want to remove member 'Jane Bloggs' from role 'Billing Administrator'?

Yes No

Figure 4.40 – Removing a role assignment

2. Click **Yes**. By doing this, the user will be removed as a member and will no longer have either permanent access or eligibility for the selected role.

Approving a role request

In the preceding example, where we made the user Jane Bloggs eligible for the Billing Administrator role, the role was automatically activated for her when she requested it. To add another layer of protection to this process, it is possible to configure the requirement for approval for each of the role settings. Let's see how this process works with the same user and role:

1. From the PIM pane in the Azure portal, navigate to **Manage | Settings**, as shown in the following screenshot:

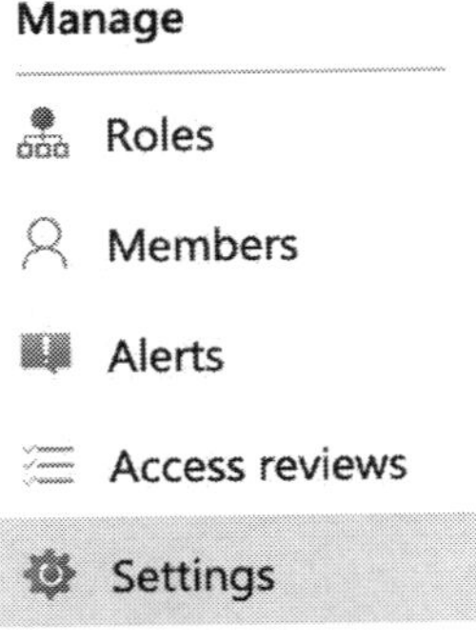

Figure 4.41 – Role settings

2. Select **Billing Administrator** from the roles list, and then click **Edit**:

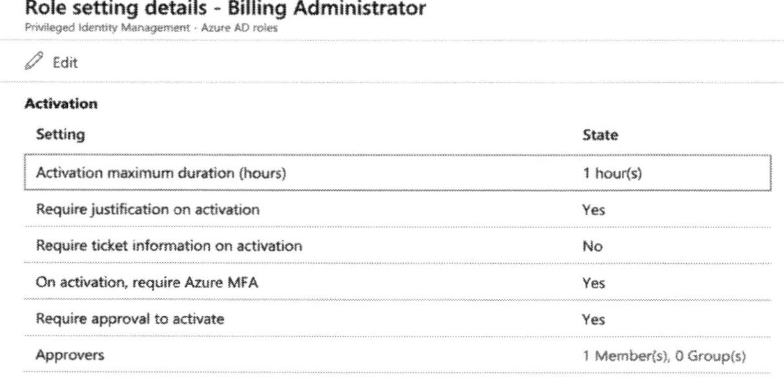

Figure 4.42 – Setting a role to require approval

3. Select the **Require approval to activate** checkbox, as shown in the following screenshot. You will have the option to select a specific user to be the approver for this role. If you do not select an approver here, the PIM administrator or Global Administrators will be set as the approvers by default:

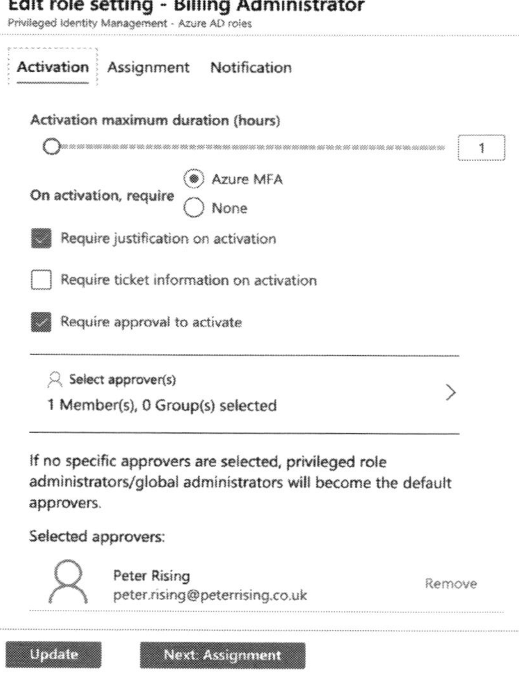

Figure 4.43 – Approver settings

4. Click **Update** to commit the changes.
5. Next, we make our user, Jane Bloggs, eligible for the Billing Administrator role again, and when she goes to activate the role.
6. The request to activate the role can be viewed by the PIM Administrator in the PIM pane of the Azure portal, under **Tasks | Approve requests**, as shown in the following screenshot:

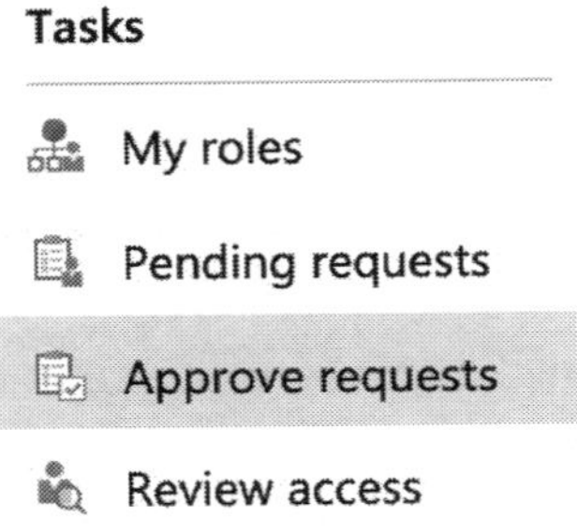

Figure 4.44 – Approve requests

7. The request will be shown as per the following screenshot:

Requests for role activations

Refresh

Role ↑↓	Requestor ↑↓	Request Time ↑↓	Reason
Billing Administrator	Jane Bloggs	4/11/2020, 10:26 AM	I need this

Figure 4.45 – Approving requests

8. The approver also receives an email alert to inform them about the user request, as shown in the following screenshot:

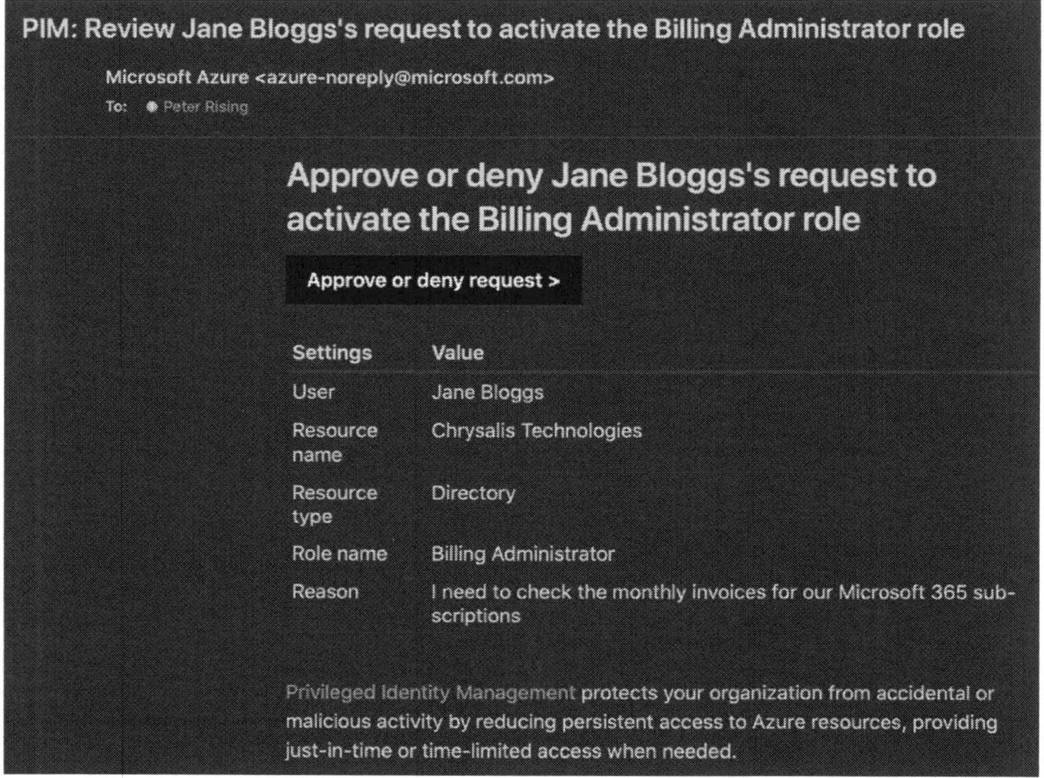

Figure 4.46 – Approval email

9. The approver can click on the link in the email to **Approve or deny the request**. Alternatively, they can go to the Azure portal, access the PIM pane, select the request, and choose **Approve**, as shown in the following screenshot:

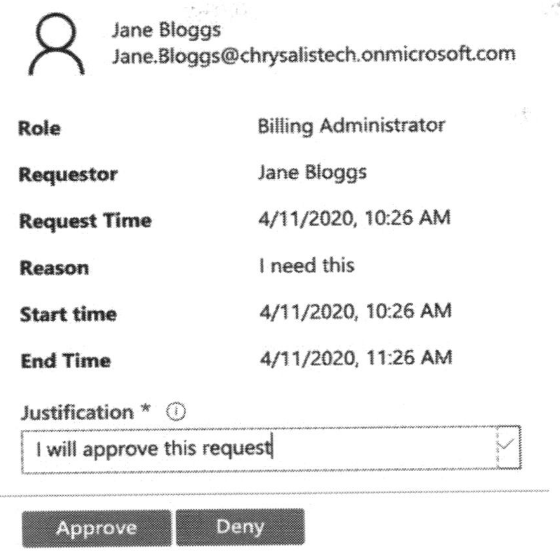

Figure 4.47 – Approving the request

10. The role has now been activated and the approver will receive an email confirming their approval action, as shown in the following screenshot:

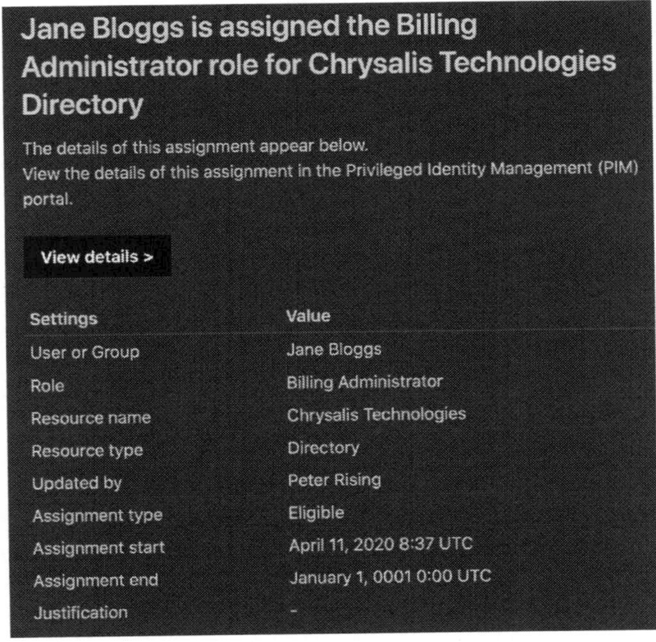

Figure 4.48 – Approver notification of activation by user

11. The user will also receive an email confirmation and can check **Azure AD roles | Active roles** to see that the role approval and activation has been successfully completed, as shown in the following screenshot:

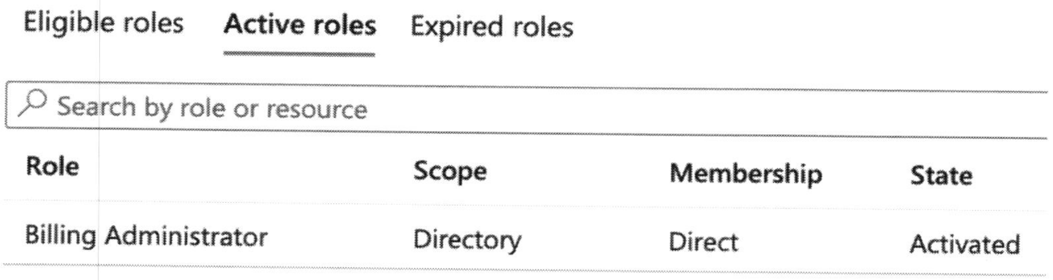

Eligible roles Active roles Expired roles

Search by role or resource

Role	Scope	Membership	State
Billing Administrator	Directory	Direct	Activated

Figure 4.49 – Role approved and activated for the user

> **Important note**
> It is also possible to use PowerShell to configure PIM. There are some references to this at the end of this chapter.

Now, you should have a good grasp of the steps required to configure PIM. You have learned how to configure PIM, as well as the Task and Manage features available within PIM. We demonstrated how to make users eligible for privileged roles, how to make the roles permanent when required, how to approve or deny user activation approval requests, and how to remove role assignments from user accounts.

To conclude this chapter, we will show you how to monitor PIM and review audit history.

Monitoring PIM

Privileged Identity Management provides several ways in which you can monitor it to ensure that it is being used in an appropriate manner. PIM administrators are able to view activity, audit trails, and activation events for roles within Azure AD.

In order to view alerts within PIM, you will need to complete the following steps:

1. Open the PIM pane from the Azure portal and choose **Azure AD roles** from the **Manage** section, as shown in the following screenshot:

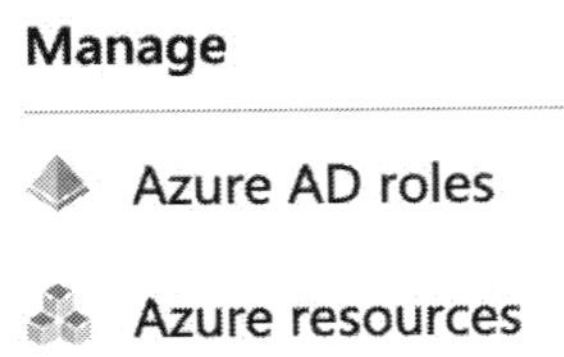

Figure 4.50 – Managing Azure AD roles

2. Select **Alerts** from the **Manage** tab, as shown in the following screenshot:

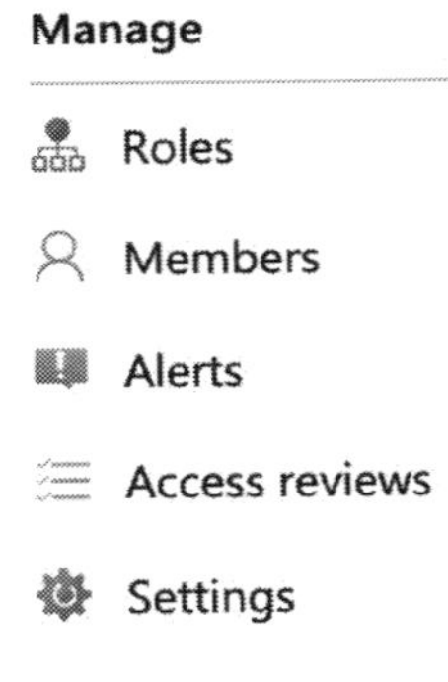

Figure 4.51 – Alerts

3. Here, you can review the recorded alerts that relate to PIM. Each alert has an alert name, as shown in the following screenshot:

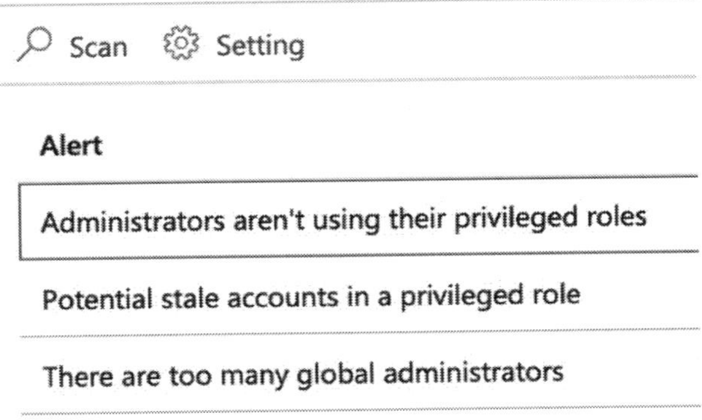

Figure 4.52 – Reviewing alerts

4. Clicking on each alert will give you more information about them, as shown in the following screenshot:

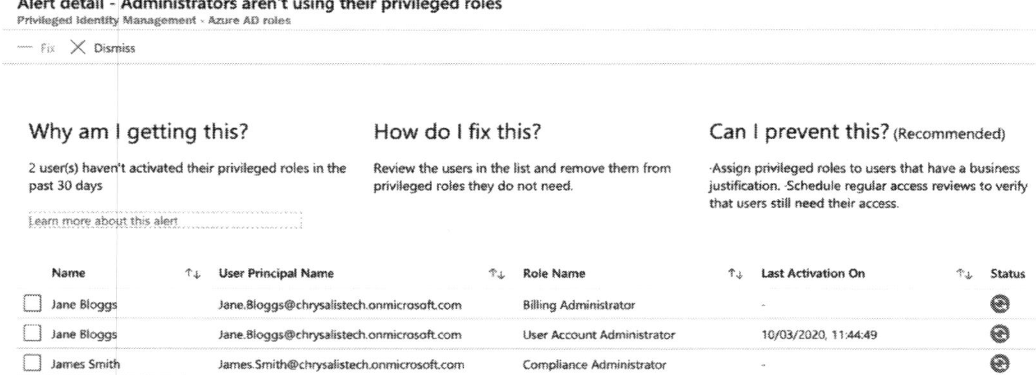

Figure 4.53 – Alert details

5. If you are comfortable with the alert, you can simply dismiss it. Alternatively, you can choose to fix it, which will resolve the alert once you have taken the corrective steps.

We are also able to review **My Audit History** from the **Activity** section. Here, we can see the recent actions that have been processed in detail:

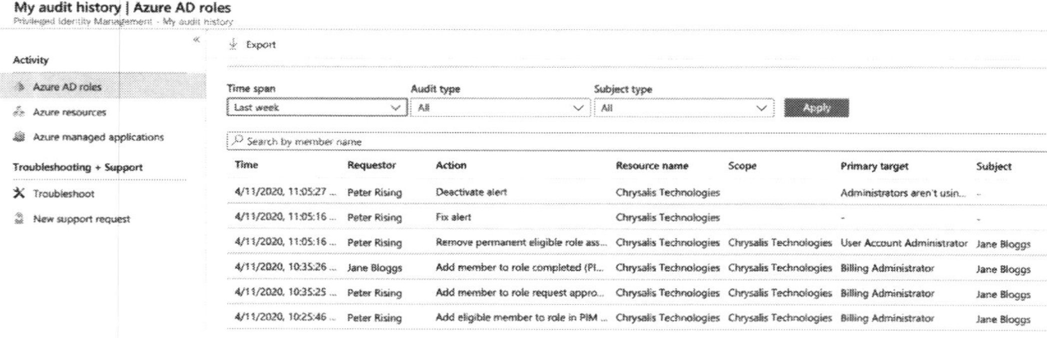

Figure 4.54 – My audit history

> **Important note**
> The audit history can be exported to a .csv file in order to make it easier to read, sort, and search.

So, in this section, we have shown you how you can monitor PIM within your Azure AD environment, as well as how you can check for stale accounts and administrators who are not using their privileged roles. It is important to constantly monitor PIM to ensure that privileged roles are being used appropriately and that the principle of least privilege is being applied where possible.

Summary

In this chapter, we have introduced you to the principles of RBAC and PIM.

We showed you how RBAC provides access management capabilities to Azure resources and enables Microsoft 365 administrators to manage access to these resources, the actions users can take, and what resources are accessible to them.

In addition, we demonstrated the steps you need to consider in order to diligently plan your PIM configuration, how to activate and license PIM on your tenant, and configure and assign roles to your users and resources with the principle of least privilege applied.

We also demonstrated how to make users eligible for privileged access roles to gain just-in-time access, how to assign permanent access to privileged roles where required, and how to remove this access when it is no longer required. Finally, we looked at the various monitoring capabilities of PIM, which enable you to keep on top of your PIM configuration and make sure that access is granted only when it's required.

In the next chapter, we will look at Identity Protection concepts in detail, along with techniques you can use to identify and protect against risky sign-in activities, such as impossible travel and non-compliant devices.

Questions

1. Which of the following is not one of the three components of an RBAC role assignment?

   a. Security principal

   b. Security reader

   c. Role definition

   d. Scope

2. True or False: You can configure Privileged Identity Management with an Azure AD Premium P1 subscription.

   a. True

   b. False

3. Where in the Azure portal would you configure RBAC for a resource?

   a. In the Access Control (IAM) option within the resource pane

   b. In the Properties option within the resource pane

   c. In the Overview option within the resource pane

   d. In the Health option within the resource pane

4. Which of the following roles are automatically granted to the first person to enable PIM in Azure AD (choose two)?

   a. Privileged Role Administrator

   b. Global Administrator

   c. Security Administrator

   d. User Management Administrator

   e. Helpdesk Administrator

5. True or False: The PIM administrator user can elevate users who are eligible for privileged roles so that they have permanent access to those roles.

   a. True

   b. False

6. When a user requires approval in order to be granted just-in-time access to a privileged role, which two methods can they use to see whether their request has been approved or denied?

   a. Wait for an email notification that contains the PIM approver's response to the request

   b. Wait for a text to arrive on their mobile device that contains the PIM approver's response to the request

   c. Log in to the Azure portal, navigate to Privileged Identity Management, and select My requests

d. Log in to the Azure portal, navigate to Privileged Identity Management, and select Review Access

e. Log in to the Azure portal, navigate to Privileged Identity Management, and select Approve requests

7. What type of license is required in order to configure RBAC?

 a. Azure AD Premium P1

 b. Azure AD Premium P2

 c. Azure AD basic

8. True or False: In RBAC, it is possible to add custom roles to a role definition.

 a. True

 b. False

9. When configuring the approval requirement to grant privileged access to an Azure resource, what will happen to the approval if you do not specify an approver?

 a. The approval will fail and the user will be notified

 b. The approval will fail and the user will not be notified

 c. The approval will complete automatically

 d. The approval will automatically be sent to the PIM administrator

10. True or False: RBAC can be managed using the Azure Cloud Shell.

 a. True

 b. False

References

Please refer to the following links for more information regarding what was covered in this chapter:

- RBAC for Azure resources: `https://docs.microsoft.com/en-us/azure/role-based-access-control/overview?wt.mc_id=4039827`
- Managing access to Azure resources using RBAC and the Azure portal: `https://docs.microsoft.com/en-us/azure/role-based-access-control/role-assignments-portal?wt.mc_id=4039827`

- Managing access to Azure resources using RBAC and Azure PowerShell: `https://docs.microsoft.com/en-us/azure/role-based-access-control/role-assignments-powershell`
- Viewing activity logs for RBAC changes to Azure resources: `https://docs.microsoft.com/en-us/azure/role-based-access-control/change-history-report?wt.mc_id=4039827`
- What is Azure AD Privileged Identity Management?: `https://docs.microsoft.com/en-us/azure/active-directory/privileged-identity-management/pim-configure?wt.mc_id=4039827`
- Getting started using Privileged Identity Management: `https://docs.microsoft.com/en-us/azure/active-directory/privileged-identity-management/pim-getting-started?wt.mc_id=4039827`
- Viewing activity and audit history for Azure resource roles in Privileged Identity Management: `https://docs.microsoft.com/en-us/azure/active-directory/privileged-identity-management/pim-resource-roles-use-the-audit-log?wt.mc_id=4039827`

5
Azure AD Identity Protection

When you consider how key identity is when planning an Office 365 implementation, the importance of protecting those identities should be given equal priority. Azure AD Identity Protection enables Microsoft 365 administrators to protect their user identities by detecting and recording identity-based risks so that they can be analyzed and investigated, and corrective measures taken.

In this chapter, we will examine the principles of Azure AD Identity Protection, how it can be used to review risky events and flagged user accounts, and create risk-based conditional access policies to improve security. You will learn how to enable this feature within the Azure portal, identify the Identity Protection roles, and conduct investigations to detect risk events and vulnerabilities within your Microsoft 365 environment.

We will cover these topics in the following order:

- Understanding Identity Protection
- Configuring user risk and sign-in risk policies
- Configuring MFA registration policies
- Configuring alert options
- Managing and resolving risk events

Understanding Identity Protection

Azure AD Identity Protection is a feature that works on the principle of risk detection and remediation. It allows Microsoft 365 administrators to view risk events and detections in the Azure portal, and then control what happens when risks are detected. They can also configure notifications regarding alerts about risk activities and receive a weekly report via email. Identity Protection will detect and report on risk classification events based on the following categories:

- Impossible travel
- Anonymous IP addresses
- Unfamiliar sign-in behavior
- Malware- linked IP addresses
- Leaked credentials
- Azure AD threat intelligence

Whenever one of these risk classifications is matched, this will result in a remediation action being triggered, such as requiring the affected users to register for/or respond to MFA or being required to perform a password reset. If a risk is deemed significant enough, the affected user can even be blocked entirely until further notice, and administrators can review reports in the Azure AD Identity Protection dashboard to respond to and resolve matches against risky users, risky sign-ins, and risk detections.

In order to view or configure Azure AD Identity Protection, you need to be a member of one of the following groups: Security Reader, Security Operator, Global Reader, or Global Administrator.

Azure AD Identity Protection requires an **Azure AD Premium P2**, **EM+S E5**, or **Microsoft 365 E5** license (for all Azure AD users who you wish to benefit from the feature) in order to take advantage of all the included policies, reports, and notifications.

With Identity Protection, you can protect users with risk policies. These are separated into the following categories:

- User risk policies
- Sign-in risk policies

It is also possible to protect your users with an MFA registration policy.

In the following sections, we will examine each of these policies in turn. So, now that we have explained the principles of Azure AD Identity Protection, let's look at how we can start to configure user risk policies and sign-in risk policies.

Configuring user risk and sign-in risk policies

User risk policies and sign-in risk policies are more or less identical in what they do. They are both capable of allowing or blocking access to Azure AD based on risk. This difference can be seen in the following screenshot in terms of the control enforcements that can be applied:

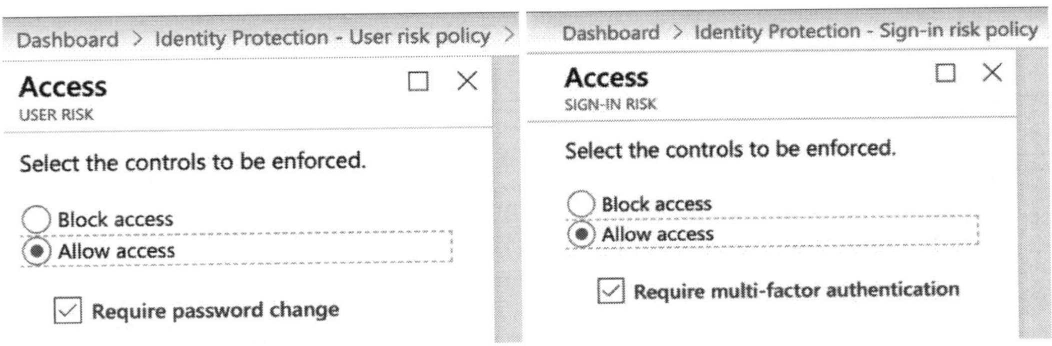

Figure 5.1 – User risk policy and Sign-in risk policy

With a user risk policy, you are able to block or allow access and require a password change, whereas with a sign-in risk policy, you are able to block or allow access and require MFA.

So, let's look at how we can configure these policies, starting with an example of a user risk policy. This will show you how a policy can be assigned to users, how conditions for the risk level can be applied, and whether or not the policy will allow the user to proceed or whether they should be blocked. Follow these steps:

1. Log in to the Azure portal (with the appropriate access, as described previously) at `https://portal.azure.com`. Search for `Azure Identity Protection` and select it. You will be taken to the following screen:

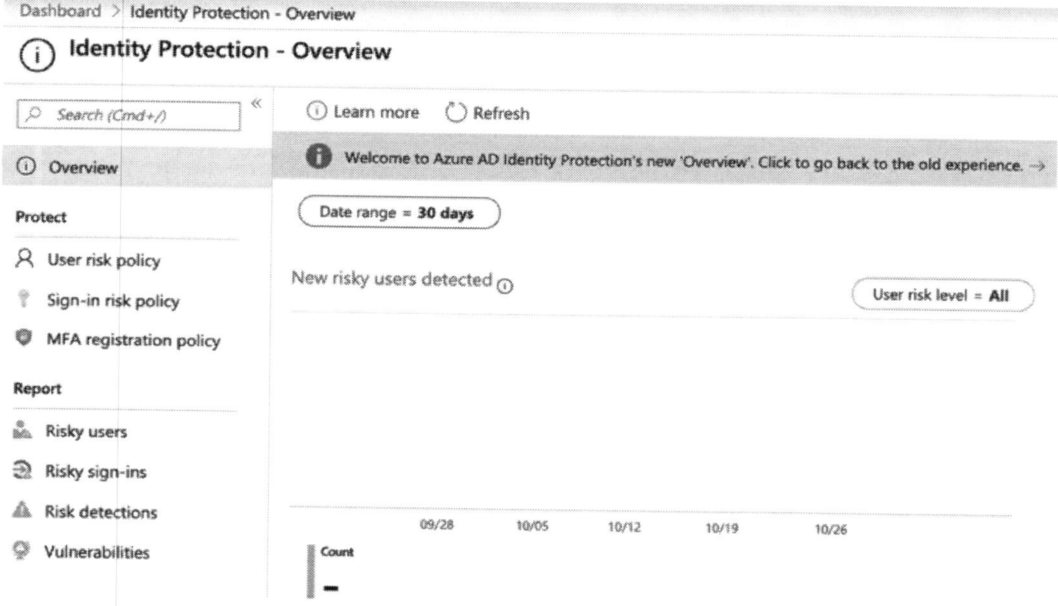

Figure 5.2 – Identity Protection - Overview

2. Under the **Protect** option, select **User risk policy**:

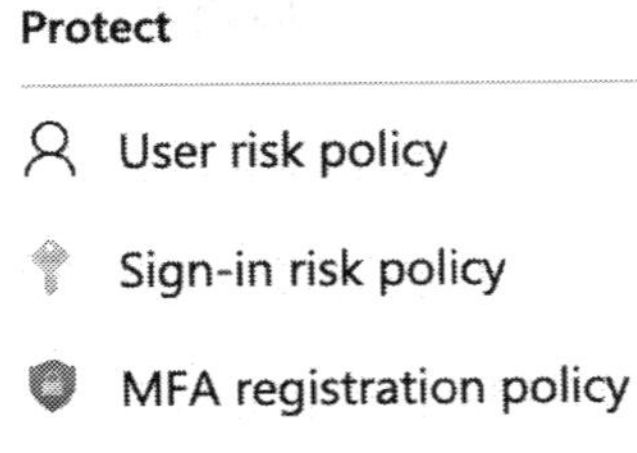

Figure 5.3 – Protect options

3. You will now see the following options for configuring the policy:

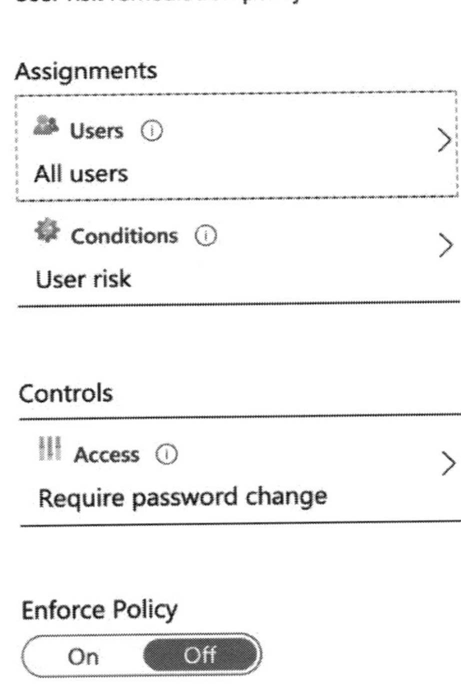

Figure 5.4 – Policy settings

4. Under **Users**, you can choose to include **All Users**, or select chosen users or groups. It is also possible to exclude specific users:

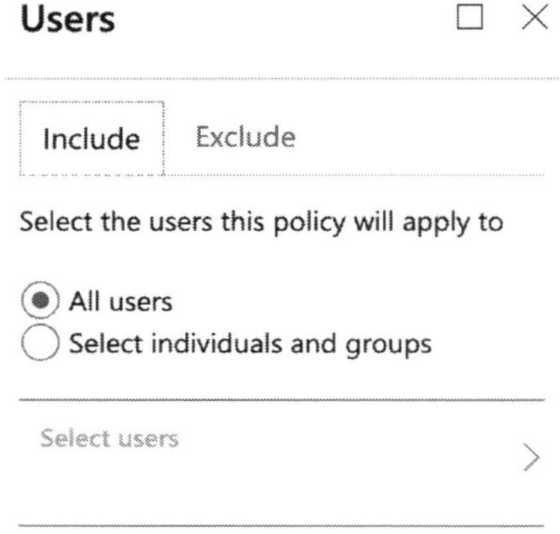

Figure 5.5 – Including or excluding users

5. Make your required selections and click **Done**.
6. Next, under **Conditions**, you have the option to **Select a risk level** that will be applied to the **User risk** policy. In the following screenshot, I have chosen **Medium and above**:

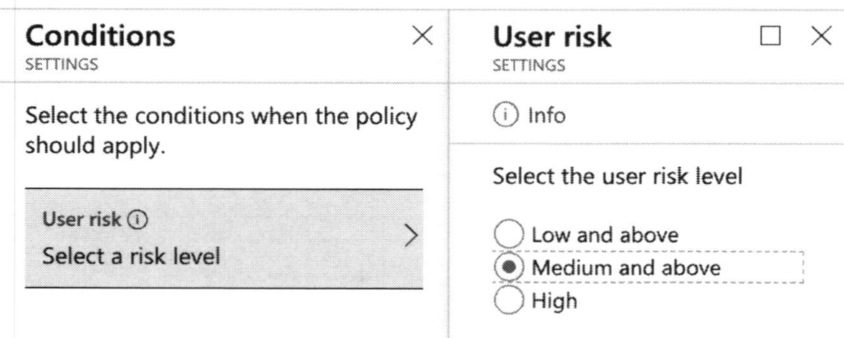

Figure 5.6 – Conditions risk level

> **Important note**
>
> Make sure that you choose an acceptable risk level when making these selections. It is important to plan for a balance between user experience and security. It is Microsoft's recommendation to set the user risk policy to **High** and the sign-in risk policy to **Medium** or higher.

7. Click **Select** and then **Done** to accept your settings.
8. Now, we need to select **Controls** and then **Access** so that we can choose whether we are going to allow or block access when this risk policy generates a match. We can also force the user to complete a password reset here:

Access
USER RISK

Select the controls to be enforced.

Block access
Allow access

Require password change

Figure 5.7 – Access options

9. Click **Select** to confirm your settings. Then, set the **Enforce Policy** option to **On** and click **Save** to commit your choices to the user risk policy:

Figure 5.8 – Enforce Policy settings

Important note

When applying a risk policy to All Users, be careful not to get locked out of your own account. Always have a break glass account that you specifically exclude from the policy to ensure you can continue to gain access. A break glass account is an emergency account that will only ever be used to regain access to your Microsoft 365 environment should you inadvertently become locked out.

With that, we have configured a user risk policy. Should you wish to configure a **Sign-in risk** policy, the process is exactly the same, with the exception of the sign-in risk access controls, which enable you to choose to **Require multi-factor authentication** alongside blocking or allowing access:

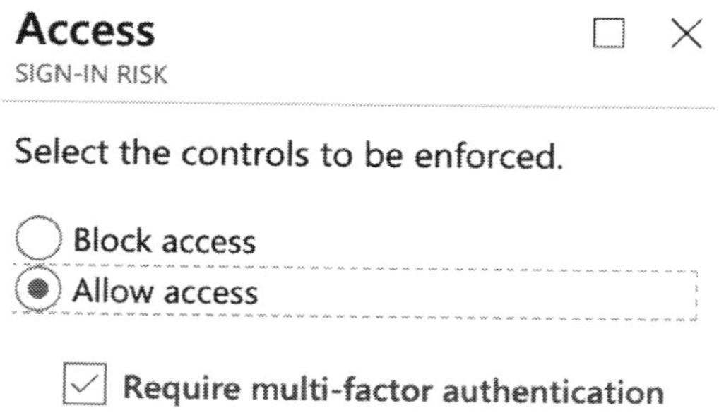

Access
SIGN-IN RISK

Select the controls to be enforced.

- ( ) Block access
- (•) Allow access
  - [x] **Require multi-factor authentication**

Figure 5.9 – Access settings

Once you have your user and sign-in risk policies configured, they will start working to automate responses based on your risk detection settings. Some further considerations when enabling these policies are as follows:

- If you wish your users to be able to respond to Identity Protection requirements such as enforcing MFA and password changes, ensure that you enable your users for MFA and self-service password reset (as described in *Chapter 2, Authentication and Security*).
- When configuring acceptable risk levels, be aware of the possible effects on your users. For example, a high threshold will minimize the number of times a risk policy is triggered. However, this will also prevent low and medium risk detections, which could lead to malicious actors being able to exploit a compromised identity within your environment.

So, now you are familiar with the best practices for configuring user risk and sign-in risk policies. We showed you how to create these policies, assign them to your users, and exclude them from certain users, along with how to set the required risk level for the policy and what actions should be taken if there is a policy match. Next, we will look at how to configure MFA registration policies with Azure AD Identity Protection.

Configuring MFA registration policies

We have already discussed MFA in *Chapter 2, Authentication and Security*, and *Chapter 3, Implementing Conditional Access Policies*, and illustrated how MFA can be enabled and enforced for your Microsoft 365 users via both the Office 365 Admin Center and by using Conditional Access policies. It is also possible to configure an Azure MFA policy for your cloud-based users from within the **Azure AD Identity Protection** pane.

In the context of Identity Protection, it is always preferable to require Azure MFA for your user sign-ins as it does the following:

- Provides strong authentication with a choice of verification methods
- Provides your users with the option to effectively take responsibility for their own risk detections and use self-remediation

In order to configure the MFA registration policy within Azure Identity Protection, we need to complete the following steps:

1. From the **Azure AD Identity Protection** pane, navigate to the **Protect** section and select **MFA registration policy**:

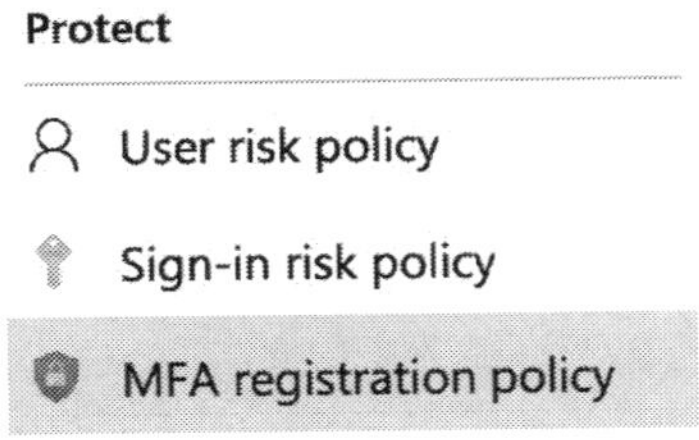

Figure 5.10 – MFA registration policy

2. Next, under **Assignments**, select **Users**:

Figure 5.11 – Assigning a policy to users

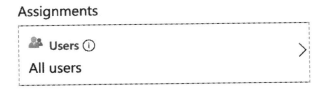

3. Here, you can decide whether you want to apply the requirement for MFA to all your users or whether to select specific users or groups. You also have the option to explicitly exclude users from the policy. When you have made your selections, click **Done**:

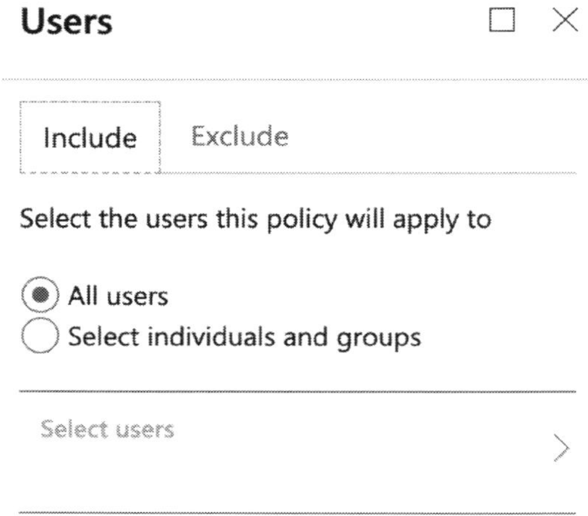

Figure 5.12 – Including or excluding users

4. Next, under **Controls** and **Access**, ensure that **Require Azure MFA** registration is selected:

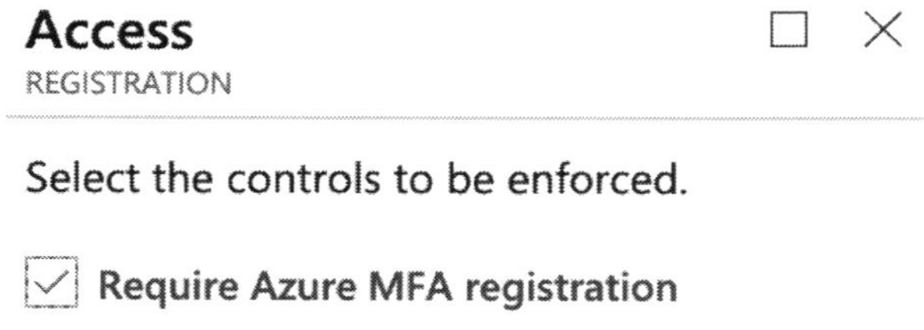

Figure 5.13 – Access controls

5. Click **Select**, and then ensure that **Enforce Policy** is set to **On**:

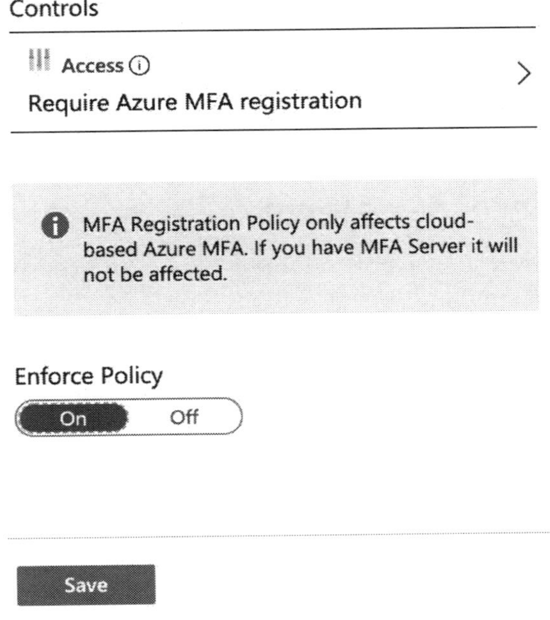

Figure 5.14 – Enforcing the policy

6. Click **Save**.

The policy will be saved, and the affected users will be prompted to register for MFA the next time they sign in with their Microsoft 365 credentials. They will be able to bypass MFA registration and continue to log in for a period of 14 days. They will then be forced to complete the registration process, or they will be unable to gain access.

> **Important note**
>
> Once again, it is important to ensure that your break glass account is explicitly excluded from the requirement to register for Azure MFA.

So, with this, we have shown you how an MFA registration policy can be configured and deployed to your Microsoft 365 users with Azure AD Identity Protection. This will force your users to register for MFA. If you have Azure AD Premium P2 licenses available to you in your tenancy, it is highly recommended to deploy the MFA registration policy.

Configuring alert options

Azure AD Identity Protection is only effective if the available alerting options are correctly configured, the alerts are being diligently reviewed by administrators, and the appropriate steps are being taken where needed. Identity Protection has two notification settings that can be configured to alert administrators of risk detections within Microsoft 365. These are **Users at risk detected alerts** and **Weekly digest**. Let's look at each of these in turn.

Users at risk detected alerts

This alert can be found under the **Notify** section of the **Azure AD Identity Protection** pane and can be used to configure an email alert that will be sent to administrators when a user at risk is detected. The benefit of this is that administrators will receive email alerts as soon as the risk event is detected:

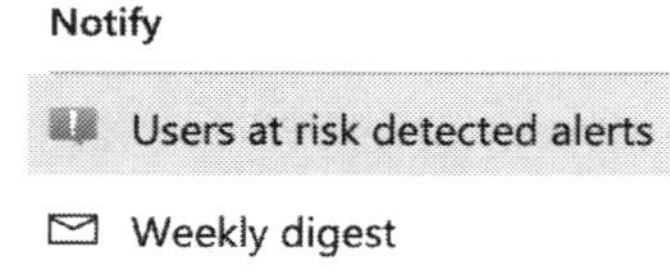

Figure 5.15 – Notification options

Clicking on this will allow you to configure the options for **Users at risk detected alerts**.

You can then complete the following steps to set the alert risk level, configure who will receive the alerts, and also download a report that will show you who has been set to receive these alerts:

1. You will see the following options (by default, the risk level is set to **High**):

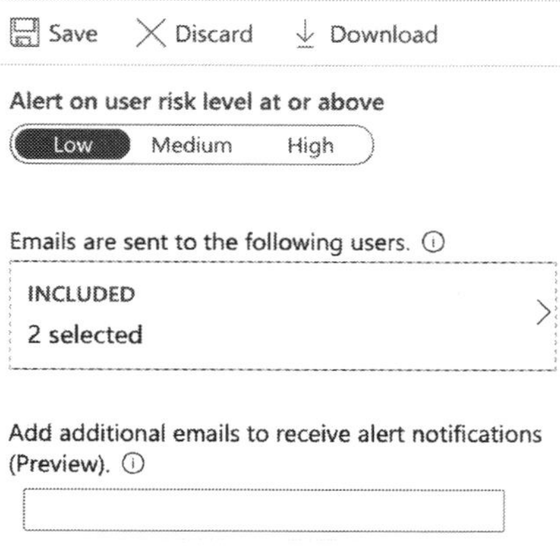

Figure 5.16 – Setting the alert level

2. Choose the alert level that you wish to configure, and then click to select which users are going to receive these alert emails:

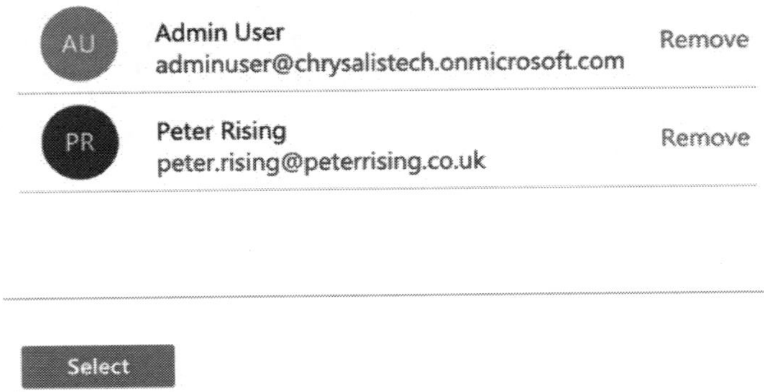

Figure 5.17 – Selecting users for alerts

3. Once you have added the required users, click **Select** and then **Save**.
4. You can also click **Download** to generate a CSV file that contains the users who have been configured to receive these alerts:

	A	B	C
1	Object ID	User	Alert Email Status
2	f208bac9-71b2-4e69-92ab-ebbe496d8515	Peter Rising	Opted In
3	176c9e8a-2245-4c56-a5b1-584ae48af066	Admin User	Opted In

Figure 5.18 – Example of a CSV report

When an alert email is triggered, the included recipients will receive a notification email in the following format:

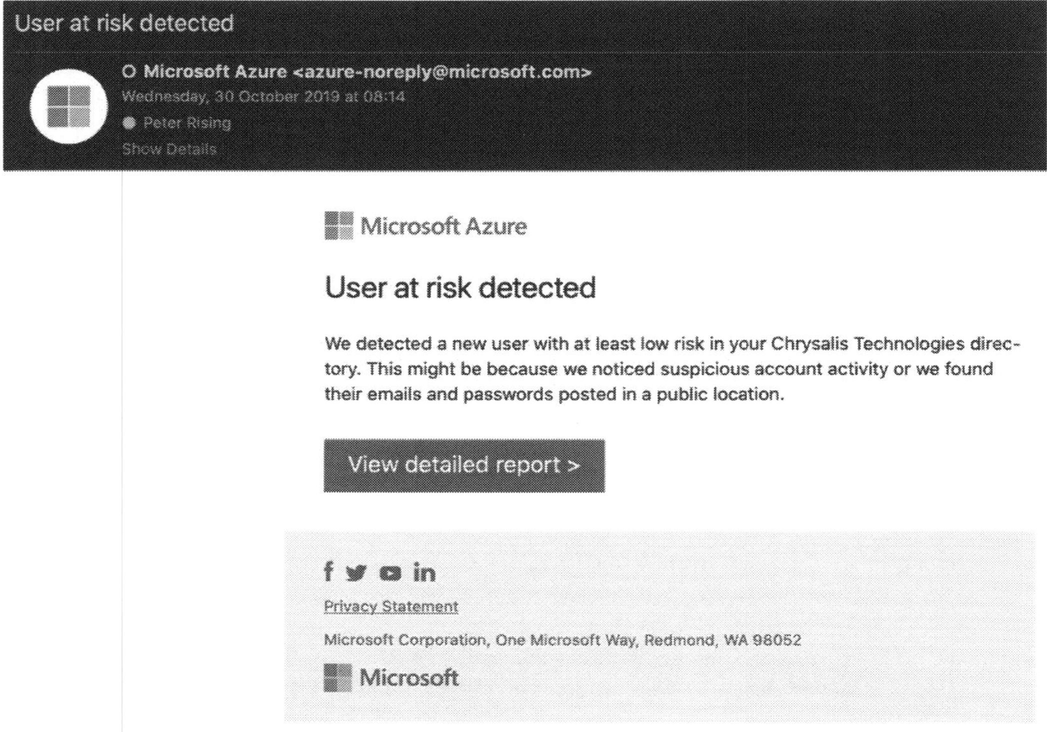

Figure 5.19 – Example of an email alert

Clicking on **View detailed report** will direct the email recipient to log in to Azure AD Identity Protection in the Azure Portal, view the alert, and take corrective action.

Weekly digest

While the users at risk detected alerts will be generated whenever Azure AD Identity Protection detects a risk, the Weekly digest works differently and will send an email on a weekly basis to show administrators how many users have been flagged for risk, how many risk events have been detected, and how many vulnerabilities have been detected.

The Weekly digest alert can also be found under the **Notify** section of **Azure AD Identity Protection** and can be configured as follows:

1. Click on **Weekly digest**; you will see the following options:

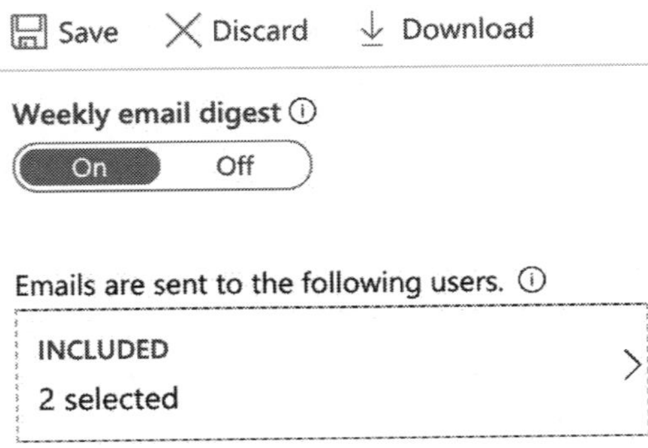

Figure 5.20 – Weekly email digest

2. Click **Included**, under **Emails are sent to the following users**, to select who the weekly digest emails will be sent to:

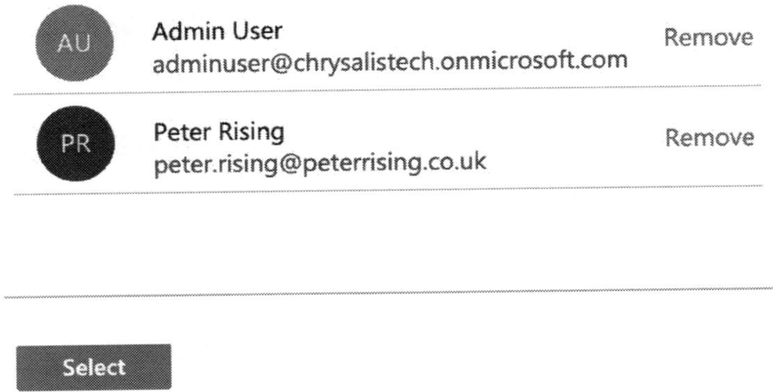

Figure 5.21 – Selecting users for the Weekly digest

3. Once you have chosen the users you wish to include when you are happy with your selections, click **Select** and then **Save**.

When the Weekly digest email has been generated, targeted users will receive a notification email in the following format:

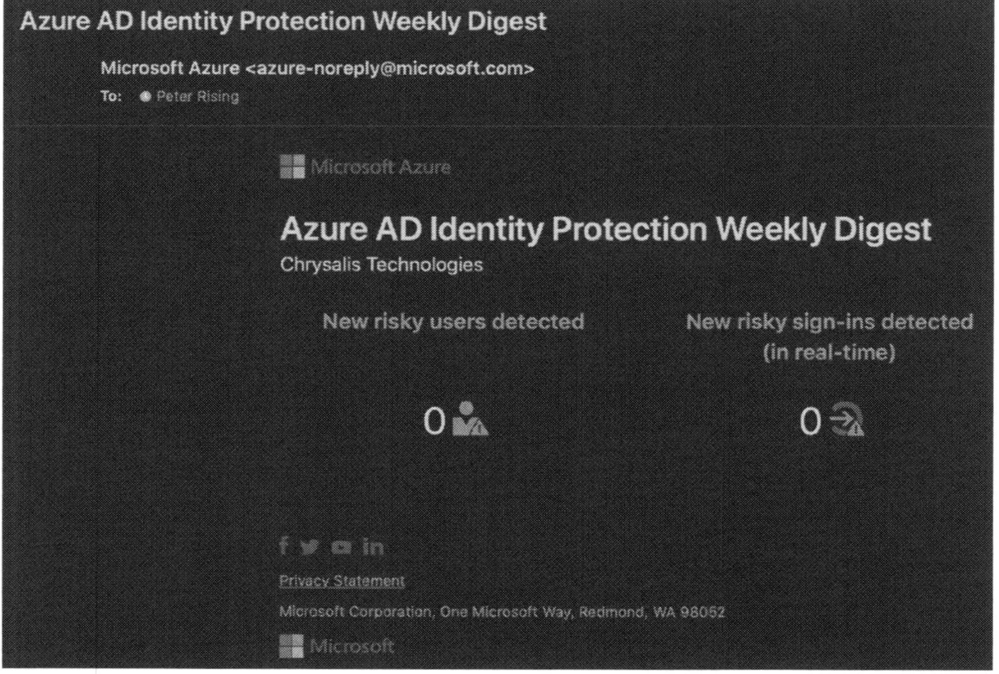

Figure 5.22 – Weekly digest email format

There are two options that the recipient can select from the email. These are as follows:

- New risky users detected
- New risky sign-ins detected (in real time)

Clicking on either of these will take the recipient directly into the **Azure AD Identity Protection** pane of the Azure portal. In the **Report** section, they can view and address the recorded incidents.

> **Important note**
>
> Configuring the users at risk alerts and the Weekly digest email will help you keep on top of your Azure AD Identity Protection. Review these regularly.

Next, we will show you how to manage and resolve risk events.

Managing and resolving risk events

The **Report** section of **Azure AD Identity Protection** provides M365 administrators with the ability to review and resolve events and detections, as shown in the following screenshot:

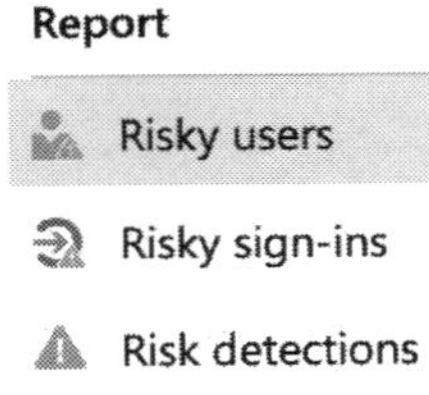

Figure 5.23 – Reports

You will be able to carry out investigations based on what is recorded in these sections and take steps to resolve any risks, as well as unblock any users who may have been blocked, provided it's safe to do so.

Let's look at each of the options within the **Report** section in detail.

Examining users at risk

A risky user is someone who's activity has matched a risk level set in Azure ID Identity Protection. When a risk is detected, alerts will be sent to administrators, as shown earlier in this chapter. However, it is important to proactively review the list of users at risk in Azure AD Identity Protection in the Azure portal and take corrective actions.

Under **Risky Users**, you will see a list of the users within your tenant who have been determined to be at risk. You will be able to see the user's name, **Risk state**, **Risk level**, and the date that the risk was last updated. An example of this is shown in the following screenshot:

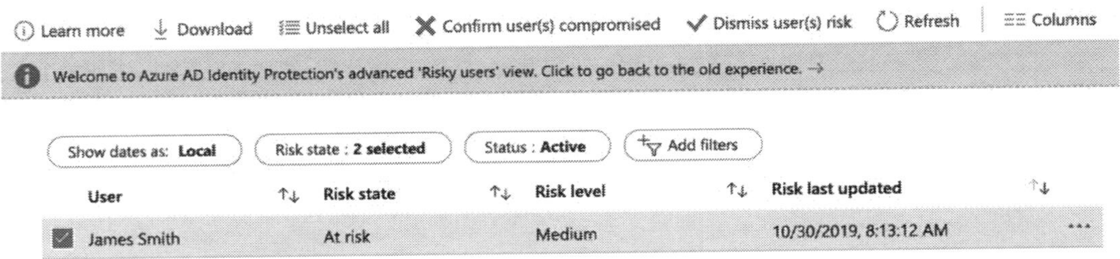

Figure 5.24 – User at risk

To further examine users at risk, we can take the following steps:

1. If you click on the ellipsis to the right of the status of the highlighted user, you will see more options, as follows:

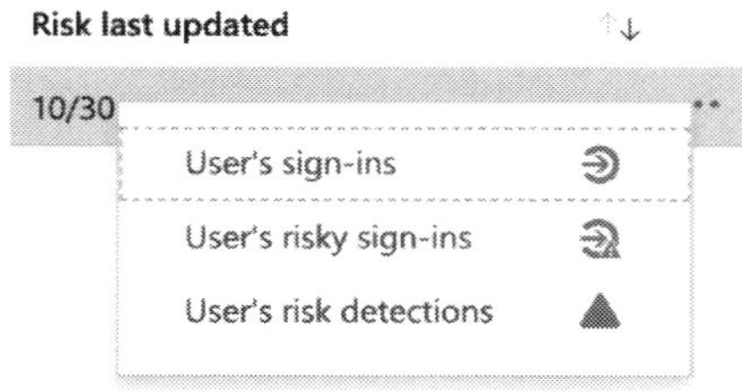

Figure 5.25 – More options

2. Highlighting an at-risk user will provide you with a detailed summary at the bottom of the **Risky Users** window, as follows:

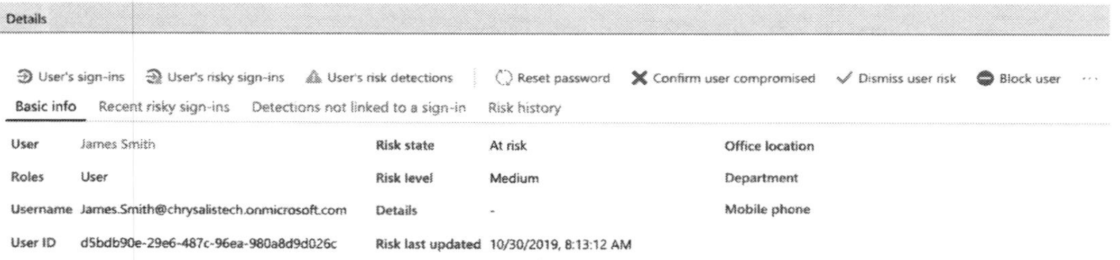

Figure 5.26 – Detail summary

Within this detail summary, you have the option to drill down and view detailed information about the user's recent activity, including the following:

- User's sign-ins
- User's risky sign-ins
- User's risk detections

Based on the information that is gathered from these events, you have the option to then apply the following actions or conditions to that user:

- Reset the user's password
- Confirm that the user is compromised
- Dismiss the user risk if you are confident that this is safe to do
- Block the user

While three of these available actions are self-explanatory, should you need to confirm that a user is compromised, then that user will be moved to the **High risk** category in order to optimize future risk assessment, as shown in the following screenshot:

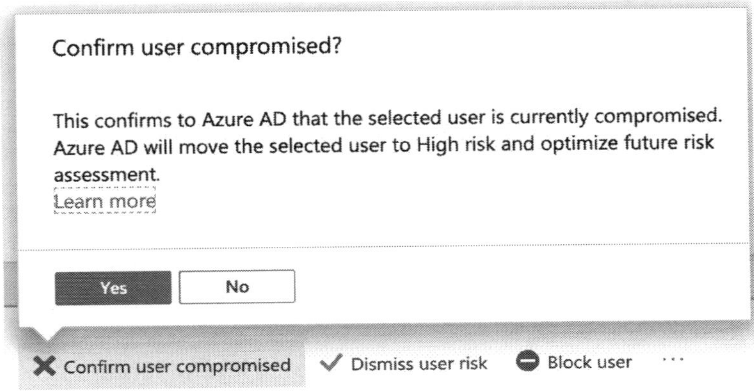

Figure 5.27 – Confirming that a user is compromised

Next, we will look at risky sign-ins.

Examining risky sign-ins

A risky sign-in is recorded in Azure ID Identity Protection when a user signs in with their Microsoft 365 account and that activity triggers a risk event.

Microsoft 365 administrators can view and manage risky sign-in activity from the **Reports** section of the **Azure AD Identity Protection** pane in the Azure portal, as follows:

- Under **Risky sign-ins**, you are able to view and manage all recorded risky sign-in activity:

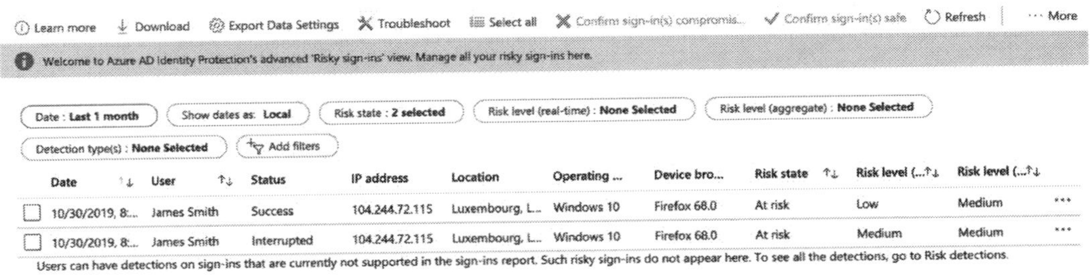

Figure 5.28 – Risky sign-ins

- Highlighting an entry in this list will provide you with additional details for the sign-in event, as shown in the following screenshot:

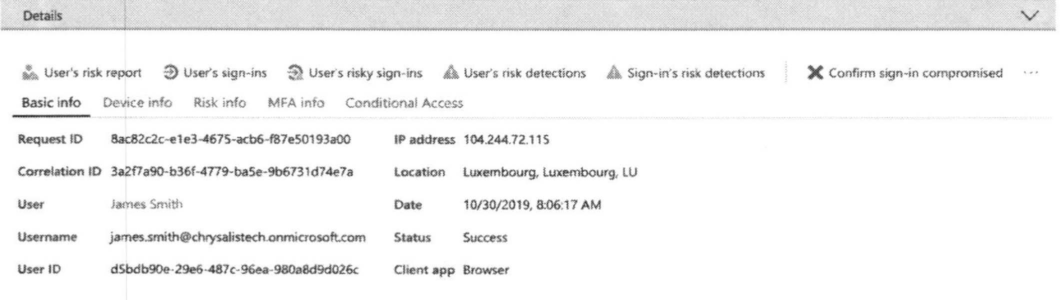

Figure 5.29 – Risk sign-in details

- Similar to Risky users, you are able to view risk reports, users' sign-ins, users' risky sign-ins, and sign-in risk detections from here. Upon examining the information presented here, you will have the option to confirm that the sign-in activity for the highlighted user was, in fact, compromised, as shown in the following screenshot:

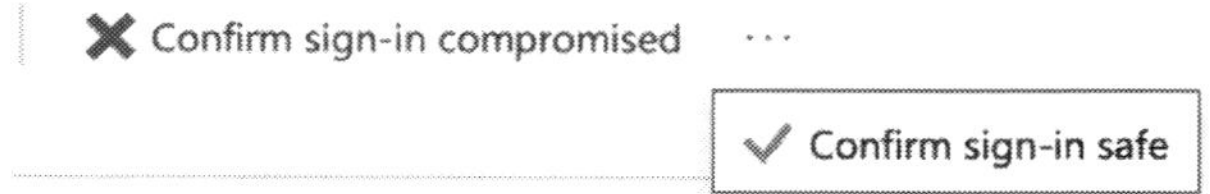

Figure 5.30 – Confirm sign-in compromised

Additionally, by clicking the ellipsis, you can confirm that the sign-in was safe.

Examining risk detections

A risk is recorded in Azure ID Identity Protection whenever any event is detected that matches a risk definition.

Microsoft 365 administrators can view and manage risk detections from the **Reports** section of the **Azure AD Identity Protection** pane in the Azure portal, as follows:

- Under **Risk detections**, you are able to view all recent recorded risk events:

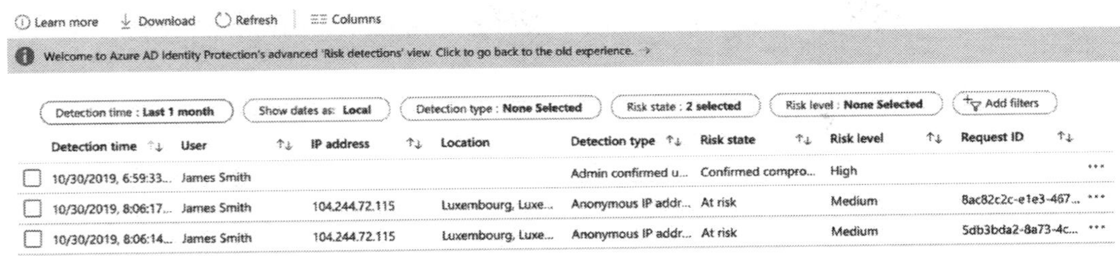

Figure 5.31 – Risk detections

- These events are broken down into the following sections:

  a. Detection Time

  b. User

  c. IP Address

  d. Location

  e. Detection Type

  f. Risk State

  g. Risk Level

  h. Request ID
- Highlighting an individual event in the list provides more details about it, as shown in the following screenshot:

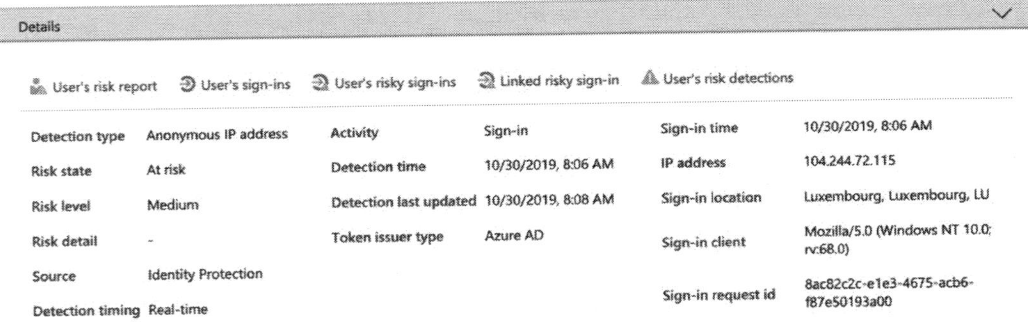

Figure 5.32 – Detected risk details

Once again, from here, you can gain access to risk reports, sign-ins and risky sign-ins, as well as risk detections.

The preceding steps provide you with the means to effectively review and manage all risk events using Azure AD Identity Protection.

> **Important note**
> Review, investigate, and remediate user risk events regularly to ensure you are keeping your Microsoft 365 tenant secure and protected. Resolve risk events as soon as you have reviewed them to keep the list of recorded events neat and manageable.

Summary

In this chapter, we examined Azure AD Identity Protection, which can be accessed from the Azure portal. We demonstrated how Identity Protection detects and records risky users, risky sign-ins, and risk events, and also provides us with the ability to review, investigate, and remediate these events with powerful preventative measures such as blocking user access, forcing password changes, or requiring MFA.

We also showed how reports and alerts can be generated and interpreted. Understanding these principles will enable you to effectively and diligently manage Azure AD Identity Protection in your Microsoft 365 environment and take the necessary steps to ensure that compromised users are identified and remediated in a timely fashion.

In the next chapter, we will examine the principles of Azure Advanced Threat Protection. We will show you how to plan for and configure ATP, as well as how to monitor and interpret the reporting features.

Questions

1. Which of the following is not a notification option that can be configured in Azure AD Identity Protection?

    a. Users at risk detected alerts

    b. Flagged users

    c. Weekly digest

2. True or False: With Identity Protection, you are able to configure an MFA registration policy.

   a. True

   b. False

3. Which of the following would not be considered an example of a sign-in risk?

   a. Impossible travel

   b. MFA authentication

   c. Anonymous IP address

   d. Leaked credentials

4. Which of these licenses is one of the possible requirements for users who need to be protected with Azure AD Identity Protection?

   a. Azure Information Protection P1

   b. Azure AD Premium P2

   c. Azure AD Premium P1

   d. Azure Information Protection P2

5. True or False: Microsoft 365 administrators can block users identified as a risk from accessing Microsoft 365 resources.

   a. True

   b. False

6. When the MFA registration policy is applied to a user, how long do they have before they are forced to complete the MFA registration process?

   a. 12 days

   b. 14 days

   c. 15 days

   d. 30 days

7. How can you best ensure that your permanent break glass account is not targeted by user risk policy and sign-in risk policy?

   a. Ensure your break glass account is synced with an on-premises AD

   b. Ensure your break glass account is a cloud-only account

   c. Ensure your break glass account is excluded from the user risk policy and the sign-in risk policy

   d. Ensure your break glass account has a complex password

8. True or False: With a user risk policy, it is possible to enforce MFA for a user.

   a. True

   b. False

9. Which of these is not a sign-in risk level?

   a. Low and above

   b. Medium and above

   c. Moderate

   d. High

10. True or False: When examining a risky user event, it is possible for administrators to confirm a suspected risky user as compromised, and in so doing, automatically raise the risk level of that user to **High**.

    a. True

    b. False

References

Please refer to the following links for more information regarding what was covered in this chapter:

- Principles of Azure AD Identity Protection and understanding how to plan for its implementation: `https://docs.microsoft.com/en-gb/azure/active-directory/identity-protection/overview-identity-protection`

- How to configure risk policies: https://docs.microsoft.com/en-gb/azure/active-directory/identity-protection/howto-identity-protection-configure-risk-policies?wt.mc_id=4039827
- How to remediate risk events and unblock users: https://docs.microsoft.com/en-gb/azure/active-directory/identity-protection/howto-identity-protection-remediate-unblock?wt.mc_id=4039827
- How to simulate risk events: https://docs.microsoft.com/en-gb/azure/active-directory/identity-protection/howto-identity-protection-simulate-risk?wt.mc_id=4039827
- How to configure notifications for Azure AD Identity Protection: https://docs.microsoft.com/en-gb/azure/active-directory/identity-protection/howto-identity-protection-configure-notifications

Section 2: Implementing and Managing Threat Protection

In this section, we will be examining how to implement and manage threat protection in Microsoft 365.

This part of the book comprises the following chapters:

- *Chapter 6, Configuring an Advanced Threat Protection Solution*
- *Chapter 7, Configuring Microsoft Defender ATP to Protect Devices*
- *Chapter 8, Message Protection in Office 365*
- *Chapter 9, Threat Intelligence and Tracking*
- *Chapter 10, Using Azure Sentinel to Monitor Microsoft 365 Security*

6

Configuring an Advanced Threat Protection Solution

When you consider the modern IT landscape, one of the biggest challenges for IT departments is how to protect your users and data from the ever-changing, ever-more-advanced complex threats that can target your environment. In the Microsoft 365 world, where you have users, email, and documents in the cloud—or on a hybrid cloud—this is particularly challenging. It is not possible to wrap a traditional firewall around your Microsoft 365 tenant or to deploy an old-style anti-virus solution, and yet it is absolutely crucial that you do everything that you can to prevent malicious actors from gaining access to and disrupting your business' data and intellectual property.

Azure Advanced Threat Protection (**Azure ATP**) provides IT departments with the means to take preventative measures against modern threats and, in this chapter, we will discuss how Azure ATP works, as well as what the prerequisites and processes for configuring and implementing Azure ATP are. We will also review the Azure ATP sensor settings, which are used to examine data within your ATP instance. We will examine the Azure ATP health center, where you can see how your Azure ATP instance is performing, as well as view alerts and reports when there are problems. Finally, we will examine how Azure ATP is monitored and how to interpret security alerts.

We will cover these topics in the following order:

- Identifying the organizational needs for Azure ATP
- Setting up an Azure ATP instance
- Managing Azure ATP activities

Identifying the organizational needs for Azure ATP

To identify your organization's needs in relation to Azure ATP, we first need to examine, in greater detail, exactly what Azure ATP is and what it can do. Essentially, Azure ATP is a security solution that is designed for use in hybrid cloud environments, where you have a mixture of on-premises and cloud users, data, and resources.

Azure ATP can monitor your on-premises domain controllers to identify and investigate advanced threats and compromised identities by using machine learning and behavioral algorithms to do the following:

- Identify suspicious activity.
- Detect and identify advanced attacks and malicious activities.
- Protect **Azure Active Directory** (**Azure AD**) identities and credentials.
- Provide incident reports.

Azure ATP can create behavioral profiles for your users and diligently analyze user activities and events to detect any advanced threats, compromised users, and malicious insiders that could threaten your organization. The information gathered by Azure ATP provides recommended security best practices and helps you significantly reduce the areas that are vulnerable to attack.

Let's look at Azure ATP in more detail, starting with how you can identify suspicious activity.

Understanding suspicious activity

Let's first examine what represents suspicious user activity from an Azure ATP perspective. To further understand this concept, you must first have an awareness of the cyber-attack kill chain, which is a series of steps to trace the progress of a cyber-attack from the beginning (which is referred to as the reconnaissance stage) to the end (which results in unauthorized data exfiltration).

Azure ATP focuses on the phases of the kill chain to detect suspicious activities, which can include the following:

- **Reconnaissance**: The attacker gathers information about the environment after gaining initial access.
- **Lateral movement**: The attacker works patiently to spread their attack and gain elevation of privileges.
- **Domain dominance (persistence)**: The attacker gains control of your environment and ensures that they have multiple points of entry to the environment.

It is crucial to understand these phases of the kill chain in order to identify suspicious activities in your Microsoft 365 environment.

Next, let's look at how we can identify advanced attacks and malicious activities.

Exploring advanced attacks and malicious activities

By focusing on the phases of the kill chain, Azure ATP can protect your environment from attack vectors before they cause any damage or disruption. Decoy accounts can be set up and used to track any malicious activities within your environment and generate security alerts that can include the following:

- Suspected identity theft using pass-the-ticket
- Suspected identity theft using pass-the-hash
- Suspected brute force attacks
- Reconnaissance using **Domain Name System** (**DNS**)
- Unusual protocols
- Suspicious service creation

The malicious activities listed here are only a few of the many that can generate security alerts within Azure ATP.

> **Important note**
>
> Please see the *References* section at the end of this chapter for links to further information and greater details on the available Azure ATP security alerts.

Understanding the Azure ATP architecture

Before you can start working with Azure ATP, it is important to have an understanding of the Azure ATP architecture. Azure ATP is a combination of services and components that work together to provide your Microsoft 365 tenant with comprehensive protection from modern threats and attacks that may target your environment. The following diagram shows the architecture of Azure ATP:

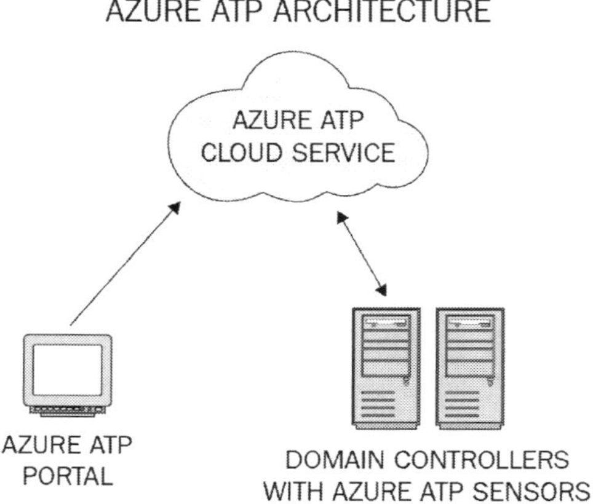

Figure 6.1 – The Azure ATP architecture

Azure ATP can function to protect your hybrid identity by leveraging three key components, as follows:

- The Azure ATP portal: This is where you create your Azure ATP instance, as well as monitor and address any threats that have been reported.
- The Azure ATP sensor: This is installed onto your on-premises domain controllers and is used to monitor domain controller traffic.
- The Azure ATP cloud service: This runs on Azure infrastructure and shares data using Microsoft's intelligent security graph. The cloud service can connect Azure ATP to Windows Defender ATP.

When you create your Azure ATP instance using the Azure ATP portal, this enables you to integrate with Microsoft security services, configure your Azure ATP sensor settings for your domain controllers, and review the data retrieved by these sensors to interpret any suspicious and malicious activities.

The Azure ATP sensor can monitor on-premises domain controller ingress and egress traffic. It receives events from domain controllers, which can include information about on-premises users and computers. The information gathered is passed on to the Azure ATP cloud service.

So, how does this information help you to understand and plan for your organization's needs for Azure ATP deployment? Essentially, we can break this down by answering the following questions:

- What do you need to protect?
- How can you protect it?
- How can you be certain that the protection you have applied is working?

The simple answers to these questions are as follows:

- You need to protect your Microsoft 365 hybrid cloud users and resources by deploying an Azure ATP instance in the Azure ATP portal.
- You can apply protection by installing Azure ATP sensors onto your on-premises domain controllers.
- You can verify that the protection is working by diligently monitoring Azure ATP events and alerts to review and respond to any potentially suspicious and malicious activities.

It is Microsoft's recommended best practice to deploy Azure ATP in three stages.

Stage 1

The following steps should be completed for stage 1 of deploying Azure ATP:

1. Set up Azure ATP to protect primary environments. Azure ATP can be deployed quickly to configure immediate protection.
2. Set sensitive accounts and honeytoken accounts (a honeytoken account is an account specifically set up to trap malicious actors).
3. Review reports and potential lateral movement paths.

Stage 2

The following steps should be completed for stage 2 of deploying Azure ATP:

1. Protect all domain controllers and forests in your organization.
2. Monitor all alerts and investigate any lateral movement or domain dominance.
3. Use the security alert guide to understand threats.

Stage 3

The following step should be completed for stage 3 of deploying Azure ATP: Integrate Azure ATP alerts into your security operation's workflows if applicable.

> **Important note**
>
> For detailed guidance on implementing Azure ATP in line with Microsoft best practice, please refer to the *An overview of Azure ATP* link that is included in the *References* section at the end of this chapter

So, the preceding steps will help you understand the principles of Azure ATP and show you how you can prepare to configure it. Now, you are ready to set up your Azure ATP instance and start taking advantage of the various features and capabilities of the product.

Setting up an Azure ATP instance

In order to set up Azure ATP for the first time, you must first ensure that you have the required licenses. Azure ATP requires an Enterprise Mobility + Security E5 or Microsoft 365 E5 license in order to function. Azure ATP data centers are set up in the following locations:

- Europe
- North America/Central America
- The Caribbean and Asia

Your Azure ATP instance will be automatically provisioned in the data center that is geographically closest to your Azure AD tenant. To begin setting up Azure ATP, log in to the Azure ATP portal, which can be accessed at `https://portal.atp.azure.com`, as a global administrator (or with the appropriate **Role-Based Access Control** (**RBAC**)) and complete the following steps:

1. Check to ensure that the domain controller or server can connect to the Azure ATP cloud service endpoints for the appropriate regions. These are as follows:

   `https://triprd1wceuw1sensorapi.atp.azure.com` (for Europe)

   `https://triprd1wcuse1sensorapi.atp.azure.com` (for the US)

   `https://triprd1wcasse1sensorapi.atp.azure.com` (for Asia)

2. Click **Create**, as in the following screenshot:

Azure Advanced Threat Protection

Welcome,
You're about to create your instance of Azure Advanced Threat Protection.

Create

Figure 6.2 – The Azure ATP welcome screen

3. Next, select the **Provide a username and password** option to connect to your on-premises AD forest, as follows:

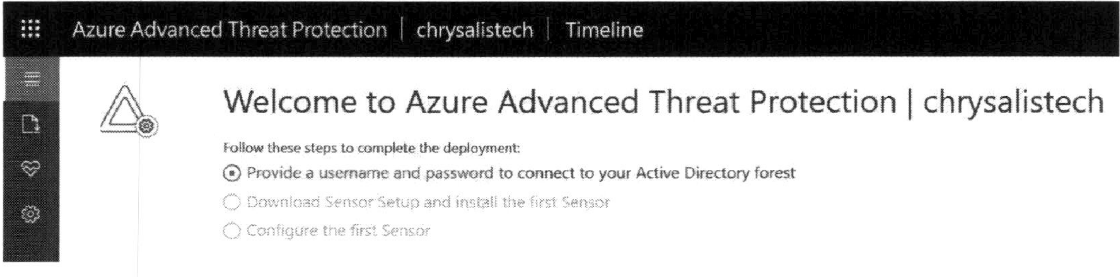

Figure 6.3 – Providing a username and password

4. Enter the administrative credentials for AD into the **Directory Services** dialogue box, as shown:

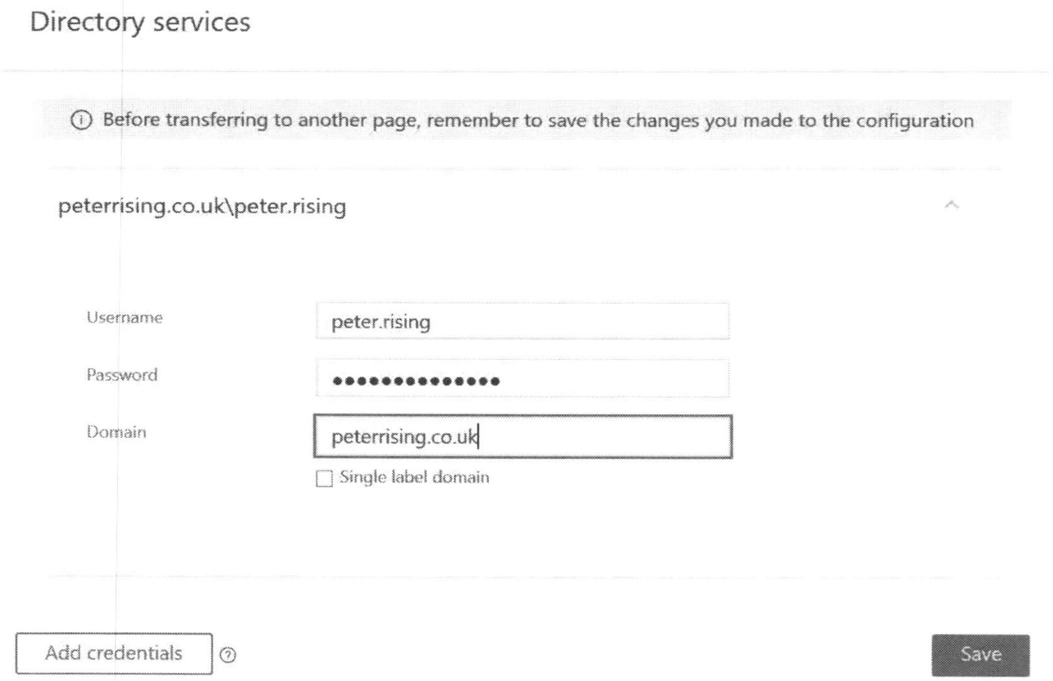

Directory services

Before transferring to another page, remember to save the changes you made to the configuration

peterrising.co.uk\peter.rising

Username peter.rising

Password ••••••••••••••

Domain peterrising.co.uk

Single label domain

Add credentials

Save

Figure 6.4 – Entering the on-premises credentials

5. Once you have entered your credentials, click **Save**.

6. Now, we need to download and install the sensor setup to your first domain controller. Click **Download Sensor Setup**, as in the following screenshot:

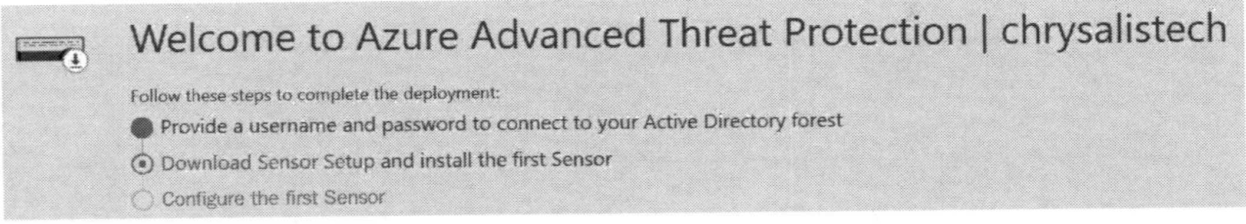

Figure 6.5 – Downloading the sensor setup

7. Click **Download** and save the ZIP file to a location where you will be able to access it to install the sensor to your domain controller. You will also need to copy your access key as this will also be required during setup:

> **Important note**
> Should you ever need to regenerate your access key, as in the following screenshot, you can do so without affecting the previous Azure ATP sensor installations.

Sensors

No Azure ATP sensors were detected.

Sensor setup Download

Access key TIWbkQFU/Akdfsvh Regenerate

NAME	TYPE	DOMAI...	VERSION	SERVICE STATUS	HEALTH

No Sensors registered

Figure 6.6 – Sensors

8. Next, from your domain controller or dedicated server, extract the installation files from the ZIP file that you saved in *Step 6*, then run the `setup.exe` Azure ATP sensor to start the installation wizard. You will see the following:

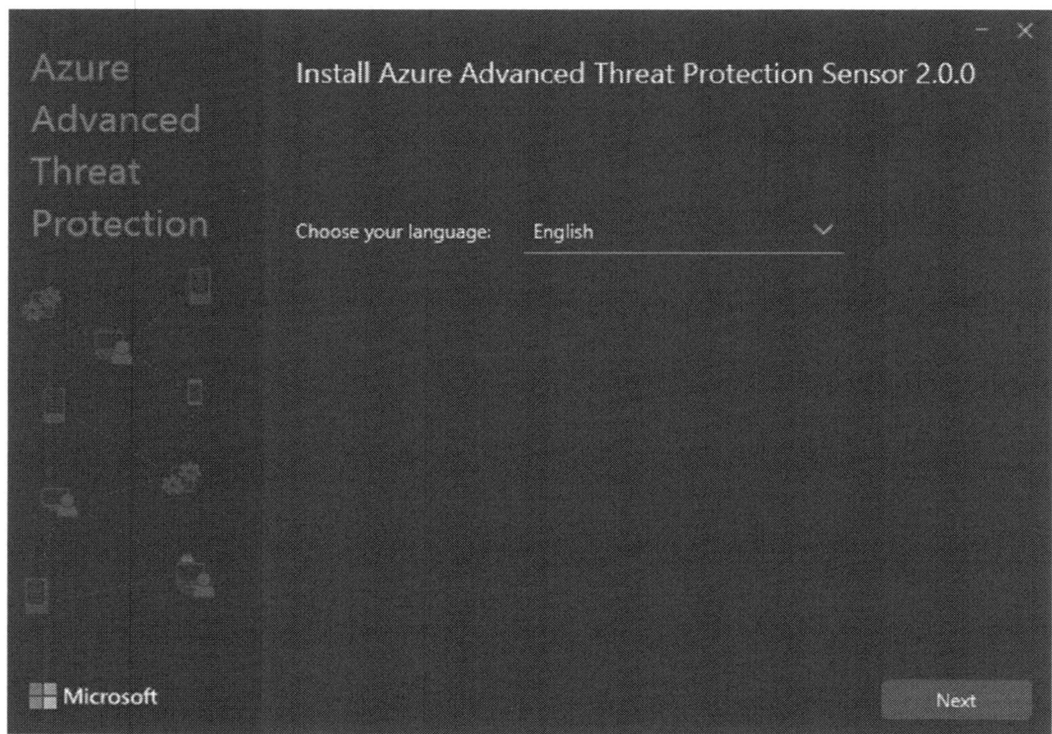

Figure 6.7 – Choosing the language

9. Select your chosen language and click **Next**. This will take you to the following screen. The wizard will detect whether you are installing the sensor to a domain controller or a dedicated server. Click **Next** again:

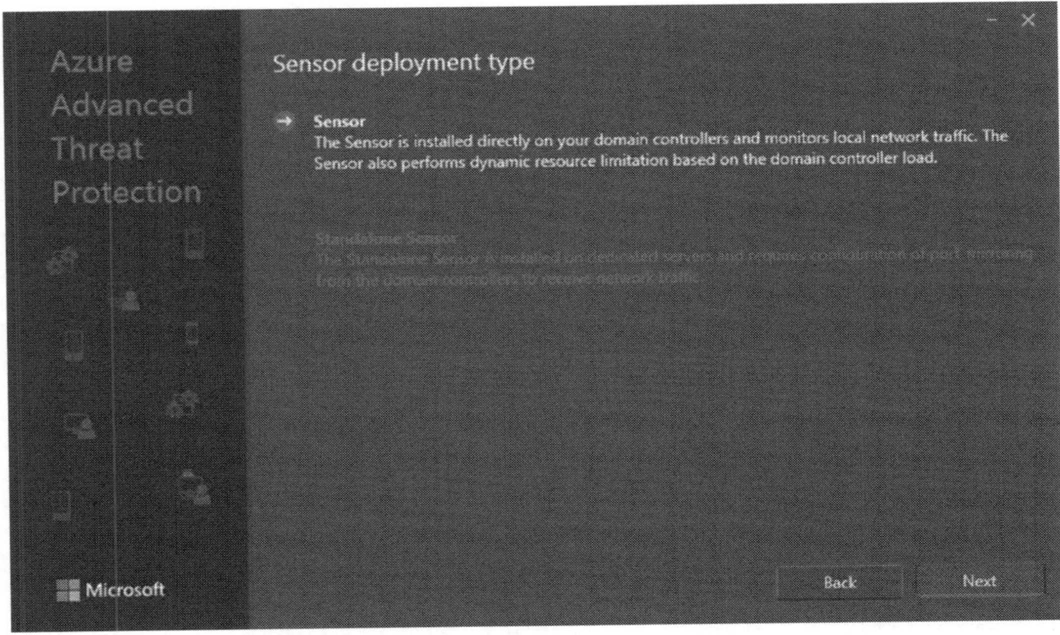

Figure 6.8 – Sensor deployment type

Choose the installation path, as in the following screenshot. The wizard will alert you, at this point, if any of the prerequisites for installing the sensor are not met, such as insufficient disk space:

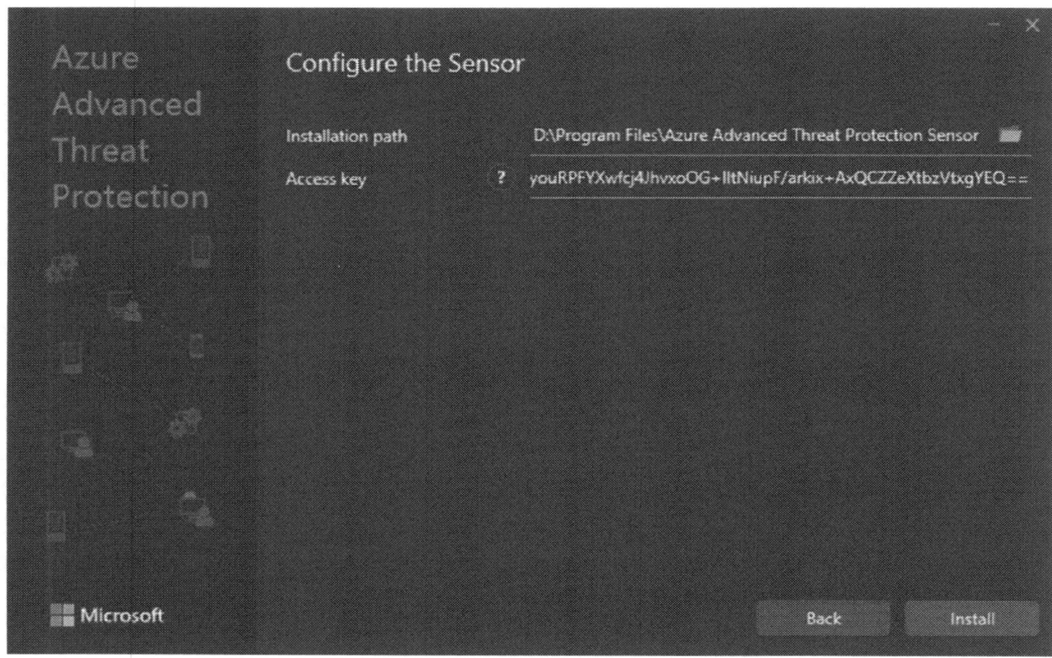

Figure 6.9 – Configuring the sensor

10. Click **Install** and the installation will start, as follows:

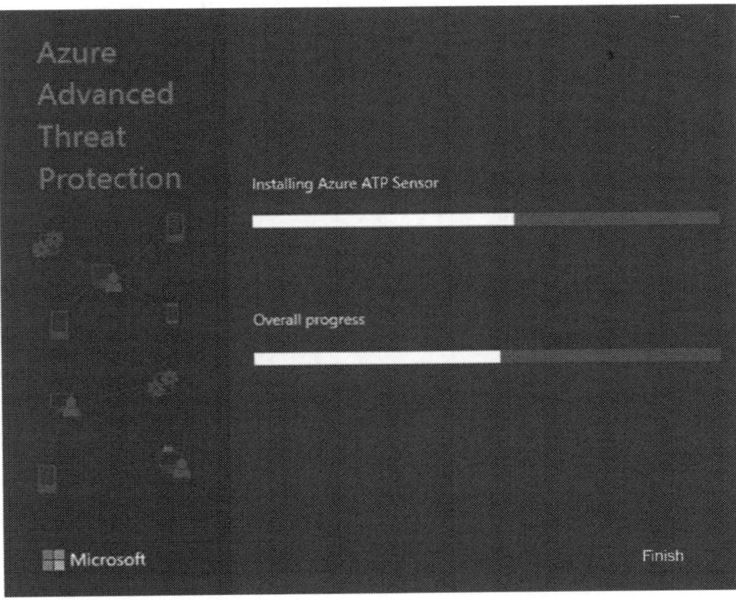

Figure 6.10 – Installation progress

11. When the installation is complete, you will see the following message. Click **Finish** to complete the setup wizard:

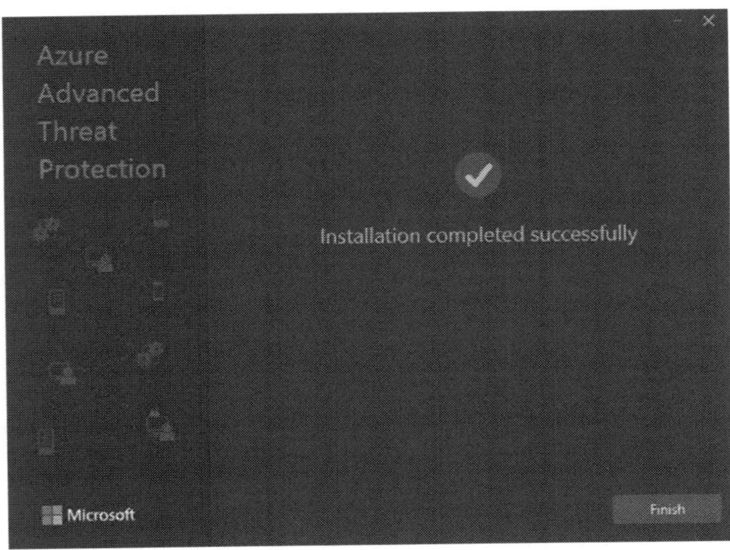

Figure 6.11 – Installation is complete

12. Once the wizard has completed, you can click on **Sensors** from the **Configuration** menu of the Azure ATP portal and you will see the first installed sensor, as in the following screenshot:

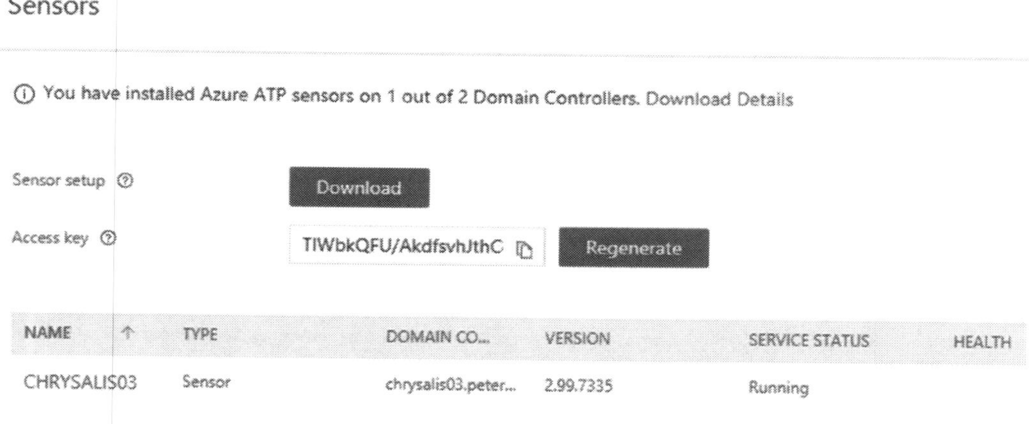

Figure 6.12 – Sensors

The preceding steps complete the initial setup of your Azure ATP instance. Should you need more sensors, you can repeat the preceding steps to do so.

> **Important note**
>
> It is possible to install a sensor onto both a domain controller and a dedicated server. When you deploy a sensor to a domain controller, it is installed as an Azure ATP sensor. However, when you deploy a sensor to a dedicated server and use port mirroring, it is installed as an Azure ATP standalone sensor.

Additional configuration options

By logging into the Azure ATP portal at `https://portal.atp.azure.com` and choosing the **Configuration** tab in the left menu, you can see all of the configuration options available to you within Azure ATP, as shown:

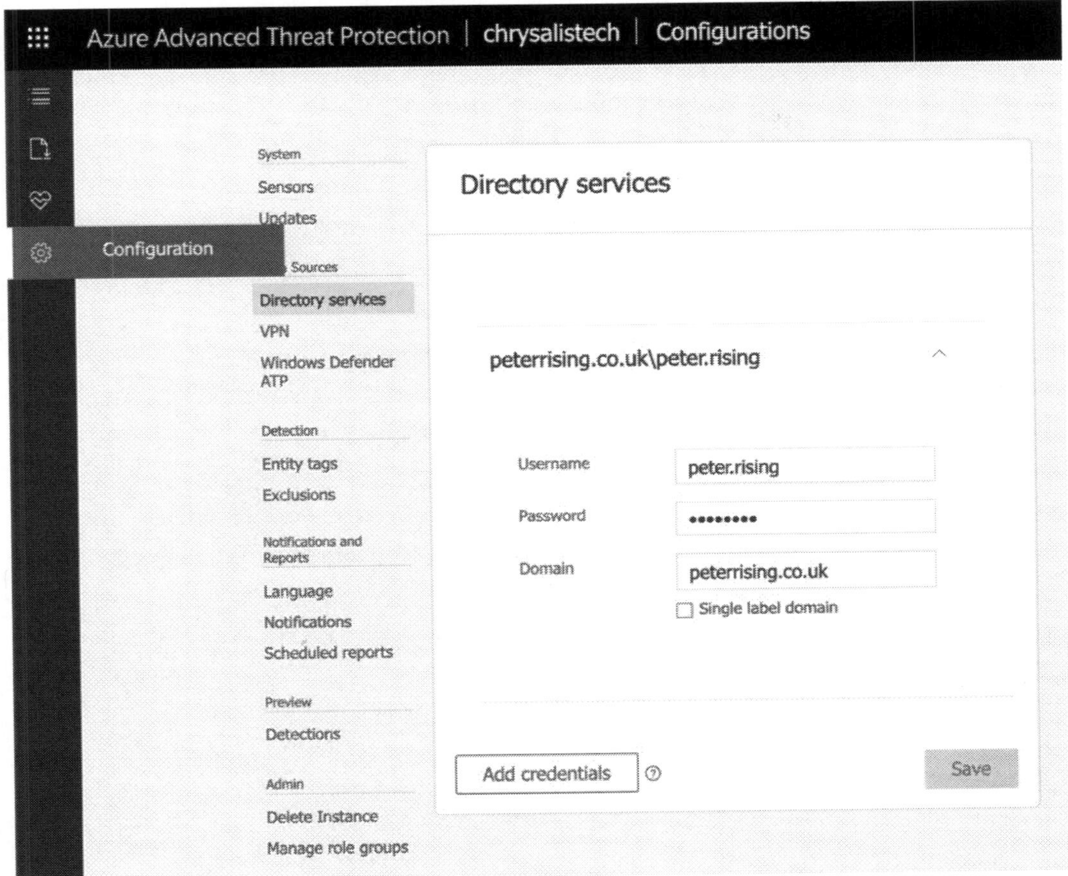

Figure 6.13 – The configuration options

The **Configuration** section is divided into the following sub-sections:

- **System**
- **Data Sources**
- **Detection**
- **Notifications and Reports**
- **Preview**
- **Admin**

> **Important note**
>
> Depending on your organizational requirements for Azure ATP, you may not need to configure all of the features within the preceding sub-sections. However, it is recommended that you familiarize yourself with all of the available options as you may be tested on these in the MS-500 exam.

So, we have now configured our Azure ATP instance and deployed the first Azure ATP sensor to a domain controller. Now that we have Azure ATP up and running in a basic form, we will look at how you can manage your Azure ATP instance and carry out monitoring and reporting tasks.

Managing Azure ATP activities

Now that we have deployed our Azure ATP instance, we can start managing and monitoring the service. It is important to review the Azure ATP portal regularly, in addition to creating alerts, to keep on top of all potential suspicious and malicious activities that may target your hybrid cloud identities.

There are a number of ways to manage and monitor the Azure ATP instance. Some of them are as follows:

- Through the security alerts timeline in the Azure ATP portal
- Through Azure ATP reports
- Through the Azure ATP workspace health center

We will now look at each of these in greater detail, starting with the security alerts timeline.

The security alerts timeline in the Azure ATP portal

When you first launch the Azure ATP portal, it opens the security alerts timeline, as follows:

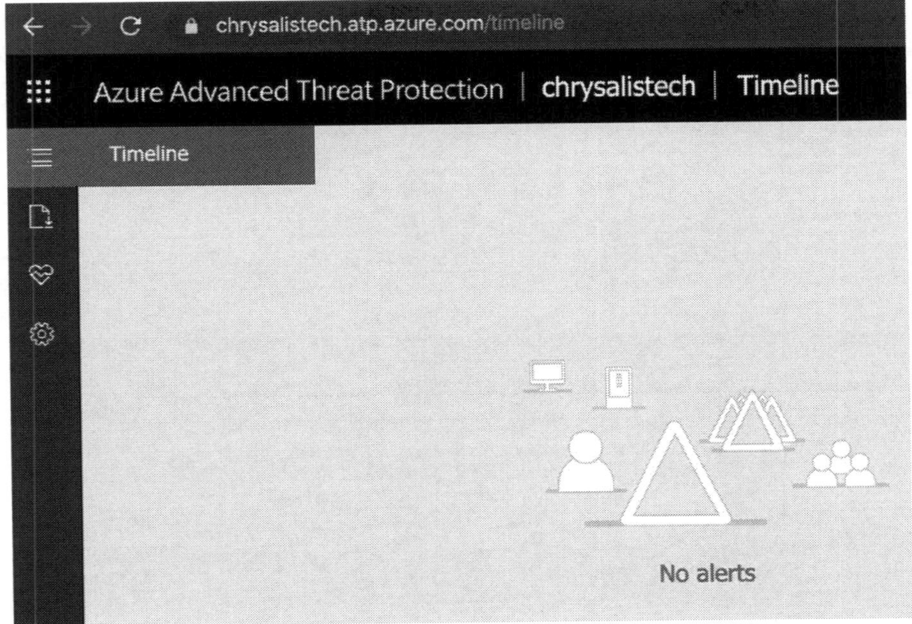

Figure 6.14 – The security alerts timeline

> **Important note**
> There are no alerts in my own timeline at the moment because the Azure ATP instance has just been generated on my tenant.

In the security alerts timeline, you can see any security alerts that have been detected in chronological order.

Security alerts contain events relating to the following information:

- Compromised users, devices, and resources
- Timeframes associated with suspicious activities
- Alert severity
- Alert status

You can share any security alerts via email with other users in your organization and you can also export a security alert to Excel. Some examples of the types of activities you could see in your timeline are as follows:

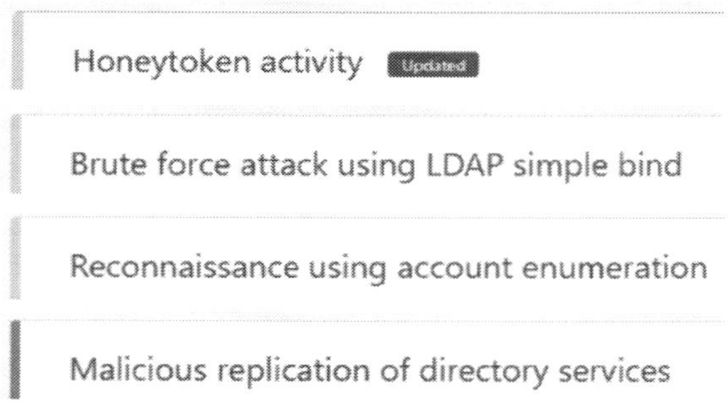

Figure 6.15 – Timeline activity types

You should review the security alerts timeline regularly in order to respond to and classify any recorded alerts. Microsoft has the following classifications for security alerts:

- **True Positive**: This is a genuine malicious action detected by Azure ATP.
- **Benign True Positive**: This is a non-malicious action detected by Azure ATP, such as a penetration test.
- **False Positive**: This is a false alarm.

If you have a large number of security alerts to review on your timeline, you can filter the alerts by **All**, **Open**, **Closed**, or **Suppressed**. You can also filter further by **High**, **Medium**, or **Low**.

Azure ATP reports

The Azure ATP **Reports** section is the second option visible on the sidebar from the Azure ATP portal, as follows:

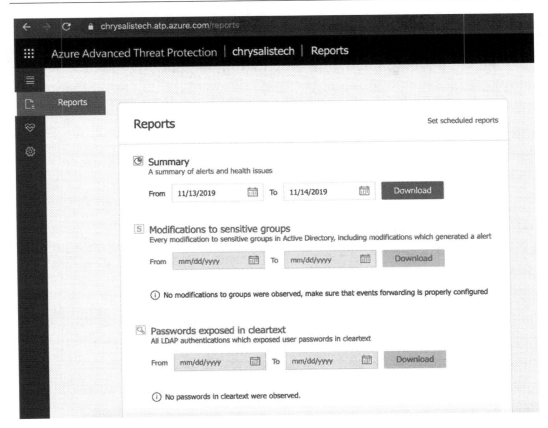

Figure 6.16 – Azure ATP reports

In **Reports**, you can generate and download reports relating to suspicious activities and system health. You can also schedule regular reports from the top-right corner of the screen, as follows:

Figure 6.17 – See scheduled reports

> **Important note**
>
> You can also access **Scheduled reports** from the **Notifications** and **Reports** section of the **Configuration** screen within Azure ATP.

When you choose to schedule a report, you will see the following options for the built-in reporting options of Azure ATP:

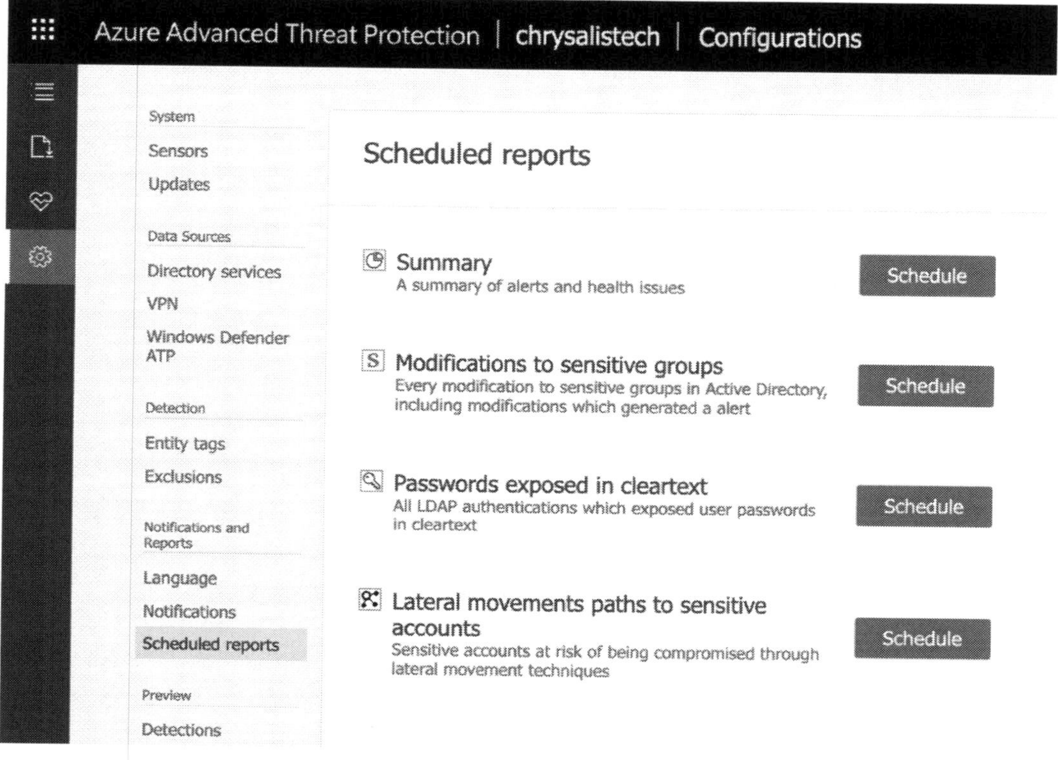

Figure 6.18 – Available scheduled reports

The reports available within Azure ATP are as follows:

- **Summary**
- **Modifications to sensitive groups**
- **Passwords exposed in cleartext**
- **Lateral movements paths to sensitive accounts**

When scheduling one of these reports, you have the following configuration options:

Summary

Send the report Daily

At (UTC) 12:00 AM

To user@domain.com

Save Cancel

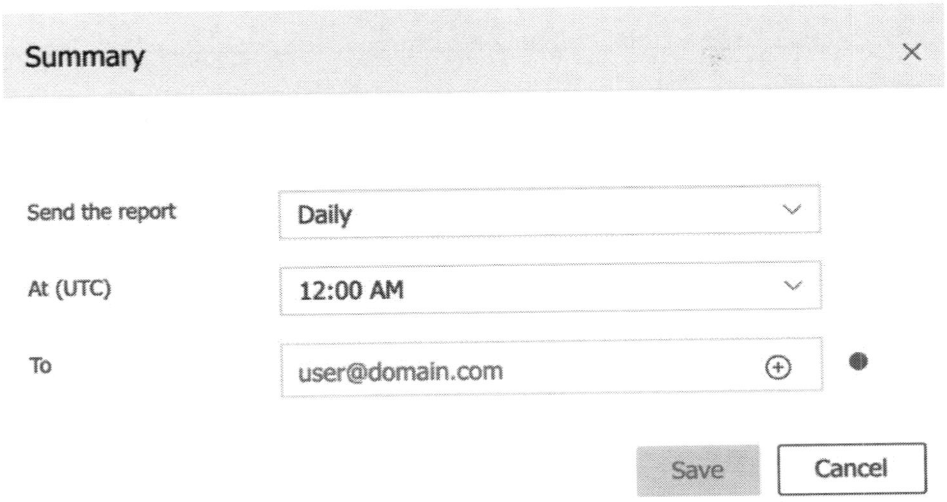

Figure 6.19 – Configuration options

You can choose to send a report on a daily, weekly, or monthly basis. You can also choose the time of day that the report will be sent and you can choose the recipients who should receive the report via email.

When you have configured your report schedule settings, they will be shown on the **Scheduled reports** page, as follows:

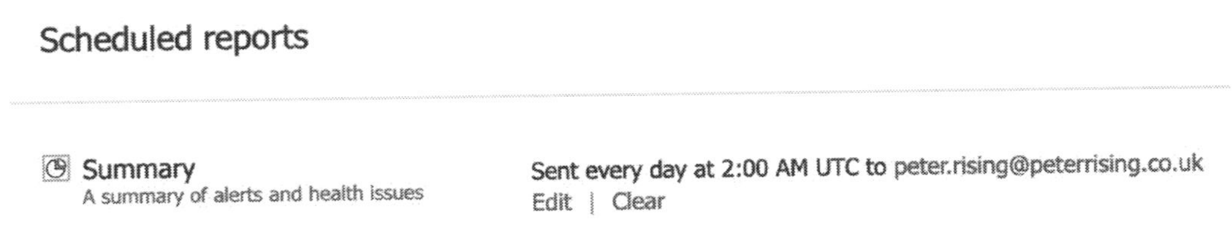

Figure 6.20 – Scheduled reports

If you choose to download one of the reports from the Azure ATP portal, the report is exported to Microsoft Excel, as in the following example, which shows the downloaded **Summary** report. There are two tabs available:

- The **Summary** tab:

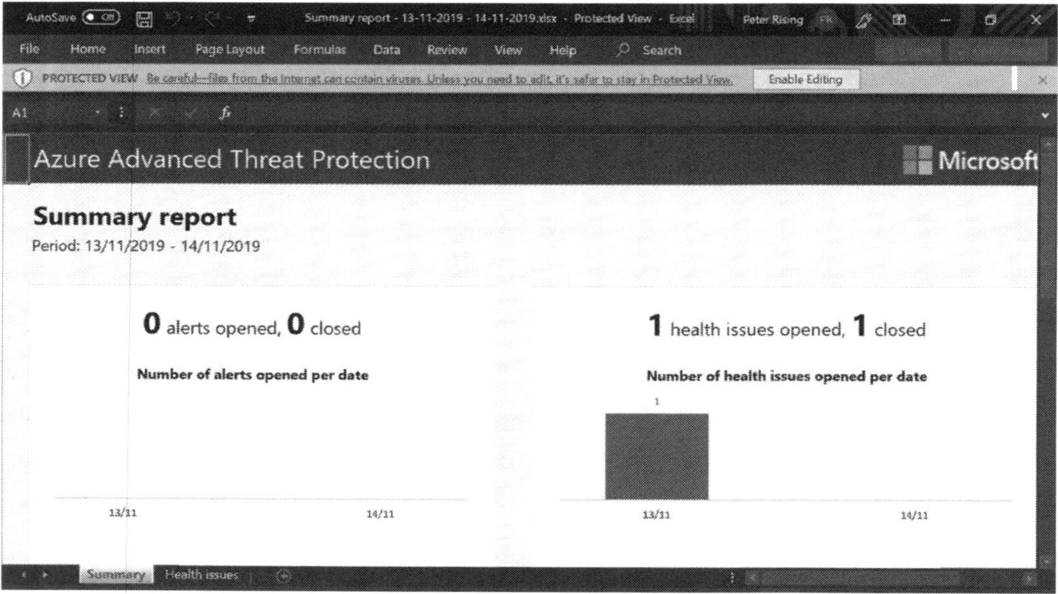

Figure 6.21 – The Summary tab

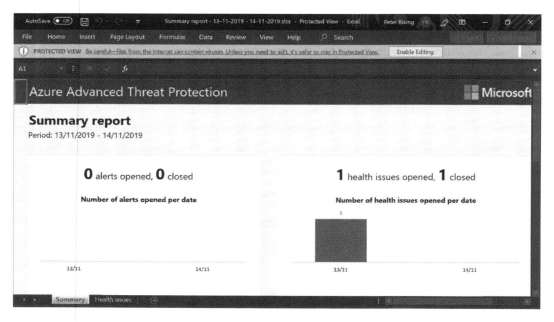

- The **Health issues** tab:

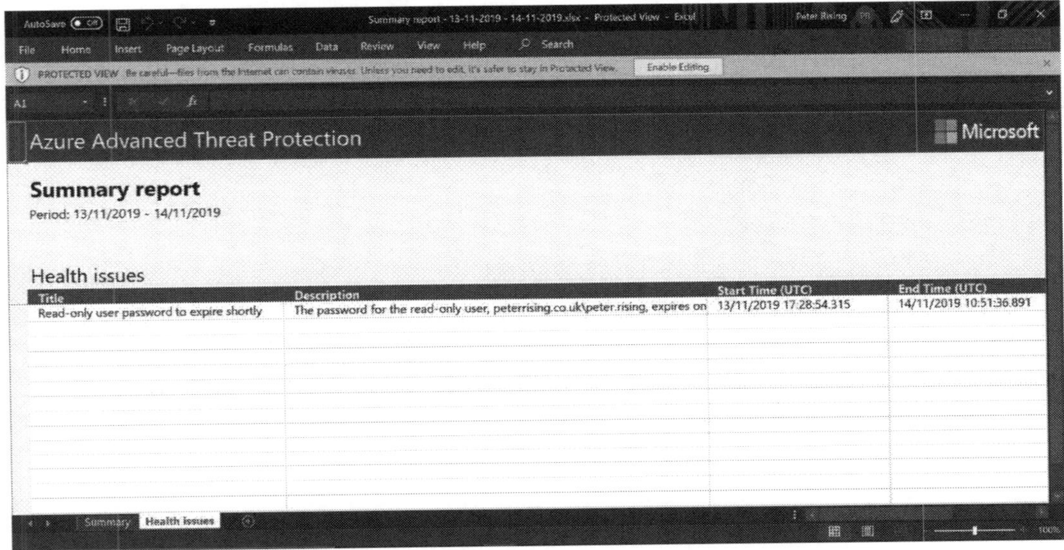

Figure 6.22 – The Health issues tab

When using Azure ATP in your environment, reports are an excellent way for you to diligently and proactively assess activities within your Azure ATP instance. It is highly recommended that you schedule regular reports to be emailed to administrators.

The Azure ATP workspace health center

The Azure ATP workspace health center can be accessed from the Azure ATP portal by clicking on the heart icon, as follows:

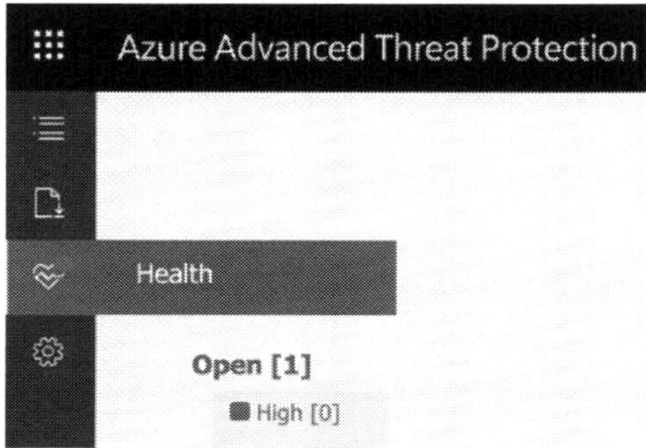

Figure 6.23 – Azure ATP portal

The health center shows you the performance information that relates to your Azure ATP workspace and alerts you on any issues. Should there be any potential problems, the health center icon will display a red dot, as in the preceding screenshot, so you have a clear visual indication when there are health issues that require your attention.

In the following example (which shows the health center of the Azure ATP instance that we set up in the previous section of this chapter), we can see that there is already a reported issue that requires attention. When we set up the Azure ATP instance on this tenant, we purposely selected an AD user account whose password is soon to expire, knowing that this would generate an alert:

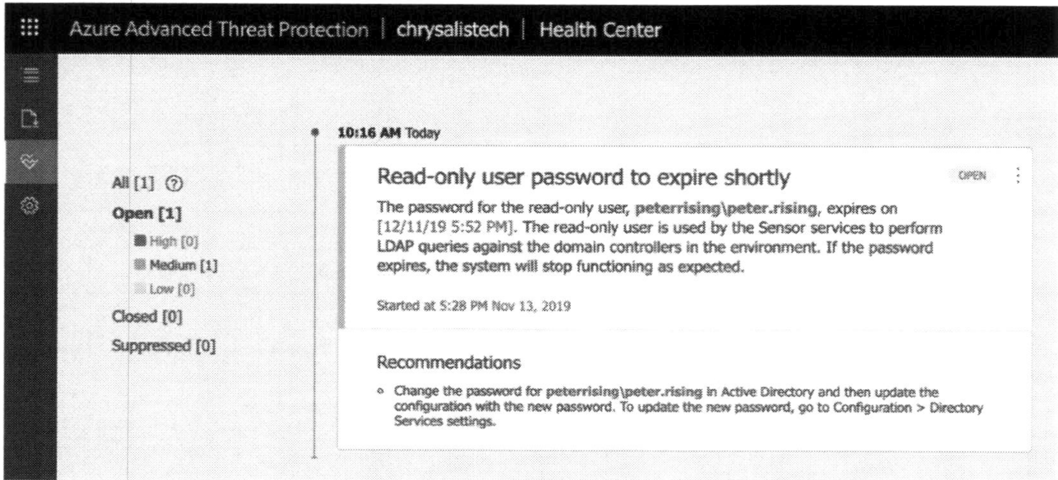

Figure 6.24 – The Azure ATP health center

There are three alert types in the Azure ATP health center, which are as follows:

- **Open**: These are new or current alerts that require attention.
- **Closed**: These are alerts that have been successfully and definitively resolved.
- **Suppressed**: These are alerts that have been identified as safe to ignore, but that may reoccur.

Alerts provide you with a lot of detail as to what the issue is and also suggest corrective measures that can be taken. Any open issues that appear in your Azure ATP instance can be addressed by clicking on the ellipsis in the right-hand corner of the alert, as follows:

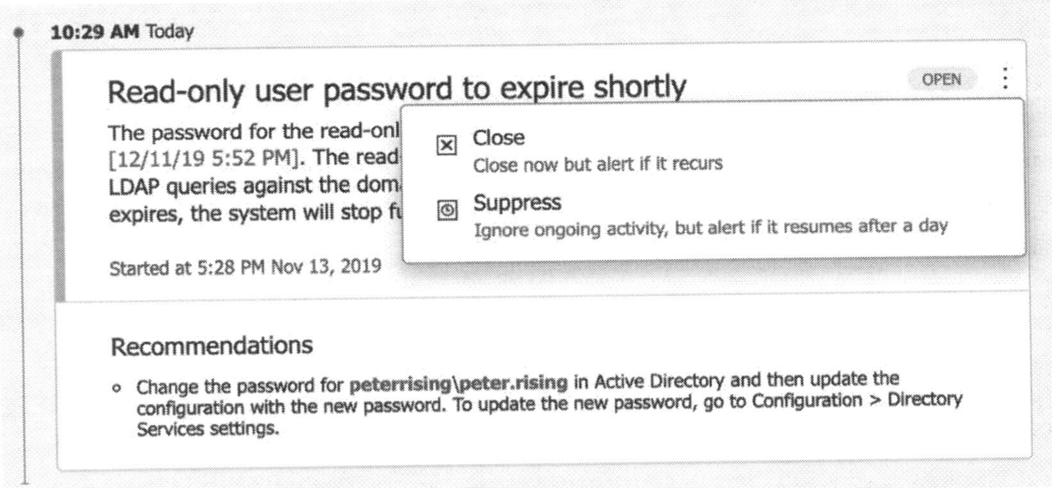

Figure 6.25 – Alert details

From the open alert, you can select from one of the available options, as follows:

- **Close**: Select **Close** if you are certain that you have diligently addressed and resolved the issue described in the activity.
- **Suppress**: Select **Suppress** if you are certain that the activity can safely be ignored at this time.

In the previous example, we closed the alert that was detected in the Azure ATP health center and it now shows in the **Closed** alerts section:

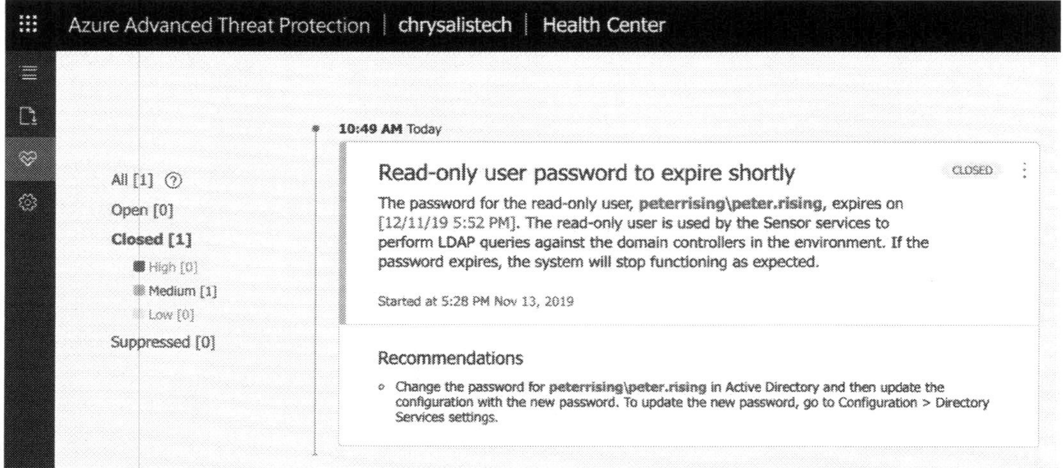

Figure 6.26 – Alert shown as closed

If we click on the ellipsis, we can reopen the alert if we need to, as follows:

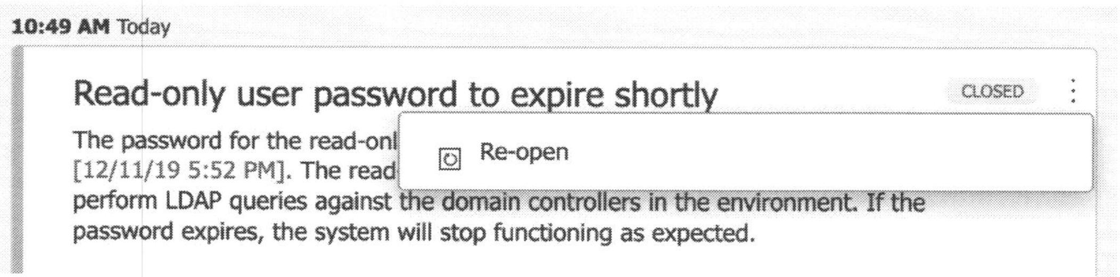

Figure 6.27 – Re-opening an alert

If we chose to suppress the activity instead of closing it, the activity would move to the **Suppressed** alerts section. We would have the same option to re-open the alert from the **Suppressed** section as we did from the **Closed** section, if required.

> **Important note**
> If you close an activity and Azure ATP detects a reoccurrence within a short time frame, Azure ATP may automatically reopen the activity.

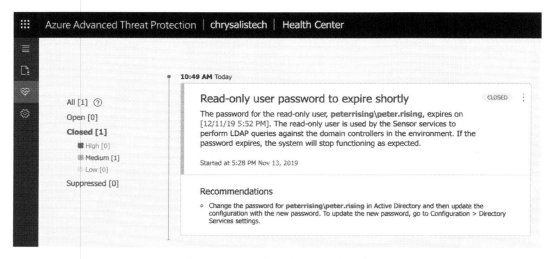

There are three levels of activity that detection can be assigned to depending on the severity of the issue. They are as follows:

- A high-level alert: This is the most severe type of alert and requires urgent attention. High-level alerts can indicate activities that can lead to high-impact attacks, such as identity theft or elevation of privilege.
- A medium-level alert: This can indicate that there has been an activity that could put identities at risk and result in a more serious attack.
- A low-level alert: This can indicate that a malicious actor could be attempting to gain initial access to your environment.

The Azure ATP health center is an extremely useful tool for Microsoft 365 administrators and will enable you to diligently and proactively respond to any suspicious or malicious activities detected in your environment. We have shown you how it can be used to monitor alerts recorded by Azure ATP and how to understand the different levels of alerts and their varying severity. You have also learned how to change the status of alerts by closing or suppressing them.

Summary

In this chapter, we examined Azure ATP, which is a feature included with Enterprise Mobility + Security E5 that enables you to protect your Microsoft 365 hybrid cloud environment against malicious actors who are attempting to access vulnerable user accounts and conduct reconnaissance activities in order to gain elevation of privilege and achieve domain dominance.

We showed you how to configure your Azure ATP instance in the Azure ATP portal and install sensors onto domain controllers or dedicated servers. We then examined how the Azure ATP portal establishes a timeline of suspicious and malicious activities, the steps you can take to review and resolve these within the Azure ATP health center, and how to use reports and report schedules.

In the next chapter, we will examine the principles of Windows Defender ATP. We will show you how to plan for and configure Windows Defender ATP, and how it can be used to protect your Windows devices.

Questions

1. Which of the following can you not install an Azure ATP sensor onto?

    a. A domain controller

    b. A Windows 10 workstation

    c. A dedicated Windows server

2. Which of the following is not an option when scheduling Azure ATP reports?

    a. Hourly

    b. Daily

    c. Weekly

    d. Monthly

3. True or false – in order to use Azure ATP, you need to have an Enterprise Mobility + Security E5 license or a standalone Azure ATP license.

    a. True

    b. False

4. Which of the following are the components that make up Azure ATP (choose three)?

    a. The Azure ATP portal

    b. The Azure ATP sensor

    c. The Azure ATP configuration manager

    d. The Azure ATP cloud service

    e. The Azure ATP cloud app security

5. True or false – your Azure ATP instance is automatically created in the closest geographical data center.

    a. True

    b. False

6. Which of the following are not types of alerts displayed in the Azure ATP health center (choose two)?

    a. Open

    b. Pending

    c. Suppressed

    d. Closed

    e. Deferred

7. Which of the following is not a built-in Azure ATP report?

    a. Modifications to sensitive groups report

    b. Directory services report

    c. Summary report

    d. Lateral movements paths to sensitive accounts report

8. True or false – Azure ATP can integrate with Windows Defender ATP.

    a. True

    b. False

9. When you export and download an Azure ATP report, what format is the report sent as?

    a. Excel (`.xlsx`)

    b. Word (`.docx`)

    c. `.txt`

    d. `.xml`

10. True or false – when setting up Azure ATP for the first time, it creates some Azure AD groups.

    a. True

    b. False

References

Please refer to the following links for more information:

- Azure ATP prerequisites: `https://docs.microsoft.com/en-us/azure-advanced-threat-protection/atp-prerequisites`
- Azure ATP documentation: `https://docs.microsoft.com/en-us/azure-advanced-threat-protection/`
- An overview of Azure ATP: `https://docs.microsoft.com/en-us/azure-advanced-threat-protection/what-is-atp`
- Creating an Azure ATP instance: `https://docs.microsoft.com/en-us/azure-advanced-threat-protection/install-atp-step1`
- Connecting Azure ATP to an on-premises AD: `https://docs.microsoft.com/en-us/azure-advanced-threat-protection/install-atp-step2`
- Downloading the Azure ATP sensor package: `https://docs.microsoft.com/en-us/azure-advanced-threat-protection/install-atp-step3`
- Installing and configuring an Azure ATP sensor: `https://docs.microsoft.com/en-us/azure-advanced-threat-protection/install-atp-step4`
- Working with Azure ATP security alerts: `https://docs.microsoft.com/en-us/azure-advanced-threat-protection/working-with-suspicious-activities`
- Azure ATP FAQs: `https://docs.microsoft.com/en-us/azure-advanced-threat-protection/atp-technical-faq#licensing-and-privacy`
- The cyber-attack kill chain: `https://www.microsoft.com/security/blog/2016/11/28/disrupting-the-kill-chain/`

7
Configuring Microsoft Defender ATP to Protect Devices

In the modern IT landscape, malicious actors who attack environments and devices use methods that are becoming more and more sophisticated, and unfortunately, the average time before a threat is detected is believed to be approximately 200 days. While traditional anti-virus and anti-malware software can still play an important role in defending against these threats, they are sadly not enough to effectively defend against modern attackers that are determined to cause disruption and implement malicious activities.

This is where Microsoft Defender **Advanced Threat Protection** (**ATP**) comes in. Microsoft Defender ATP is a cloud-based online service that provides prevention, detection, and investigation methods that you can use to respond to advanced threats within your organization. In this chapter, you'll learn how to configure and manage the Microsoft Defender ATP features to provide the best protection for your organization, as well as how to enable and configure always-on protection and monitoring.

In addition, we will examine how **Microsoft Defender Application Guard** can be used to protect your environment. You will also learn how **Microsoft Defender Application Control** can help administrators plan and implement control of specific applications, how BitLocker can be configured to manage Windows 10 device encryption, and how app protection policies for non-Windows device encryption can be applied. Finally, we will examine how the protection of enterprise data can be accomplished with **Windows Information Protection** (**WIP**).

We will cover these topics in the following order:

- Implementing Microsoft Defender ATP
- Managing and monitoring Microsoft Defender ATP
- Implementing additional Microsoft Defender features
- Managing device encryption for your Windows 10 devices

Technical requirements

Microsoft Defender ATP has a number of minimum requirements that must be met in order to use the service.

Licensing requirements

You will need one of the following licenses in order to use Microsoft Defender ATP:

- Windows 10 Enterprise E5
- Microsoft 365 E5
- Microsoft 365 E3 (with the Microsoft 365 E5 Security add-on)

Supported operating systems

The following operating systems are capable of supporting Microsoft Defender ATP:

- Windows 7 SP1 Enterprise
- Windows 7 SP1 Pro
- Windows 8.1 Enterprise
- Windows 8.1 Pro
- Windows 10 Enterprise
- Windows 10 Pro

- Windows Server 2008 R2 SP1
- Windows Server 2012 R2
- Windows Server 2016
- Windows Server 2019
- macOS X
- Linux
- Android

Implementing Microsoft Defender ATP

Microsoft Defender ATP enables organizations to investigate and respond to advanced threats that target their enterprise networks by providing information about advanced attack detections based on behavioral patterns. The threats detected by Microsoft Defender ATP are interpreted into a forensic timeline that is then used to build and maintain a threat intelligence knowledge base.

This is achieved by using **endpoint behavioral sensors**, which collect signals from the Windows 10 operating system and send that data to Microsoft Defender ATP.

Cloud security analytics then uses machine learning techniques to translate the collected data into insights and provide recommendations on how to resolve advanced threats.

Finally, **threat intelligence** activities are carried out by Microsoft hunters and security experts, which allows Microsoft Defender ATP to recognize the tools and methods employed by malicious actors and to alert administrators when this behavior is detected.

Microsoft Defender ATP provides both preventative and post-breach detection; it comprises the following features and components:

- Reduces the attack surface
- Provides next-generation protection
- Conducts endpoint detection and response
- Conducts automated investigation and remediation
- Provides a Secure Score reporting tool
- Carries out advanced hunting to provide custom threat intelligence

The Microsoft Defender ATP service can be installed and configured via a dedicated Windows Security Center cloud portal. Next, we will look at how we can configure Microsoft Defender ATP.

> **Important note**
> In many of the following screenshots, you will see references to Windows Defender ATP as opposed to Microsoft Defender ATP. The product was renamed when other platforms, such as macOS X, also became compatible. However, some of the installation experiences have not yet caught up with the name change.

Configuring Microsoft Defender ATP

Once you have acquired the required licenses to run Microsoft Defender ATP, you can start to configure the service by using the cloud portal:

1. Go to `https://securitycenter.windows.com/` and log in with your Microsoft 365 Global Administrator credentials. The portal will look as follows:

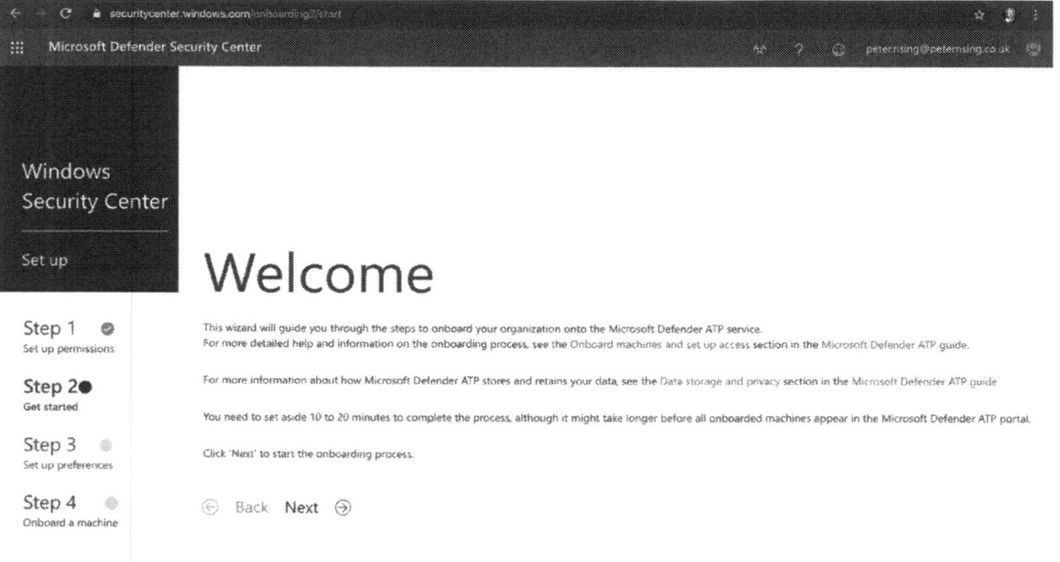

Figure 7.1 – Microsoft Defender Security Center

2. Click **Next** to proceed to the next step of the setup wizard, where you will be asked to configure your preferred data storage location, data retention policy, and organization size. Retention can be set between 30 and 180 days. **180 days** is the default setting:

Step 1
Set up permissions
Step 2
Get started
Step 3
Set up preferences
Step 4
Onboard a machine

Select data storage location

This option cannot be changed without completely offboarding from Microsoft Defender ATP and completing a new enrollment process.
For more information, see the Data storage and privacy section in the Microsoft Defender ATP guide.

US UK Europe

Select the data retention policy

This will determine the period of time we retain your data in your cloud instance.
Note this does not refer to expiration or cancellation of your Microsoft Defender ATP contract.
For more information, see the Data storage and privacy section in the Microsoft Defender ATP guide.

180 days

Select your organization size

Select the estimated number of machines you have in your organization.

Up to 1,000

Preview features

This section allows you to turn preview features on/off.
Turn on to be among the first to try upcoming features.
It is turned on by default to allow you to experience the latest features as they become available.

On

Back Next

Figure 7.2 – Data storage location

3. When prompted to create your cloud instance, click **Continue**:

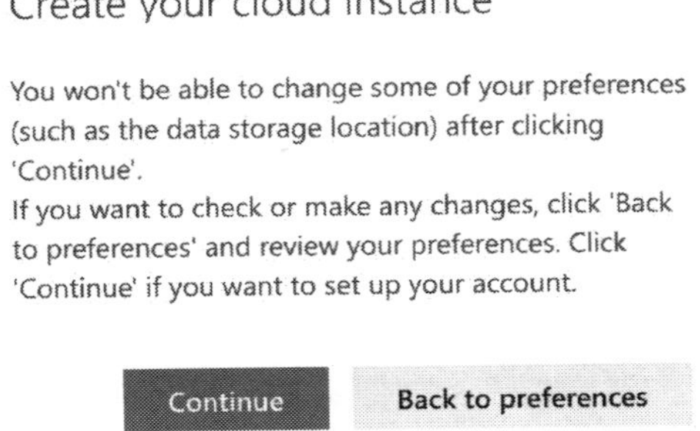

Create your cloud instance
You won't be able to change some of your preferences (such as the data storage location) after clicking 'Continue'.
If you want to check or make any changes, click 'Back to preferences' and review your preferences. Click 'Continue' if you want to set up your account.
Continue
Back to preferences

Figure 7.3 – Creating your cloud instance

4. The wizard will proceed to create your Microsoft Defender ATP account, as follows:

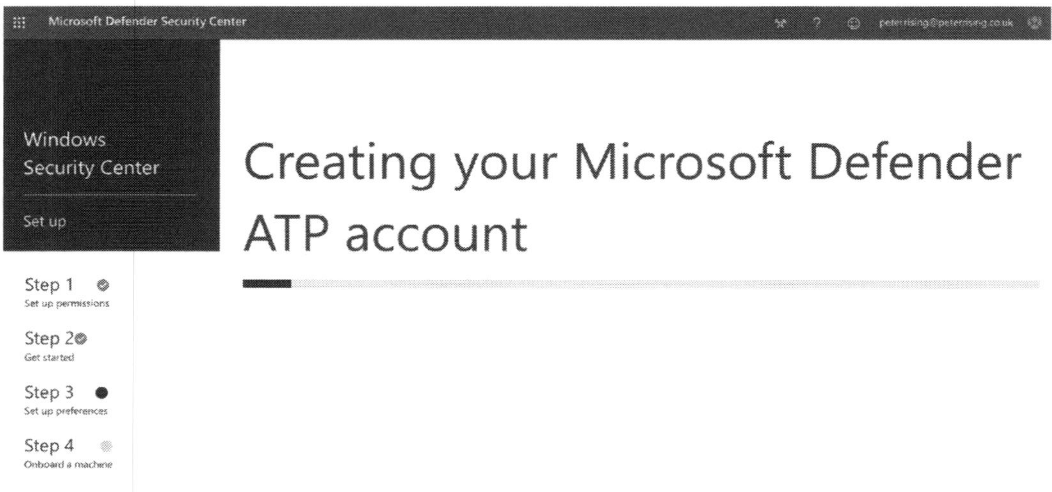

Figure 7.4 – Creating your Microsoft Defender ATP account

5. Next, you will see the following screen:

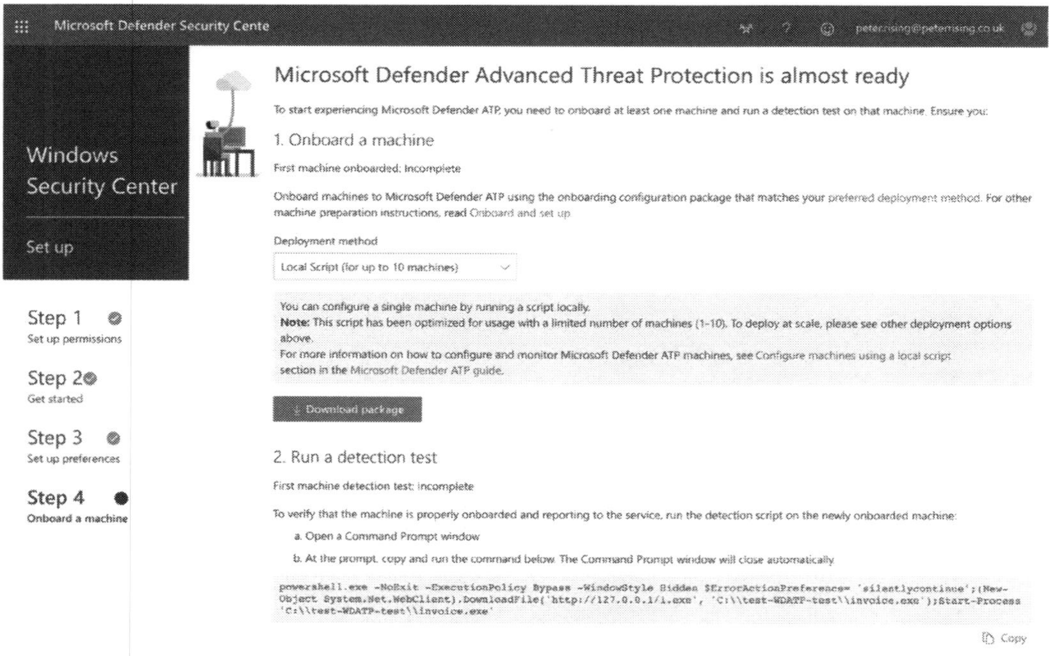

Figure 7.5 – The next steps

6. In this step, you need to choose your preferred deployment method. The options for deployment are shown in the following screenshot:

Microsoft Defender Advanced Threat Protection is almost ready

To start experiencing Microsoft Defender ATP, you need to onboard at least one machine and run a detection test on that machine. Ensure you:

1. Onboard a machine

First machine onboarded: Incomplete

Onboard machines to Microsoft Defender ATP using the onboarding configuration package that matches your preferred deployment method. For other machine preparation instructions, read Onboard and set up.

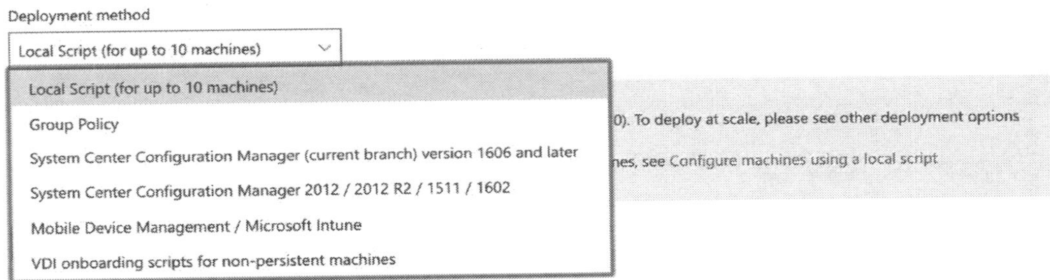

Figure 7.6 – Onboarding a machine

7. For the purposes of this demonstration, we have chosen to deploy Microsoft Defender ATP to a Windows 10 computer using the **Local Script (for up to 10 machines)** option by clicking on the **Download Package** option. In a production environment, you will more likely choose one of the other options for bulk deployment of Microsoft Defender ATP.

8. The downloaded package provides you with a ZIP file that contains a file named `WindowsDefenderATPLocalOnboardingScript.cmd`. This must be executed on the target workstation via an administrative command prompt, as in the following screenshot:

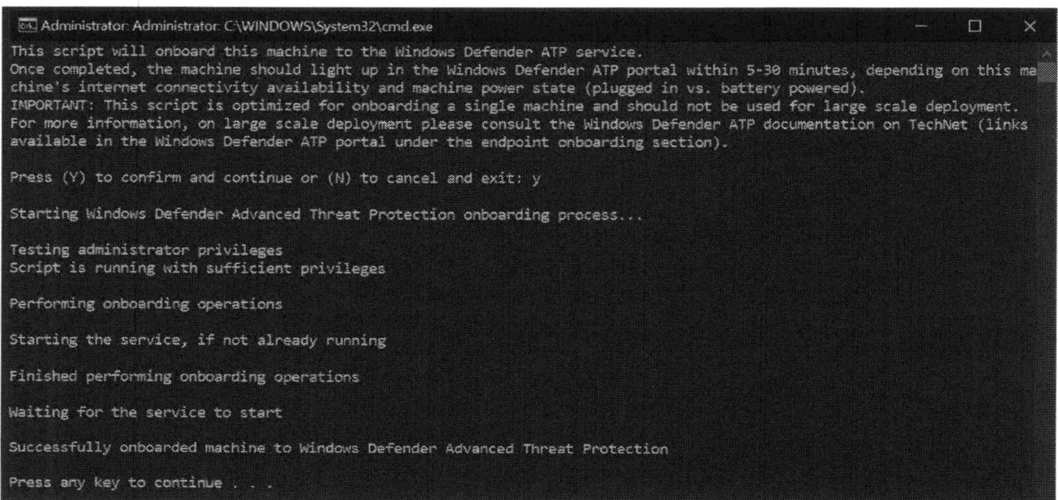

Figure 7.7 – Onboarding script

9. Once the installation is successfully executed, you can verify the installation in the Microsoft Defender ATP service by executing the following command:

2. Run a detection test

First machine detection test: Incomplete

To verify that the machine is properly onboarded and reporting to the service, run the detection script on the newly onboarded machine:

a. Open a Command Prompt window

b. At the prompt, copy and run the command below. The Command Prompt window will close automatically.

```
powershell.exe -NoExit -ExecutionPolicy Bypass -WindowStyle Hidden $ErrorActionPreference= 'silentlycontinue';(New-Object System.Net.WebClient).DownloadFile('http://127.0.0.1/1.exe', 'C:\\test-WDATP-test\\invoice.exe');Start-Process 'C:\\test-WDATP-test\\invoice.exe'
```

Copy

If successful, the detection test will be marked as completed and a new alert will appear in few minutes.

Figure 7.8 – Running a detection test

10. Once completed, you will see the following message displayed in the setup wizard:

2. Run a detection test

First machine detection test: Completed

Figure 7.9 – Detection test completed

11. You can now click on **Start using Windows ATP**, as shown:

Start using Windows ATP

Figure 7.10 – Start using Windows ATP

12. You will now be taken to the cloud-based **Microsoft Defender Security Center** page, as shown in the following screenshot:

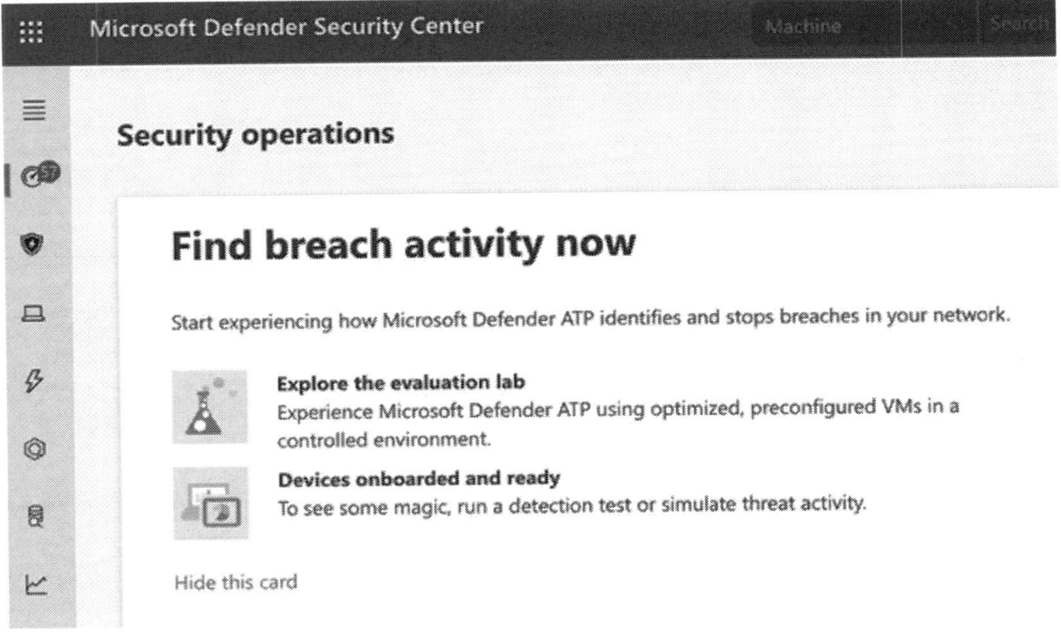

Figure 7.11 – Microsoft Defender Security Center

13. By expanding the left-side menu, we can see the workstation where we deployed Microsoft Defender ATP by clicking on **Machines list**:

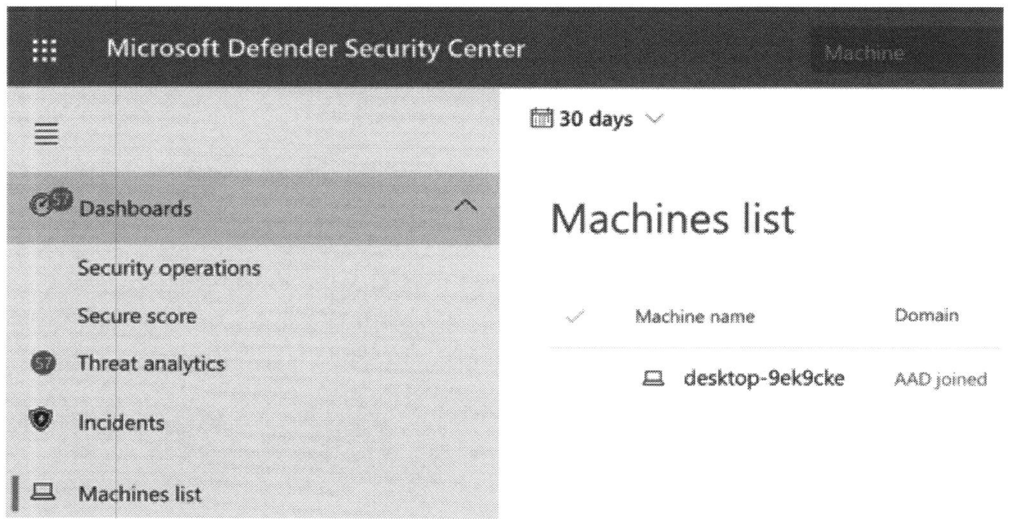

Figure 7.12 – Machines list

14. If we click to select that workstation, we are presented with a dashboard that is specific to the machine, where we can view and assess any detected risks on the device and respond to them. This is shown in the following screenshot:

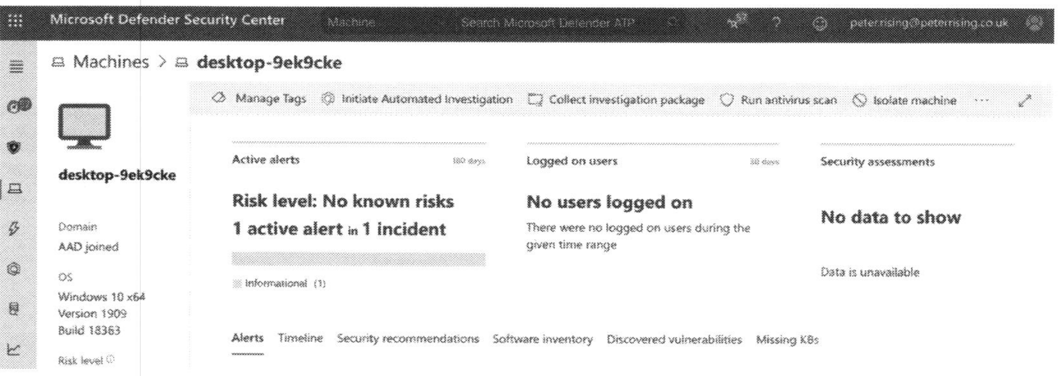

Figure 7.13 – Machine details

So, to recap what we have learned, we have now set up the Microsoft Defender ATP cloud service with our preferred settings and deployed Microsoft Defender ATP to a single Windows 10 Azure **Active Directory** (**AD**)-joined workstation.

We can see a vast amount of information and activities for the device. We also learned that there are a number of ways in which Microsoft Defender ATP can be deployed to both Windows and other devices in your organization.

Next, we will look at how you can use Microsoft Defender ATP to monitor and manage the protection and detection of threats in your environment.

Managing and monitoring Microsoft Defender ATP

Now that we have the Microsoft Defender ATP instance set up and deployed to one or more workstations, there are a number of capabilities that can be fine-tuned in Microsoft Defender Security Center.

It is hugely important to regularly and diligently monitor and manage your Microsoft Defender ATP instance in order to maximize security protection in your environment. Let's look at how you can make the most of some of the available options.

Attack surface reduction capabilities

From Security Center, selecting **Configuration Management** will show you the following options, where you can configure your Microsoft Defender ATP instance to connect to Intune:

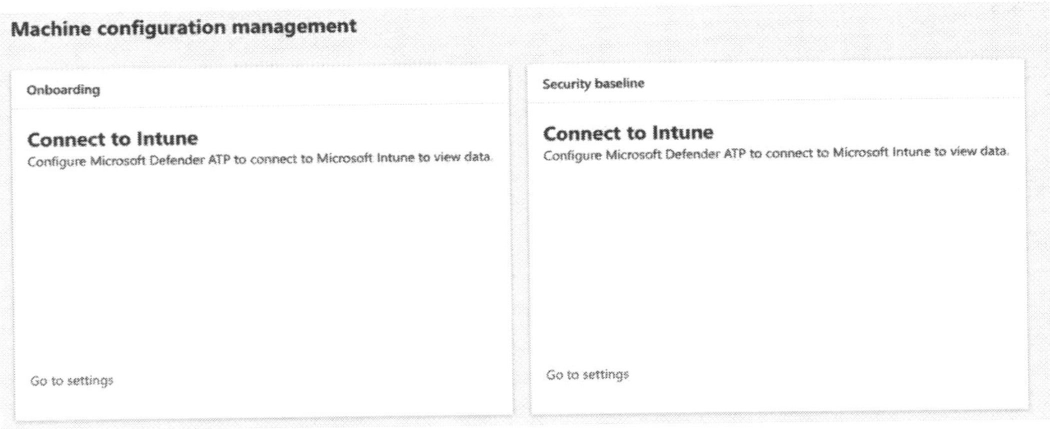

Figure 7.14 – Machine configuration management

By clicking on **Go to settings** on either of the preceding options, you will be taken to **Advanced features**, where you can connect Microsoft Defender ATP to Microsoft Intune, as follows:

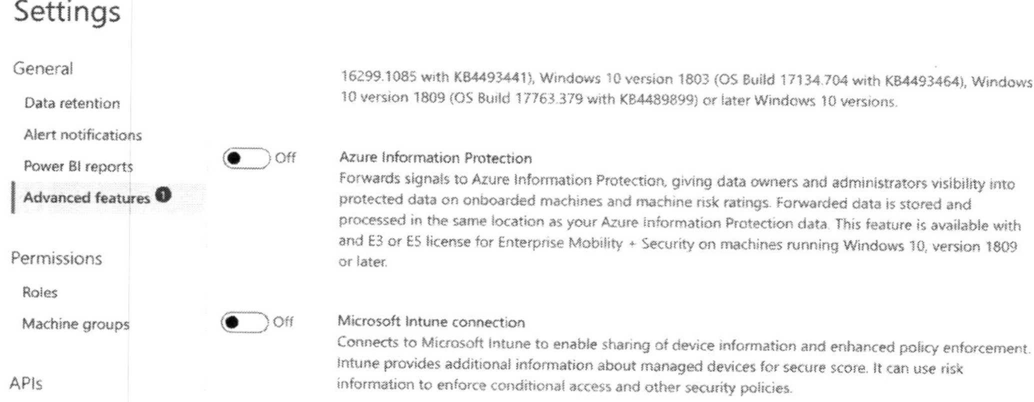

Figure 7.15 – The Advanced features settings

Once you have enabled the connection, the **Machine configuration management** options for Intune will change, as follows:

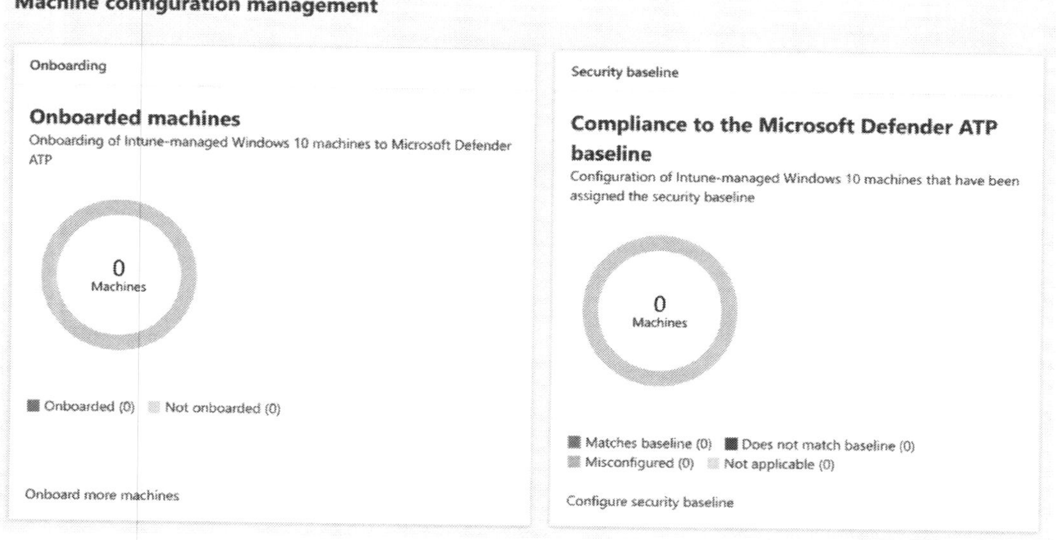

Figure 7.16 – Machine configuration management

You can also select the **Machine attack surface management** option from the configuration management settings, as follows:

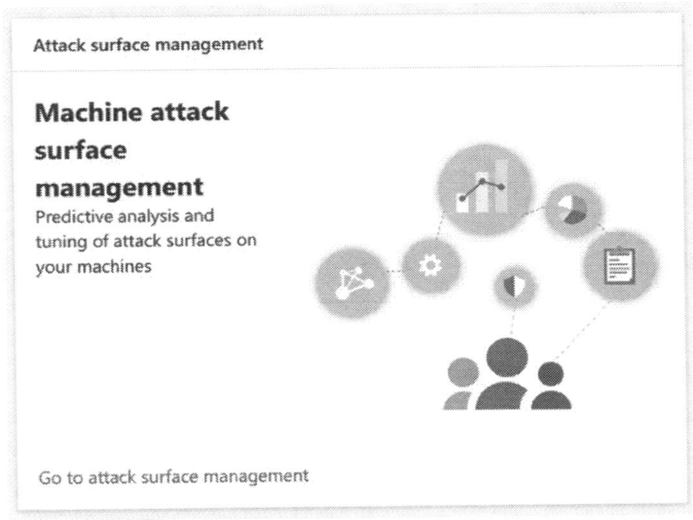

Figure 7.17 – Machine attack surface management

By clicking on **Go to attack surface management**, you will be taken to the following page, where you will be able to view reports on attack surface reduction rules:

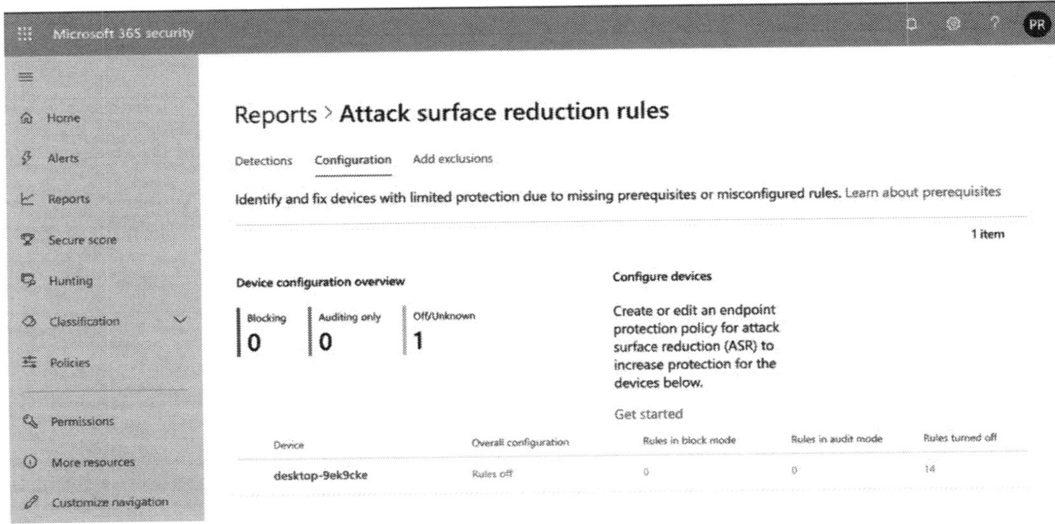

Figure 7.18 – Attack surface reduction rules

You can use the reports to identify and fix devices that may have limited protection due to missing prerequisites or misconfigured rules.

Now that you understand the attack surface reduction capabilities, let's look at the **Secure score** dashboard.

The Secure score dashboard

The **Secure score** dashboard can be used to view and filter a list of security recommendations, as follows:

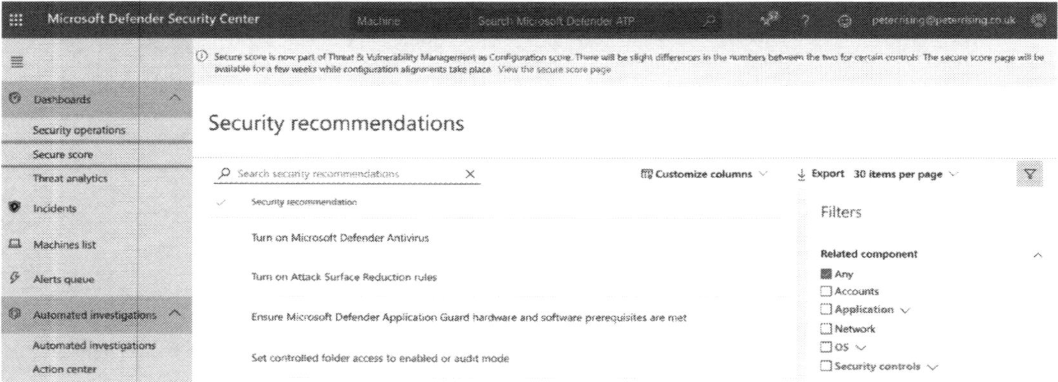

Figure 7.19 – Security recommendations

By selecting an individual item from the list, you can see detailed information on risk and remediation options, as follows:

Turn on Microsoft Defender Antivirus

Open software page | Remediation options | Exception options | ...

Description

Determines whether Microsoft Defender Antivirus is configured to run and scan for malware and other potentially unwanted software.
This feature is available for machines on Windows 10, version 1607 or later.

Potential risk

Not having a current, updated antivirus product scanning each computer for malicious file activity exposes the organization to malware or other potentially unwanted software.

Recommendation insights

- No machines in your organization are configured as recommended

Configuration ID	**CCE**
scid-2010	N/A
Category	**Exposed machines**
Security controls (Antivirus)	1 / 1

Impact

▾ 3.33 | + 10.00

Figure 7.20 – Remediation options

You should diligently review the **Secure score** section regularly and act on the recommendations to improve your score.

Next, let's look at how we can integrate Microsoft Defender ATP with Azure ATP.

Integrating with Azure ATP

It is also possible to integrate your Microsoft Defender ATP instance with your Azure ATP instance (which we discussed in *Chapter 6, Configuring an Advanced Threat Protection Solution*). This can be achieved from the **Settings** menu, as follows:

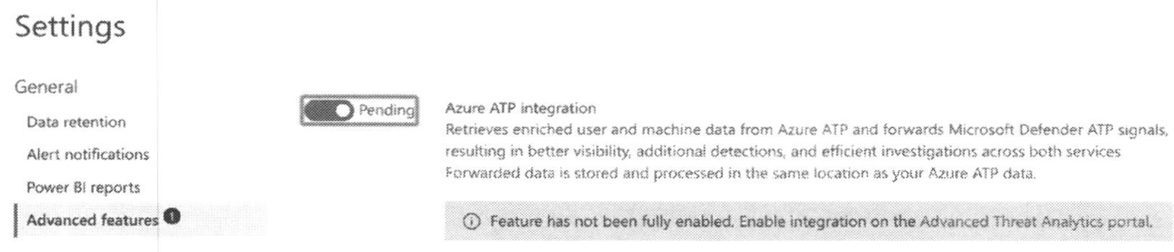

Figure 7.21 – Azure ATP integration

When you activate the integration, you will be directed to activate the feature from the Azure ATP portal as well, if it has not already been enabled. Log in to the Azure ATP portal at `https://portal.atp.azure.com` and activate the feature, as follows:

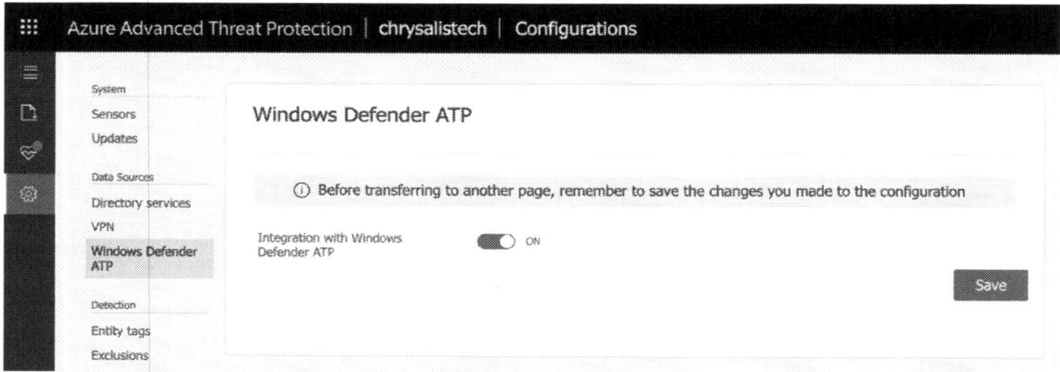

Figure 7.22 – Activating integration from the ATP portal

Click to save your changes, then return to the **Settings** section of Microsoft Defender Security Center, and then click to enable integration with Azure ATP once again. It should now activate without any problems, as in the following screenshot:

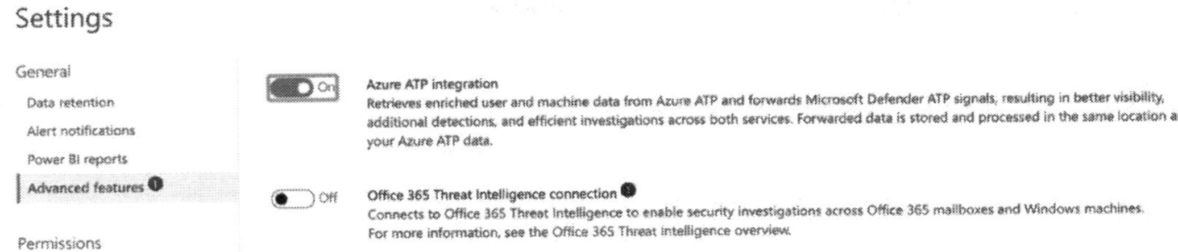

Figure 7.23 – Enabling integration

Enabling integration with Azure ATP retrieves user and machine data from Azure ATP and sends information from Microsoft Defender ATP in the other direction. This results in increased visibility and detections across both of these services.

The Microsoft Defender Security Center settings

There are a vast number of settings that you can review and leverage within the security center to effectively manage and monitor your Microsoft Defender ATP instance. The available options are as follows:

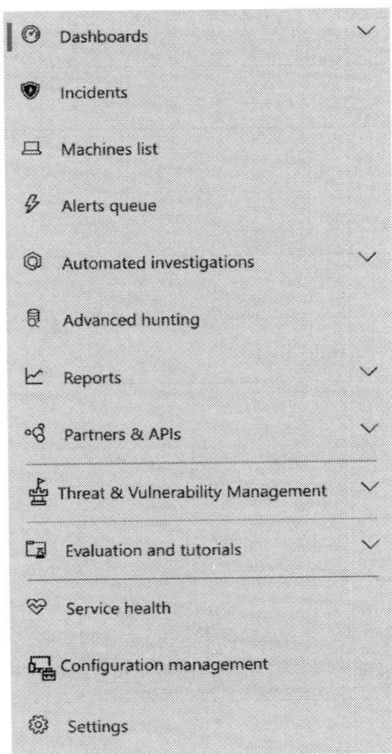

Figure 7.24 – The Security Center settings

The available options are described in greater detail in the following table:

Setting	Features included
Dashboards	• Security Operations • Secure Score • Threat Analytics
Incidents	A list of incidents over the last 30 days.
Machines list	A list of devices that have Microsoft Defender ATP deployed to them.
Alerts queue	A list of detected alerts over the last 30 days.
Automated investigations	• Automated investigations • Action center
Advanced hunting	Runs custom queries and detections.
Reports	• Threat Protection • Machine health and compliance • Web protection
Partners and APIs	• Partner applications • Connected applications • API Explorer • Data export settings
Threat and Vulnerability Management	• Dashboard • Security recommendations • Remediation • Software inventory • Weaknesses
Evaluation and tutorials	• Evaluation lab • Simulations and tutorials
Service health	Shows current status and status history for the Microsoft Defender ATP service.
Configuration management	Provides machine configuration management capabilities.
Settings	Enables you to configure a number of settings, including alerts and notifications, advanced features, and rules and permissions.

> **Important note**
> Further details on all the settings described in the preceding table can be found in many of the links included in the *References* section at the end of this chapter.

So, to recap what we have learned so far in this chapter, we showed you how to install, configure, and monitor the Microsoft Defender ATP service within your Microsoft 365 environment. Next, we will show you how to further refine the service by implementing additional features, which include Windows Defender Application Guard, Application Control, Exploit Guard, and Secure Boot.

Implementing additional Microsoft Defender features

Now that we know how to manage and monitor Microsoft Defender ATP, let's look at some of its associated features, which are designed to complement Microsoft Defender ATP

Configuring Microsoft Defender Application Guard

Microsoft Defender Application Guard is a system designed to isolate devices in such a way that malicious actors are unable to use their attack methodologies against them. It protects your company's users on Windows 10, specifically on the Microsoft Edge browser, by providing isolation of untrusted sites when users browse the internet.

Microsoft Defender Application Guard empowers Microsoft 365 security administrators to explicitly define the following categories:

- Trusted web sites
- Trusted cloud resources
- Trusted networks

A zero-trust methodology is employed to ensure that anything that is not defined in the preceding categories is considered untrusted and is blocked. So, how does this work? Essentially, when a user who is protected by Microsoft Defender Application Guard attempts to access a website that is not trusted via Microsoft Edge or Internet Explorer, the site is opened in an isolated container.

The result of this is that if the website contains malicious code or content, then the user's PC is not affected in any way. Subsequently, a potential attack is prevented and malicious actors cannot carry out any reconnaissance that could lead to the elevation of privileges and domain dominance.

Microsoft Defender Application Guard can be deployed to domain-joined computers on your organization's network by using either System Center Configuration Manager or Microsoft Intune.

It is also possible to deploy Microsoft Defender Application Guard to **Bring Your Own Device** (**BYOD**) or personal Windows devices. While these devices are not domain-joined, it is possible to protect them with Application Guard if they are managed by Intune.

When you configure Microsoft Defender Application Guard to be deployed to your Windows devices, it enables the following features, which can be found under **Control Panel | Programs and Features | Install Windows Features**:

Windows Features

Turn Windows features on or off

To turn a feature on, select its checkbox. To turn a feature filled box means that only part of the feature is turned on

- [x] Telnet Client
- [ ] TFTP Client
- [ ] Virtual Machine Platform
- [x] Windows Defender Application Guard
- [ ] Windows Hypervisor Platform
- [ ] Windows Identity Foundation 3.5

Figure 7.25 – Turning Windows features on or off

Once enabled, clicking on the menu bar within Microsoft Edge will show the following options:

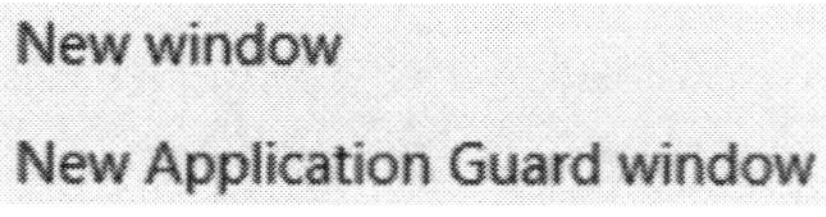

Figure 7.26 – The Edge browser experience

When a user selects the **New Application Guard window** option, they can browse safely and any malicious code or content lurking on a website will not be able to harm the workstation as the browser session will be completely isolated.

Configuring Microsoft Defender Application Control

Microsoft Defender Application Control can restrict the applications on your network from accessing the system kernel. Microsoft Defender Application Control can also block scripts that are unsigned, as well as MSIs.

You can create Application Control policies directly on Windows 10 Enterprise computers or Windows Server 2016. It is also possible to deploy Microsoft Defender Application Control to any Windows 10 edition or Windows Server 2016 via a **Mobile Device Management** (**MDM**) solution, such as Microsoft Intune. It is also possible to use Group Policy to deploy Application Control policies to Windows 10 Enterprise computers or Windows Server 2016.

To create a Microsoft Defender Application Control policy using Intune, follow these steps:

1. Open the Intune portal, click on **Device Configuration** | **Profiles**, and select **Create profile**. You will see the following:

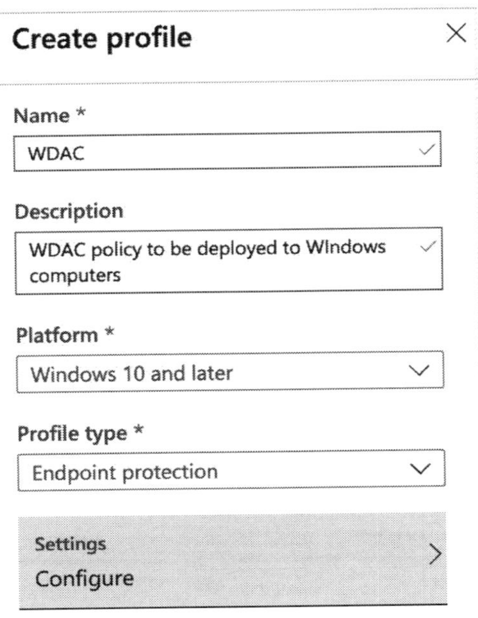

Figure 7.27 – Creating a profile

2. Fill in the **Name**, **Description**, **Platform**, and **Profile type** fields, as in the preceding screenshot, and then click on **Configure** under the **Settings** menu. Then, click on **Microsoft Defender Application Control**, as in the following screenshot:

Figure 7.28 – Microsoft Defender Application Control

3. This feature can be configured as follows:

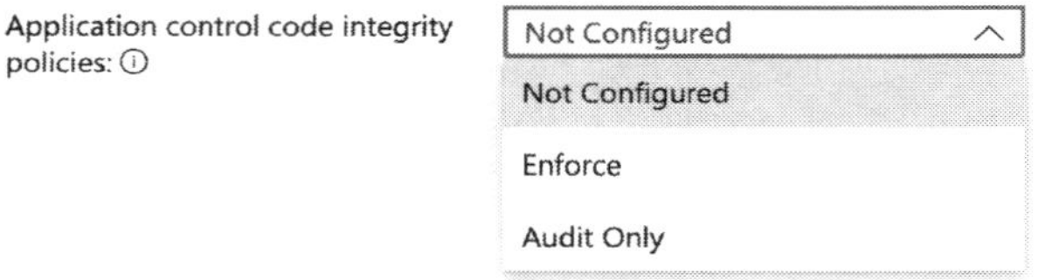

Figure 7.29 – Policy options

4. In this example, we will set the Application Control policy to **Enforce** and **Trust apps with good reputation** to **Enable**:

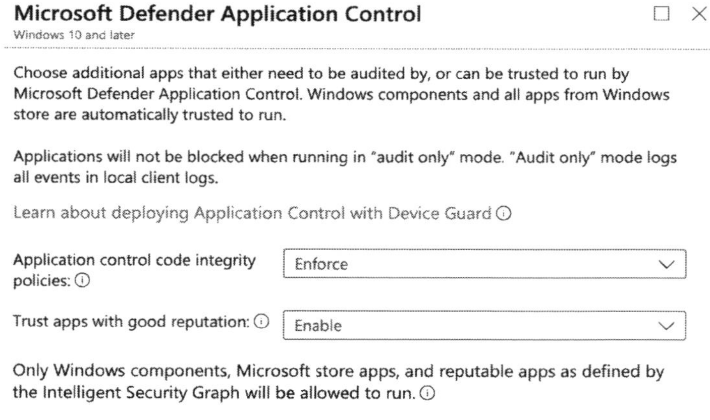

Figure 7.30 – Policy settings

5. Click **OK**, then **OK** again, and finally, click **Create** to save the profile. The profile is now ready and can be assigned to users or groups, as in the following screenshot:

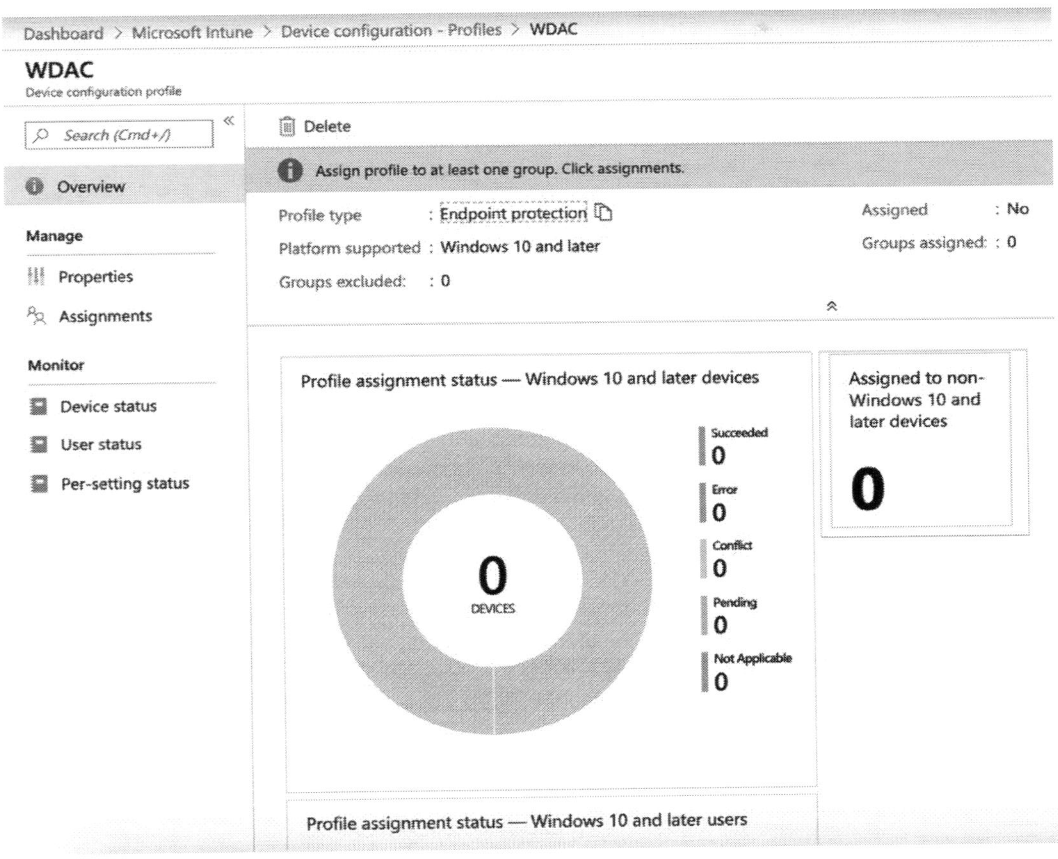

Figure 7.31 – Profile overview

You can monitor your Microsoft Defender Application Control profile from the **Monitor** section on the left-hand side of the profile.

Configuring Microsoft Defender Exploit Guard

Microsoft Defender Exploit Guard provides intrusion detection capabilities in Windows 10. You can use Microsoft Defender Exploit Guard to protect your apps and to reduce the attack surface of your apps by using rules that are designed to prevent malware attacks.

You can also use Microsoft Defender Exploit Guard to protect your users against social engineering attacks by using Windows Defender SmartScreen within the Microsoft Edge browser. Additionally, you can use **Controlled folder access** to protect files within your system folders to prevent them from being changed by malicious actors.

As with Application Control, Microsoft Defender Exploit Guard can be enabled and deployed by using the same method shown for Application Control, and the available configuration settings are as follows:

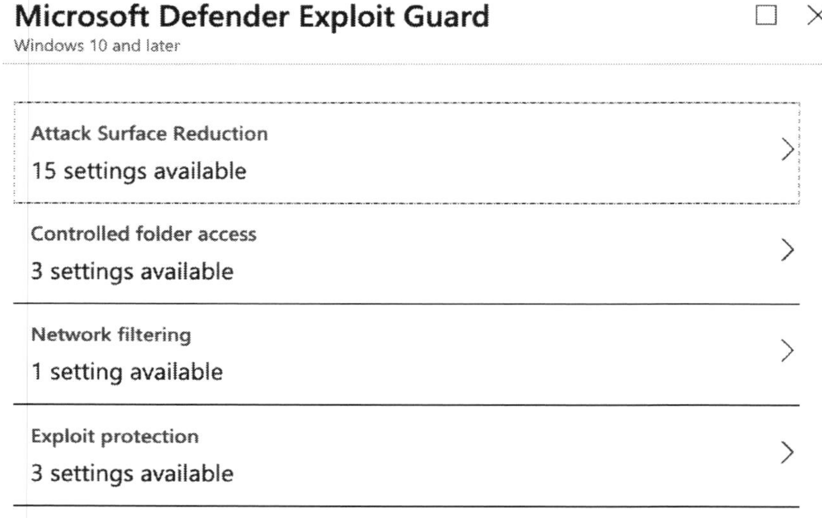

Figure 7.32 – Microsoft Defender Exploit Guard via Intune

There are a number of configuration settings that can be applied to your devices for Microsoft Defender Application Guard, Microsoft Defender Application Control, and Microsoft Defender Exploit Guard. You will find links to articles on how you can configure these features in the *References* section at the end of this chapter.

Next, let's look at how WIP can be used to protect data.

Using WIP to configure WIP policies and protect data

WIP is a feature that is designed to protect against the accidental leakage of data from both business and personal devices. WIP works alongside Azure Rights Management to control the data that leaves devices.

WIP is deployed by configuring policies in Microsoft Intune. This is shown in the following steps:

1. Log in to the Azure portal and go to **Intune**, and then select **Client Apps**. You will see the following:

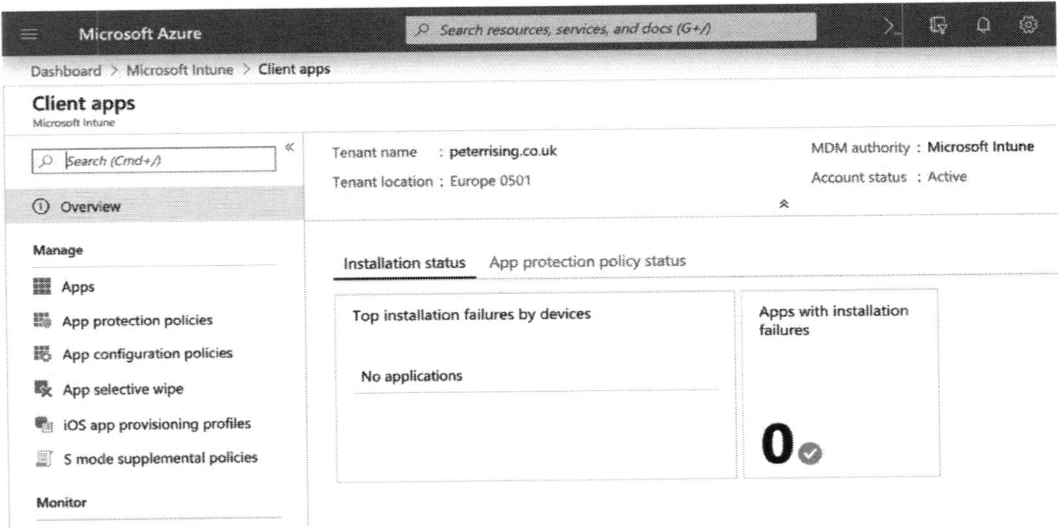

Figure 7.33 – Client apps

2. Click on **App protection policies**, and then select **Create policy**, as in the following screenshot:

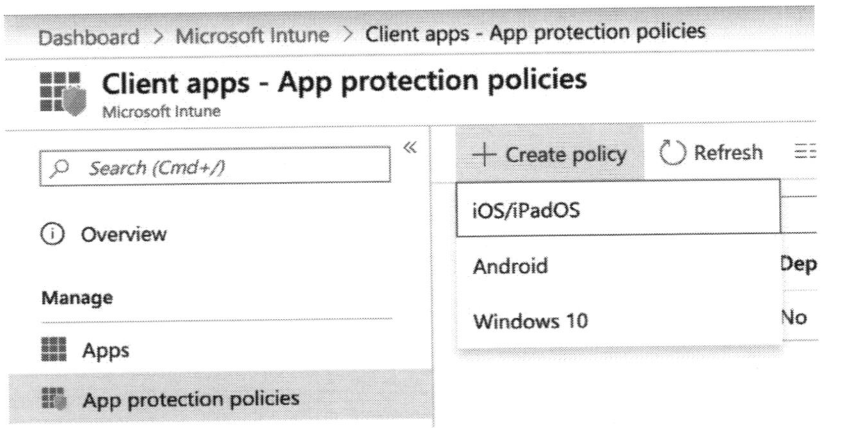

Figure 7.34 – App protection policies

3. Choose **Windows 10**, and then complete the required fields as in the following screenshot:

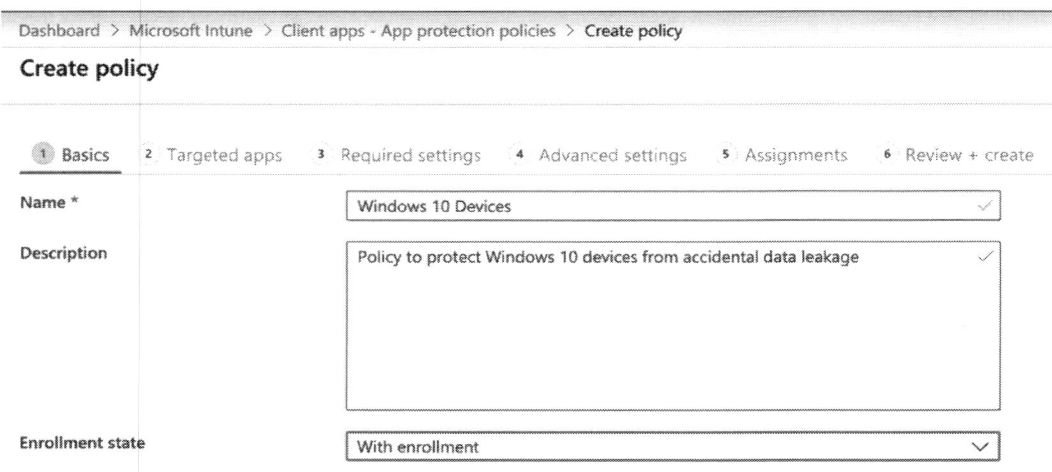

Figure 7.35 – Policy settings

4. Click **Next**, and then complete the setup wizard to include any targeted apps and required settings and to apply them to targeted users. Click **Create** to complete the setup of your policy.

You can use WIP to protect both recommended apps and apps from the Microsoft store.

WIP is a feature that can be applied in numerous ways. To learn more about WIP and how you can configure it to protect devices in your organization, please use the links included in the *References* section at the end of this chapter.

So, to recap, the features of Microsoft Defender Application Guard, Microsoft Defender Application Control, and Microsoft Defender Exploit Guard are available to complement the settings you configure for your environment using Microsoft Defender ATP. Next, we will look at how you can manage device encryption.

Managing device encryption for your Windows 10 devices

In the modern IT landscape, it is more crucial than ever to protect your organization's devices against data theft in case a device is stolen or lost. In this section, we will examine how BitLocker can be used to encrypt Windows 10 devices.

Introduction to BitLocker

BitLocker Drive Encryption provides integrated data protection features for your Windows 10 devices to combat the threat of stolen, lost, or poorly decommissioned Windows devices.

BitLocker is most effective when used with **Trusted Platform Module** (**TPM**) version 1.2 or later. However, it also works on computers that do not have TPM version 1.2 or later by using a USB start up key. You can also apply a form of multi-factor authentication with BitLocker with the ability to block device startup until one of the following responses has been provided:

- A user PIN number
- A removable device that contains a start up key

These methods help to ensure that the device doesn't start until the appropriate challenge has been issued and answered.

So, how is BitLocker configured? It can be deployed to devices using either Group Policy or Microsoft Intune. For deployment via Intune, you need to create a profile by taking the following steps:

1. Go to `portal.azure.com` and go to the Intune portal. Then, go to **Device Configuration | Profiles | Create Profile** and fill in the fields, as in the following screenshot:

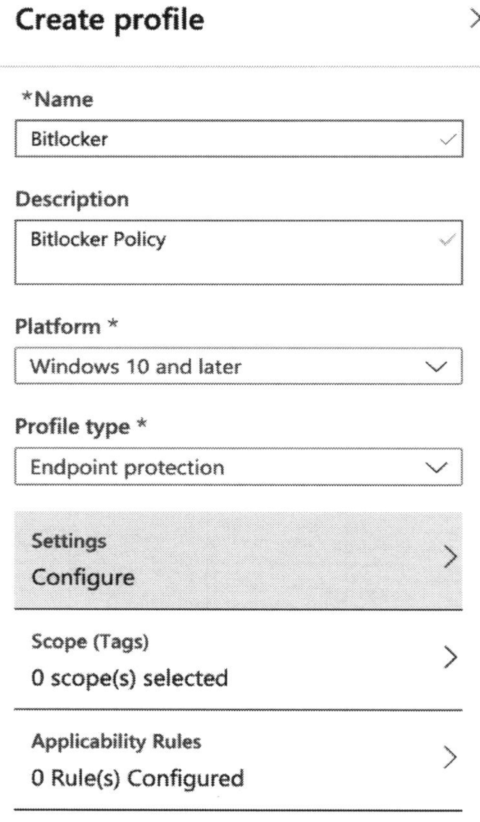

Figure 7.36 – Creating a profile

2. Next, click on **Settings | Configure | Windows Encryption** and you will see the following options:

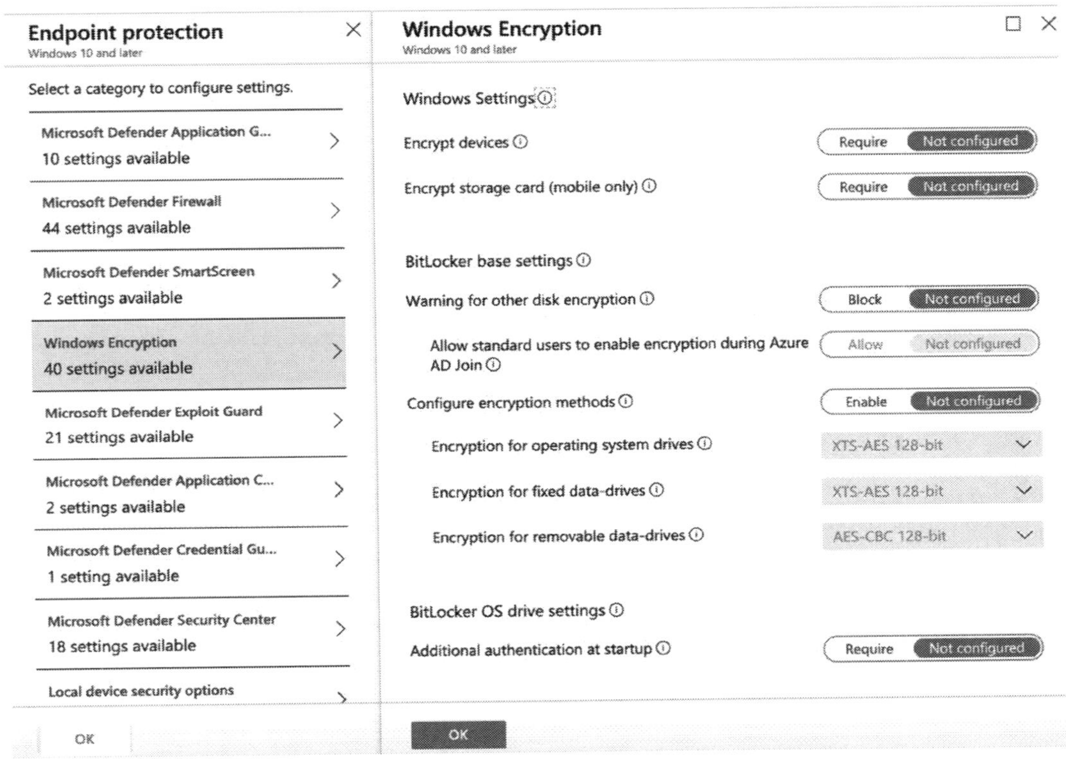

Figure 7.37 – Windows Encryption

There are a number of options to encrypt your Windows devices available in this section, and how you choose to configure these will depend on the security requirements of your organization.

Once you have configured the required settings for your BitLocker policy, click on **OK**, then **OK** again, and finally, click on **Create**.

The policy is now created and you can assign the policy to the required users and devices, as follows:

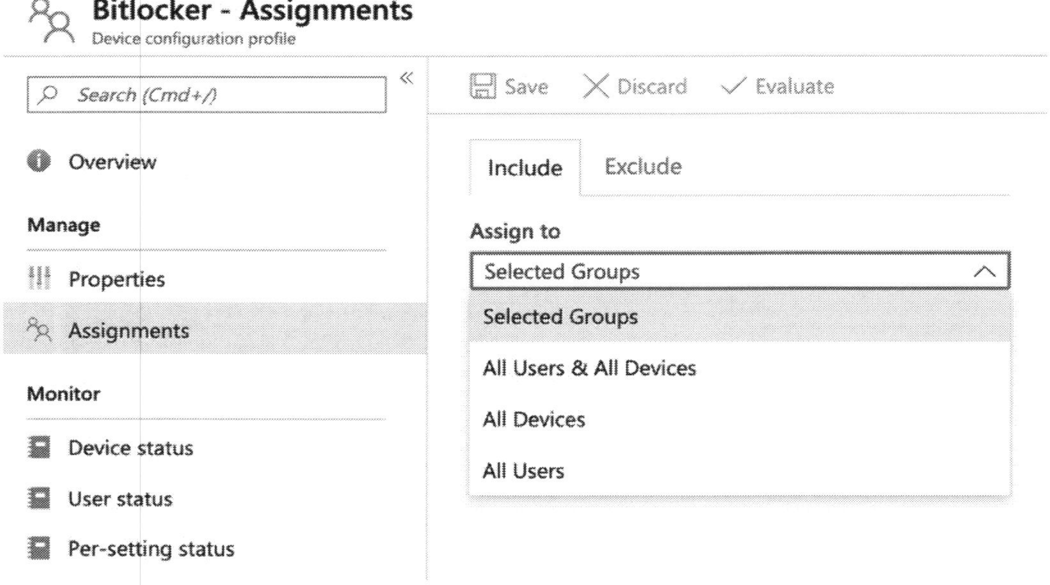

Figure 7.38 – BitLocker assignments

BitLocker is now deployed to your targeted devices and you will be able to monitor device and user status from within Intune to ensure that all required devices have the appropriate BitLocker data encryption settings applied.

So, to recap, BitLocker protects your Windows devices against loss or theft by ensuring that the devices are encrypted by settings that can be deployed by either Group Policy or Microsoft Intune.

Summary

In this chapter, we examined how Microsoft Defender ATP can be used to protect your organization's devices.

We showed you how to plan your Microsoft Defender ATP implementation, how to create your Microsoft Defender ATP instance, and how to manage and monitor the service.

We also examined how Microsoft Defender ATP can be integrated with Azure ATP and how the additional features of Microsoft Defender Application Guard, Microsoft Defender Application Control, and Microsoft Defender Exploit Guard can complement the core features, as well as how these features can be deployed by different methods, including System Center Configuration Manager, Group Policy, and Microsoft Intune.

Finally, we looked at how BitLocker can apply data protection and encryption to your Windows devices in order to safeguard them from loss, theft, or poor decommissioning practices.

In the next chapter, we will discuss message protection in Microsoft 365. We will show you how you can protect your emails in Exchange Online and apply anti-spoofing and anti-impersonation settings and anti-spam and anti-malware policies, as well as how to configure safe attachments and safe links within the Microsoft 365 Security & Compliance Center.

Questions

1. Which of the following licenses are required to use Microsoft Defender ATP (choose two)?

   a. Microsoft 365 E5

   b. Microsoft 365 E3

   c. Windows 10 Enterprise E5

   d. Windows 10 Enterprise E3

   e. Enterprise Mobility + Security E3

2. True or false: Windows Defender Application Control can be deployed by Intune.

   a. True

   b. False

3. Which of the following URLs are used to access Microsoft Defender ATP Security Center (choose two)?

   a. `securitycenter.windows.com`

   b. `securitycenter.microsoft.com`

   c. `securitycenter.windows.net`

   d. `securitycenter.microsoft.net`

4. Which profile type do you need to configure in Intune in order to configure BitLocker deployment?

   a. Network Boundary

   b. Endpoint Protection

   c. Identity Protection

   d. Administrative Templates

   e. Domain Join

5. Where would you go on a Windows 10 device to enable Windows Defender Application Guard?

   a. **Control Panel | Windows Features**

   b. **Access work or school**

   c. **Settings**

6. True or false: Windows Defender Application Guard can be configured using System Center Configuration Manager.

   a. True

   b. False

7. Where in the Microsoft Defender ATP Security Center would you go to configure Advanced Features?

   a. **Configuration Management**

   b. **Settings**

   c. **Advanced Hunting**

   d. **Automated Investigations**

8. What is the minimum number of days that retention settings can be set in relation to Microsoft Defender ATP?

   a. 30 days

   b. 60 days

   c. 90 days

   d. 120 days

9. True or false: You can download a package to manually onboard a limited number of machines to Microsoft Defender ATP.

    a. True

    b. False

10. Which two options are available from the **Service Health** menu within Microsoft Defender ATP Security Center?

    a. Current Status

    b. Archived Events

    c. Status History

    d. Updates

    e. Alerts

References

Please refer to the following links for more information:

- Microsoft Defender Advanced Threat Protection: `https://docs.microsoft.com/en-us/windows/security/threat-protection/microsoft-defender-atp/microsoft-defender-advanced-threat-protection`
- An overview of the Microsoft Defender ATP capabilities: `https://docs.microsoft.com/en-us/windows/security/threat-protection/microsoft-defender-atp/overview`
- Configuring attack surface reduction: `https://docs.microsoft.com/en-us/windows/security/threat-protection/microsoft-defender-atp/configure-attack-surface-reduction`
- Integrating Azure ATP and Microsoft Defender ATP: `https://docs.microsoft.com/en-us/azure-advanced-threat-protection/integrate-wd-atp`
- Microsoft Defender Credential Guard: `https://docs.microsoft.com/en-us/windows/security/identity-protection/credential-guard/credential-guard`
- Microsoft Defender Application Control: `https://docs.microsoft.com/en-us/windows/security/threat-protection/windows-defender-application-control/windows-defender-application-control`

- Microsoft Defender Exploit Guard: `https://www.microsoft.com/security/blog/2017/10/23/windows-defender-exploit-guard-reduce-the-attack-surface-against-next-generation-malware/`
- BitLocker Encryption: `https://support.microsoft.com/en-gb/help/4028713/windows-10-turn-on-device-encryption`
- WIP: `https://docs.microsoft.com/en-us/windows/security/information-protection/windows-information-protection/create-wip-policy-using-intune-azure`

8
Message Protection in Office 365

Exchange Online is one of the core features of the Microsoft 365 platform, and the majority of businesses with an Office 365 tenant will rely heavily on email as one of their primary methods of communication, both internally and also with customers, suppliers, and other external senders and recipients. In an ever-changing security landscape where attackers are becoming more sophisticated and ever more determined to cause chaos and disruption, it is absolutely crucial to provide as much protection and security as possible to your users when they are sending and receiving emails using Exchange Online.

Office 365 Message Protection is designed to address these challenges. In this chapter, you will learn the steps required to implement and manage Office 365 messaging protection.

We will show you how to protect domains and users within your Microsoft 365 environment by creating an anti-phishing policy, how to prevent spoofing and impersonation, what are the best practices for anti-spam protection, and how to protect your users from malicious and unsafe links and attachments with **Advanced Threat Protection** (**ATP**) **Safe Links** and ATP **Safe Attachments.**

We will cover these topics in the following order:

- Protecting users and domains with ATP anti-phishing protection and policies
- Configuring Office 365 anti-spam protection
- Exploring Office 365 ATP **Safe Attachments** options and policies
- Exploring Office 365 ATP **Safe Links** options, blocked **Uniform Resource Locators** (**URLs**), and policies

Protecting users and domains with ATP anti-phishing protection and policies

Phishing is a practice utilized by malicious actors designed to trick email users into revealing personal or sensitive information, such as passwords or credit card numbers. Phishing is a form of what is known as social engineering, during which emails will be sent by what appear to be genuine and reputable email domains from well-known and trusted organizations, but, in fact, originate from malicious sources.

It is extremely difficult to prevent phishing attacks, as the average email user is not trained to look for clues and signs that would alert trained IT professionals that an email is not genuine. Educating your users on the principals of phishing, and what they need to be aware of, is certainly a good start in trying to minimize phishing attacks within your environment. However, education alone is not enough, and this is where Office 365 ATP comes in.

Office 365 ATP includes ATP anti-phishing protection. ATP anti-phishing policies can be set up by **global administrators** or **security administrators** to protect your Office 365 email domains and users from malicious, impersonation-based, phishing attacks.

Office 365 ATP is available within the following Microsoft 365 subscriptions:

- Office 365 ATP Plan 1
- Office 365 ATP Plan 2
- Microsoft 365 Business
- Microsoft 365 Enterprise E5
- Office 365 Enterprise E5

Office 365 anti-phishing policies can be configured from the Microsoft 365 Security and Compliance Center, which can be accessed at `https://protection.office.com`.

> **Important note**
>
> A limited anti-phishing policy is also available within the **Exchange admin center (EAC)** and can be configured using **Exchange Online Protection (EOP)**.

We will now take a look at how you can set up an ATP anti-phishing policy in the Security and Compliance Center.

Setting up an ATP anti-phishing policy

Configuring an ATP anti-phishing policy is crucial for protecting your domains and users against phishing attacks. To do this, we need to take the following steps:

1. Go to the Microsoft 365 Security and Compliance Center at `https://protection.office.com`, which is shown as follows:

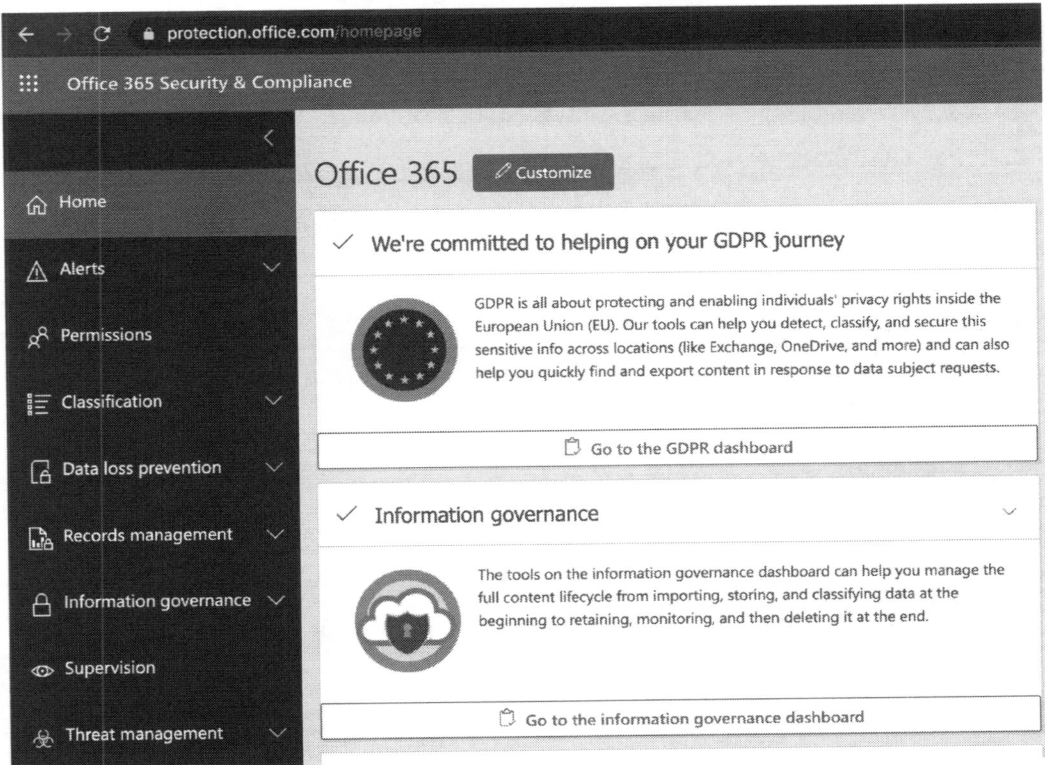

Figure 8.1 – Security and Compliance Center

2. Navigate to **Threat management** and choose **Policy**, as shown in the following screenshot:

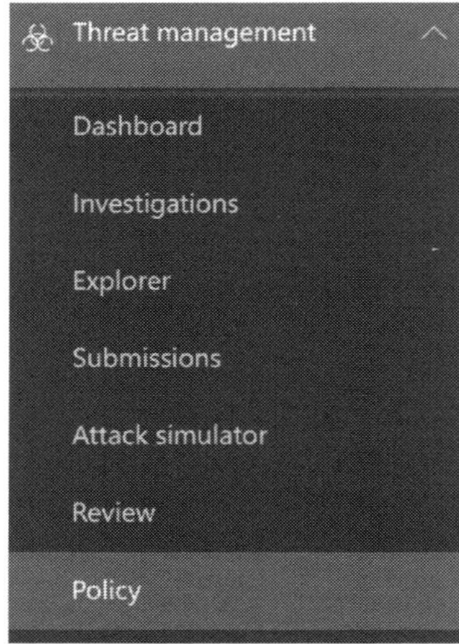

Figure 8.2 – Threat management | Policy

3. You will now see the following options:

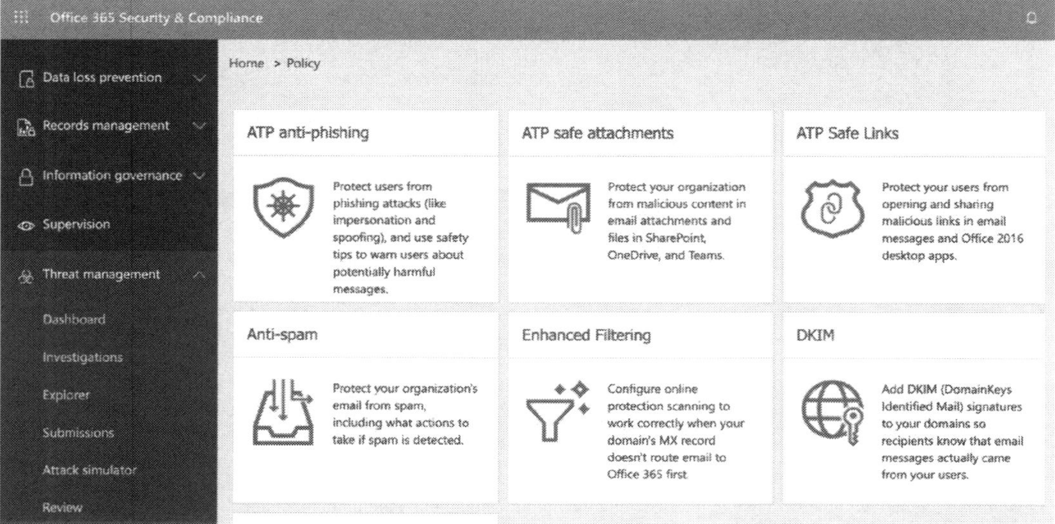

Figure 8.3 – Policy features

4. Click on **ATP anti-phishing** and then select **Create** to set up a new policy. This takes you to the following policy setup wizard:

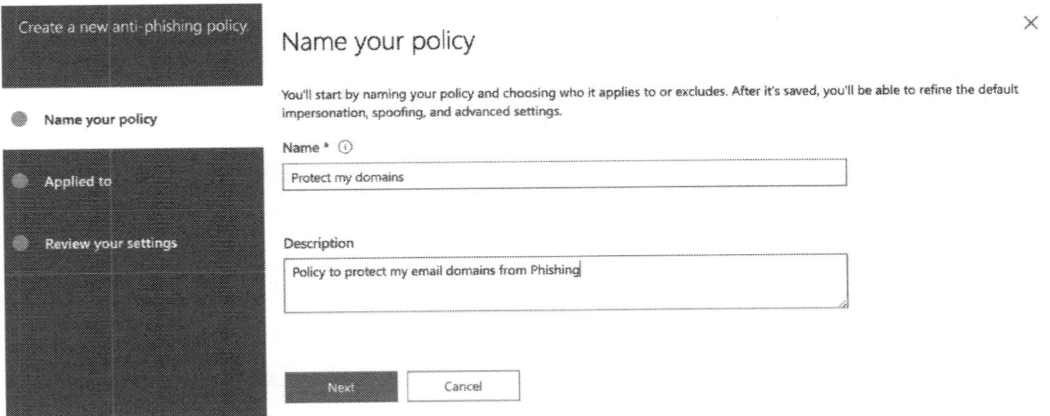

Figure 8.4 – Naming your policy

5. Enter a name and description for your policy, and click **Next**. This takes you to the following screen:

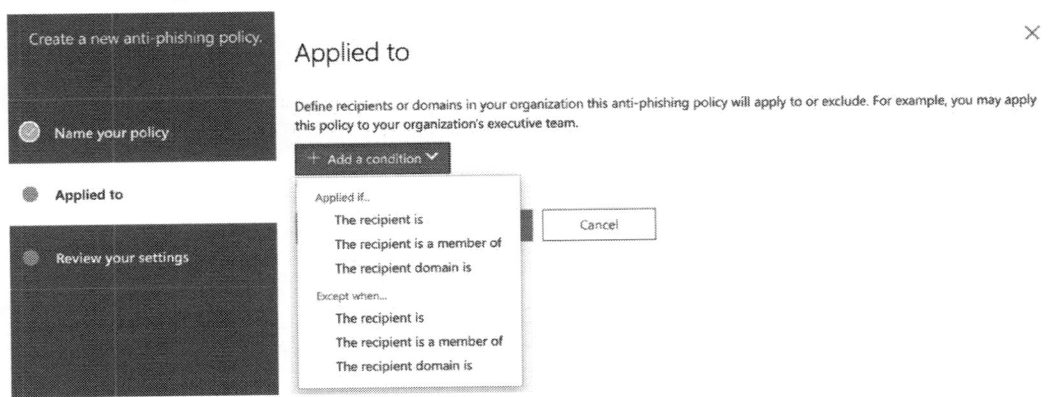

Figure 8.5 – Policy description

6. In the **Applied to** dialog shown in the preceding screenshot, you may now choose the **Add a condition** option to choose when this policy will be applied. In this example, we will apply the policy to the email domain in our tenant, so we will choose **The recipient domain is** option. This will take you to the following screen:

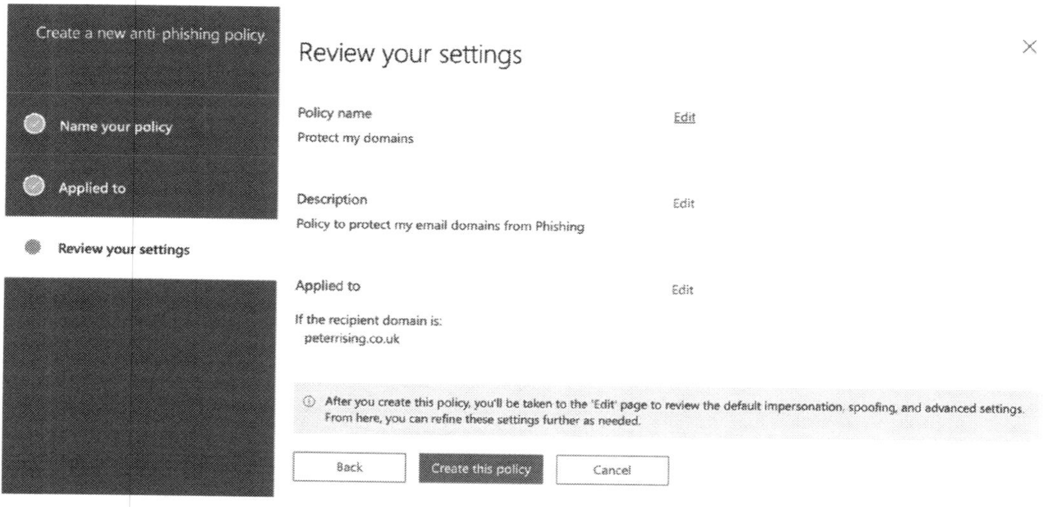

Figure 8.6 – Reviewing the settings

7. Add the domain that you wish to protect. In the example shown in the preceding screenshot, we have added a single domain from our tenant. Once you have reviewed your settings, click **Create this policy**. The policy is now created and can be seen as shown in the following screenshot:

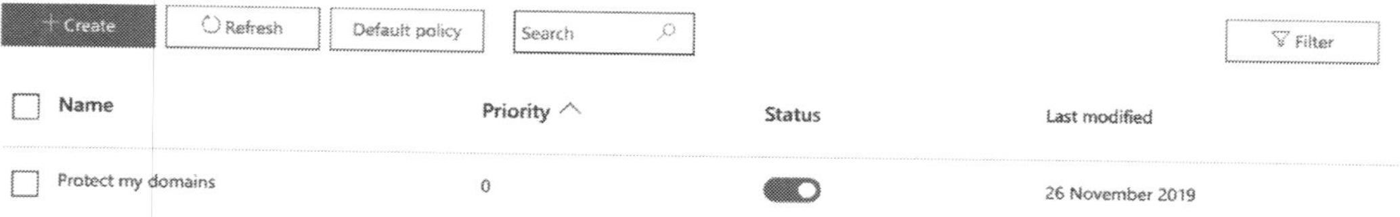

Figure 8.7 – New policy created

8. Click on the policy in order to edit the available settings within the policy, as per the following screenshot:

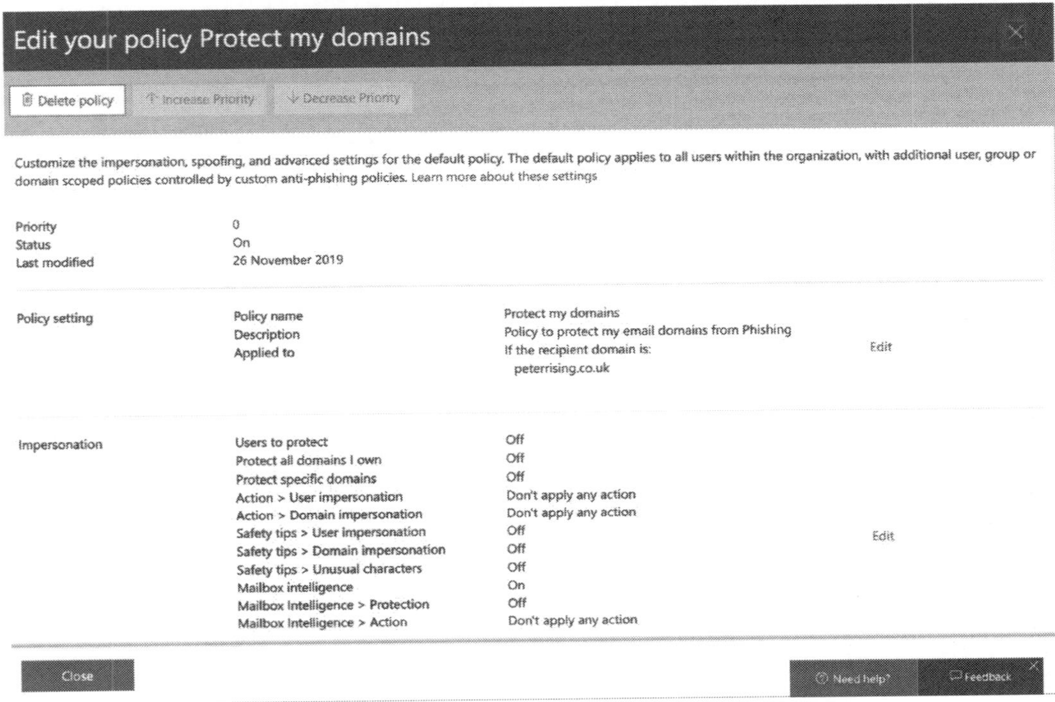

Figure 8.8 – Editing the policy

9. Edit each of the settings within the policy editor to configure the preferred settings for your policy. The settings that you can modify are **Policy setting**, **Impersonation**, **Spoof**, and **Advanced settings**.

The preceding steps that we have completed were taken to configure the policy settings, to apply protection to a single recipient domain. Now, let's take a look at the other settings we can configure in turn, starting with **Impersonation**.

Configuring Impersonation settings

When you select the newly created policy that we set up in the preceding steps, clicking on **Edit** under the **Impersonation** section of the policy takes you to the **Edit impersonation policy** options, as shown in the following screenshot:

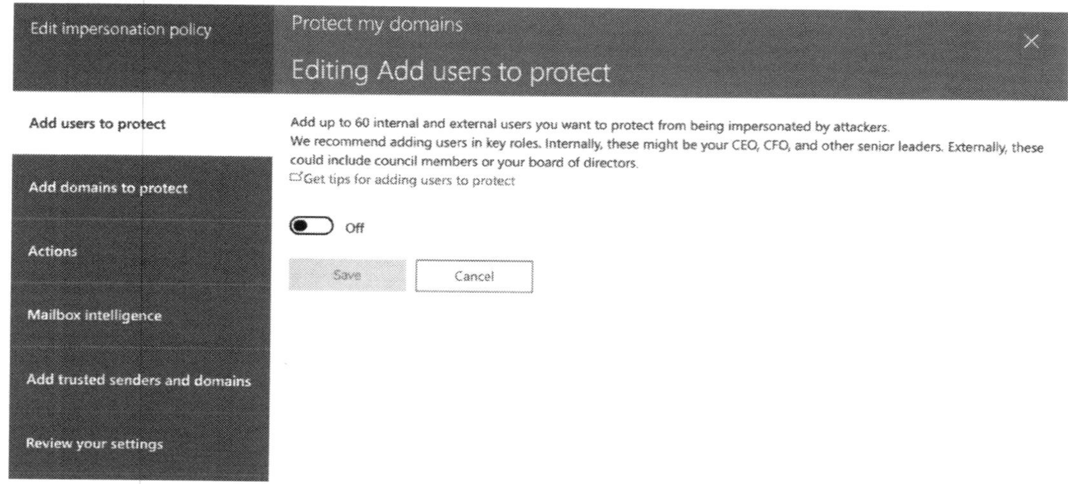

Figure 8.9 – Adding users to protect

The following settings may be configured in the impersonation policy editor:

Setting	Options
Add users to protect	Here, you may add up to 60 internal or external users for whom you wish to configure impersonation protection. It is common practice to add high-level targets to this setting, such as **chief executive officer** (**CEO**), **chief operations officer** (**COO**), and **chief financial officer** (**CFO**). This setting needs to be set to **On** before users can be added.

Setting	Options
Add domains to protect	Here, you may add any email domains for which you wish to configure impersonation protection. You can choose to add either only the domains that you own or custom domains, or both.
Actions	Here, you may choose the actions that are taken when an email is sent by an impersonated user or domain. The available options are as follows: • Redirect message to other email addresses • Move message to the recipient's junk email folder • Quarantine the message • Deliver the message and add other addresses to the **blind carbon copy** (**BCC**) line • Delete the message before it's delivered • Don't apply any action You may also turn on impersonation safety tips from here, which will show a warning in the recipient's email if an impersonation attack is detected.
Mailbox intelligence	Here, you may enable mailbox intelligence to analyze your users' mail flow patterns. This will show which of your users' contacts they communicate with most frequently, which enables easier identification of an attacker who may be attempting to impersonate one of those contacts.
Add trusted senders and domains	Here, you may add email addresses and domains that are deemed to be trustworthy and that will not be affected by this policy.
Review your settings	Here, you may quickly review all of the preceding settings to ensure they are appropriate for your organizational needs.

Once you are certain that your **Impersonation** settings are configured appropriately, click on **Save** to apply them to the policy. Next, let's look at the spoof settings.

Configuring spoof settings

Before we explain how to configure your spoofing filter settings, we need to explain exactly what spoofing is. Spoofing is a process whereby domain users are allowed to send messages on behalf of another domain or email address. An example of this would be the shared mailbox feature within Exchange Online. Because spoofing is a recognized and often necessary and legitimate process, the **Simple Mail Transfer Protocol** (**SMTP**) supports spoofing by default.

However, spoofing may also be used for malicious purposes, and attackers will frequently use spoofing techniques to try to initiate impersonation attacks. This is why it is important to configure spoofing protection settings within your Microsoft 365 environment.

You may configure the spoof settings for your policy in exactly the same way as the **Impersonation** settings, by clicking on your policy. In this case, however, you need to click on **Edit** under the **Spoof** section. This will take you to the **Spoofing filter settings** editor, as shown in the following screenshot:

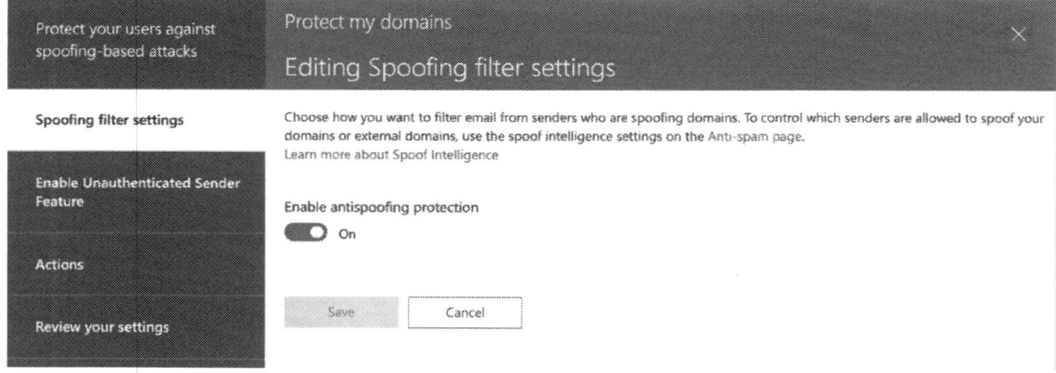

Figure 8.10 – Editing Spoofing filter settings

The following settings may be configured in the **Spoofing filter settings** editor:

Setting	Options
Spoofing filter settings	Here, you may choose how you wish to filter emails from users who are spoofing domains. You can enable or disable anti-spoofing protection from here.
Enable Unauthenticated Sender Feature	Here, you may enable or disable the Unauthenticated Sender Feature. If enabled, this feature will apply a ? symbol in Outlook's sender card if the sender fails authentication checks.
Actions	Here, you may choose from the following actions that are taken when a person spoofing your domain is not an allowed sender: • Move the message to the recipient's junk email folder • Quarantine the message
Review your settings	Here, you may quickly review all of the preceding settings to ensure they are appropriate for your organizational needs.

Once the appropriate settings have been configured, you may click to save the spoofing filter settings. Finally, let's look at the advanced settings for our anti-phishing policy.

Configuring Advanced settings

The advanced settings available for your policy may be configured by once again clicking to select your policy, where you will see the following available settings:

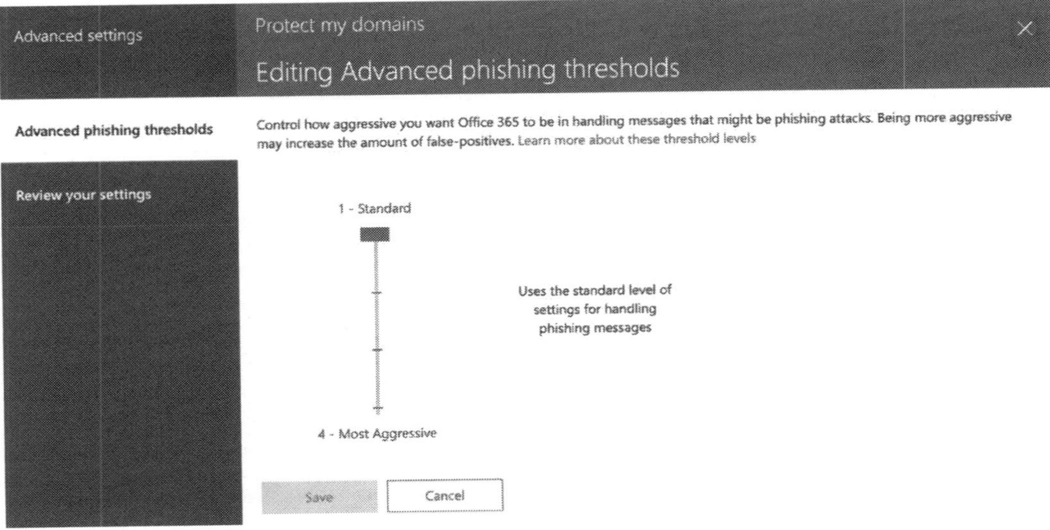

Figure 8.11 – Editing Advanced phishing thresholds

The following settings may be set under **Advanced settings**:

Setting	Options
Advanced phishing thresholds	Here, you may choose the aggression level for handling advanced phishing incidents. These are as follows: • **Standard** • **Aggressive** • **More Aggressive** • **Most Aggressive**
Review your settings	Here, you can review your chosen settings before applying any changes to the policy.

Once again, you may click on **Save** when the settings are configured for your organizational requirements.

> **Important note**
> When configuring anti-phishing policies for your Office 365 tenant using Office 365 ATP, it is recommended to protect either domains or emails, but not both. Configuring domains will provide more complete protection.

In this section, we have shown you how to configure an Office 365 ATP anti-phishing policy for your domains and users in Office 365. Next, we will look at how anti-spam protection can be applied by configuring anti-spam policies for your Office 365 users.

Configuring Office 365 anti-spam protection

Office 365 includes built-in anti-spam protection, which can help you to control inbound and outbound spam emails that are flowing through Exchange Online. Anti-spam protection has long been available via the Exchange Online portal, but in line with Microsoft recommended practices for implementing security and compliance features within your Microsoft 365 environment, Office 365 anti-spam protection is now more logically configured via the security and compliance center.

Let's take a look at how you can configure your Office 365 anti-spam settings. To do this, proceed as follows:

1. We need to log in to the Office 365 Security and Compliance Center.
2. Navigate to **Threat management**.
3. Then, go to **Policy**, and choose **Anti-spam**. You will see the options shown in the following screenshot:

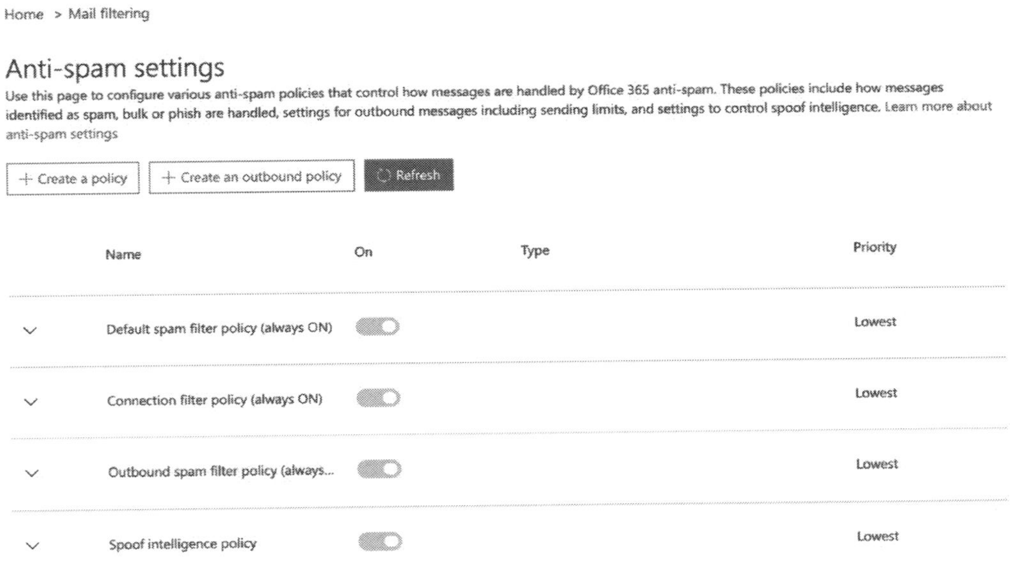

Home > Mail filtering

Anti-spam settings

Use this page to configure various anti-spam policies that control how messages are handled by Office 365 anti-spam. These policies include how messages identified as spam, bulk or phish are handled, settings for outbound messages including sending limits, and settings to control spoof intelligence. Learn more about anti-spam settings

+ Create a policy   + Create an outbound policy   Refresh

Name	On	Type	Priority
Default spam filter policy (always ON)			Lowest
Connection filter policy (always ON)			Lowest
Outbound spam filter policy (always...			Lowest
Spoof intelligence policy			Lowest

Figure 8.12 – Anti-spam settings

There are four built-in policies available in the **anti-spam settings**, which you can configure and apply to your environment. It is also possible to create new policies. Let's take a look at the built-in policies first.

Default spam filter policy

The **Default spam filter policy** option is automatically enabled. It identifies and processes messages identified as spam by applying the settings and actions shown in the following screenshot:

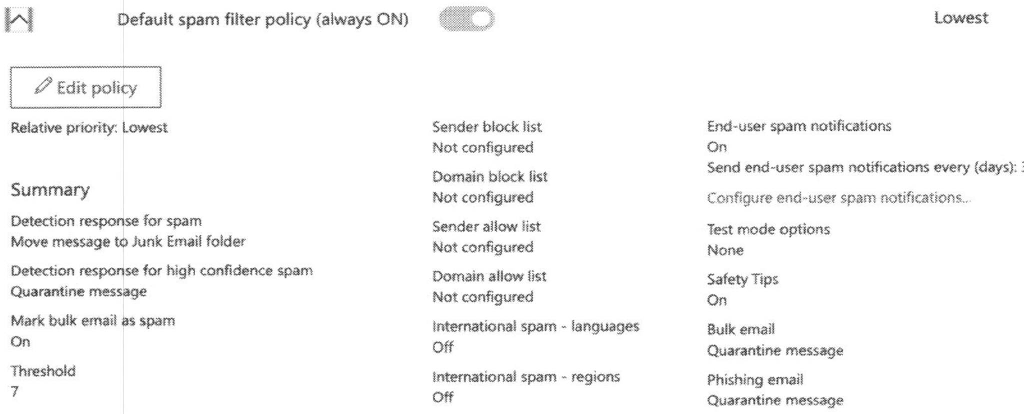

Figure 8.13 – Default spam filter policy

It is recommended that you either customize the **Default spam filter policy** to meet your organizational needs or create specific policies that can be targeted to your Office 365 users. Next, let's look at the connection filter policy.

Connection filter policy

The default **Connection filter policy** option is automatically enabled and will check the reputation of senders before allowing a message through. Allow lists and safe sender lists may be configured within this policy to ensure that any messages sent from a specific **Internet Protocol** (**IP**) address or IP address range will be successfully delivered. Block lists can be configured in the same way.

The default **Connection filter policy** option can be configured by editing the settings, as shown in the following screenshot:

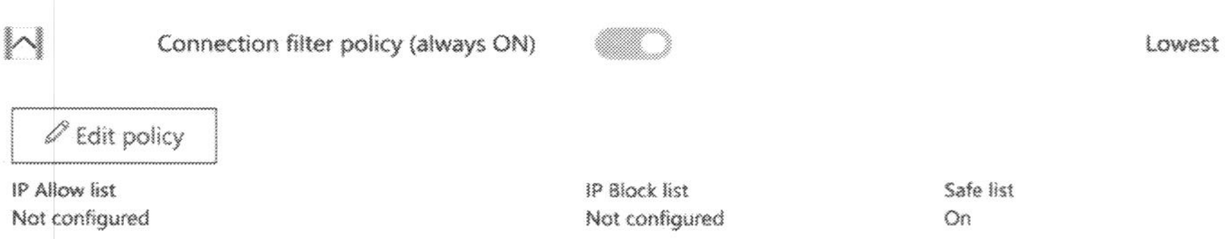

Figure 8.14 – Connection filter policy

It is not possible to create a separate connection filter policy; therefore, the default **Connection filter policy** must be used to maintain your lists of allowed and blocked IP addresses and IP ranges.

Next, we will look at the **Outbound spam filter policy**.

Outbound spam filter policy

The default **Outbound spam filter policy** option is automatically enabled and allows you to configure settings for outbound spam detections, as shown in the following screenshot:

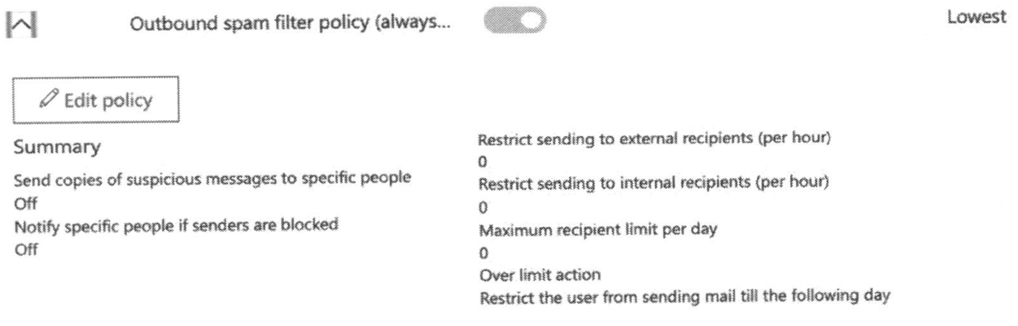

Figure 8.15 – Outbound spam filter policy

You can use this policy to send notifications of suspicious messages to specific people, and also for when senders are blocked. This policy also allows you to set the maximum number of recipients per user. Specify **0** to use the defaults, or enter a value between 0 and 10,000.

In addition to the default **Outbound spam filter policy**, you may also configure a custom outbound policy that can be targeted to specific users and groups.

Spoof intelligence policy

The default **Spoof intelligence policy** option is automatically enabled and allows you to review any senders who may be spoofing your domains. You have the option to review spoofing activity, as shown in the following screenshot:

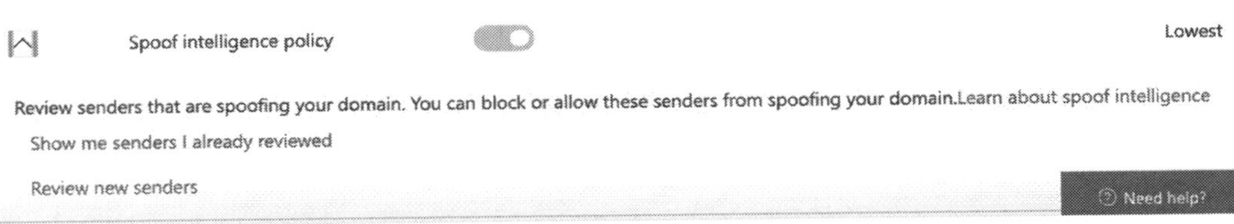

Figure 8.16 – Spoof intelligence policy

> **Important note**
>
> If your users have Office 365 E5 or Office 365 ATP licenses, connection filtering will automatically create, allow, and block lists of senders who are spoofing your domains.

Additional email authentication protection

In addition to setting the spoofing filter settings within the Office 365 Security and Compliance Center, it is also Microsoft's recommended practice to configure the following email authentication techniques for any custom email domains you may have in your Office 365 tenant:

- **Sender Policy Framework** (**SPF**) – A **Domain Name System** (**DNS**) record to validate the origin of email messages, and prevent spoofing and phishing
- **DomainKeys Identified Mail** (**DKIM**) – Adds a digital signature to email message headers to prevent spoofers from sending messages that appear to be coming from your domain
- **Domain-based Message Authentication, Reporting, and Compliance** (**DMARC**) – An authentication technique that protects from phishers who have spoofed the `5322.From` email address, which is displayed in mail clients

Configuring these features will add another layer of protection to your email domains and help to protect you against phishing and spoofing attempts.

> **Important note**
>
> Further information on the additional email authentication settings described previously may be found in the *References* section at the end of this chapter.

Configuring Office 365 anti-spam settings and policies with PowerShell

In addition to using the Office 365 Security and Compliance Center to configure your anti-spam settings and policies, it is also possible to use PowerShell. Some of the most commonly used PowerShell commands are shown as follows:

- `Get-HostedContentFilterPolicy` – You may use this command in order to see the spam filter settings.
- `Set-HostedContentFilterPolicy` – You may use this command in order to edit the spam filter settings.

- `New-HostedContentFilterPolicy` – You may use this command in order to create an entirely new and custom spam filter policy.
- `Remove-HostedContentFilterPolicy` – You may use this command in order to delete any custom policies that you may have set up.

The following is an example of creating a custom spam filter policy using PowerShell:

```
New-HostedContentFilterPolicy -Name 'New Content Filter
Policy' -HighConfidenceSpamAction Redirect -SpamAction
Redirect -RedirectToRecipients user1@domain.com
-FalsePositiveAdditionalRecipients user2@domain.com
```

This example will create a new content filter policy called **New Content Filter Policy**, which has the following settings:

- Redirects spam messages (or messages that may be spam) to `user1@domain.com`
- Sends a copy of spam quarantine false-positive submissions to `user2@domain.com`

Further examples of PowerShell commands relevant to configuring anti-spam settings in Office 365 can be found in the *References* section at the end of this chapter.

So, to recap on what we have learned in this section, we have shown you how you can use the Office 365 Security and Compliance Center to edit the default policies for anti-spam within Office 365, and also how to create new policies that can be targeted to specific users and groups. We also looked at how PowerShell can be used to create and edit anti-spam settings and policies.

Next, we will look at Office 365 ATP **Safe Attachments**, and how this feature can be used to protect your users from suspicious attachments within email messages.

Exploring Office 365 ATP Safe Attachments options and policies

Safe Attachments is an Office 365 ATP feature that allows you to protect your users from opening attachments that may contain malicious code.

In this section, we will show you how to manage **Safe Attachments** in Office 365 by setting up policies in the Microsoft 365 Security and Compliance Center, and also by using Windows PowerShell.

In order to create a **Safe Attachments** policy, you must be a member of one of the following role groups:

- **Organization Management**
- **Hygiene Management**

> **Important note**
> It is also possible to configure and manage **Safe Attachments** from the **Exchange Admin Center** (EAC). However, it is Microsoft's recommendation to use the Office 365 Security and Compliance Center.

Creating a Safe Attachments policy from the Security and Compliance Center

To create a new **Safe Attachments** policy, we need to complete the following steps:

1. From the Microsoft 365 Security and Compliance Center, navigate to **Threat management**, choose **Policy**, and then click on **ATP Safe Attachments**. This will show you the following screen:

Home > Safe attachments
Safe attachments
Use this page to protect your organization from malicious content in email attachments and files in SharePoint, OneDrive, and Microsoft Teams.
Protect files in SharePoint, OneDrive, and Microsoft Teams
If a file in any SharePoint, OneDrive, or Microsoft Teams library is identified as malicious, ATP will prevent users from opening and downloading the file. Learn more about ATP for SharePoint, OneDrive, and Microsoft Teams
Turn on ATP for SharePoint, OneDrive, and Microsoft Teams
Protect email attachments
Set up an ATP safe attachments policy for specific users or groups to help prevent people from opening or sharing email attachments that contain malicious content. Learn more about ATP safe attachments for email
Reports for this feature just got better. Check out the new report in the Security and Compliance Center for an enhanced reporting experience.
ENABLED
NAME
PRIORITY
Default Policy
0
Default Policy
Enabled
1 selected of 1 total
Save

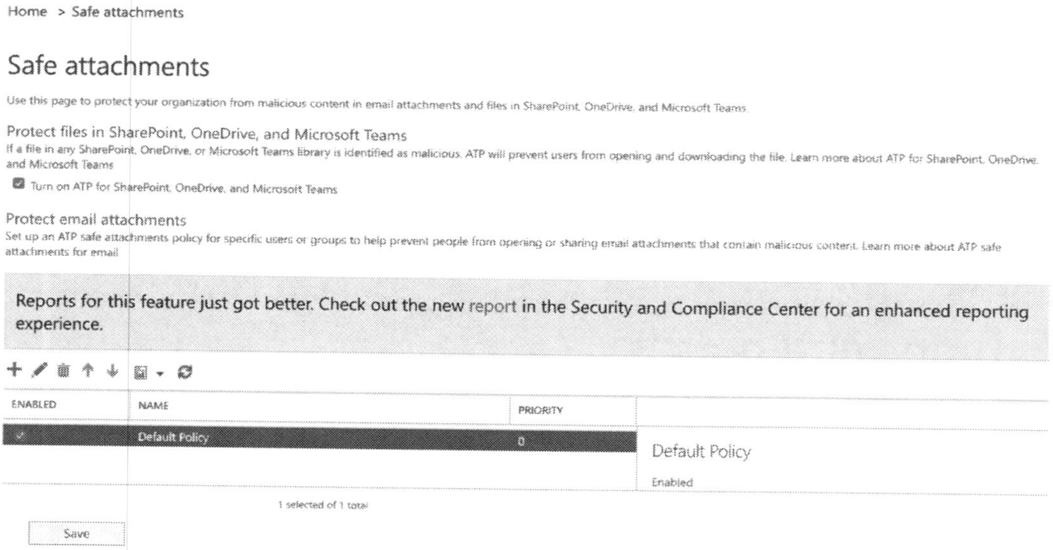

Figure 8.17 – Safe attachments

2. You can edit the default policy from here, if required. However, in this example, we will create a new policy by clicking on the + icon. Enter a **Name** and **Description** for your policy, as shown in the following screenshot:

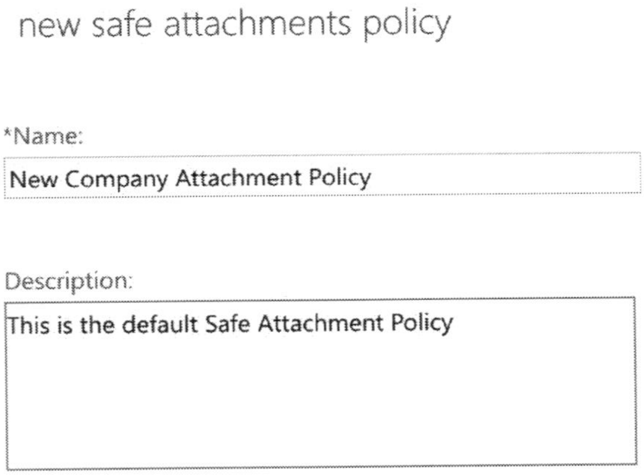

new safe attachments policy
*Name:
New Company Attachment Policy
Description:
This is the default Safe Attachment Policy

Figure 8.18 – New safe attachments policy

3. Next, we need to choose the action that will be applied when threats are detected in attachments. In this example, we will configure the option for **Dynamic Delivery**, which will deliver the email message to the end user without any delay and will detonate the attachment in Microsoft's sandbox environment when the user chooses to open it. This is shown as follows:

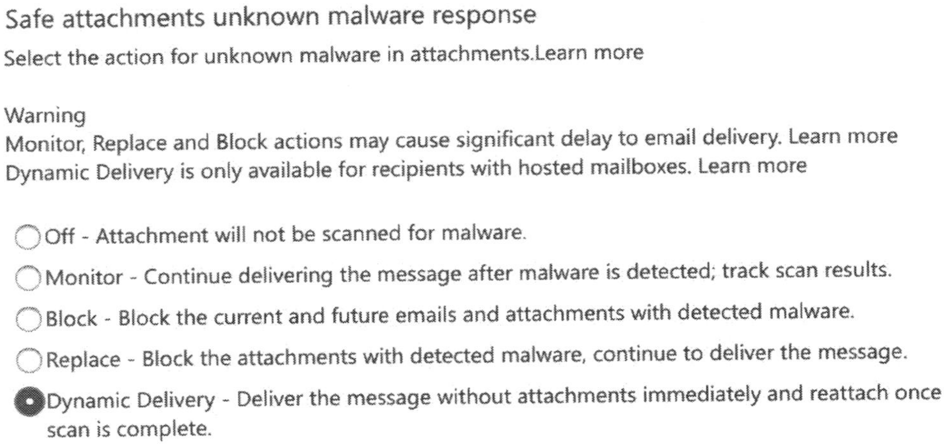

Safe attachments unknown malware response
Select the action for unknown malware in attachments.Learn more
Warning
Monitor, Replace and Block actions may cause significant delay to email delivery. Learn more
Dynamic Delivery is only available for recipients with hosted mailboxes. Learn more
Off - Attachment will not be scanned for malware.
Monitor - Continue delivering the message after malware is detected; track scan results.
Block - Block the current and future emails and attachments with detected malware.
Replace - Block the attachments with detected malware, continue to deliver the message.
Dynamic Delivery - Deliver the message without attachments immediately and reattach once scan is complete.

Figure 8.19 – Malware response setting

4. Next, we can choose an email recipient for any blocked, monitored, or replaced attachments to be sent to, as shown in the following screenshot:

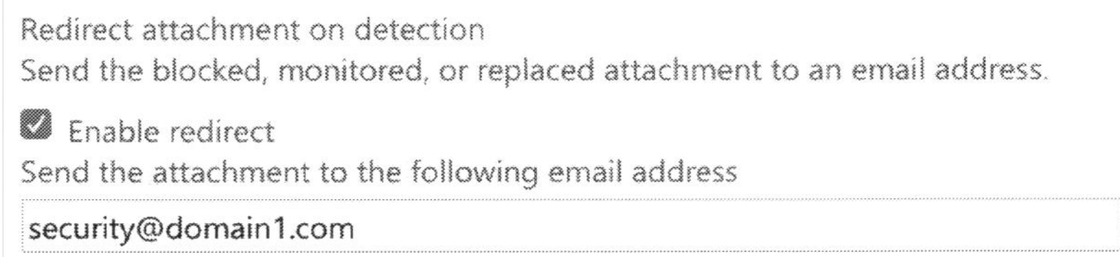

Figure 8.20 – Attachment redirection options

5. Finally, we will apply our **Safe Attachments** policy to the targeted users, groups, or domains within Office 365, along with any required conditions or exceptions, as the following screenshot shows:

Apply the above selection if malware scanning for attachments times out or error occurs.

Applied To

Specify the users, groups, or domains for whom this policy applies by creating recipient based rules:

*If...

Select one

add condition

Except if...

add exception

Figure 8.21 – Conditions and exceptions

6. Click **Save** to finalize your policy.

Now, let's take a look at some of the PowerShell commands that can be used to create a **Safe Attachments** policy.

Creating a Safe Attachments policy using Windows PowerShell

Safe Attachments policies may also be configured with the following PowerShell commands once connected to Exchange Online PowerShell:

- `Get-SafeAttachmentPolicy` – You may use this command in order to examine the **Safe Attachments** policy settings.

- `Set-SafeAttachmentPolicy` – You may use this command in order to modify the existing **Safe Attachments** policy settings.
- `New-SafeAttachmentPolicy` – You may use this command in order to set up an entirely new and custom **Safe Attachments** policy.
- `Remove-SafeAttachmentPolicy` – You may use this command in order to remove any custom **Safe Attachments** policies you may have configured.

You may also apply rules to your **Safe Attachments** policies using PowerShell. A rule defines the conditions, and a policy defines the actions. The following PowerShell commands are available for **Safe Attachments** rules:

- `Get-SafeAttachmentRule` – You may use this command in order to examine the **Safe Attachments** rule settings.
- `Set-SafeAttachmentRule` – You may use this command in order to modify the current **Safe Attachments** rule settings.
- `New-SafeAttachmentRule` – You may use this command in order to set up an entirely new and custom **Safe Attachments** rule.
- `Remove-SafeAttachmentRule` – You may use this command in order to remove any custom **Safe Attachments** rules you may have configured.

> **Important note**
>
> **Safe Attachments** policies must be created before you can create **Safe Attachments** rules.

In this section, we have shown you how you can configure **Safe Attachments** by using Office 365 ATP. You have learned that **Safe Attachments** policies can be created and applied for your Office 365 users, groups, and domains, and that rules, conditions, and exceptions may be applied to these policies.

We showed you that you can manage **Safe Attachments** by using the Microsoft 365 Security and Compliance Center, and by connecting to the Exchange Online PowerShell tool.

Next, we will show you how the Office 365 ATP **Safe Links** feature can be used to protect your Office 365 users from suspicious links within emails and within Microsoft Office applications.

Exploring Office 365 ATP Safe Links options, blocked URLs, and policies

Safe Links is an Office 365 ATP feature that allows you to protect your users from links they receive that may contain malicious code.

In this section, we will show you how you can manage **Safe Links** in Office 365 by modifying the default **Safe Links** policy, or by setting up a new **Safe Links** policy that will be targeted to specific users. **Safe Links** policies can be managed in the Microsoft 365 Security and Compliance Center and by using Windows PowerShell.

Viewing or modifying the default Safe Links policy from the Security and Compliance Center

In order to view or modify the default **Safe Links** policy, you need to complete the following steps:

1. From the Microsoft 365 Security and Compliance Center, navigate to **Threat management**, choose **Policy**, and then click on **ATP Safe Links**. This will show you the following screen:

Home > Safe links
Safe links
Safe links help prevent your users from following links in email and documents that go to web sites recognized as malicious. Use this page to set up policies that determine how all or specific users in your organization interact with safe links. Learn more about safe links
Reports for this feature just got better. Check out the new report in the Security and Compliance Center for an enhanced reporting experience.
Policies that apply to the entire organization
NAME
Default
Summary
Settings:
Do not track when users click safe links:
Enabled
Do not let users click through safe links to original URL:
Enabled
Applied to:
Office 2016 on Windows:
Enabled

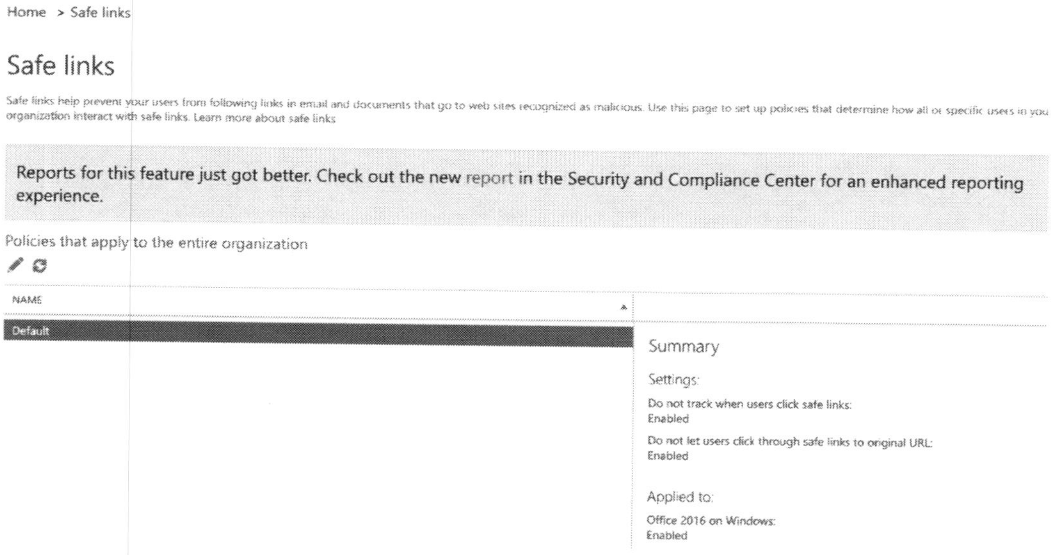

Figure 8.22 – Safe links

2. You will see a default policy that applies to the entire organization. Double-click on **Default**, and you will see the following screen:

Safe links policy for your organization

Settings that apply to content across Office 365

When users click a blocked URL, they're redirected to a web page that explains why the URL is blocked.

Block the following URLs:

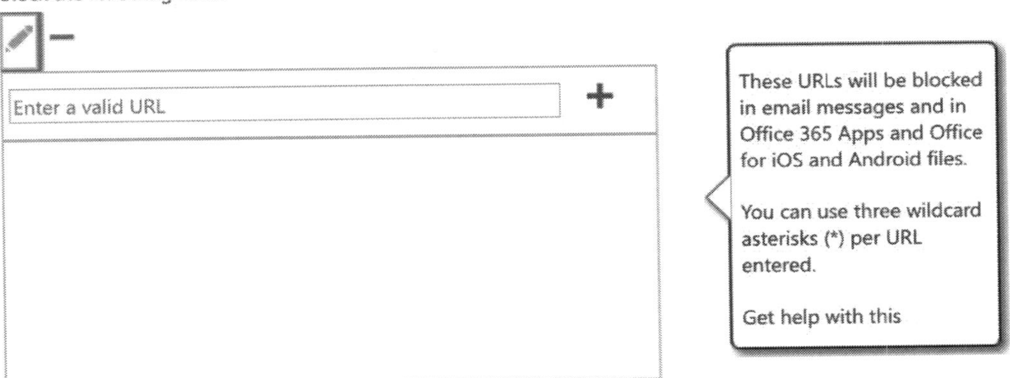

Enter a valid URL
These URLs will be blocked in email messages and in Office 365 Apps and Office for iOS and Android files.
You can use three wildcard asterisks (*) per URL entered.
Get help with this

Settings that apply to content except email

These settings don't apply to email messages. If you want to apply them for email, create a safe links policy for email recipients.

Use safe links in:

- [x] Office 365 applications

For the locations selected above:

- [x] Do not track when users click safe links
- [x] Do not let users click through safe links to original URL

Figure 8.23 – Default safe links policy

3. Here, you are able to choose the **Block the following URLs** option shown in the preceding screenshot, should you wish to explicitly prevent access to any URLs that you know to be malicious or unsuitable. There are also some additional settings that you can select if you wish to apply **Safe Links** to content in applications other than email.

You can return to your default **Safe Links** policy should you need to add or modify the list of blocked URLs.

Creating a new Safe Links policy from the Security and Compliance Center

With **Safe Links** in Office 365, you can also create policies that apply to specific recipients. The default **Safe Links** policy has a few settings that you are able to configure. This option gives you far greater control over the behavior of **Safe Links** and the experience your Microsoft 365 users will have.

In order to create a new **Safe Links** policy, you need to complete the following steps:

1. From the Microsoft 365 Security and Compliance Center, navigate to **Threat management**, choose **Policy**, and then click on **ATP Safe Links**. This will show you the following screen:

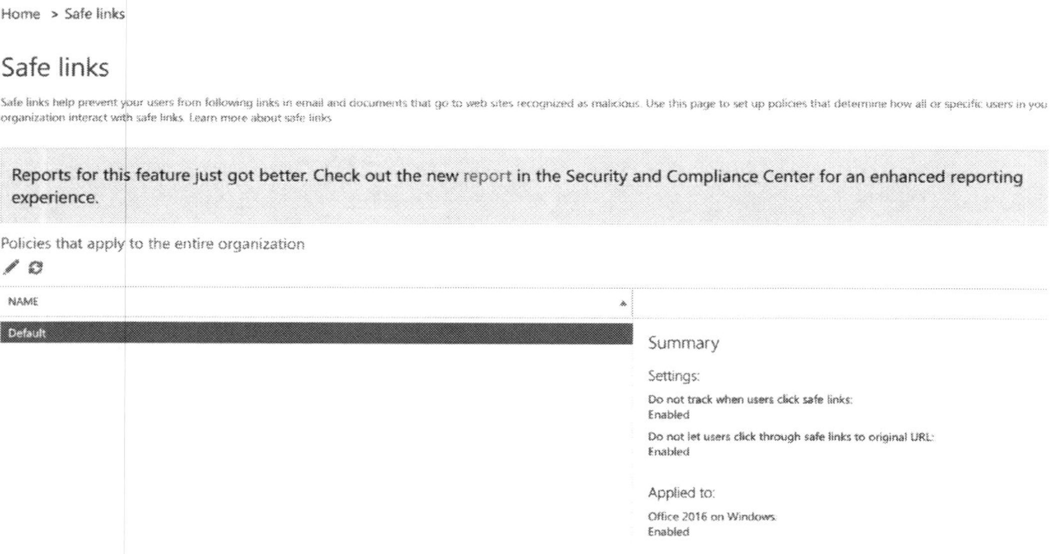

Figure 8.24 – Safe links

2. You will again see the default policy that applies to the entire organization. In this example, however, we will create a new policy to be applied to specific recipients. Scroll down the page, and you will see the following:

Policies that apply to specific recipients

ENABLED	NAME	PRIORITY

There are no items to show in this view.

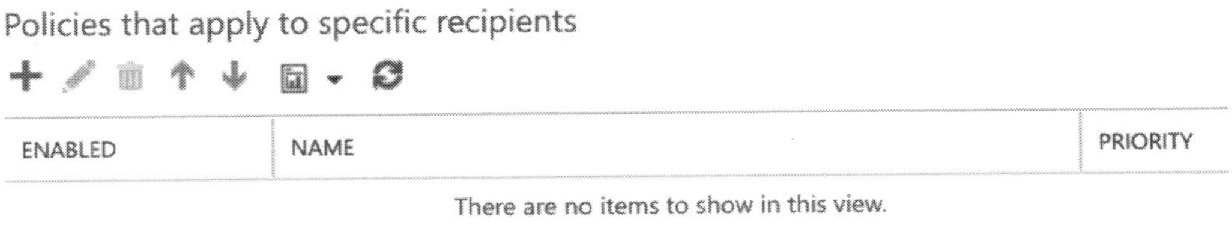

Figure 8.25 – Creating a custom policy

3. Click the + icon to create a new policy. You will see the following:

new safe links policy

*Name:

Targeted Safe Links Policy

Description:

This safe links policy is targeted to all Office 365 users

Select the action for unknown potentially malicious URLs in messages.

Off

On - URLs will be rewritten and checked against a list of known malicious links when user clicks on the link.

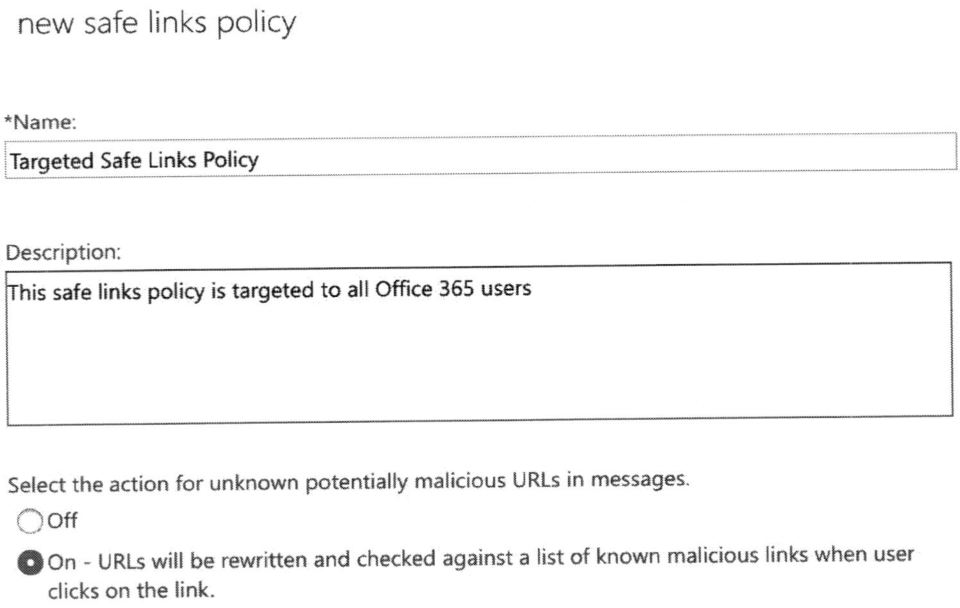

Figure 8.26 – New safe links policy

Enter a **Name** and **Description** for your policy, and select the action you wish the policy to take for malicious URLs. Next, complete the following settings:

- [x] Apply real-time URL scanning for suspicious links and links that point to files.
  - [x] Wait for URL scanning to complete before delivering the message.
- [x] Apply safe links to email messages sent within the organization.
- [ ] Do not track when users click safe links.
- [ ] Do not let users click through safe links to original URL.

Figure 8.27 – Policy setting options

4. Next, create a list of any URLs you wish to exclude from URL rewrites, as shown in the following screenshot:

Do not rewrite the following URLs:

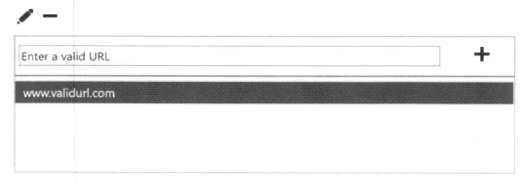

Figure 8.28 – Excluding URLs

5. Finally, set the policy to apply to the targeted users, groups, or domains, and add any required conditions or exceptions, shown as follows:

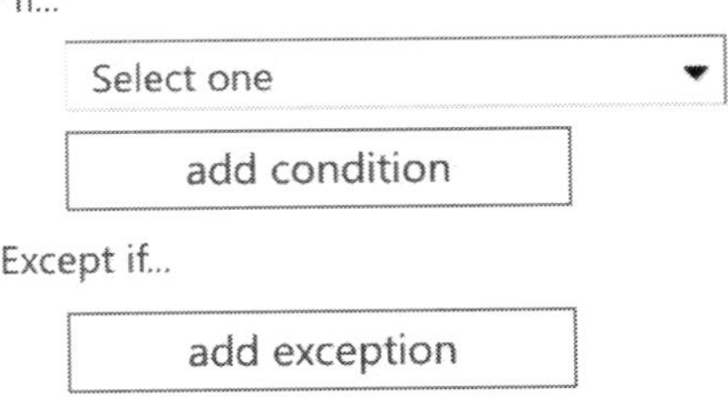

Figure 8.29 – Conditions and exceptions

6. Click **Save** to complete the creation of your policy.

Now, let's take a look at some of the PowerShell commands that can be used to create a **Safe Links** policy.

Creating a Safe Links policy using Windows PowerShell

Safe Links policies may also be configured with the following PowerShell commands, once connected to Exchange Online PowerShell:

- `Get-SafeLinksPolicy` – View **Safe Links** policy settings
- `Set-SafeLinksPolicy` – Edit existing **Safe Links** policy settings
- `New-SafeLinksPolicy` – Create a custom **Safe Links** policy
- `Remove-SafeLinksPolicy` – Delete a custom **Safe Links** policy

In the same way you can use **Safe Attachments**, you may also apply rules to your **Safe Links** policies using PowerShell. Once again, the rule defines the conditions, and the policy defines the actions. The following PowerShell commands are available for **Safe Links** rules:

- `Get-SafeLinksRule` – View **Safe Links** rule settings
- `Set-SafeLinksRule` – Edit existing **Safe Links** rule settings
- `New-SafelinksRule` – Create a custom **Safe Links** rule
- `Remove-SafelinksRule` – Delete a custom **Safe Links** rule

In this section, we have shown you how you can configure **Safe Links** by using Office 365 ATP. You have learned about the default **Safe Links** policy that will apply to all users in your tenant, and that additional **Safe Links** policies can be created with more customized settings and applied to specific Office 365 users, groups, and domains.

In addition, we showed you that rules, conditions, and exceptions may be applied to these policies. We also showed you that you can manage **Safe Links** by using the Microsoft 365 Security and Compliance Center, and also by connecting to the Exchange Online PowerShell tool.

Summary

In this chapter, we examined how Office 365 ATP can be used to protect your organization's users, groups, and domains from malicious content.

We showed you how ATP anti-phishing policies can be created to protect your users from spoofing and impersonation attacks. We also examined how Office 365 anti-spam settings can be created and applied to determine what happens when spam emails are detected.

In addition, we created Office 365 **Safe Attachments** and **Safe Links** policies to protect Office 365 users, groups, and domains by using the Microsoft 365 Security and Compliance Center, and also by using Exchange Online PowerShell.

In the next chapter, we will examine the principles of Office 365 threat investigation and tracking, and how administrators are able to protect users by using the Threat Dashboard, Threat Explorer, and by viewing incidents.

We will also show how the Office 365 Attack Simulator can be used for testing purposes.

Questions

1. Office 365 ATP is not included with which of the following subscriptions?

   a. Office 365 Enterprise E5

   b. Office 365 ATP Plan 2

   c. Office 365 Enterprise E3

   d. Microsoft 365 Enterprise

2. True or false: Office 365 **Safe Attachments** policies can be created via Windows PowerShell.

   a. True

   b. False

3. Which of the following is a valid PowerShell command for creating a **Safe Links** rule?

   a. `Set-SafeLinksRule`

   b. `New-SafeLinksRule`

   c. `Get-SafeLinksRule`

   d. `Start-SafeLinksRule`

4. What is the default option for the bulk email threshold?

   a. 1

   b. 9

   c. 7

   d. 5

5. True or false: The default spam filter policy is enabled by default.

   a. True

   b. False

6. Which section of the Microsoft 365 Security and Compliance Center would you access to manage Office 365 message protection features?

   a. **Threat management | Security**

   b. **Threat management | Compliance**

   c. **Threat management | Settings**

   d. **Threat management | Policy**

7. Which of the following is not a valid setting for threat detection action for spam?

   a. Move message to junk email folder

   b. Add X-header

   c. Prepend subject line with text

   d. Move message to the **Deleted Items** folder

e. Redirect message to email address

f. Quarantine message

8. True or false: Spoofing is supported by the SMTP protocol by default.

   a. True

   b. False

9. Which of the following are valid actions that can be applied to the **Safe Attachments** unknown malware response (choose three)?

   a. Block

   b. Dynamic delivery

   c. Edit

   d. Monitor

   e. Scan

10. True or false: SPF can be used to control whether your Office 365 users can send emails to external recipients.

    a. True

    b. False

References

Please refer to the following links for more information:

- Office 365 ATP anti-phishing protection: `https://docs.microsoft.com/en-us/microsoft-365/security/office-365-security/anti-phishing-protection`
- Setting up up anti-phishing policies: `https://docs.microsoft.com/en-us/microsoft-365/security/office-365-security/set-up-anti-phishing-policies`
- Office 365 anti-spam protection: `https://docs.microsoft.com/en-us/microsoft-365/security/office-365-security/anti-spam-protection`
- SPF: `https://en.wikipedia.org/wiki/Sender_Policy_Framework`

- DKIM: https://en.wikipedia.org/wiki/DomainKeys_Identified_Mail
- DMARC: https://en.wikipedia.org/wiki/DMARC
- Anti-spam policies with PowerShell: https://docs.microsoft.com/en-us/powershell/module/exchange/antispam-antimalware/new-hostedcontentfilterpolicy?view=exchange-ps
- Office 365 ATP safe attachments: https://docs.microsoft.com/en-us/powershell/module/exchange/antispam-antimalware/new-hostedcontentfilterrule?view=exchange-ps
- Office 365 ATP Safe Attachments: https://docs.microsoft.com/en-us/microsoft-365/security/office-365-security/atp-safe-attachments
- Office 365 ATP Safe Links: https://docs.microsoft.com/en-us/microsoft-365/security/office-365-security/atp-safe-links

9

Threat Intelligence and Tracking

As a Microsoft 365 administrator, it is important to dedicate time and effort to analyzing and responding to any events or alerts that are detected and shown in the Microsoft 365 Security & Compliance Center. The key to maintaining a safe and secure environment is to be proactive in monitoring your Microsoft 365 tenant.

The threat investigation and response capabilities within Microsoft 365 enable administrators to maximize the effectiveness of the features that they enable within their Microsoft 365 environment. This means that you can diligently protect your users from suspicious behavior and malicious actors.

In this chapter, you will learn about the threat management dashboard and Threat Explorer, as well as how to view and interpret incidents. You will also learn how to view reports and threat trackers, manage quarantined messages and files, and use the Office 365 attack simulator to conduct tests on your environment.

We will cover these topics in the following order:

- Understanding the Office 365 threat management security dashboard
- Using Office 365 Threat Explorer and threat trackers
- Managing quarantined messages and files
- Performing controlled simulated attacks

Understanding the Office 365 threat management security dashboard

In previous chapters, we demonstrated that the Microsoft 365 Security & Compliance Center is a powerful tool used by administrators to diligently and effectively manage data protection and compliance within their organization. Threat management is a crucial part of keeping your environment protected and secure, and Microsoft has provided a useful security dashboard to help you review your threat protection status from a high level and respond to security alerts.

By accessing the security dashboard, you can view a color-coded chart that shows global, weekly threat detections; a graph showing malware families that are detected and malware trends; and insights on spoofed domains that failed authentication. You can also view security trends, which provide you with information on Trojan-Downloader scripts, spambots, and email flooders, as well as a quick list of the top targeted users in your organization.

Reviewing and analyzing **Insights**, **Threat Intelligence**, and **Trends** within the security dashboard will provide you with visibility on the origin of potential threats and the affected users, as well as guide you on remediation practices and how to protect your environment from further instances.

The security dashboard can be accessed by going to the Microsoft 365 Security & Compliance Center at `https://protection.office.com` and navigating to **Threat management | Dashboard**.

The dashboard is shown in the following screenshot:

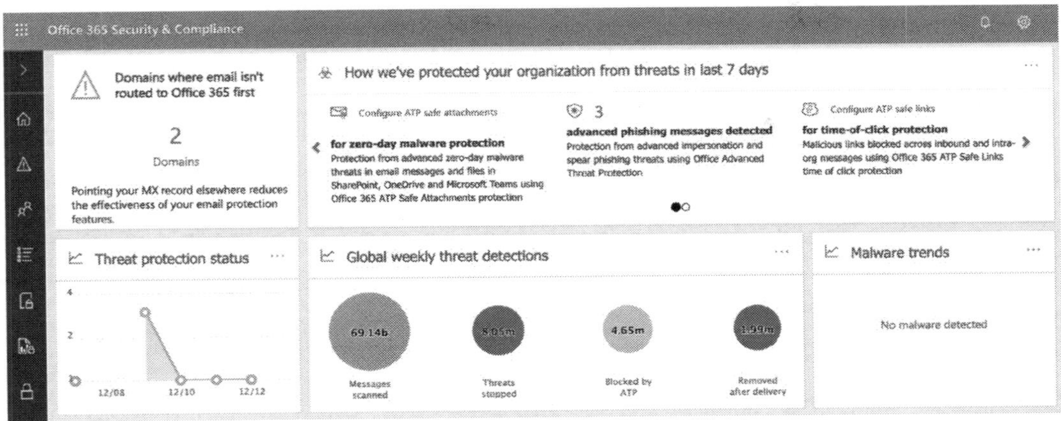

Figure 9.1 – The threat management dashboard

> **Important note**
> To access the security dashboard, you must be an Office 365 global administrator, a security administrator, or a security reader.

The information available on the security dashboard depends on your Office 365 subscription, but will typically include the following widgets:

- **Threat protection status**
- **Insights**
- **Threat Intelligence**
- **Trends**

Let's look at each of these widgets in turn, starting with **Threat protection status**.

Threat protection status

The **Threat protection status** widget provides you with information on any threats that have been detected and blocked by Office 365 Exchange Online Protection and Office 365 Advanced Threat Protection.

By selecting the **Threat protection status** widget, you will be able to access the report shown in the following screenshot:

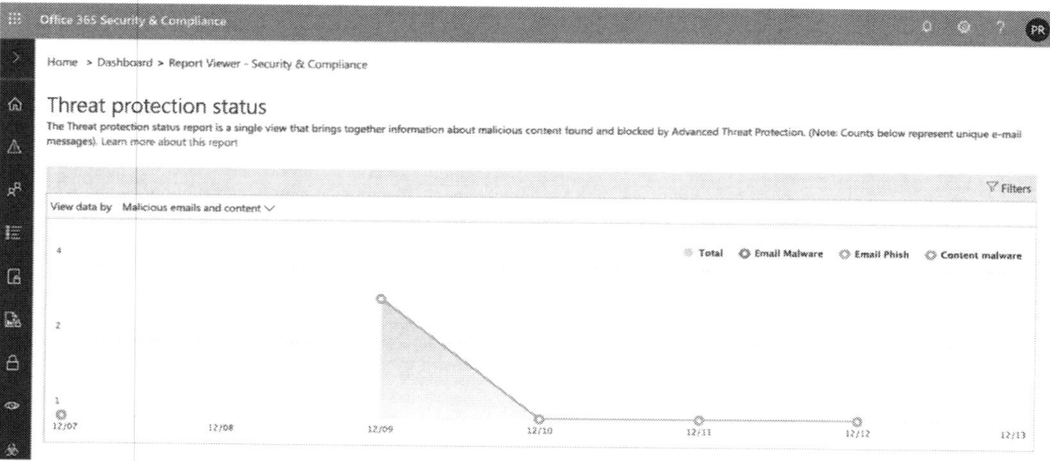

Figure 9.2 – Threat protection status

This report can be filtered as required to view the data by specific content, as in the following screenshot:

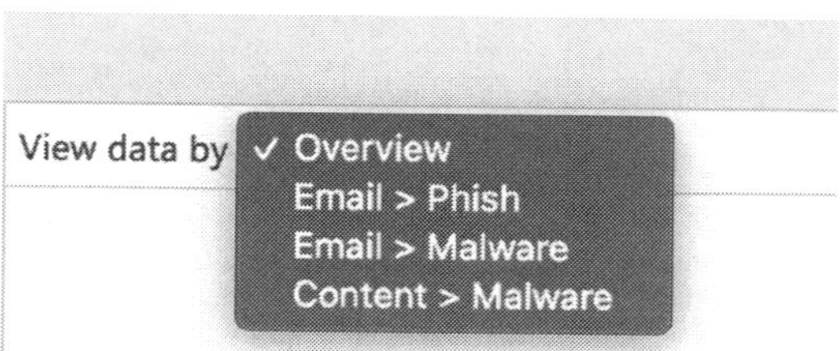

Figure 9.3 – The Threat protection status filter

The data can also be filtered by date range to view data from up to 90 days or by detection criteria, as the following screenshot shows:

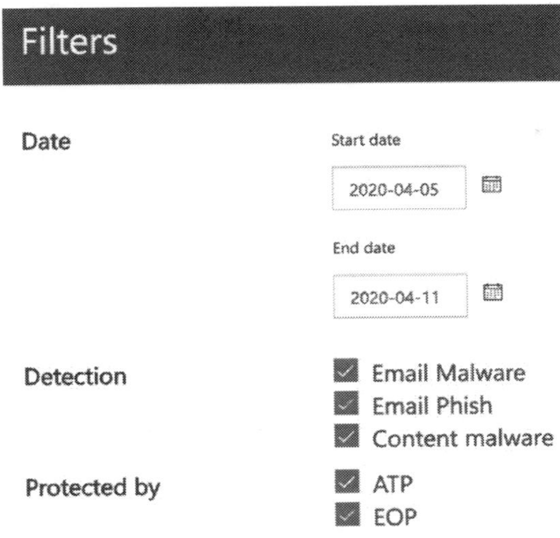

Figure 9.4 – The available filters

When you choose some of the different data views, it is also possible to create schedules, request reports, and view the details in a table format. Next, let's look at **Insights**.

Insights

With **Insights**, you can quickly view key issues that need attention, such as attacks or other suspicious activities.

In the following screenshot, we have an example where we can see some insights that have been highlighted for attention by the Microsoft 365 administrators.

These include some suspicious domain spoofing activity and a recommendation to enable impersonation policies to protect users and domains:

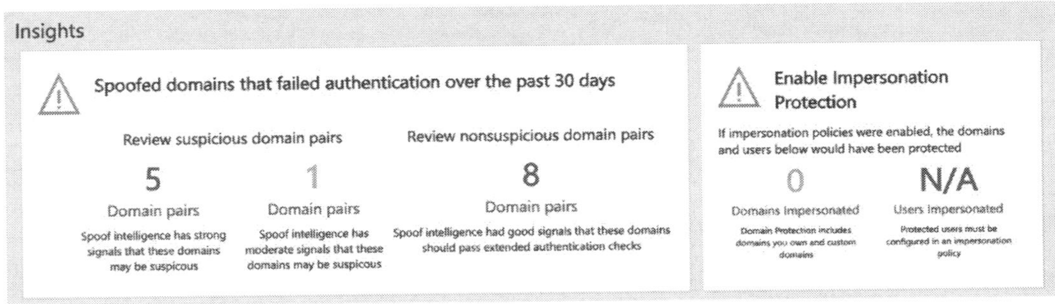

Figure 9.5 – Insights

Insights should be reviewed proactively and regularly in order to maximize security and protection within your Microsoft 365 tenant.

Threat Intelligence

This section provides you with information that can help you to prepare for and understand emerging threats and security trends, as you can see in the following screenshot:

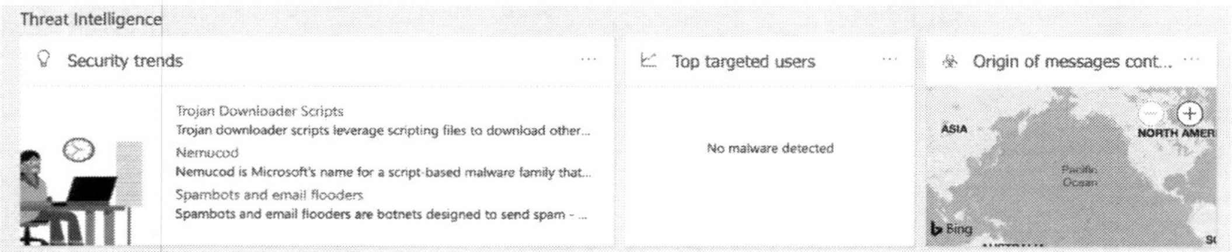

Figure 9.6 – Threat Intelligence

It is important to understand the ever-changing threat landscape, and reviewing **Threat Intelligence** will help you maintain a good awareness of any emerging threats.

Trends

The **Trends** widget shows you a summary of mail flow trends. By selecting the **Sent and received email** report, you can acquire information relating to spam detection, malware, and rule messages:

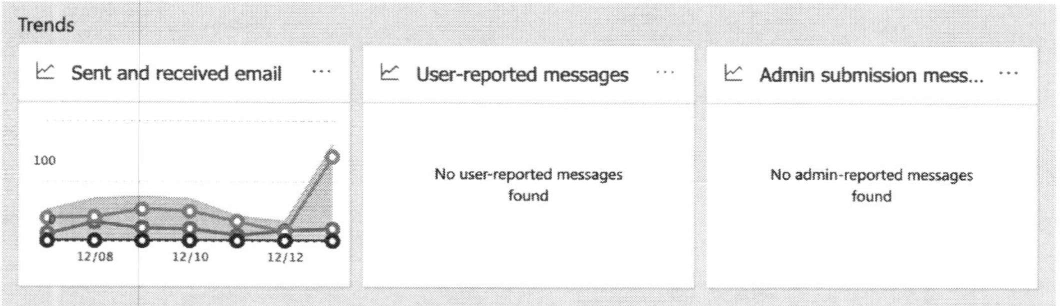

Figure 9.7 – Trends

Within the **Trends** widget, you can drill down by category and filter by date, message direction, and message type, as in the following screenshot, which shows the available filters under the **Sent and received email** section:

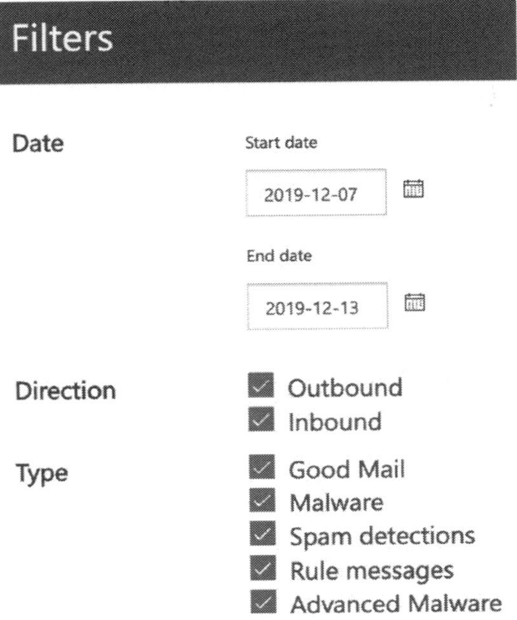

Figure 9.8 – Filters

Reviewing the trends within the security dashboard is an important way of being able to understand and analyze the activities of your users.

So, you have now learned about the security dashboard and how you can use it to quickly assess threats within your Microsoft 365 environment with a broad executive-level view. Next, we will examine how Threat Explorer and threat trackers can enable administrators to drill deeper into the threats that are detected in the Security & Compliance Center.

Using Office 365 Threat Explorer and threat trackers

In this section, we will examine how Threat Explorer and threat trackers can be used by Microsoft 365 administrators to review and interpret threats that may be targeting their environment. First, we will look at Threat Explorer.

Using Threat Explorer

Threat Explorer provides Microsoft 365 administrators with detailed information on threats detected within their environment, including malware and phishing. You can access Threat Explorer from the Security & Compliance Center by navigating to **Threat Management | Explorer**. Threat Explorer shows you a chart that is color-coded and includes attacks that have targeted your Microsoft 365 environment, as in the following screenshot:

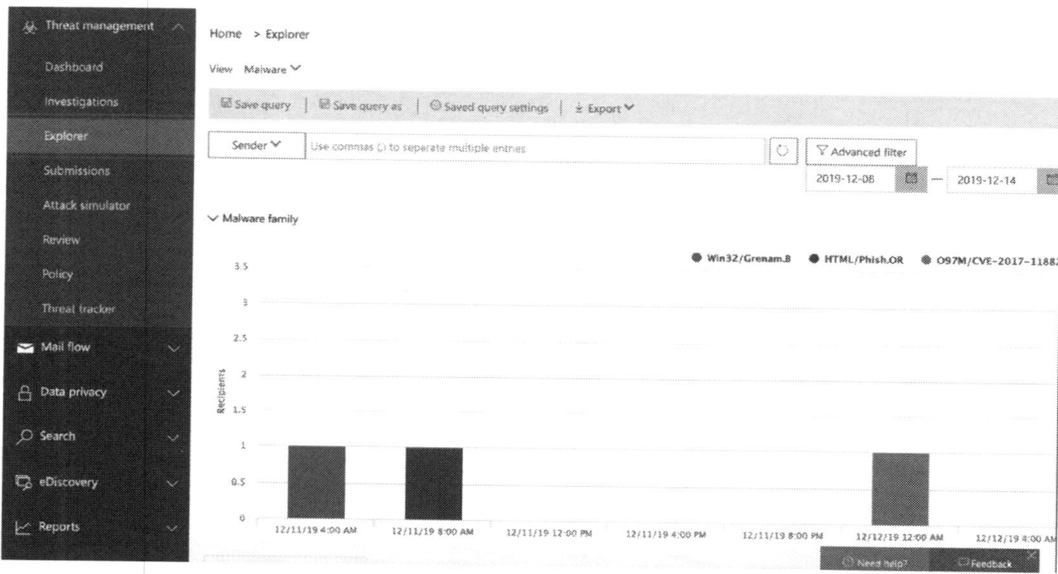

Figure 9.9 – Threat management explorer

Directly beneath the chart, you will see three tabs, where you can view the top malware families, a list of emails with malware that has been received, and a map that shows the origins of these emails:

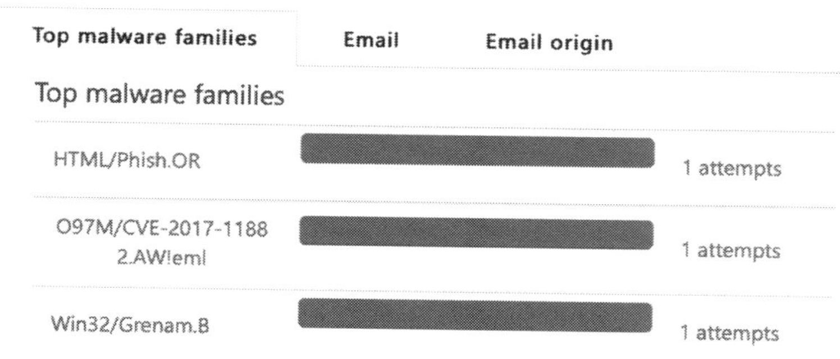

Figure 9.10 – Top malware families

You can also modify the **Threat explorer** views within your tenant. The default view within Threat Explorer is set to **Malware**, but you can select other views, as in the following screenshot:

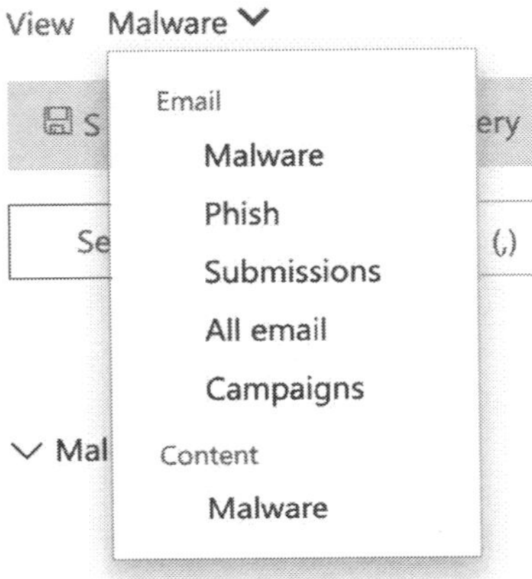

Figure 9.11 – Threat explorer views

You can also drill down further to view it by specific senders and you can explore other categories, such as **Malware family**, **Sender domain**, **Delivery action**, and **Detection technology**, as the following screenshot shows:

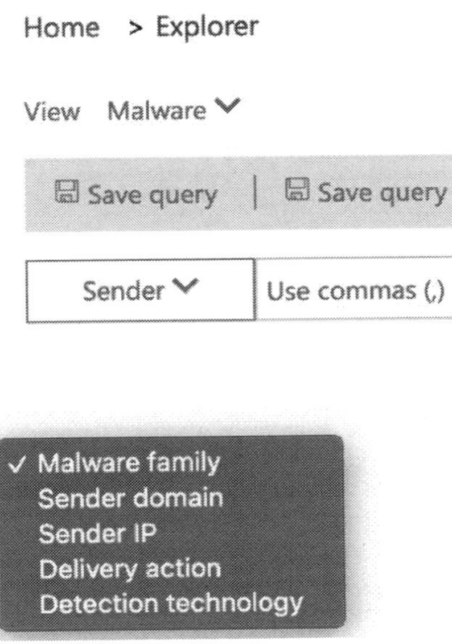

Figure 9.12 – The filter options

> **Important note**
>
> With Threat Explorer, you can view reports and recommendations from Microsoft partners, who can advise you on how to interpret and act on the Threat Explorer detections.

Next, let's look at threat trackers.

Using threat trackers

You can also access threat trackers from the Security & Compliance Center by navigating to **Threat Management | Threat tracker**. The **Threat tracker** page displays widgets that show intelligence on potential cybersecurity threats, such as **Trending campaigns**, as in the following screenshot:

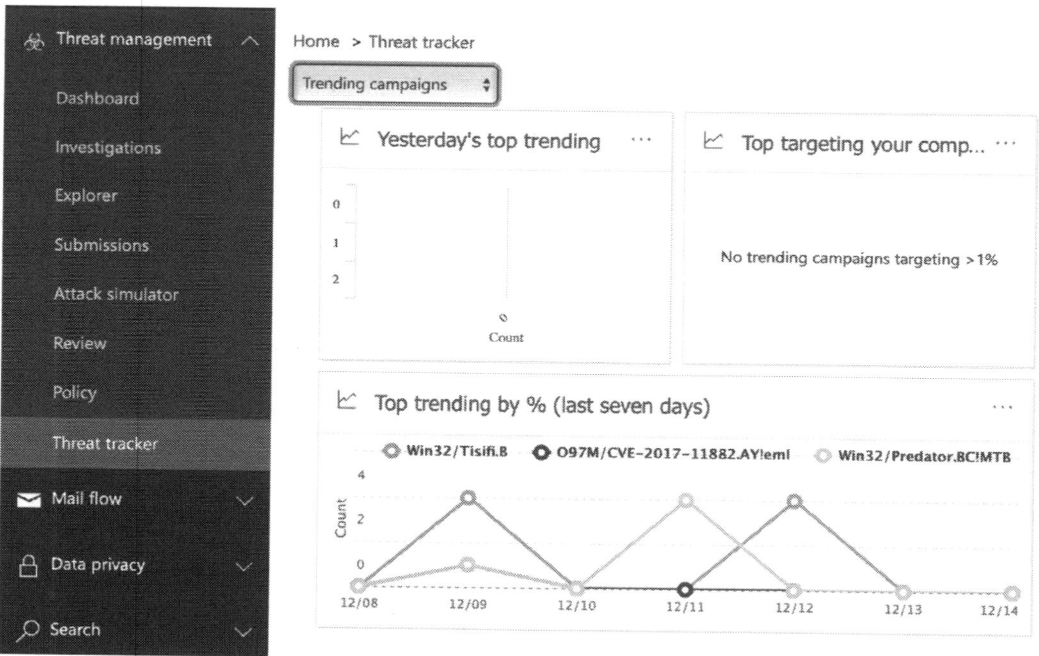

Figure 9.13 – Threat tracker

Beneath the widgets is a list of targeted and trending or noteworthy attacks, with a link to the right of each entry that allows you to open each option in Threat Explorer to view the threat in greater detail. This is shown in the following screenshot:

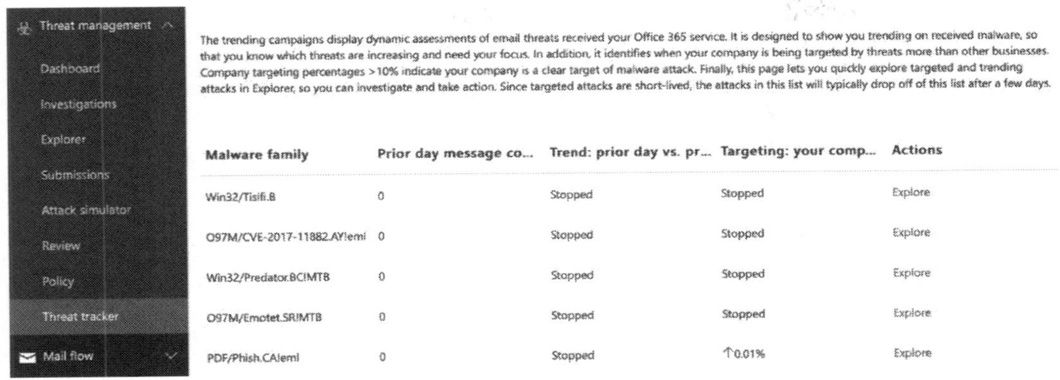

Threat management
Dashboard
Investigations
Explorer
Submissions
Attack simulator
Review
Policy
Threat tracker
Mail flow
The trending campaigns display dynamic assessments of email threats received your Office 365 service. It is designed to show you trending on received malware, so that you know which threats are increasing and need your focus. In addition, it identifies when your company is being targeted by threats more than other businesses. Company targeting percentages >10% indicate your company is a clear target of malware attack. Finally, this page lets you quickly explore targeted and trending attacks in Explorer, so you can investigate and take action. Since targeted attacks are short-lived, the attacks in this list will typically drop off of this list after a few days.
Malware family
Prior day message co...
Trend: prior day vs. pr...
Targeting: your comp...
Actions
Win32/Tisifi.B
0
Stopped
Stopped
Explore
O97M/CVE-2017-11882.AY!eml
0
Stopped
Stopped
Explore
Win32/Predator.BC!MTB
0
Stopped
Stopped
Explore
O97M/Emotet.SR!MTB
0
Stopped
Stopped
Explore
PDF/Phish.CA!eml
0
Stopped
↑0.01%
Explore

Figure 9.14 – Trending campaigns

There are a number of different threat trackers that can be viewed. In the preceding example, we showed you the trending trackers. However, you can drill down and choose others, as in the following screenshot:

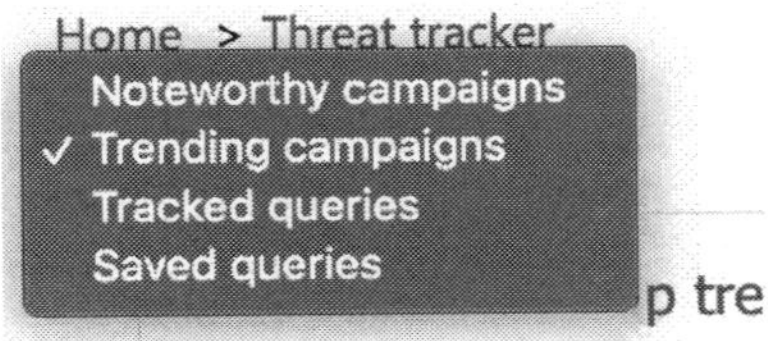

Figure 9.15 – The filter options

Further information on the available threat trackers and how you can use them is included in the *References* section at the end of this chapter.

> **Important note**
>
> You should monitor the **Threat tracker** page to keep an eye out for any new threats that appear.

In this section, we introduced you to Threat Explorer and threat trackers in the Microsoft 365 Security & Compliance Center. We showed you how you can view more detailed information in Threat Explorer than you can in the threat management security dashboard.

We also looked at how threat trackers are widgets containing information on cybersecurity threats and how these link to Threat Explorer.

Next, we will show you how to manage quarantined messages in Office 365.

Managing quarantined messages and files

As a Microsoft 365 administrator, you can use the Office 365 quarantine feature to view and take action on emails and files that have been placed there due to having been identified as one of the following:

- Spam
- Bulk email
- Phishing email
- Contains malware
- Matches a transport rule

The following steps show you how to access **Quarantine** from the Microsoft 365 Security & Compliance Center and describe the actions and responses that are available to you:

1. **Quarantine** can be accessed from the Microsoft 365 Security & Compliance Center by navigating to **Threat Management** | **Review**, as in the following screenshot:

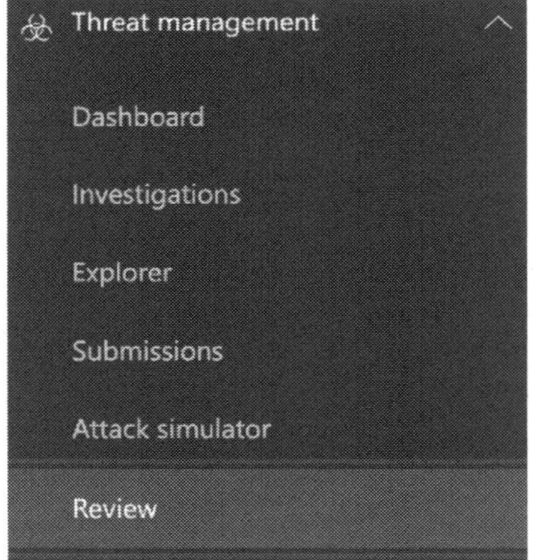

Figure 9.16 – Reviewing the Quarantine section

2. Select the **Quarantine** tile, as in the following screenshot:

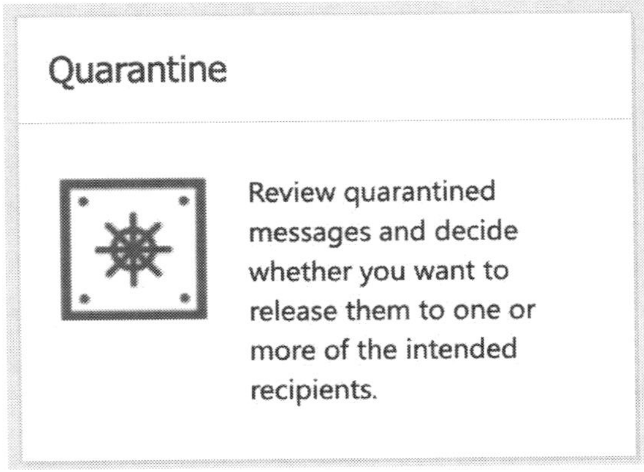

Figure 9.17 – The Quarantine tile

3. You will now be taken to **Quarantine**, as in the following screenshot:

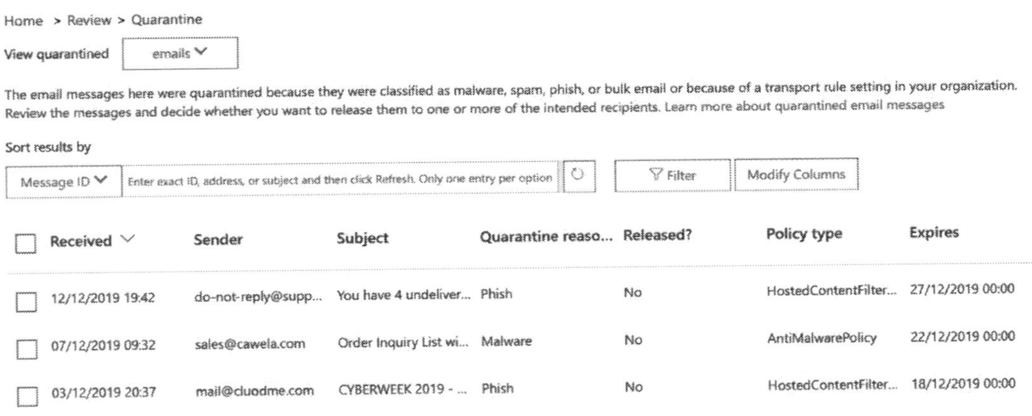

Figure 9.18 – Quarantine

In the preceding example, we can see that three email items have been directed to **Quarantine**. By selecting one of the quarantined items, you can take action in relation to the message, as in the following screenshot:

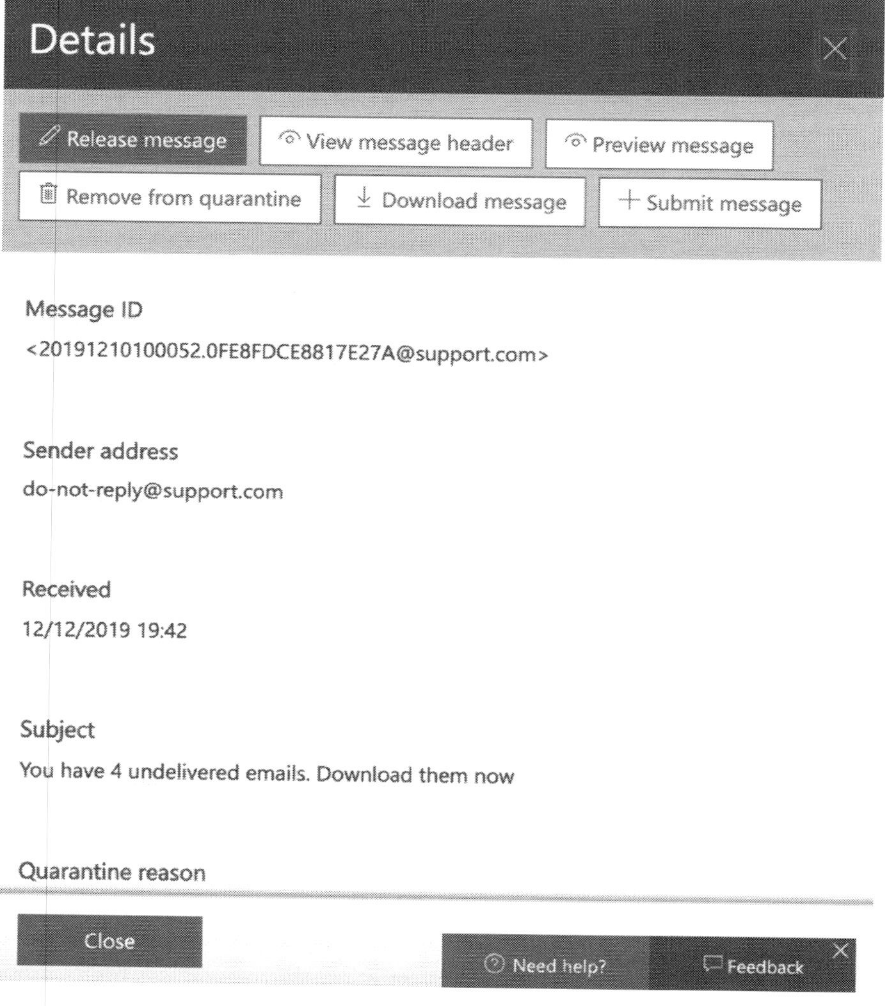

Figure 9.19 – Quarantined item details

The available actions from within the quarantined item details are as follows:

Action	Options and result
Release message	Admins can choose which recipients to release the message to and whether to report the message to Microsoft for analysis.
View message header	Shows the message headers so that admins can check the source of the message to assess its authenticity.
Preview message	Shows a preview of the quarantined message in a choice of Source view or Text view.
Remove from quarantine	Removes the message entirely from quarantine and does not deliver the message to the original recipient or anyone else.
Download message	The administrator can download the message. This option should be used with great caution.
Submit message	This will submit the quarantined message to Microsoft for analysis.

It is also possible to select more than one quarantined item at a time and apply **Bulk actions** to your selections, as shown:

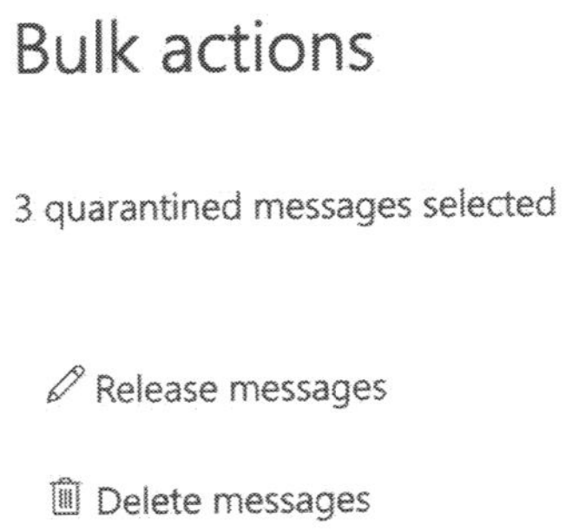

Bulk actions

3 quarantined messages selected

Release messages

Delete messages

Figure 9.20 – Bulk actions

The default retention setting for items within the Office 365 **Quarantine** section is 30 days (this is also the maximum setting). However, this can be changed by modifying the **Default Spam Filter** policy in the Security & Compliance Center.

> **Important note**
>
> You must be a global administrator or be assigned to one or more of the Security & Compliance Center role groups in order to manage quarantined messages or files.

In this section, we showed you how you can access the Office 365 **Quarantine** section to view quarantined email messages and files. You have learned how you can release quarantined items to the intended recipients or alternative recipients, as well as how to view message headers and preview messages, how to remove items permanently from quarantine, and how to submit quarantined items for analysis to Microsoft. We also explained the default retention settings for items in the **Quarantine** section. Next, we will examine how you can simulate attacks within your Microsoft 365 tenant.

Performing controlled simulated attacks

One of the great features available to global administrators and security administrators within the **Threat Management** section of the Security & Compliance Center is the ability to carry out simulated attacks using the attack simulator. The attack simulator can also be accessed directly from `https://protection.office.com/attacksimulator`, which is shown in the following screenshot:

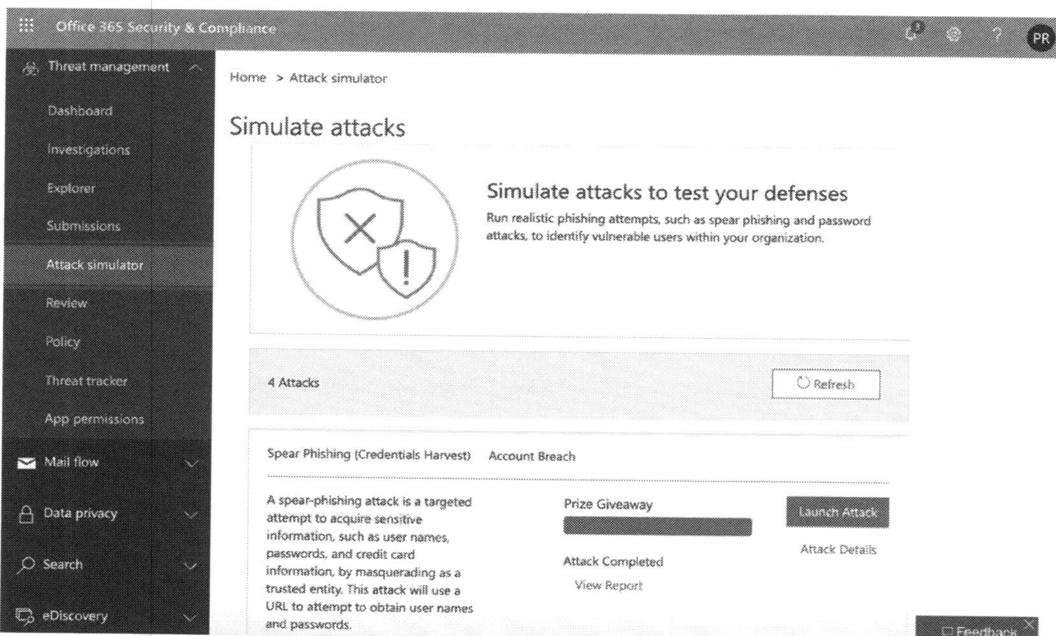

Figure 9.21 – Simulating attacks

> **Important note**
>
> In order to use the attack simulator, the account you are using to log in to the Security & Compliance Center must have multi-factor authentication enabled. All emails must be hosted in Exchange Online and an Office 365 Advanced Threat Protection (Plan 2) subscription must be assigned to all users.

The attack simulator allows you to target users within your organization to test how they respond to a realistic attack scenario. It is a powerful tool that can provide visibility to you as an administrator on the most vulnerable users in your environment and enable you to provide training and education to these users to increase their awareness of the threats they could potentially encounter. The attack simulator currently has the following available simulations:

- **Spear Phishing (Credentials Harvest)**
- **Spear Phishing (Attachment)**
- **Brute force password (dictionary attack)**
- **Password Spray attack**

Let's look at how we can execute one of these attacks using the **Spear Phishing (Credentials Harvest)** attack as an example.

Launching an attack

The first of the two available spear phishing attacks is an attempt to harvest credentials and is shown in the following screenshot:

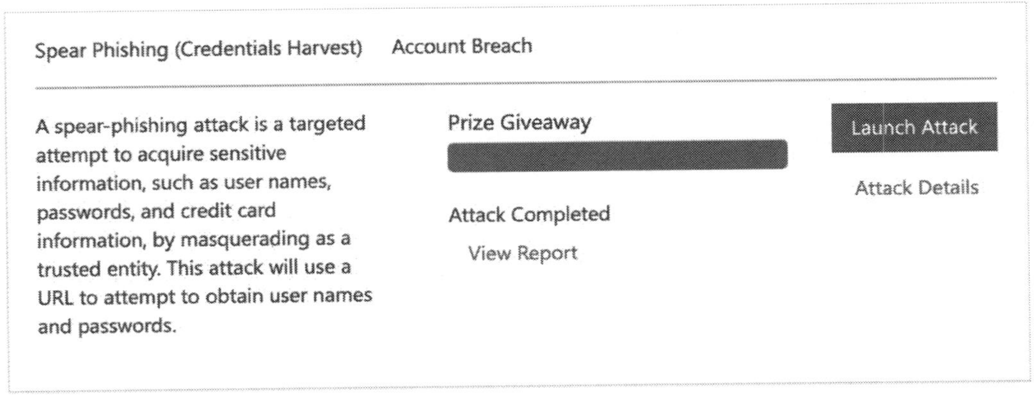

Figure 9.22 – Launching an attack

The following steps show you how to view the settings of the attack and how to launch an attack campaign:

1. By clicking on **Attack Details**, you can expand the information on what this attack is designed to do. As you can see from the following screenshot, this attack will attempt to trick recipients into performing an action and/or revealing some form of confidential information:

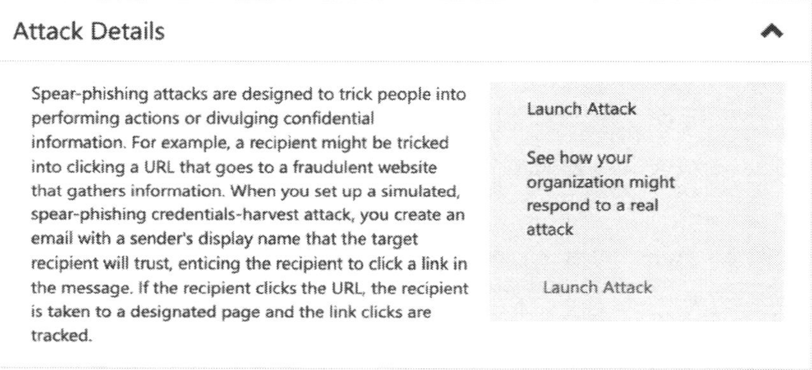

Figure 9.23 – Attack details

2. If you have executed this attack simulation before, you can view the attack history and historic attacks by date range, as well as export the results to a `.csv` file, as shown:

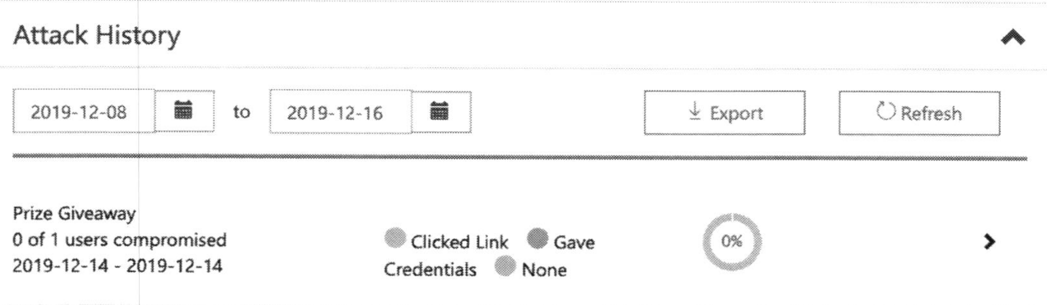

Figure 9.24 – Attack history

3. You also have the option to create new phishing email templates that you can use in future simulated attacks. This enables you to change the format of the email that the targeted users will receive in these attacks so that they do not recognize it as an attack:

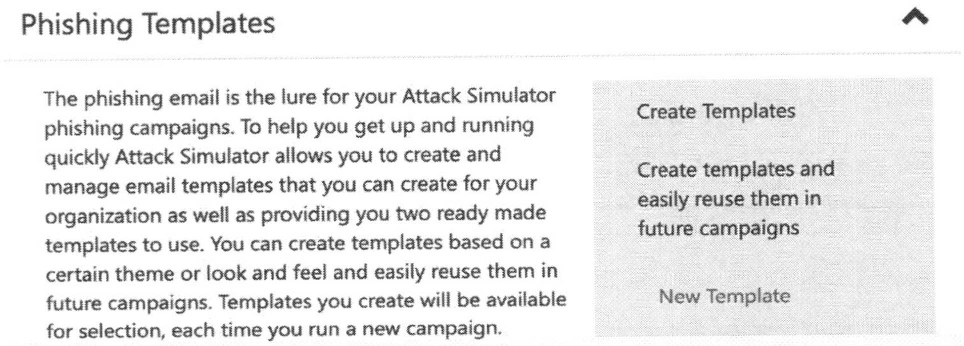

Figure 9.25 – Phishing templates

4. If you wish to run this simulation, click on **Launch Attack** and you will be taken to the wizard, as in the following screenshot, where you will need to provide a name, under the **Start** page, for your attack and decide whether or not to use a template (which, in this example, we will do). Then, click **Next**:

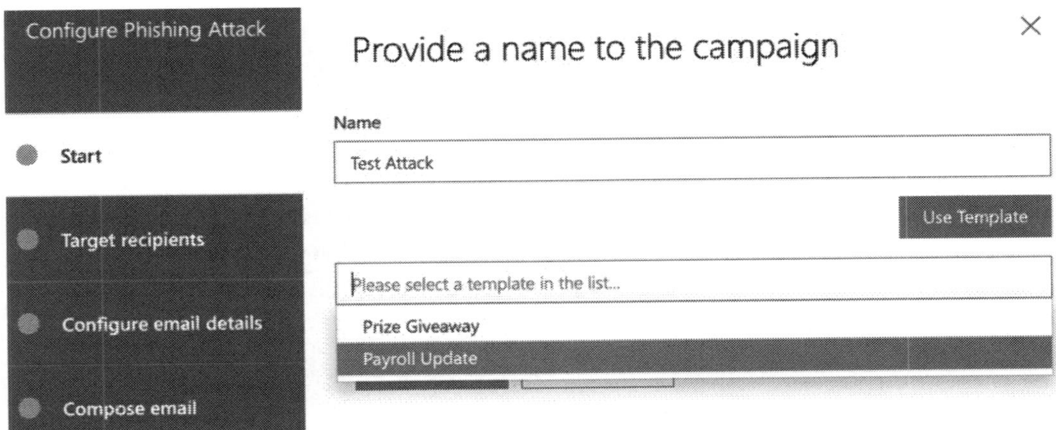

Figure 9.26 – Naming your campaign

5. Under the **Target recipients** page, you will need to choose the recipients, as in the following screenshot, where I selected **James Smith** and **Jane Bloggs**. Then, click **Next**:

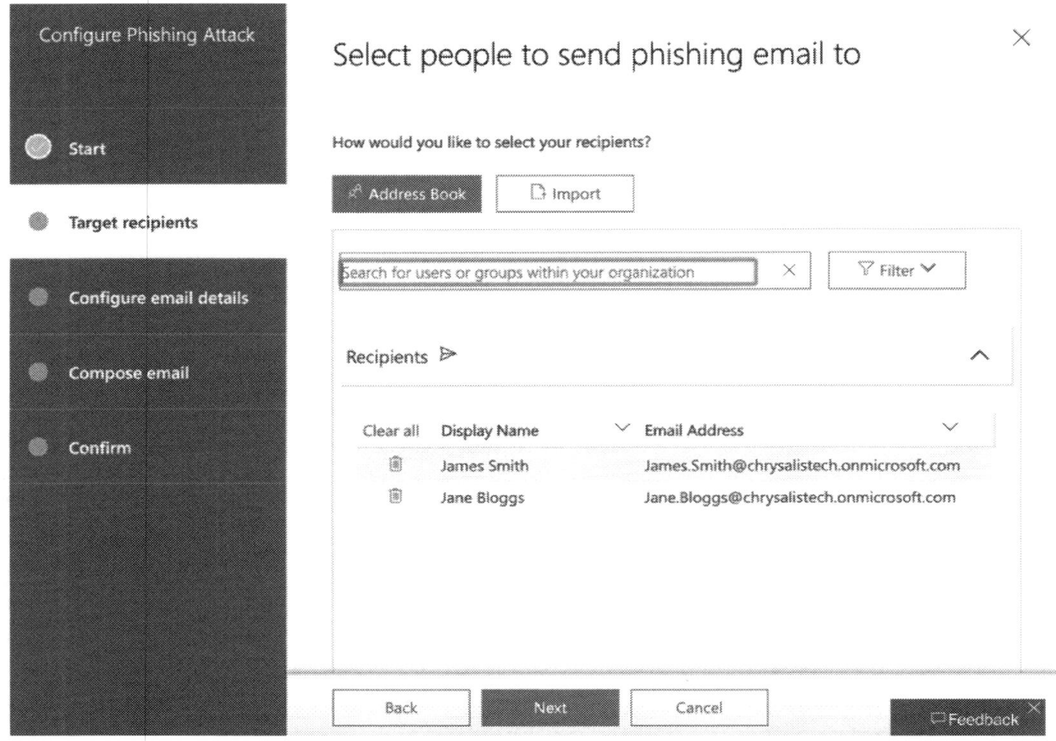

Figure 9.27 – Choosing the target recipients

6. If you have chosen a template, as we did in this example, the **Configure email details** section will be pre-populated, as the following screenshot shows. If you are not using a template, however, you will need to complete this section yourself. When you are happy with the content in this section, click **Next**:

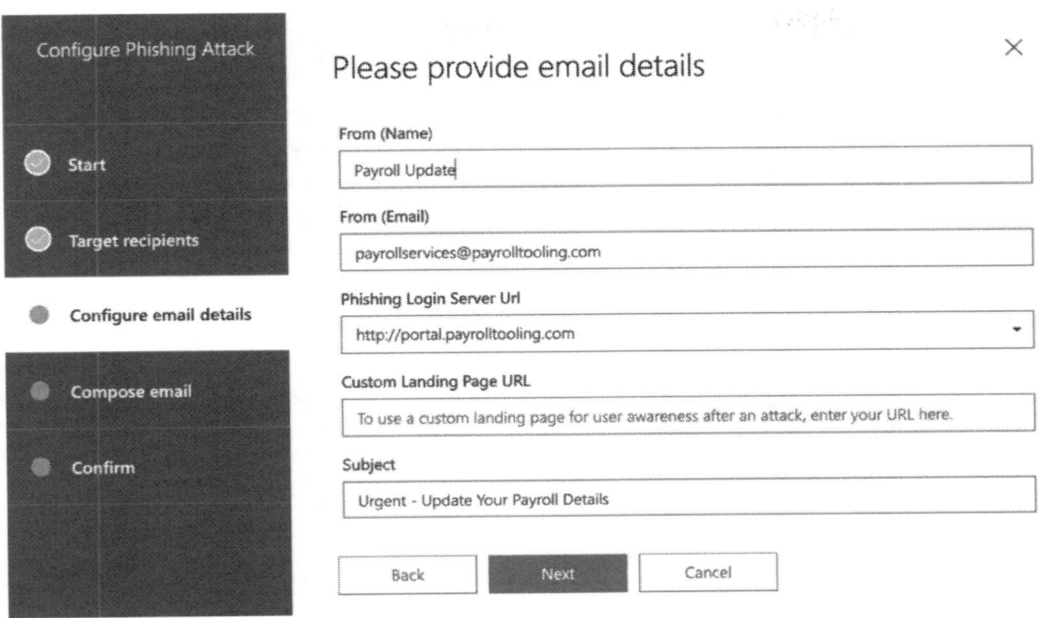

Figure 9.28 – Entering the email details

7. Under the **Compose email** section, if you have selected a template as we did, your email details will be pre-populated. If not, you will need to enter the body of the email body and then click **Next**, as shown:

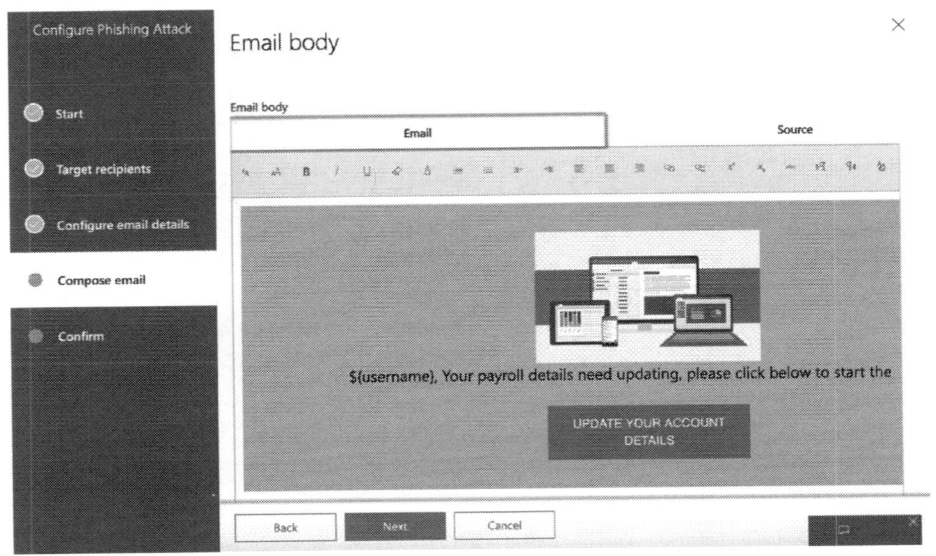

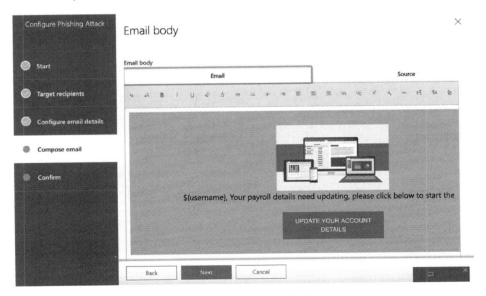

Figure 9.29 – The email body

8. Finally, click on **Finish** to launch the attack, as follows:

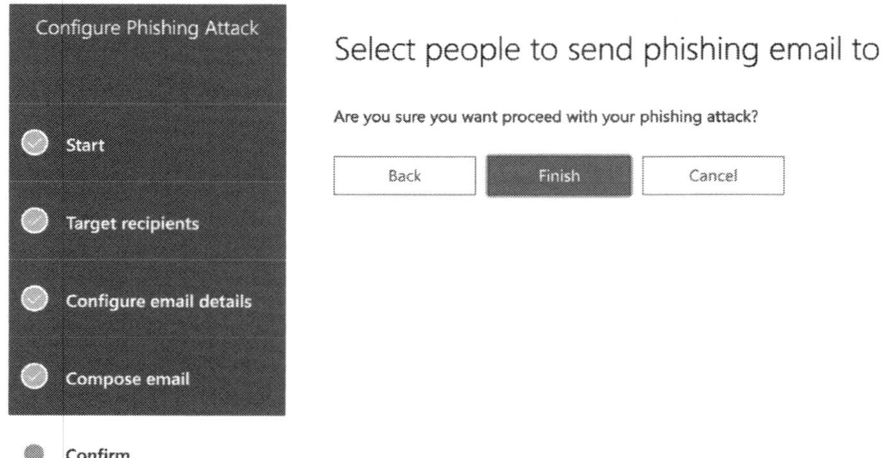

Figure 9.30 – Completing the phishing attack configuration

9. To illustrate how the targeted users will receive the email, we can log in to Jane Bloggs' mailbox and we can see that she has received the email:

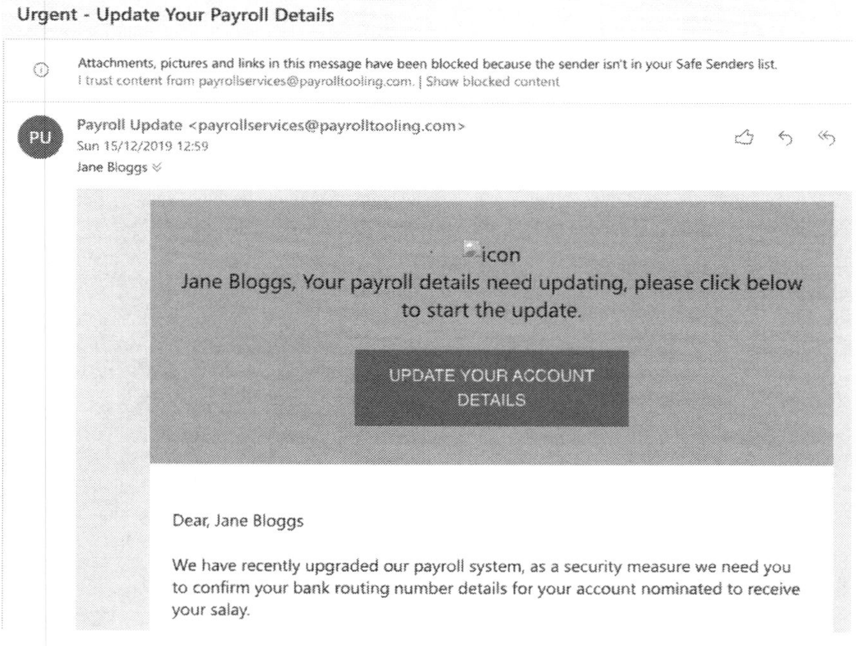

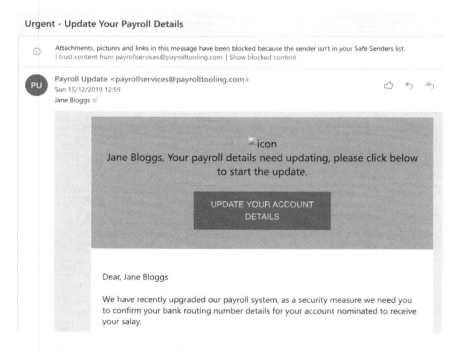

Figure 9.31 – An example of the email received by the targeted user

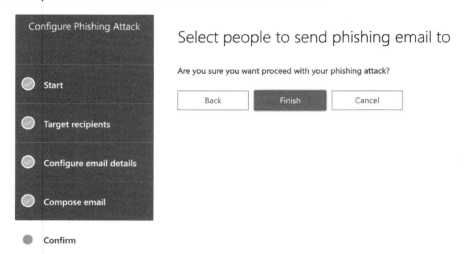

10. If the user clicks on the **UPDATE YOUR ACCOUNT DETAILS** link, they will be taken to the following page, which appears to be an Office 365 login screen:

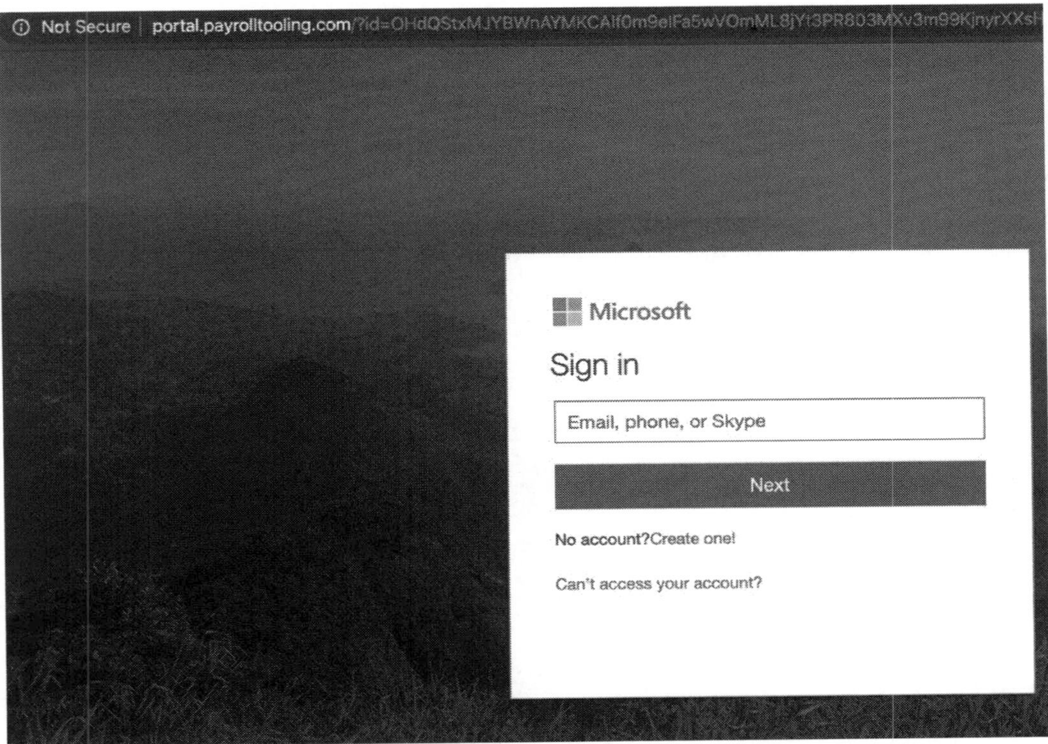

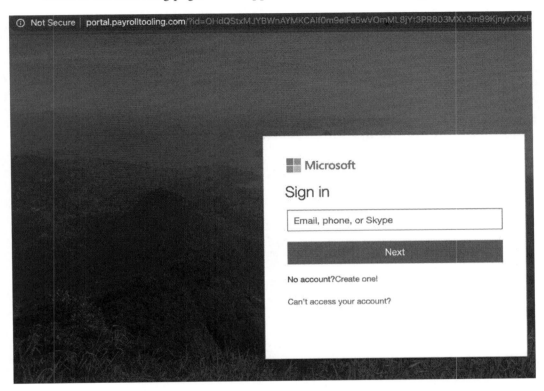

Figure 9.32 – The user is directed to a sign-in page

11. The action of clicking on the link is enough to generate a response to the attack simulation and when we return to the attack simulator in the Security & Compliance Center, we can view the attack and select the **View Report** option, as we can see in the following screenshot:

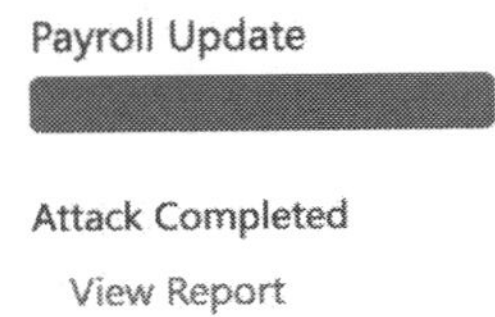

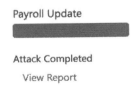

Figure 9.33 – Viewing the attack report

12. We can see in the report in the following screenshot that the user has opened the email but has not provided any credentials:

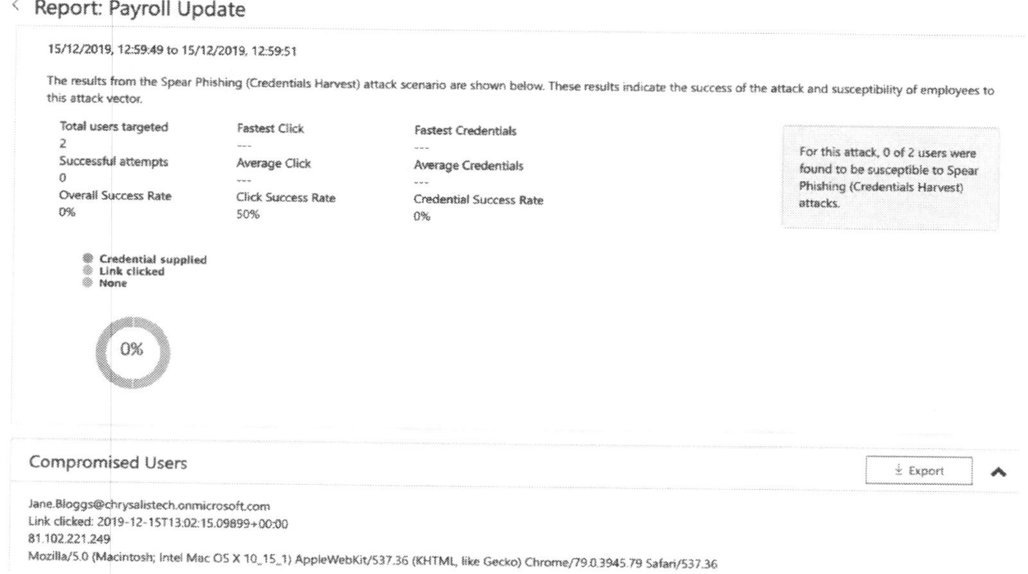

Figure 9.34 – Viewing the attack details

13. Should the user provide their credentials, they will be directed to the following web page, which explains to them that this was a simulation:

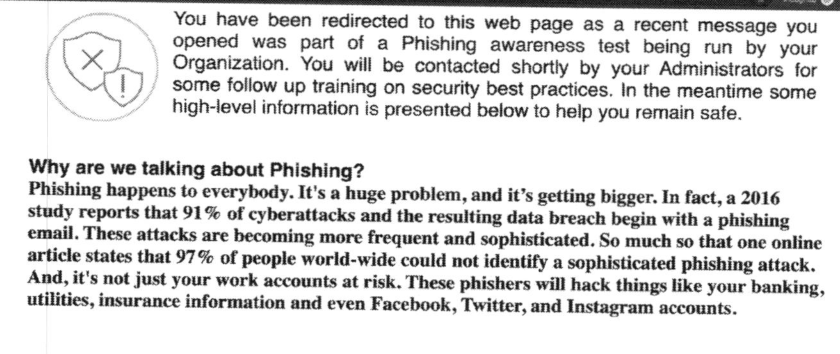

Figure 9.35 – The user simulation warning

14. The act of providing credentials also shows up in the attack report, as the following screenshot shows:

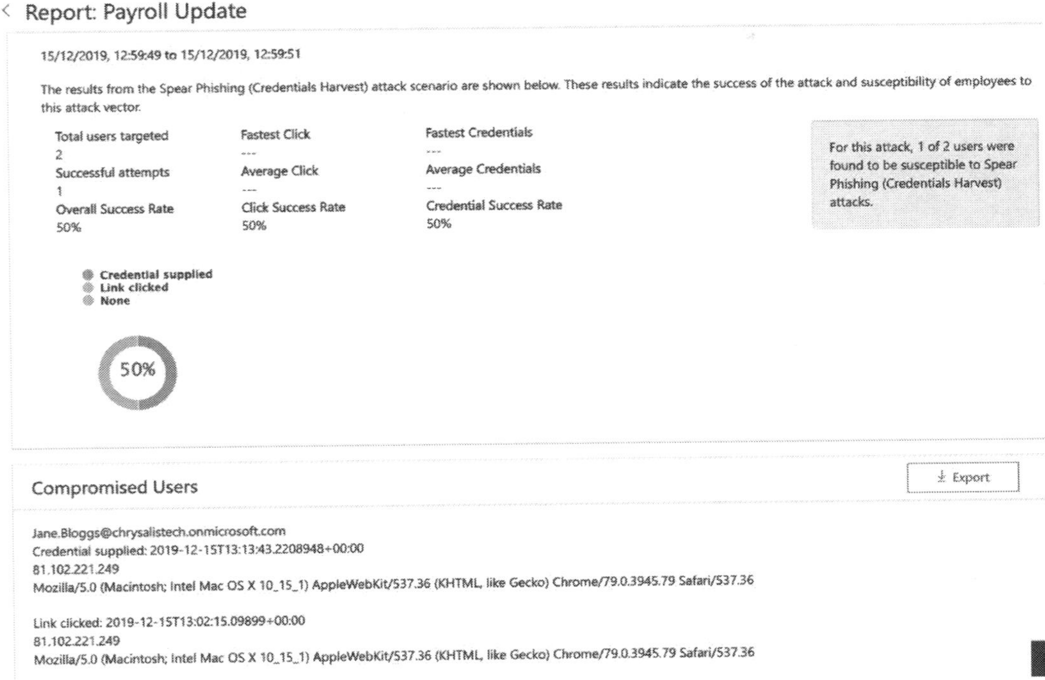

Figure 9.36 – Compromised user details based on an attack simulation

So, you can see how this is a very powerful tool that can be used to educate users and gain visibility on those users in your organization who may be most at risk of being compromised.

In this section, we demonstrated the results of launching a simulated attack for only one of the four attack types included in the Security & Compliance Center. The other attacks can be executed in exactly the same way described in the preceding steps, and it is highly recommended that you leverage this feature to promote awareness of security and compliance principles to educate your user base.

Summary

In this chapter, we introduced you to the principles of threat intelligence and threat tracking within your Microsoft 365 environment. You have learned how to access the threat management dashboard, where you can see high-level information relating to threats. Additionally, we showed you how to gain more granular visibility of threats, such as malware, by accessing Threat Explorer, as well as how to use the **Threat tracker** page, which consists of widgets that provide information on cybersecurity threats.

We also examined how you can view quarantined emails and files and take appropriate actions and finally, we saw how the attack simulator is a powerful feature of threat management that allows you to simulate attacks by generating emails designed to test the awareness of your users within your Microsoft 365 environment.

In the next chapter, we will introduce you to Azure Sentinel, which is a cloud-based security information and event manger (SIEM) tool that enables analysis of vast quantities of data both within Microsoft 365 and from external sources using artificial intelligence technology.

Questions

1. Which of the following roles cannot be used to access the security dashboard?

   a. Security administrator

   b. Service administrator

   c. Security reader

   d. Global administrator

2. True or false: To run simulated attacks with the Office 365 attack simulator, multi-factor authentication must be enabled on the account that you intend to launch the attack from.

   a. True

   b. False

3. What is the default retention period for the Office 365 message quarantine feature?

   a. 15 days

   b. 20 days

   c. 30 days

   d. 50 days

4. Which section of the Security & Compliance Center contains the Office 365 **Quarantine** area?

    a. **Threat management | Review**

    b. **Threat management | Dashboard**

    c. **Threat management | Investigations**

    d. **Threat management | Submissions**

5. True or false: The maximum number of days that the quarantine retention period may be set to is 60 days.

    a. True

    b. False

6. Which of the following is not one of the built-in simulated attacks?

    a. Spear phishing

    b. Brute force password

    c. Password spray

    d. Whale phishing

7. True or false: An Office 365 Advanced Protection Plan 1 license is required for all users in order to generate simulated attacks with the attack simulator?

    a. True

    b. False

8. Which of the following is not an action available for a quarantined message?

    a. Release message

    b. Open message

    c. Remove from quarantine

    d. Preview message

    e. View message header

9. True or false: The global weekly threat detections report consists of a color-coded chart showing information on the messages that have been scanned and the threats that have been prevented.

    a. True

    b. False

10. Where on the threat management dashboard would you access information on Trojan-Downloader scripts, spambots, and email flooders?

    a. The **Malware Trends** widget

    b. The **Security Trends** widget

    c. **Top targeted users**

    d. **Insights**

References

Please refer to the following links for more information:

- The threat management dashboard: `https://docs.microsoft.com/en-us/microsoft-365/security/office-365-security/security-dashboard`
- Threat Explorer: `https://docs.microsoft.com/en-us/microsoft-365/security/office-365-security/threat-explorer`
- Threat trackers: `https://docs.microsoft.com/en-us/microsoft-365/security/office-365-security/threat-trackers`
- Managing quarantined messages: `https://docs.microsoft.com/en-us/microsoft-365/security/office-365-security/manage-quarantined-messages-and-files`
- Performing controlled simulated attacks: `https://docs.microsoft.com/en-us/microsoft-365/security/office-365-security/attack-simulator`

10

Using Azure Sentinel to Monitor Microsoft 365 Security

Azure Sentinel is a cloud-based **security information and event management** (**SIEM**) tool that enables the analysis of vast quantities of data both within Microsoft 365 and from external sources using artificial intelligence technology. Azure Sentinel allows you to gather data, detect potential threats, and then investigate and respond to those threats. In this chapter, we will show you how to plan and configure your Azure Sentinel instance, explain the process of using Azure Sentinel playbooks, and finally how to monitor and manage Azure Sentinel on an ongoing basis.

After reading this chapter, you will be able to access and enable Azure Sentinel in the Azure portal, set up a Log Analytics workspace, and connect to Microsoft and third-party data sources. You will learn how to use playbooks to automate responses to security issues and understand how to manage and monitor Azure Sentinel on an ongoing basis.

In this chapter, we will cover the following topics:

- Planning and configuring Azure Sentinel
- Using Azure Sentinel playbooks
- Managing and monitoring Azure Sentinel

Planning and configuring Azure Sentinel

The first steps you need to take when planning to use Azure Sentinel for your organization is to enable Azure Sentinel itself, and then connect it to your organization's data sources. Azure Sentinel has several native Microsoft connectors that enable integration with other Microsoft services, such as *Azure Active Directory*, *Office 365*, *Microsoft Defender for Identity*, *Microsoft Cloud App Security*, and many more.

It is also possible to configure Azure Sentinel to connect to non-Microsoft services, and use connection methods such as **Syslog**, **REST API**, or the **Common Event Format** (**CEF**).

Knowing what you are looking to achieve by deploying Azure Sentinel within your Microsoft 365 environment will help you to plan which connectors you need in order to achieve your objectives.

Once you know which data sources you need to connect to, you can connect to them and use several available workbooks that provide insights on your data.

So how do we enable Azure Sentinel? Let's take a look!

Enabling Azure Sentinel

The first step we need to take in order to enable Azure Sentinel is to connect to an existing workspace or create a new workspace in the Azure portal. In this instance, we will create a new workspace as part of the process of enabling Azure Sentinel.

> **Important note**
>
> You must have contributor permissions for the Azure subscription where you plan to deploy your Azure Sentinel workspace.

To enable Azure Sentinel, you need to complete the following steps:

1. Go to the Azure portal at `https://portal.azure.com` and search for and select **Azure Sentinel**:

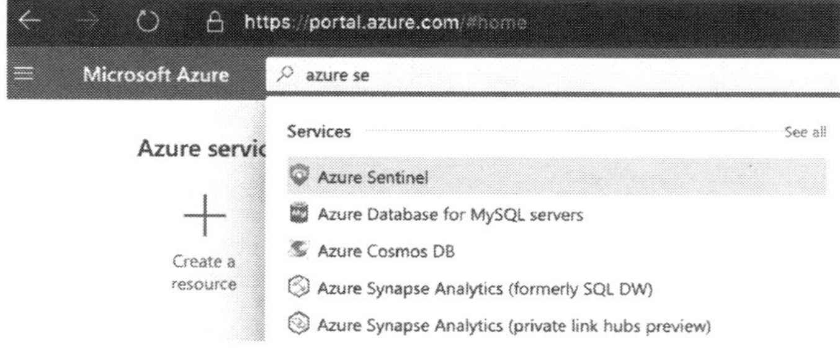

Figure 10.1 – Searching for Azure Sentinel in the Azure portal

You will now see the **Azure Sentinel workspaces** screen, as shown in the following screenshot:

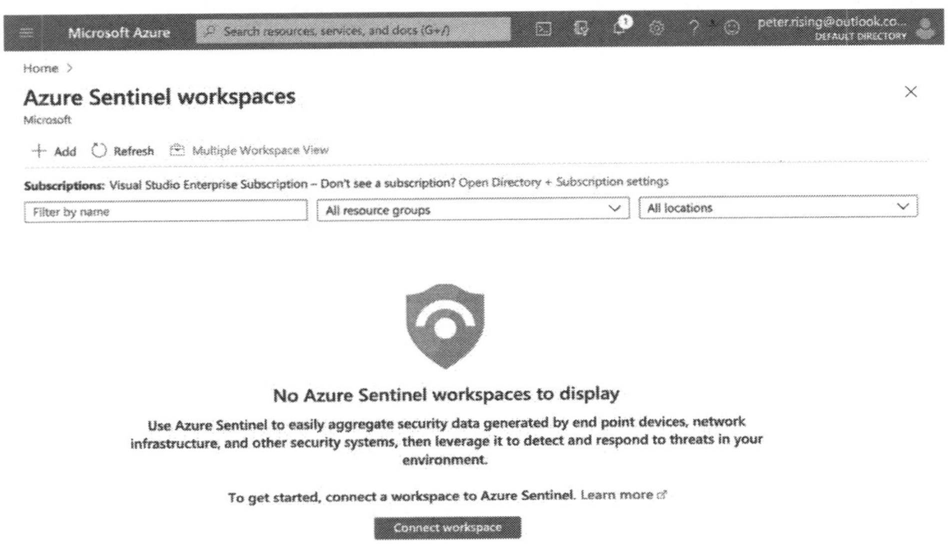

Figure 10.2 – Azure Sentinel workspaces

2. Click on **Connect workspace**. If any suitable workspaces were available, they would be visible here:

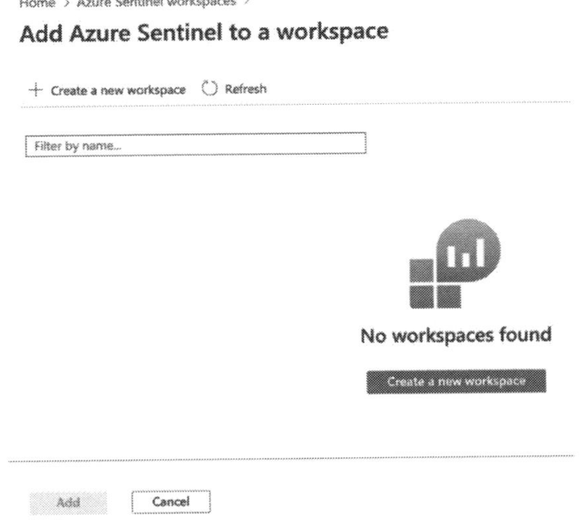

Figure 10.3 – Choosing your workspace for Azure Sentinel

3. There are no available workspaces, so we need to click on **Create a new workspace** and we will see a page as shown in the following screenshot:

Home > Azure Sentinel workspaces > Add Azure Sentinel to a workspace >
Create Log Analytics workspace
A Log Analytics workspace is the basic management unit of Azure Monitor Logs. There are specific considerations you should take when creating a new Log Analytics workspace. Learn more
With Azure Monitor Logs you can easily store, retain, and query data collected from your monitored resources in Azure and other environments for valuable insights. A Log Analytics workspace is the logical storage unit where your log data is collected and stored.
Project details
Select the subscription to manage deployed resources and costs. Use resource groups like folders to organize and manage all your resources.
Subscription *
Visual Studio Enterprise Subscription
Resource group *
RG1
Create new
Instance details
Name *
Workspace200
Region *
East US
Review + Create
« Previous
Next : Pricing tier >

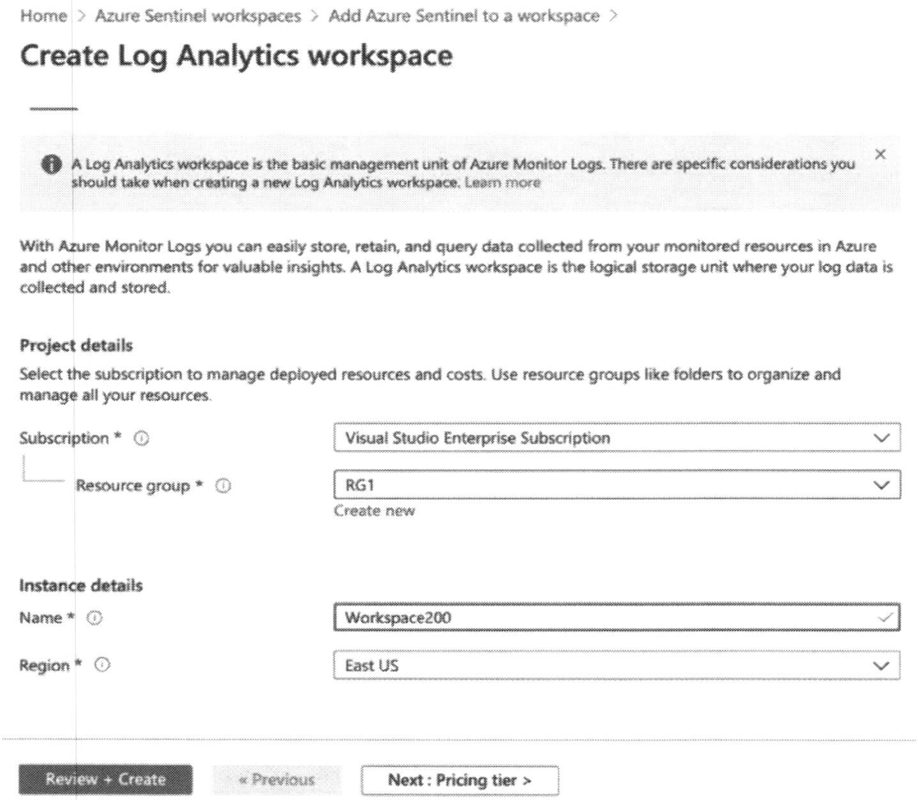

Figure 10.4 – Creating a Log Analytics workspace

4. Choose **Subscription** and **Resource group**, give your instance a name, select a region, and then click on **Next: Pricing tier** >. Then, select **Pricing tier** and click **Next: Tags** >, as shown in the following screenshot:

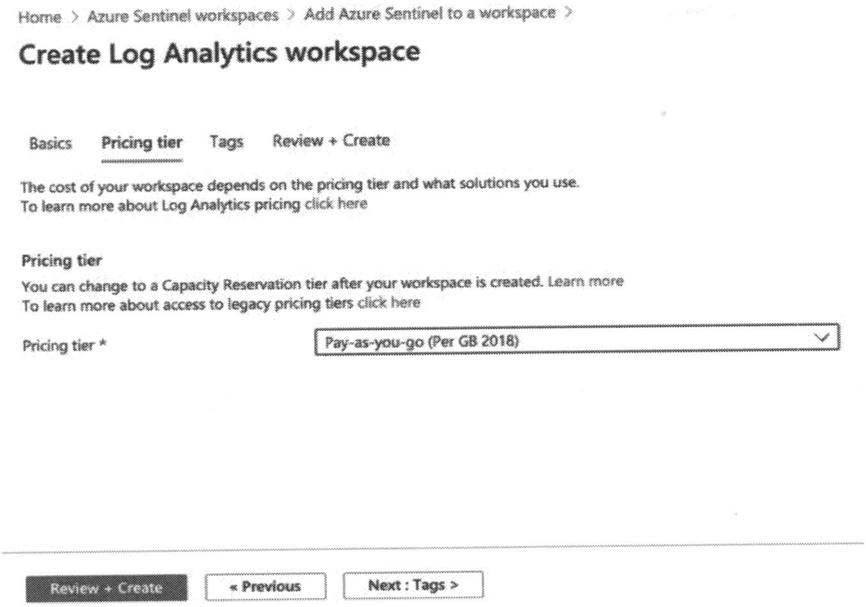

Home > Azure Sentinel workspaces > Add Azure Sentinel to a workspace >

Create Log Analytics workspace

Basics | **Pricing tier** | Tags | Review + Create

The cost of your workspace depends on the pricing tier and what solutions you use.
To learn more about Log Analytics pricing click here

Pricing tier

You can change to a Capacity Reservation tier after your workspace is created. Learn more
To learn more about access to legacy pricing tiers click here

Pricing tier * | Pay-as-you-go (Per GB 2018)

Review + Create | « Previous | Next : Tags >

Figure 10.5 – Selecting a pricing tier for your workspace

5. Optionally, add **Tags** to help you categorize resources:

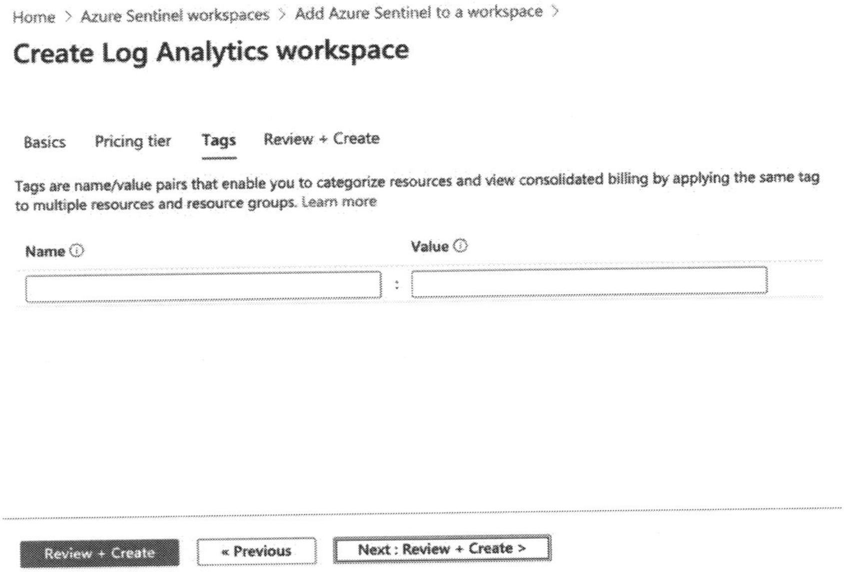

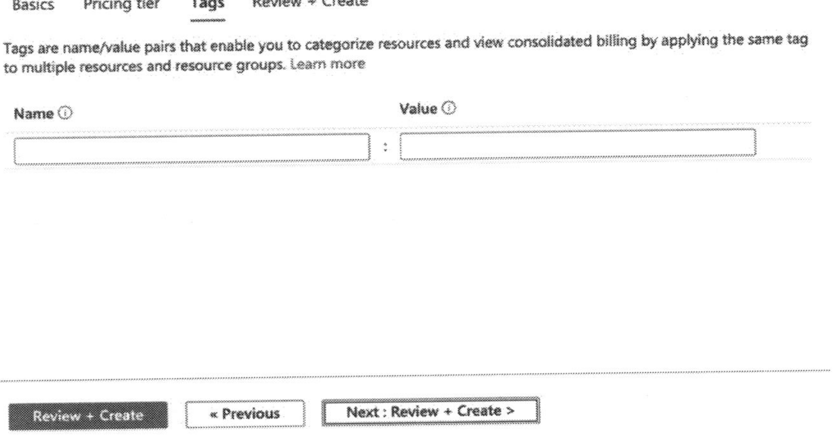

Figure 10.6 – Optionally adding tags to your workspace

6. Then, click **Next: Review + Create** >. Review your selections and then click on **Create**, as shown in the following screenshot:

Home > Azure Sentinel workspaces > Add Azure Sentinel to a workspace >

Create Log Analytics workspace

Validation passed

Basics Pricing tier Tags **Review + Create**

Log Analytics workspace
by Microsoft

Basics

Subscription	Visual Studio Enterprise Subscription
Resource group	RG1
Name	Workspace200
Region	East US

Pricing

Pricing tier	Pay-as-you-go (Per GB 2018)

Tags

(none)

Create « Previous Download a template for automation

Figure 10.7 – Reviewing settings and creating your workspace

The new workspace is shown as seen in the following screenshot:

Figure 10.8 – The Azure Sentinel workspace has now been created

7. Select your new workspace and then click **Add**. This process can take a few minutes to complete:

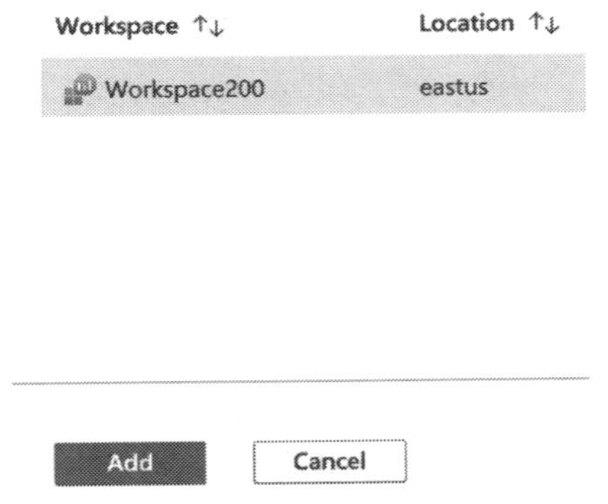

Figure 10.9 – Adding Sentinel to the workspace

Azure Sentinel will now be enabled and connected to your chosen workspace, as shown in the following screenshot:

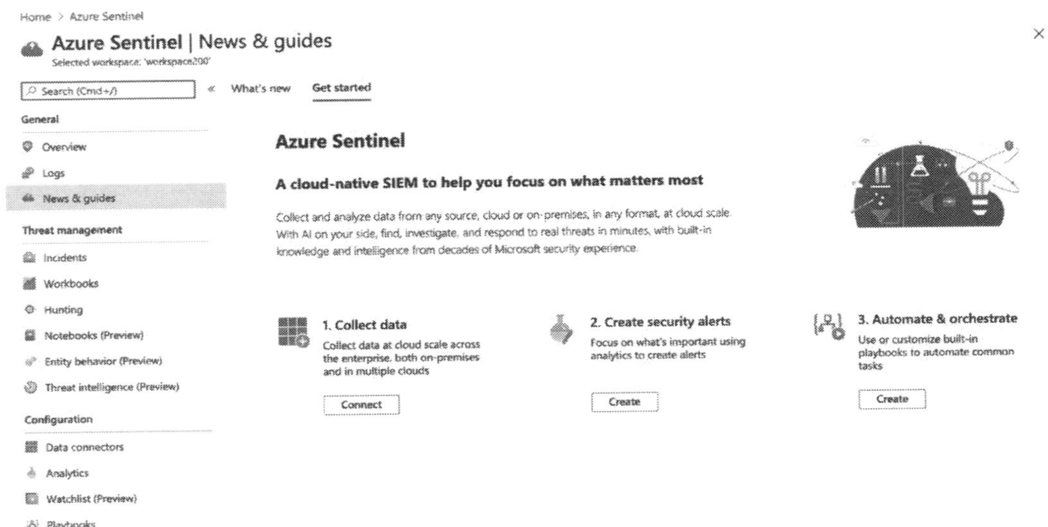

Figure 10.10 – Azure Sentinel is enabled and connected to the workspace

Now that we have enabled **Azure Sentinel** within the Azure portal and connected it to our chosen workspace, the next step is to connect Sentinel to some data sources.

Connecting Azure Sentinel to data sources

Now that Azure Sentinel is enabled, let's go through the process of collecting data by connecting it to data sources. This is achieved by completing the following steps:

1. Go to **Azure Sentinel** in the Azure portal and select **Configuration | Data connectors**, as shown in the following screenshot:

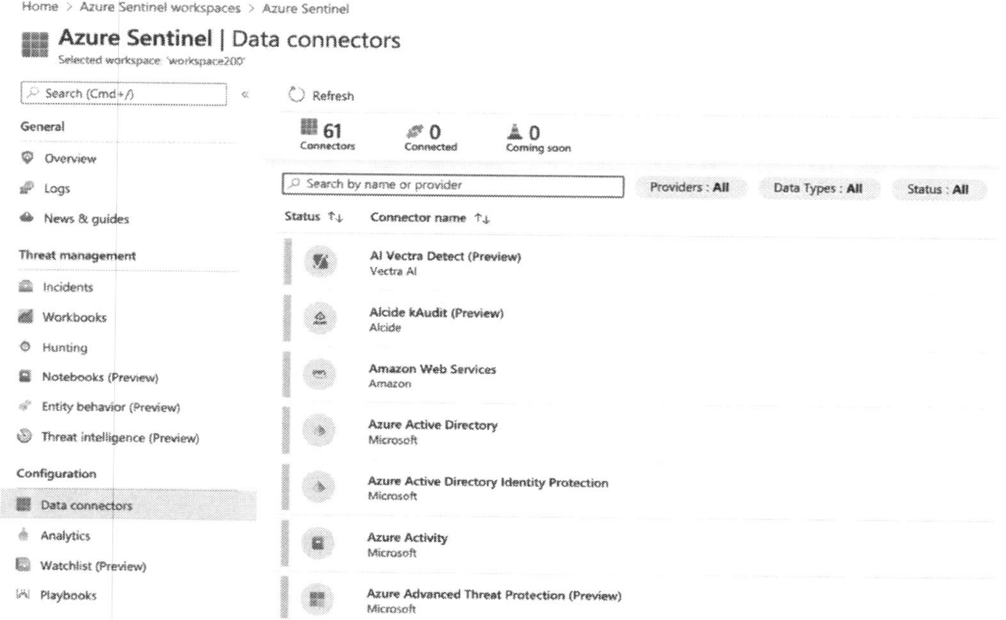

Figure 10.11 – Using Data connectors

2. As *Figure 10.11* shows, you will see an extensive list of data source connectors that you can configure with **Azure Sentinel**. There are connectors for both Microsoft and third-party data sources. You may filter these connectors by **Providers**, **Data Types**, and **Status**. For this example, we will filter and select a Microsoft data source:

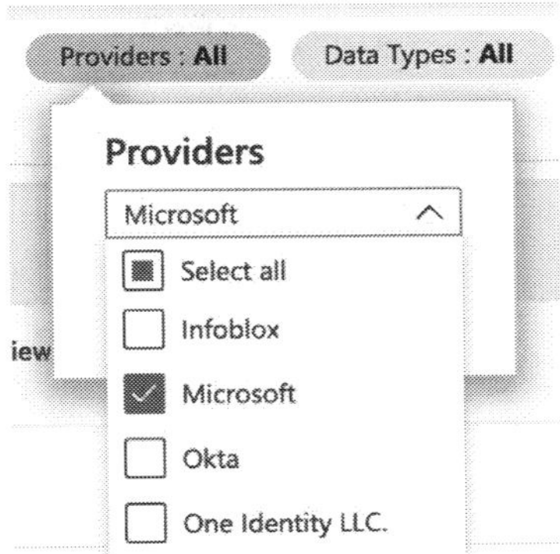

Figure 10.12 – Filtering the data source by provider

3. You will now see the list of Microsoft data connectors. Let's choose the **Office 365** connector. Doing so will open the connector description on the right side of the screen and you will see that this connector provides you with insights into ongoing user activities, as shown in the following screenshot:

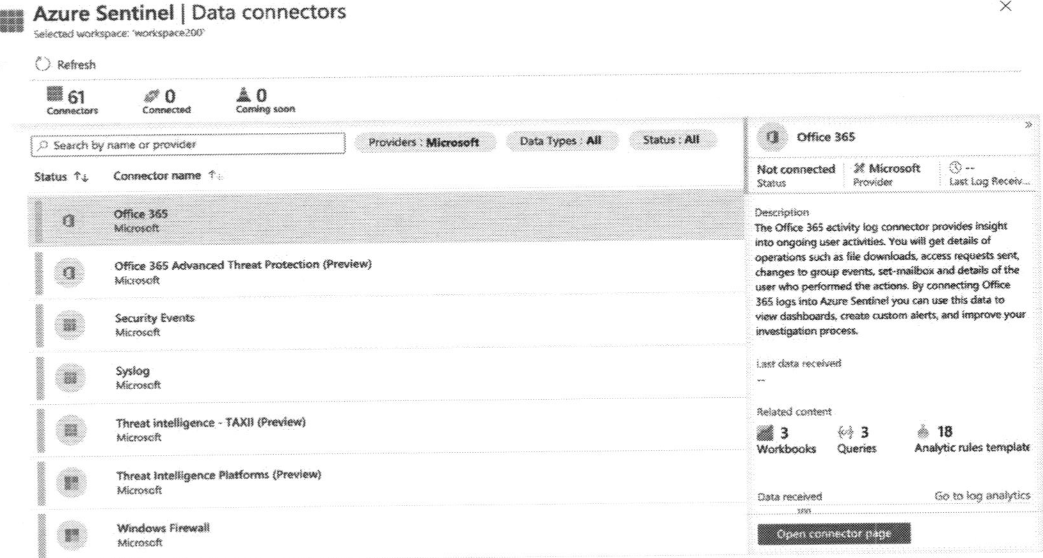

Figure 10.13 – Choosing the Office 365 connector

4. Click on **Open connector page**. Under **Instructions**, you will see some **Prerequisites** for using the connector:

Figure 10.14 – Prerequisites for using the connector

5. Scrolling down, you will next see the **Configuration** options for the connector. In this example, we will select all three options, which are **Exchange**, **SharePoint**, and **Teams (Preview)**. Then, click **Apply Changes**:

Configuration
Connect Office 365 activity logs to your Azure Sentinel.
Select the record types you want to collect from your tenant and click Apply Changes.
Exchange
SharePoint
Teams (Preview)
Apply Changes

Figure 10.15 – Connector configuration options

Scroll down further and you will see that the final option allows you to search for any **Previously connected tenants**. This feature provides the ability to search for and view any Office 365 tenants that you may have previously had connected to Azure Sentinel, and you may view and modify which logs you collect from each tenant:

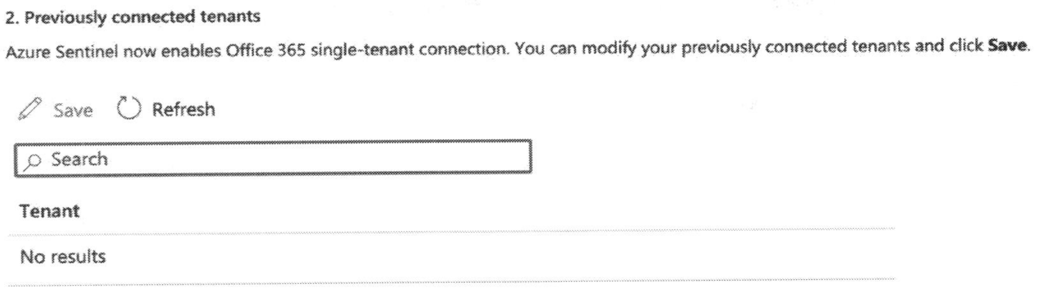

2. Previously connected tenants

Azure Sentinel now enables Office 365 single-tenant connection. You can modify your previously connected tenants and click **Save**.

Save Refresh

Search

Tenant

No results

Figure 10.16 – Previously connected tenants option

6. From the **Next steps** tab, you are shown some **Recommended workbooks**, which you can use to view logs relating to your data connector. Workbooks provide you with a way to monitor your data in Office 365. There are several built-in workbook templates that you can choose from, or you may create your own custom workbooks:

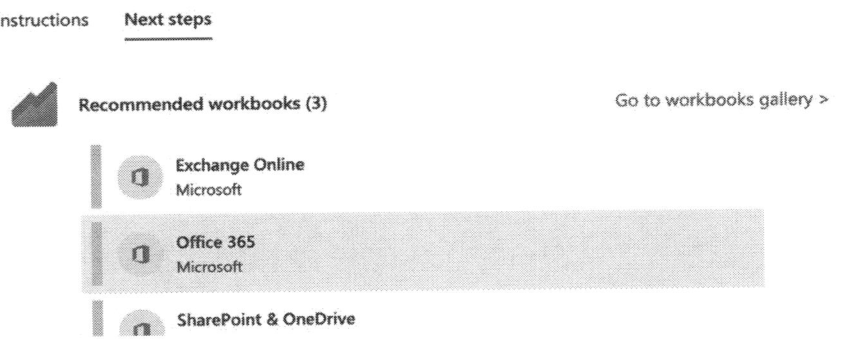

Figure 10.17 – Viewing recommended workbooks

7. Scroll down and you will see some useful **Query samples**, which can be used to investigate data gathered by your connector:

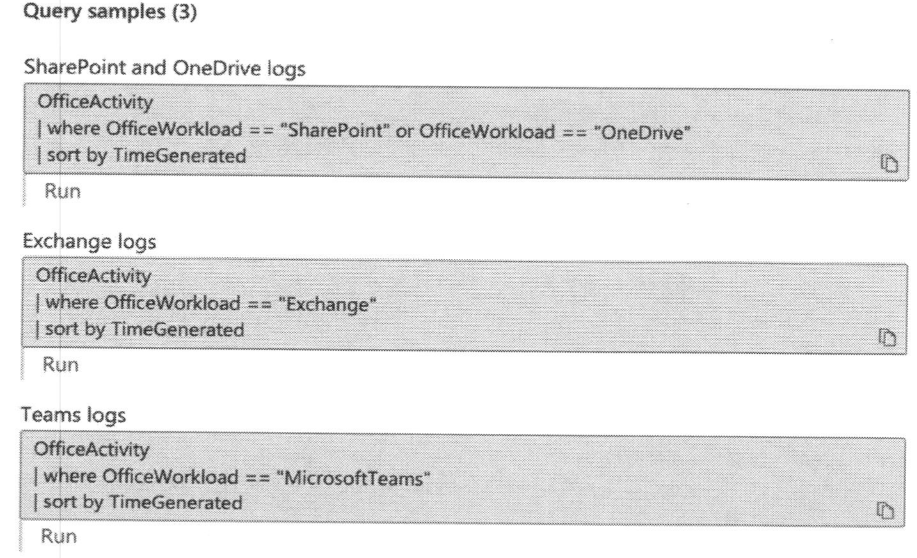

Query samples (3)
SharePoint and OneDrive logs
OfficeActivity
| where OfficeWorkload == "SharePoint" or OfficeWorkload == "OneDrive"
| sort by TimeGenerated
Run
Exchange logs
OfficeActivity
| where OfficeWorkload == "Exchange"
| sort by TimeGenerated
Run
Teams logs
OfficeActivity
| where OfficeWorkload == "MicrosoftTeams"
| sort by TimeGenerated
Run

Figure 10.18 – Viewing recommended query samples

8. Finally, scroll down further and you will see some analytics rule templates:

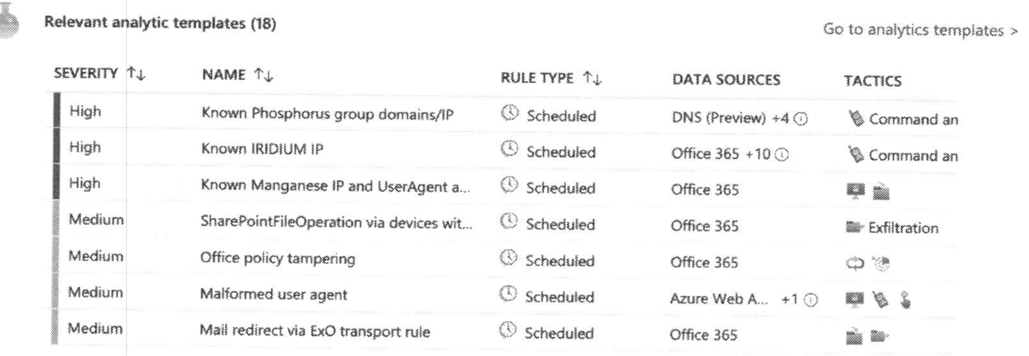

Relevant analytic templates (18)
Go to analytics templates >
SEVERITY
NAME
RULE TYPE
DATA SOURCES
TACTICS
High
Known Phosphorus group domains/IP
Scheduled
DNS (Preview) +4
Command an
High
Known IRIDIUM IP
Scheduled
Office 365 +10
Command an
High
Known Manganese IP and UserAgent a...
Scheduled
Office 365
Medium
SharePointFileOperation via devices wit...
Scheduled
Office 365
Exfiltration
Medium
Office policy tampering
Scheduled
Office 365
Medium
Malformed user agent
Scheduled
Azure Web A... +1
Medium
Mail redirect via ExO transport rule
Scheduled
Office 365

Figure 10.19 – Viewing recommended analytics rule templates

9. By selecting one of the available workbooks, we can see what the workbook is designed to do. If we want to add it to **Azure Sentinel**, we just need to click **Save**, as shown in the following screenshot, where we are looking at the **Exchange Online** workbook:

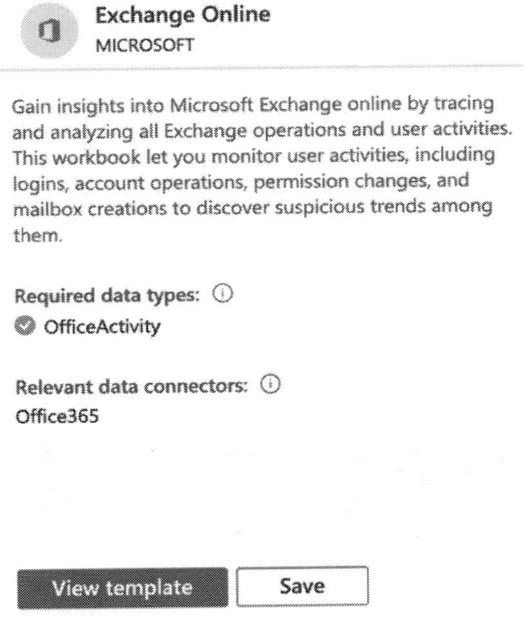

Figure 10.20 – Exchange Online workbook

10. Next, choose the location where you wish to save the workbook:

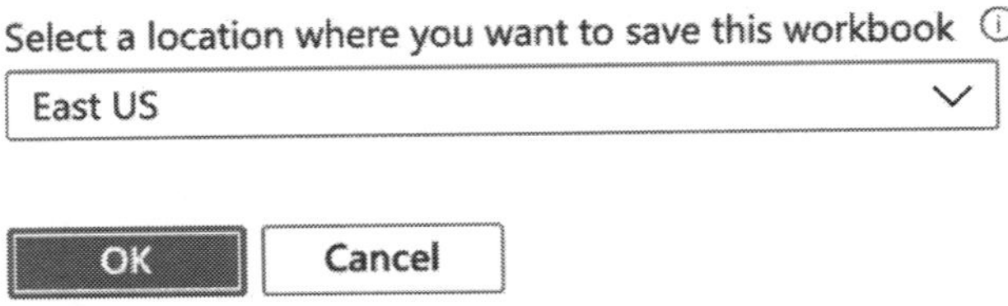

Figure 10.21 – Choosing your workbook location

11. Now, click on **View saved workbook** (you may also view any workbooks that you save via the **Azure Sentinel** portal under **Workbooks | My workbooks**):

Figure 10.22 – Click to view your saved workbook

The workbook is opened and, as shown in the following screenshot, you will not see any matched activities immediately:

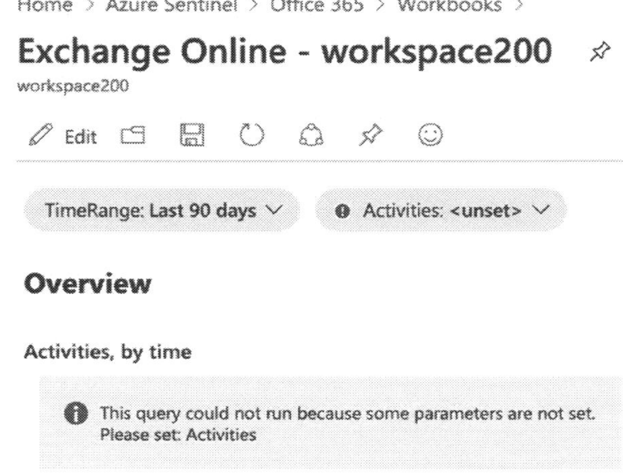

Figure 10.23 – A new Azure Sentinel workbook

12. Click the **Activities** drop-down menu to check the **All** option, and then click the **Save** icon:

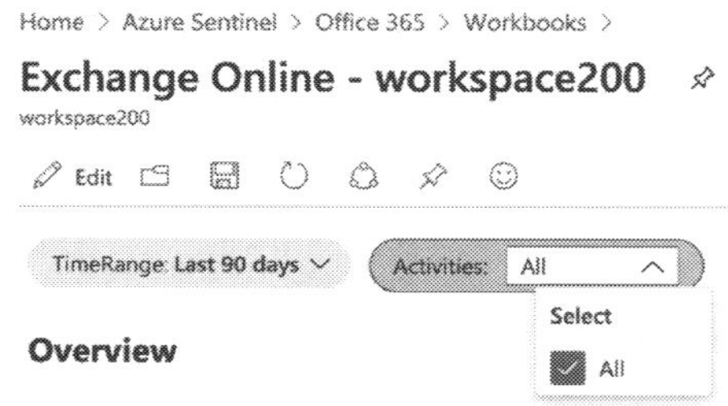

Figure 10.24 – Selecting all activities

13. The workbook will now appear as shown in the following screenshot:

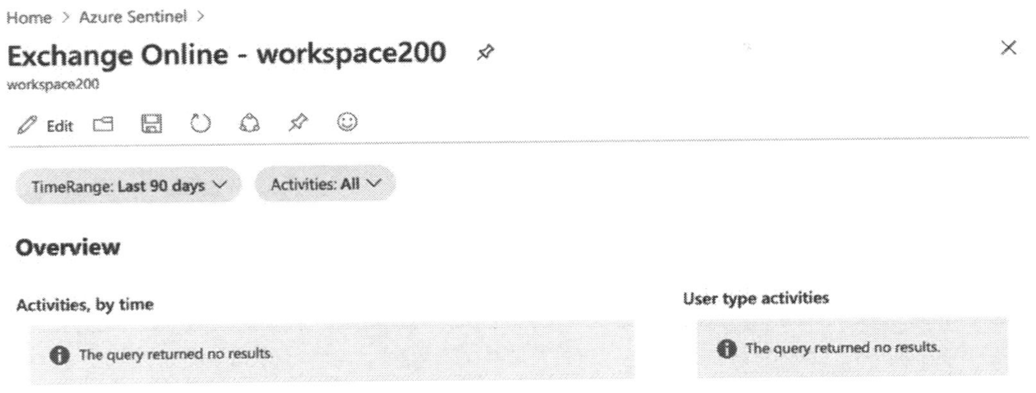

Figure 10.25 – Workbook saved with all activities targeted for analysis by the data connector

So, that is how you enable Azure Sentinel in your Microsoft 365 tenant and connect it to a workspace and data connectors.

> **Important note**
> Azure Sentinel is an extremely complex service within the Microsoft Azure portal. This chapter will only cover the basic principles of Azure Sentinel, which are sufficient in the context of the MS-500 certification. Should you wish to gain a more advanced understanding of Azure Sentinel, there are several references you may consult that are included at the end of this chapter.

Next, we will look at Azure Sentinel playbooks.

Using Azure Sentinel playbooks

Azure Sentinel includes a feature called **playbooks**. These can be used to create automated responses where Sentinel detects security issues. For example, should one of the workbooks we configured in the previous section detect an issue, a playbook could be configured to respond to that, either manually or automatically.

> **Important note**
> Playbooks are based on Azure Logic apps, and therefore should you wish to use them, you will need to be aware of additional charges that you will incur.

Let's look at how to create a security playbook in Azure Sentinel. Here, we will connect a playbook to the Logic Apps designer and trigger an email alert when a SharePoint list is modified. This is achieved by completing the following steps:

1. From the **Azure Sentinel** portal, select **Configuration** | **Playbooks**:

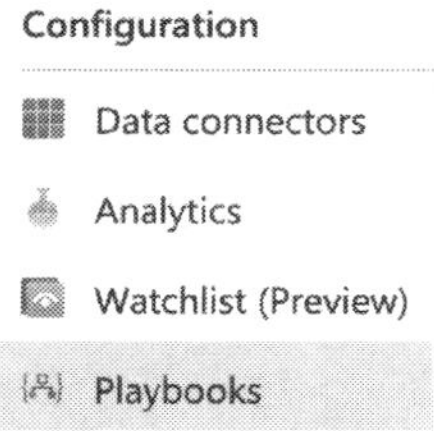

Figure 10.26 – Configuring a security playbook

2. Click on **Add Playbook**:

Figure 10.27 – Adding a playbook

3. In this example, we will set up a simple playbook, which I have set as shown in the following screenshot:

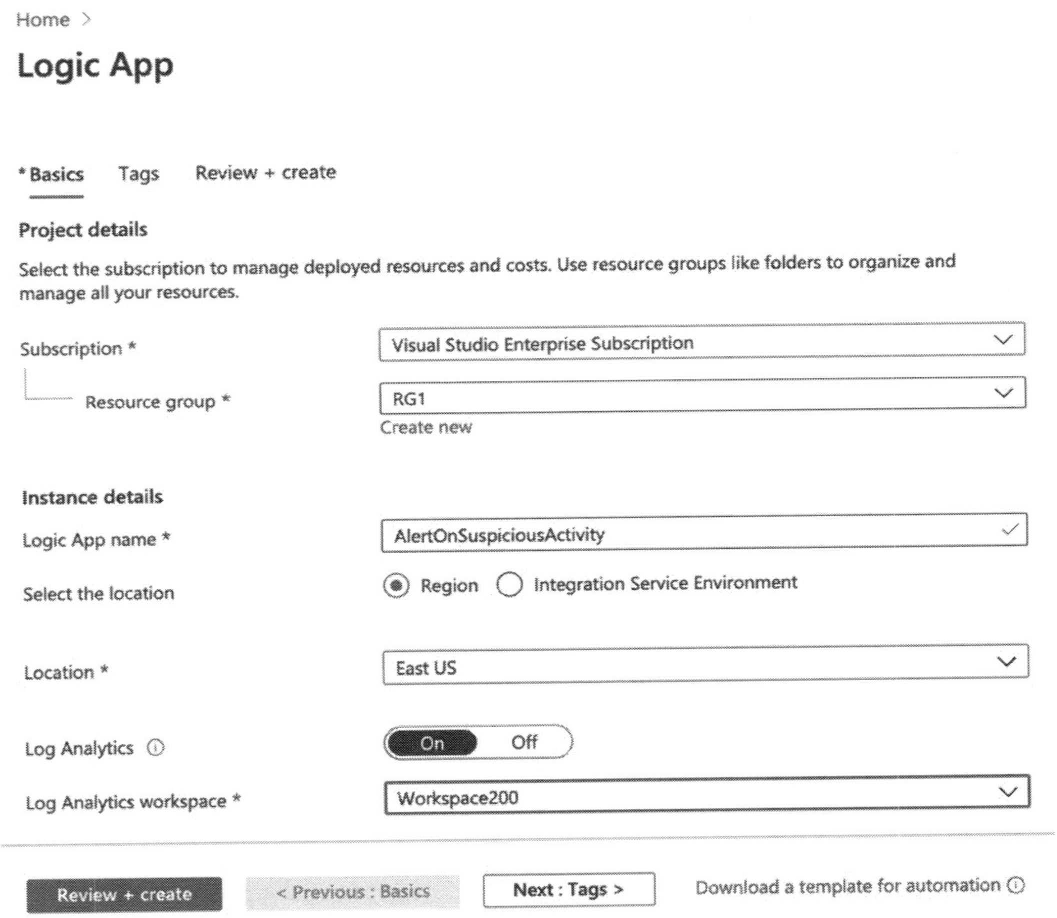

Home >

Logic App

*Basics Tags Review + create

Project details

Select the subscription to manage deployed resources and costs. Use resource groups like folders to organize and manage all your resources.

Subscription * Visual Studio Enterprise Subscription

Resource group * RG1

Create new

Instance details

Logic App name * AlertOnSuspiciousActivity

Select the location Region Integration Service Environment

Location * East US

Log Analytics On Off

Log Analytics workspace * Workspace200

Review + create < Previous : Basics Next : Tags > Download a template for automation

Figure 10.28 – Configuring your logic app

4. You may optionally add some tags. However, we will skip that process here and select **Review + create**:

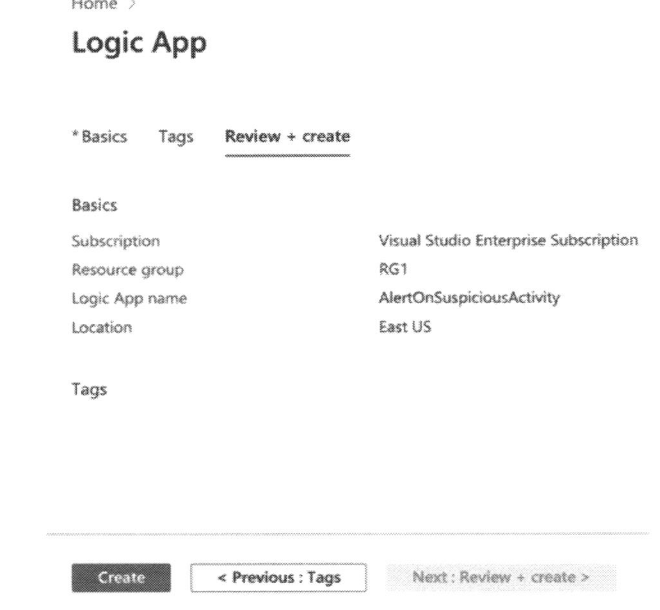

Figure 10.29 – Creating your logic app

5. Now click **Create**, and you will see that your deployment is complete, as shown in the following screenshot:

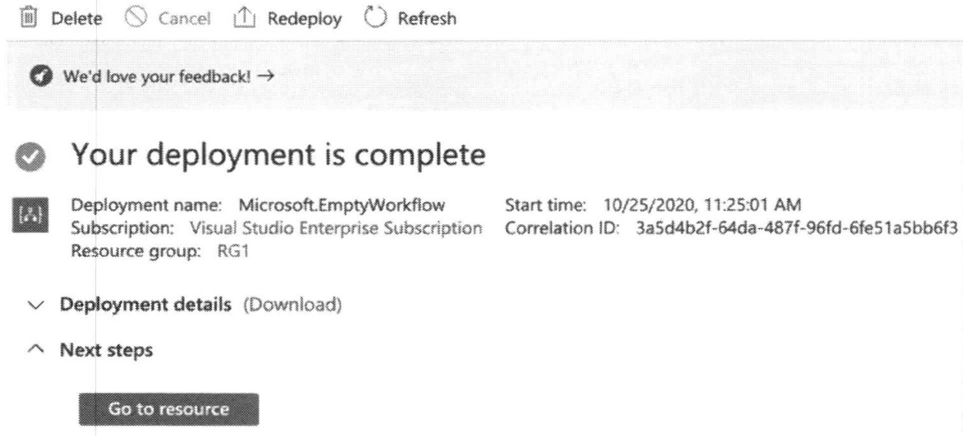

Figure 10.30 – Logic app deployed

6. Now, click on **Go to resource**, and you will see a page as shown in the following screenshot:

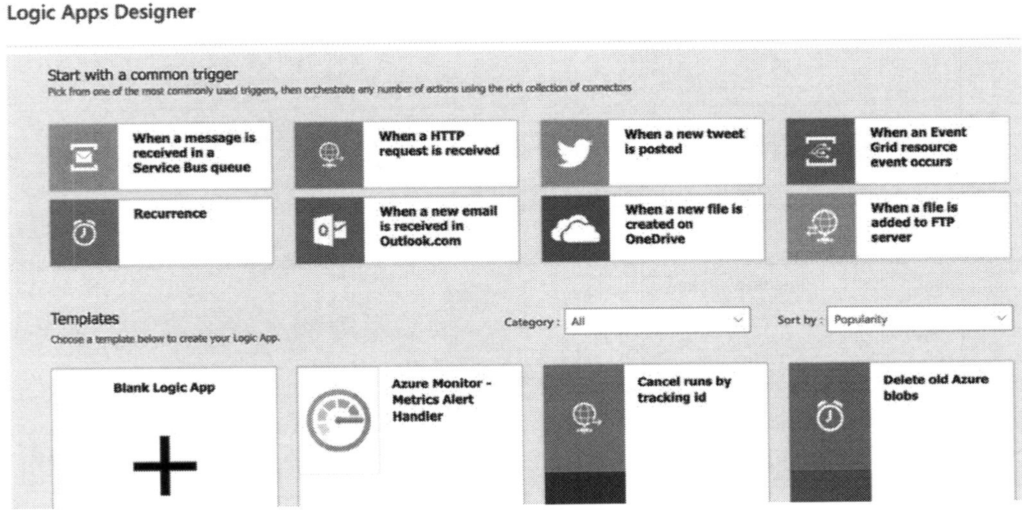

Figure 10.31 – Logic Apps Designer

7. From the **Logic Apps Designer** screen, you can choose to create your logic app, which will form your playbook from either a built-in template, or by using a **Blank Logic App**. In this example, we will select a simple built-in template called **Send an email when an item in a Sharepoint list is modified**:

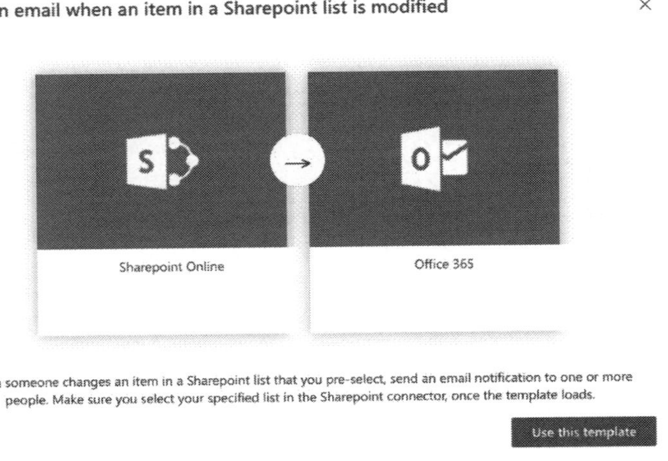

Figure 10.32 – Send an email when an item in a SharePoint list is modified

8. You will see that there are two steps in this logic app connection. You will need to select each of these steps to authenticate to the services, and then click on **Continue**:

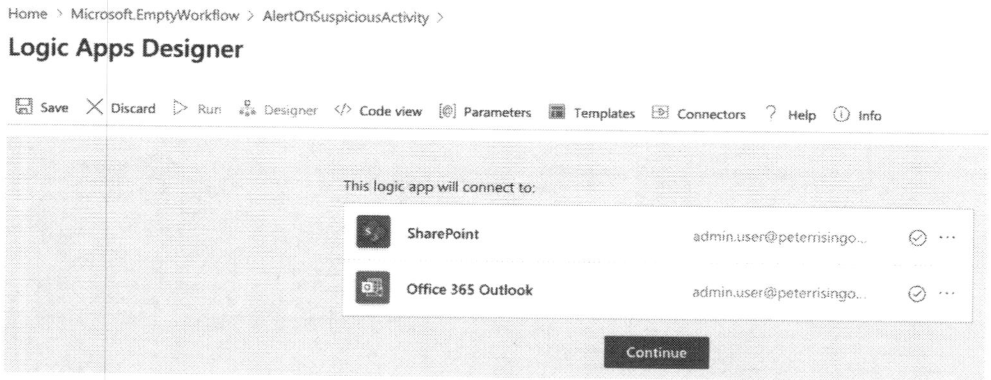

Figure 10.33 – Setting the logic app connections

9. The options shown in *Figure 10.34* are displayed. In this example, we are setting our playbook to check every 3 minutes to see whether a new item is created in a SharePoint list. Should this be the case, the next stage of the playbook will send an email to the creator of the list, and the person who modified the list:

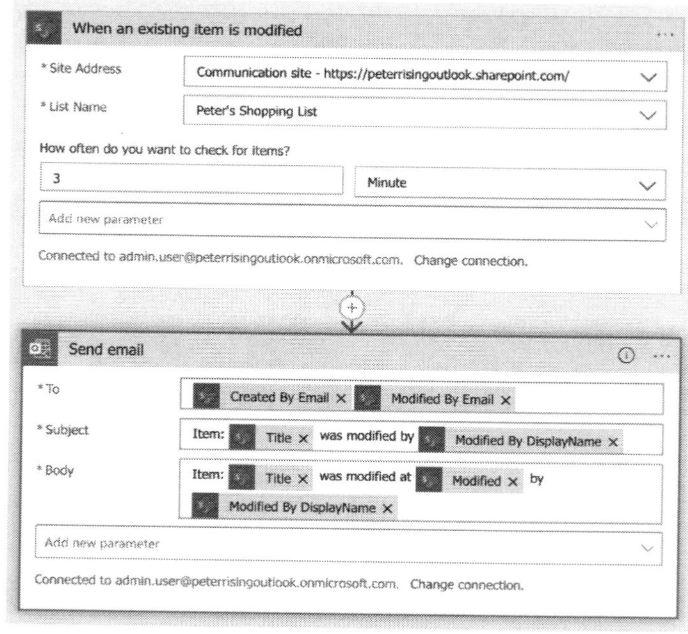

Figure 10.34 – Configuring the logic app connections

10. The SharePoint list in question is a shopping list, and to test the playbook, we will add a new list item, in this case **Biscuits**, as shown in *Figure 10.35*:

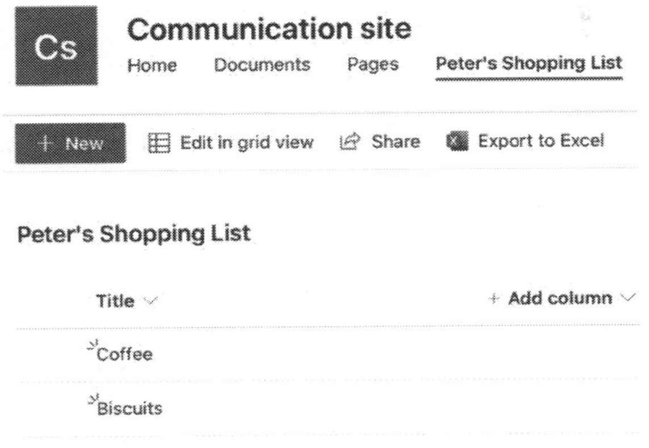

Figure 10.35 – Biscuits added to shopping list

11. Almost immediately after adding our new list item, we can see that an email is sent to the mailboxes targeted in the playbook. This is shown in *Figure 10.36*:

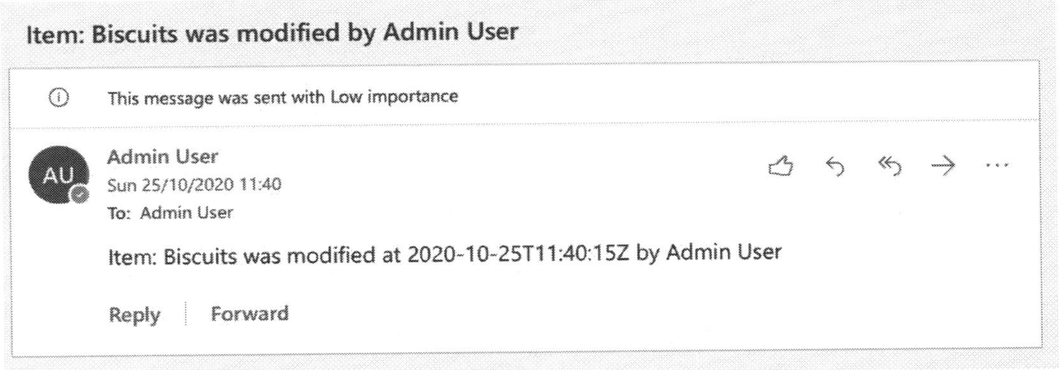

Figure 10.36 – Email alert generated by the playbook

The playbook we have just created is a very simple example, and we set it to be triggered automatically. The playbook could also be triggered manually if required from within the logic app.

Next, we will show you how you can manage and monitor Azure Sentinel on an ongoing basis.

Managing and monitoring Azure Sentinel

Now that you have configured your Azure Sentinel instance and set up some workbooks and playbooks, it is important to manage and monitor Azure Sentinel in order to ensure that you are regularly reviewing and responding to any threats and taking any corrective action that may be required.

Some of the methods available to manage and monitor Azure Sentinel are described as follows.

Azure Sentinel Overview

From the **Azure Sentinel | Overview** section, you are able to review a selection of alerts and metrics, as shown in the following screenshot:

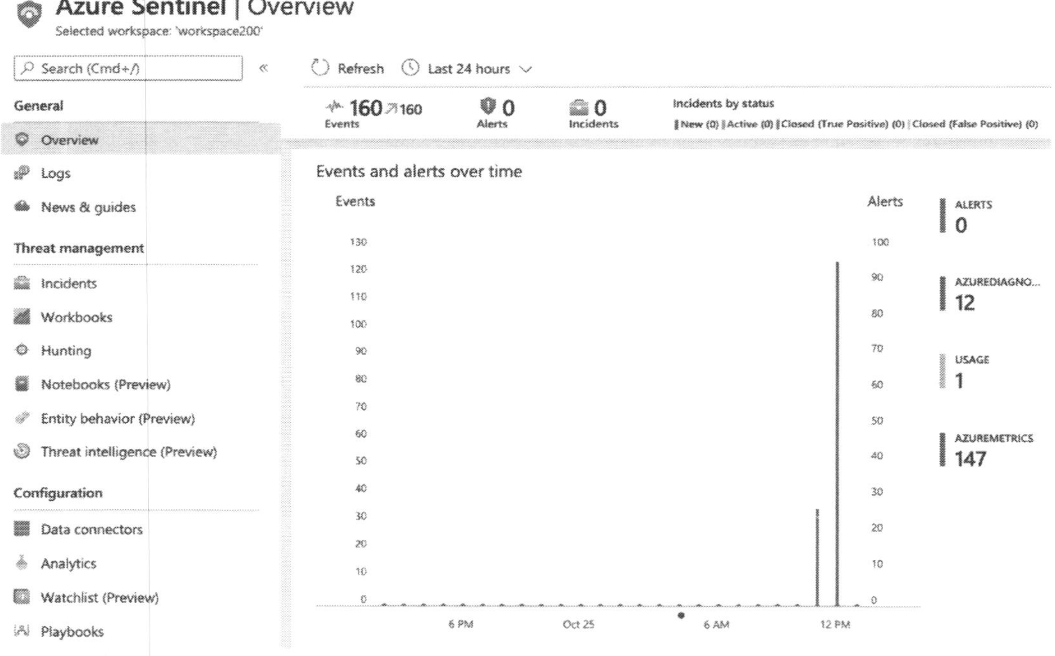

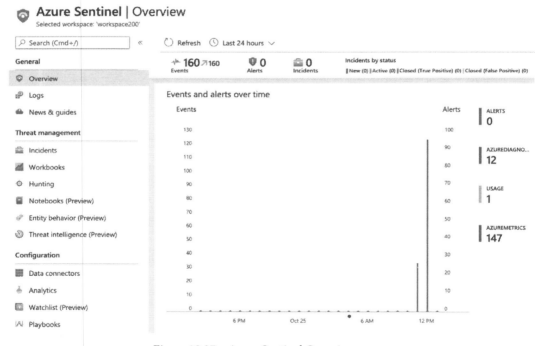

Figure 10.37 – Azure Sentinel Overview screen

Here you will be able to review events and alerts, usage, and metrics.

Azure Sentinel Logs

From the **Azure Sentinel | Logs** section, you may choose from a large number of built-in queries under **Log Analytics workspaces** and see information on things such as **Unauthorized Users** and **Throttled Users**, as shown in the following screenshot:

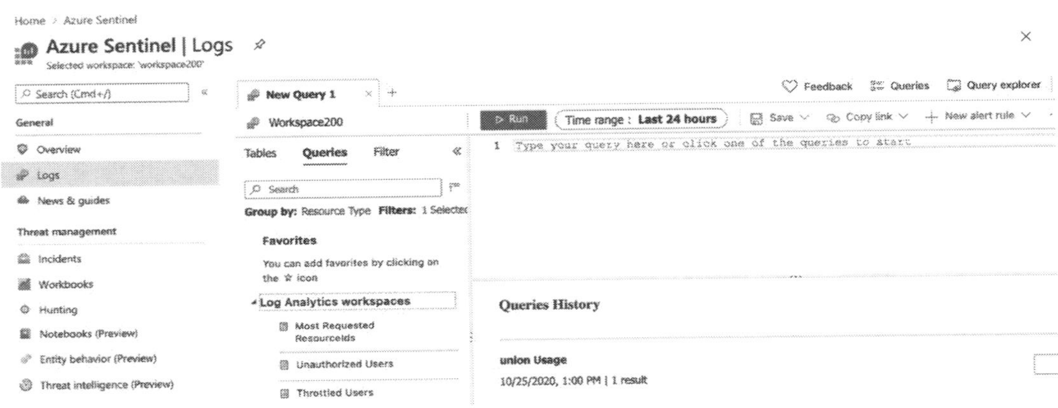

Figure 10.38 – Azure Sentinel Logs

From the **Logs** page, you can access tables, queries, and filters. You can also choose from a list of **Log Analytics workspaces** to run any queries you may require.

Threat management tools

Threat management tools will help you to manage and monitor activities within Azure Sentinel. From the Azure Sentinel portal, you may also leverage a number of threat management tools, which include the following:

- **Incidents**
- **Workbooks**
- **Hunting**
- **Notebooks (Preview)**
- **Entity behavior (Preview)**
- **Threat intelligence (Preview)**

These features are shown in the **Azure Sentinel** portal in the following screenshot:

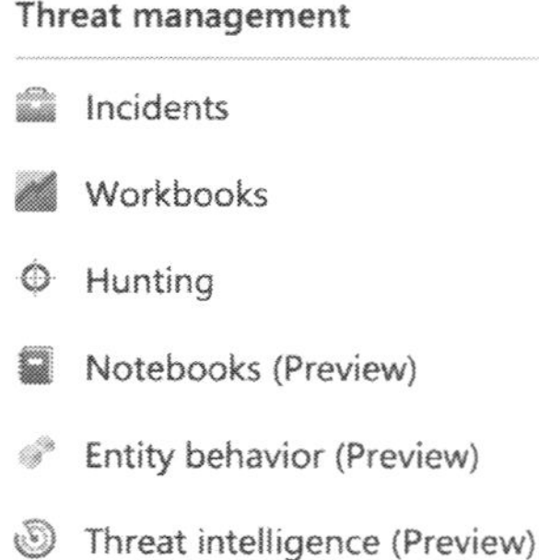

Figure 10.39 – Azure Sentinel Threat management options

It is highly recommended that Azure Sentinel administrators regularly review the events and alerts that are reported in the **Overview** section, along with the Azure Sentinel logs and the tools that are included in the **Threat management** section of the Azure Sentinel portal.

Summary

In this chapter, we introduced you to Azure Sentinel. You learned that Azure Sentinel is a cloud-based SIEM tool that allows you to analyze large amounts of data from both Microsoft and third-party sources. We demonstrated how to enable Azure Sentinel and connect it to a new or existing workspace. Then we showed you how to set up and configure Azure Sentinel security playbooks, which can be set to respond manually or automatically when Sentinel detects security issues.

In the next chapter, we will show you how you can control secure access to information stored within your Microsoft 365 tenant by examining features such as implementing guest access with Azure B2B, securing privileged accounts, and customer lockbox features.

Questions

1. True or False: Azure Sentinel can connect to both Microsoft native and third-party data sources?

    a. True

    b. False

2. Where in the Azure Sentinel portal would you configure security playbooks?

   a. **General | Playbooks**

   b. **Threat Management | Playbooks**

   c. **Configuration | Playbooks**

   d. **Settings | Playbooks**

3. What is the first thing you need to configure when you enable Azure Sentinel?

   a. Create a playbook.

   b. Set up a data connector.

   c. Connect to a playbook.

   d. Connect to a workspace.

4. When deploying your Azure Sentinel workspace, what role permissions do you need?

   a. Global reader

   b. Contributor

   c. Security operator

   d. Reviewer

5. True or False: A security playbook is used to create automated responses when Sentinel detects security issues?

   a. True

   b. False

6. Which Microsoft portal must you access to configure Azure Sentinel?

   a. `https://portal.office.com`

   b. `https://portal.azure.com`

   c. `https://security.microsoft.com`

   d. `https://compliance.microsoft.com`

7. True or False: Azure Sentinel is not a SIEM tool?

   a. True

   b. False

References

Please refer to the following links for more information regarding what was covered in this chapter:

- What is Azure Sentinel?: `https://docs.microsoft.com/en-us/azure/sentinel/overview`
- Onboarding Azure Sentinel: `https://docs.microsoft.com/en-us/azure/sentinel/quickstart-onboard`
- Azure Sentinel – Collecting logs from Microsoft Services and Applications: `https://techcommunity.microsoft.com/t5/azure-sentinel/azure-sentinel-collecting-logs-from-microsoft-services-and/ba-p/792669`
- Connecting data sources to Azure Sentinel: `https://docs.microsoft.com/en-us/azure/sentinel/connect-data-sources`
- Creating a log analytics workspace: `https://docs.microsoft.com/en-us/azure/azure-monitor/learn/quick-create-workspace`
- Investigating incidents with Azure Sentinel: `https://docs.microsoft.com/en-us/azure/sentinel/tutorial-investigate-cases`
- Running a playbook in Azure Sentinel: `https://docs.microsoft.com/en-us/azure/sentinel/tutorial-respond-threats-playbook`

Section 3: Information Protection in Microsoft 365

In this section, we will be examining how to protect information in Microsoft 365.

This part of the book comprises the following chapters:

- *Chapter 11, Controlling Secure Access to Information Stored in Office 365*
- *Chapter 12, Azure Information Protection*
- *Chapter 13, Data Loss Prevention*
- *Chapter 14, Cloud App Discovery and Security*

11
Controlling Secure Access to Information Stored in Office 365

In the previous chapters, we have discussed the importance of securing and protecting a Microsoft 365 environment and shown you the various methods of protection that are available to you as an administrator. These include Multi-Factor Authentication, Conditional Access, Role-based access control, Azure AD Identity Protection, and **Privileged Identity Management** (**PIM**).

In this chapter, we will examine some additional features that you can use to protect user and device access within Office 365. We will show you how **Privileged Access Management** (**PAM**) enables the principle of **just enough access** (**JEA**) and grants permissions to users for functions at the task level, as opposed to a collection of tasks that are combined to make up a role (such as in PIM).

You will also learn the principles of the **Customer Lockbox** and how to turn Customer Lockbox requests on or off. Additionally, we will explain how to configure external sharing with **Azure B2B** while also demonstrating how this process differs from the external sharing capabilities of OneDrive and SharePoint Online.

We shall cover these topics in the following order:

- Understanding PIM
- Understanding Customer Lockbox
- Protecting access to the collaboration components of Office 365
- Allowing external user access with B2B sharing

Understanding privileged access management

PAM is a Microsoft 365 feature that provides more granular capabilities by granting users access to functions at a task level, as opposed to via roles. This is best explained by comparing PAM to PIM. We examined PIM earlier in this book in *Chapter 4, Role Assignment and Privileged Identities in Microsoft 365*, and explained how it can be used to grant JIT access to the administrative roles within Microsoft 365 (such as Global Administrator or Exchange Administrator). These roles are made up of a collection of functions. PAM differs in that it enables the principle of JEA instead, which means that access can be granted to specific individual functions instead of a collection of functions that make up a role. For example, with PAM, you can grant your users access to a single function, such as creating a new Exchange Online Transport rule.

> **Important note**
>
> At the time of writing this book, Privileged Access Management is limited only to functions available within Exchange Online. It is expected that functions from other services within Office 365 will be added to PAM in the coming months.

Let's take a look at how to enable PAM in a Microsoft 365 tenant and start using it, both from the Microsoft 365 Admin Center and from Windows PowerShell.

Enabling PAM

To enable PAM within your Microsoft 365 tenant, you need to have the Exchange Management Administrator role. You can enable and configure this feature by logging into the Microsoft 365 Admin Center at `https://admin.microsoft.com/` and completing the following steps:

1. Create a mail-enabled security group in Office 365 and add members to this group who you wish to be able to approve PAM requests. In the following example, we have created a group called **PAM**:

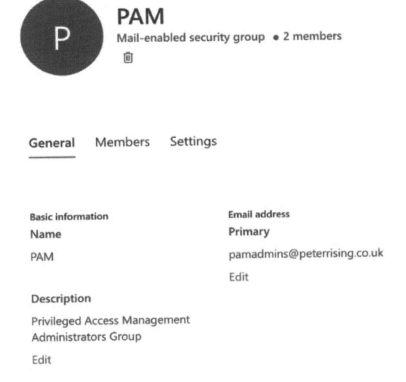

Figure 11.1 – Mail-enabled security group

2. Next, navigate to **Settings | Org settings**, as shown in the following screenshot:

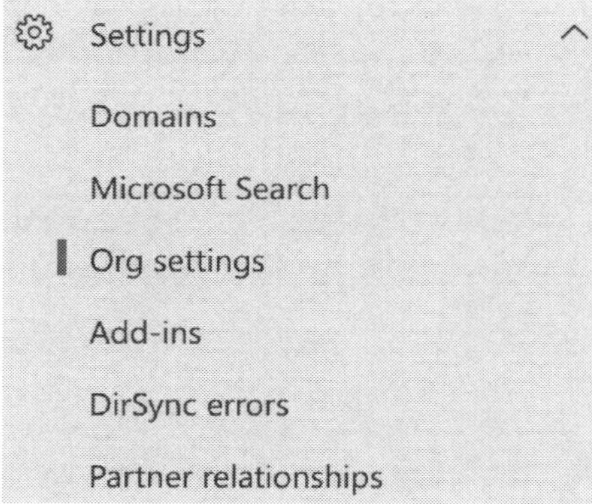

Figure 11.2 – Settings

3. Select the **Security & privacy** option, as shown in the following screenshot:

Settings

Services Security & privacy Organization profile

Figure 11.3 – Security and privacy

4. Scroll down to **Privileged Access**. You will see the following screen. Click on **Edit**:

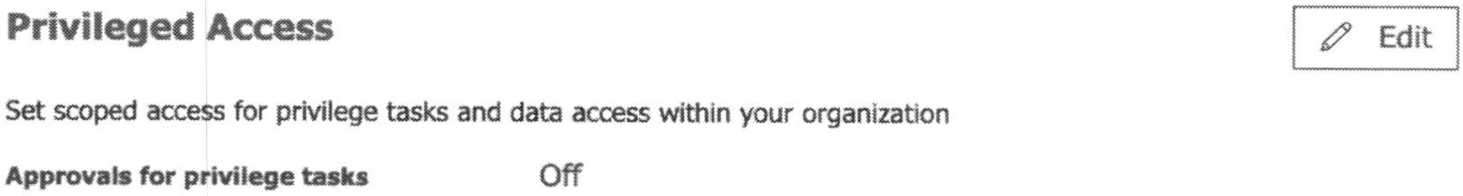

Privileged Access

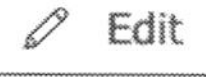

Set scoped access for privilege tasks and data access within your organization

Approvals for privilege tasks Off

Figure 11.4 – Privileged Access

5. Set **Require approvals for privilege tasks** to **On** and choose the group we created in *step 1*. Then, click on **Save**, as shown in the following screenshot:

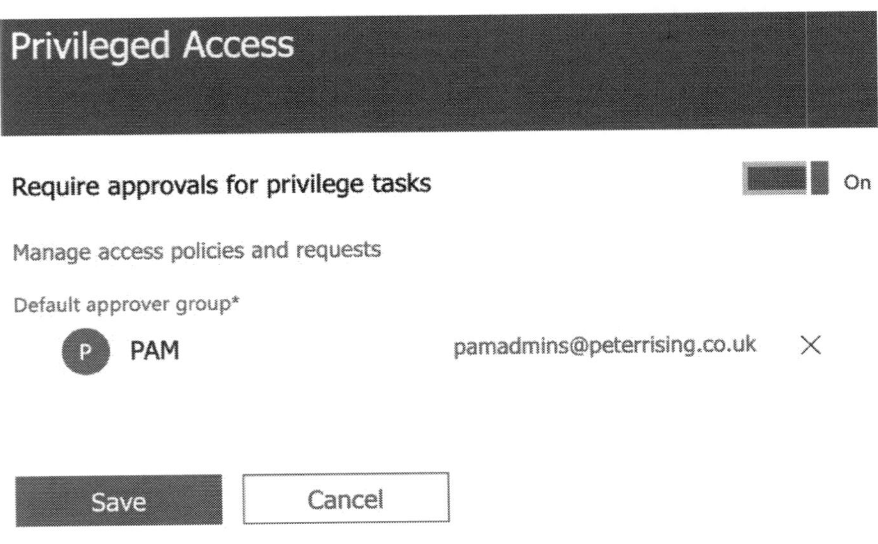

Figure 11.5 – Privileged Access

This page will now look as follows:

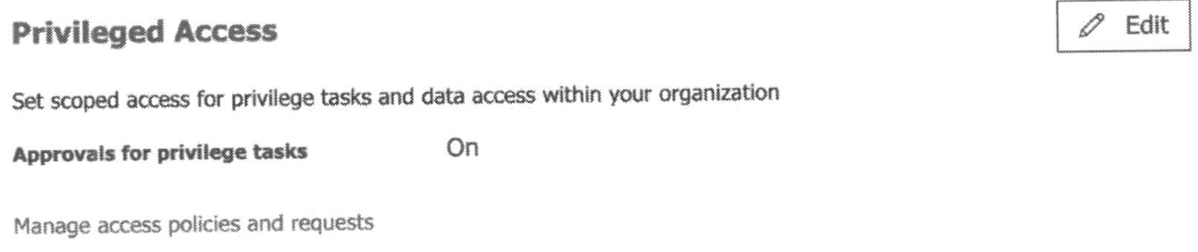

Figure 11.6 – Privileged Access

6. To enable PAM using Exchange Online PowerShell, enter the following command:

```
Enable-ElevatedAccessControl -AdminGroup 'pamadmins@
peterrising.co.uk'
```

Now that we have enabled the PAM feature, let's look at creating access policies.

Creating access policies for PAM

To create an access policy for PAM, we need to complete the following steps:

1. From the Microsoft 365 Admin Center, navigate to **Settings | Security & privacy** and choose **Privileged Access**. Then, select **Manage access policies and requests**, as shown in the following screenshot:

Privileged Access

Set scoped access for privilege tasks and data access within your organization

Approvals for privilege tasks On

Manage access policies and requests

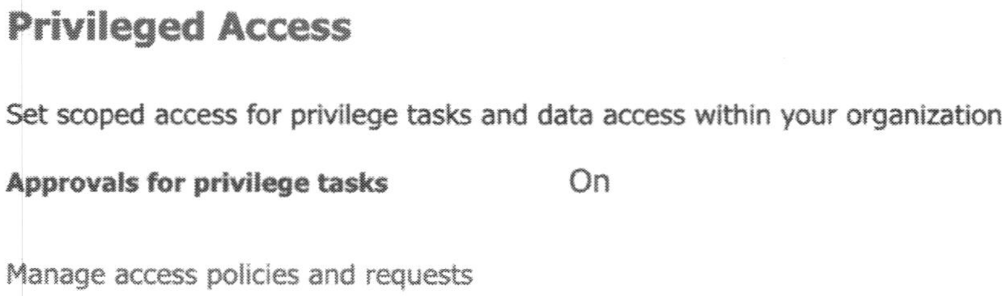

Figure 11.7 – Manage access policies and requests

2. Next, click on **Configure Policies** at the top right-hand side of the screen, as shown in the following screenshot:

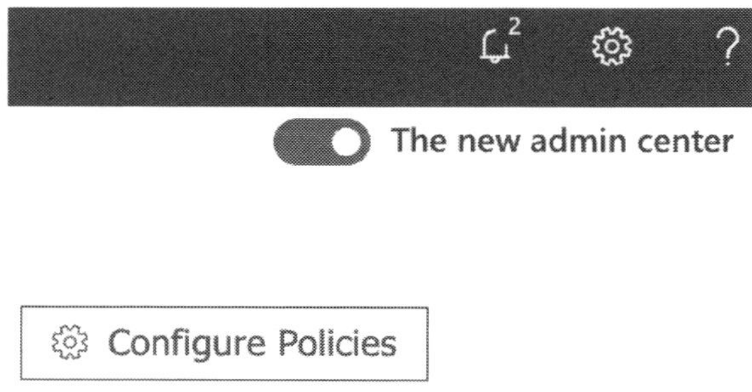

Figure 11.8 – Configure Policies

3. You will see a list of policies. As shown in the following screenshot, we have already created some policies:

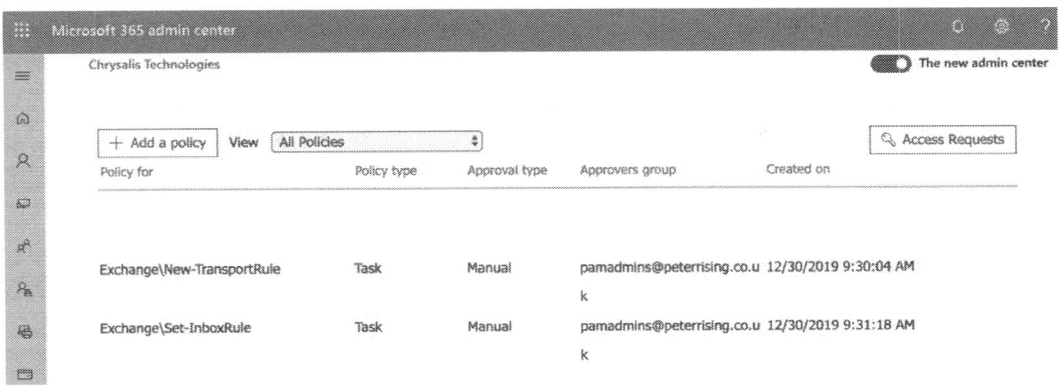

Figure 11.9 – Policies

4. To create a new policy, click on **Add a policy**. Here, you will see the options shown in the following screenshot:

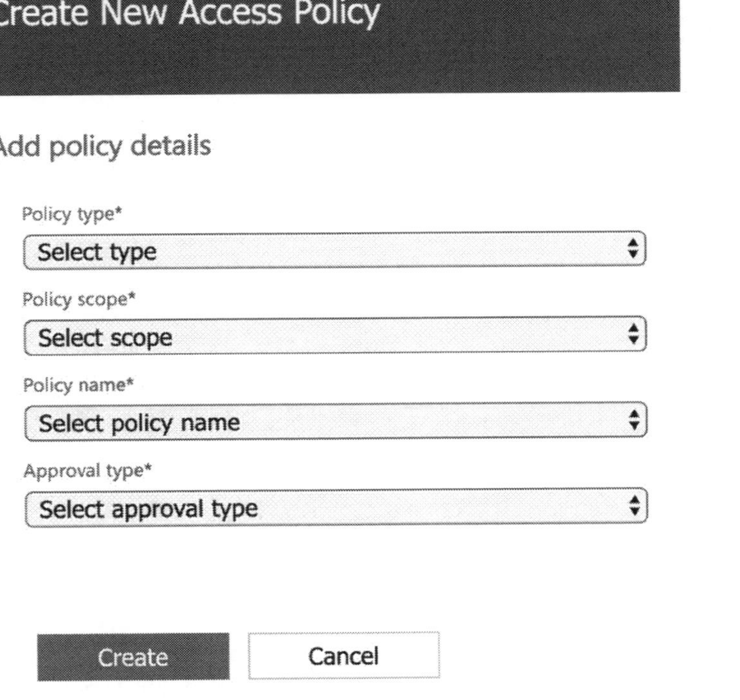

Figure 11.10 – Create New Access Policy

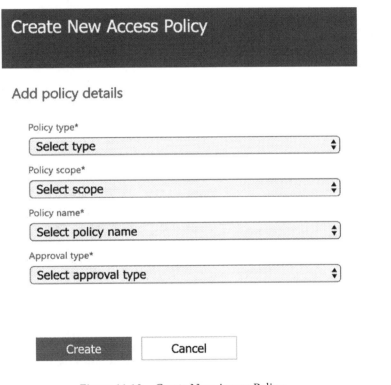

You have the following options to choose from for each of the available fields:

Field	Options
Policy type	Task. Role. Role Group.
Policy scope	Exchange.
Policy name	Here, you have a choice of built-in policies relevant to the type chosen.
Approval type	Manual (if selected, an additional field will be displayed where you will need to choose the mail enabled security group you created earlier in this chapter). Auto.

5. Once you have made the required field selections for your policy, click on **Create**.
6. To create a new access policy using Exchange Online PowerShell, we can run the following command:

```
New-ElevatedAccessApprovalPolicy -Task 'Exchange\
New-MailboxSearch' -ApprovalType Manual -ApproverGroup
'pamadmins@peterrising.co.uk'
```

The previous command creates a new policy with the following settings:

Field	Options
Policy type	Task
Policy scope	Exchange
Policy name	New-MailboxSearch
Approval type	Manual
Approval Group	pamadmins@peterrising.co.uk

So, to recap, we have now enabled PAM in our Microsoft 365 tenant and created some example access policies. Next, let's look at submitting and approving PAM requests.

Submitting and approving PAM requests

Now that we have PAM enabled and some access policies set up, users are able to submit privileged access requests that can then be approved by members of the approval group, which we set up earlier in this chapter.

> **Important note**
>
> At the time of writing this book, the ability for standard users to submit PAM requests from the Microsoft 365 Admin Center is oddly not yet available, and only users with existing admin role assignments are able to access the submission request page.

In order to submit and approve requests from the Microsoft 365 Admin Center, we need to complete the following steps:

1. From the Microsoft 365 Admin Center, navigate to **Settings | Security & privacy** and choose **Privileged Access**.
2. Select **Manage access policies and requests**. You will see the following screen:

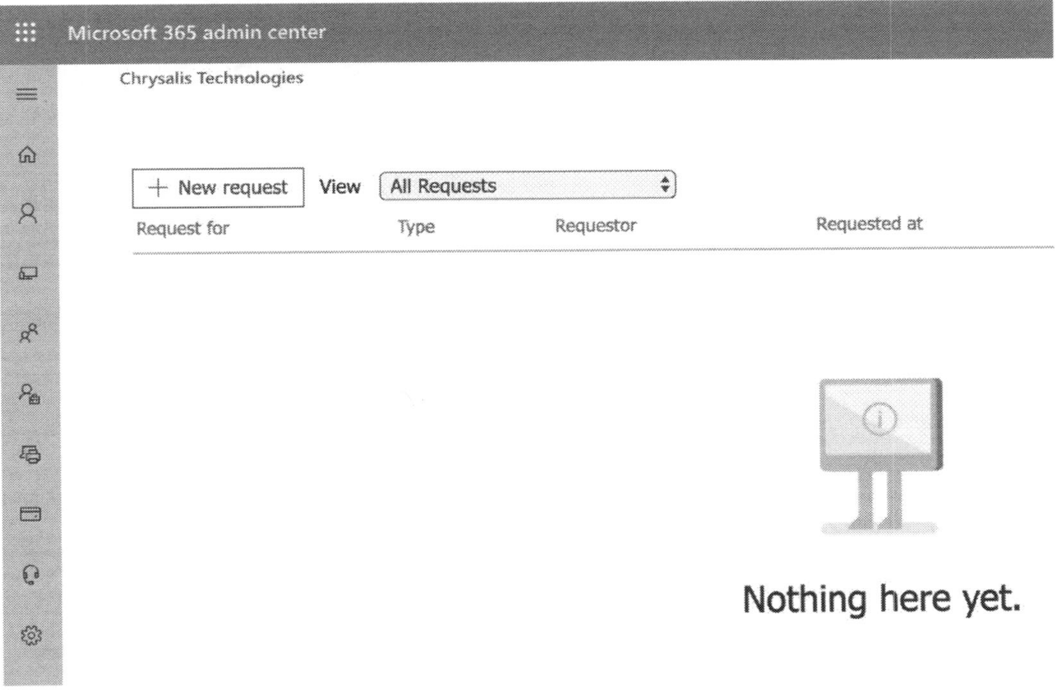

Figure 11.11 – Managing access policies and requests

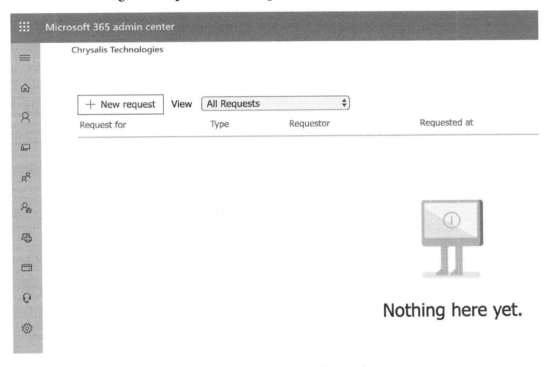

3. Users with existing admin access are able to click on **New request** and choose from the options shown in the following screenshot:

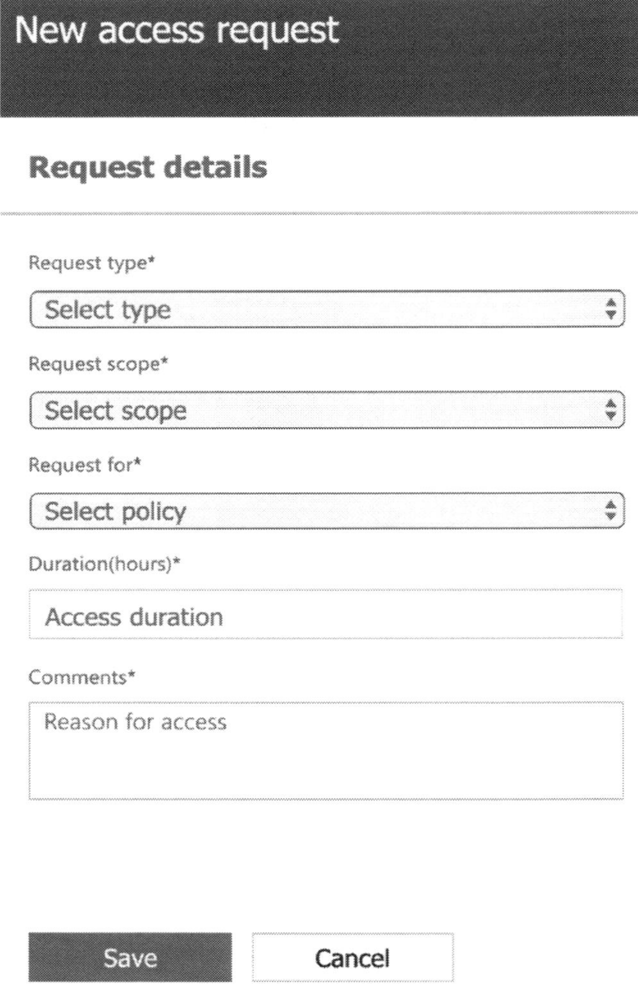

Figure 11.12 – New access request

4. Once the details have been filled in, the user will click on **Save** to complete the request.

The request will then appear in the list and be visible to approvers, who may then open and approve or deny the request for access.

> **Important note**
> Users should be able to submit PAM requests, and then get them approved or denied by the approvers by using Exchange Online PowerShell. As the functionality for this process is limited at the time of writing this book and cannot be accessed by users yet, we are not able to cover this process in detail. Please take a look at the Privileged Access Management link that's included in the *References* section at the end of this chapter for more details.

In this section, we have shown you how PAM can be used in Microsoft 365 to provide users with access to elevated privileges at the task level using the principle of JEA. Next, we will examine how the Customer Lockbox feature allows you to control the level of access that Microsoft support engineers will have to your environment when troubleshooting issues on your behalf.

Understanding Customer Lockbox

On occasion, you may need to contact Microsoft for support in relation to your Office 365 tenant. This is usually achieved via the use of troubleshooting tools or other means.

However, on some occasions, it may be necessary for a Microsoft Engineer to request access to your tenant.

In order to ensure that this is carried out in a secure and controlled manner, Microsoft provide the Customer Lockbox feature, which, when enabled, will require any Microsoft support representatives to complete a request and approval process in order to gain access.

> **Important note**
> Customer Lockbox is only available for organizations with Microsoft 365 E5, Office 365 E5, Information Protection and Compliance, or Advanced Compliance add-on subscriptions. Customer Lockbox currently works only with Exchange Online, OneDrive, and SharePoint Online.

Enabling Customer Lockbox

The Customer Lockbox feature can be enabled in the Microsoft 365 Admin Center by Office 365 Global Administrators (or by any user who has been assigned the Customer Lockbox access approver admin role). Once the feature has been activated, Microsoft is obliged to seek permission from an organization before accessing any content within their tenant.

Enabling the Customer Lockbox feature can be done by completing the following steps:

1. From the Microsoft 365 Admin Center, navigate to **Settings | Org settings | Security & privacy** and choose **Edit** from the **Customer Lockbox** section, as shown in the following screenshot:

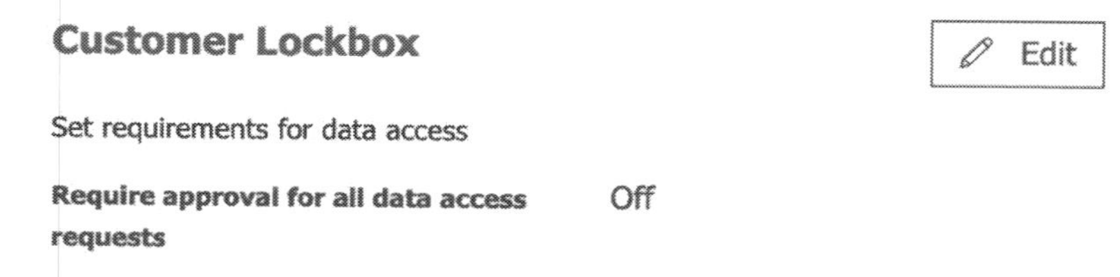

Figure 11.13 – Customer Lockbox

2. Click the check box next to **Require approval for all data access requests** and click **Save changes**.

The Customer Lockbox feature is now enabled for the tenant. Next, we will examine the process of approving or denying a Customer Lockbox request from Microsoft.

Responding to Customer Lockbox requests

Whenever Microsoft make a Customer Lockbox request for access to your tenant, Global Administrators can respond to this by completing the following steps:

1. Log into the Microsoft 365 Admin Center and navigate to **Support | Customer Lockbox Requests**, as shown in the following screenshot:

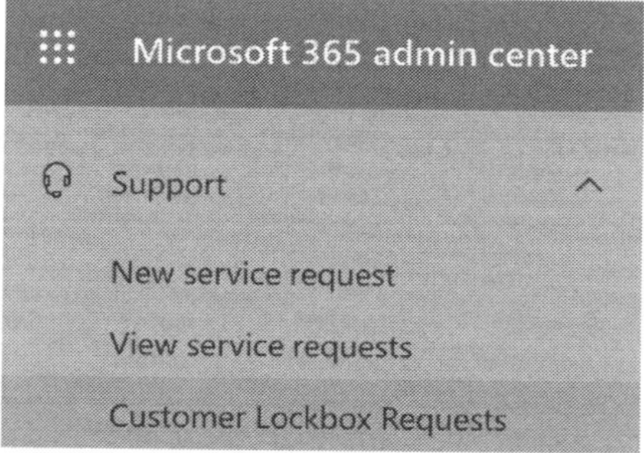

Figure 11.14 – Customer Lockbox Requests

2. Any **Customer Lockbox Requests** will be shown here and will include a reference number, date of the request, the identity of the requestor, and the status of the request (which will initially be set to **Pending**).

3. By clicking on a request, the Global Administrator can review further details about the nature of the request, and then choose to **Approve** or **Deny** access.
4. If the request is approved, the Microsoft Engineer will then be granted a 4-hour window of access to troubleshoot the issue. After this 4-hour period, access will be automatically removed.

All Customer Lockbox activity is recorded in the Office 365 audit log and can be accessed from the Microsoft 365 Security and Compliance Center at `https://protection.office.com`.

> **Important note**
> Further information on auditing Customer Lockbox activity is included in the *References* section at the end of this chapter.

In this section, we have introduced you to the Customer Lockbox feature of Office 365, which allows Global Administrators to enable a setting that requires Microsoft support engineers to request approval for access to your environment in order to troubleshoot issues related to Exchange Online, OneDrive, and SharePoint Online.

In the next section, we will show you how it is possible to protect the collaboration components within your Office 365 environment by configuring policies to protect and secure your SharePoint Online Team Sites and document libraries, as well as OneDrive document libraries.

Protecting access to the collaboration components of Office 365

With more and more documents being stored in the cloud, it is important, as a Microsoft 365 Administrator, to ensure that access to files and folders in services such as SharePoint Online and OneDrive are effectively protected.

There are some simple settings within the SharePoint Online Admin Center that you can configure to apply access control settings for your users, which will help to ensure that only authorized personnel are able to access the content that is hosted in your Microsoft 365 tenant.

In order to configure these settings, we need to take the following steps:

1. Log into the Microsoft 365 Admin Center at `https://admin.microsoft.com/`. Then, under **Admin Centers**, select **SharePoint**, as shown in the following screenshot:

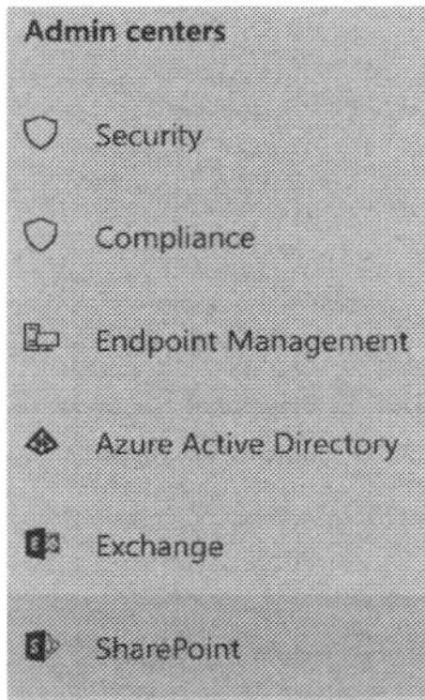

Figure 11.15 – SharePoint

2. From the SharePoint Admin Center, select **Access Control** from the left-hand side menu, which will make the following options appear:

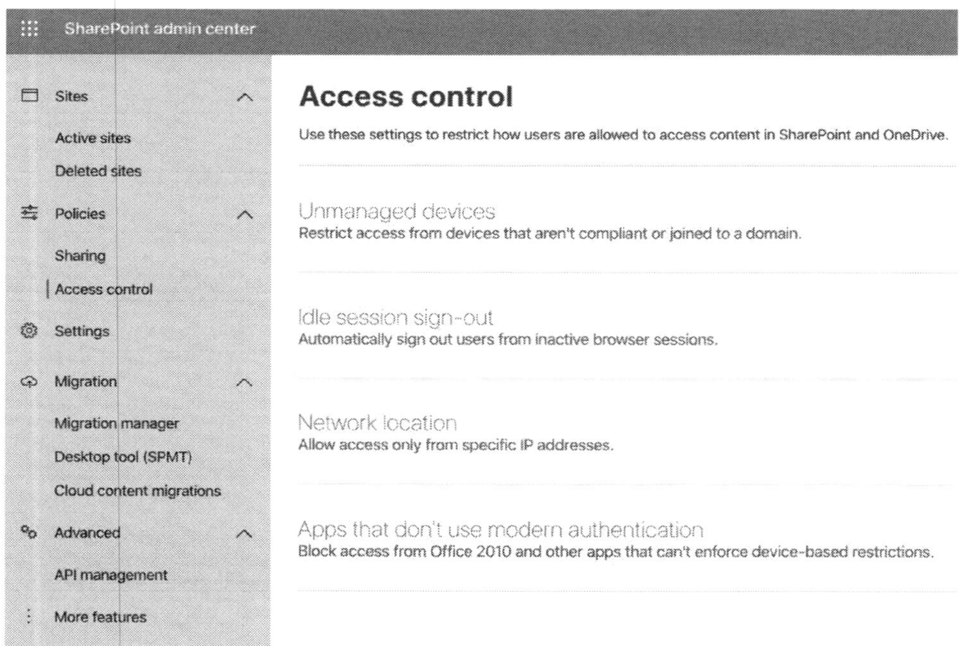

Figure 11.16 – Access control

3. The **Unmanaged devices** option enables you to set tenant-wide settings to control the level of access from any unmanaged devices, as shown in the following screenshot:

Unmanaged devices

The setting you select here will apply to all users in your organization. To customize conditional access policies, save your selection and go to the Azure AD admin center.

- (•) Allow full access from desktop apps, mobile apps, and the web
- ( ) Allow limited, web-only access
- ( ) Block access

If you don't want to limit or block access organization-wide, you can do so for specific sites. Learn how

Save Cancel

Figure 11.17 – Unmanaged devices

4. The **Idle session sign-out** option can be set as follows to automatically sign out users after a period of inactivity:

Idle session sign-out

Warn and then sign out users on unmanaged devices after a period of inactivity. This setting applies when users don't select to stay signed in.

Sign out inactive users automatically

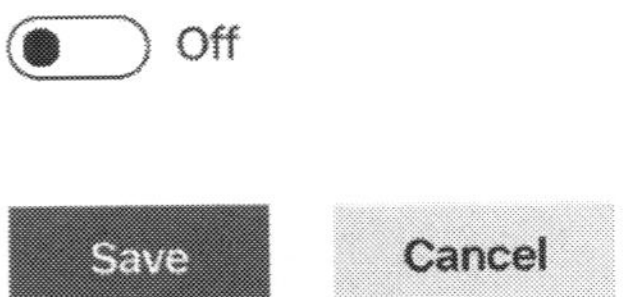

Figure 11.18 – Idle session sign-out

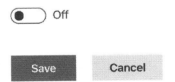

5. Under **Network location**, you have the option to allow access only from IP ranges that you have specified, as shown in the following screenshot:

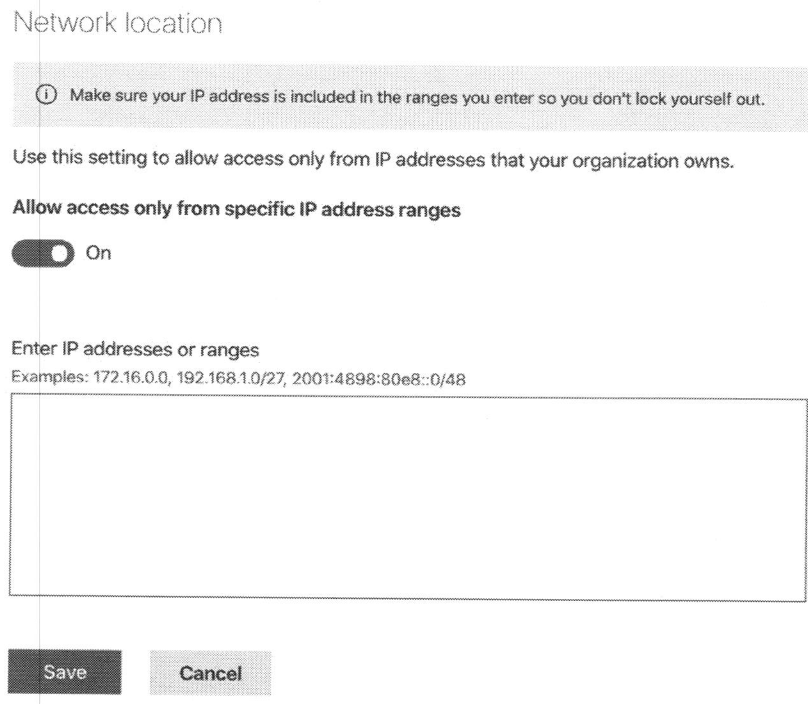

Figure 11.19 – Network location

6. Finally, you can set the option to allow or block access for **Apps that don't use modern authentication**, as shown in the following screenshot:

Apps that don't use modern authentication

Some third-party apps and previous versions of Office can't enforce device-based restrictions. Use this setting to block all access from these apps.

Allow access

Block access

Save Cancel

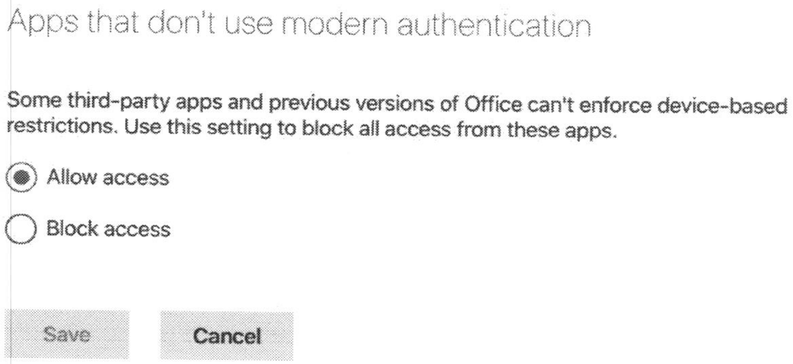

Figure 11.20 – Apps that don't use modern authentication

It is highly recommended that Microsoft 365 Administrators review these settings where they have users accessing content within SharePoint Online and OneDrive.

Organizational needs and policies will, of course, differ, but it is good practice to use these settings as a baseline to protect access to your Office 365 documents and data.

> **Important note**
>
> The access control settings described here are a good starting point for protecting and securing access to your data within Microsoft 365. In order to apply more advanced protection, consider configuring Conditional Access Policies and Azure AD Identity Protection, as described in the earlier chapters of this book.

In this section, we have shown you some quick and easy ways to protect your files and folders stored in SharePoint Online and OneDrive Sites and Document Libraries.

We showed you how the access control settings in the SharePoint Online Admin Center can be used to apply policies for unmanaged devices, idle session timeout settings, and allow access only from specified IP address ranges. We also showed you how to allow or block apps that do not use modern authentication.

In the final section of this chapter, we will examine the principles of allowing external user access to your Microsoft 365 environment by using Azure Active Directory B2B collaboration.

Allowing external user access with B2B sharing

With **Azure AD B2B**, Microsoft 365 administrators have the ability to enable and control cross-organization collaboration. This allows you to invite external users to access apps and resources within your Office 365 environment, while also requiring these external users to comply with the security principles that you have defined for your organization, such as Multi-Factor Authentication or Conditional Access.

There are some licensing requirements that relate to Azure AD B2B, and you can allow up to five guest users per Azure AD license.

Inviting external users is a very straightforward process, and is shown in the following steps:

1. Log into the Azure portal at `https://portal.azure.com` and navigate to **Azure Active Directory | Users**:
2. Select the **New guest user** option, as shown in the following screenshot:

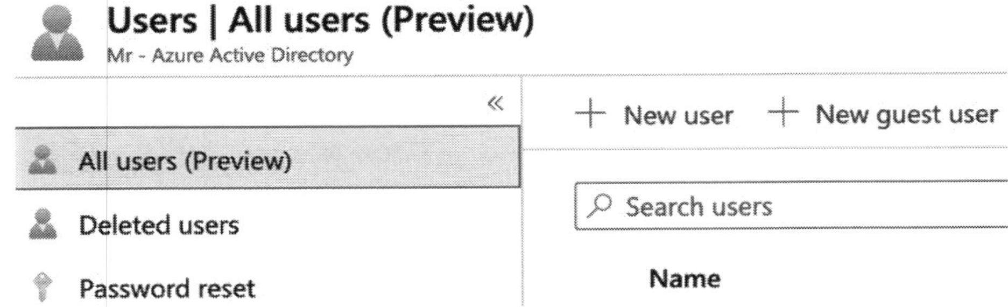

Figure 11.21 – New guest user

3. You will see the following options, where you can either create the user yourself or send an invitation to the user:

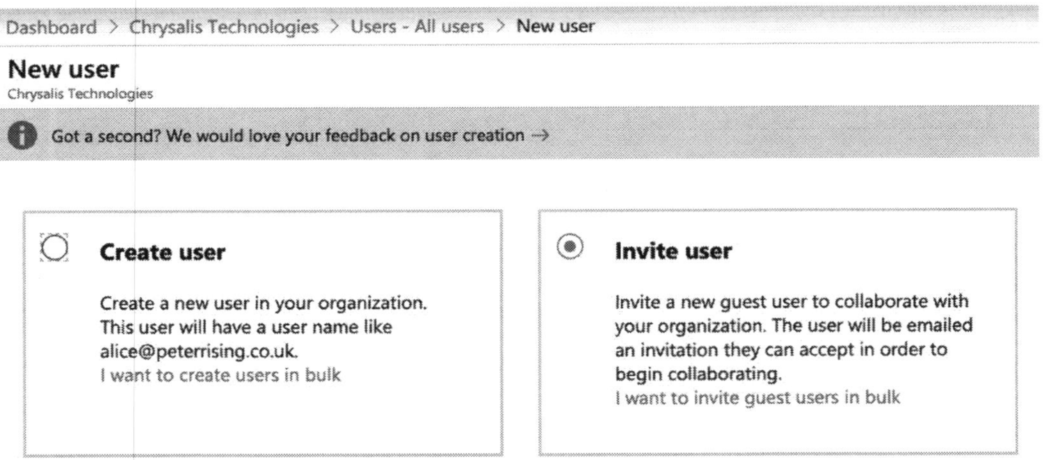

Figure 11.22 – New guest user

4. In this example, we will choose to send an invitation to an external user who is using a personal **Google account**, as shown in the following screenshot:

Identity

Name ⓘ — Crispin Delaney

Email address * ⓘ — crispin.delaney@gmail.com

First name — Crispin

Last name — Delaney

Personal message

Please accept this invitation to access our Office 365 resources

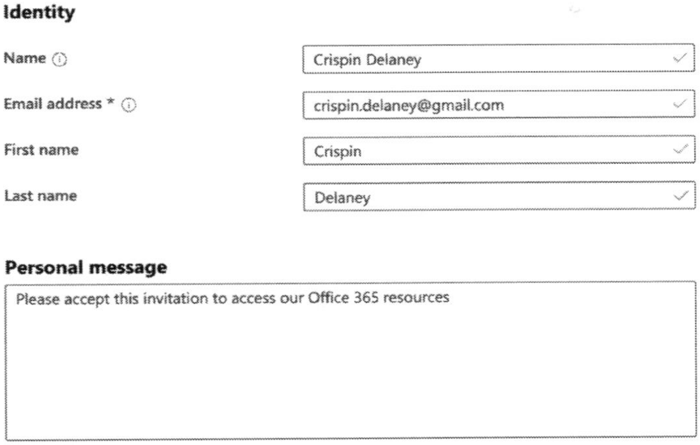

Figure 11.23 – User details

5. Further down the guest user creation dialog, we can control what the new guest user will be able to access by assigning them to groups, allowing or blocking sign in, setting a country usage location, and assigning roles, as shown in the following screenshot:

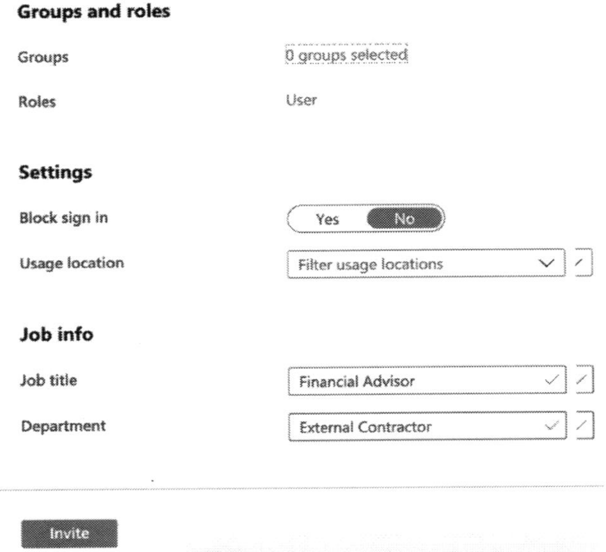

Figure 11.24 – Groups and roles

6. Once you have made the required selections for your external user, click on **Invite**. The invitation will be generated, as follows:

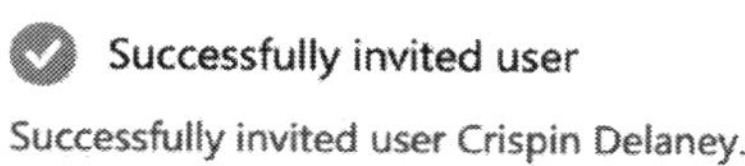

Figure 11.25 – Successful invitation

7. Now, our target guest user will receive an invitation email in their Gmail account, as shown in the following screenshot:

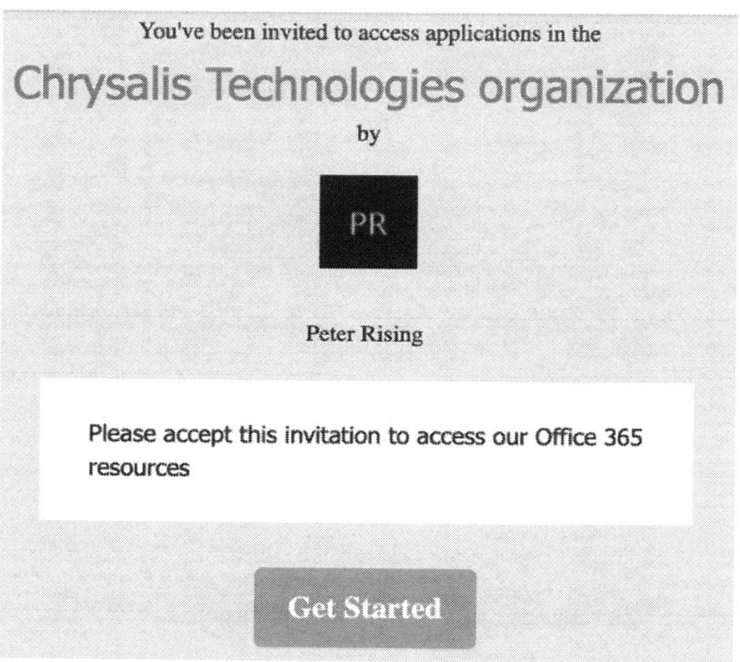

Figure 11.26 – Guest user invitation

8. By clicking on the **Get Started** link in the invitation email, the guest user will be prompted to click **Next** to create an account, as shown in the following screenshot:

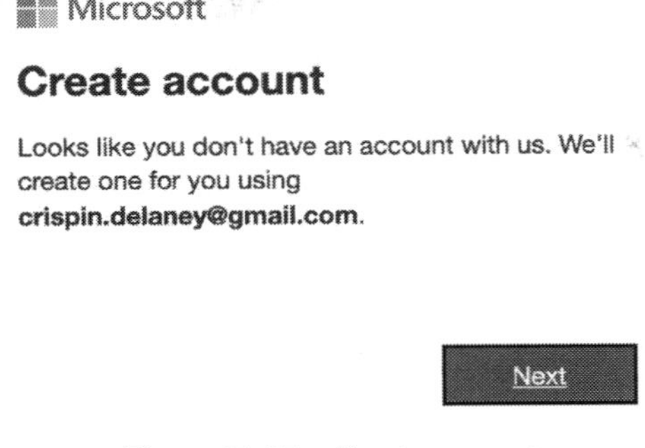

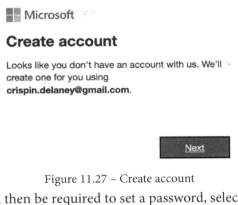

Figure 11.27 – Create account

The guest user will then be required to set a password, select a region, and provide their date of birth. They will also receive a further verification email with a code they will need to enter.

9. Once this has all been completed, they will see the permissions review dialog, as shown in the following screenshot. They must click on **Accept** to complete the process:

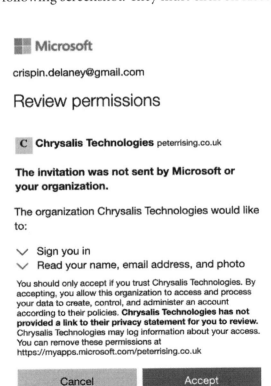

Figure 11.28 – Review permissions

The user is now logged into your organization's Office 365 environment and will be able to access any apps or resources you have assigned to them. In this example, we have not assigned the user to any apps yet, but this can easily be done via group memberships:

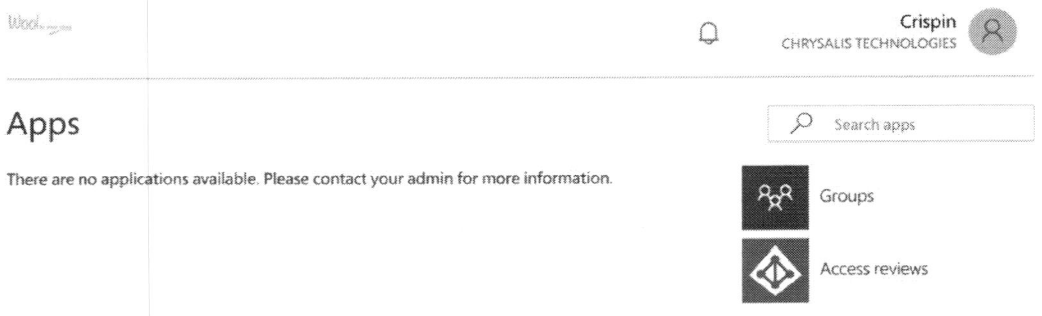

Figure 11.29 – Apps

10. Back in the Azure portal, you will now be able to see the new **Guest user** object, as shown in the following screenshot:

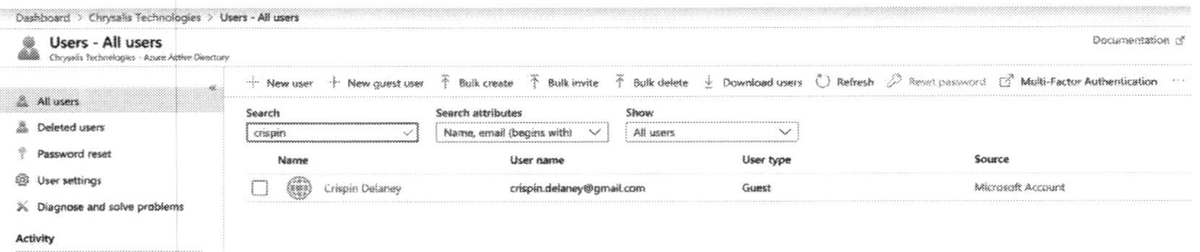

Figure 11.30 – Guest user object

When we select the user, we can see that they retain their own identity. However, we can also apply our organizational requirements to them in order for them to be able to access the apps and resources within our environment:

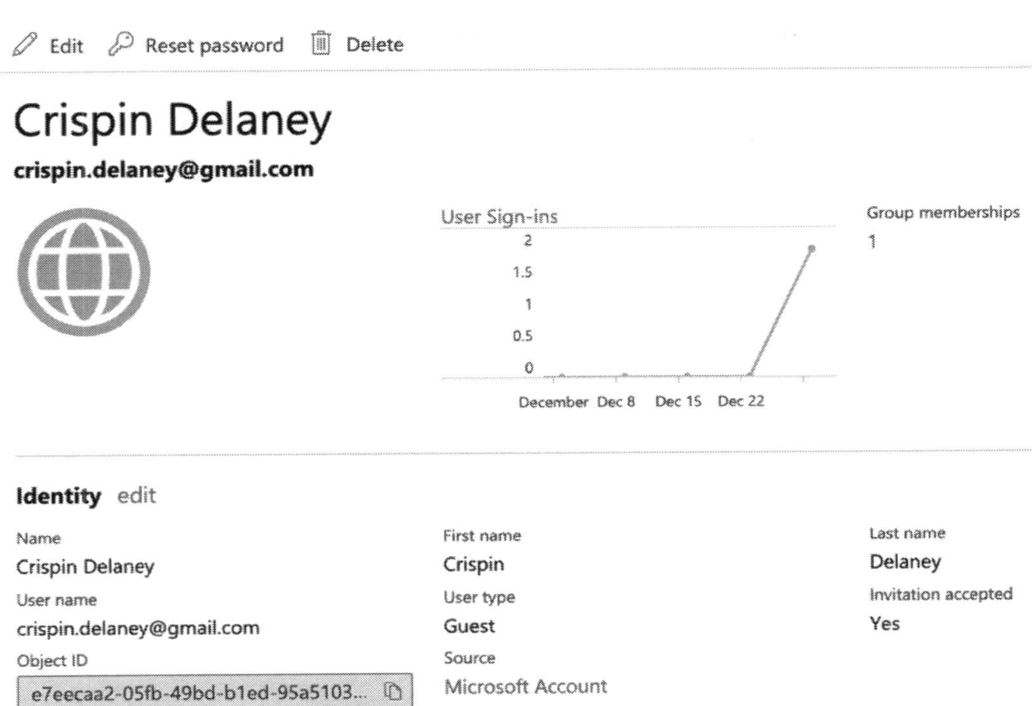

Figure 11.31 – Guest user details

Azure B2B is a simple yet powerful way to allow external parties access to the apps and resources in your Microsoft 365 environment, all while retaining control of what they are allowed to do and the security principles they must adhere to in order to gain access.

> **Important note**
>
> SharePoint Online and OneDrive have slightly different invitation mechanisms for external/guest users. The options for external access can be found in the **SharePoint Admin Center**, under the **Sharing** section.

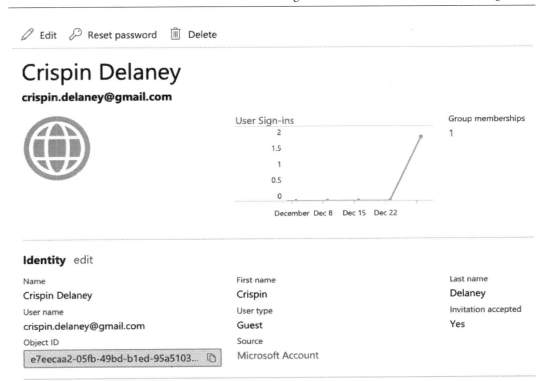

Summary

In this chapter, we examined the principles of securing access to your Microsoft 365 environment by using features such as privileged access management to grant users just enough access to specific tasks within Microsoft 365, instead of assigning them to roles that have additional capabilities.

We also showed you how the Customer Lockbox is used to ensure that Microsoft support engineers must specifically request permission to access your tenant, and that their activities will be recorded in an audit log. In addition, we demonstrated how access controls can easily be applied for SharePoint and OneDrive via the SharePoint Admin Center, as well as how Azure B2B sharing allows you to invite external users into your organization to access your apps and resources in a secure and controlled manner.

In the next chapter, we will introduce you to Azure Information Protection, which is a powerful Azure AD Premium feature that allows Microsoft 365 administrators to configure labels and policies in the Azure portal and synchronize these to the Microsoft 365 Admin Center using unified labeling.

Users are then able to apply label classifications to emails and documents in order to protect them and ensure that only authorized recipients can access the content.

Questions

1. True or False: Privileged Access Management is currently supported only for Exchange Online.

   a. True

   b. False

2. With Azure B2B, how many guest users can be licensed to a single Azure AD license?

   a. 3

   b. 5

   c. 10

   d. 15

3. When a Customer Lockbox access request is made by Microsoft, how long does the representative have access to the Microsoft 365 environment?

    a. 1 hour

    b. 2 hours

    c. 4 hours

    d. 6 hours

    e. 1 day

4. Which of the following is not an available policy type in Privileged Access Management?

    a. Task

    b. Role Group

    c. Role

    d. Task Group

5. Which of the following is not an option when configuring access controls in the SharePoint Admin Center?

    a. Unmanaged devices

    b. Unmanaged users

    c. Idle session timeout

    d. Network Location

    e. Apps that don't use modern authentication

6. Where in the Microsoft 365 Admin Center would you configure Privileged Access Management?

    a. Settings | Services and Add-ins

    b. Settings | Domains

    c. Settings | Security and Privacy

    d. Settings | Organization Profile

7. What are the methods of setting up Azure B2B guest users (choose two)?

    a. Invite User

    b. Delegate User

    c. Create User

    d. Synchronize User

    e. Add existing user to a group

8. True or False: The SharePoint Online external sharing setting is the same as for Azure AD B2B.

    a. True

    b. False

9. Which of the following subscriptions will provide the Customer Lockbox functionality (choose two)?

    a. Microsoft 365 E5

    b. Microsoft 365 E3

    c. Office 365 E3

    d. Office 365 E5

    e. Office 365 Business Premium

10. True or False: Azure B2B guest users can be forced to register for Multi-Factor Authentication in order to gain access to your Microsoft 365 environment.

    a. True

    b. False

References

Please refer to the following links for more information regarding what was covered in this chapter:

- Privileged Access Management: `https://docs.microsoft.com/en-us/microsoft-365/compliance/privileged-access-management-overview`
- Configuring Privileged Access Management: `https://docs.microsoft.com/en-us/microsoft-365/compliance/privileged-access-management-configuration`

- Customer Lockbox (and auditing Customer Lockbox requests) in Office 365: `https://docs.microsoft.com/en-us/microsoft-365/compliance/customer-lockbox-requests`
- Securing SharePoint Sites and files: `https://docs.microsoft.com/en-gb/microsoft-365/enterprise/sharepoint-file-access-policies`
- Azure Active Directory B2B: `https://docs.microsoft.com/en-us/azure/active-directory/b2b/`
- Troubleshooting Azure Active Directory B2B: `https://docs.microsoft.com/en-us/azure/active-directory/b2b/troubleshoot`

12
Azure Information Protection

With **data governance** (**DG**) becoming more and more important, Microsoft 365 administrators need to consider how to identify and classify all of the data stored in their organization and take steps to protect against any sort of data loss, whether it be accidental or malicious.

Microsoft provides **Azure Information Protection (AIP)** to respond to these requirements. AIP enables the use of labels and policies to allow your users to classify and protect the data they are working with. This includes documents and emails. When you protect an email or document, encryption is applied, ensuring that the email or document may only be accessed by those who have permission. An example of AIP would be to apply a **Do not forward** label to an email, meaning that the recipient of that email is unable to forward the email to other parties who are not authorized to look at that content.

In this chapter, we will introduce the features of AIP. You will learn how to plan your organization's AIP deployment and activate the Azure Rights Management service, and how to use classifications, labeling, and protection. In addition, we will show you how to create labels and label policies, use the AIP scanner to identify and protect on-premises data, deploy the AIP client where required, and track and revoke protected documents using the document tracking site, Microsoft Office, or File Explorer.

We shall cover these topics in the following order:

- Planning and implementing an AIP deployment for your organization
- Setting up AIP labels and policies
- Use the AIP scanner to detect and protect on-premises content
- Tracking and revoking protected documents

Planning and implementing an AIP deployment for your organization

In order to effectively plan for an AIP deployment in your organization, you need to have an understanding of how AIP is licensed in order to decide which Microsoft 365 subscriptions you are going to require for your users.

There are four subscription options available for AIP. These are described in the following table:

Name	Included in License plans	Features
Free	Any Azure AD account	Users are able to view or read any protected content.
AIP for Office 365	Office 365 Enterprise E3 Office 365 Enterprise E5	Users may apply Information Rights Management features and apply email message encryption.
AIP Premium P1	Standalone plan Microsoft 365 Business EM+S E3 Microsoft 365 E3	Users may manually apply label classifications to emails and documents to protect content.
AIP Premium P2	Standalone plan EM+S E5 Microsoft 365 E5	Automatic labeling may be applied to emails and documents when sensitive content is detected. Additionally, the AIP scanner may be deployed to detect and protect on-premises content.

To summarize this, should you need to encrypt emails and documents, but not apply label classifications, then AIP for Office 365 is going to work just fine. If you need to take this a step further and require label classification capabilities, then AIP Premium P1 is the way to go. Finally, if you require all of the features mentioned in the preceding table, but also need to be able to automatically apply label classifications to sensitive content and use the on-premises AIP scanner, then you will need to use AIP Premium P2.

Once you have determined your AIP licensing requirements and acquired the necessary licenses for your users, you may proceed and check the activation settings for AIP within your Microsoft 365 tenant. Tenants that were provisioned after 2018 will have AIP activated by default. However, activation can be checked or completed by using any of the following methods:

- Office 365 Admin Center
- Azure portal
- Azure AD Rights Management PowerShell

Let's look at each of these methods.

Checking AIP activation status using the Office 365 Admin Center

In order to manage the activation status of AIP from the Office 365 Admin Center, you must be a Global Administrator, Security Administrator, or Azure Information Protection Administrator. You will need to navigate to `https://admin.microsoft.com` and complete the following steps:

1. Select **Settings | Services & add-ins | Microsoft Azure Information Protection**, as shown in the following screenshot:

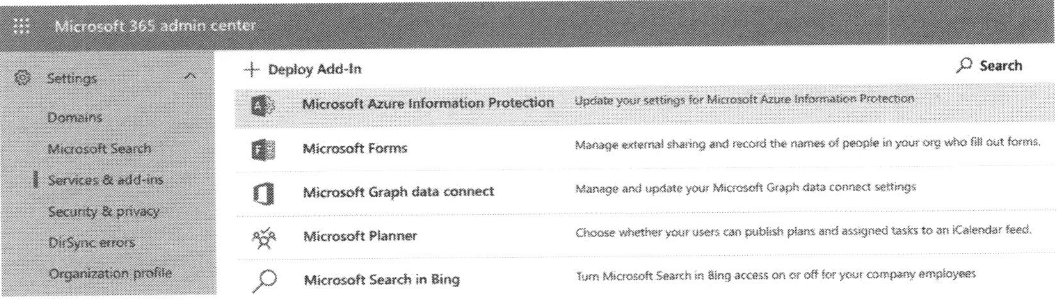

Figure 12.1 – Services and add-ins

2. Click on **Manage Microsoft Azure Information Protection Settings**. You will see the option to **activate** or **deactivate** rights management, as shown in the following screenshot:

rights management

Rights management is activated

Rights Management safeguards your emails and documents and helps you securely share this data with your colleagues.

To disable Rights Management, click deactivate.

deactivate

additional configuration

You can configure advanced features for Rights Management using Microsoft Azure.

This requires a one-time sign-up for a free Azure subscription to access Azure Active Directory.

advanced features

resources

- What is Rights Management?
- Rights Management Deployment roadmap
- Using Rights Management
- FAQs for Rights Management

Figure 12.2 – Rights management

The preceding screenshot also shows you an option for **advanced features**. If you select this option, you will be taken to the AIP page within the Azure portal. Next, we will take a look at the Azure portal options for AIP.

Checking AIP activation status using the Azure portal

In order to manage the activation status of AIP from the Azure portal, you must be a Global Administrator, Security Administrator, or Azure Information Protection Administrator.

You will need to navigate to `https://portal.azure.com` and complete the following steps:

1. Select **All services | Azure Information Protection**, as shown in the following screenshot:

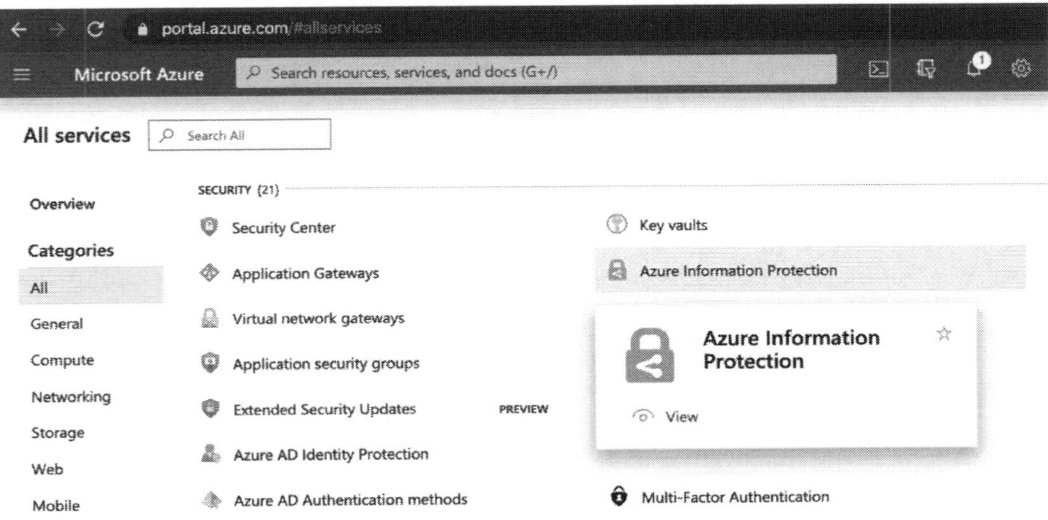

Figure 12.3 – Azure Information Protection

2. You will be taken the Azure Information Protection section. From the left-hand side menu, click on **Protection activation** from the **Manage** section, as shown in the following screenshot:

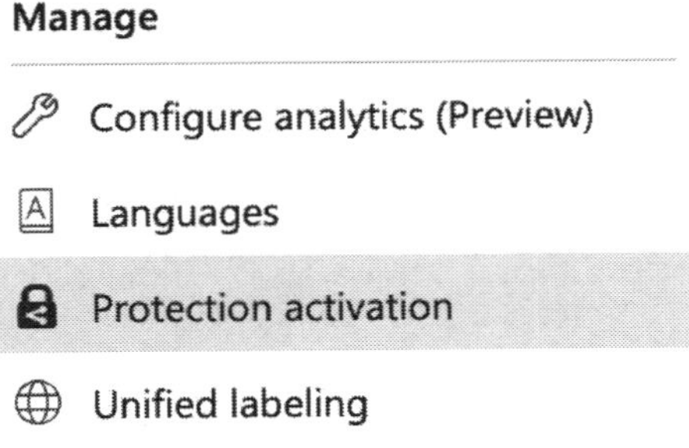

Figure 12.4 – Protection activation

3. Next, you will see the activation status for AIP in your tenant, as the following screenshot illustrates:

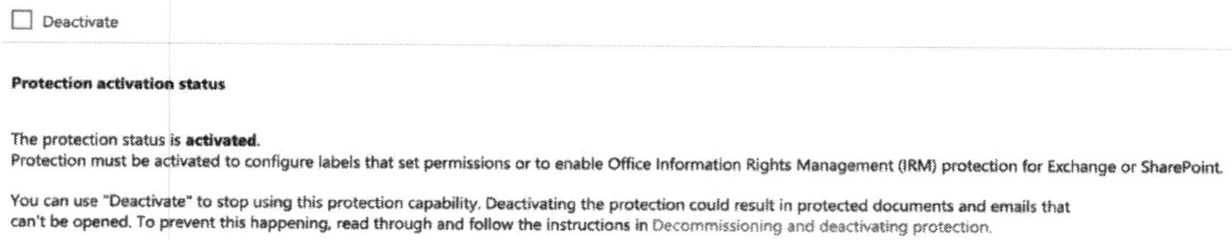

☐ Deactivate

Protection activation status

The protection status is **activated**.
Protection must be activated to configure labels that set permissions or to enable Office Information Rights Management (IRM) protection for Exchange or SharePoint.

You can use "Deactivate" to stop using this protection capability. Deactivating the protection could result in protected documents and emails that can't be opened. To prevent this happening, read through and follow the instructions in Decommissioning and deactivating protection.

Figure 12.5 – Activation status

As with the Office 365 Admin Center, you have the same options to **Activate** or **Deactivate** the AIP feature for your tenant. Finally, let's look at how you can check the AIP activation status using the Azure `AIPService` PowerShell module.

Checking AIP activation status using the Azure AIPService PowerShell

In order to manage the activation status of AIP from Windows PowerShell, you will need to install the `AIPService` module. The `AIPService` module replaces an older module called the `AADRM` module. The `AADRM` module must be uninstalled on the computer that you are using PowerShell on before you can install the newer `AIPService` module. This process is detailed in the following steps:

1. Run PowerShell as an administrator on your computer and run the following command to uninstall the older module, if you have it installed already:

```
Uninstall-Module -Name AADRM
```

2. Now, you may proceed and install the new `AIPService` module by running the following command:

```
Install-Module -Name AIPService
```

3. Next, we need to connect to the service. This is done by running the following command:

```
Connect-AIPService
```

4. When prompted, enter your Azure AD Global Administrator credentials to authenticate to Office 365. Once connected, run the following command to check whether AIP is activated for your tenant:

```
Get-AIPService
```

5. This command will show you the current activation status for AIP. The following screenshot shows all of the preceding commands running in sequence and illustrates that AIP is enabled for this example:

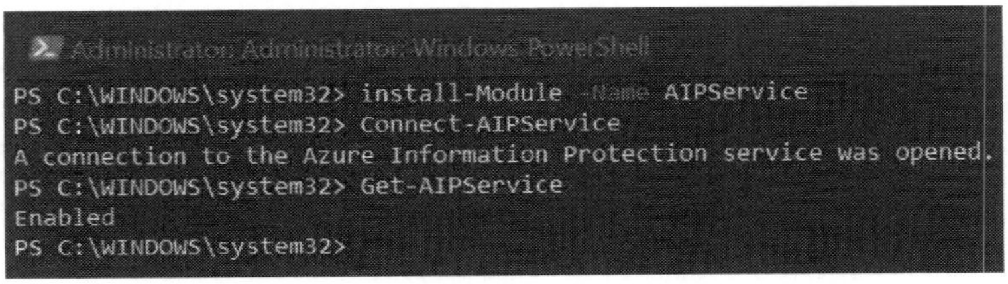

```
Administrator: Administrator: Windows PowerShell
PS C:\WINDOWS\system32> install-Module -Name AIPService
PS C:\WINDOWS\system32> Connect-AIPService
A connection to the Azure Information Protection service was opened.
PS C:\WINDOWS\system32> Get-AIPService
Enabled
PS C:\WINDOWS\system32>
```

Figure 12.6 – AIP activation status in PowerShell

6. If the status had been set to disabled, AIP could be activated for the tenant by running the following command:

```
Enable-AIPService
```

Now that we have ensured that AIP is activated, we are one step closer to being able to start using the AIP service to create labels and policies. One additional step that is important to complete at this point is configuring one of more superusers for AIP. This requirement will be described in the next section.

Configuring AIP superusers

AIP uses the **Azure Rights Management service** to protect organizational data. One or more AIP superusers can be created in order to ensure that there is always someone authorized to read or inspect AIP protected data. This is important in the event that a user leaves the business and they have applied protection to documents. In this situation, AIP superusers have the ability to alter or completely remove the protection.

The superuser feature is not enabled by default, and no users are assigned to the role. In order to enable this feature, we need to complete the following steps:

1. Run Windows PowerShell as an administrator and connect to `AIPService`, as demonstrated in the previous section.
2. Run the following command:

```
Enable-AIPServiceSuperUserFeature
```

In the following screenshot, we can see the successful activation of the `super user feature`:

```
Administrator: Administrator: Windows PowerShell
PS C:\WINDOWS\system32> Enable-AIPServiceSuperUserFeature
The super user feature is enabled for the Azure Information Protection service.
PS C:\WINDOWS\system32>
```

Figure 12.7 – Enabling the super user feature in PowerShell

3. Now that the feature is enabled, we can assign the AIP superuser role to either individual users or to a group of users who are to be trusted with this role. Do this by executing the following PowerShell commands:

```
Add-AipServiceSuperuser
Set-AipServiceSuperUserGroup
```

> **Important note**
> It is good practice to assign superusers individually as opposed to using groups. This is due to the fact that Azure Rights Management will cache group content, which can result in delays when adding or removing members of a group.

4. In order to see which individual users are set as AIP superusers, use the following command:

```
Get-AIPServiceSuperUser
```

> **Important note**
>
> You can limit the number of Global Administrators in your Microsoft 365 tenant by adding users as AIP Service Administrators. This can be done by using the `Add-AIPServiceRoleBasedAdministrator` command from within Windows PowerShell. Users assigned this role are able to enable the superuser feature and also assign other users the superuser role.

So, to recap what we have learned in this section, we have shown you the various methods you can use to check whether AIP has been enabled in your Microsoft 365 tenant, along with how to activate or deactivate the AIP feature as required. Now that you know how to access and enable AIP and set up super users, we can look at how to create labels and label policies, as well as how to enable unified labeling.

Setting up AIP labels and policies

The core functionality of Azure Information Protection is based on labels and policies. Microsoft 365 Administrators can define **sensitivity labels** in the Azure portal. These labels can be configured with protection settings, visual markings (such as watermarks), and, depending on your subscriptions, they may also include conditions so that a label can be automatically applied.

Once the AIP labels have been created, policies may then be defined in order to determine which users will be able to see and use the labels within their Microsoft Office applications.

> **Important note**
>
> At the time of writing this book, sensitivity labels are available within Microsoft Office applications for Windows, Mac, Office Online, and iOS and Android.

Historically, AIP labels have been controlled and deployed from the Azure portal. More recently, however, the **Unified labeling** feature has been included, which allows you to synchronize and manage your labels from the Microsoft 365 Security and Compliance Center.

Let's take a look at how this works, starting with setting up labels from the Azure portal.

Setting up labels

Once you have activated Azure Information Protection for your tenant, you will have some predefined labels already present. These can be found in the Azure portal, under **All services | Azure Information Protection | Classifications | Labels**, as shown in the following screenshot:

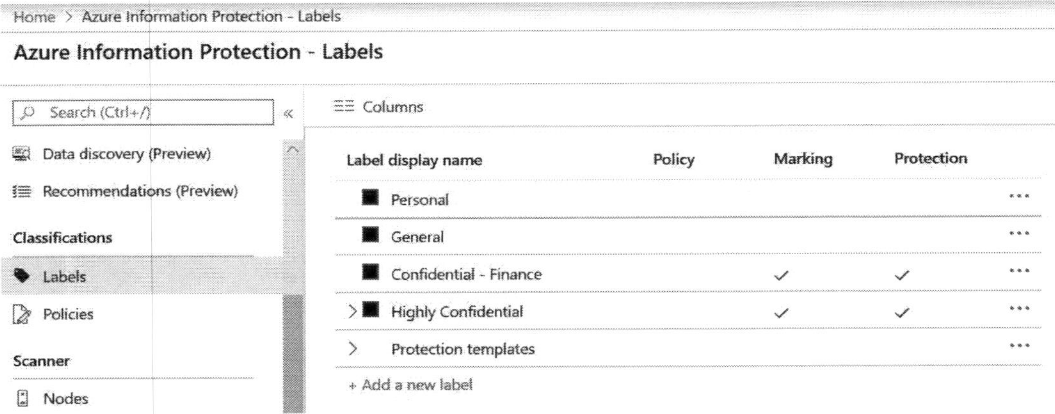

Figure 12.8 – AIP labels

These default labels may be suitable for many organizations and are often a good starting point when considering an AIP deployment pilot to a small group of users. As you will note from the preceding screenshot, the labels have different settings related to protection and marking.

The **Highly Confidential** label may also be expanded to show available sublabels. Let's take a look at the various options you have for labels by going through the process of setting up a new label. To do this, we need to complete the following steps:

1. Click on **Add a new label**. You will see the following screen:

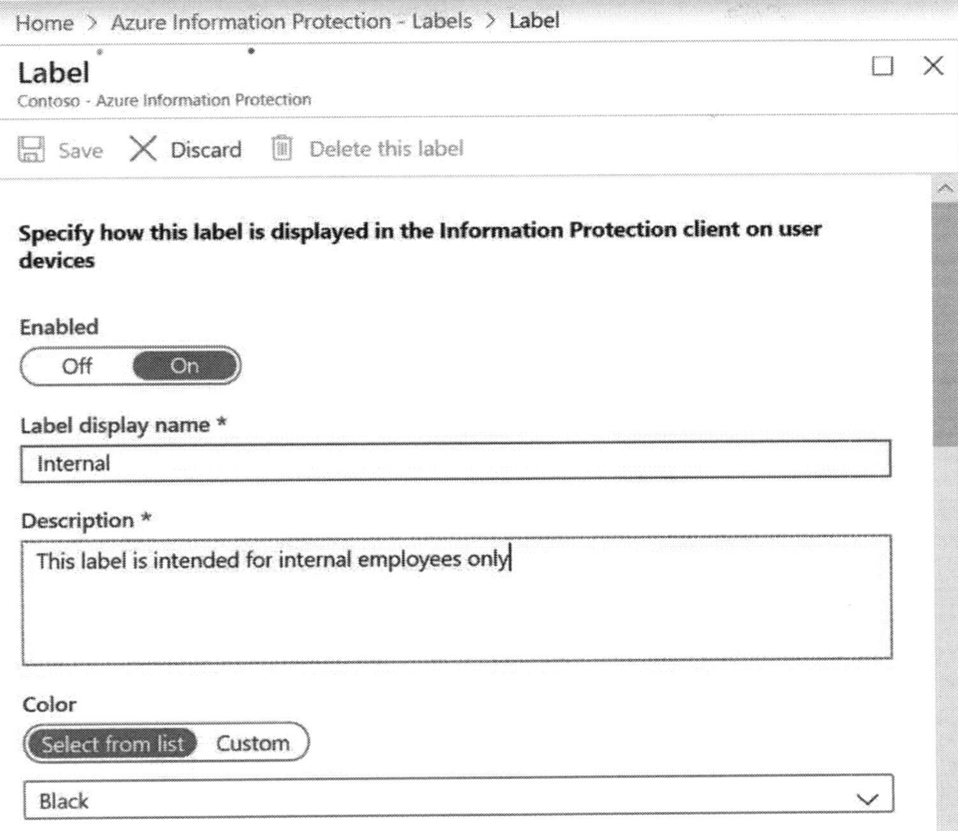

Figure 12.9 – Adding a new label

In this example, we will create a label called **Internal**, which is only intended for use by internal tenant users. We need to enter a **Label display name**, a **Description**, and choose a label **Color**, if required, as the preceding screenshot illustrates. Additionally, we can set the **Enabled** slider to **On** or **Off**, depending on whether we wish the label to be activated immediately. Alternatively, we can choose to activate it at a later time.

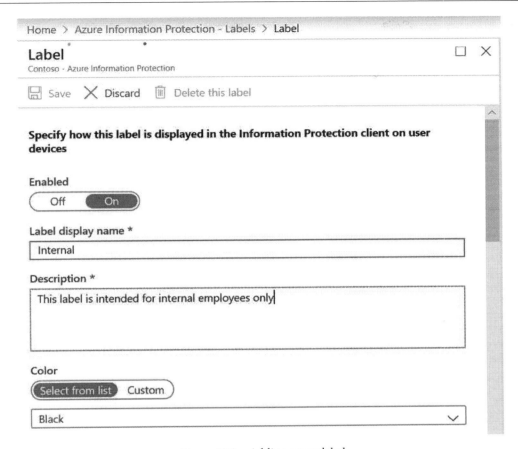

2. Next, we need to scroll down and select the option to **Protect**, which can be found under **Set permissions for documents and emails containing this label**, as shown in the following screenshot:

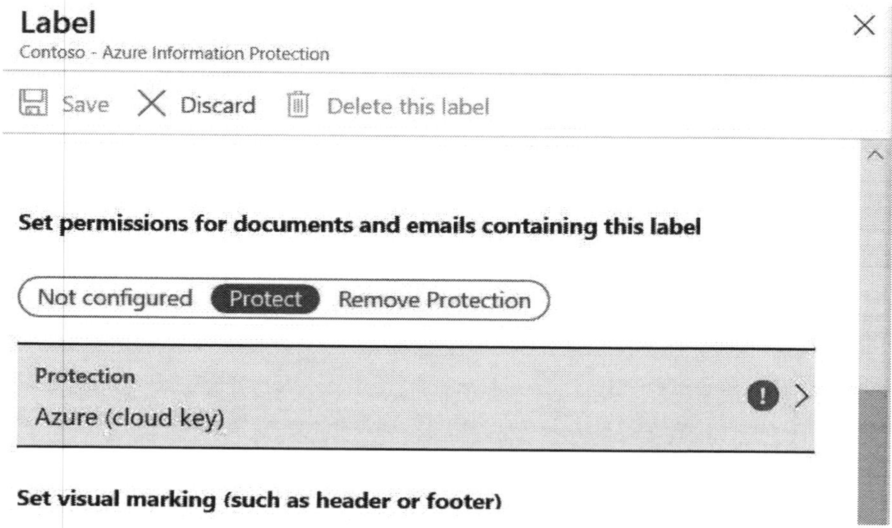

Figure 12.10 – Protection settings

3. Next, under **Protection**, click on **Azure (cloud key)**. You will see the protection options shown in the following screenshot:

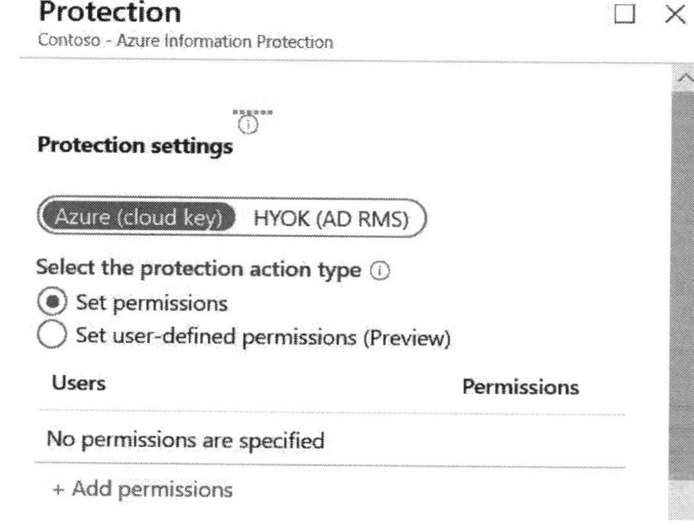

Figure 12.11 – Cloud key settings

4. From the **Label protection** settings, you can choose between an **Azure (cloud key)** or the option to hold your own key with **HYOK (AD RMS)**. In most cases, and for the purposes of this example, **Azure (cloud key)** is the recommended option.
5. You then have the option to **select the protection action type**. We have two options here. These are **Set permissions** and **Set user-defined permissions (Preview)**. We are going to set up this label with traditional permissions by leaving the **Set permissions** option selected.

> **Important note**
>
> The **Set user-defined permissions (Preview)** option allows you to configure email-only labels so that you can apply the *Do not forward* option to emails.

6. Next, with **Set permissions** selected, click on **Add permissions**. You will see the options shown in the following screenshot:

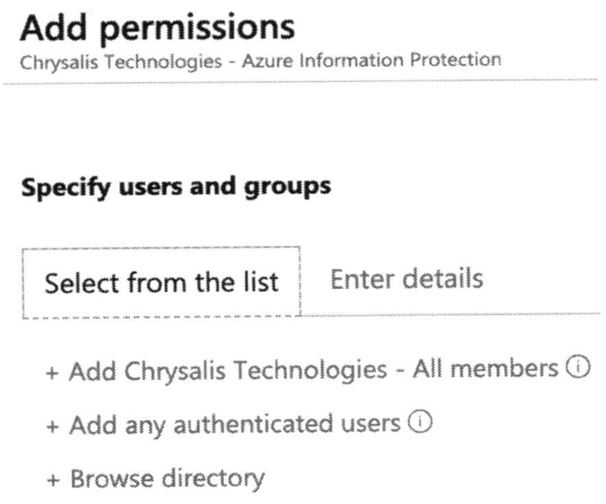

Add permissions
Chrysalis Technologies - Azure Information Protection

Specify users and groups

Select from the list | Enter details

+ Add Chrysalis Technologies - All members ⓘ
+ Add any authenticated users ⓘ
+ Browse directory

Figure 12.12 – Setting label permissions

7. From the **Add permissions** options, you can choose to add all tenant members, any authenticated users, or you may browse the directory to search for specific Azure AD Users and Groups. The **Enter details** tab is also available, should you wish to specify any external users or domains who should have permissions. In this example, however, we will choose the first available option, which is to add **All Members**.

8. Next, if we scroll down the **Add permissions** options, we will see the available permissions options for the users we are assigning to the label. We will leave the default setting of **Co-Owner** as-is, which means that users have full permission to access any content that this label may be applied to. This is shown in the following screenshot:

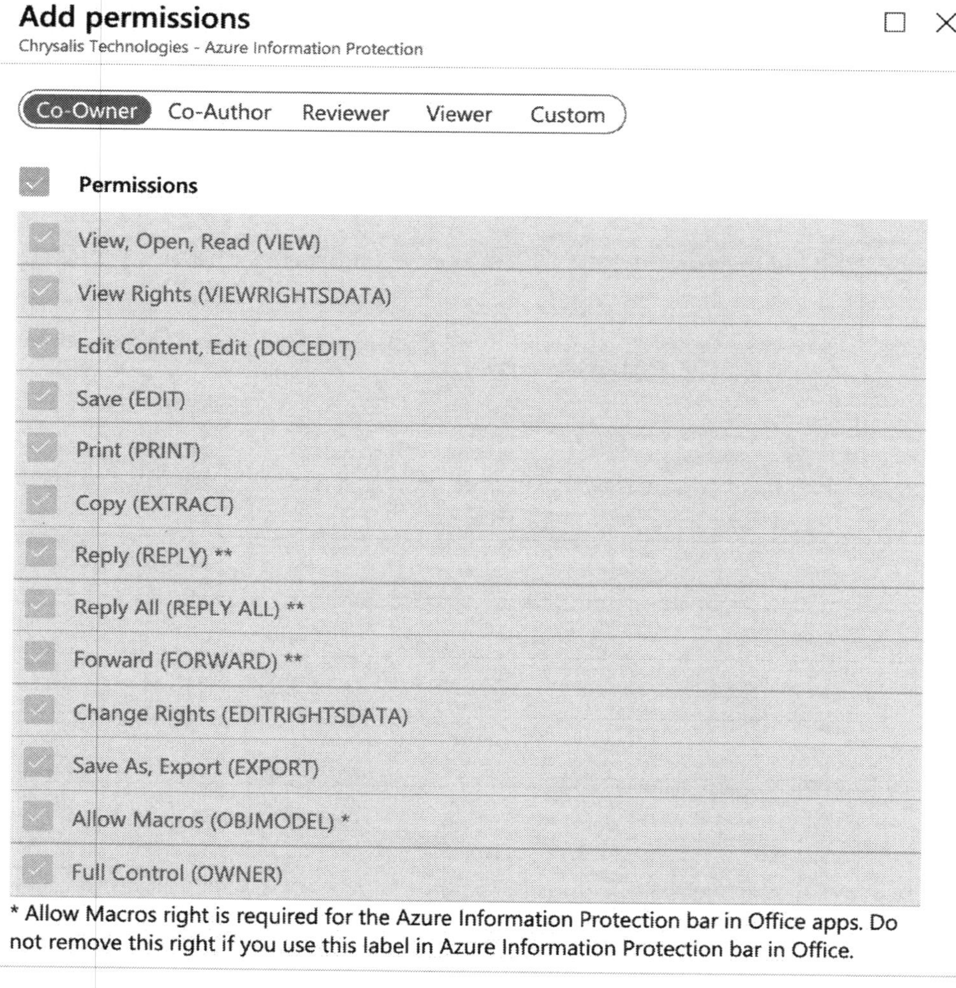

Figure 12.13 – Permissions options

9. Click on **OK** to finish setting up the permissions. This will take you back to the **Protection settings** screen, as shown in the following screenshot:

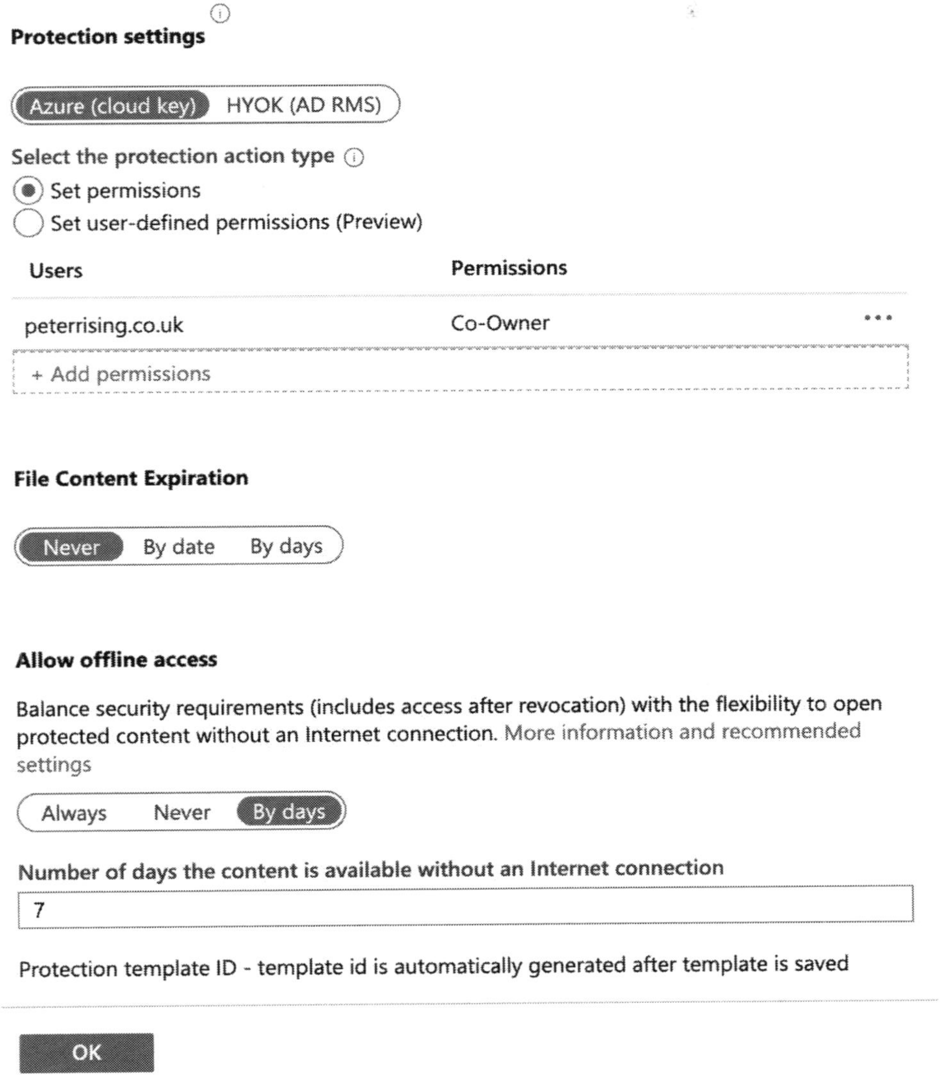

Protection settings

Azure (cloud key) HYOK (AD RMS)

Select the protection action type

Set permissions

Set user-defined permissions (Preview)

Users	Permissions
peterrising.co.uk	Co-Owner

+ Add permissions

File Content Expiration

Never By date By days

Allow offline access

Balance security requirements (includes access after revocation) with the flexibility to open protected content without an Internet connection. More information and recommended settings

Always Never By days

Number of days the content is available without an Internet connection

7

Protection template ID - template id is automatically generated after template is saved

OK

Figure 12.14 – Protection settings

You will see additional options for **File Content Expiration** in this section, as illustrated in the preceding screenshot. You can set expiry dates for access, configure offline access, and also set a number of days for which access can be granted without an internet connection. Click **OK** to complete these settings. This takes you back to the main label creation dialog, as shown in the following screenshot:

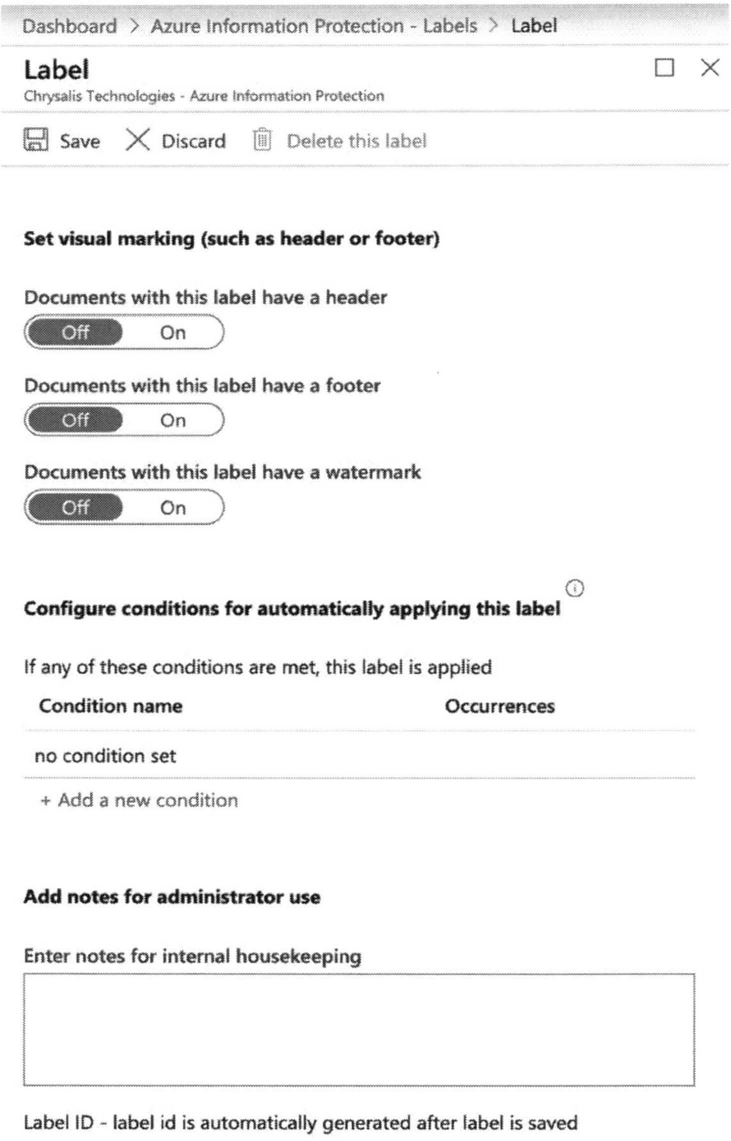

Dashboard > Azure Information Protection - Labels > Label

Label

Chrysalis Technologies - Azure Information Protection

Save | Discard | Delete this label

Set visual marking (such as header or footer)

Documents with this label have a header

Off | On

Documents with this label have a footer

Off | On

Documents with this label have a watermark

Off | On

Configure conditions for automatically applying this label

If any of these conditions are met, this label is applied

Condition name	Occurrences
no condition set	

+ Add a new condition

Add notes for administrator use

Enter notes for internal housekeeping

Label ID - label id is automatically generated after label is saved

Figure 12.15 – Additional options

Here, you can set some additional options, such as applying visual markings to content protected by this label.

10. Additionally, you have some options to **Configure conditions for automatically applying this label**. Selecting **Add a new condition** will take you to the following screen, where you can choose from a selection of built-in sensitive information types or define your own:

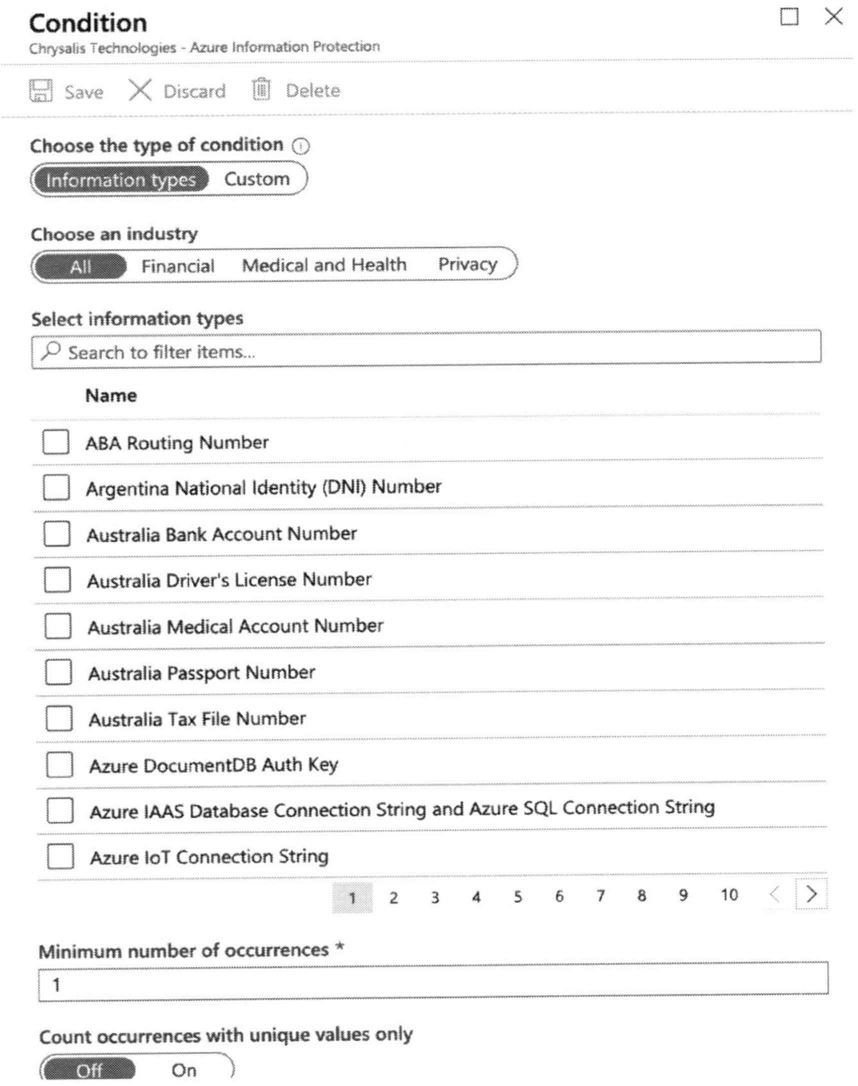

Figure 12.16 – Applying conditions

11. When you have made your selections, click **Save**.

> **Important note**
>
> In order to apply enforced conditions to a label, you will need either an Azure Information Protection P2 license, an EM+S E5 license, or a Microsoft 365 E5 license.

12. You may then choose to have the label applied automatically or recommended this to your users, as shown in the following screenshot:

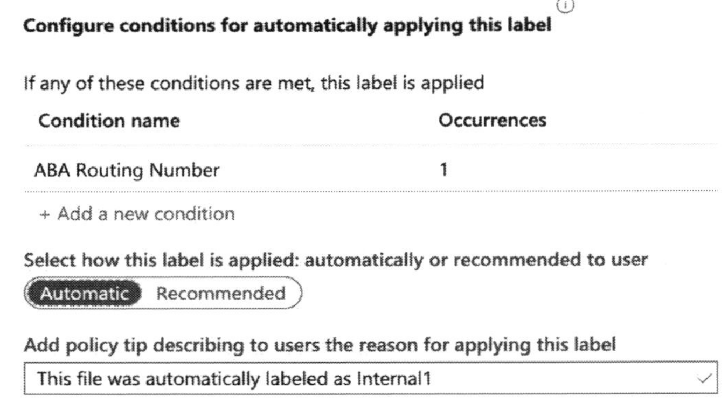

Figure 12.17 – Applying conditions

13. Finally, you can optionally add notes to your label for administrator use. All of the required settings for the new label have now been completed. Click on **Save** to finish creating your label. You will now see your new label in the list of labels, as shown in the following screenshot:

Label display name	Policy	Marking	Protection	
■ Personal				...
■ General				...
■ Confidential - Finance		✓	✓	...
> ■ Highly Confidential		✓	✓	...
■ Internal			✓	...
> Protection templates				...
+ Add a new label				

Figure 12.18 – Labels

> **Important note**
> Note that for this label, we have applied Protection settings, but no visual markings.

So, now that we have shown you how to create a label in Azure Information Protection, let's look at setting up a label policy.

Setting up label policies

Once you have one or more labels defined, the next step is to set up or apply an existing label policy to your users and groups in Azure AD. Label policies can be found in the Azure portal, under **All services | Azure Information Protection | Classifications | Policies**, as shown in the following screenshot:

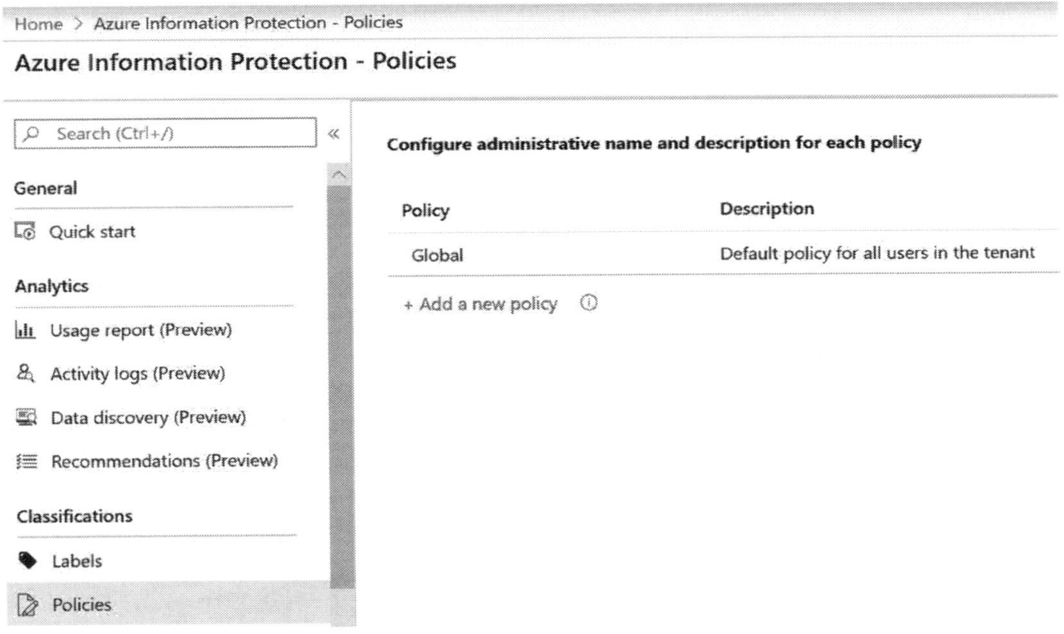

Figure 12.19 – Label policies

You will see one existing policy here named **Global**, which is the **Default policy for all users in the tenant**. Here, you may modify the default policy or add your own. We will show you this process in the following steps:

1. Double-click the **Global** policy to review the settings that have been configured for it, as shown in the following screenshot:

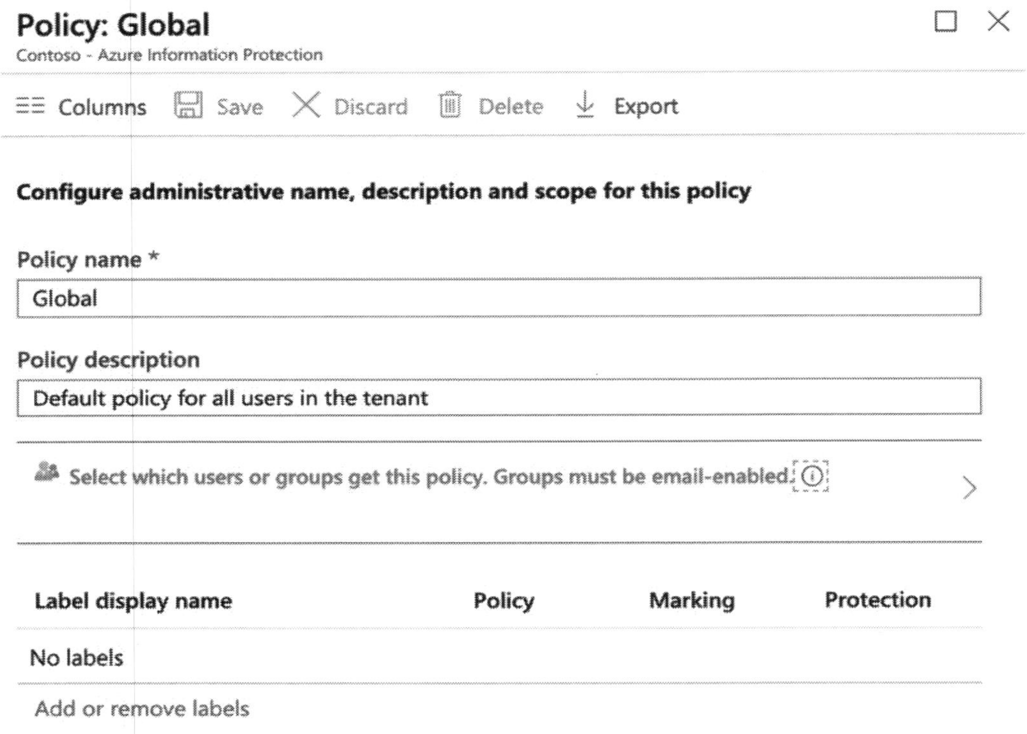

Figure 12.20 – Editing the global policy

We can see the name and description that have been assigned to the policy, and also that we are unable to modify the users or groups that this policy applies to. By default, no labels are assigned to the default Global Policy.

2. We can choose to include some labels by clicking **Add or remove labels**. This will provide us with the options shown in the following screenshot:

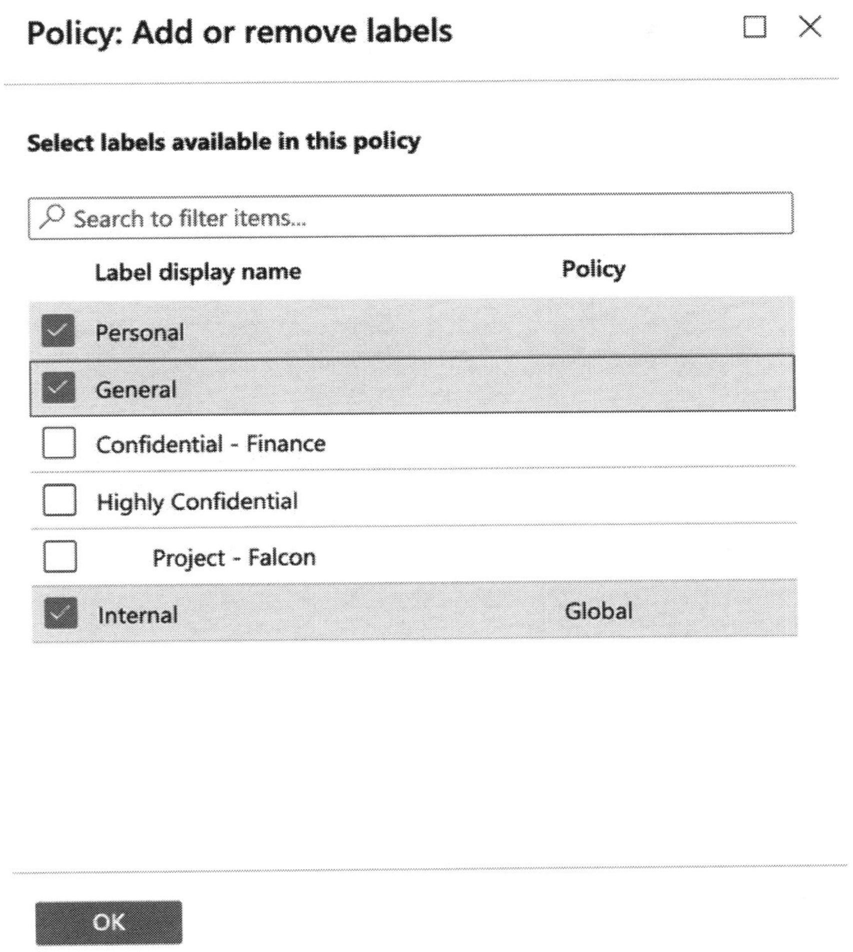

Policy: Add or remove labels

Select labels available in this policy

Search to filter items...

	Label display name	Policy
☑	Personal	
☑	General	
☐	Confidential - Finance	
☐	Highly Confidential	
☐	Project - Falcon	
☑	Internal	Global

OK

Figure 12.21 – Choosing labels for the policy

In this example, we have chosen to add three labels to the default policy (including the **Internal** label, which we set up in the previous step).

3. After clicking **OK**, we can see that our three chosen labels are now included in the policy settings.
4. We are also able to enter a **Title** and **Tooltip**, along with a default label for the policy. In this example, we have set the default label to the **Internal** label, as shown in the following screenshot:

Label display name	Policy	Marking	Protection
Personal	Global		
General	Global		
Internal	Global		✓

Add or remove labels

Configure settings to display and apply on Information Protection end users

Title *

Sensitivity

Tooltip

The current label for this content. This setting identifies the risk to the business if this content is shared with unauthorized people inside or outside the organization.

Select the default label

Internal

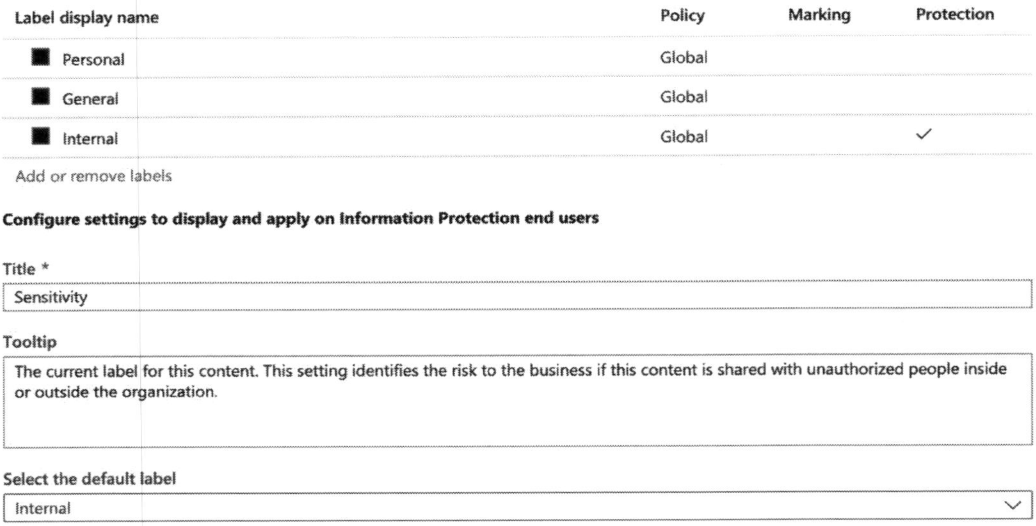

Figure 12.22 – Setting the default label

5. If we scroll down further, we have some additional options we can configure. In this example, we will set the remaining options as per the following screenshot:

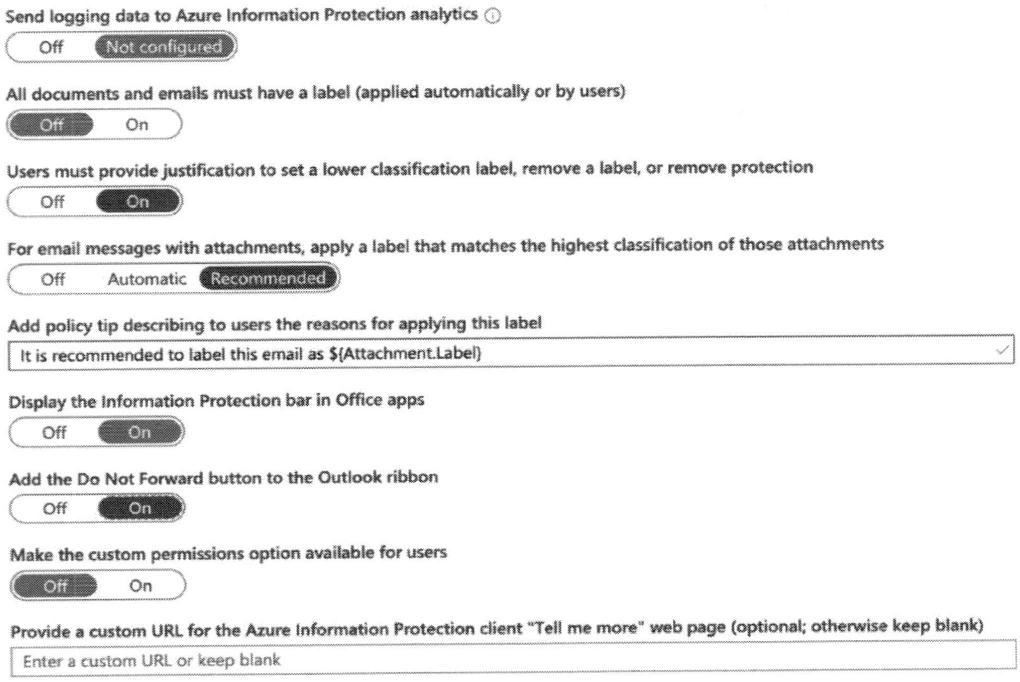

Send logging data to Azure Information Protection analytics
Off | Not configured

All documents and emails must have a label (applied automatically or by users)
Off | On

Users must provide justification to set a lower classification label, remove a label, or remove protection
Off | On

For email messages with attachments, apply a label that matches the highest classification of those attachments
Off | Automatic | Recommended

Add policy tip describing to users the reasons for applying this label
It is recommended to label this email as ${Attachment.Label}

Display the Information Protection bar in Office apps
Off | On

Add the Do Not Forward button to the Outlook ribbon
Off | On

Make the custom permissions option available for users
Off | On

Provide a custom URL for the Azure Information Protection client "Tell me more" web page (optional; otherwise keep blank)
Enter a custom URL or keep blank

Figure 12.23 – Additional options

6. Once you have applied the desired changes to the policy, click on **Save**, and then click on **OK**.

The preceding steps have shown you how to modify the default Global Policy, which, as we have stated, will apply to all users. You will likely want to consider creating your own custom label policy and applying it to selected users or groups in order to roll out labels to your users in a phased approach. You can click **Add a new policy** in order to create your own custom policy. The settings within your custom policy can be configured in exactly the same way as shown in the preceding steps.

Now that we have shown you how to set up or modify AIP labels and label policies from the Azure portal, let's look at how to enable unified labeling in order to manage sensitivity labels from the Microsoft 365 Security and Compliance Center.

Enabling Unified labeling

With Azure Information Protection, you also have the option to use **Unified labeling**. In newer Microsoft 365 tenants, you will find that **Unified labeling** is activated by default. You may can the status of your own tenant by completing the following steps:

1. Navigate to **All services | Azure Information Protection | Manage | Unified labeling**, as shown in the following screenshot:

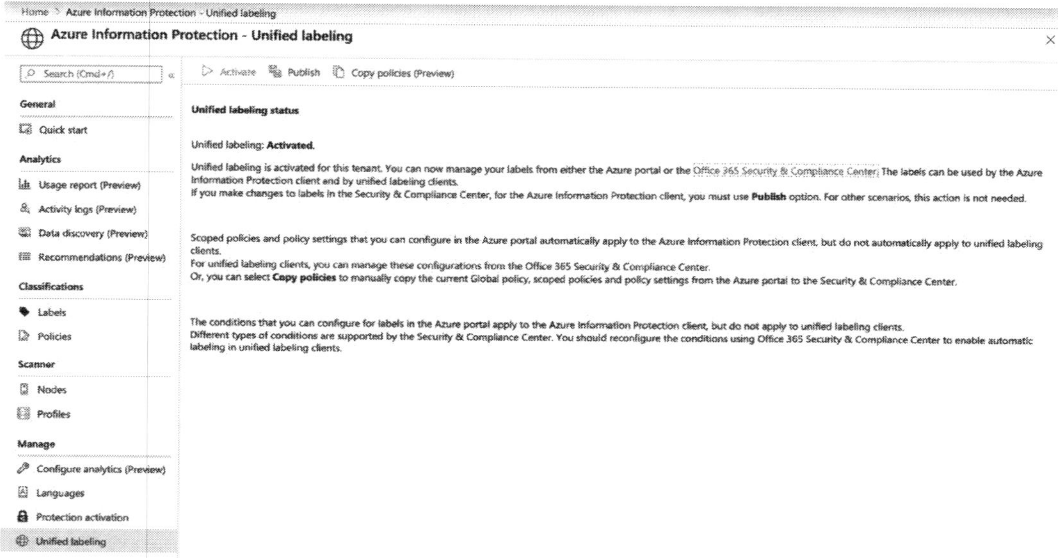

Figure 12.24 – Unified labeling

2. If **Unified labeling** is not already activated, you can click on **Activate** to do so.
3. Once enabled, the labels that you have defined in your Azure portal will be published to the Security and Compliance Center. You can trigger the option to publish the labels manually if you wish this to take place immediately by clicking on **Publish**.

4. While it is not possible to publish your label policies to the Security and Compliance Center at this time, there is now a preview feature included, called **Copy policies (Preview)**, where you can choose to copy the **Global** default policy to the Security and Compliance Center, as shown in the following screenshot:

Figure 12.25 – Copy policies (Preview) feature

5. Once you have chosen this option, you will see that the policy is successfully published, as shown in the following screenshot:

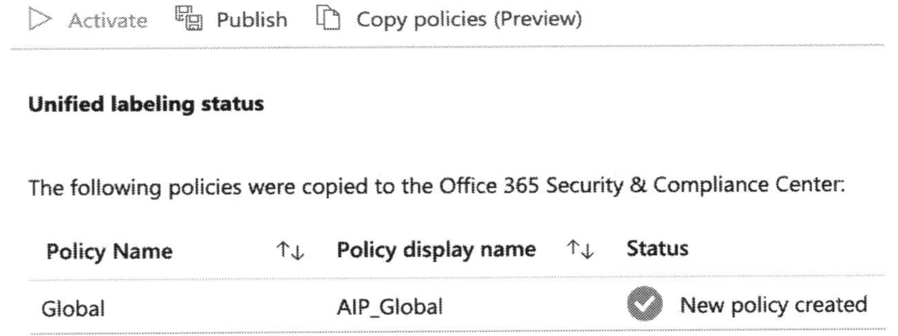

Figure 12.26 – New policy created

6. Now that we have checked that **Unified labeling** is activated and published, we can switch over to the Security and Compliance Center at `https://protection.office.com` and check the labels by choosing **Sensitivity Labels | Labels**.

As shown in the following screenshot, all of the labels from the Azure portal have been successfully published, including the **Internal** label, which we set up earlier in this chapter:

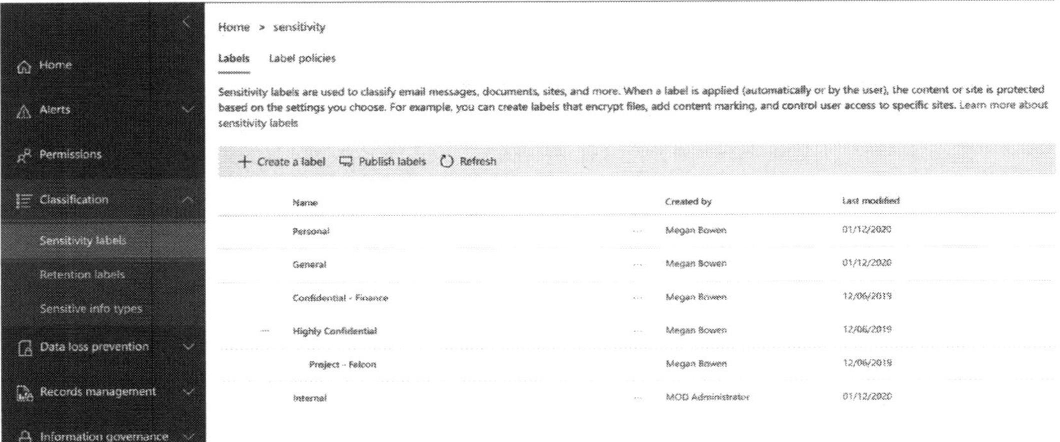

Figure 12.27 – Labels in the Security and Compliance Center

7. If we click on **Label policies**, we will also see that the AIP Global policy that we published using the preview feature in the previous step is visible, as shown in the following screenshot:

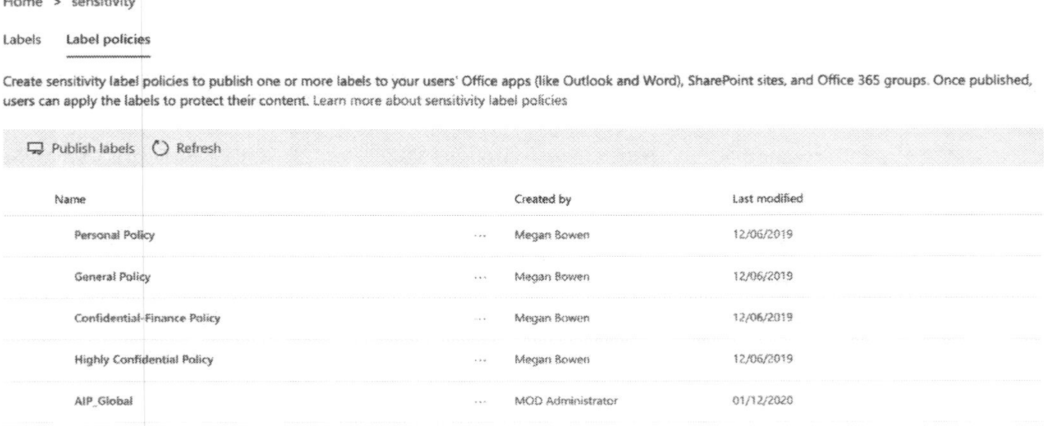

Figure 12.28 – Label policies in the Security and Compliance Center

New policies can also be created manually from the Security and Compliance Center. Some examples that have been created can be seen in the preceding screenshot. If you create label policies from here, you will need to use the **Publish labels** setting to apply the labels to selected users and groups.

> **Important note**
>
> The **Unified labeling** client is required on devices so that you can use sensitivity labels and policies published from the Security and Compliance Center. Details on the **Unified labeling** client and the more traditional AIP client can be found in the *References* section at the end of this chapter.

Now that we have configured the settings for **Unified labeling** within the Azure portal and the Microsoft 365 Security and Compliance Center, we can look at how our users will experience these features.

User experience

When your users are targeted by label policies, they will see the sensitivity bar available within their Microsoft Office applications, as shown in the following screenshot:

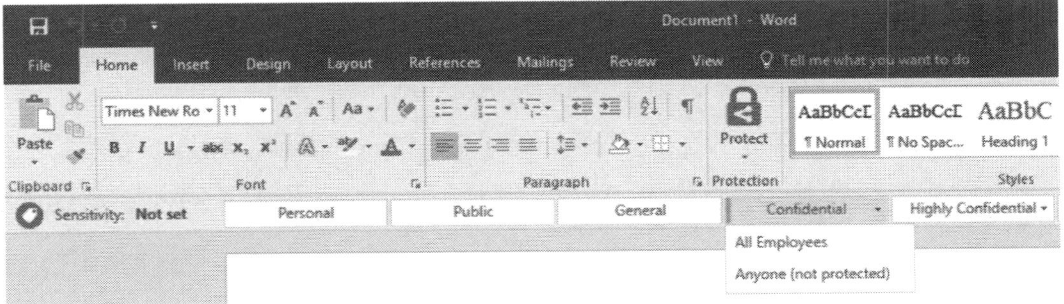

Figure 12.29 – Sensitivity bar in Microsoft Office

The experience will differ slightly, depending on the platform or operating system. In addition, there is a distinct difference between the experience of the traditional AIP labeling client and the newer **Unified labeling** client. If you have the traditional client installed, your users will see the **Protect** button, as shown in the preceding screenshot. However, should they have the **Unified labeling** client, they will see the **Sensitivity** button instead.

In this section, we have shown you how to configure AIP labels and policies, how to enable **Unified labeling**, and demonstrated the user experience.

Next, we will explore how to use the AIP Scanner to search for on-premises content and apply protection to it.

Using the AIP Scanner to detect and protect on-premises content

If you have an Azure Information Protection Premium P2 subscription, you can use the AIP Scanner tool to automatically classify and label documents that are stored within on-premises file shares or SharePoint servers. The AIP Scanner is a tool that can be installed on a Windows Server.

Once installed in your environment, the AIP Scanner uses the AIP client to index the on-premises content that it detects. Microsoft 365 sensitive information types (which are included in Data Loss Prevention) are used to determine whether the scanned content needs to be labeled.

Installing the AIP Scanner

To install the AIP Scanner, we need to use Windows PowerShell on the server that was chosen to host the service. This can be achieved by completing the following steps:

1. Run Windows PowerShell as an administrator and run the following command:

```
Connect-AIPService
```

2. Enter your administrator credentials when prompted.

> **Important note**
>
> In order to configure the AIP Scanner, you will need to have an AIP superuser already configured. The process of enabling superusers was described earlier in this chapter, in the *Configuring AIP superusers* section.

Use the following command to install the scanner:

```
Install-AIPScanner
```

3. When prompted, enter some credentials to create a SQL database for the context of the service to run in.

Once installed, we need to create a profile in the Azure portal. This can be done by completing the following steps:

1. Log into the Azure portal and navigate to **All services | Azure Information Protection | Scanner | Profiles**, as shown in the following screenshot:

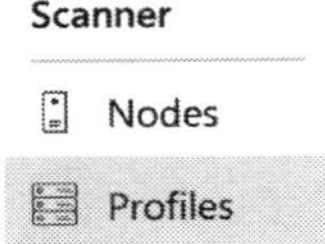

Figure 12.30 – AIP scanner profiles

2. Choose **Add**. Enter a **Profile name** and **Description** and configure your chosen profile settings, as shown in the following screenshot:

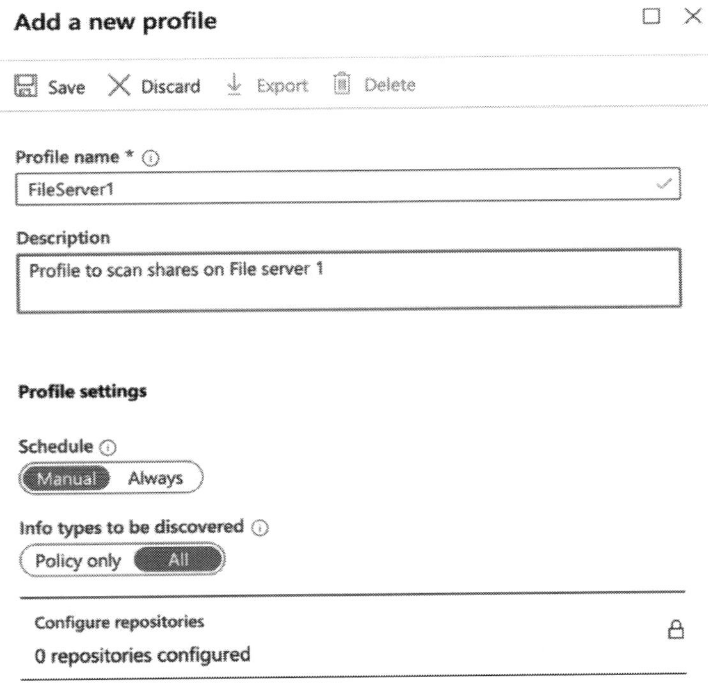

Figure 12.31 – Adding a new profile

> **Important note**
> You will be unable to click on **Configure repositories** to enter a UNC path for the content you wish to scan until you have saved your new profile.

3. Scroll down to **Policy enforcement**. You will see the options shown in the following screenshot:

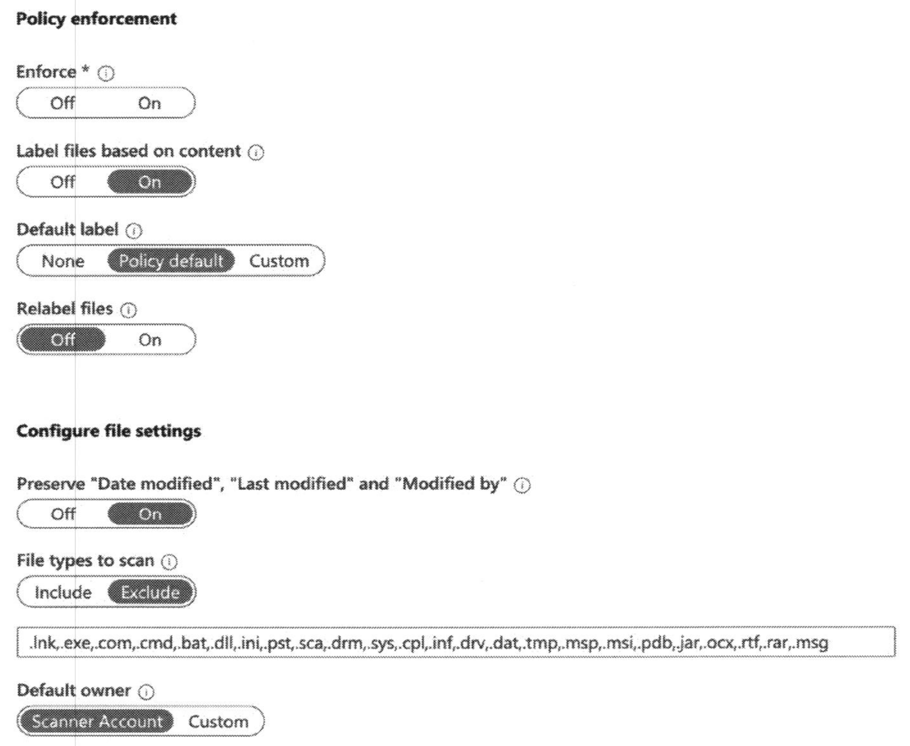

Figure 12.32 – Policy enforcement

4. Choose the appropriate options and click **Save**. Once saved, you will have the ability to click on **Configure Repositories** and enter the UNC paths of the content you wish to scan. You will see that the profile has been created, as shown in the following screenshot:

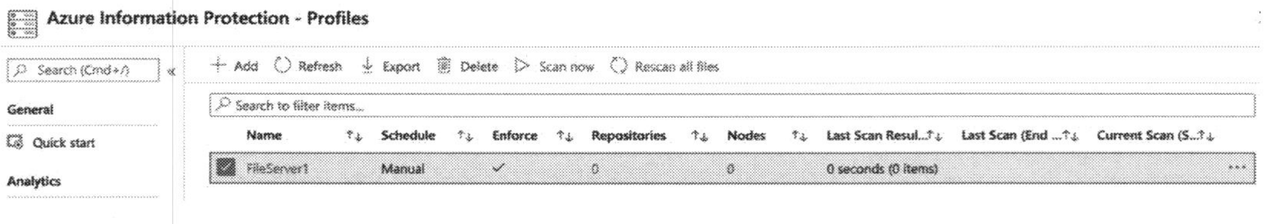

Figure 12.33 – New profile created

Note that you will be unable to run the profile at this time and that the **Scan now** option remains grayed out. In order to enable the profile for use, you must ensure that the AIP client is fully installed on the server that you are scanning, and you must also create two applications registered in Azure Active Directory. These will be used for the `Set-AIPAuthentication` cmdlet. The applications required are as follows:

- A web app/API application
- A native application

Instructions on how to configure the required applications are included in the *References* section at the end of this chapter.

In this section, we have explained the purpose of the AIP Scanner. We have shown you how to install the scanner and configure a profile for the scanner, which will enable it to interrogate an on-premises data repository, as well as how to apply classifications and labels based on the profile settings you create.

In the final section of this chapter, we will show you how to track and revoke protected documents.

Tracking and revoking protected documents

Once you have your AIP configuration defined and rolled out to your Microsoft 365 users, as well as started applying labels to documents, you can access the document tracking site in order to view and, if necessary, revoke access to content, should it no longer be deemed appropriate. We will demonstrate this process in the following steps:

1. You can access the document tracking site from the following URL: `https://portal.azurerms.com/#/admin`.
2. If you are logging in for the first time, you will be prompted to download and install the app. You will need to download the version that's appropriate for your operating system.

3. Once installed, you can launch the **Azure Information Protection Viewer** and then click **Open** on a protected file, as the following screenshot illustrates:

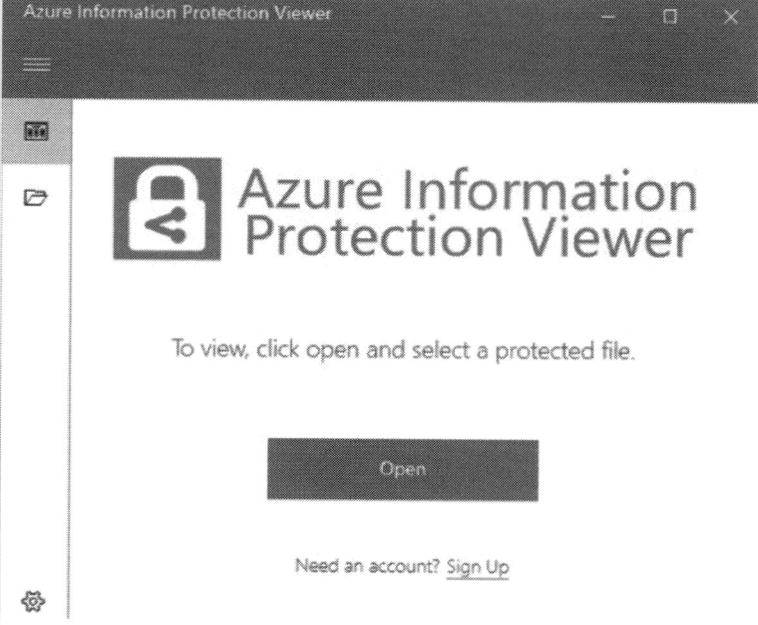

Figure 12.34 – Azure Information Protection Viewer

4. Alternatively, you can perform the same steps from within your Microsoft Office applications. Click on the **Protect** icon from the sensitivity bar (or the **Sensitivity** icon, if you're using the **Unified labeling** client). Next, click on **Track and Revoke**.

Using both the Azure Information Protection Viewer and the sensitivity bar options within your Microsoft Office applications, you will be able to track access to your content and either export the list to a CSV file or **Revoke access**, as shown in the following screenshot:

Figure 12.35 – Revoke access

> **Important note**
> Links to the tracking and revocation options for your protected documents can be found in the *References* section at the end of this chapter.

In this section, we demonstrated how to track and revoke access to content in your organization that has been protected with Azure Information Protection. We showed how this can be done from within your Microsoft Office applications, and also how to do this by downloading and installing the Azure Information Protection viewer. Both methods provide quick and easy access for users and administrators so that they can inspect their documents and revoke any access that may no longer be appropriate.

Summary

In this chapter, we introduced you to **Azure Information Protection** (**AIP**). We showed you how AIP is a powerful feature of Azure AD Premium that allows you to apply labels and label policies to your emails and documents within Microsoft 365.

We illustrated how to activate AIP for your tenant, as well as how to synchronize your labels to the Security and Compliance Center using Unified Labeling. In addition, we showed you how to use the AIP Scanner to interrogate your on-premises content and apply classifications to this content automatically.

Finally, we showed you how to track and revoke the content you have protected with AIP labels using the in-built sensitivity bar in your Microsoft Office applications, or by using the Azure Information Protection Viewer.

In the next chapter, we will be looking at **Data Loss Prevention** (**DLP**) and how it can be used to safeguard your users from accidentally sharing sensitive content.

Questions

1. Which of the following subscriptions can't be used to automatically classify and protect content with Azure Information Protection?

   a. Azure Information Protection Premium P2

   b. EM+S E3

   c. EM+S E5

   d. Microsoft 365 E5

2. You can activate AIP for your Microsoft 365 tenant using PowerShell.

   a. True

   b. False

3. Which PowerShell module was replace by the newer `AIPService` module?

   a. AIP

   b. AADRM

   c. Activedirectory

   d. ADRMS

4. Which of the following is not a visual marking setting available for an AIP label?

   a. Watermark

   b. Highlight

   c. Header

   d. Footer

5. AIP labels can be published to the Microsoft 365 Security and Compliance Center using the **Unified labeling** feature.

   a. True

   b. False

6. Which of the following commands is used to install the AIP Scanner?

   a. `Import-AIPScanner`

   b. `Install-AIPScanner`

   c. `Set-AIPScanner`

   d. `Get-AIPScanner`

7. Which of the following two methods can be used to track and revoke content protected with AIP?

   a. The Azure Information Protection Scanner

   b. The Azure Information Protection client

   c. The Azure Information Protection unified client

   d. The Azure Information Protection viewer

   e. The track and revoke option within Microsoft Office applications

8. The Azure Information Protection Scanner does not require a dedicated Windows Server.

   a. True

   b. False

9. Which of the following PowerShell commands is a valid method for assigning the AIP superuser role, without needing to grant full Global Administrator access?

   a. `Add-AIPServiceRoleBasedAdministrator`

   b. `EnableAIPServiceSuperUserFeature`

   c. `EnableAIPService`

   d. `Set-AIPServiceSuperUserGroup`

10. Which of the following Azure AD roles is unable to activate the Azure Information Protection Service in a Microsoft 365 tenant?

    a. User Administrator

    b. Global Administrator

    c. Azure Information Protection Administrator

    d. Security Administrator

References

Please refer to the following links for more information:

- Activating the protection service with AIP: `https://docs.microsoft.com/en-us/azure/information-protection/activate-service`
- Installing the `AIPService` PowerShell Module: `https://docs.microsoft.com/en-us/azure/information-protection/install-powershell`
- Configuring an AIP super user: `https://docs.microsoft.com/en-us/powershell/module/aipservice/add-aipservicesuperuser?view=azureipps`
- Using PowerShell with the AIP client: `https://docs.microsoft.com/en-au/azure/information-protection/rms-client/client-admin-guide-powershell`
- Deploying the AIP Scanner: `https://docs.microsoft.com/en-us/azure/information-protection/deploy-aip-scanner`

- Using the AIP scanner to label files, and creating and configuring the Azure AD applications for `Set-AIPAuthentication`: `https://docs.microsoft.com/en-us/azure/information-protection/rms-client/client-admin-guide-powershell#how-to-label-files-non-interactively-for-azure-information-protection`
- Configuring and using document tracking: `https://docs.microsoft.com/en-us/azure/information-protection/rms-client/client-admin-guide-document-tracking`
- Track and revoke documents in AIP: `https://docs.microsoft.com/en-us/azure/information-protection/rms-client/client-track-revoke`

13
Data Loss Prevention

Data Loss Prevention (**DLP**) in Microsoft 365 is designed to allow administrators to protect users from accidentally sharing sensitive information from your organization. This is achieved by creating policies that can be applied to your users and groups across multiple Microsoft 365 services. These policies use built-in or custom sensitive information types that can then be detected within the emails or documents that your users are working on, as well as trigger user policy tips to provide guidance on sharing information. These policies can also block any such emails or documents more aggressively when a policy match is detected and alert and report on such instances.

In this chapter, we will show you how to effectively plan and implement your sensitive information types and DLP policies. We will also demonstrate how you can manage the reporting features and alert settings available to you, along with creating policies from built-in templates or creating custom policies to meet your requirements using simple or advanced settings.

We shall cover these topics in the following order:

- Planning and implementing DLP
- Creating DLP policies and assigning them to Office 365 locations
- Managing sensitive information types
- DLP reporting and alerting capabilities

Planning and implementing DLP

In order to effectively plan for your Microsoft 365 DLP deployment, you need to understand any existing or potential data leakage within your organization. DLP can initially be configured with policies that run in test mode only. This is a good starting point for acquiring the information you need to determine your DLP strategy.

Before you go ahead and create your test policies, it is important that you understand how DLP works, what sort of information can be detected, and which Microsoft 365 services can be protected.

A good starting point is to examine the **Sensitive info types** that are used by DLP policies. There are a number of built-in sensitive information types available in Microsoft 365. These can be viewed from the Microsoft 365 Security and Compliance Center, which can be accessed by administrators at `https://protection.office.com`, or by navigating to **Classification | Sensitive info types**, as shown in the following screenshot:

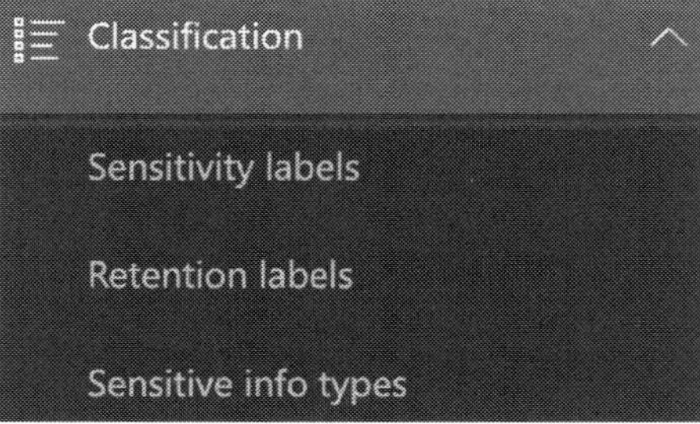

Figure 13.1 – Sensitive info types

These **Sensitive info types** can be associated with the DLP policies that you create. It is also possible to create your own custom **Sensitive info types**. The following screenshot shows some of the built-in **Sensitive info types**:

Home > Sensitive info types

The sensitive info types here are available to use in your security and compliance policies. These include a large collection of types we provide, spanning regions around the globe, as well as any custom types you have created.

+ Create

Name	Publisher
ABA Routing Number	Microsoft Corporation
Argentina National Identity (DNI) Number	Microsoft Corporation
Australia Bank Account Number	Microsoft Corporation
Australia Driver's License Number	Microsoft Corporation
Australia Medical Account Number	Microsoft Corporation
Australia Passport Number	Microsoft Corporation
Australia Tax File Number	Microsoft Corporation

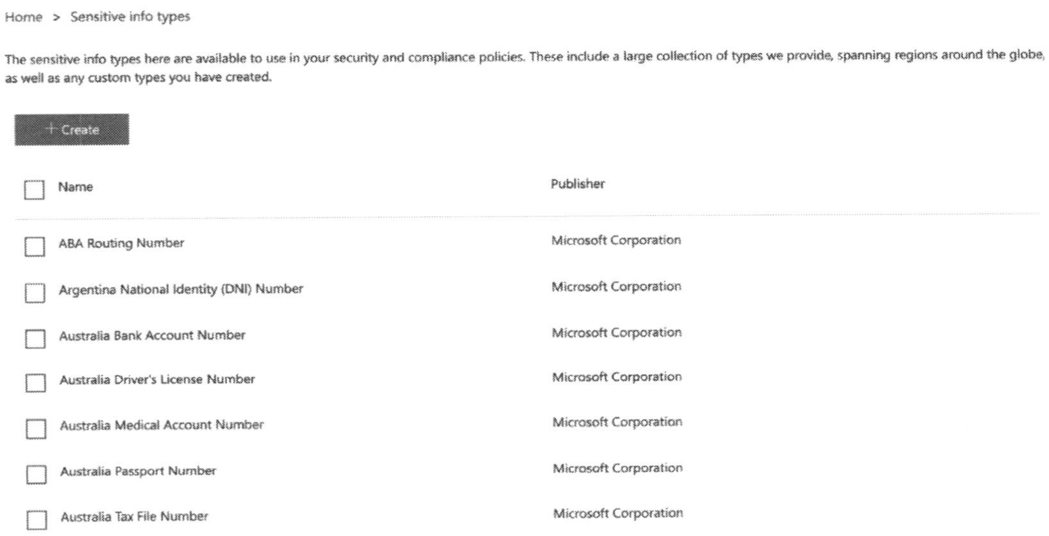

Figure 13.2 – Built-in Sensitive info types

The DLP policies that you create in the Security and Compliance Center can be applied to the following Microsoft 365 locations:

- **Exchange email**
- **SharePoint sites**
- **OneDrive accounts**
- **Teams chat and channel messages**

In the following screenshot, you can see that you have the option to protect all available locations or only those you wish to select:

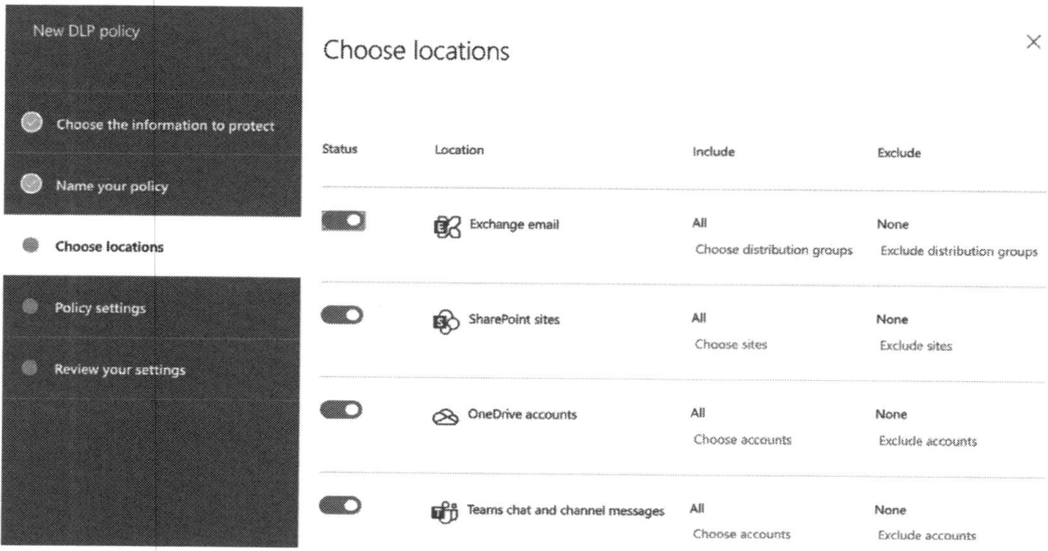

Figure 13.3 – Protecting Office 365 locations

DLP policies can be configured with conditions and actions, including the following:

- Notify users when content matches the policy settings
- Detect when a specific amount of information is being shared at one time
- Send incident reports to Global Admins
- Restrict access or encrypt the content

Choosing only the option to **Notify users when content matches the policy settings** is a good way of testing your DLP policies. Users will receive policy tips in their Microsoft Office applications, and a corresponding alert will be generated in the Security and Compliance Center. However, no further action will be taken, and no encryption or access restrictions will be applied.

When you've finished setting up your DLP Policy, select the option shown in the following screenshot. This will place the policy in test mode, and users will see policy tips when there is a match:

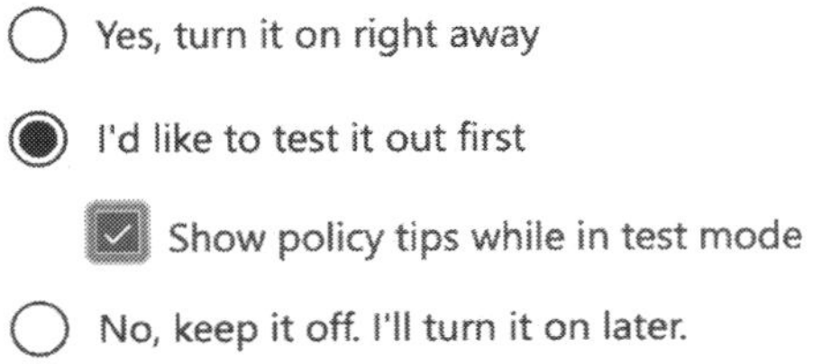

Yes, turn it on right away

I'd like to test it out first

Show policy tips while in test mode

No, keep it off. I'll turn it on later.

Figure 13.4 – Setting the policy in test mode

Important note

Policy tips are currently only available for users with Microsoft Office applications running on Windows computers, Outlook on the web, documents in SharePoint Online or OneDrive for Business, and Excel, PowerPoint, and Word (when the document is stored on a site targeted by a DLP policy).

In this section, we have explained how DLP works in Microsoft 365. We showed you that DLP policies can be created in the Microsoft 365 Security and Compliance Center to protect your Microsoft 365 locations. This is done by identifying the sensitive information types in these locations that are defined in the policy. We also explained that it's good practice to set your DLP policies in test mode initially and show policy tips to your users. This will help your users become familiar with the principles of DLP before you fully enable it, and will also help administrators experience typical alerts and matches, and how to take corrective measures.

Next, we will show you how to create DLP policies and assign them to your users and groups in Microsoft 365.

Creating DLP policies and assigning them to Office 365 locations

Now that you understand the core components that make up a DLP policy and that enabling your policies in test mode is a good way to begin, let's go ahead and create an actual DLP policy using a template and assign it to the chosen Office 365 locations. To do this, we need to complete the following steps:

1. Log into the Microsoft 365 Security and Compliance Center, which can be accessed by administrators at `https://protection.office.com`, and navigate to **Data loss prevention** | **Policy**, as shown in the following screenshot:

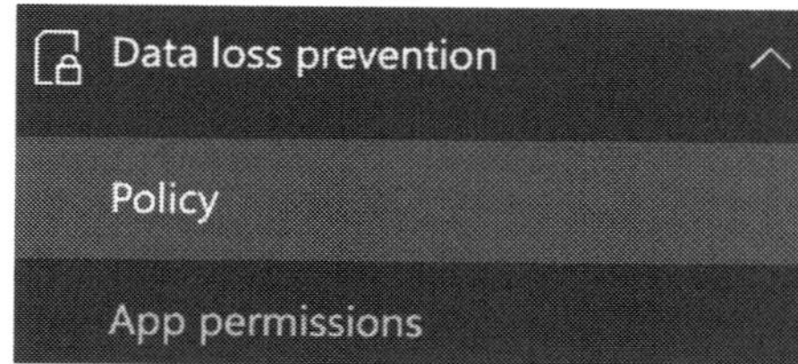

Figure 13.5 – Policy

2. Click on **Create a policy**, as shown in the following screenshot:

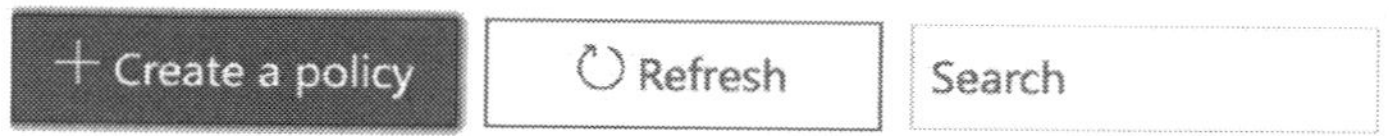

Figure 13.6 – Create a policy

3. For this example, we will configure a **Financial** policy from a template for a business in the **United Kingdom**. Choose **Financial** and select **United Kingdom**, as shown in the following screenshot:

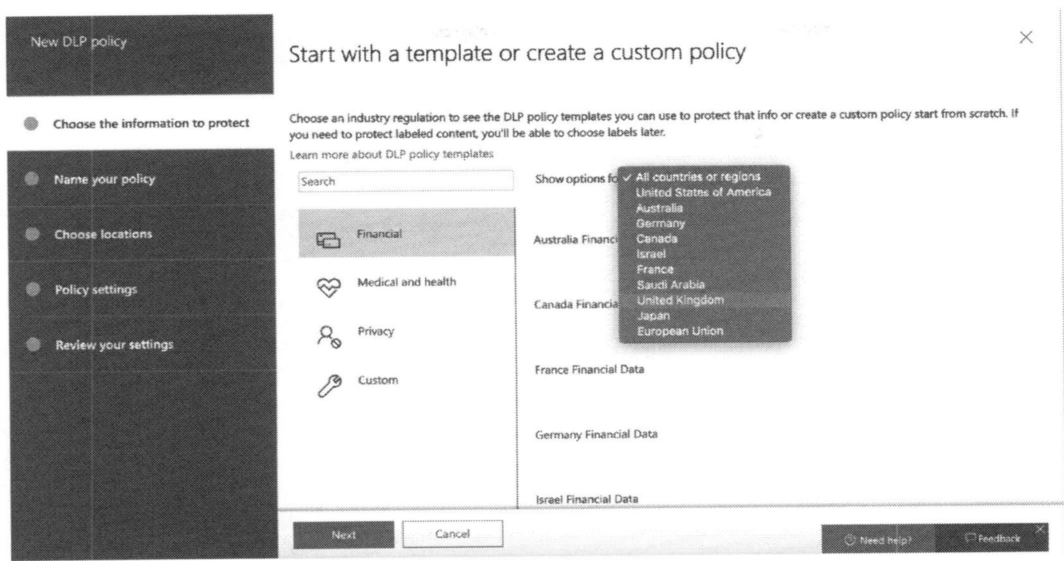

Figure 13.7 – Creating a policy from a template

4. There are two options for UK under the financial templates. For this example, we will select **U.K. Financial Data** and then **Next**, as shown in the following screenshot:

Choose an industry regulation to see the DLP policy templates you can use to protect that info or create a custom policy start from scratch. If you need to protect labeled content, you'll be able to choose labels later.
Learn more about DLP policy templates

Search

Show options for United Kingdom

Financial
Medical and health
Privacy
Custom

PCI Data Security Standard (PCI DSS)
U.K. Financial Data

U.K. Financial Data

Description
Helps detect the presence of information commonly considered to be financial information in United Kingdom, including information like credit card, account information, and debit card numbers.

Protects this information:
Credit Card Number
EU Debit Card Number
SWIFT Code

Next Cancel Need help? Feedback

Figure 13.8 – Creating a policy from a template

5. Next, enter a **Name** and **Description** for your policy and click **Next**, as shown in the following screenshot:

Name your policy

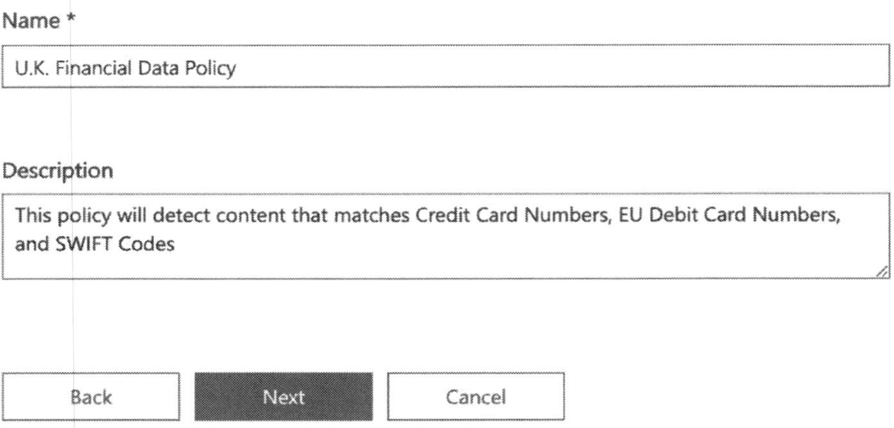

Figure 13.9 – Setting a Name and Description for the policy

6. Next, you have the option to choose the locations you wish to protect. In this example, we will choose the default option, which is to protect all content. Once selected, click **Next**, as shown in the following screenshot:

Choose locations

We'll protect content that's stored in the locations you choose. *

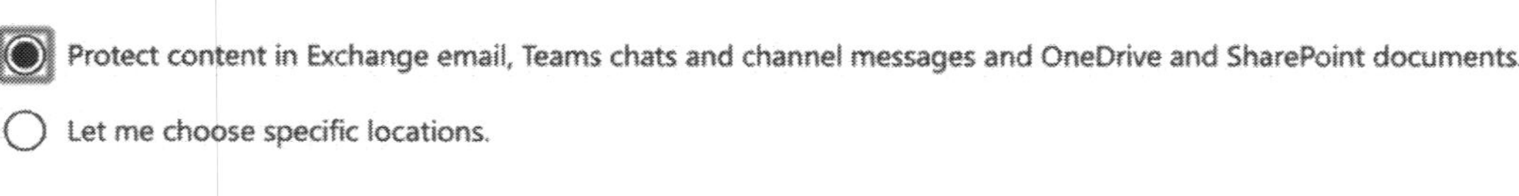

Figure 13.10 – Choosing which Office 365 locations to protect

7. Now, we have the option to customize the protection settings. For this example policy, we will leave the default settings as-is, as shown in the following screenshot:

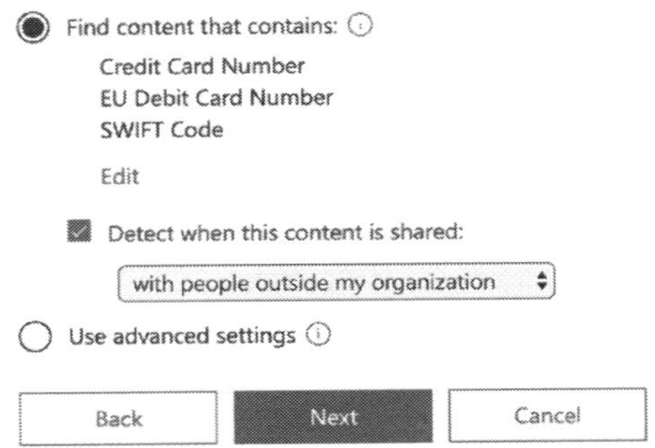
Customize the type of content you want to protect
Select 'Find content that contains' if you want to quickly set up a policy that protects only sensitive info or labeled content. Use advanced settings for more options, such as protecting content in email messages sent to specific domains, attachments with specific file extensions, and more.
Find content that contains:
Credit Card Number
EU Debit Card Number
SWIFT Code
Edit
Detect when this content is shared:
with people outside my organization
Use advanced settings
Back
Next
Cancel

Figure 13.11 – Customizing the content to protect

8. Once you have clicked **Next**, you can choose what you wish the policy to do if sensitive information is detected. There are a number of options that can be set at this point, as follows:

   a. Showing policy tips to users and sending them an email notification

   b. Detecting a specific amount of sensitive info being shared at one time

   c. Sending reports in an email

   d. Restricting access to the content

For this example, we will configure these settings like so:

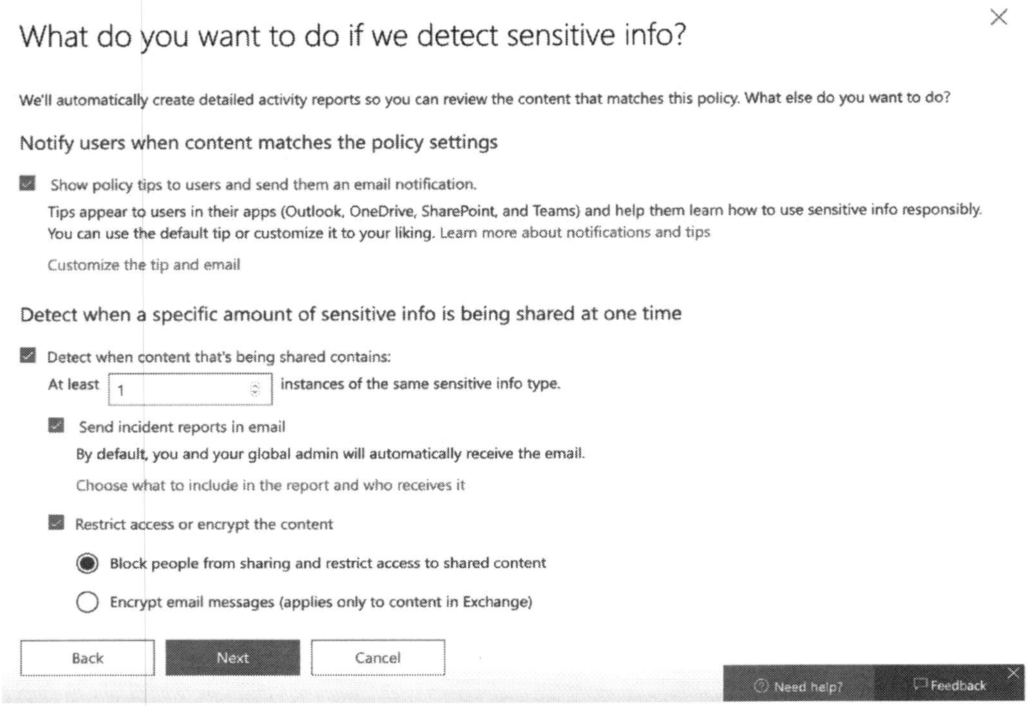

What do you want to do if we detect sensitive info?

We'll automatically create detailed activity reports so you can review the content that matches this policy. What else do you want to do?

Notify users when content matches the policy settings

- [x] Show policy tips to users and send them an email notification.

Tips appear to users in their apps (Outlook, OneDrive, SharePoint, and Teams) and help them learn how to use sensitive info responsibly. You can use the default tip or customize it to your liking. Learn more about notifications and tips

Customize the tip and email

Detect when a specific amount of sensitive info is being shared at one time

- [x] Detect when content that's being shared contains:

At least 1 instances of the same sensitive info type.

- [x] Send incident reports in email

By default, you and your global admin will automatically receive the email.

Choose what to include in the report and who receives it

- [x] Restrict access or encrypt the content

(•) Block people from sharing and restrict access to shared content

( ) Encrypt email messages (applies only to content in Exchange)

Back Next Cancel Need help? Feedback

Figure 13.12 – Settings for when sensitive information is detected

9. By selecting the option to **Choose what to include in the report and who receives it**, we have the option to choose the settings for our incident report, as shown in the following screenshot:

Customize the incident report

Use email incident reports to notify you when a policy match occurs.

Send notifications to these people

SiteAdmin
adminuser@chrysalistech.onmicrosoft.com

Add or remove people

All incident reports include information about the item that was matched, where the match occurred, and the rules and policies it triggered.

You can also include the following information in the report:

- [x] The name of the person who last modified the content
- [x] The types of sensitive content that matched the rule
- [x] The rule's severity level
- [x] The content that matched the rule, including the surrounding text
- [x] The item containing the content that matched the rule

OK Cancel

Figure 13.13 – Customize the incident report screen

10. Click on **OK** and then **Next**. You will see the following options for customizing access and override permissions. In this example, we will set the option for an override of the policy to be allowed by users who see the policy tip. A justification for the override must be provided, as shown in the following screenshot:

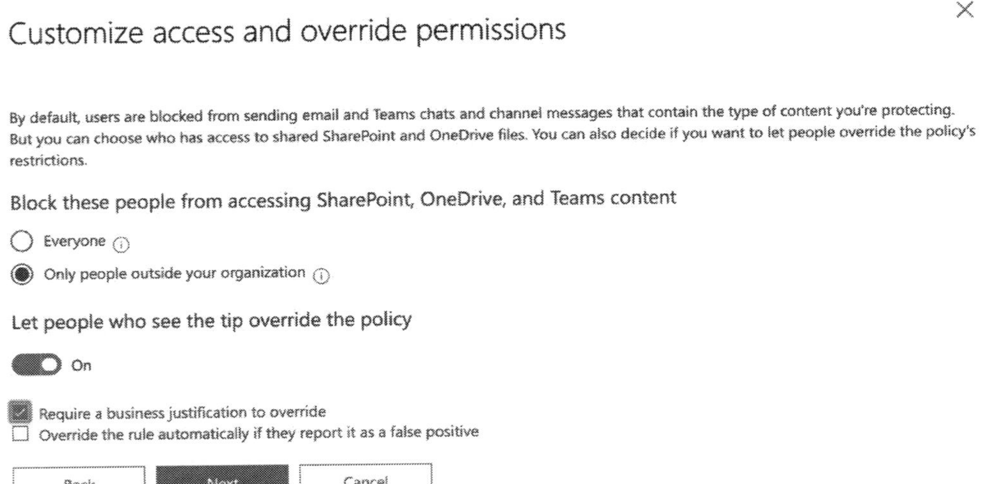

Figure 13.14 – Customize access and override permissions screen

11. Next, we can choose how we wish the policy to be applied. It can be enabled immediately, placed in test mode, or turned off for later use. In this example, we will choose the option to test our new policy first, and also enable policy tips for our users while in test mode, as shown in the following screenshot:

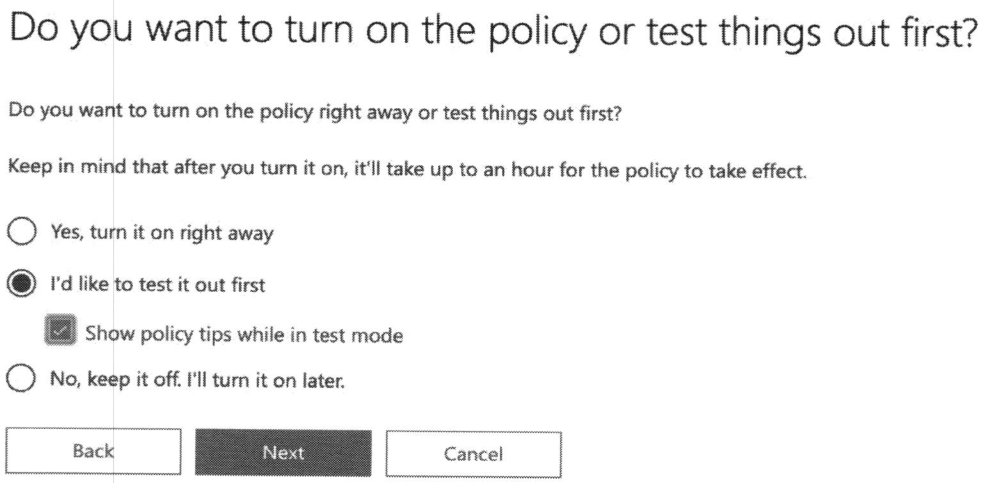

Do you want to turn on the policy or test things out first?

Do you want to turn on the policy right away or test things out first?

Keep in mind that after you turn it on, it'll take up to an hour for the policy to take effect.

Yes, turn it on right away

I'd like to test it out first

Show policy tips while in test mode

No, keep it off. I'll turn it on later.

Back Next Cancel

Figure 13.15 – Turning on the policy

12. Click **Next**. You will see the following screen, where you can review the settings you have configured for your policy and make any last-minute changes if required:

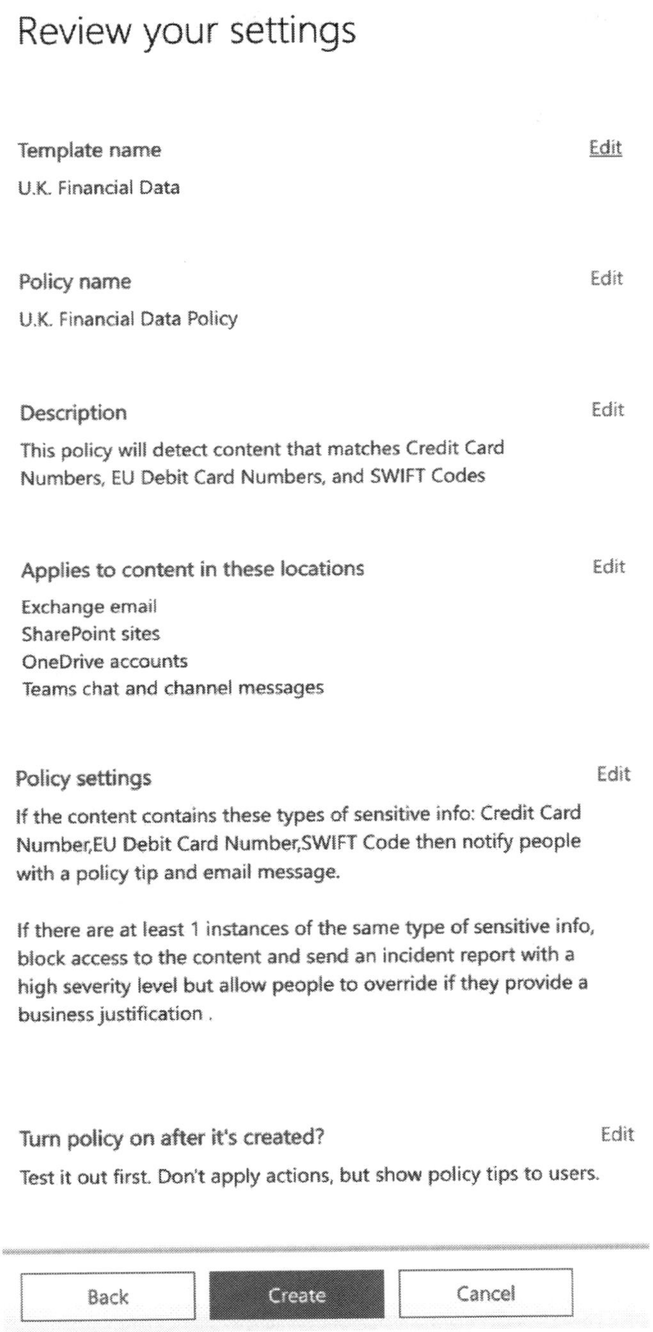

Review your settings

Template name Edit

U.K. Financial Data

Policy name Edit

U.K. Financial Data Policy

Description Edit

This policy will detect content that matches Credit Card Numbers, EU Debit Card Numbers, and SWIFT Codes

Applies to content in these locations Edit

Exchange email
SharePoint sites
OneDrive accounts
Teams chat and channel messages

Policy settings Edit

If the content contains these types of sensitive info: Credit Card Number,EU Debit Card Number,SWIFT Code then notify people with a policy tip and email message.

If there are at least 1 instances of the same type of sensitive info, block access to the content and send an incident report with a high severity level but allow people to override if they provide a business justification .

Turn policy on after it's created? Edit

Test it out first. Don't apply actions, but show policy tips to users.

Back Create Cancel

Figure 13.16 – Reviewing the settings

13. Once you are happy with your policy settings, click **Create** to finish creating your policy.

Testing your DLP policy

Now that your DLP policy has been created, it should take effect after approximately 1 hour and start detecting genuine policy matches. It is also possible to attempt to manually trigger the policy by sending an email from an account that is bound by the policy containing a match.

In our example policy, we created conditions to apply the policy when UK financial data was detected. It is important to point out that DLP is intelligent enough to know when a random set of numbers are entered to represent a debit or credit card number. However, there are some websites available where genuine test card numbers can be found in order to conduct successful testing.

In the following screenshot, we can see that a policy tip appears when a user in our tenant tries to send an email to an external recipient that contains a credit card number:

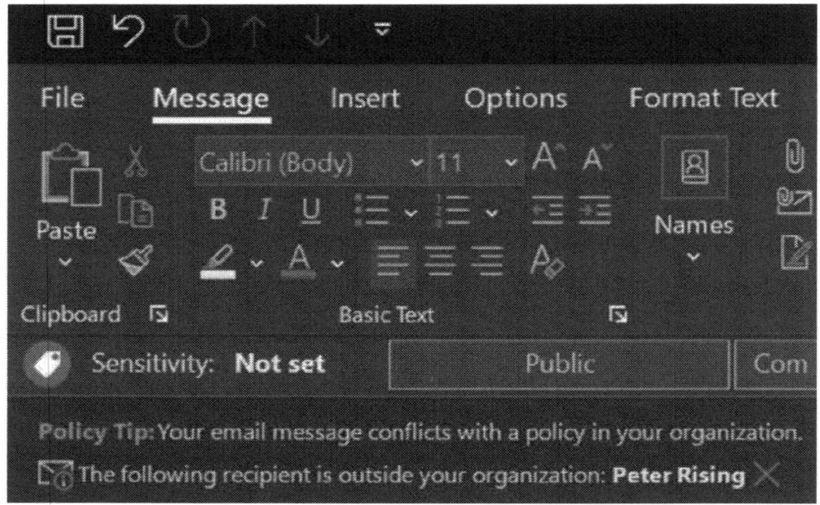

Figure 13.17 – Policy tip in Outlook

Since we set up the policy so that it only runs in test mode at this time, the user will still be able to successfully send the email.

Once the user has sent the email, an alert will be sent to them, as shown in the following screenshot:

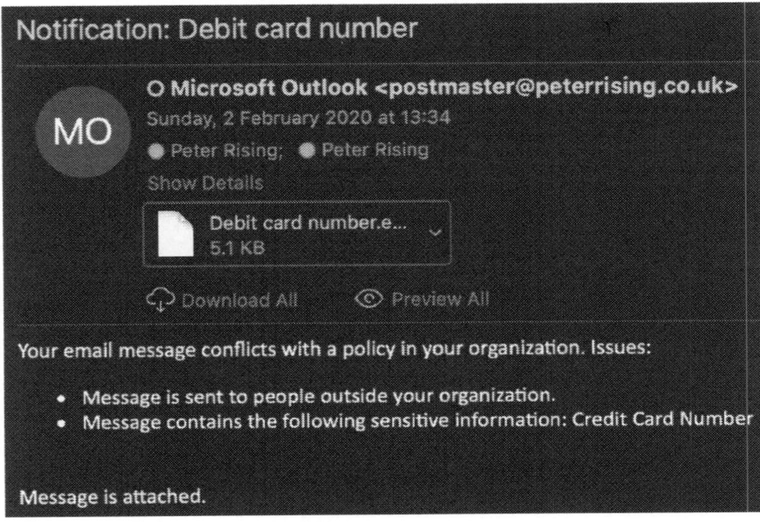

Figure 13.18 – Email notification of policy match

A copy of the original email is also attached to the alert.

So, if you initially configure your DLP policies in test mode in this way, this will give you a good opportunity to assess the accuracy and effectiveness of your policies when you make the decision to fully activate and enforce them.

Editing your DLP policy

When testing your DLP policy, you may find that you need to go back and make some changes if the results are not as expected. You can change the conditions, actions, user notifications, user overrides, and incident report settings within your policy while editing.

To edit the policy, you need to complete the following steps:

1. Highlight the policy and select **Edit policy**, as shown in the following screenshot:

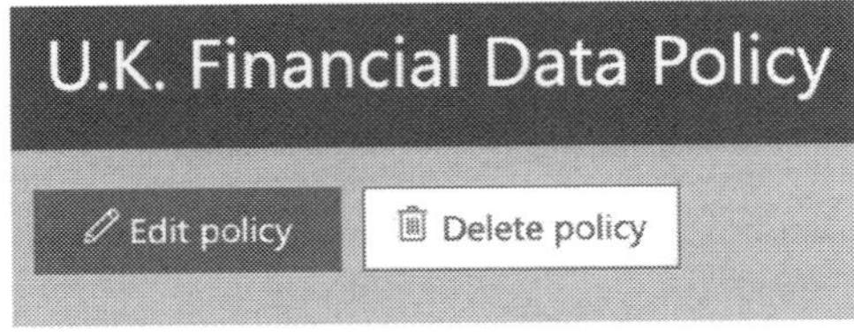

Figure 13.19 – Edit policy

2. You will see that this policy has been set up with both low and high volume detected content settings, as shown in the following screenshot:

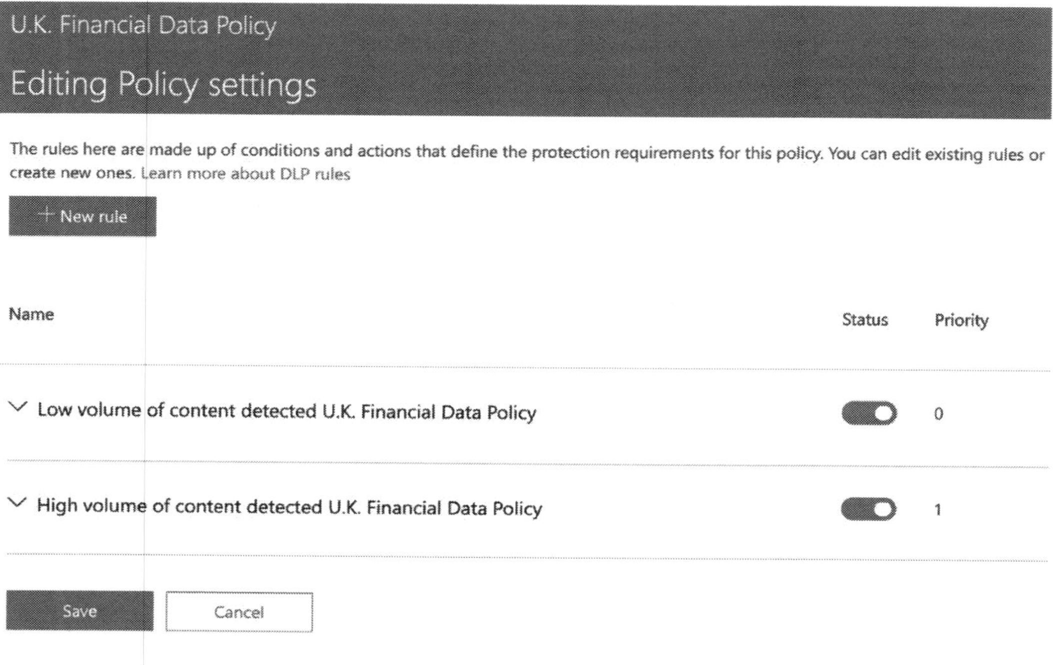

Figure 13.20 – Low and high volume content options

It is important to modify both of these settings with any changes to the policy you wish to make.

3. For this example, we will select the low volume option and click **Edit rule**, as shown in the following screenshot:

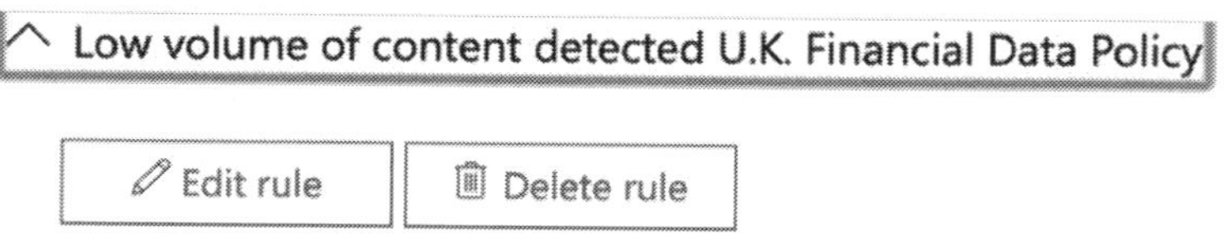

Figure 13.21 – Editing the low volume content rule

4. Editing the rule will open the advanced edit options, as shown in the following screenshot:

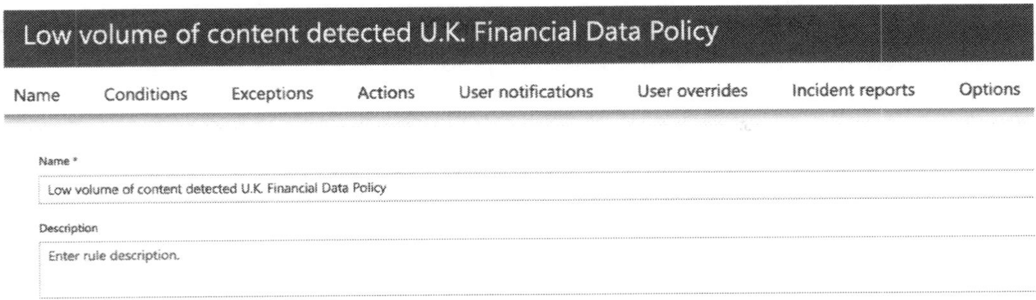

Figure 13.22 – Advanced edit options

5. You will need to navigate through all of the sections within the advanced policy settings and, once you are happy with your changes, click **Save**.

The changes to your policy will be saved and should take effect in a short period of time.

> **Important note**
>
> DLP policies can also be created and managed via the **Exchange Online Management Center** at `https://outlook.office.com/ecp`. However, policies that are created here will only apply to Exchange Online. It is a Microsoft recommended practice that you create your DLP policies from the Microsoft 365 Security and Compliance Center, as detailed in the steps laid out in the previous section.

In this section, we showed you how to create a DLP policy and assign it to all or a selection of Office 365 locations. We demonstrated how you can keep your new policy turned off until you are ready to test or activate it, as well as how to enable it in test mode with user notifications and policy tips.

We also showed you how you can edit your DLP policies after creating them and how you can modify them with the advanced policy settings.

Next, we will look at the sensitive information types included in the Security and Compliance Center.

Managing sensitive information types

As we have already discussed, DLP is able to use the many built-in sensitive information types that are available in the Microsoft 365 Security and Compliance Center. However, there may also be occasions where it is necessary for a business to add one or more custom sensitive information types to allow the identification and protection of information, which is not covered by the built-in options.

To create a custom sensitive information type in the Security and Compliance Center, you will need to have either Global Administrator or Compliance Administrator permissions. Then, complete the following steps:

1. Select **Classification** | **Sensitive info types** and click **Create**, as shown in the following screenshot:

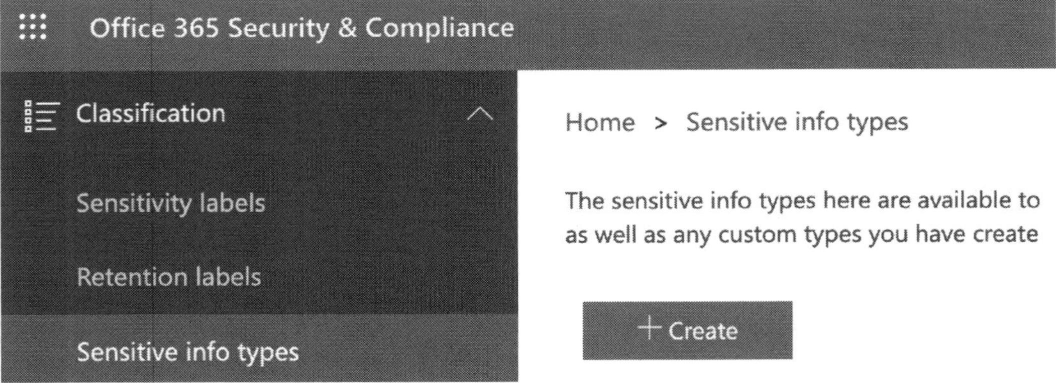

Figure 13.23 – Creating a sensitive information type

2. Enter a **Name** and **Description** for your new sensitive information type and then click on **Next**, as shown in the following screenshot. Here, we are creating an entry for an employee ID:

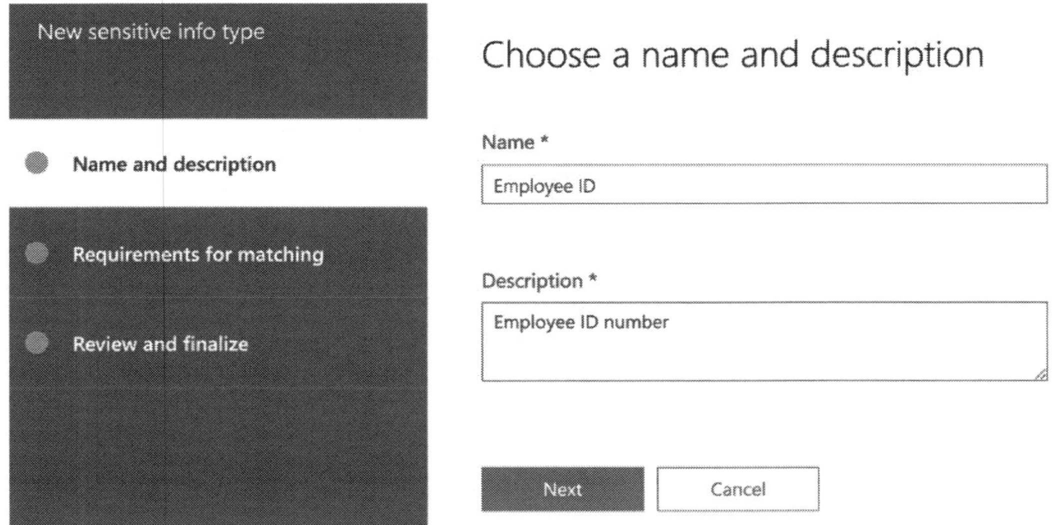

Figure 13.24 – Choosing a name and description

3. On the **Requirements for matching** section, click on **Add an element**, as shown in the following screenshot:

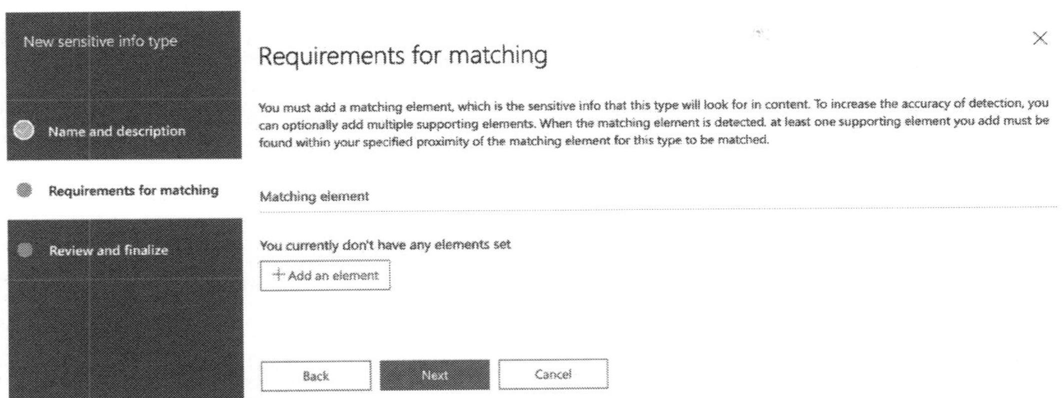

Figure 13.25 – Setting the requirements for matching

4. You can choose from **Keywords**, **Regular expression**, or **Dictionary (Large keywords)**. In this example, we will choose **Keywords**. The following screenshot shows **Keywords** as one of the available options for this setting:

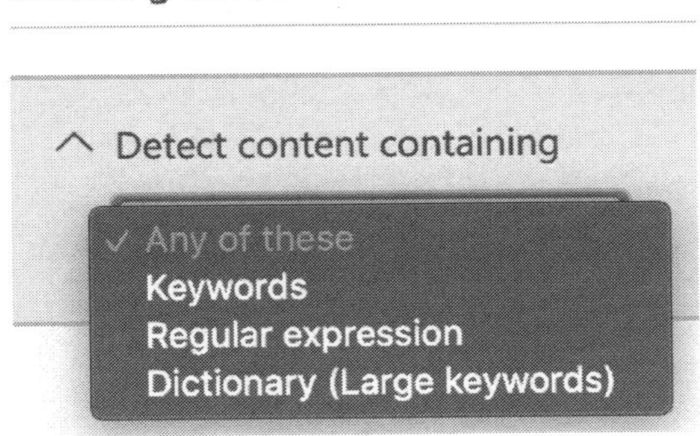

Figure 13.26 – Setting the matching element

5. For our example, we will add an entry called **CTECHOP** (which will represent the Chrysalis Technologies operative), as shown in the following screenshot:

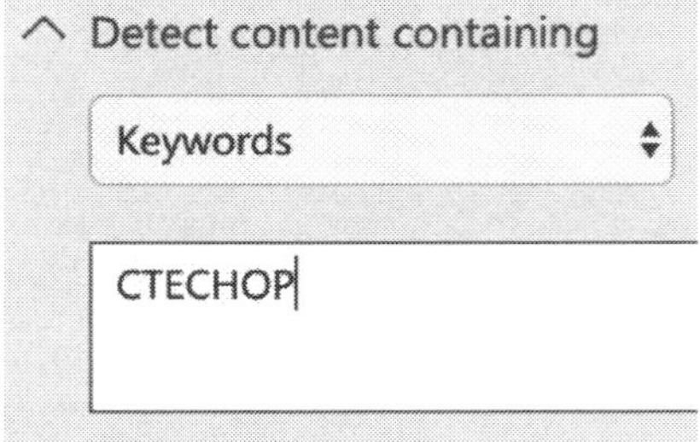

Figure 13.27 – Setting the keyword

6. Supporting elements can also be added to the sensitive information type, as shown in the following screenshot. For this example, we will not add any **Supporting elements**:

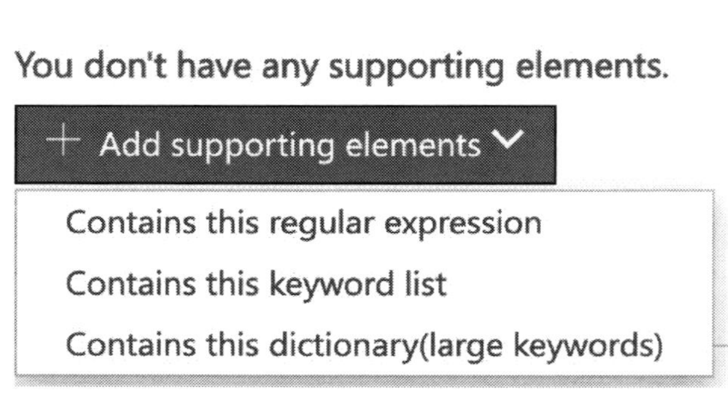

Figure 13.28 – Add supporting elements

7. You can also change the **Confidence level** and **Character proximity** settings for the sensitive information type. In this example, we will leave the default settings as-is, as shown in the following screenshot:

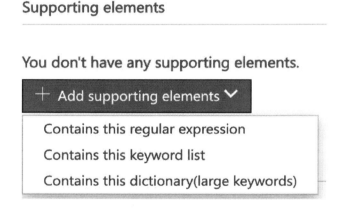

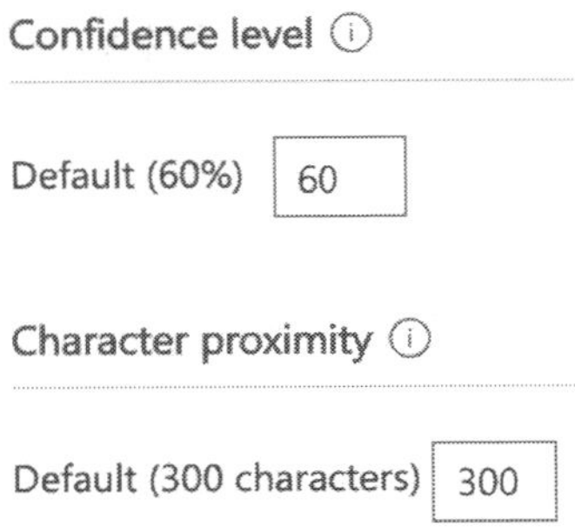

Figure 13.29 – Confidence level settings

8. Click **Next** to be taken to the **Review and finalize** options. If you are happy with the settings you have configured, click on **Finish**, as shown in the following screenshot:

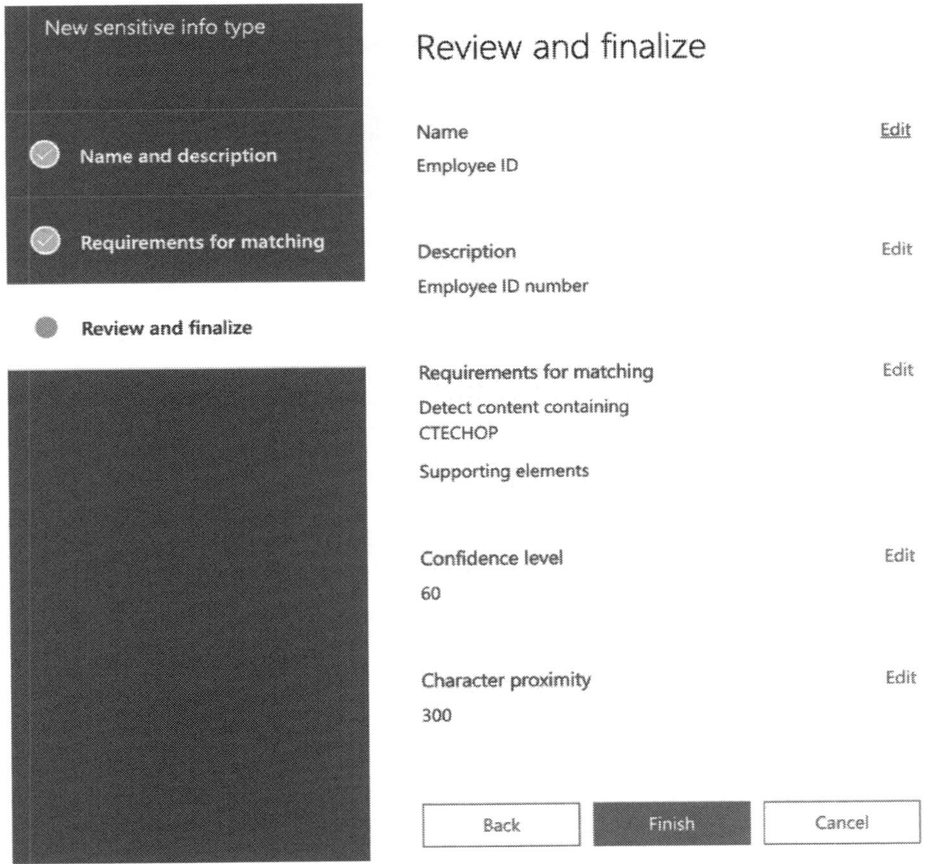

Figure 13.30 – Review and finalize page

9. You will receive the message as shown in the following screenshot. Click **Yes**:

Security & Compliance

Sensitive type is successfully saved. It is recommended to test the sensitive type before use. Do you want to test created sensitive type?

Figure 13.31 – Notification of sensitive information type creation

Your custom sensitive information type is now set up and available. It is recommended that you test this before advising your Microsoft 365 users that it is available to them. A custom sensitive information type can be added to a new or existing DLP policy by searching for the sensitive information type when creating or editing a policy, as shown in the following screenshot:

Sensitive info types

Choose which sensitive info types to add from the list below.

employ

Added (0)

Sensitive info types (1)

Name	Publisher
Employee ID	Chrysalis Technologies

Figure 13.32 – Adding a custom sensitive information type to a DLP policy

> **Important note**
>
> It is also possible to configure custom sensitive information types by using **Security and Compliance Center PowerShell**, as well as **Exact Data Match Based Classification**. Information related to these methods can be found in the references section at the end of this chapter.

In this section, we demonstrated that while the built-in sensitive information types included in the Microsoft 365 Security and Compliance Center will usually fulfill most requirements, it may also be necessary, on some occasions, to create one or more custom sensitive information types.

We showed you how to create a custom sensitive information type by using a keyword and also demonstrated that other methods are available, such as **Regular expression** and **Dictionary (Large keywords).**

Next, we will review the reporting and alerting capabilities that are available within your Microsoft 365 environment.

DLP reporting and alerting capabilities

There are a number of reporting and alerting capabilities for DLP that are available within the Microsoft 365 Security and Compliance Center. Regularly reviewing these will give Microsoft 365 administrators valuable insights into how effectively DLP is configured and working. The reports that are available are as follows:

- **DLP policy matches**
- **DLP incidents**
- **DLP false positives and overrides**

You can view the available DLP reports from the Security and Compliance Center by navigating to **Reports** | **Dashboard** and choosing **DLP policy matches**, as shown in the following screenshot:

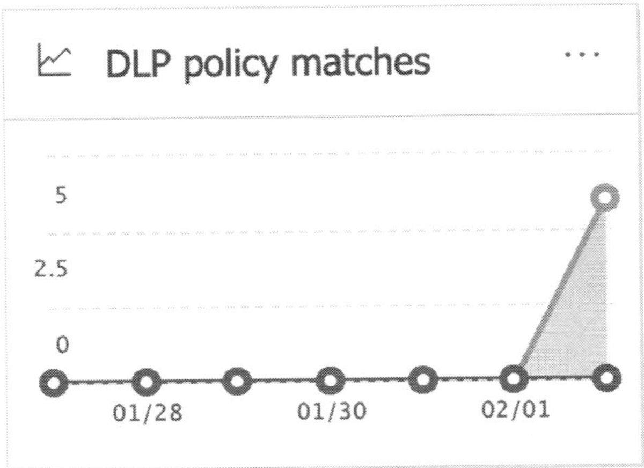

Figure 13.33 – DLP policy matches

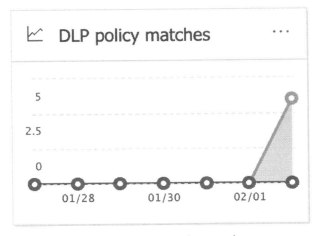

The **DLP policy matches** section shows a count of recent policy matches, all of which you can filter by date, location, policy, or action.

Clicking into the tile will give you a broader view of the DLP policy match activity, along with related reports on **DLP incidents** and **DLP false positives and overrides**, as shown in the following screenshot:

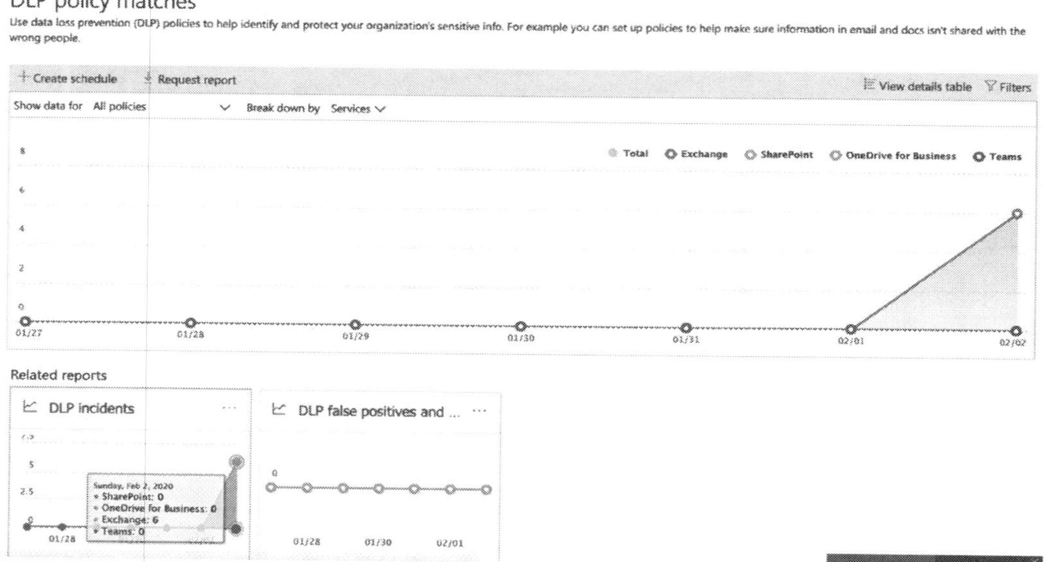

Figure 13.34 – DLP policy match activity

The **DLP incident** reports shows us that, in this case, there have been *six* recent DLP incidents in our tenant related to Exchange Online. You can choose the **Request report** option in order to send an email to yourself or others that contains further details on these incidents so that you can analyze further and take any corrective measures.

DLP false positives and overrides will show you a count of any detected false positives and overrides (if allowed). This report can be filtered and examined in the same way as the DLP incident reports so that you can analyze this activity and, once again, apply any required corrective measures. For example, if DLP policy overrides are allowed in your organization and you are seeing a high volume of overrides and user justifications, this may need to be addressed.

All of the DLP reports available in the Security and Compliance Center can contain information for up to 4 months prior to the current date. However, the most recent DLP activity may take up to 24 hours to be included in these reports.

> **Important note**
> It is also possible to acquire reporting information related to DLP by using Windows PowerShell. Details on how to run these reports is included in the references section at the end of this chapter.

Summary

In this chapter, we explained how DLP in Microsoft 365 can help you create policies based on built-in and custom sensitive information types. This prevents the users in your organization accidentally sharing sensitive information.

We demonstrated how to set up and modify a DLP policy and apply it to all or selected Office 365 locations. We also showed you how to effectively plan your DLP rollout by creating policies in test mode only, as well as how to view and interpret the reports that are available in the Security and Compliance Center.

In addition, we showed you how to view and interpret the available reports and alerts related to DLP from the Security and Compliance Center, along with how to set up your own custom sensitive information types using regular expressions, keywords, and dictionary (large keywords) settings.

In the next chapter, we will be looking at Cloud App Discovery and Security and how this can be used to gain visibility of SaaS applications within our Microsoft 365 environment.

Questions

1. DLP helps to prevent the accidental sharing of data from Office 365 locations by using policies that look for matches against both built-in and custom sensitive information types.

   a. True

   b. False

2. Which of the following locations in Office 365 can't be protected by a DLP policy (choose two)?

   a. SharePoint sites

   b. PowerApps

   c. OneDrive accounts

   d. Exchange email

   e. Yammer groups

   f. Teams chat and channel messages

3. Where in the Microsoft 365 Security and Compliance Center would you view the available DLP reports?

   a. **Data Loss Prevention | Policy**

   b. **Threat Management | Dashboard**

   c. **Reports | Dashboard**

   d. **Classification | Sensitive info types**

4. Which of the following is not an example of a custom sensitive information type?

   a. Dictionary (large keyword)

   b. Regular expression

   c. Dictionary (regular expression)

   d. Keyword

5. The rules within DLP Policies are made up conditions and actions.

   a. True

   b. False

6. Other than the Security and Compliance Center, where can you also configure DLP policies?

   a. Teams Admin Center

   b. Exchange Admin Center

   c. The Azure Portal

   d. The Microsoft 365 Admin Center

7. When a DLP policy is set to test with policy tips, the policy and its rule will be enforced.

a. True

b. False

8. What can DLP protect within Microsoft Teams (select two)?

a. Calendar

b. Teams chat

c. Channel messages

d. Apps

9. When including or excluding Exchange email content from a DLP policy, this is based on which of the following?

a. Security Groups

b. Distribution Groups

c. Office 365 Groups

d. Users

10. Policy tips are available to users who are working with Microsoft Office 2016 for Mac.

a. True

b. False

References

Please refer to the following links for more information regarding what was covered in this chapter:

- Overview of DLP: `https://docs.microsoft.com/en-gb/microsoft-365/compliance/data-loss-prevention-policies`
- Setting up a DLP policy from a template: `https://docs.microsoft.com/en-gb/microsoft-365/compliance/create-a-dlp-policy-from-a-template`
- DLP reporting using PowerShell: `https://docs.microsoft.com/en-us/powershell/module/exchange/policy-and-compliance-dlp/Get-DlpDetectionsReport?redirectedfrom=MSDN&view=exchange-ps`
- Viewing reports for DLP: `https://docs.microsoft.com/en-gb/microsoft-365/compliance/view-the-dlp-reports`

- Connecting to Security and Compliance PowerShell: `https://docs.microsoft.com/en-us/powershell/exchange/office-365-scc/connect-to-scc-powershell/connect-to-scc-powershell?view=exchange-ps`
- Creating a custom sensitive information type using Security and Compliance PowerShell: `https://docs.microsoft.com/en-us/microsoft-365/compliance/create-a-custom-sensitive-information-type-in-scc-powershell`
- Creating a custom sensitive information type using exact data match-based classification: `https://docs.microsoft.com/en-us/microsoft-365/compliance/create-custom-sensitive-information-types-with-exact-data-match-based-classification`

14
Cloud App Discovery and Security

When you move your organization's apps and services to the cloud, you are provided with greater flexibility and agility for your users. However, this is a double-edged sword as a traditional firewall cannot be wrapped around the Microsoft 365 platform. However, the need to protect your Microsoft 365 apps and services remains absolutely crucial. Finding the right balance between user convenience and security is a challenge faced by modern workplace administrators; Microsoft Cloud App Security can help to address this challenge.

In this chapter, we will explain the principles of Cloud App Security and its licensing requirements. You will then learn how to configure Cloud App Security for your Microsoft 365 environment, as well as how to create snapshot Cloud Discovery reports and discover cloud apps. In addition, we will show you how to use app connectors to enable visibility and control over the apps you connect with and apply policies to.

We will cover these topics in the following order:

- Understanding Cloud App Security
- Configuring Cloud App Security
- Using the Cloud App Security dashboard, reports, and logs

Understanding Cloud App Security

Cloud App Security is a **Cloud Access Security Broker** (**CASB**) solution designed to provide Microsoft 365 administrators with visibility of all **Software as a Service** (**SaaS**) applications within their organization and alert them to risky cloud app usage.

The framework of Cloud App Security enables you to discover shadow IT activities, as well as identify, classify, and protect sensitive information stored in the cloud. It also detects anomalous behavior within cloud apps to protect you against cyber threats and ensure that industry standards for security and compliance are applied to your cloud apps to protect them against data leakage.

Cloud App Security is available in two versions. They are as follows:

- **Office 365 Cloud App Security**: Available with **Office 365 Enterprise E5**
- **Microsoft Cloud App Security**: Available with **EM+S E5** and **Microsoft 365 E5**

Office 365 Cloud App Security provides visibility and control over native Office 365 cloud apps only, whereas Microsoft 365 Cloud App Security contains a wider set of features that provide enhanced visibility and control across a wider range of third-party SaaS solutions.

> **Important note**
> In this chapter, we will only focus on the wider feature set available in Microsoft 365 Cloud App Security.

With Microsoft 365 Cloud App Security, administrators can complete the following tasks:

- Use Cloud Discovery to identify cloud apps used by their organization
- Allow or disallow cloud apps
- Use app connectors to gain visibility of, and control over, third-party apps
- Use **Azure Active Directory** (**Azure AD**) Conditional Access App Control in conjunction with Cloud App Security
- Use built-in policies or create custom policies to control SaaS app usage

Let's look at each of these tasks in greater detail, starting with Cloud Discovery.

Cloud Discovery

Cloud Discovery allows you to discover the cloud apps used in your organization by uploading logs from your edge devices, which are analyzed by Cloud App Security, to detect cloud app usage. This can be achieved by manually uploading the logs from firewalls or proxies or by configuring log collectors to automate regular log reports.

Sanctioning or unsanctioning cloud apps

The Cloud App Security app catalog consists of over 16,000 cloud apps, which are available for use within your Microsoft 365 environment. Microsoft ranks these apps based on industry standards and applies a risk score to each app. This helps you assess how risky an app may be for your organization and allows you to make informed decisions as to whether you sanction these apps on your tenant.

Using app connectors to gain visibility and control of third-party apps

If you wish to approve and use non-Microsoft cloud apps in your organization, app connectors allow you to integrate third-party cloud apps with Cloud App Security and extend Microsoft 365 security and protection to these additional apps. This is achieved with APIs issued from the cloud app provider, which allows the app to be accessed and controlled by Cloud App Security.

Using Azure AD Conditional Access App Control in conjunction with Cloud App Security

Cloud App Security can also leverage the powerful capabilities of Azure AD Conditional Access to control cloud apps by using reverse-proxy architecture. Conditional Access App Control allows you to avoid data leakage, enforce encryption, monitor activities on unmanaged devices, and control any access from external networks or IP ranges that may constitute a risk.

Using built-in policies or creating custom policies to control SaaS app usage

Cloud App Security comes with a selection of pre-configured policy templates that can be applied to users in your organization when risky activity or behavior is detected within the SaaS apps allowed by your Microsoft 365 tenant.

One example of this kind of policy is detecting multiple failed user login attempts to a cloud app. You can set these templates or create your own custom policies to detect single-instance or repeated behavior, select filters and alerts, and apply governance actions when cloud app activity matches a policy.

> **Important note**
> Further information on the principles of Cloud App Security can be found in the *References* section at the end of this chapter.

In this section, we introduced you to Cloud App Security. We explained how Office 365 Cloud App Security comprises a subset of the features of Microsoft Cloud App Security and that Cloud App Discovery can discover SaaS app usage within your organization. We also discussed how over 16,000 apps in the app catalog can be allowed or disallowed for your users based on a Microsoft risk score and how app connectors can be used to enable third-party apps by using APIs. Finally, we talked about how Conditional Access App Control and Cloud App Security policies can be used to control the activity of the cloud apps you allow in your Microsoft 365 environment.

Next, we will show you how to configure Cloud App Security.

Configuring Cloud App Security

Now that you understand the principles of Cloud App Security, let's take a look at how you can configure it to gain visibility of your SaaS applications. First, we need to be aware of some prerequisites for using Cloud App Security. They are as follows:

- A valid license to use the Cloud App Security service. Microsoft Cloud App Security is available with a variety of Microsoft 365 subscriptions. For more information, please refer to the *References* section at the end of this chapter.
- A Global Administrator or Security Administrator role.

Once you have fulfilled these prerequisites, you can proceed to configure your Cloud Discovery settings.

> **Important note**
> Once access has been assigned with the required licenses and roles, you may need to wait approximately 15 minutes before you are able to log in to the Cloud App Security portal.

Configuring Cloud Discovery

With Cloud Discovery, you can manually upload traffic logs from your firewall and proxies and analyze them for cloud app activity. Additionally, you can automate regular log collection. This is done by completing the following steps:

1. Log in to the Cloud App Security portal at `https://portal.cloudappsecurity.com` as a Global Administrator or a Security Administrator. This will take you to the portal, as in the following screenshot:

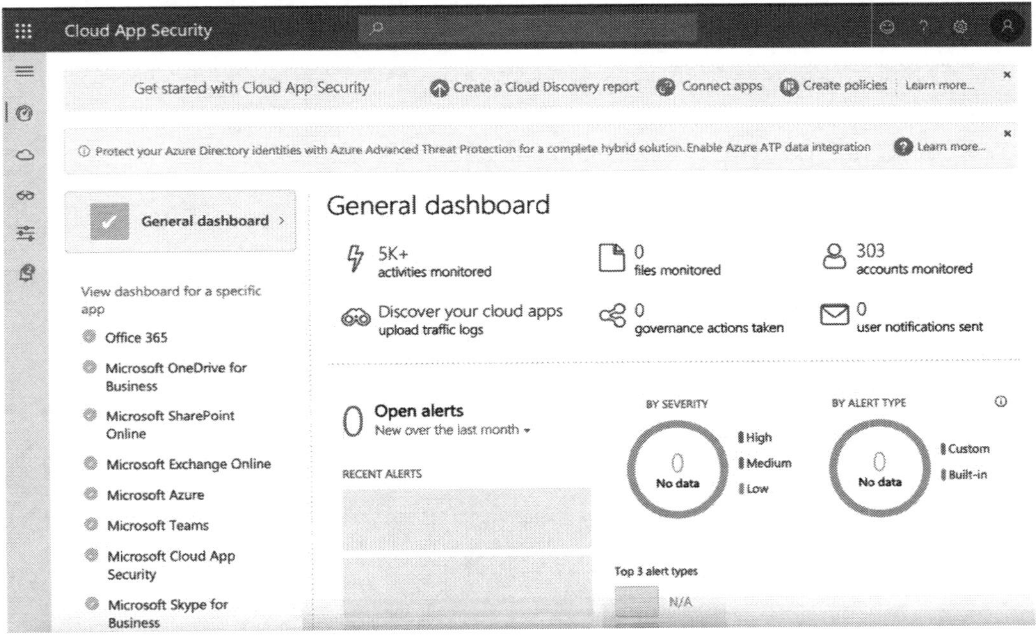

Figure 14.1 – The Cloud App Security portal

2. Click on the **Discover** option from the left-hand side menu and select **Create snapshot report**, as in the following screenshot:

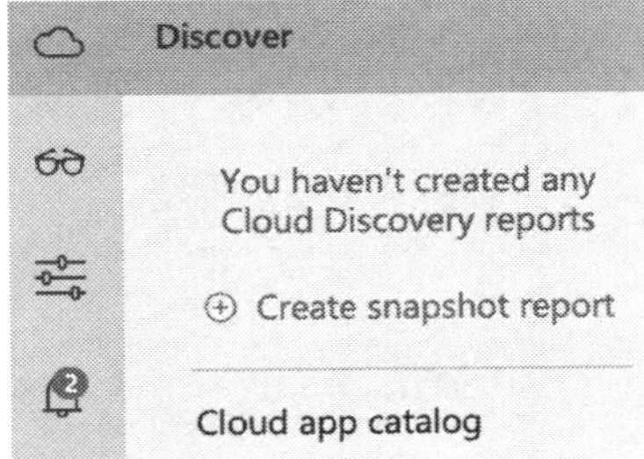

Figure 14.2 – Creating a snapshot report

3. You will need to enter a report name and description for your report. You also have the **Anonymize private information** option, as shown:

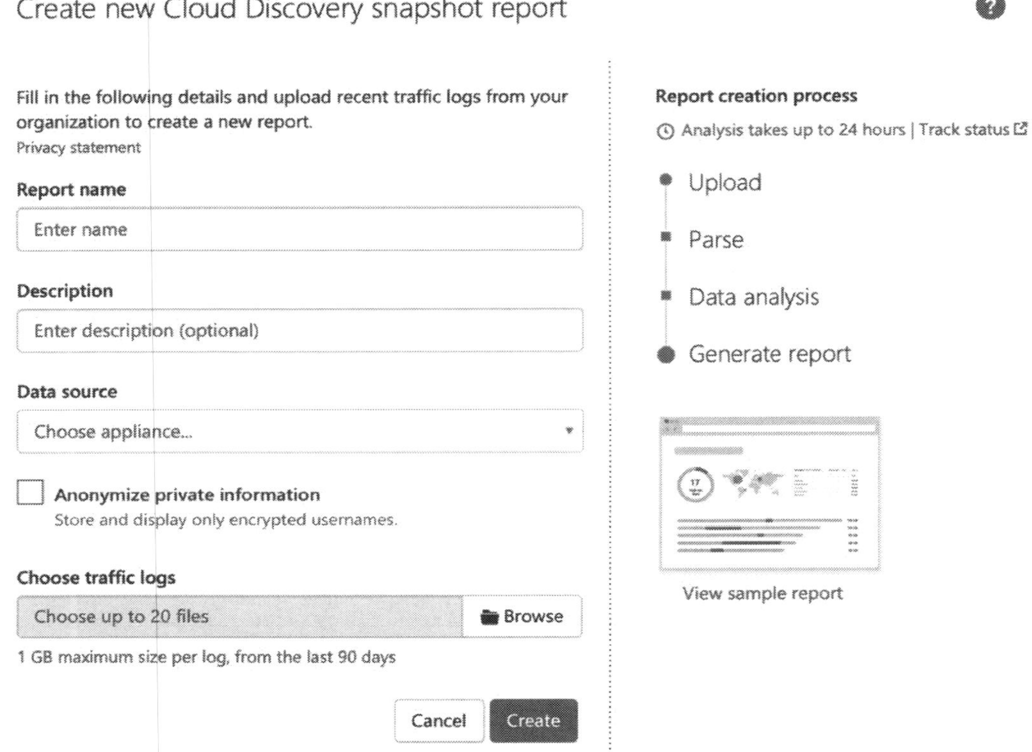

Figure 14.3 – The details for creating a snapshot report

4. Click **Browse** to choose your traffic logs and you will be able to select your appliance from the list, as shown:

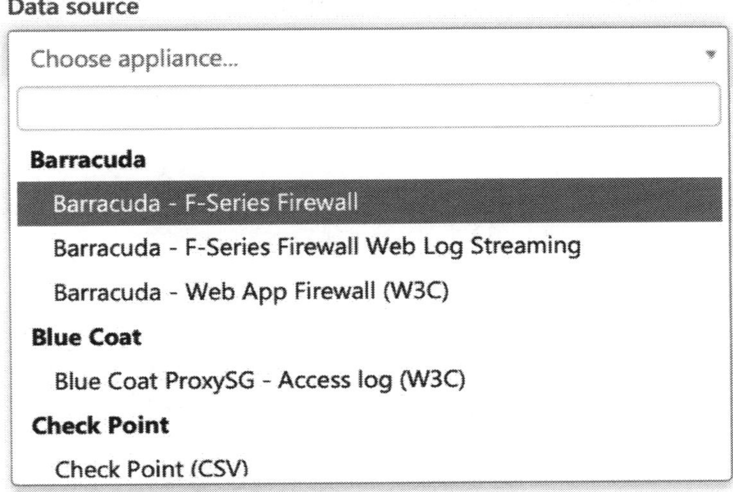

Figure 14.4 – Choosing your appliance

5. For this example, no appliance was available for demonstration. However, if you click on **View sample report** (shown in *Figure 14.3*), you can see how the snapshot report is presented. This is shown in the following screenshot:

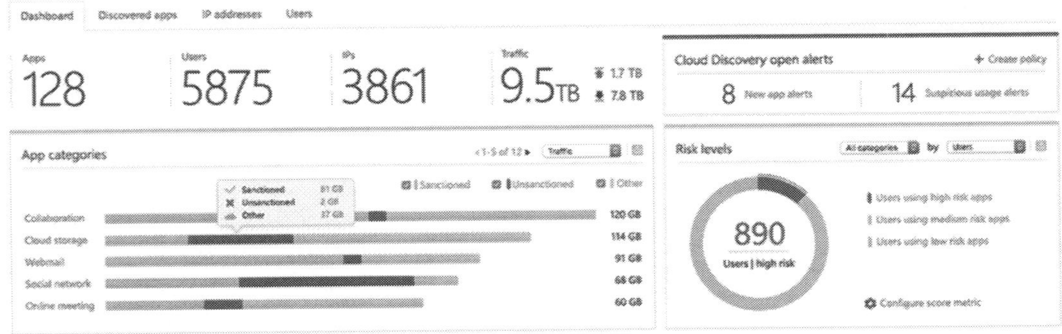

Figure 14.5 – A sample report

6. You can also automatically collect and upload traffic logs at regular intervals. This is done by clicking on the cogwheel at the top right of the screen, and selecting **SOURCES | Log collectors**, as shown:

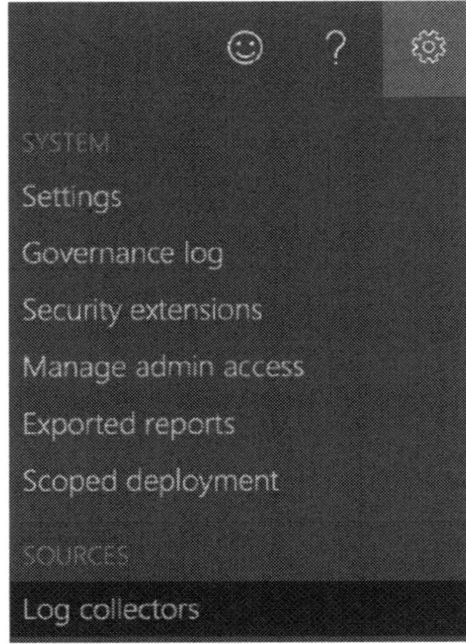

Figure 14.6 – Log collectors

7. Click on the **Add data source...** button to add your data source, as in the following screenshot:

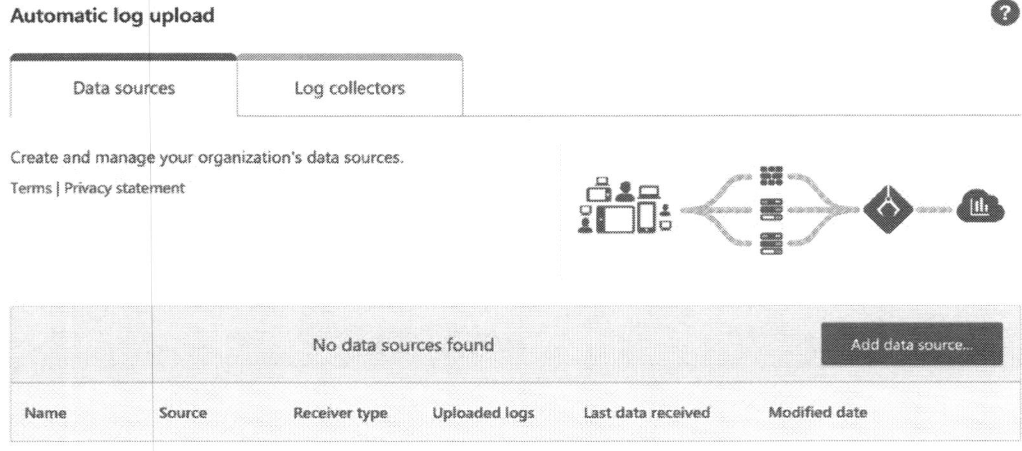

Figure 14.7 – Adding a data source

8. Then, click on the **Add log collector...** button to add your log collector settings, as in the following screenshot:

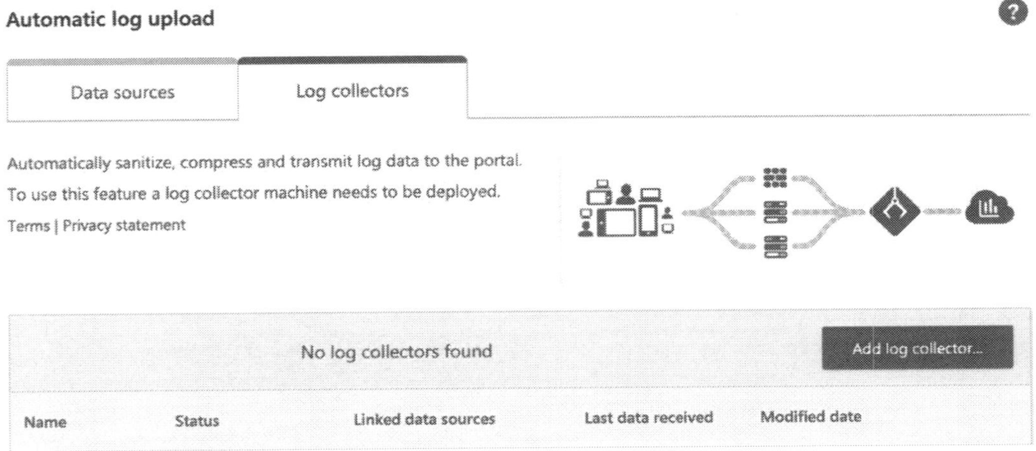

Figure 14.8 – Adding the log collector settings

Uploading your traffic logs will provide you with valuable intelligence on your cloud app usage. Next, let's look at how you can sanction and unsanction cloud apps.

Sanctioning and unsanctioning apps

Cloud App Security includes a vast app catalog consisting of both native Office 365 and third-party cloud applications. Microsoft assigns a risk score to each of these cloud apps, which you can assess to decide whether to sanction an app for use within your Microsoft 365 environment.

To access the app catalog, we need to carry out the following steps in the Cloud App Security portal:

1. Click on **Discover**, and then select **Cloud app catalog**:

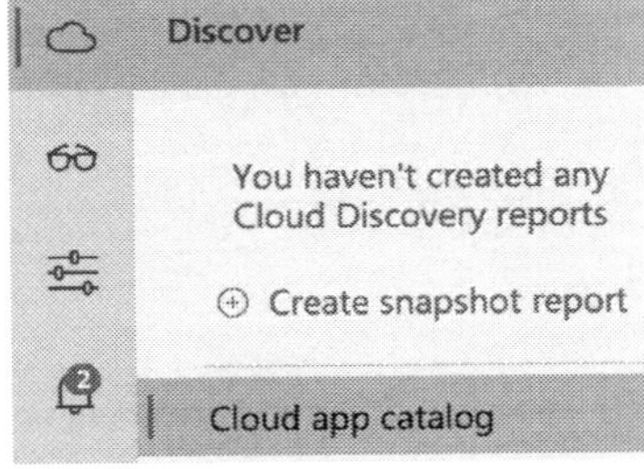

Figure 14.9 – Cloud app catalog

2. A list of apps is displayed, as in the following screenshot:

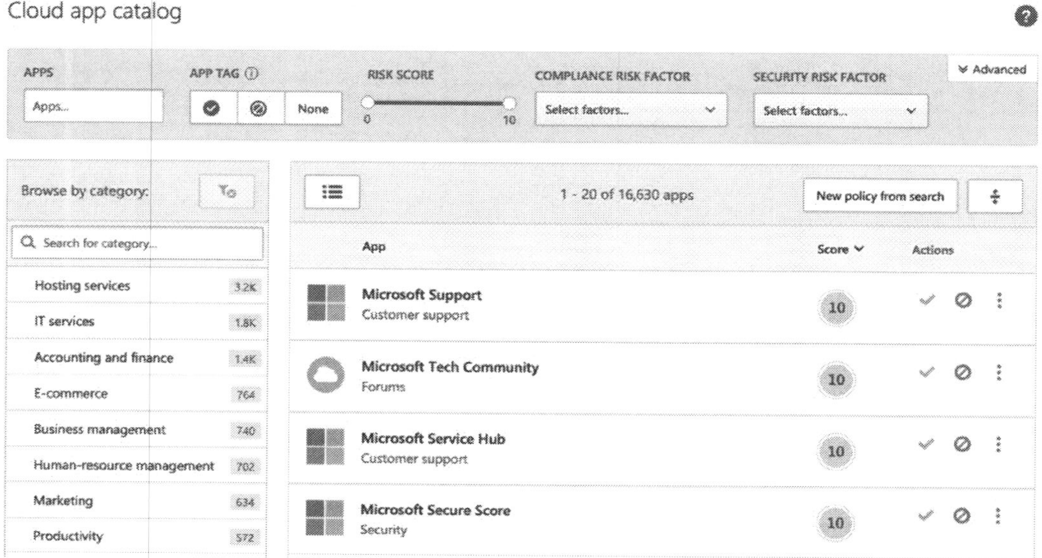

Figure 14.10 – A list of cloud apps

3. Each app has a risk score and you can quickly mark an app as sanctioned or unsanctioned from the two icons to the right of each app listing. Clicking on the three dots will also provide you with further actions that you can take in relation to the apps in the app catalog. This is shown in the following screenshot:

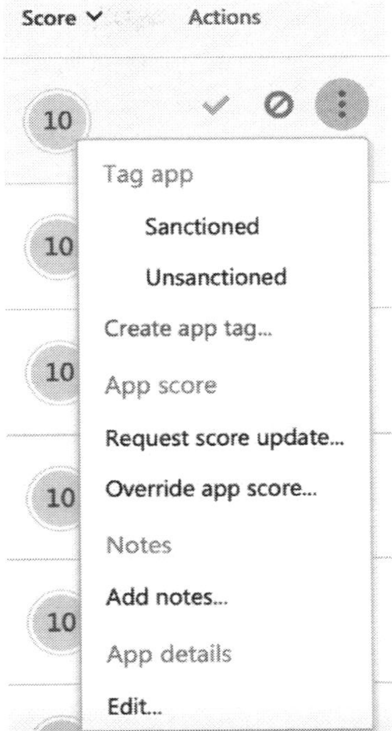

Figure 14.11 – Further actions

Next, let's examine how to connect an app using the Cloud App Security dashboard.

Connecting apps

We can connect apps in the Cloud App Security dashboard to provide greater visibility by taking the following steps:

1. From the Cloud App Security portal, which can be accessed from `https://portal.cloudappsecurity.com`, click on the cogwheel and select **App connectors**, which will take you to the **Connected apps** section, as in the following screenshot:

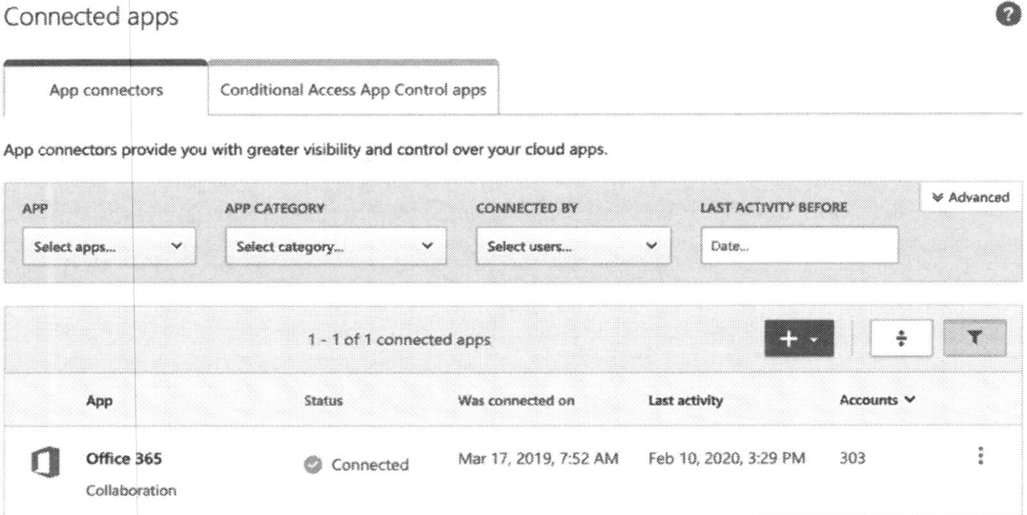

Figure 14.12 – Connected apps

2. When you click on the plus sign, you are given the option to add connected apps, as shown:

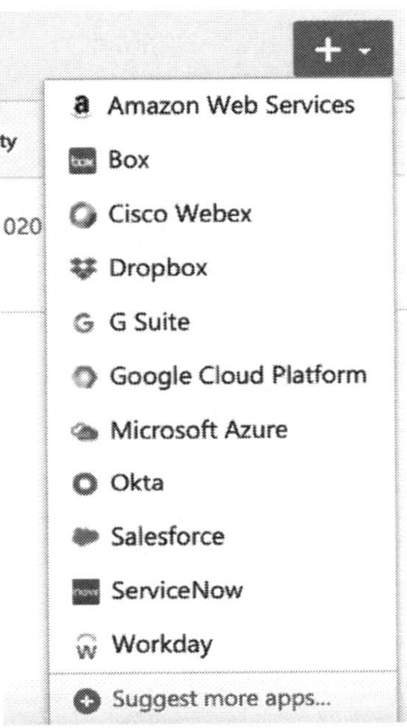

Figure 14.13 – Adding connected apps

3. We will connect **Dropbox** to Cloud App Security for this example:

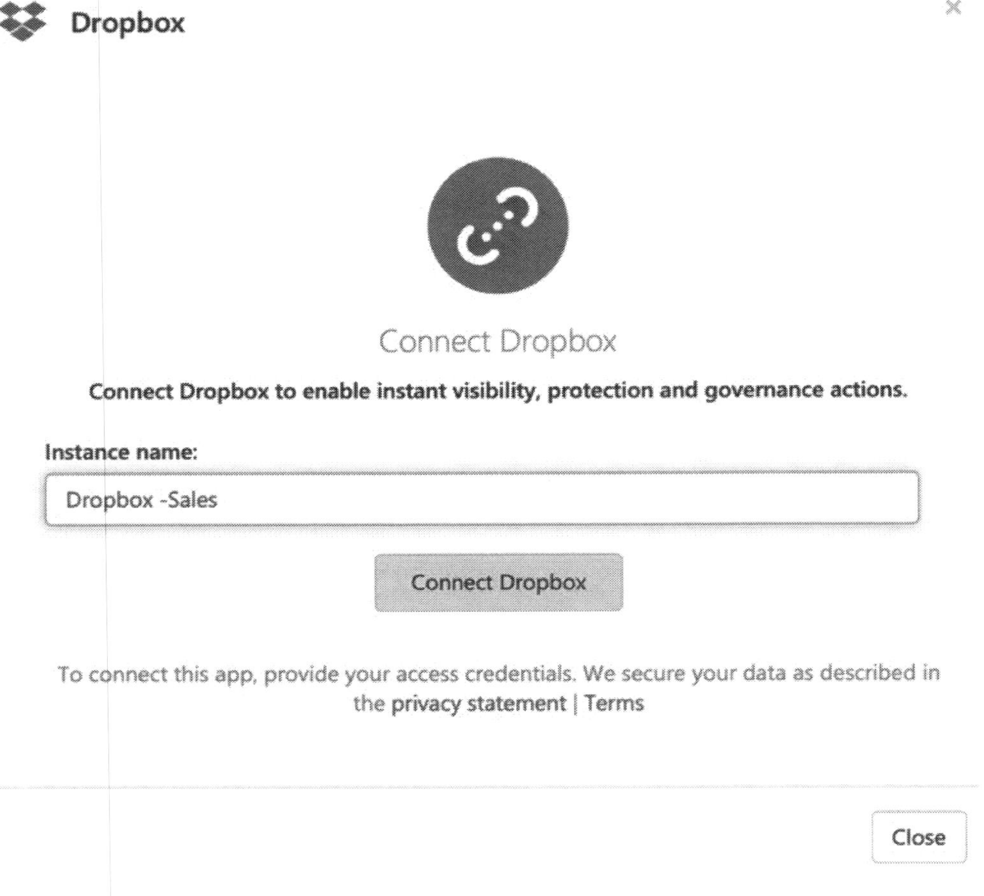

Figure 14.14 – Connecting an app

4. Enter your Dropbox account details, click **Save settings**, and then click on **Follow the link**, as shown:

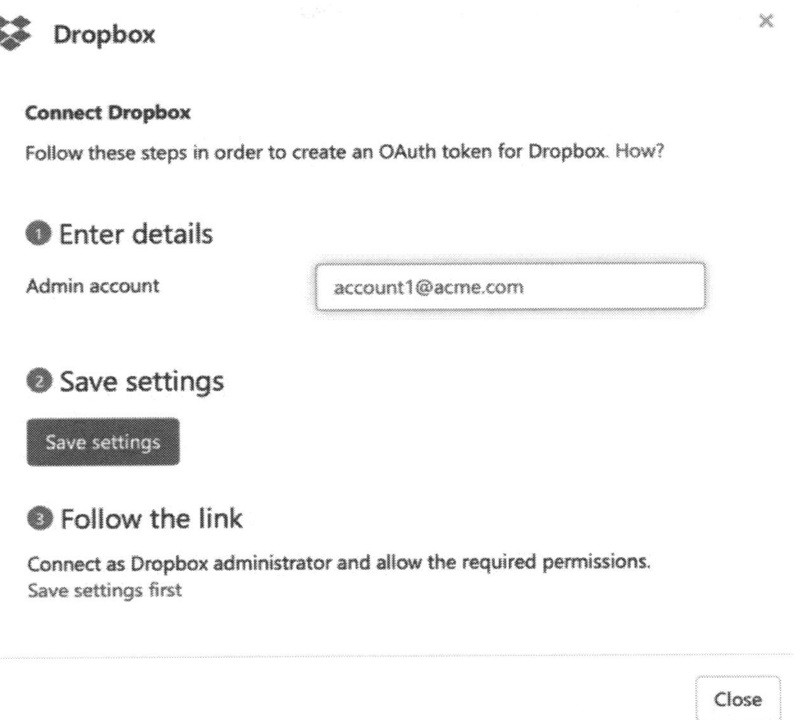

Figure 14.15 – Entering account details

5. Once completed, you will see your connected app in the list, as in the following screenshot:

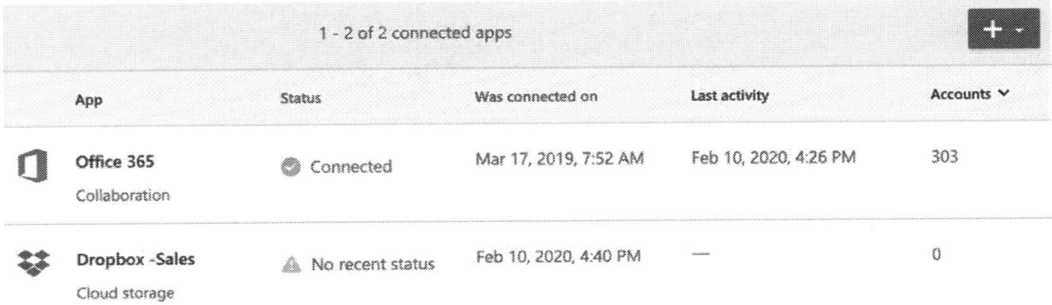

1 - 2 of 2 connected apps

App	Status	Was connected on	Last activity	Accounts
Office 365 Collaboration	Connected	Mar 17, 2019, 7:52 AM	Feb 10, 2020, 4:26 PM	303
Dropbox -Sales Cloud storage	No recent status	Feb 10, 2020, 4:40 PM	—	0

Figure 14.16 – The list of connected apps

Next, let's look at how Cloud App Security allows us to control our cloud apps by applying built-in or custom policies.

Controlling apps with policies

With Cloud App Security policies, you can control your cloud apps with governance and compliance actions. This can be achieved by completing the following steps:

1. From the Cloud App Security dashboard, select **Control | Templates**, as in the following screenshot:

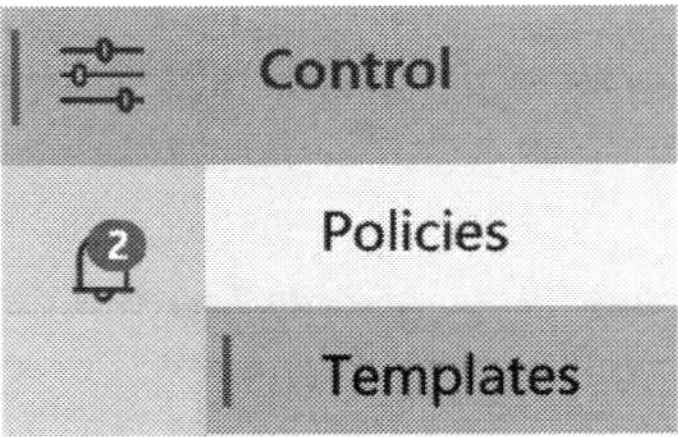

Figure 14.17 – Policy templates

2. You will see a list of available policy templates that you can create a policy from. In this example, we will choose the policy named **Mass download by a single user**. Click on the plus sign, as in the following screenshot:

Figure 14.18 – The list of policy templates

3. In the policy settings, you can configure your preferences for the policy, such as the **Policy severity** option, as shown:

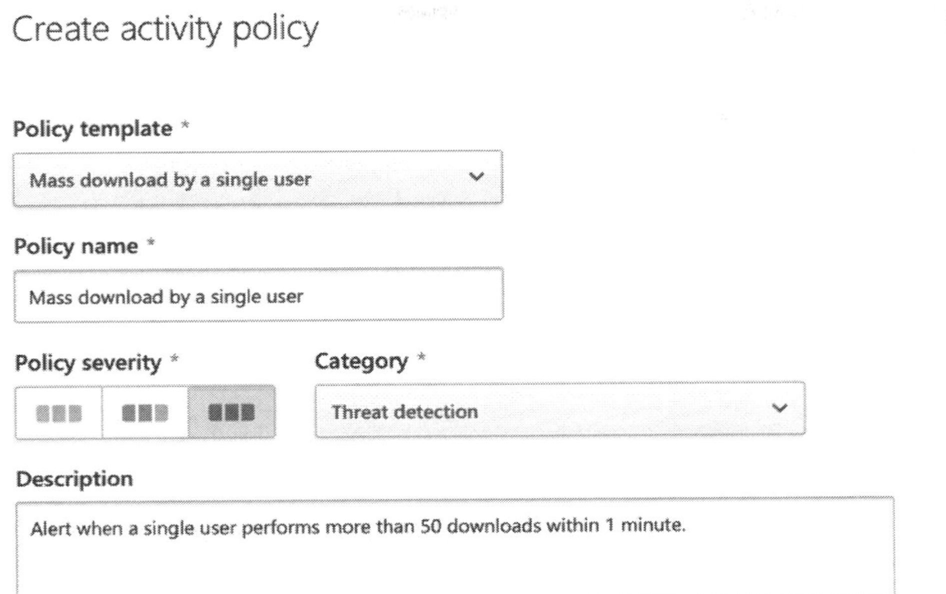

Figure 14.19 – Creating an activity policy

4. As you scroll through the policy settings options, you can also configure filtering settings for your policy, as in the following screenshot:

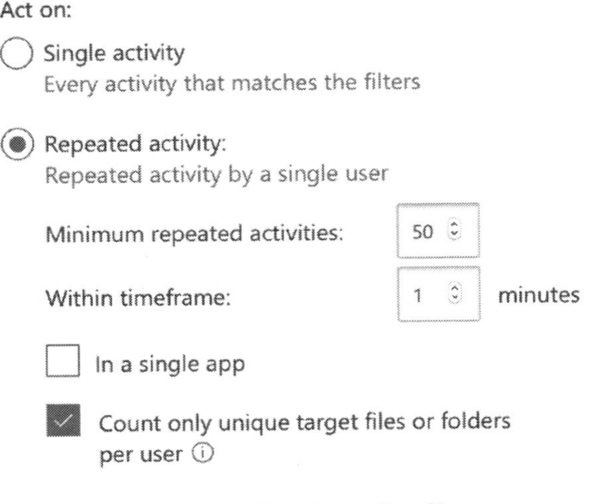

Figure 14.20 – Creating policy filters

5. Next, you can view and modify the activity matching settings for your policy, as in the following screenshot:

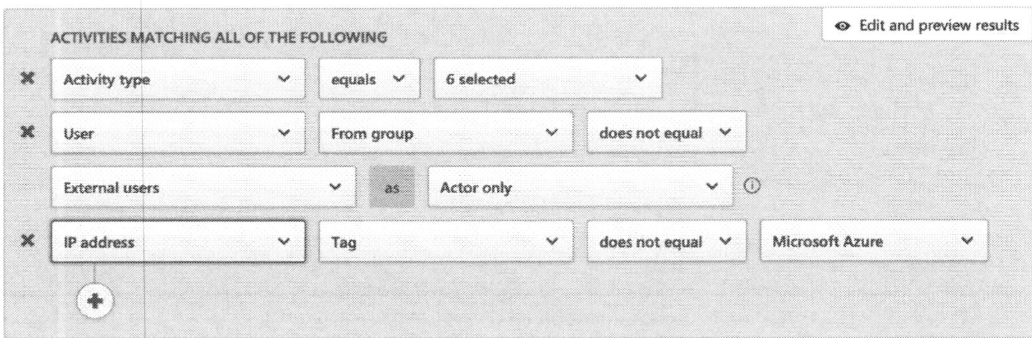

Figure 14.21 – Modifying the activity matching settings

6. You can also configure alerts to notify users or administrators when there is a policy match, as shown:

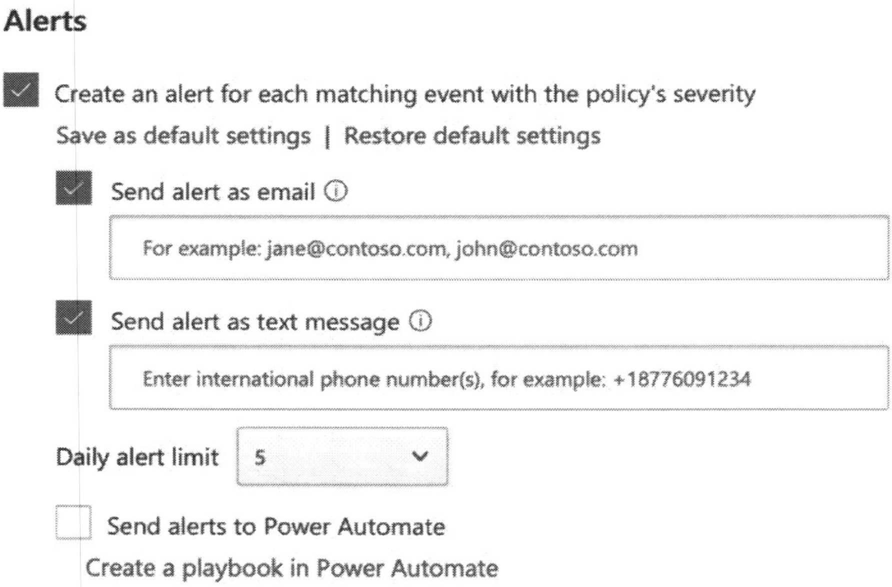

Alerts

Create an alert for each matching event with the policy's severity

Save as default settings | Restore default settings

Send alert as email

For example: jane@contoso.com, john@contoso.com

Send alert as text message

Enter international phone number(s), for example: +18776091234

Daily alert limit 5

Send alerts to Power Automate

Create a playbook in Power Automate

Figure 14.22 – Configuring alerts

7. Finally, you can choose which governance actions are applied when a policy match occurs. These can either be set for all apps or just for Office 365 apps. The **Governance actions** options are shown in the following screenshot:

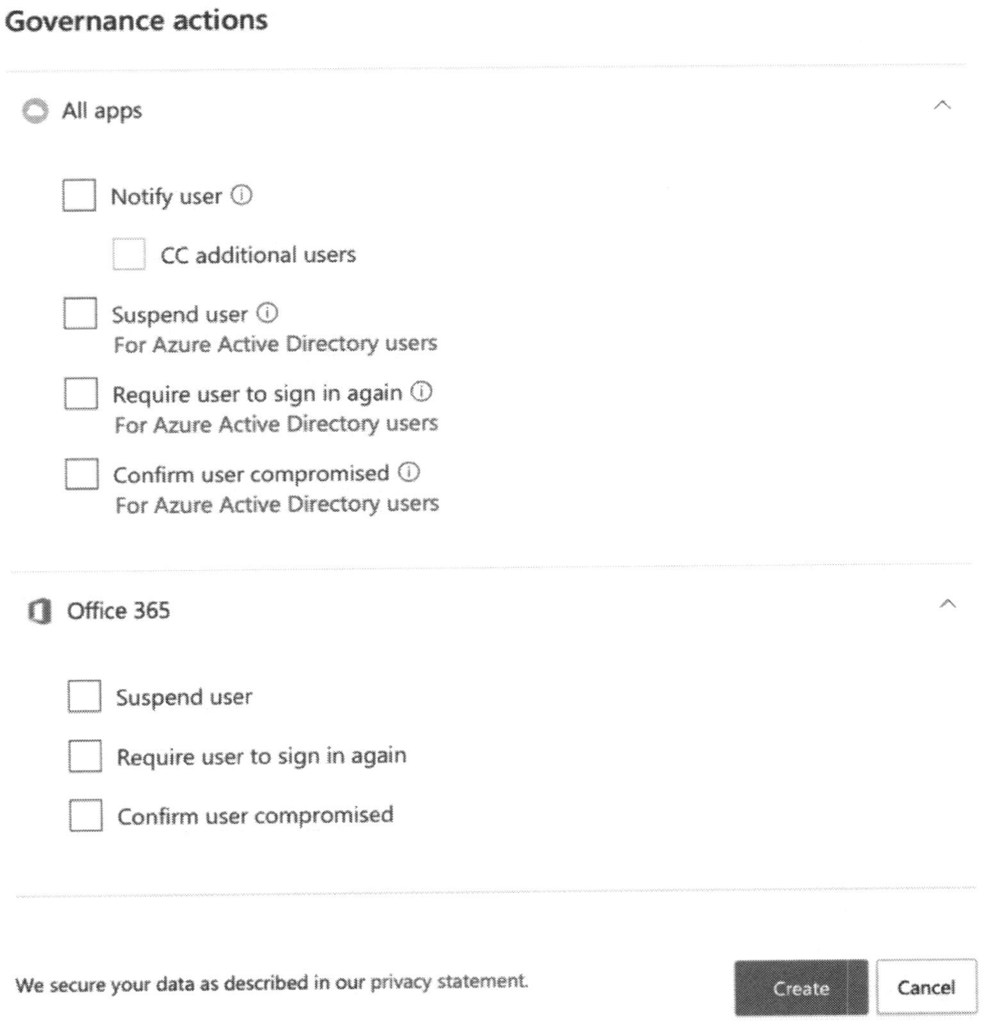

Governance actions

All apps

Notify user

CC additional users

Suspend user
For Azure Active Directory users

Require user to sign in again
For Azure Active Directory users

Confirm user compromised
For Azure Active Directory users

Office 365

Suspend user

Require user to sign in again

Confirm user compromised

We secure your data as described in our privacy statement.

Create Cancel

Figure 14.23 – Setting the Governance actions options

8. When you are happy with your policy settings, click on **Create** to complete the setup of your policy. Your policy is created and you can search for it in the Cloud App Security portal under **Control** | **Policies**. You can then modify the policy if required, as well as click on **View all matches** to see any instances where your policy has been triggered:

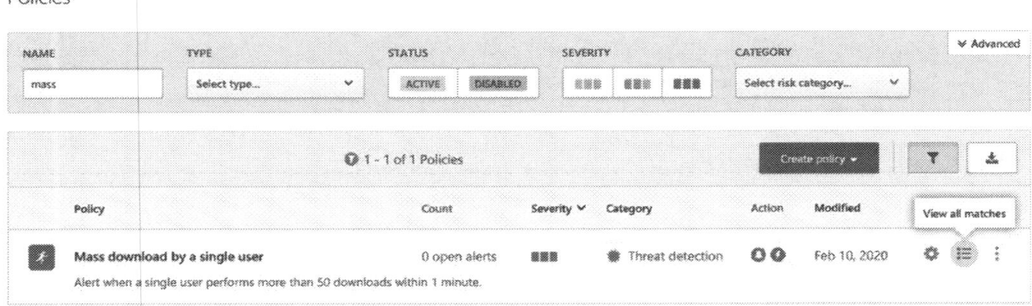

Figure 14.24 – Viewing all matches

The policy templates available to you in Cloud App Security provide you with many useful options to alert you to cloud app activity and respond by applying governance actions.

Next, we will examine how Conditional Access App Control can be used with Cloud App Security to prevent data leakage, enforce encryption, and control access to your cloud applications in Microsoft 365.

Using Conditional Access App Control with Cloud App Security

Cloud App Security can integrate with Azure AD Conditional Access to control access to your Microsoft 365 cloud apps.

This can be configured by completing the following steps:

1. From the Cloud App Security portal, click on the cogwheel and select **Conditional Access App Control**, as in the following screenshot:

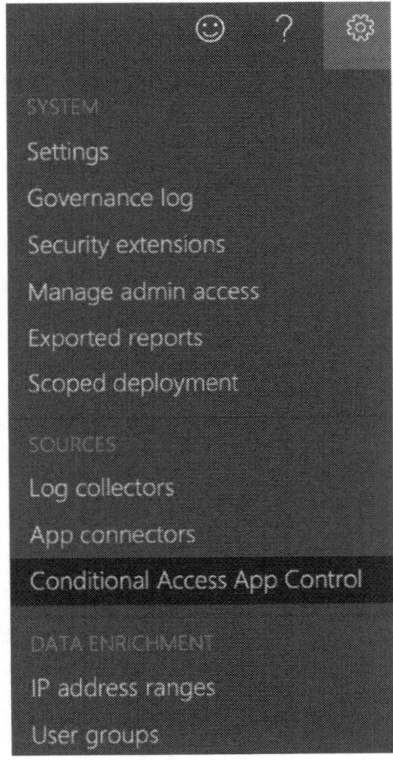

Figure 14.25 – Conditional Access App Control

2. When you first log in to the **Conditional Access App Control apps** section, there will be no apps available to you. This is because you need to enable session controls for your Conditional Access policies from the Azure portal first:

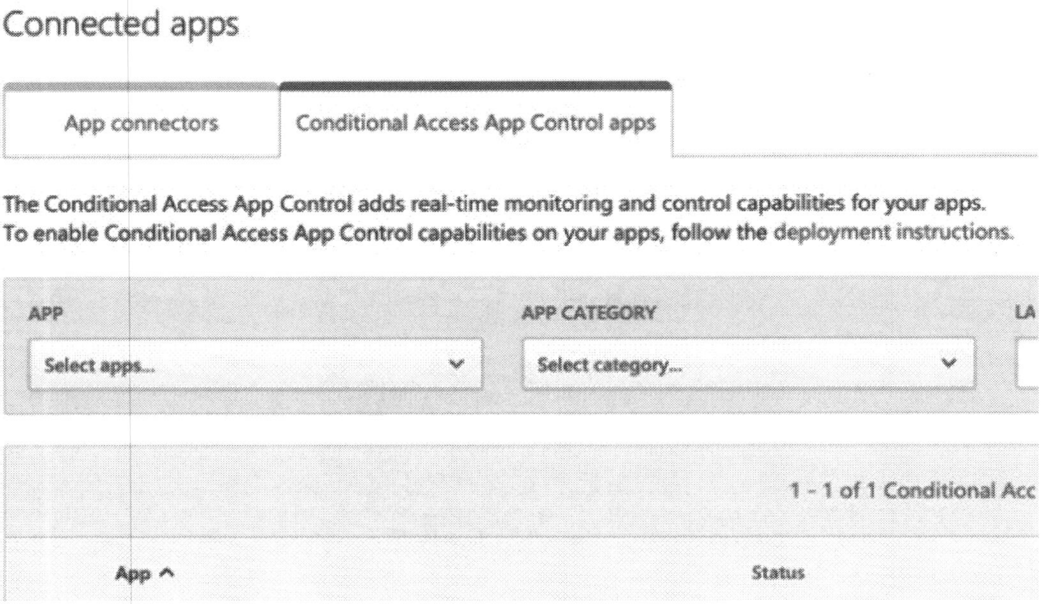

Figure 14.26 – Conditional Access App Control apps

3. In order to enable the session controls, go to `https://portal.azure.com` and navigate to **Azure Active Directory | Security | Conditional Access**. In the following example, we have a policy scoped to a user in our tenant called **James Smith** that is set to prompt for **Multi-Factor Authentication** (**MFA**) when accessing **Exchange Online**.

4. In order to set this up, click on **New Policy**, or edit an existing policy. By clicking on **Access Control | Session** within the policy settings, we can choose our session controls. Under the **Use Conditional Access App Control** option, there are three available settings. For this example, we will set it to **Monitor Only (Preview)**. The session control settings are shown in the following screenshot:

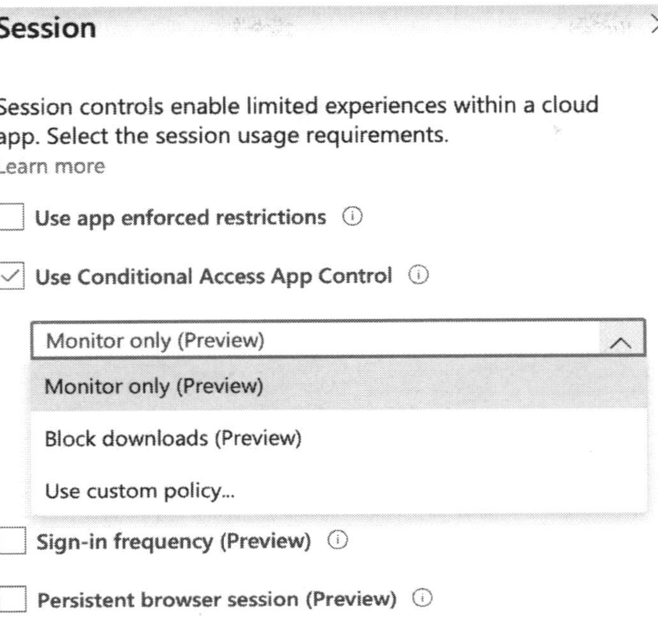

Figure 14.27 – Session controls

5. After saving our modification to the Conditional Access policy, we now need to sign in to Exchange Online as our user, James Smith, by going to `https://outlook.office.com` and entering the user credentials.
6. Now that we have enabled session controls on the Conditional Access policy, we are prompted to accept a certificate when logging in to the Exchange Online service, as in the following screenshot:

Figure 14.28 – The certificate prompt

7. After accepting the certificate, you are warned that access to Exchange Online is monitored:

Access to Microsoft Exchange Online is monitored

For improved security, your organization allows access to **Microsoft Exchange Online** in monitor mode.

Access is only available from a web browser.

Figure 14.29 – User warning of monitoring activity

8. Now that you have completed the process of logging in and completing the conditional access requirements, we can return to the **Conditional Access App Control apps** setting within the Cloud App Security portal. Now, we can see that **Microsoft Exchange Online - General** has been added as an available app in this section:

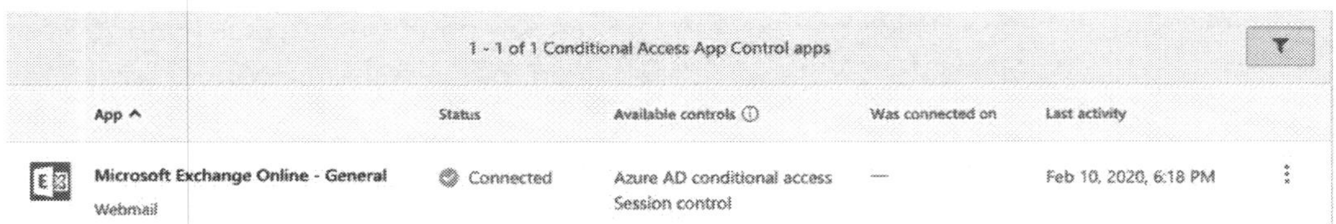

Figure 14.30 – The new Conditional Access App Control apps page

9. By clicking on the app, we can inspect the available tabs, which contain information relating to this cloud app. By clicking on **Activity log**, we can see that our user, James Smith, was redirected to a session control in order to successfully log on to Exchange Online:

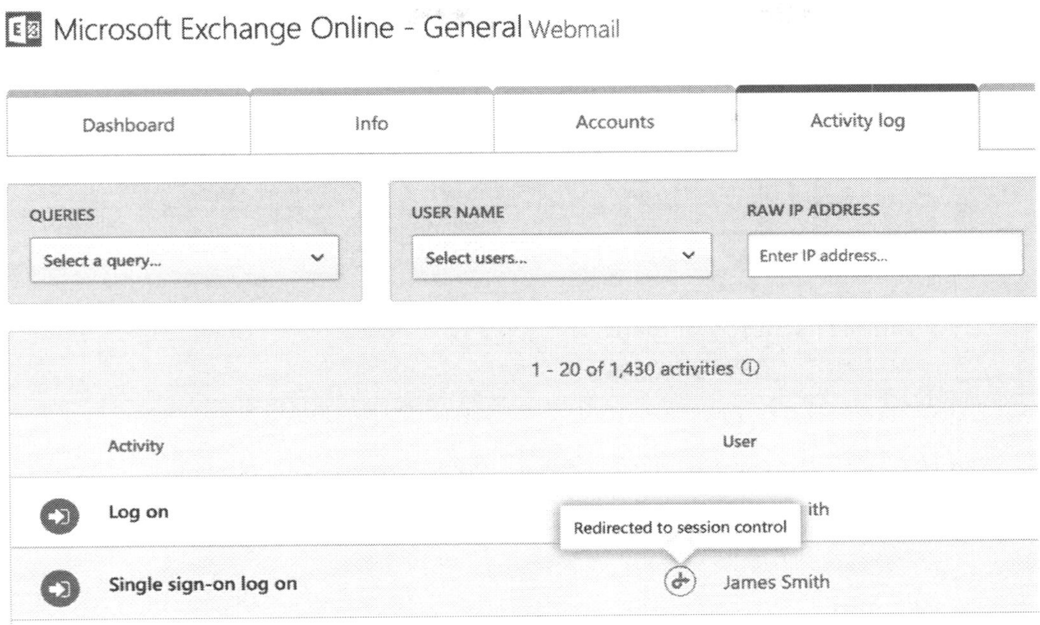

Figure 14.31 – The app control settings

So, as we have demonstrated, Condition Access App Control empowers Microsoft 365 Cloud App Security with controls to help you monitor and protect your Office 365 cloud apps. In the preceding example, we used Exchange Online in a Conditional Access policy and enforced session controls to make the activities visible in the Cloud App Security portal.

In this section, we showed you how to configure Cloud App Security for your organization. You learned how Cloud App Security can identify cloud app activity in your organization by uploading traffic logs from your edge devices.

We also showed you how you can sanction cloud apps and use app connectors to gain more visibility on your cloud app usage, as well as how policies and Conditional Access App Control are powerful tools to bring additional visibility and control.

In the final section of this chapter, we will review the Cloud App Security dashboard and explain how reports and logs can be used to gather vital intelligence on cloud app activity within your Microsoft 365 environment.

Using the Cloud App Security dashboard, reports, and logs

With Cloud App Security, you are also able to generate and review reports that contain information on file activity within your cloud applications. There are three key reports available that relate to file activity in Cloud App Security. They are as follows:

- **Data sharing overview**: This report lists all the files stored in your cloud apps, sorted by app.
- **Outbound sharing by domain**: This report lists the domains in which files are shared by users in your cloud apps.
- **Owners of shared files**: This report lists users who own files that are shared externally.

In order to generate and review these reports, we need to complete the following steps:

1. From the Cloud App Security dashboard, go to **Investigate | Files**, as in the following screenshot:

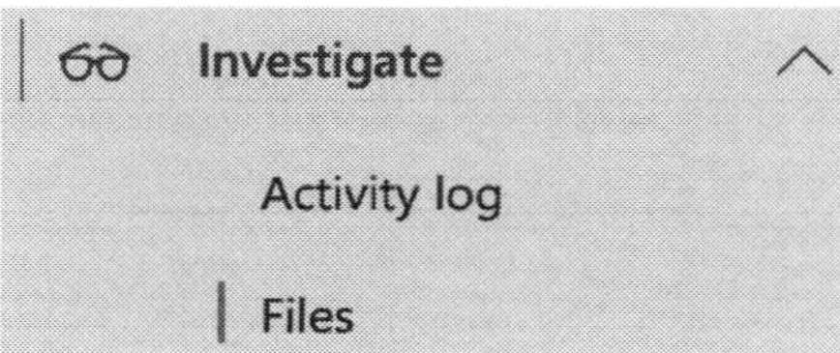

Figure 14.32 – Investigating files

2. By clicking on the three dots next to an individual file item, you can see recent file activity in this area for your cloud apps and apply the following actions:

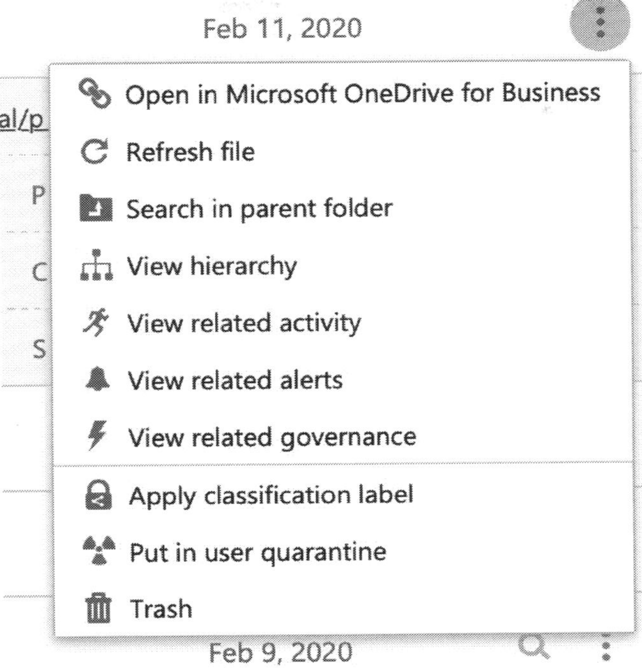

Figure 14.33 – The available file actions

3. At the top right of the dashboard, you can click on the three dots and you will see the available reports described previously:

Figure 14.34 – The available reports

4. Clicking on any of these reports will take you directly to that report, where you can see more details about the recorded activities, as in the following example of **Data sharing overview**:

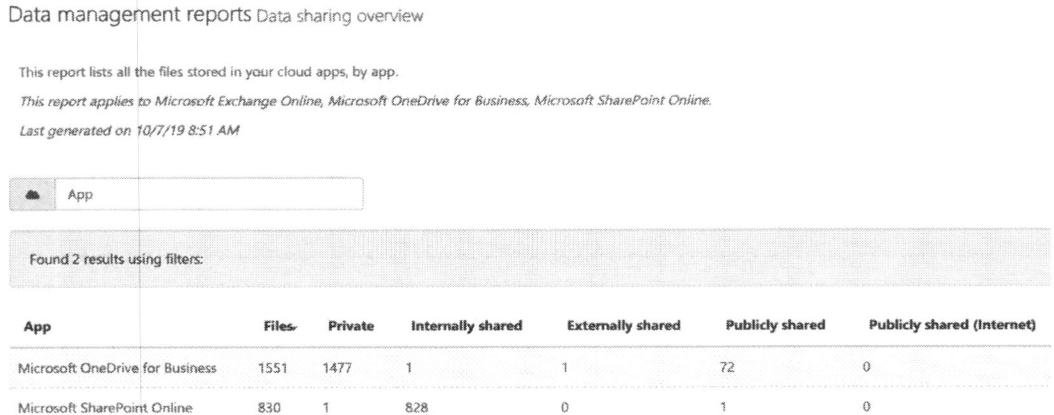

Figure 14.35 – A data management report

In addition to the preceding reports, we can also view the activity log. This is also available from the Cloud App Security portal, under **Investigate**.

5. Clicking on **Activity log** will show you the following:

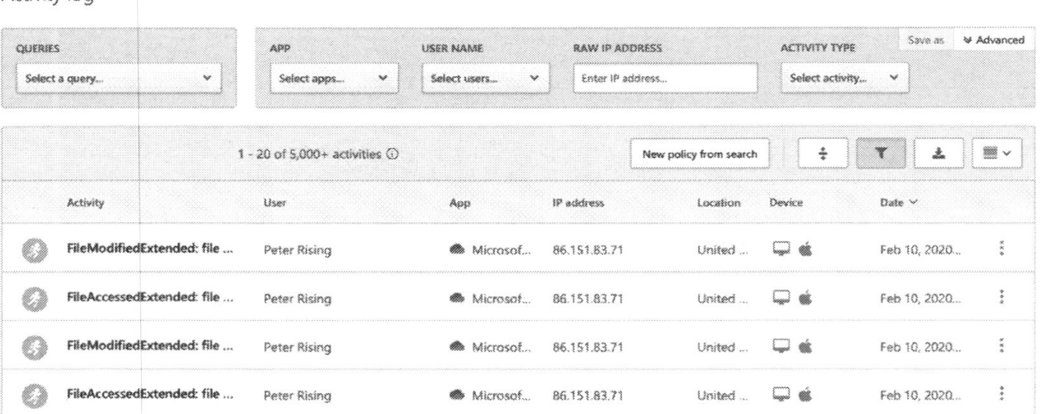

Figure 14.36 – Activity log

6. You can use the queries and filters at the top of the activity log to view specific log activity. Expanding each log entry displays additional details relating to the recorded activity.

The additional options available under the **Investigate** section are as follows:

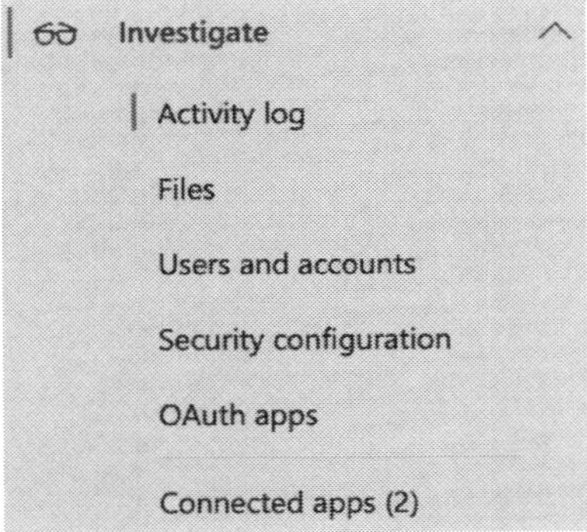

Figure 14.37 – Additional investigation options

You can also review and manage alerts within Cloud App Security. The **Alerts** page can be accessed from the bottom of the left-hand side menu. This is shown in the following screenshot:

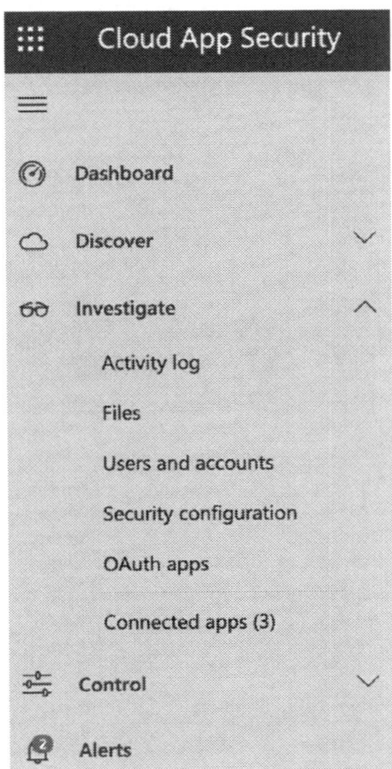

Figure 14.38 – Selecting Alerts from the menu

Once you have clicked on **Alerts**, you will see the list of alerts, as in the following screenshot:

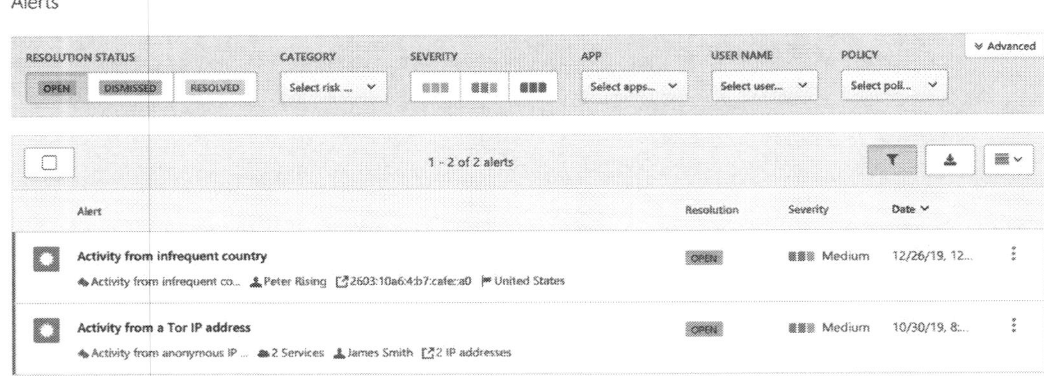

Figure 14.39 – Alerts

Analyzing the alerts recorded by Cloud App Security will give you a deeper understanding of your cloud environment. Any suspicious alerts can be remediated by creating policies to block any further instances of that activity.

When opening an alert, you can apply the following options to dismiss or resolve the alert as appropriate:

Figure 14.40 – Resolving alerts

In this section, we examined the available options in Microsoft 365 Cloud App Security to navigate the dashboard, as well as view reports, activity logs, and alerts. We showed you how you can interpret these alerts and apply remediation where required by adjusting policies to prevent any reoccurrence.

Summary

In this chapter, we introduced you to Cloud App Security. We explained the two variations of Cloud App Security and how Office 365 Cloud App Security is a subset of the wider features available in Microsoft 365 Cloud App Security.

You learned how Cloud App Security can provide visibility of your cloud app usage within your Microsoft 365 environment, both with native Office 365 apps and third-party cloud apps. We showed you how to discover cloud activity by uploading traffic logs from your edge devices, along with how to sanction and unsanction cloud apps and connect third-party cloud apps using the app connector.

We also demonstrated how policies can be applied from built-in templates and custom creation to control cloud app usage. Finally, we showed you how Azure AD Conditional Access can integrate with Cloud App Security by using session controls.

The topics we have covered in this chapter will enable you to plan and configure your Cloud App Security deployment from the Cloud App Security portal, which can be accessed from `https://portal.cloudappsecurity.com`.

In the next chapter, we will introduce you to the principles of data governance and compliance in your Microsoft 365 environment with security analytics and reporting features. You will learn about Windows analytics, the configuration of Windows diagnostic data, telemetry in Microsoft Office, and additional features, such as Office 365 Secure Score and the Microsoft Graph Security API.

Questions

1. Which of the following is not a version of Cloud App Security?

   a. Office 365 Cloud App Security

   b. Advanced Cloud App Security

   c. Microsoft Cloud App Security

2. True or false: Cloud App Security can only be used with an Office 365 E3 license.

   a. True

   b. False

3. Which of the following is not one of the available reports in Cloud App Security?

    a. Owners of shared files

    b. Administrator overview

    c. Data sharing overview

    d. Outbound sharing by domains

4. True or false: Conditional Access App Control allows you to apply session controls to your Conditional Access policies to integrate with Cloud App Security.

    a. True

    b. False

5. Where in the Cloud App Security portal would you go to sanction or unsanction an app?

    a. **Control | Policies**

    b. **Investigate | Connected Apps**

    c. **Investigate | Security Configuration**

    d. **Discover | Cloud app catalog**

6. When configuring a policy template, which of the following alerts can be configured (choose three)?

    a. Send alert as email

    b. Send alert via Microsoft Flow

    c. Send alert as text message

    d. Send alert via RSS feed

    e. Send alert to Power Automate

7. Which of the following Microsoft 365 admin roles can be used to configure Cloud App Security (choose two)?

    a. Security Administrator

    b. Global Reader

    c. Global Administrator

    d. User Administrator

    e. Service Administrator

8. True or false: With Cloud Discovery, you can upload traffic logs from your firewalls and proxy servers both manually and by automation, and view the results in Cloud App Security.

   a. True

   b. False

9. Which of the following URLs would you use to access the Cloud App Security dashboard?

   a. `https://portal.clouddiscovery.com`

   b. `https://admin.cloudappsecurity.com`

   c. `https://microsoft.cloudappsecurity.com`

   d. `https://portal.cloudappsecurity.com`

10. Where would you go on the Cloud App Security dashboard to view recent file activity within your Microsoft 365 environment?

   a. **Investigate | Users and accounts**

   b. **Investigate | Security Configuration**

   c. **Investigate | Files**

   d. **Discover | Users**

References

Please refer to the following links for more information:

- Comparing Office 365 Cloud App Security and Microsoft 365 Cloud App Security: `https://docs.microsoft.com/en-us/cloud-app-security/editions-cloud-app-security-o365?wt.mc_id=4039827`
- Setting up Cloud App Security: `https://docs.microsoft.com/en-us/cloud-app-security/general-setup?wt.mc_id=4039827`
- Cloud App Discovery: `https://docs.microsoft.com/en-us/office365/securitycompliance/create-app-discovery-reports-in-ocas?wt.mc_id=4039827`
- Connecting apps: `https://docs.microsoft.com/en-us/cloud-app-security/enable-instant-visibility-protection-and-governance-actions-for-your-apps?wt.mc_id=4039827`

- Cloud App Security policies: `https://docs.microsoft.com/en-us/cloud-app-security/control-cloud-apps-with-policies?wt.mc_id=4039827`
- Reports: `https://docs.microsoft.com/en-us/cloud-app-security/built-in-reports?wt.mc_id=4039827`
- Alerts: `https://docs.microsoft.com/en-us/cloud-app-security/managing-alerts?wt.mc_id=4039827`

Section 4: Data Governance and Compliance in Microsoft 365

In this section, we will be examining how to implement data governance and compliance principles within Microsoft 365.

This part of the book comprises the following chapters:

- *Chapter 15, Security Analytics and Auditing Capabilities*
- *Chapter 16, Personal Data Protection in Microsoft 365*
- *Chapter 17, Data Governance and Retention*
- *Chapter 18, Search and Investigation*
- *Chapter 19, Data Privacy Compliance*

15
Security Analytics and Auditing Capabilities

When you consider the importance of security, compliance, and best practice configuration in your Microsoft 365 environment, the configuration of your Microsoft 365 services is only as effective as the analytical, auditing, and reporting capabilities that are available to Microsoft 365 administrators. When you configure, review, and take any required actions by using these capabilities, you can gain vital intelligence on the activities within your environment.

In this chapter, we will introduce you to the concepts of analytics and intelligence within Microsoft 365. You will learn about desktop analytics, the configuration of Windows diagnostic data, and Telemetry in Microsoft Office.

We will also examine some additional features on the subject of auditing and discuss how you can enable auditing, search audit logs, view audit search results, and create and use alert policies to trigger alerts against specific activities.

By the end of this chapter, you will be able to confidently implement and manage the features that we will examine.

We will cover these topics in the following order:

- Understanding Desktop Analytics, Windows diagnostics, and Office Telemetry
- Configuring Office 365 auditing
- Performing an audit log search
- Configuring an audit alert policy

Understanding Desktop Analytics, Windows diagnostics, and Office Telemetry

In this section, we will examine three of the key features that relate to analytics and diagnostic information within Microsoft 365. We will begin by looking at **Desktop Analytics** (formerly known as Windows Analytics).

Desktop Analytics

This cloud-based service integrates more tightly with System Center Configuration Manager than its predecessor to provide you with intelligence on the Windows clients in your organization and show you information on their readiness for updates.

From the Desktop Analytics portal, which can be accessed by navigating to `https://devicemanagement.portal.azure.com`, you can complete the following tasks and activities:

- Set up an inventory of your organization's apps.
- Gain visibility on app compatibility.
- Target driver and app updates to specific users in a pilot group.
- Deploy Windows 10 to managed devices.

In order to set up, configure, and run Desktop Analytics on your environment, you will need a **Global Administrator** account and one of the following licenses:

- Windows 10 Enterprise E3
- Windows 10 Enterprise E5
- Microsoft 365 F3

- Microsoft 365 E3
- Microsoft 365 E5
- Windows Virtual Desktop Access E3
- Windows Virtual Desktop Access E5

To set up Desktop Analytics for the first time, you will need to open the Desktop Analytics portal and complete the following steps:

1. From the **Set up Desktop Analytics** screen, click **Start**, as in the following screenshot:

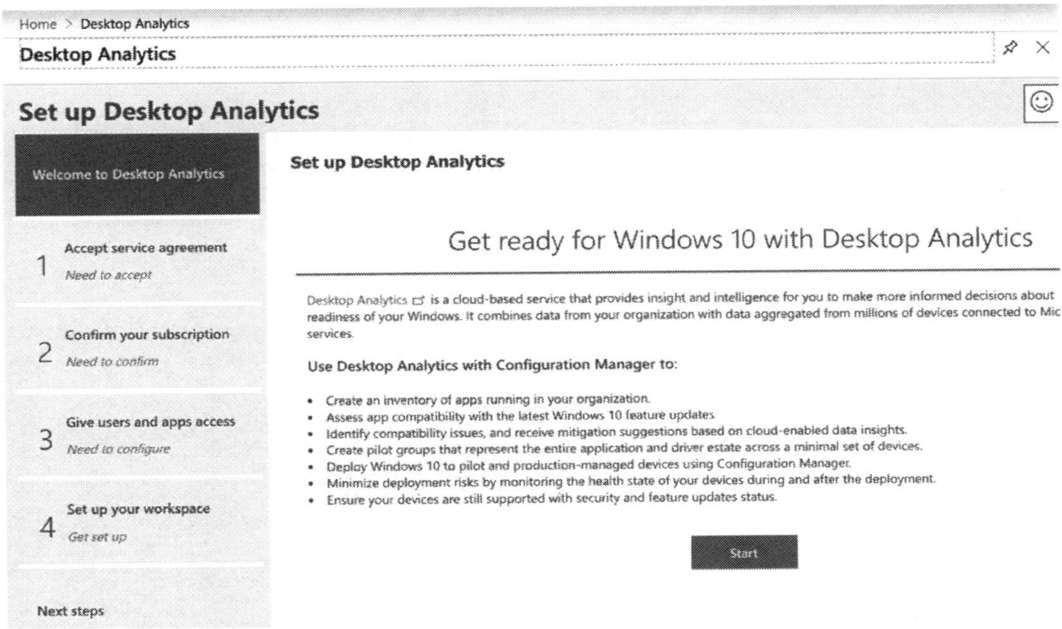

Figure 15.1 – Setting up Desktop Analytics

2. You will now progress through a four-step wizard. Under step 1, which is titled **Accept service agreement**, click **Next**:

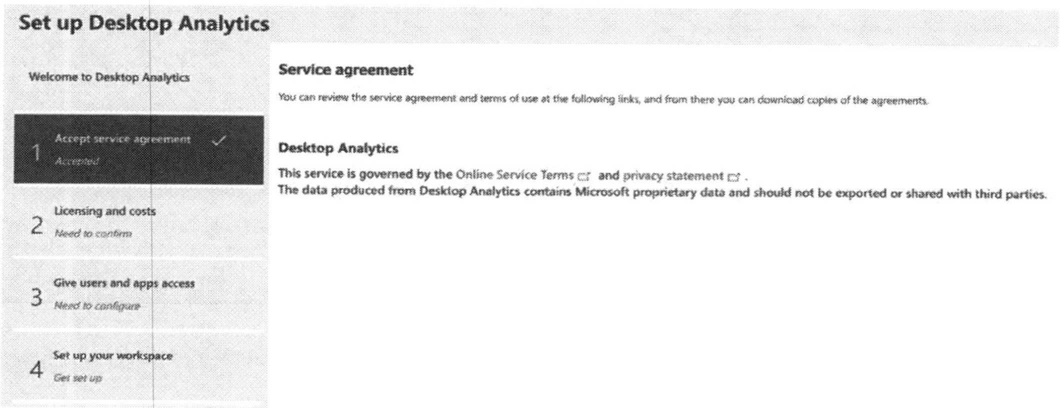

Figure 15.2 – Accepting the service agreement

3. Under step 2, you need to confirm that you have a valid subscription. Next to the **Do you have one of the supported subscriptions?** option, move the slider from **No** to **Yes**, as in the following screenshot:

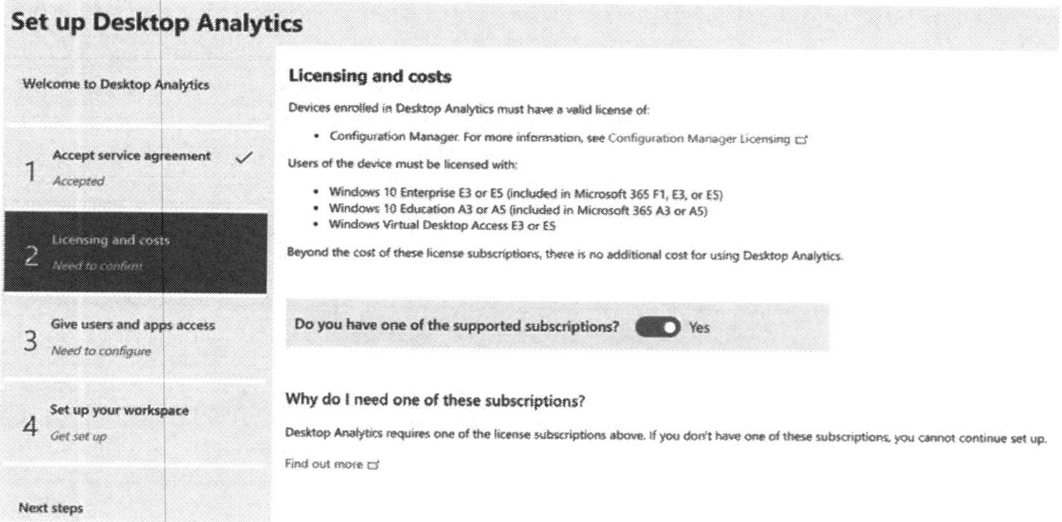

Figure 15.3 – Confirming your subscription

4. Under the **Give users and apps access** option, set **Allow Desktop Analytics to manage Directory roles on your behalf** to **Yes**, as in the following screenshot:

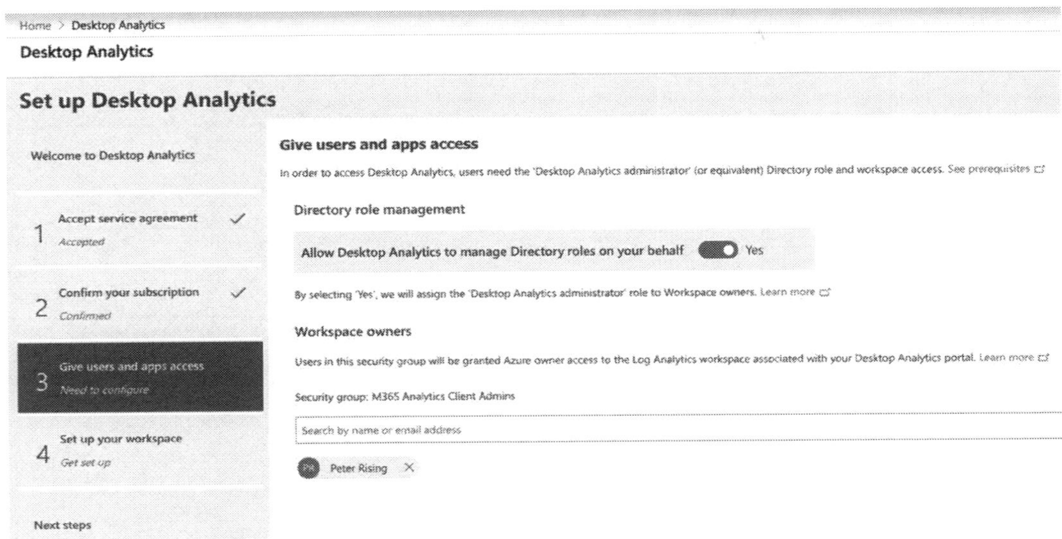

Figure 15.4 – Giving users and apps access

5. Click **Next** and you will see the **Set up your workspace** options, as shown in the following screenshot:

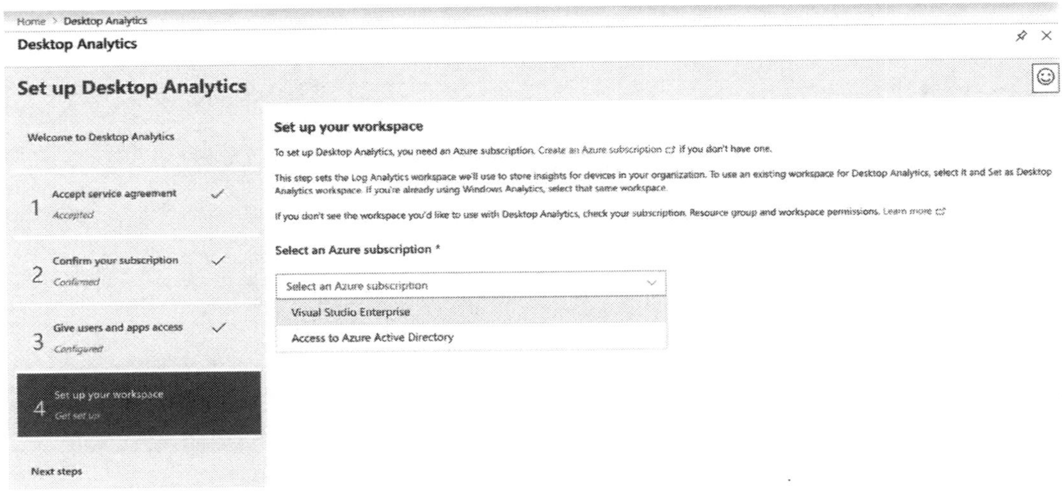

Figure 15.5 – Setting up your workspace

6. Click the drop-down option under **Select an Azure subscription** and choose an available subscription. In this example, I selected **Visual Studio Enterprise**, but you can select any subscription that you wish. This will take you to the **Add a workspace** option, as in the following screenshot:

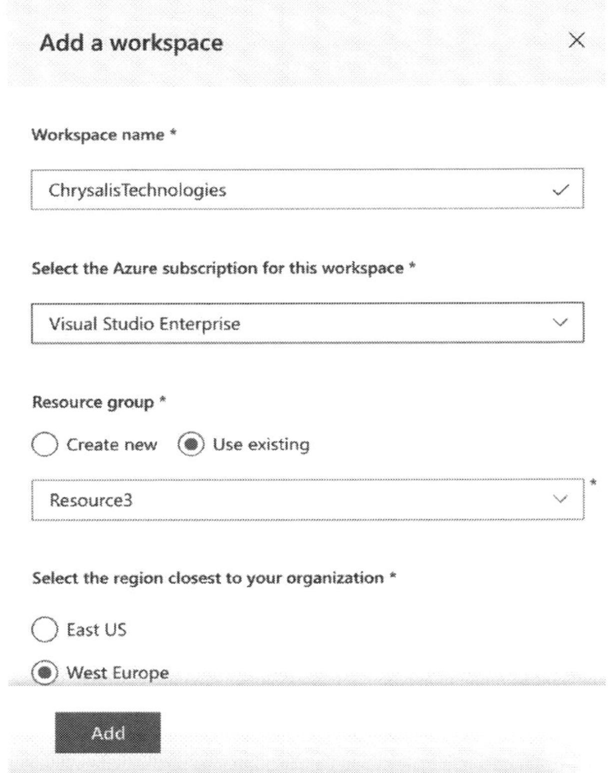

Figure 15.6 – Adding a workspace

7. Enter your workspace name, select your Azure subscription, choose an Azure resource group, then select the region closest to your organization. Then, click **Add**. This will take you to the option shown in the following screenshot:

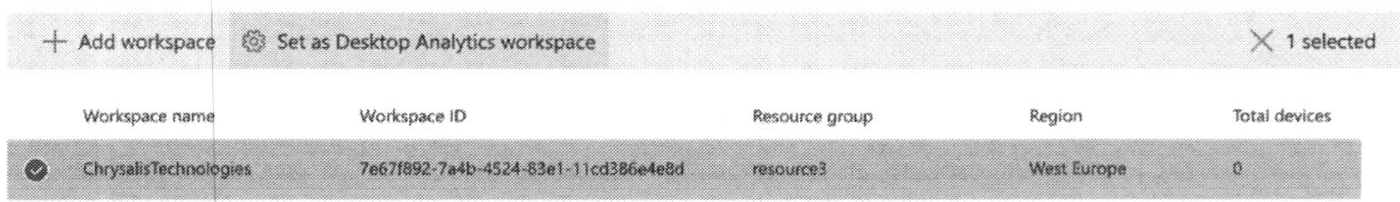

Figure 15.7 – Setting your Desktop Analytics workspace

8. Select the workspace that you just added, then click on **Set as Desktop Analytics workspace**. You will then be asked to confirm and grant access. Click **Continue** when prompted.
9. Next, you will be asked to accept a Microsoft permissions access request. Click on the **Consent on behalf of your organization** option, then click on **Accept**.
10. You will now see the **Next steps** option, as in the following screenshot. Click on **Go to Desktop Analytics**:

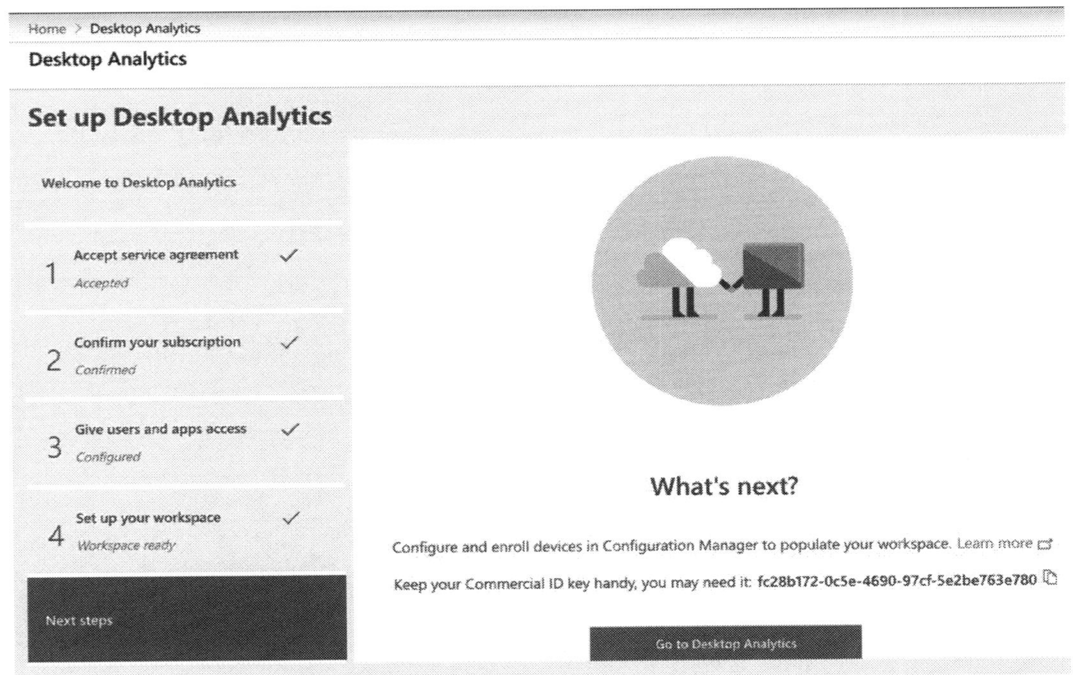

Figure 15.8 – Next steps

11. You are now taken to the Desktop Analytics portal, as shown:

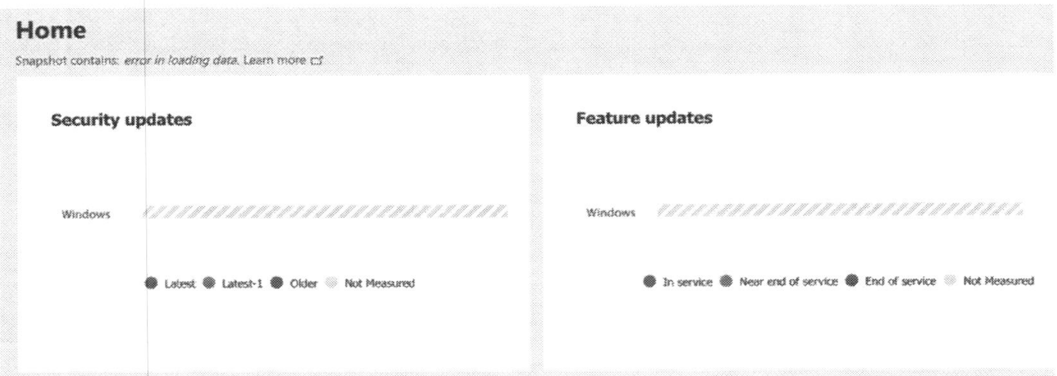

Figure 15.9 – The Desktop Analytics portal

Now that you have configured Desktop Analytics for your organization, you can navigate the portal to gain intelligence on the security and feature updates, along with your organizational assets.

The portal will assist you in overcoming the challenge of keeping your Windows 10 devices up to date, as well as help you to remove time-consuming manual processes, such as testing applications.

> **Important note**
>
> In this section, we have introduced you to the principles of Desktop Analytics and shown you how to set it up for your Microsoft 365 environment. However, fully configuring and using Desktop Analytics and integrating it with Configuration Manager is a complex process that is beyond the scope of this book. For more detailed information, please refer to the *Desktop Analytics deployment plans* link provided in the *References* section at the end of this chapter.

Next, we will look at Windows diagnostics.

Windows diagnostics

Windows diagnostics provide you with the ability to collect data from the Windows devices in your environment. Once Windows diagnostics are configured on a device, they publish events and data gathered from event logging and tracing APIs, which can be examined in **Diagnostic Data Viewer**.

It is possible to configure the diagnostic settings using the following methods:

- Group Policy
- The Registry settings
- **Mobile Device Management** (**MDM**) policies

To configure via Group Policy, we need to complete the following steps:

1. Open **Group Policy Management Console** by clicking on the Windows Start button and searching `Group Policy Management`.
2. Navigate to **Computer Configuration** | **Administrative Templates** | **Windows Components** | **Data Collection** | **Preview Builds**.
3. Click on **Allow Telemetry**.
4. Under **Options**, choose the telemetry level.
5. Click **OK**.

To configure via Registry settings, do the following:

1. Click on the Windows Start button and type in `regedit`, then click **OK**.
2. Navigate to `HKEY_LOCAL_MACHINE\Software\Policies\Microsoft\Windows\DataCollection`.
3. Right-click on **DataCollection**, click **New**, then select the **DWORD (32-bit)** option.
4. Enter `AllowTelemetry`, then press **Enter**.
5. Double-click on your new entry and set the value for **DataCollection**.
6. Click **OK**.

Once you have configured the preceding settings, you can click on **File** and then **Export** to save it as a `.reg` file, which you can then use to run the preceding settings as a script on the devices in your organization.

To use MDM to set the Windows diagnostics, you need to use **Policy Configuration Service Provider**, which enables you to apply the `AllowTelemetry` MDM policy.

> **Important note**
>
> Configuring Windows diagnostics and Telemetry is a useful process, but while it is valuable to have an awareness of the capabilities and deployment methods described here, this is not a core subject in the scope of the MS-500 certification. Further details on how to configure Windows diagnostics can be found in the *References* section at the end of this chapter.

Next, we will examine Office Telemetry.

Office Telemetry

Office Telemetry consists of a dashboard that is viewed in an Excel workbook. It is used to view information relating to Office files and add-ins based on usage, health data, compatibility, and the inventory.

There are two main components of Office Telemetry—the Telemetry dashboard and the Telemetry logs. Both of these are installed automatically with Office 365 Pro Plus. The Telemetry dashboard consists of the following components:

- Telemetry logging
- The Telemetry agent
- The shared folder
- The Telemetry processor
- The database

When Office Telemetry is in use in an organization, data is collected as users log in to their computers, and a scheduled task is triggered to upload data from the agent on the computer to the shared folder. The agent uploads data to the shared folder every 8 hours.

The Telemetry processor then sends the uploaded data from the shared folder to the database.

Once the data is in the database, it can be viewed in the Telemetry dashboard spreadsheet and examined by Microsoft 365 administrators.

So, the process of collecting Office Telemetry is as follows:

1. The agent collects Telemetry data and sends it to the shared folder.
2. The processor collects the data from the shared folder and sends it to the database.
3. Finally, the data placed in the database is presented on the dashboard.

Telemetry data can be collected for up to 100,000 users and can consist of up to 10 processors and shared folder pairs, and up to 30 users can access the Office Telemetry dashboard.

> **Important note**
>
> Like Windows diagnostics, Office Telemetry is a useful tool for Microsoft 365 administrators and while it is not a core subject on MS-500, an understanding of what it does and how it works is relevant to this exam guide. Further information on Office Telemetry can be found in the *References* section at the end of this chapter.

In this section, we discussed Desktop Analytics, Windows diagnostics, and Telemetry, as well as how they can be useful tools to a Microsoft 365 administrator.

You learned that Desktop Analytics provides visibility on security and feature updates on your Windows 10 devices and how Windows diagnostics collect data from your devices that can be viewed and interpreted in **Diagnostic Data Viewer**. Finally, we explained how Office Telemetry collects data relating to files and add-ins and transmits it to the dashboard at regular intervals, which can then be viewed and interpreted by administrators.

Next, we will look at the available security reporting features, dashboards, and auditing capabilities available within your Microsoft 365 environment.

Configuring Office 365 auditing

The auditing feature within Microsoft 365 provides administrators with the crucial ability to monitor and keep track of the activities of both users and administrators. By accessing the available security and compliance centers, you can assess and mitigate potential risks, manage and control your users, and ensure that you are fulfilling any business and regulatory compliance requirements.

In the previous chapters of this book, we referred to the Microsoft 365 Security & Compliance Center. This can be accessed from `https://protection.office.com` and is a powerful and comprehensive portal where administrators can quickly access information relating to Microsoft 365 services, such as Exchange Online or OneDrive, and interpret that information to plan and implement controls and policies to protect Microsoft 365 users and services. The Microsoft 365 Security & Compliance portal is shown in the following screenshot:

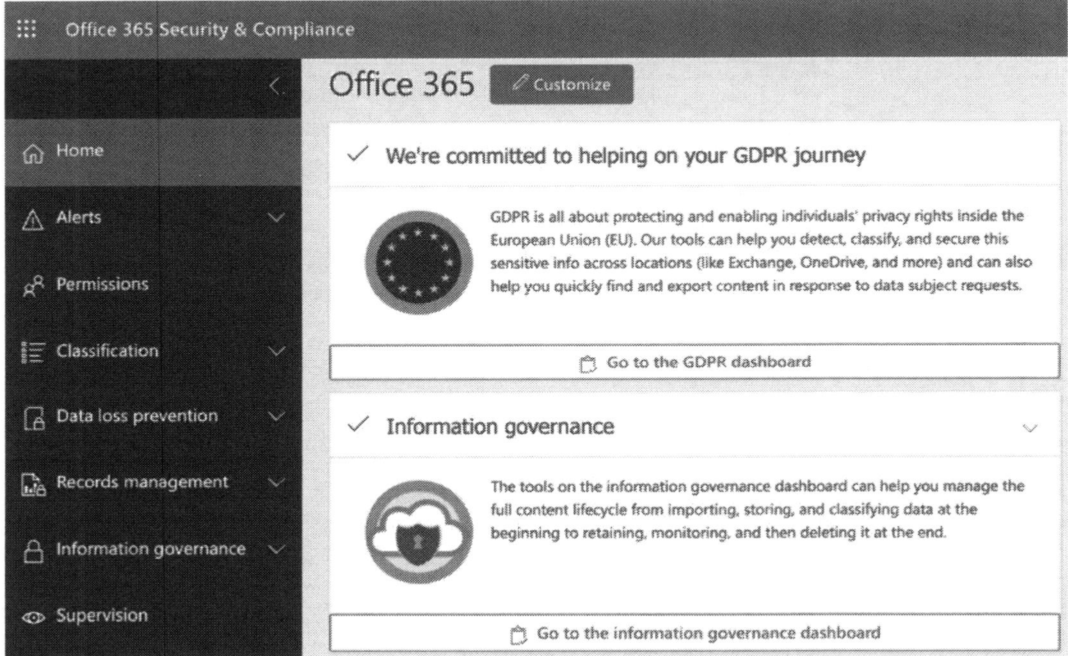

Figure 15.10 – The Security & Compliance portal

Also available are the Microsoft 365 security center, which can be accessed via `https://security.microsoft.com/`, and the Microsoft 365 compliance center, which can be accessed via `https://compliance.microsoft.com/`

These separate portals are aimed at more specialized roles and provide security administrators and compliance administrators with information, settings, and controls that are more focused on these particular areas.

By accessing these portals, administrators can navigate through many features, which include the following:

- **Alerts**
- **Permissions**
- **Classification**
- **Data loss prevention**
- **Records management**
- **Information governance**
- **Supervision**
- **Threat management**
- **Mail flow**
- **Data privacy**
- **Search and investigation**
- **Reports**
- **Service assurance**

Now, let's look at how you turn on auditing within your Microsoft 365 tenant.

Turning on the audit log

The Office 365 audit logging capability cannot be enabled by default in some Microsoft 365 tenants; it might need to be explicitly enabled by a Microsoft 365 administrator. In order to enable audit logging, you need to complete the following steps:

1. Open the Security & Compliance Center and navigate to **Search | Audit log search**. You will see the banner shown in the following screenshot:

Audit log search

! To use this feature, turn on auditing so we can start recording user and admin activity in your organization. When you turn this on, activity will be recorded to the Office 365 audit log and available to view in a report. Turn on auditing

Figure 15.11 – Turning on auditing

2. Click on **Turn on auditing** and you will see a message advising you that auditing is being enabled and will be available to you within a few hours.

3. Alternatively, you can enable auditing by connecting to **Exchange Online PowerShell** and entering the following command:

```
Set-AdminAuditLogConfig -UnifiedAuditLogIngestionEnabled
$true
```

4. Should you, for any reason, wish to turn off auditing, this must be completed via **Exchange Online PowerShell** by running the following command:

```
Set-AdminAuditLogConfig -UnifiedAuditLogIngestionEnabled
$false
```

> **Important note**
>
> In order to turn auditing on or off, you must be a global administrator or a member of the compliance management or organization management role groups.

Once auditing has been enabled, you will be able to search for user and administrator activities within your tenant for a period of up to 90 days.

So, we have now shown you how to enable auditing within your Microsoft 365 environment. Let's now take a look at how we can perform an audit log search.

Performing an audit log search

Now that we have auditing log searches enabled on our Microsoft 365 tenant, we can search a unified audit log to view a wide range of user or administrator actions. Some examples of these actions include the following:

- A user renames a file.
- A user creates a list in SharePoint.
- An administrator changes a device's access policy.
- A user removes a sensitivity label from a file.

These are only a few examples from an extremely comprehensive list of possible activities that can be interrogated using the audit log.

In the following example, we will interrogate the audit log to show us when a user has downloaded files to their computer. In order to do this, we need to carry out the following steps:

1. From the Security & Compliance Center, navigate to **Search** | **Audit log search**. You will see the **Audit log search** tool, as in the following screenshot:

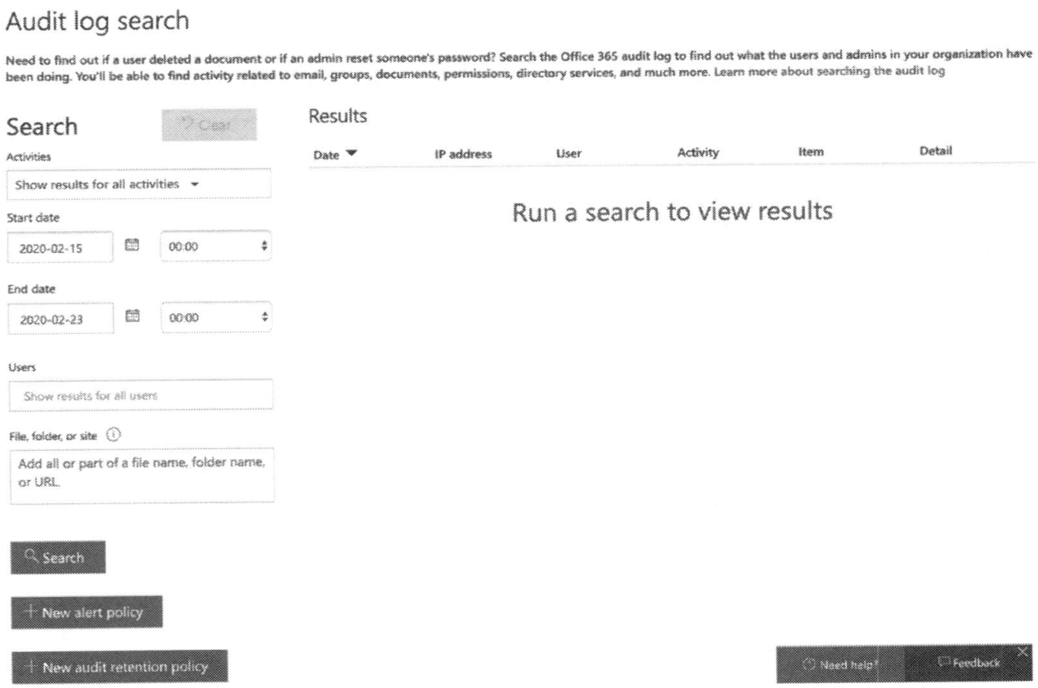

Figure 15.12 – Audit log search

2. Under **Activities**, click on the dropdown next to **Show results for all activities**. You will see the full list of activities to choose from, as in the following screenshot:

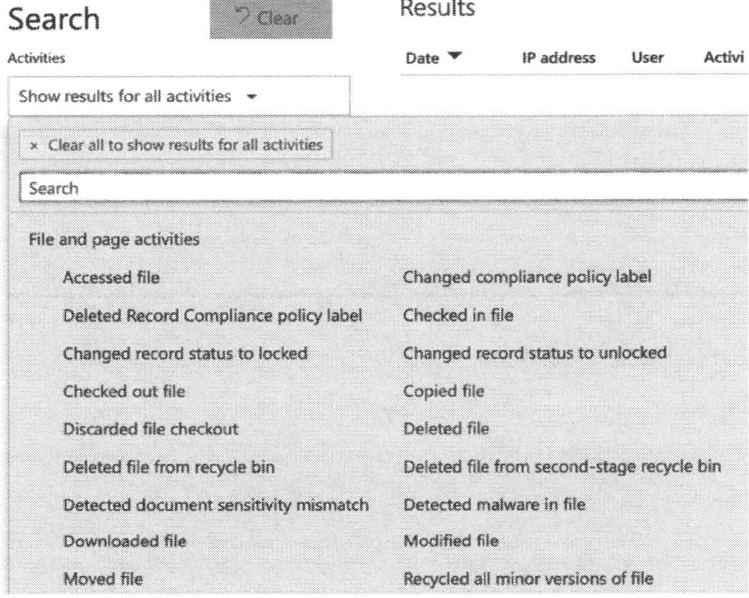

Figure 15.13 – Activity results

3. Scroll down to **Synchronization activities | Downloaded files to computer**, as in the following screenshot:

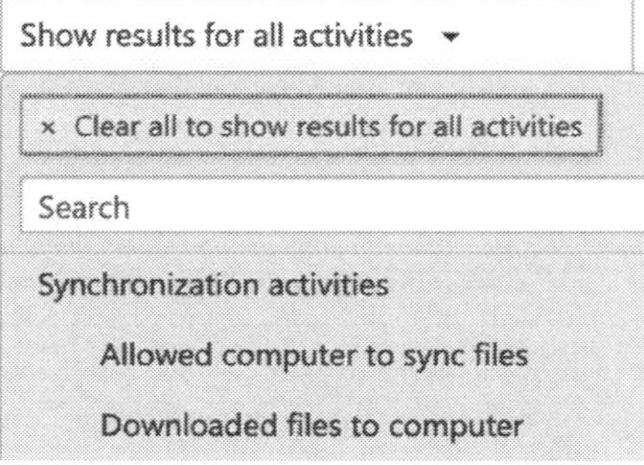

Figure 15.14 – Selecting an activity

4. Next, select the date range for your search (remember that auditing only extends to 90 days, or 1 year for Office 365 E5 and Microsoft 365 E5 subscriptions) and select a specific user to search against if required. You can also add a URL or part of a filename, as shown:

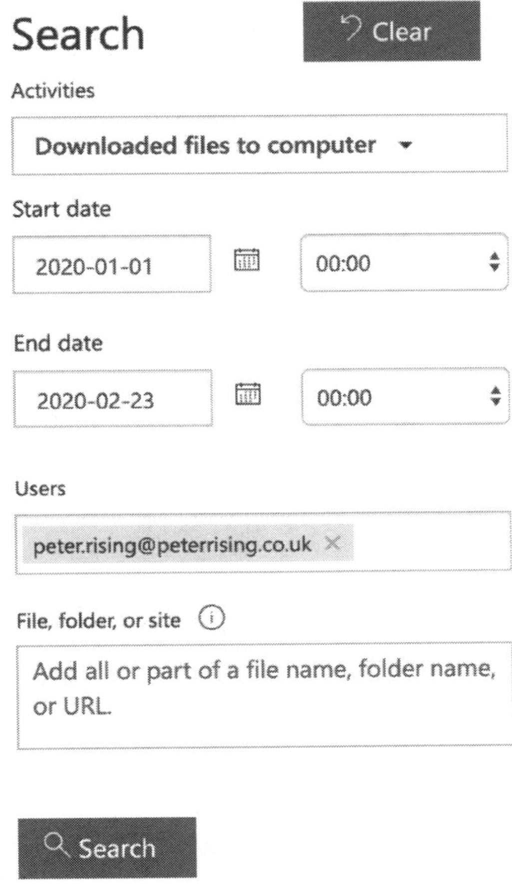

Figure 15.15 – Searching parameters

5. Click on **Search** and your results will appear as follows:

Results 16 results found

Filter results | Export results

Date	IP address	User	Activity	Item	Detail
2020-02-19 17:53:38	185.201.60.254	peter.rising@peter...	Downloaded files t...	MS-500_14.docx	
2020-02-19 17:07:06	185.201.60.254	peter.rising@peter...	Downloaded files t...	MS-500_14.docx	
2020-02-09 08:54:09	86.151.83.71	peter.rising@peter...	Downloaded files t...	MS-500_12final.do...	
2020-02-09 08:52:16	86.151.83.71	peter.rising@peter...	Downloaded files t...	MS-500_11_RK_Fo...	
2020-02-09 08:50:40	86.151.83.71	peter.rising@peter...	Downloaded files t...	MS-500_10_ForRe...	
2020-02-09 08:46:17	86.151.83.71	peter.rising@peter...	Downloaded files t...	B15082_09_1st Dra...	
2020-02-09 08:44:02	86.151.83.71	peter.rising@peter...	Downloaded files t...	B15082_08_1stDra...	
2020-02-09 08:42:00	86.151.83.71	peter.rising@peter...	Downloaded files t...	B15082_07_2nd Dr...	
2020-02-09 08:40:57	86.151.83.71	peter.rising@peter...	Downloaded files t...	B15082_06_1stDra...	
2020-02-09 08:36:58	86.151.83.71	peter.rising@peter...	Downloaded files t...	B15082_05_2ndDr...	

Figure 15.16 – Search results

6. We can see all the matches for downloaded files for the selected user during the dates selected. Clicking on a specific result will show you specific details about it, as in the following screenshot:

Details

Date:

IP address:

User:

Activity:

Item:

Detail:

Id:

Object Id:

Record Type:

Source Relative Url:

User Agent:

More information

Figure 15.17 – Detailed individual result categories

7. The results of your search can also be filtered or exported to a `.csv` file if desired.

So, as you can see, searching the audit log is both a simple yet powerful action. Based on the results of your audit log searches, you can also create alert policies if required. We will discuss the audit alert policy capabilities in the final section of this chapter.

Configuring an audit alert policy

As we demonstrated in the previous section, searching the audit log is a quick and effective way to view user and administrator activities within your Microsoft 365 environment. However, should you find yourself repeatedly carrying out the same types of audit log searches, then you may wish to consider minimizing your administrative effort on this activity by instead configuring an alert policy that automatically alerts you whenever the activity you wish to search for occurs.

Alert policies can be categorized and applied to your users and a threshold is set to trigger an alert. Alerts can be sent to administrators via an email notification or can be viewed in the Security & Compliance Center under **Alerts | View alerts**.

Alert policies are triggered by user or administrator actions that match conditions within an alert policy. In order to create alert policies, you must be a member of the **Manage Alerts** or **Organization Configuration** roles, which can be set from the Security & Compliance Center.

To set up an alert policy, we need to complete the following steps:

1. From the Security & Compliance Center, navigate to **Alerts | Alert policies**, as in the following screenshot:

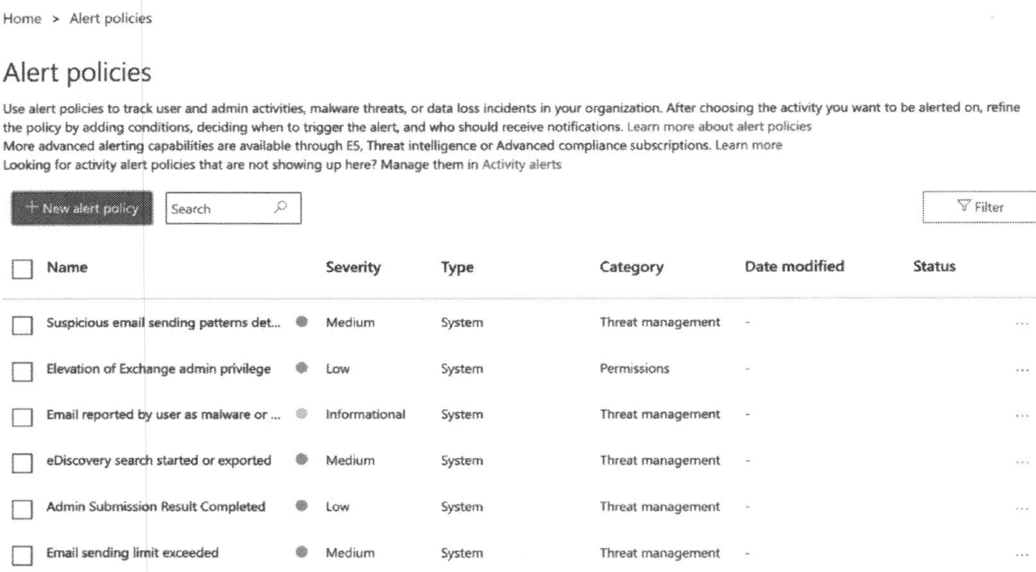

Figure 15.18 – Alert policies

2. A number of built-in default policies are included here and you can edit some, but not all, of the settings of these policies, as the following screenshot shows:

Figure 15.19 – Editing a default policy

3. To create a new alert policy, click on **New policy** and enter a name, description, severity level, and category for your policy. For this example, we will create a policy that will alert us whenever a user shares a file or folder from an Office 365 location, as shown in the following screenshot:

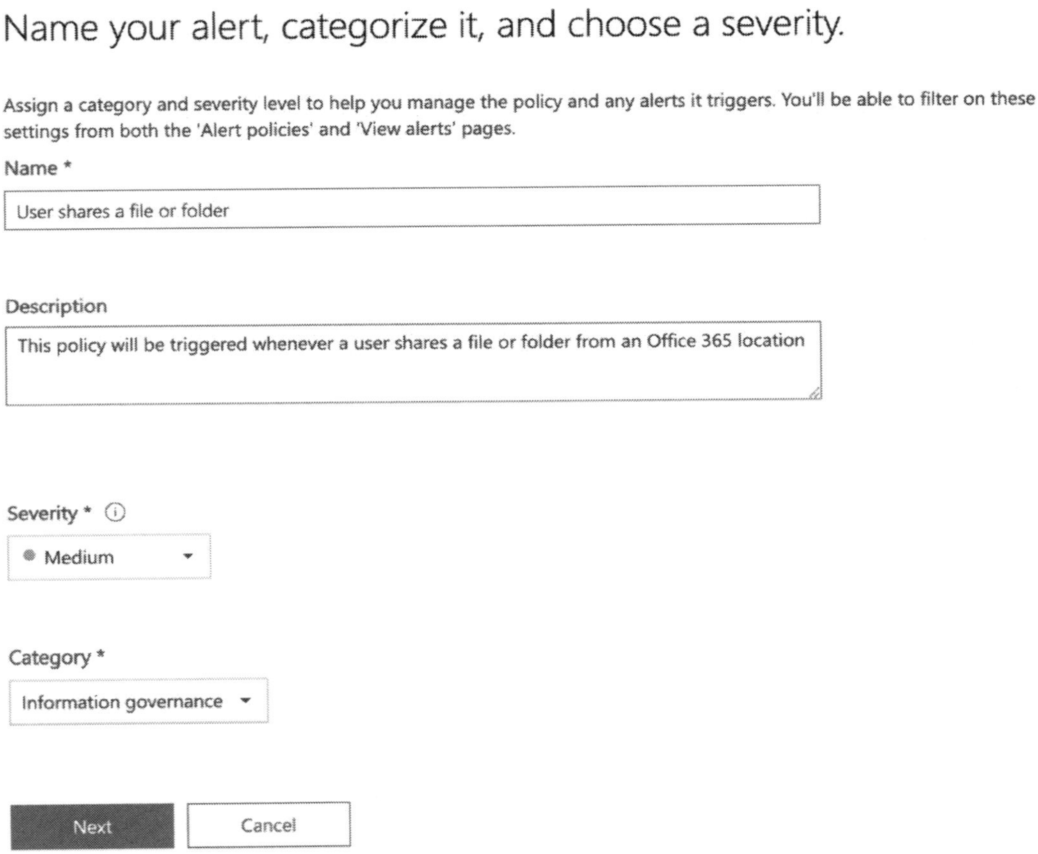

Name your alert, categorize it, and choose a severity.

Assign a category and severity level to help you manage the policy and any alerts it triggers. You'll be able to filter on these settings from both the 'Alert policies' and 'View alerts' pages.

Name *

User shares a file or folder

Description

This policy will be triggered whenever a user shares a file or folder from an Office 365 location

Severity *

Medium

Category *

Information governance

Next Cancel

Figure 15.20 – New policy details

4. Click **Next** and you will be prompted to choose an activity for your alert policy and set how you wish the alert to be triggered. For our example policy, we will choose the settings displayed in the following screenshot:

Choose an activity, conditions and when to trigger the alert

You can only choose one activity but you can add conditions to refine what we'll detect.

What do you want to alert on?

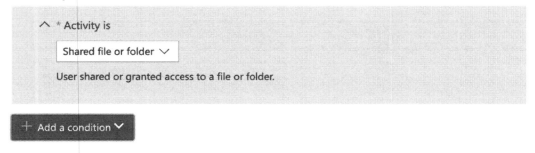

User shared or granted access to a file or folder.

How do you want the alert to be triggered?

Every time an activity matches the rule

Figure 15.21 – Alert and trigger settings

5. You can apply more conditions to your alert policy if desired by clicking on the **Add a condition** option. Selecting this option provides you with the options shown in the following screenshot:

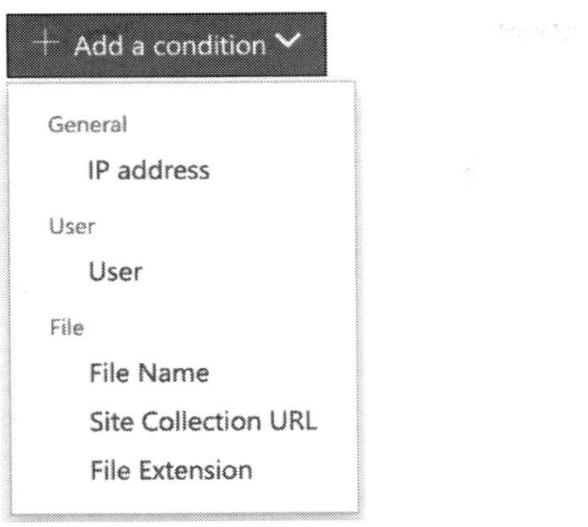

Figure 15.22 – Further conditions

6. Click **Next** and you will be prompted to choose the settings for the notification you receive whenever there is a policy match. We can set **Send email notifications** to one or more users and set the **Daily notification limit** option, which is useful if you are expecting a large number of policy matches and you do not wish the alert recipients to be bombarded with too many emails. These options are shown in the following screenshot:

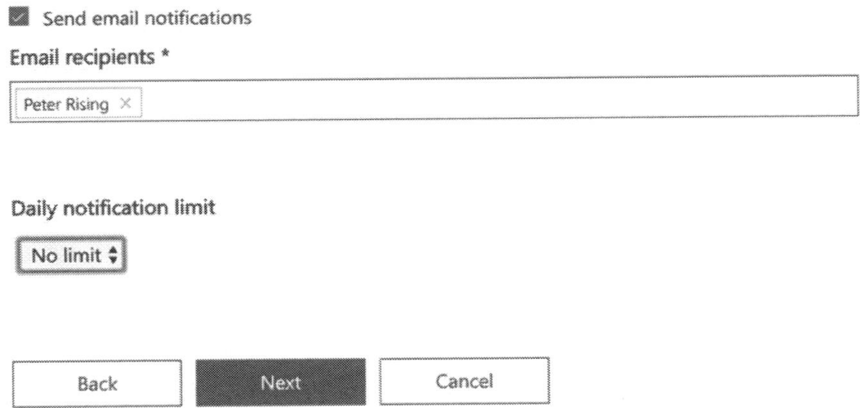

Figure 15.23 – Notification settings

7. Click **Next** and you will see the **Review your settings** dialog, where you can make any last-minute changes to your policy. You can also choose whether to turn your policy on immediately or leave it turned off until you are ready to activate it. These options are shown in the following screenshot:

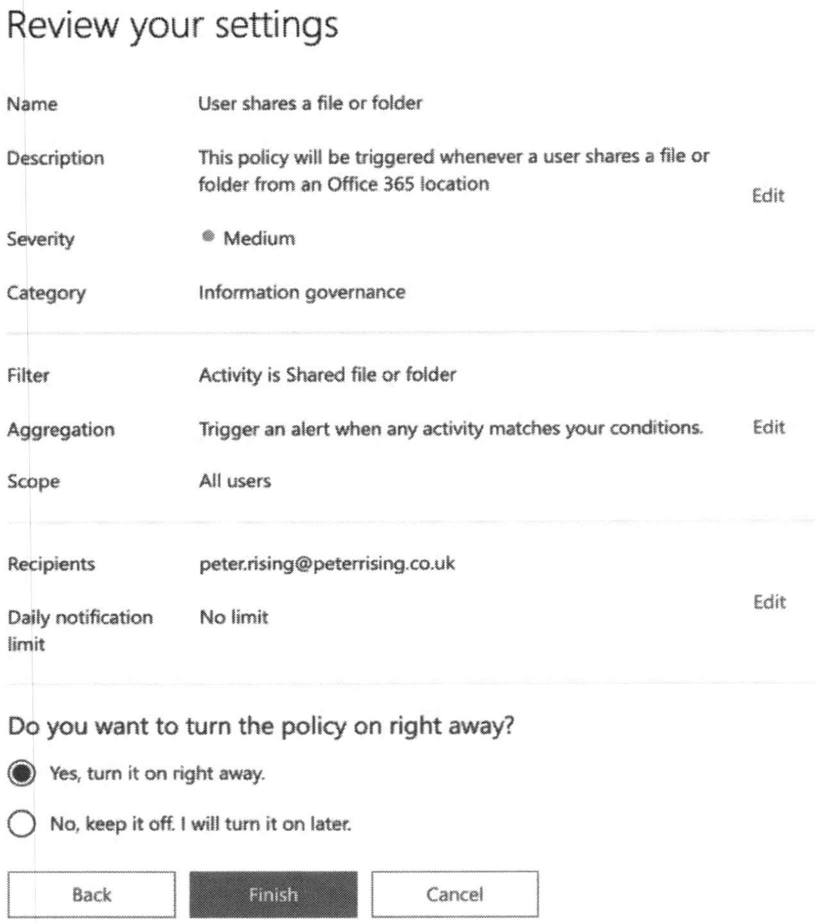

Review your settings

Name User shares a file or folder

Description This policy will be triggered whenever a user shares a file or folder from an Office 365 location

Edit

Severity Medium

Category Information governance

Filter Activity is Shared file or folder

Aggregation Trigger an alert when any activity matches your conditions. Edit

Scope All users

Recipients peter.rising@peterrising.co.uk

Edit

Daily notification limit No limit

Do you want to turn the policy on right away?

Yes, turn it on right away.

No, keep it off. I will turn it on later.

Back Finish Cancel

Figure 15.24 – Reviewing your policy settings

8. Click on **Finish** and your policy will be created. You will be able to view and edit it immediately from the **Alert policies** list, as shown:

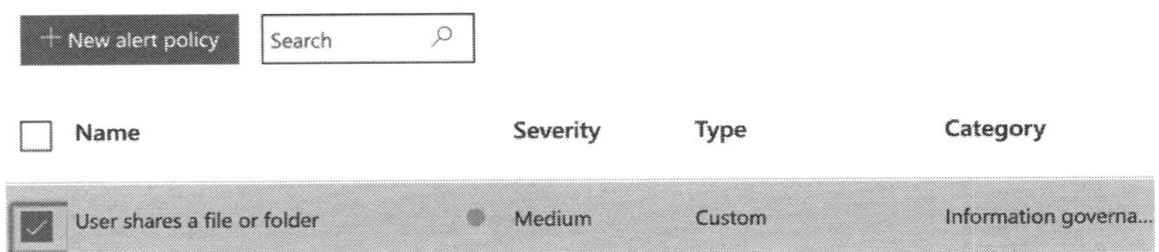
Alert policies
Use alert policies to track user and admin activities, malware threats, or data loss incidents in your organization. After choo
the policy by adding conditions, deciding when to trigger the alert, and who should receive notifications. Learn more abou
More advanced alerting capabilities are available through E5, Threat intelligence or Advanced compliance subscriptions. Le
Looking for activity alert policies that are not showing up here? Manage them in Activity alerts
+ New alert policy
Search
Name
Severity
Type
Category
User shares a file or folder
Medium
Custom
Information governa...

Figure 15.25 – The new custom policy shown in the policy list

Now that the preceding policy has been created; this results in a policy match being visible in the **View alerts** section in the Security & Compliance Center, which will also trigger an email alert to the included recipients within the policy whenever there is a policy match.

In this section, we showed you how to configure audit alert policies from the Security & Compliance Center. You learned that custom alert policies can be configured and set with conditions and triggers to generate alerts and notifications against any policy matches.

Summary

In this chapter, we introduced you to the principles of security analytics, auditing, and reporting within Microsoft 365. You learned how you can use Desktop Analytics to access intelligence on your Windows 10 clients and how Windows diagnostics can be used to collect data from the devices in your environment.

In addition, we explained how Office Telemetry is a powerful dashboard where you can view information about Office files, add-ins, and the inventory. Finally, we showed you how to enable audit logging within your Microsoft 365 environment from both the Security & Compliance Center and Windows PowerShell, along with how to perform audit log searches and create alert policies to notify administrators via email or the Security & Compliance Center whenever a policy match is triggered.

In the next chapter, we will talk about personal data protection in Office 365 and how you can identify and protect personal user data using content searches. We will also look at how to apply sensitivity labels to protect your personal data.

Questions

1. How can you view Office Telemetry data in Office 365?

   a. From email notifications

   b. From the Excel Telemetry dashboard workbook

   c. From the Security and Compliance Center

   d. From the Office 365 admin portal

2. True or false – the audit logging feature can be turned off from the Security & Compliance Center.

   a. True

   b. False

3. Which of the following URLs grants you access to the Desktop Analytics portal?

   a. `https://admin.microsoft.com`

   b. `https://devicemanagement.portal.azure.com`

   c. `https://portal.office365.com`

   d. `https://portal.azure.com`

4. Which of the following PowerShell commands is used to enable audit logging in your tenant?

   a. `Set-AdminAuditLogConfig -UnifiedAuditLogIngestionEnabled $yes`

   b. `Set-AdminAuditLogConfig -UnifiedAuditLogIngestion $enabled`

   c. `Set-AdminAuditLog -UnifiedAuditLogIngestionEnabled $true`

   d. `Set-AdminAuditLogConfig -UnifiedAuditLogIngestionEnabled $true`

5. True or false – in Office Telemetry, the Telemetry processor sends telemetry data to the database.

   a. True

   b. False

6. Where in the Security & Compliance Center would you set up an audit alert policy?

    a. **Alerts | Alert Policies**

    b. **Alerts | View Alerts**

    c. **Alerts | Manage Advanced Alerts**

    d. **Alerts | Dashboard**

7. Which of the following licenses will not allow you to configure Desktop Analytics?

    a. Microsoft 365 E3

    b. Microsoft 365 E5

    c. EM+S E3

    d. Windows Virtual Desktop Access E3

8. For up to how many days can the audit log can provide information?

    a. 70

    b. 30

    c. 90

    d. 60

9. Which of the following methods cannot be used to deploy Windows diagnostics?

    a. Group Policy

    b. MDM policies

    c. The Office deployment tool

    d. The Registry settings

10. True or false – the Security & Compliance Center contains a number of default alert policies.

    a. True

    b. False

References

Please refer to the following links for more information:

- What is Desktop Analytics?: https://docs.microsoft.com/en-us/configmgr/desktop-analytics/overview#prerequisites
- Setting up Desktop Analytics: https://docs.microsoft.com/en-us/configmgr/desktop-analytics/tutorial-windows10
- Desktop Analytics deployment plans: https://docs.microsoft.com/en-us/configmgr/desktop-analytics/about-deployment-plans
- Connecting Desktop Analytics to Configuration Manager: https://docs.microsoft.com/en-us/configmgr/desktop-analytics/connect-configmgr
- Configuring Windows diagnostic data for Windows Telemetry: https://docs.microsoft.com/en-us/windows/privacy/configure-windows-diagnostic-data-in-your-organization
- An overview of Diagnostic Data Viewer: https://docs.microsoft.com/en-us/windows/privacy/diagnostic-data-viewer-overview
- Configuring diagnostic data using MDM: https://docs.microsoft.com/en-us/windows/client-management/mdm/policy-configuration-service-provider
- Office Telemetry: https://docs.microsoft.com/en-us/DeployOffice/compat/compatibility-and-telemetry-in-office?wt.mc_id=4039827
- Planning deployment of Office Telemetry: https://docs.microsoft.com/en-us/DeployOffice/compat/plan-telemetry-dashboard-deployment
- Deploying the Office Telemetry dashboard: https://docs.microsoft.com/en-us/DeployOffice/compat/deploy-telemetry-dashboard
- Turning Office 365 auditing on or off: https://docs.microsoft.com/en-us/microsoft-365/compliance/turn-audit-log-search-on-or-off
- Searching the Office 365 audit log: https://docs.microsoft.com/en-us/microsoft-365/compliance/auditing-troubleshooting-scenarios
- Managing alert policies: https://docs.microsoft.com/en-us/microsoft-365/compliance/alert-policies

16
Personal Data Protection in Microsoft 365

One of the challenges faced by Microsoft 365 compliance administrators is to be aware of their responsibilities concerning any personal data that resides within their environment. The **General Data Protection Regulations** (**GDPR**) describes personal data as any information that relates to an identified or identifiable natural person.

In this chapter, we will demonstrate how you can identify and protect personal data within your Microsoft 365 environment by using content searches to find personal data, and then we will look at how to protect that data using retention or sensitivity labels. We will also explain how **Data Loss Prevention** (**DLP**) reports, audit logs, alert policies, and Cloud App Security can be used to monitor leaks of personal data.

We will cover these topics in the following order:

- Conducting searches for personal data
- Using retention labels to protect personal data
- Accessing logs and reports to search for and monitor personal data leaks

Conducting searches for personal data

Under GDPR, compliance administrators are obliged to respond to any requests by users for access to any personal data relating to them that is stored in the Microsoft 365 tenant. In order to provide the required information, the **Content search** feature can be used. Content searches use built-in sensitive information types, which can be found in the Security & Compliance Center under **Classification | Sensitive info types**.

We have discussed these sensitive information types in previous chapters of this book when we talked about DLP and **Azure Information Protection** (**AIP**). DLP is particularly useful in protecting your organization against personal data loss as it is capable of detecting personal data in transit in an Exchange Online email and can act accordingly with policy tips, and DLP policies and rules. We will examine this in further detail later on in this chapter.

First, let's take a look at how you can use content searches to find personal data in your Microsoft 365 environment. This requires you to complete the following steps:

1. Sign in to the Security & Compliance Center at `https://protection.office.com` and navigate to **Search | Content search**. This will take you to the eDiscovery page, as in the following screenshot:

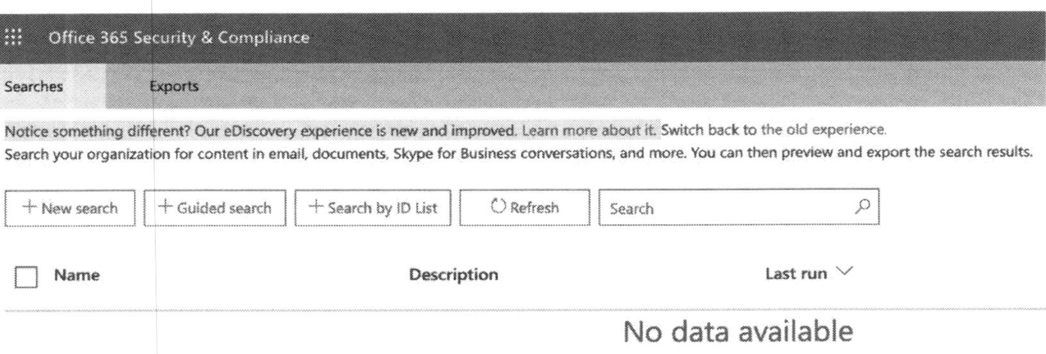

Figure 16.1 – The content search page

2. You have three options to choose from here, which are as follows:

   a. **New search**: This is the default option, which we will use in the following steps.

   b. **Guided search**: This option is a wizard-based guide that helps you through the search process.

   c. **Search by ID List**: The final option allows you to search for Exchange Online mailbox items. This process was formerly known as targeted search and requires a CSV file to identify the mailbox items that should be targeted by the search.

3. For this example, we will select the default **New search** option, as in the following screenshot:

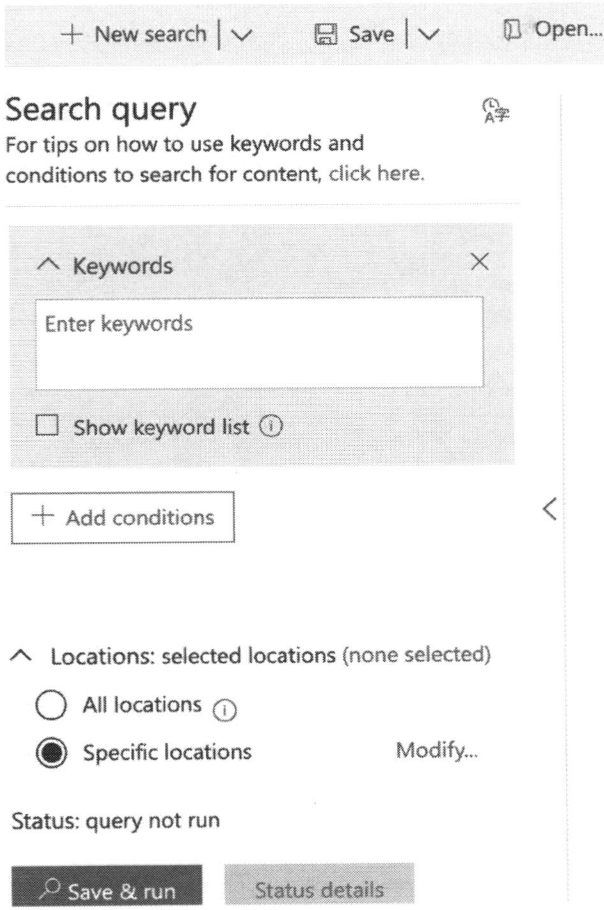

Figure 16.2 – New search

4. The first **Search query** option is **Keywords**. In this section, you can enter any keywords that you wish your content search to look for, along with other properties such as the date, author, or subject. You can also use the **Show keyword list** option to display all of the keywords you enter on individual rows.

5. Once you have set your keywords, you can also choose to add conditions to your search. Conditions help you to narrow down your search parameters and get the specific results that you are searching for. When you click on **Add conditions**, you will see a list of conditions that you can select from, as shown:

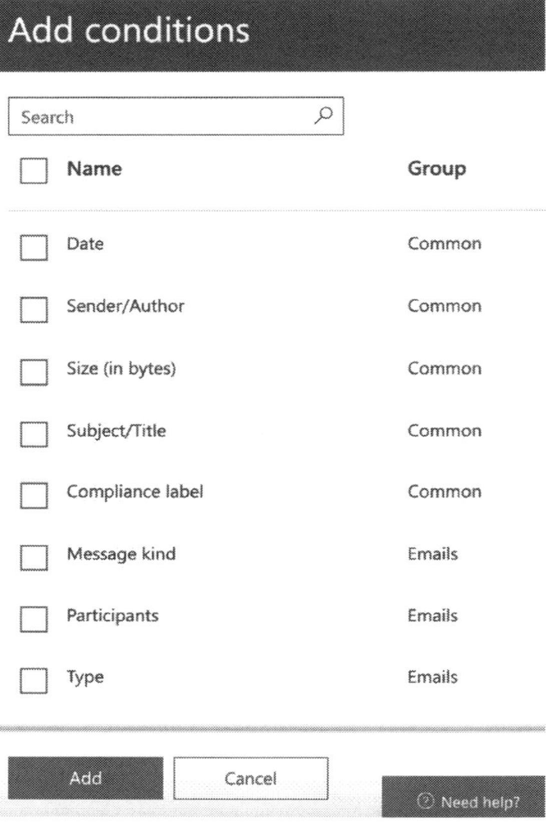

Figure 16.3 – Adding conditions to your content search

6. Once you have added any conditions you require to your search, you can choose the Microsoft 365 locations that you wish to search against. By default, **Specific locations** is selected. By clicking on **Modify**, you will see the location options, as in the following screenshot:

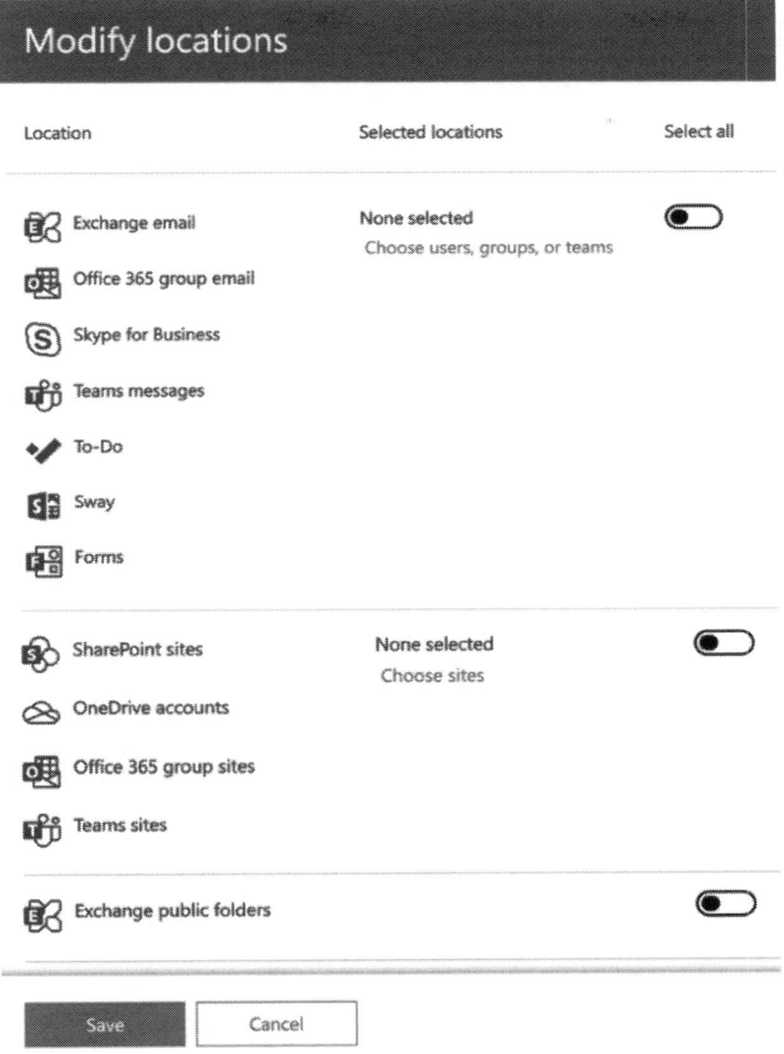

Figure 16.4 – Modifying the search locations

7. Use the toggle switches to select which areas you wish to include in your search; you can then filter your choices further by choosing specific users, groups, teams, or sites. When you have made your selections, click **Save**. Alternatively, if you wish to search through all the locations, choose the **All locations** option.
8. Now that you have made your selections, you are ready to run your content search. Click on **Save & run** to start the search.

9. Next, you will see the **Save search** page, where you need to enter a name for your search and an optional description, as in the following screenshot:

Figure 16.5 – Saving your search

10. Click on **Save** and your content search will now start. Depending on the keywords, conditions, and locations you configured for your search, the results may take some time to display. You will see the search in progress, as in the following screenshot:

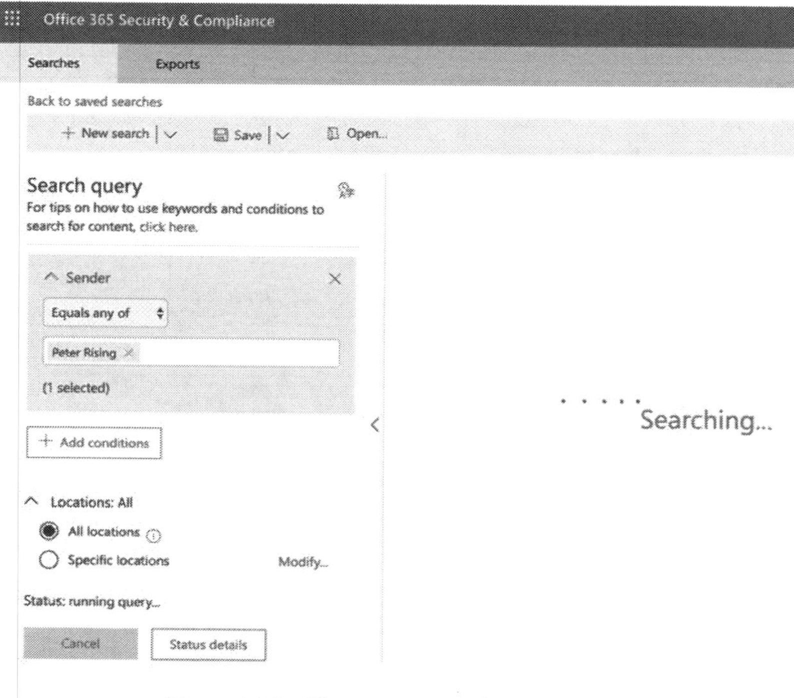

Figure 16.6 – The content search in progress

11. Once the search is complete, you can access the results by clicking on the relevant search in the list of searches, as in the following screenshot:

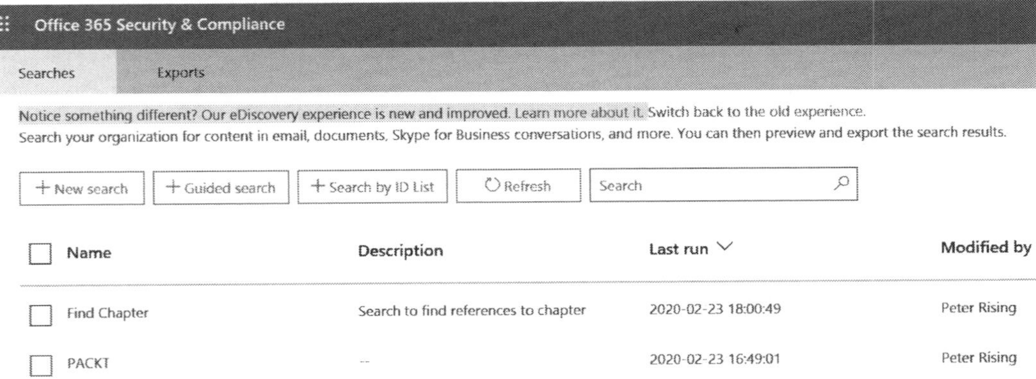

Figure 16.7 – Completed searches

12. When you open your search, you can choose to preview your search results by clicking on **View results**, or you can choose the **Export report** option to generate a report that can be viewed in more detail in Excel. You can also re-run the search if required:

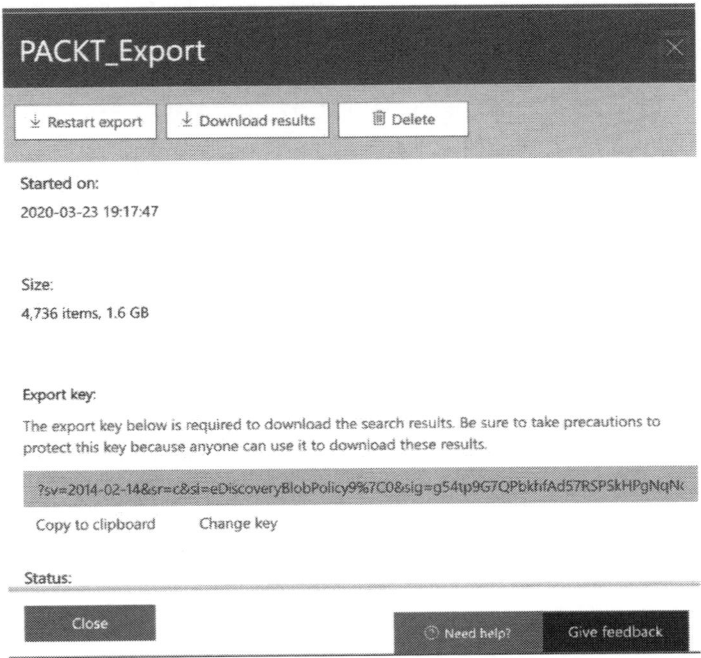

Figure 16.8 – Viewing or exporting the search results

13. If you choose the **Export report** option, **eDiscovery Export Tool** will open, as shown:

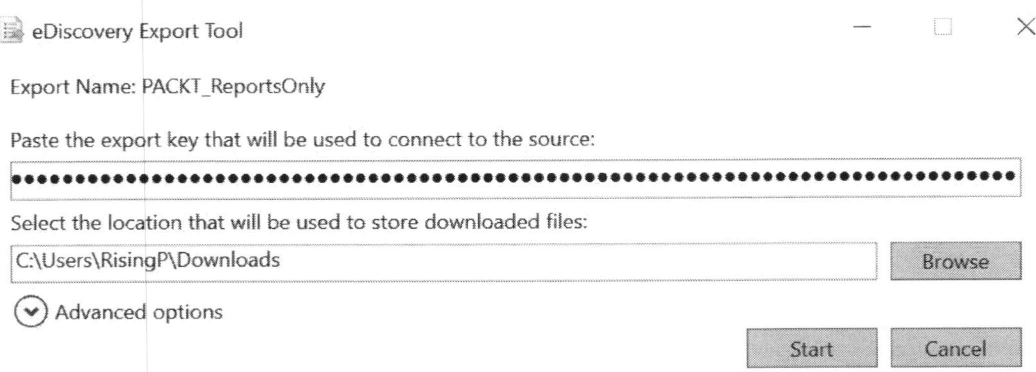

Figure 16.9 – eDiscovery Export Tool

14. Copy and paste the export key (which we can see in *Figure 16.8*), and then choose a folder to download the report to. Then, click **Start**. The following files will be created in the folder you selected:

Name	Date modified	Type
Export Summary 03.23.2020-1925PM.csv	23/03/2020 19:25	Microsoft Excel Com...
manifest.xml	23/03/2020 19:25	XML Document
Results.csv	23/03/2020 19:25	Microsoft Excel Com...
trace.log	23/03/2020 19:22	Text Document

Figure 16.10 – Exported content

15. In the following screenshot, we can see the `Export Summary` CSV file. The `Results` CSV file shows more detailed information exported from the search:

	A	B	C	D
1	Export Name	PACKT_ReportsOnly		
2	Export ID	76192d39-fb91-4e8d-a3c1-08d7cf5ee3cb		
3	Status	The export completed successfully.		
4	De-Duplication Enabled	No		
5	Export Location	C:\Users\RisingP\Downloads\PACKT_ReportsOnly\03.23.2020-1920PM		
6	Remove RMS Protection	NO		
7	Location with Results	7		
8	Location that successfully downloaded	7		
9	Locations that failed to download	0		
10				
11		Items	Size(GB)	Size(Bytes)
12	Estimated	497	1.589	1,706,418,303
13	SharePoint Estimated	497	1.589	1,706,418,303
14	Downloaded	497	1.589	1,706,418,303
15				
16	Item Downloaded Errors	0		
17	Item Downloaded Warnings	0		
18	Item Skipped	0		
19				

Figure 16.11 – The CSV export

> **Important note**
>
> At the time of writing this book, sensitive information types cannot be selected to search for data contained in Exchange Online mailboxes at rest.

In this section, we showed you how to run a content search from the Security & Compliance Center to look for personal data within your Microsoft 365 locations. You learned how content searches can be set up with one or more keywords to search against and how conditions can narrow down your search results and provide you with the content you are searching for. Finally, we showed you how you can choose to search through specific Microsoft 365 locations or search through all locations during your search.

Next, we will show you how labels can be used to help you protect personal data in your Microsoft 365 environment.

Using retention labels to protect personal data

In *Chapter 11, Controlling Secure Access to Information Stored in Office 365*, we showed you how to use sensitivity labels and policies to protect emails and documents in your Microsoft 365 environment. Retention labels can also be used to apply protection to personal data within Microsoft 365. With retention labels, you can automatically apply labels when sensitive information types are detected or allow your users to manually apply retention labels. Your retention labels can be set up to force the retention of the content you are applying the policy to for a specified retention period.

The way that retention labels are set to be published determines which Office 365 locations the labels will be applied to.

When a retention label is published to your end users, or auto-applied based on a query, your retention label policy can apply to the following locations:

- Exchange Online
- SharePoint Online
- OneDrive
- Office 365 groups

When a retention label is auto-applied based on sensitive information types, your retention label policy can apply to the following locations:

- Exchange Online (all mailboxes only)
- SharePoint Online
- OneDrive

Microsoft recommends that you use retention labels for any personal data. In the following example steps, we will show you how to set up retention labels and policies using sensitive information types:

1. Open the Security & Compliance Center from `https://protection.office.com` and navigate to **Classification | Retention labels**, as in the following screenshot:

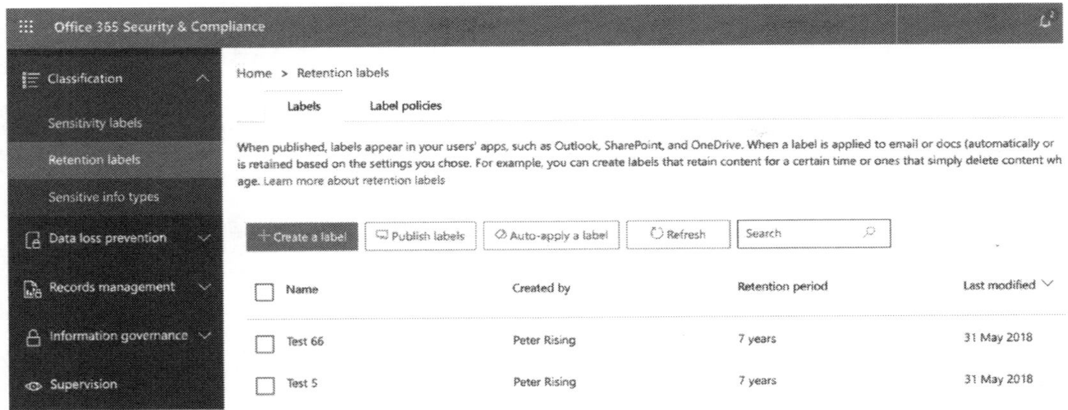

Figure 16.12 – Retention labels in the Security & Compliance Center

2. Click on **Create a label** and you will see the following options:

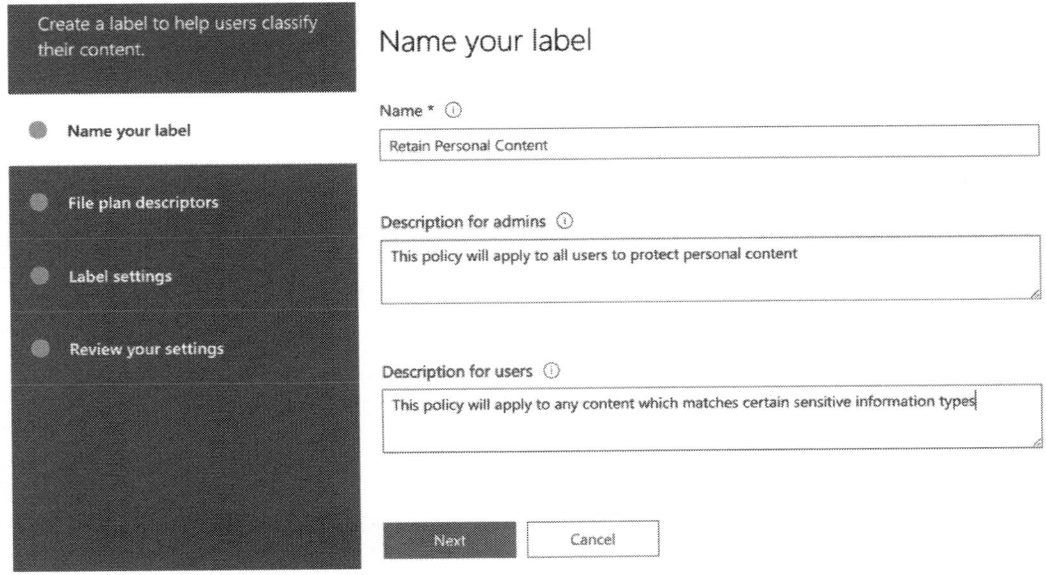

Figure 16.13 – Naming your label

3. Enter a name and description for admins and users, and then click on **Next**. You will see the **File plan descriptors** options. If you choose to set file plan descriptors, then, based on the conditions you set, your retention label will automatically apply, as the following screenshot illustrates:

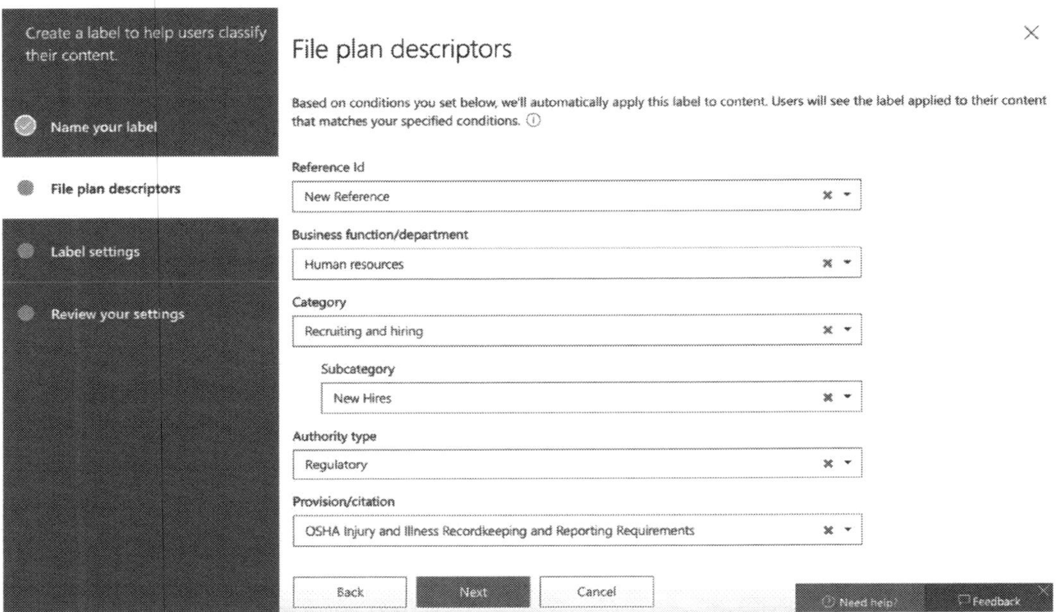

Figure 16.14 – Setting file plan descriptors to automatically apply retention labels

4. Click **Next** and you will see the **Label settings** options. If you set file plan descriptors, then the option to manually set retention is not available. However, if you left **File plan descriptors** blank, then you can choose to apply retention by configuring the settings, as shown:

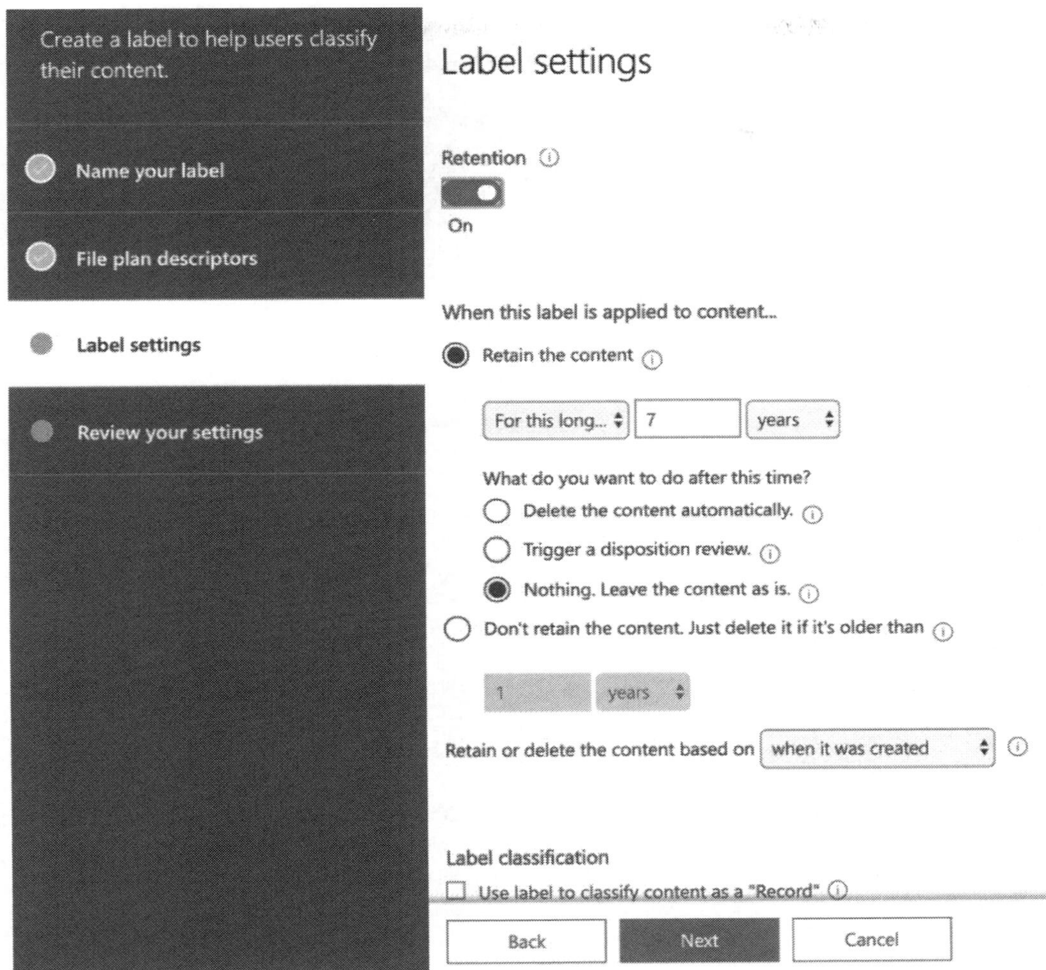

Figure 16.15 – Manually setting the retention settings

5. Here, you can choose to set **Retention** to **On** or **Off**, as well as set how long the content is to be retained for and what actions are taken at the end of the retention period. You can also choose to use your label to classify the content as a record. When you have completed the required settings, click **Next** to review the settings of your label, and then click **Create this label** to complete the setup of your new retention label.

6. Your new label will appear in the list of retention labels and if you select it, you can choose to edit, publish, or auto-apply your label, as follows:

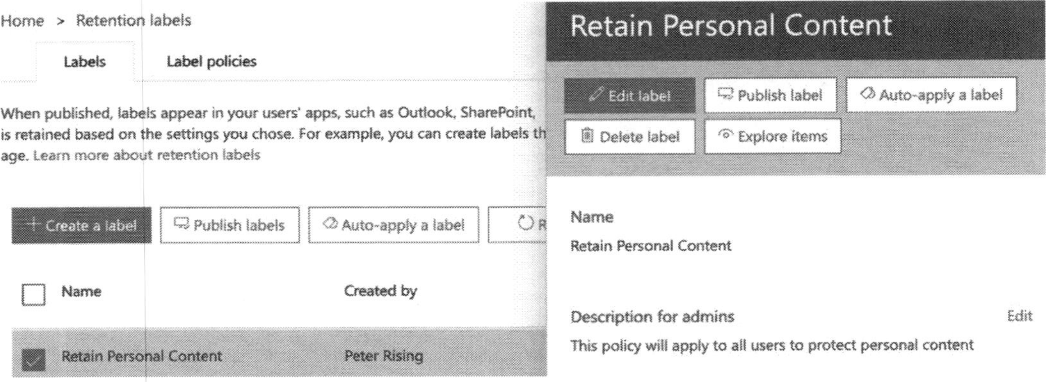

Figure 16.16 – A new retention label

7. Publishing your label creates a label policy that allows you to target the Office 365 locations where the label will be available. Once you have published your labels to a policy, you can view the new policy under the **Label policies** section.
8. Auto-applying a label will enable you to set the conditions for when you want a label to apply, as shown:

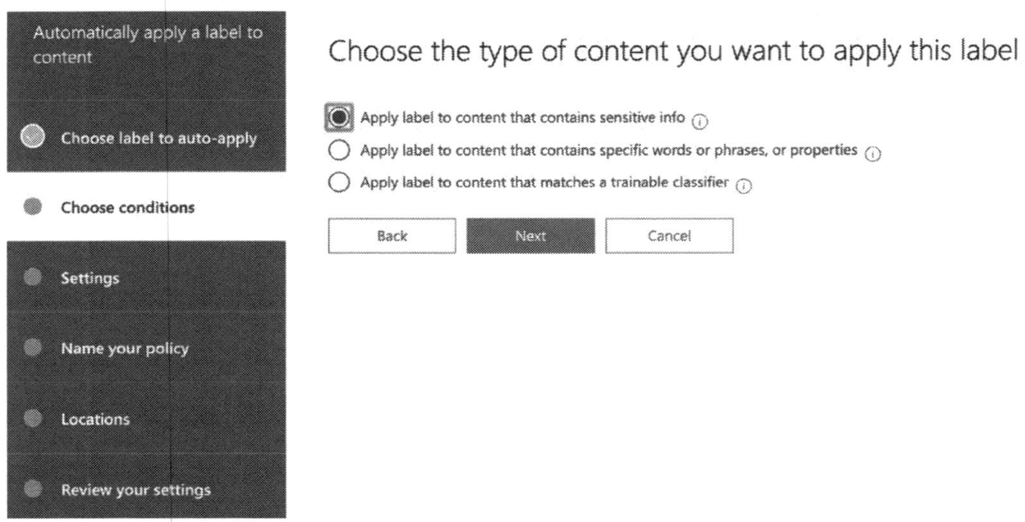

Figure 16.17 – Conditions for auto-applying a retention label

9. Once you set the sensitive information types that trigger that label to be automatically applied, you can continue to **Name your policy** and apply it to the required Office 365 locations.
10. Users can manually apply a label from Outlook on the web by right-clicking on the email, selecting **Assign policy**, and then selecting the desired label, as shown:

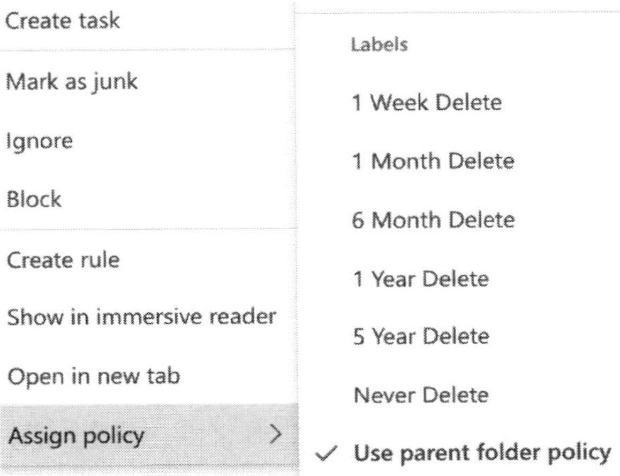

Figure 16.18 – Assigning a label

11. Once the chosen label is applied to the email, you can see this by clicking on the email, where you will notice that the label is visible, as shown:

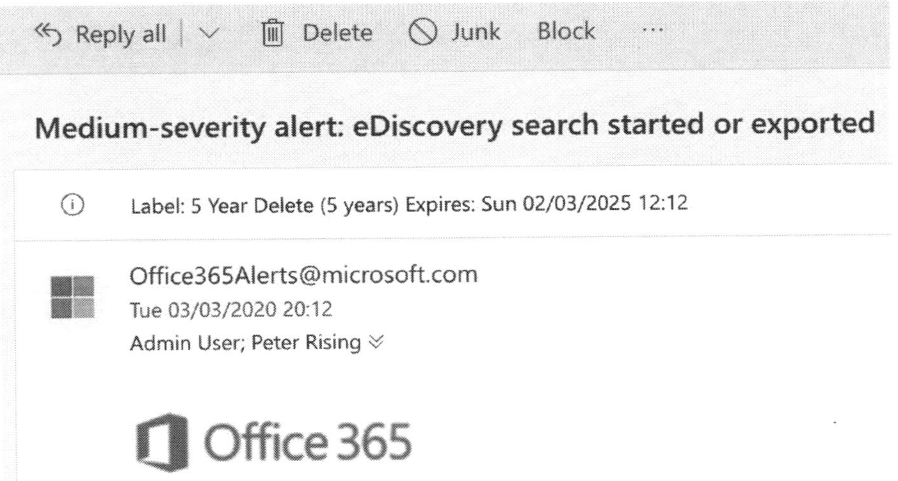

Figure 16.19 – The label

> **Important note**
>
> You can apply retention labels to Outlook, SharePoint, OneDrive, and Office 365 groups in a similar way. Further details on applying retention labels to your Office 365 content can be found in the *References* section at the end of this chapter.

In this section, we showed you how retention labels can be applied to emails and documents within your Microsoft 365 environment. You learned that labels can be created with file plan descriptors to automatically apply a label to content, as well as by manually setting the retention label settings.

We also showed you how retention labels can then be published to Office 365 locations using label policies or by auto-application. Finally, we showed you how your end users can view and apply retention labels in their applications and how they would appear.

In the final section of this chapter, we will show you how to use logs and reports within your Microsoft 365 environment to search for any potential personal data leaks.

Accessing logs and reports to search for and monitor personal data leaks

Now that you are aware of some of the tools and methods that can be used to prevent personal data loss, it is equally important to diligently monitor the use of personal data in your organization. There are a number of methods available to assist Microsoft 365 compliance administrators to achieve this. They include the following:

- Data loss prevention reports
- Alert policies
- Microsoft Cloud App Security

Let's examine each of these methods.

Data loss prevention reports

With data loss prevention reports, you can monitor any personal data contained in OneDrive or SharePoint Online, along with any email that is in transit, by viewing policy matches and trends within the Security & Compliance Center.

To view the data loss prevention reports, you need to complete the following steps:

1. Go to the Security & Compliance Center and navigate to **Reports | Dashboard**, as shown:

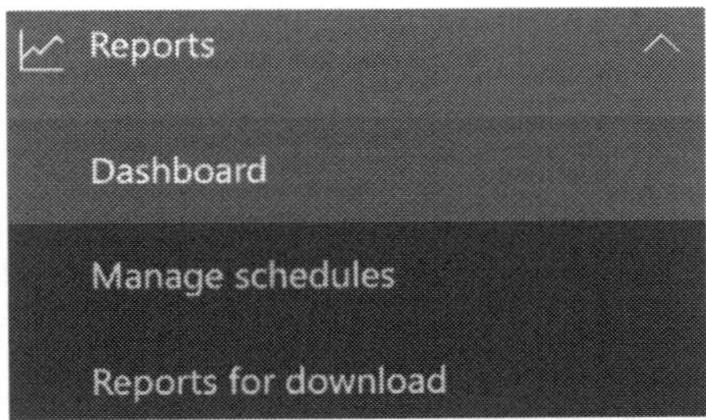

Figure 16.20 – The Reports dashboard

2. Locate the **DLP policy matches** tile and click on it to open it. This will take you to the Security & Compliance report viewer, as the following screenshot shows:

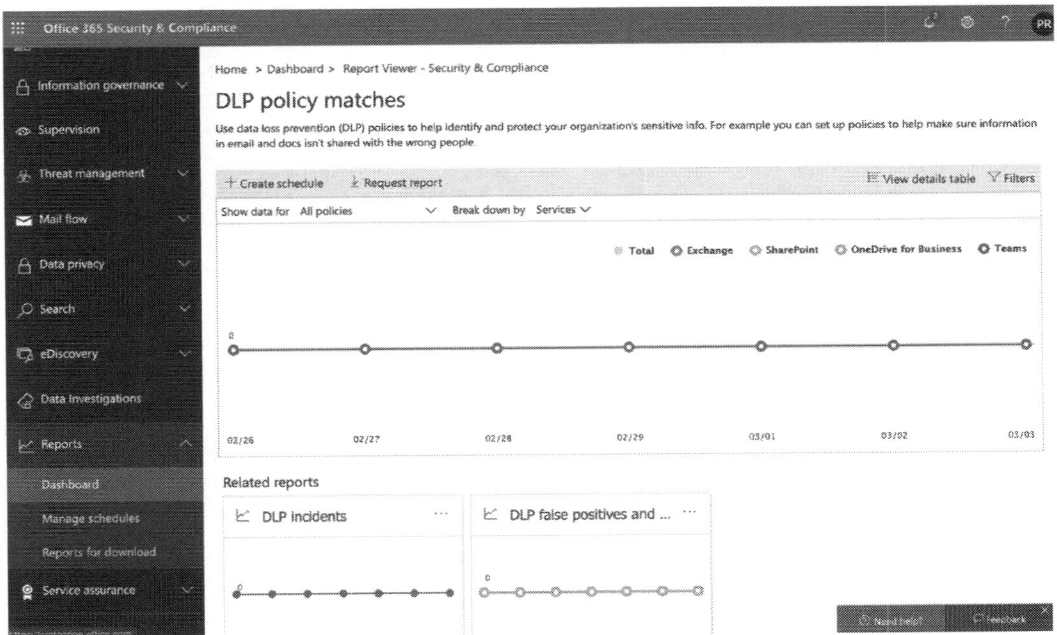

Figure 16.21 – The Security & Compliance report viewer

3. Within the report viewer, you can navigate through **DLP policy matches**, **DLP Incidents**, and **DLP false positives and overrides**.

4. In order to generate a report, click on the **Request report** button and you will see the options to create your report, as in the following screenshot:

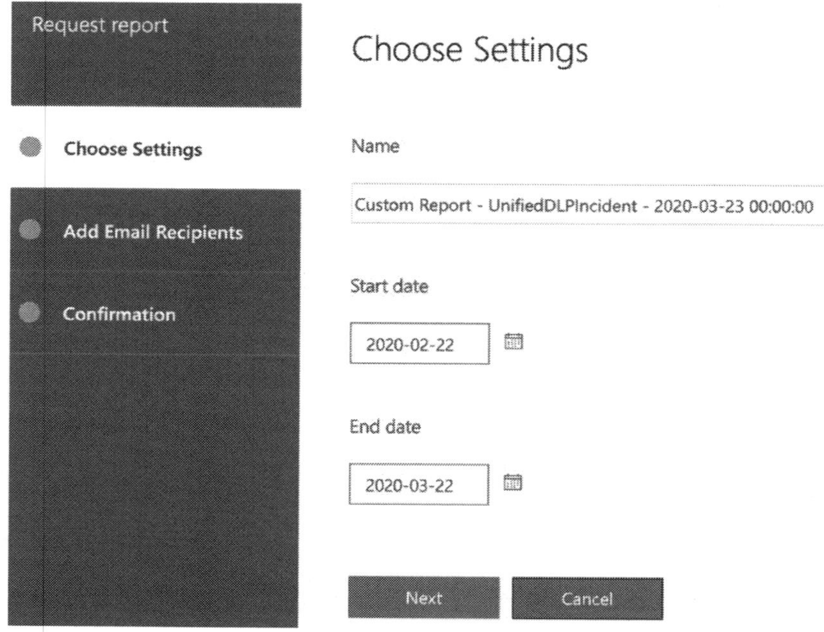

Figure 16.22 – Requesting a report

5. Click **Next** and enter an email recipient that you want to send this report to:

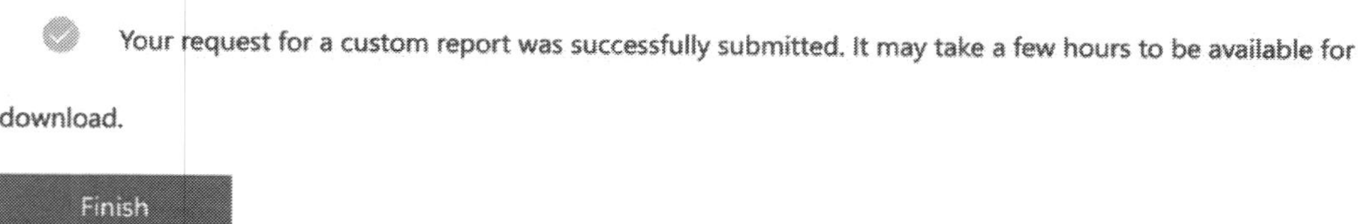

Confirmation
Your request for a custom report was successfully submitted. It may take a few hours to be available for download.
Finish

Figure 16.23 – Successful report request submission

6. Click **Finish** and wait for the report to be emailed to you. The email will appear in your inbox, as shown:

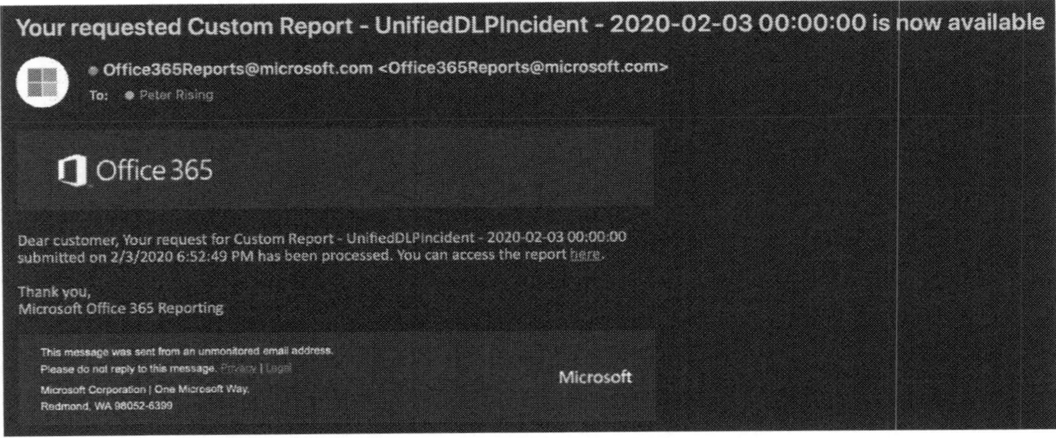

Figure 16.24 – Custom email report

7. Within the email, you can click on the **You can access the report here** option and it will open the report for you.
8. Alternatively, you can access the report from the Security & Compliance Center under **Reports | Reports for download**.

It may take a number of hours for the report to be emailed to you. The information included in these reports will help you to detect and view any personal data leakage occurrences.

Alert policies

Alert policies can also be used in conjunction with the Office 365 audit log to review both user and admin activities across your Office 365 services. With alert policies, you can set up and view alerts, and with the audit log, you can carry out manual searches to look for events based on specific criteria or time frames.

Alert policies can be created and viewed by completing the following steps:

1. Open the Security & Compliance Center from `https://protection.office.com` and navigate to **Alerts | Alert policies**, as shown:

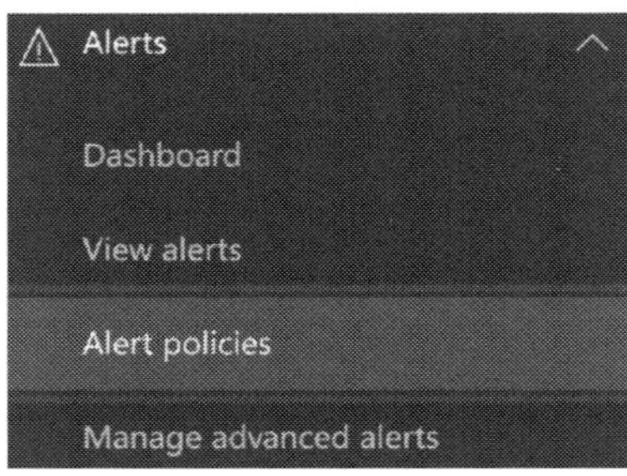

Figure 16.25 – Alert policies

2. You will see the list of alert policies, as in the following screenshot, and you can set up new alert policies or edit existing alert policies to notify you when a specific activity occurs:

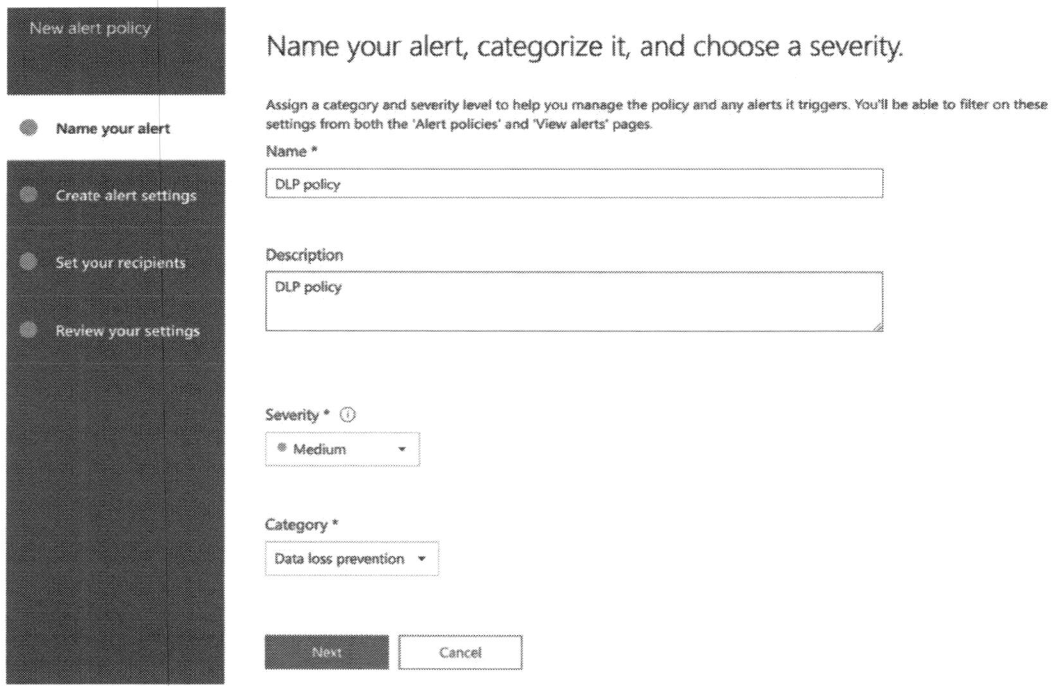

Figure 16.26 – The New alert policy wizard

3. Next, choose the alert settings for your policy and select the activities that will trigger the policy. Set the recipients and then, finally, review and create the policy.
4. The users you select to be targeted by the policy will start to receive email alerts when a policy match is detected. An example of this sort of email is shown in the following screenshot:

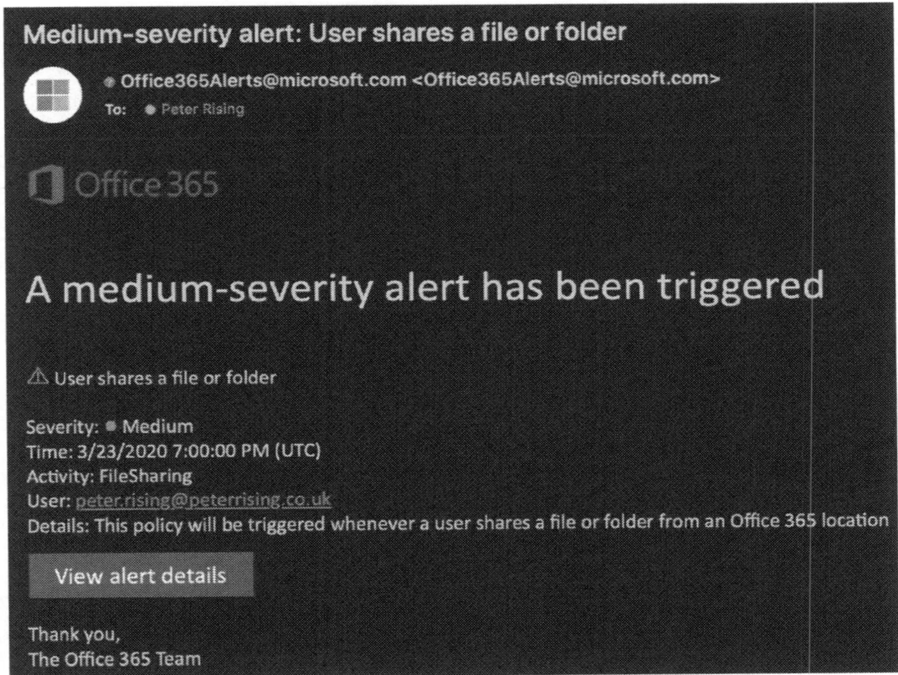

Figure 16.27 – An alert policy email notification

5. Click on **View alert details** and it will take you directly to the alert within the Security & Compliance Center, as the following screenshot shows:

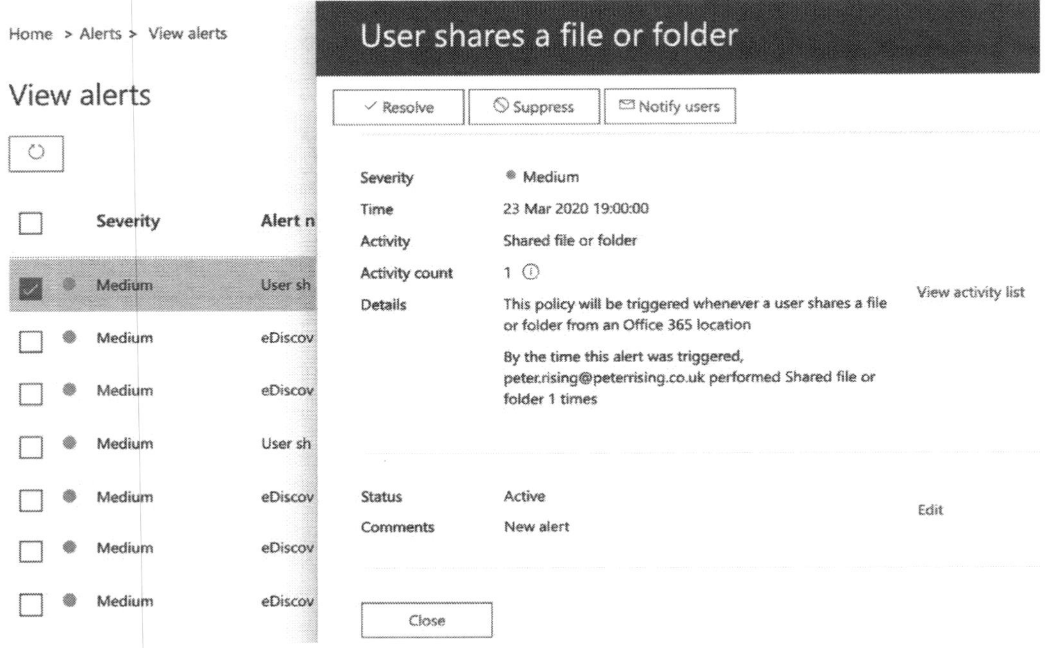

Figure 16.28 – Alert details

In addition to using these types of alerts, you can view the audit log to manually search for events relating to data loss prevention.

> **Important note**
>
> For more details on alert policies and the Office 365 audit log, please refer to *Chapter 14, Cloud App Discovery and Security*, where we covered alert policies and the audit log in greater detail.

Microsoft Cloud App Security

It is also possible to use the Microsoft Cloud App Security **Investigate** feature to view how personal data travels within cloud applications.

From the Cloud App Security portal, which is accessed via `https://portal.cloudappsecurity.com`, you can view the activity log and files to view sharing activities, which will help you to identify potentially sensitive information that is leaving the organization. The **Investigate** feature is shown in the following screenshot:

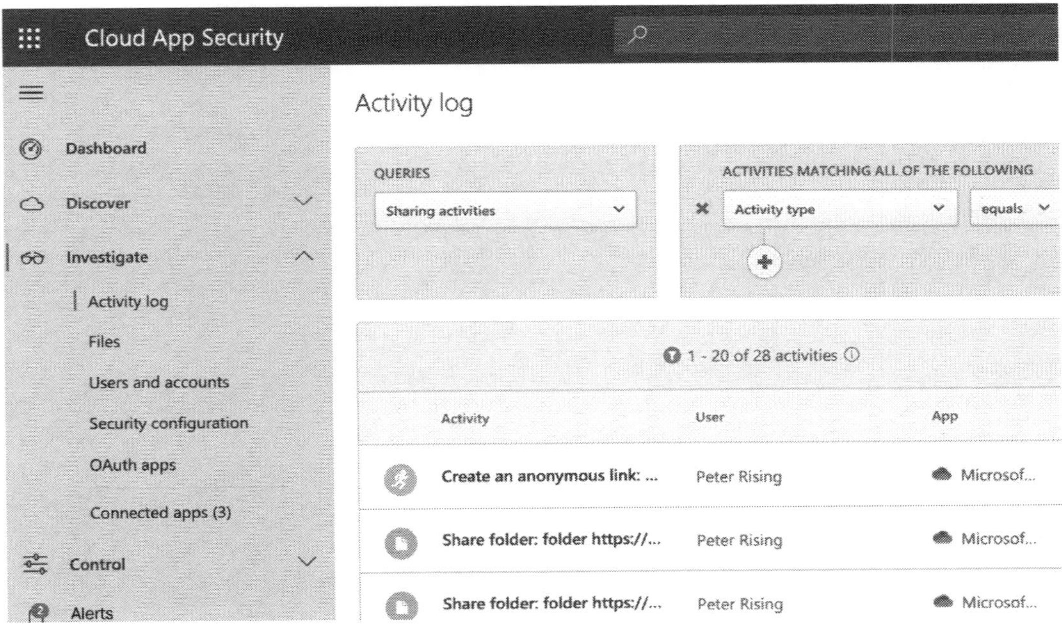

Figure 16.29 – The Cloud App Security portal

You can also configure Cloud App Security policies to assist you with managing sensitive data. We will create an example policy in the following steps:

1. Create the following policy from the Cloud App Security dashboard by going to **Control | Templates** and creating a new policy based on the **File containing PII detected in the cloud (built-in DLP engine)** template, as in the following screenshot:

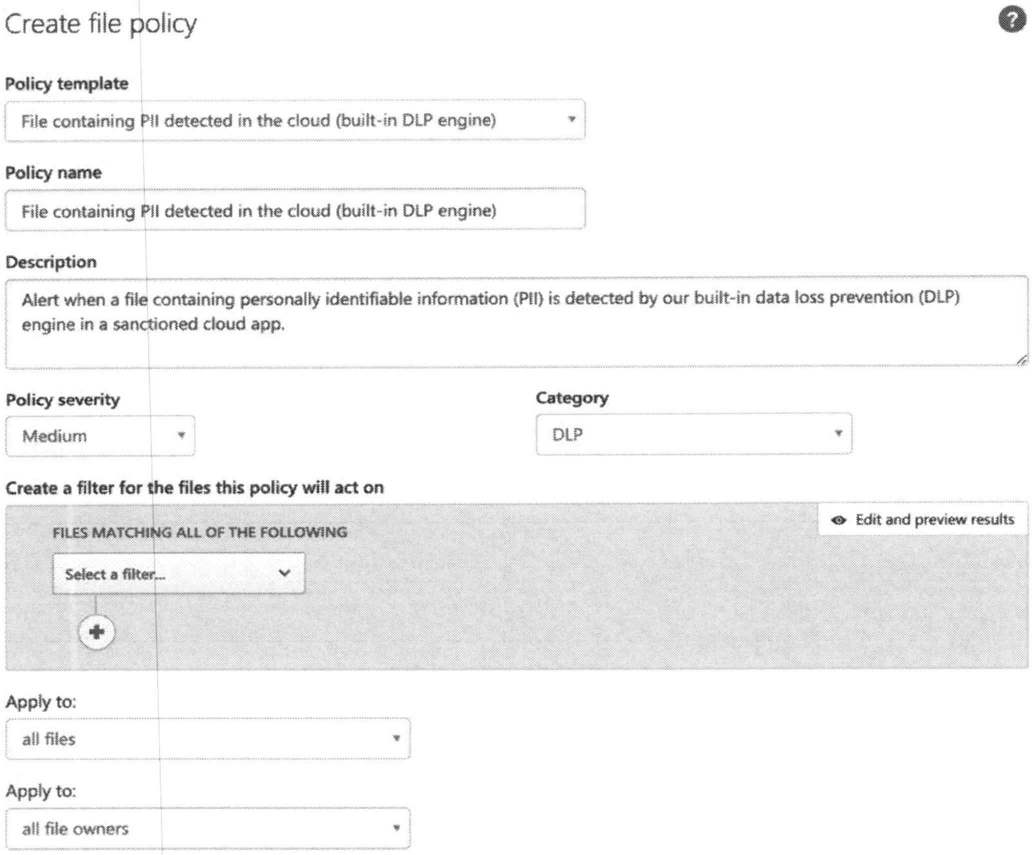

Create file policy

Policy template

File containing PII detected in the cloud (built-in DLP engine)

Policy name

File containing PII detected in the cloud (built-in DLP engine)

Description

Alert when a file containing personally identifiable information (PII) is detected by our built-in data loss prevention (DLP) engine in a sanctioned cloud app.

Policy severity

Medium

Category

DLP

Create a filter for the files this policy will act on

FILES MATCHING ALL OF THE FOLLOWING

Edit and preview results

Select a filter...

Apply to:

all files

Apply to:

all file owners

Figure 16.30 – Creating a policy from a template

2. Scroll down and select the settings shown in the following screenshot:

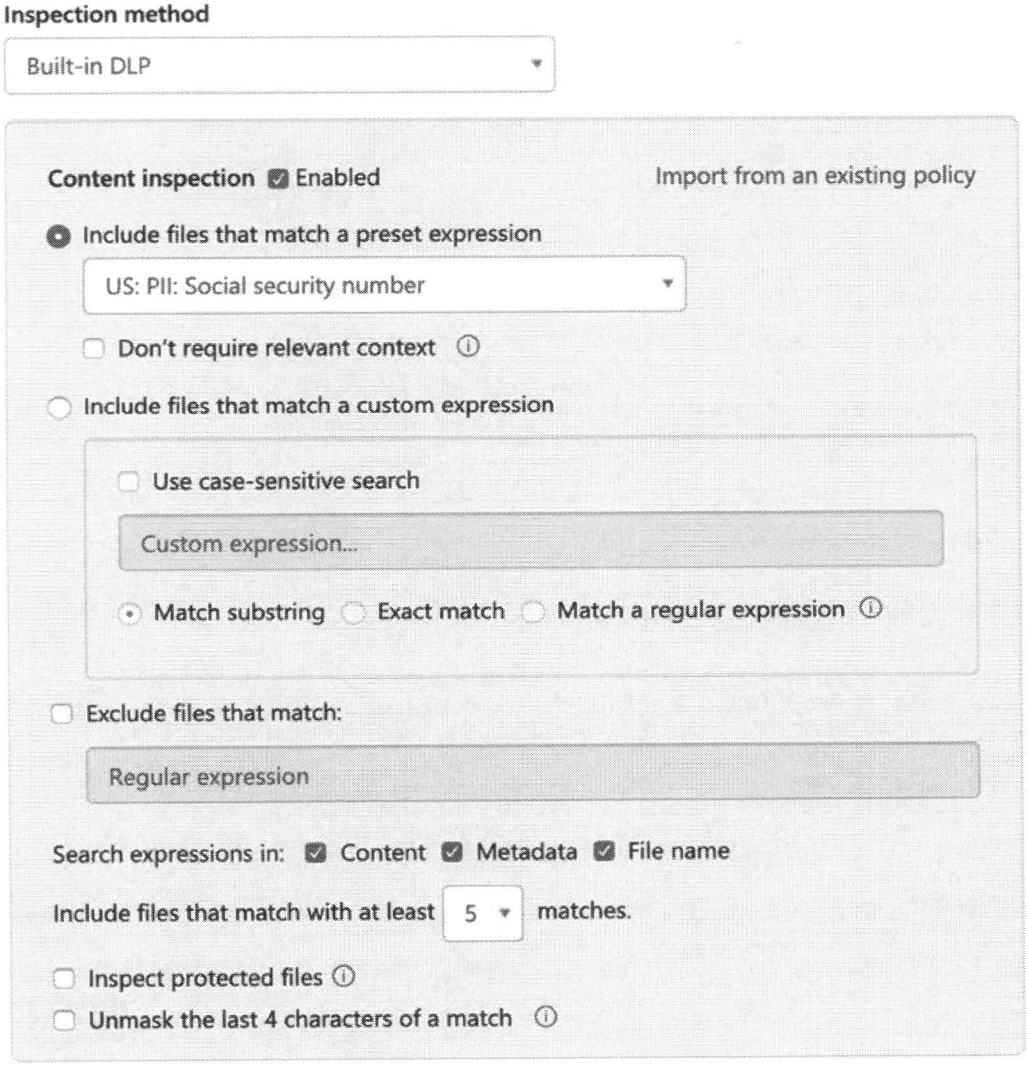

Inspection method

Built-in DLP

Content inspection Enabled

Import from an existing policy

Include files that match a preset expression

US: PII: Social security number

Don't require relevant context

Include files that match a custom expression

Use case-sensitive search

Custom expression...

Match substring Exact match Match a regular expression

Exclude files that match:

Regular expression

Search expressions in: Content Metadata File name

Include files that match with at least 5 matches.

Inspect protected files

Unmask the last 4 characters of a match

Figure 16.31 – Creating a policy from a template

3. Finally, scroll down and configure the **Alerts** and **Governance actions** options, as shown:

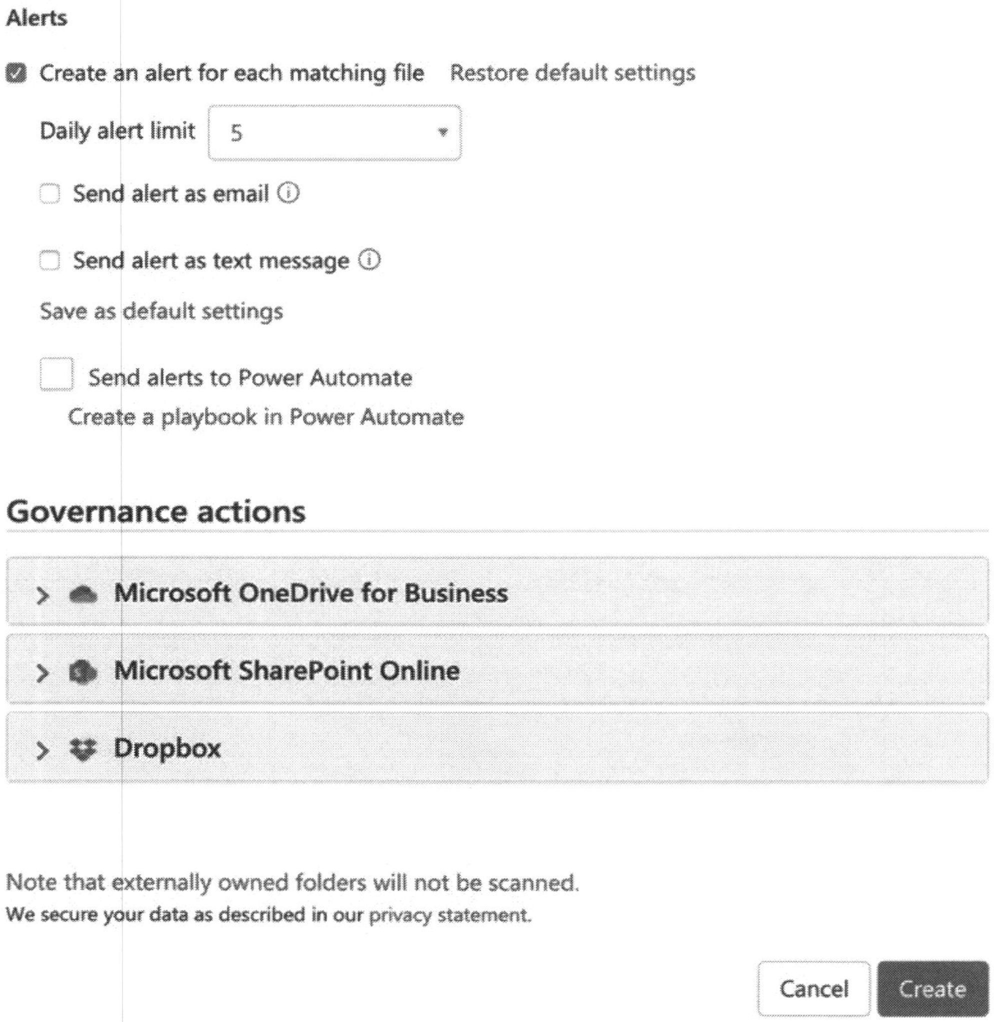

Alerts

Create an alert for each matching file Restore default settings

Daily alert limit 5

Send alert as email

Send alert as text message

Save as default settings

Send alerts to Power Automate

Create a playbook in Power Automate

Governance actions

Microsoft OneDrive for Business

Microsoft SharePoint Online

Dropbox

Note that externally owned folders will not be scanned.

We secure your data as described in our privacy statement.

Cancel Create

Figure 16.32 – Creating a policy from a template

4. Click **Create** to finalize your new policy.

The policy we created in the preceding steps will alert us when a file containing **Personally Identifiable Information** (**PII**) is detected by the built-in DLP engine within any sanctioned cloud app.

Another potentially useful policy that you could create using Cloud App Security is one to block any downloads of files within your cloud apps to unmanaged devices. Alerts for this activity would show you any cases of these download attempts.

> **Important note**
>
> Microsoft Cloud App Security was covered in greater detail in *Chapter 13, Data Loss Prevention*. Please refer to that chapter for more information on Cloud App Security.

In this section, you learned how to access and monitor logs and reports within Microsoft 365 to gain visibility on personal data activity in your organization. We demonstrated how DLP reports, including policy matches, incident reports, and false positives and overrides, can be used to detect sensitive information.

In addition, we demonstrated how alert policies within the Security & Compliance Center can be used to generate email alerts to administrators to be triggered when a match to sensitive information types is detected. The Office 365 audit log can also be interrogated to locate these activities.

Finally, we showed you how Cloud App Security can provide visibility on activities related to file and sharing activity, as well as how policies can be created to alert us about these activities.

Summary

In this chapter, we introduced you to the principles of protecting personal data within Microsoft 365. You learned how to run content searches from the Security & Compliance Center and how to preview and export the results.

We also showed you how retention labels and policies can be set up to be applied either automatically, based on matches to sensitive information types, or by manually applying your preferred retention settings.

Finally, we demonstrated the various methods of monitoring and reporting in relation to personal data within Microsoft 365. This includes configuring alert policies and viewing the Office 365 audit log activities, along with viewing and interpreting the DLP reporting options within the Security & Compliance Center and setting up policies within Cloud App Security.

In the next chapter, we will examine data governance and retention, which includes how to view data governance logs, how to plan and execute retention tags and policies, and how to use supervision policies and apply in-place and litigation holds.

Questions

1. True or false: A content search can be configured to specific Office 365 locations.

   a. True

   b. False

2. Where in the Security & Compliance Center would you go to configure retention labels?

   a. **Classification | Sensitivity Labels**

   b. **Classification | Retention Policies**

   c. **Classification | Retention Labels**

   d. **Classification | Sensitive info types**

3. True or false: With a content search, the results can be exported and viewed in Excel.

   a. True

   b. False

4. Which of the following cannot be used to view and interpret personal data within Microsoft 365?

   a. DLP reports

   b. Alert policies

   c. Cloud App Security policies

   d. Threat detection reports

5. Which of the following is an option when using content searches?

   a. Focused Search

   b. Guided Search

   c. Advanced Search

6. Which of the following options would you use if you wanted to automatically apply a retention label based on conditions?

   a. File plan descriptors

   b. Label settings

   c. Label classification

7. True or false: Retention can be manually enabled on a retention label when file plan descriptors have also been configured.

   a. True

   b. False

8. Where in the Security & Compliance Center would you go to start a content search?

   a. **eDiscovery | Advanced eDiscovery**

   b. **Search | eDiscovery**

   c. **Search | Content Search**

   d. **Investigation | Content Search**

9. Where in the Cloud App Security portal would you go to set up a new alert policy based on a template?

   a. **Control | Templates**

   b. **Control | Policies**

   c. **Investigate | Files**

   d. **Investigate | Security Configuration**

10. True or false: Retention labels can be viewed and applied by users to emails when using Outlook on the web.

    a. True

    b. False

References

Please refer to the following links for more information:

- Content search in Office 365: `https://docs.microsoft.com/en-us/microsoft-365/compliance/content-search?view=o365-worldwide`
- Keyword queries and search conditions for content search: `https://docs.microsoft.com/en-us/microsoft-365/compliance/keyword-queries-and-search-conditions?view=o365-worldwide`
- Exporting content search results: `https://docs.microsoft.com/en-us/microsoft-365/compliance/export-search-results?view=o365-worldwide`

- Exporting content search reports: `https://docs.microsoft.com/en-us/microsoft-365/compliance/export-a-content-search-report?view=o365-worldwide`
- An overview of retention labels: `https://docs.microsoft.com/en-us/microsoft-365/compliance/labels?view=o365-worldwide`
- Bulk-creating retention labels using PowerShell: `https://docs.microsoft.com/en-us/microsoft-365/compliance/bulk-create-publish-labels-using-powershell?view=o365-worldwide`
- Alert policies in the Security & Compliance Center: `https://docs.microsoft.com/en-gb/microsoft-365/compliance/alert-policies?view=o365-worldwide#default-alert-policies?wt.mc_id=4039827`

17
Data Governance and Retention

Planning for data governance and retention is a crucial task for Microsoft 365 compliance administrators and it is vital to have the correct strategy in place to ensure that your organization is protected and compliant. There are a number of ways to govern and retain data that is hosted in your Microsoft 365 environment in order to ensure that the content cannot be lost either accidentally or due to the actions of a malicious insider.

In this chapter, we will introduce you to the principles of data governance and retention. You will learn how to configure retention tags and policies, how to use supervision policies to capture employee communications, and how litigation holds can be used to preserve electronically stored information. We will also explain how data such as user `.pst` files can be imported into Office 365 using the Security & Compliance Center, as well as show you how to configure in-place archiving and manage any inactive mailboxes.

We will cover these topics in the following order:

- Understanding data governance and the retention requirements for your organization
- Navigating data governance reports and dashboards
- Configuring retention tags, retention policies, and supervision policies

- Configuring litigation holds to preserve Office 365 data
- Importing data into Office 365 from the Security & Compliance Center
- Configuring archiving

Understanding data governance and the retention requirements for your organization

Planning for data governance in Microsoft 365 requires compliance administrators to understand any internal organizational policies that must be adhered to, along with any applicable industry regulations.

These requirements will obviously differ depending on the nature of the organization, but overall, the principles of governing your data to ensure that you can appropriately retain, or retain then delete, the content within emails and documents are essentially universal.

The logical starting point for compliance administrators when starting on this journey is retention. Having the correct set of retention policies configured and applied will enable the other components of data governance to logically fall into place. With retention policies in Microsoft 365, you can apply actions organization-wide or to specific locations or users, which will either retain or delete content in line with set retention periods.

When an email or a document is targeted by a retention policy, the user who is working on that content can make any necessary changes unimpeded, but the retention policy will make a copy of the original document and this will be retained for the duration of that retention policy. This works across the various Office 365 services, as follows:

- **SharePoint Online and OneDrive**: A copy of the original content will be retained in the Preservation Hold library.
- **Email and public folders**: A copy of the original content will be retained in the Recoverable Items folder.
- **Teams**: Chat content is stored in Exchange Online.

Should your organization be bound by more restrictive regulations, then you may be required to configure retention policies using the Preservation Lock feature. When Preservation Lock is applied to a retention policy, the policy cannot be turned off or set to lesser restriction settings by anyone (including Office 365 administrators).

Once a retention policy has been applied to OneDrive or SharePoint Online content, the following scenarios are possible.

The content is modified or deleted during the retention period

If changes or deletions are made to the content while a retention period is in effect and the retention policy is set to delete any data that is subject to that retention period at the end of the retention period, a copy of the original content is placed in the Preservation Hold library. The Preservation Hold library is scanned periodically to identify content whose retention duration is complete. That content is then moved directly to a second-stage recycle bin. Site collection administrators can restore content from here; otherwise, it is permanently deleted and unrecoverable after a period of 93 days.

The content is unchanged during the retention period

If no modifications are made to the content while a retention period is in effect and the retention policy is set to delete that content at the end of the retention period, the content is moved to a first-stage recycle bin when the retention duration is completed. Users will be able to purge the first-stage recycle bin, which moves the contents to the second-stage recycle bin. Users do not have access to the second-stage recycle bin. These two stages of recycle bins combined have a retention period of 93 days, after which the content is permanently deleted and unrecoverable.

Mailbox and public folder content

When working with retention policies concerning mailbox and public folder content, the **Recoverable Items** folder within the user's mailbox is regularly inspected and any content within it that is no longer subject to a retention period is permanently deleted 14 days after the end of the retention period that applied to that item.

> **Important note**
>
> Only users who have the eDiscovery role can view items in other users' recoverable items folder.

In this section, you have learned that retention is a core principle when it comes to data governance in Office 365. Once you have your retention policies defined and deployed, you can leverage further powerful features of Office 365 data governance, such as configuring inactive mailboxes and setting in-place and litigation holds. We will explore all of these features in detail later in this chapter, including how to configure retention tags and policies.

Next, we will show you how to view data governance reports and dashboards.

Navigating data governance reports and dashboards

Microsoft provides administrators with a great deal of information relating to data governance, which can be accessed from the Security & Compliance Center. Regularly viewing this information enables you to stay one step ahead in ensuring that your organization meets its compliance and regulatory obligations, as well as allowing you to make logical adjustments to the existing compliance settings that you have already configured. The Microsoft 365 information governance dashboard provides you with visibility on the following details:

- How the labels you have configured are applied
- The top five labels report
- Label trends over the past 90 days
- A snapshot of how much content is retained
- Information on how many users in your organization are protected by a retention policy
- Information on how many users have an online archive mailbox enabled

In order to view this information in the Security & Compliance Center, we need to take the following steps:

1. Navigate to **Information Governance | Dashboard** and you will see the dashboard shown in the following screenshot:

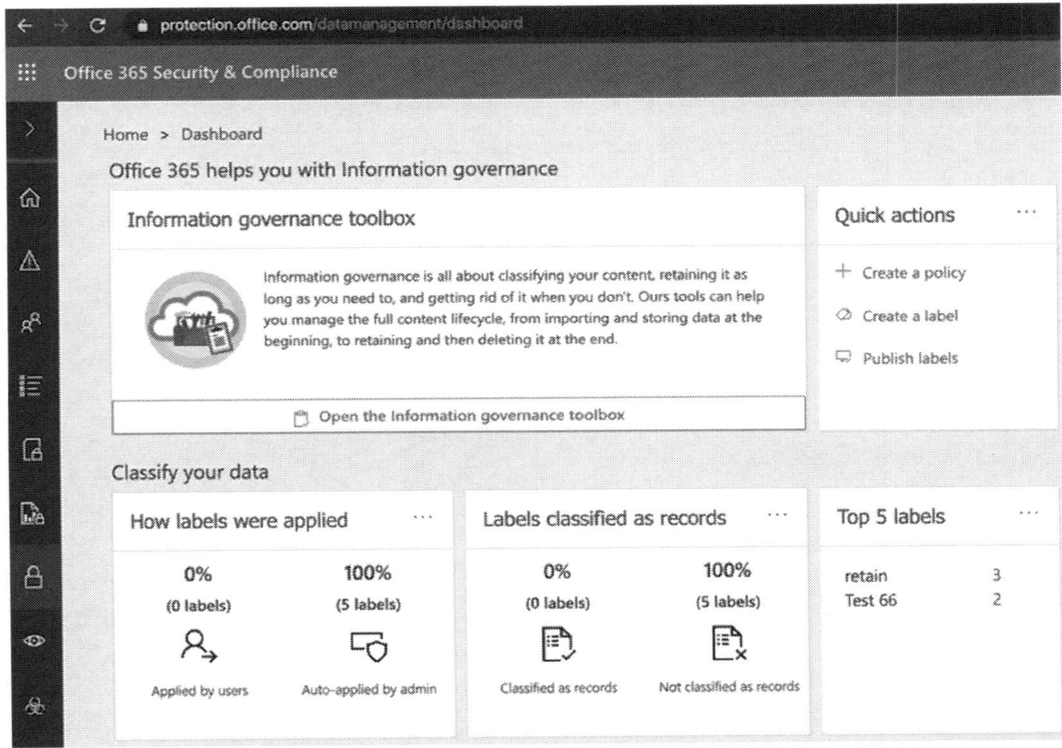

Figure 17.1 – The information governance dashboard

2. Scroll down to the **Classify your data** section to review the available reports, as in the following screenshot:

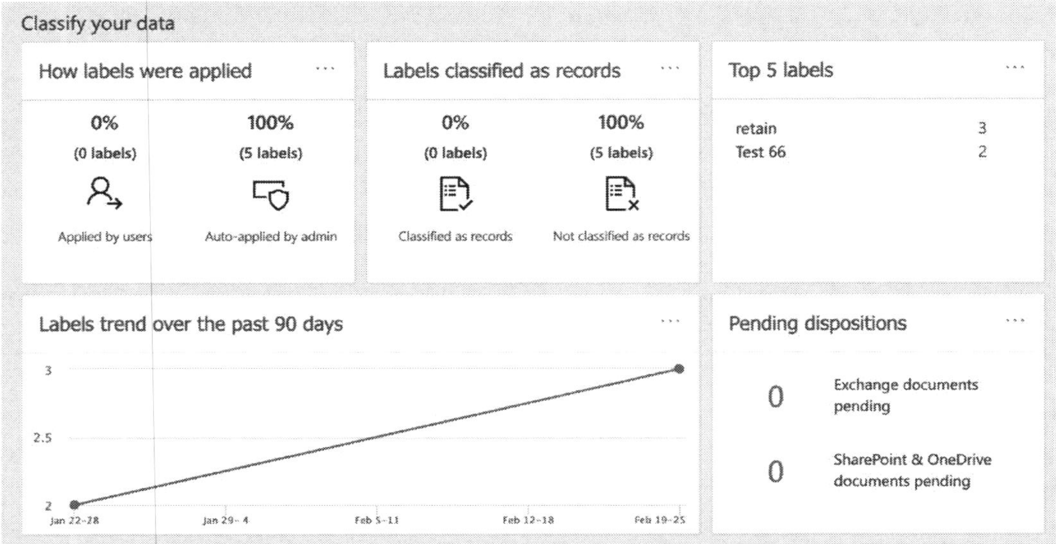

Figure 17.2 – The Classify your data reports

3. We can open each of these reports individually to view them in more detail. The following screenshot shows what this looks like for the **How labels were applied** report:

Figure 17.3 – The How labels were applied report

4. Clicking on **View details table** will show you this information, as shown:

Home > Dashboard > Report Viewer - Security & Compliance

Label auto apply report

View report | Filters

Label	Location	Apply type	Retention type	Record type	Disposition type	Count
retain	OneDrive	Auto applied	Preserve	NotRecord	AutomaticDisposition	3
Test 66	OneDrive	Auto applied	Preserve	NotRecord	AutomaticDisposition	2

Figure 17.4 – View details table

5. You can also select the **Filters** option, where you can set the date range for your reports for up to 90 days and choose to filter between manually applied or auto-applied labels, as shown:

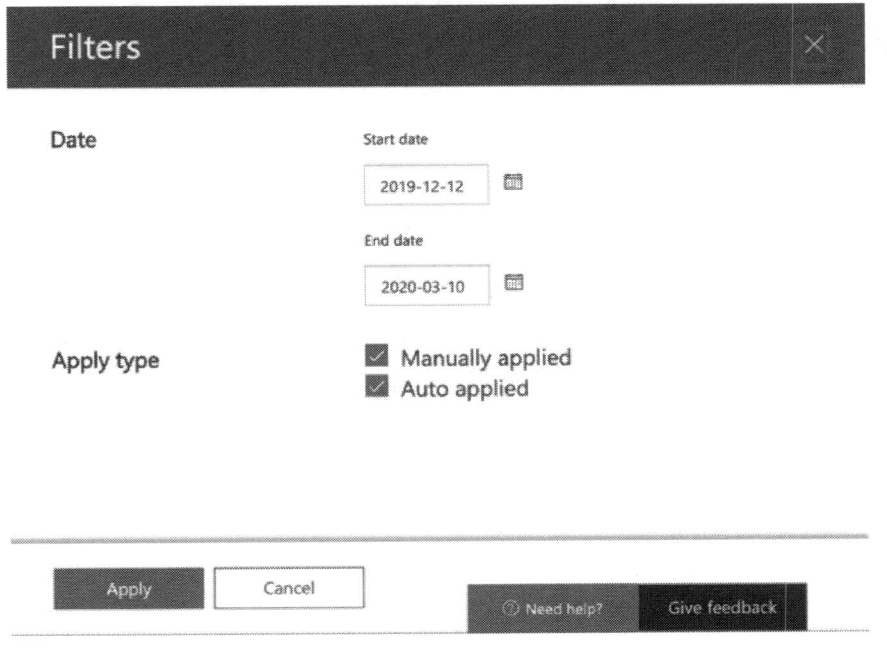

Figure 17.5 – Applying filters

6. Under the **Govern and stay compliant** section of the information governance dashboard, you can also view the tiles shown in the following screenshot:

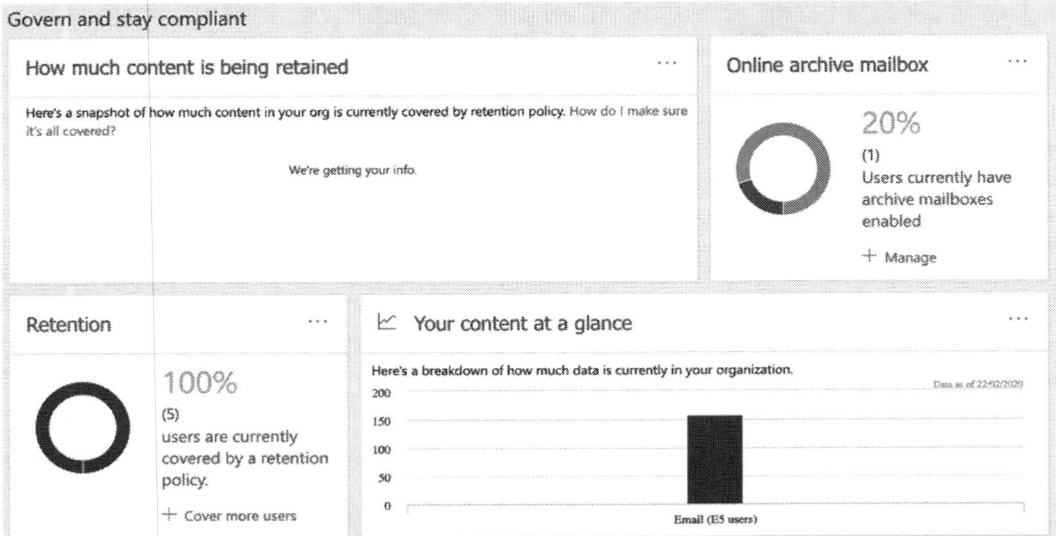

Figure 17.6 – Govern and stay compliant

7. Clicking on the ellipsis icon next to each report and selecting **Go to dashboard** will take you to the dashboard for that report, as the following screenshot illustrates:

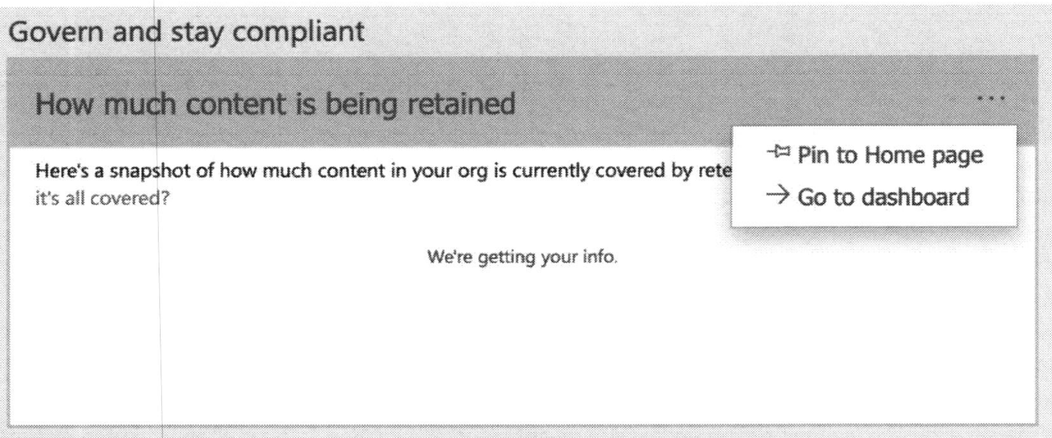

Figure 17.7 – The Go to dashboard option for each report

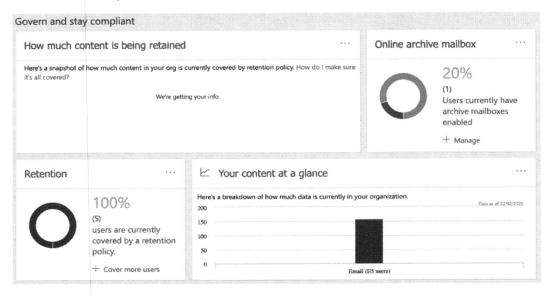

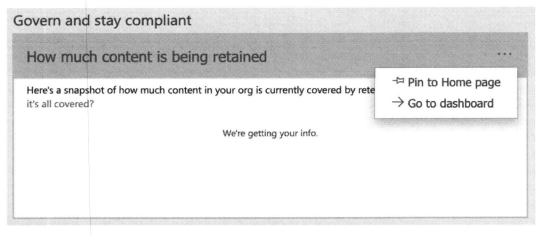

So, as you can see, there are a number of ways that you can keep track of your organization's compliance settings by accessing the reports and dashboards we described.

In this section, we introduced you to the information governance dashboard, which can be found in the Security & Compliance Center. This dashboard provides administrators with quick and easy access to a range of information and reports on how the compliance principles you applied to your Office 365 locations are enforced.

Next, we will show you how to set up retention tags and policies.

Configuring retention tags, retention policies, and supervision policies

When working with retention in Office 365, there are two distinctly different methods that you can use.

For Exchange Online email content, you can configure retention tags and retention policies using the **Compliance** section of the Exchange admin center. This method is particularly relevant to the settings that are applied to users when they have an online archive enabled for their mailbox (which we will examine in more detail later in this chapter).

It is also possible to configure retention policies for Exchange Online and other locations in Office 365, including SharePoint Online, OneDrive, and Teams, from the Security & Compliance Center.

While using the Security & Compliance Center is now the preferred method of creating retention policies, the Exchange admin center method remains important as it is the only way that retention tags can be configured. In this section, we will show you how to create a retention policy using both of the methods described here.

Creating a retention policy using the Exchange admin center

Creating a retention policy from the Exchange admin center allows you to manage the email life cycle of your Office 365 users by creating retention tags, associating these tags with retention policies that are then applied to your email users. To create retention policies using this method, you must have the **Messaging Records Management** permissions, which are assigned to the **Compliance Management**, **Organization Management**, and **Records Management** roles.

The policy can be created by first creating or using an existing retention tag by completing the following steps:

1. Log in to the Exchange admin center at `https://outlook.office.com/ecp` and navigate to **Compliance Management | Retention Tags**, as in the following screenshot:

NAME	TYPE	RETENTION PERIOD	RETENTION ACTION
1 Month Delete	Personal	30 days	Delete
1 Week Delete	Personal	7 days	Delete
1 Year Delete	Personal	365 days	Delete
5 Year Delete	Personal	1825 days	Delete
6 Month Delete	Personal	180 days	Delete
Default 2 year move to archive	Default	730 days	Archive
Deleted Items	Deleted Items	30 days	Delete
Junk Email	Junk Email	30 days	Delete
Never Delete	Personal	Unlimited	Delete
Personal 1 year move to archive	Personal	365 days	Archive
Personal 5 year move to archive	Personal	1825 days	Archive
Personal never move to archive	Personal	Unlimited	Archive

Figure 17.8 – Retention tags

2. There are a number of pre-configured retention tags in Exchange Online, as shown in the preceding screenshot. To add a new retention tag, click on the + sign and choose from the following options:

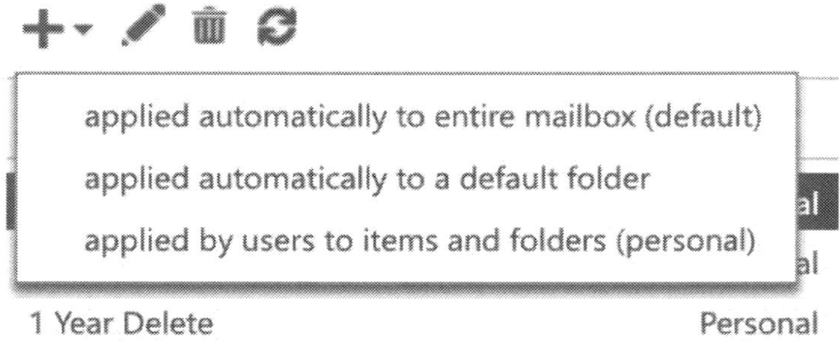

Figure 17.9 – Adding a new retention tag

For this example, we will select the option to create a personal retention tag that users can choose to apply to email items and folders. When applied, this tag moves items from the user's mailbox to their archive mailbox (if enabled) after a period of 2 years. This, and the other available retention tag options (such as **Delete and Allow Recovery** and **Permanently Delete**), are shown in the following screenshot:

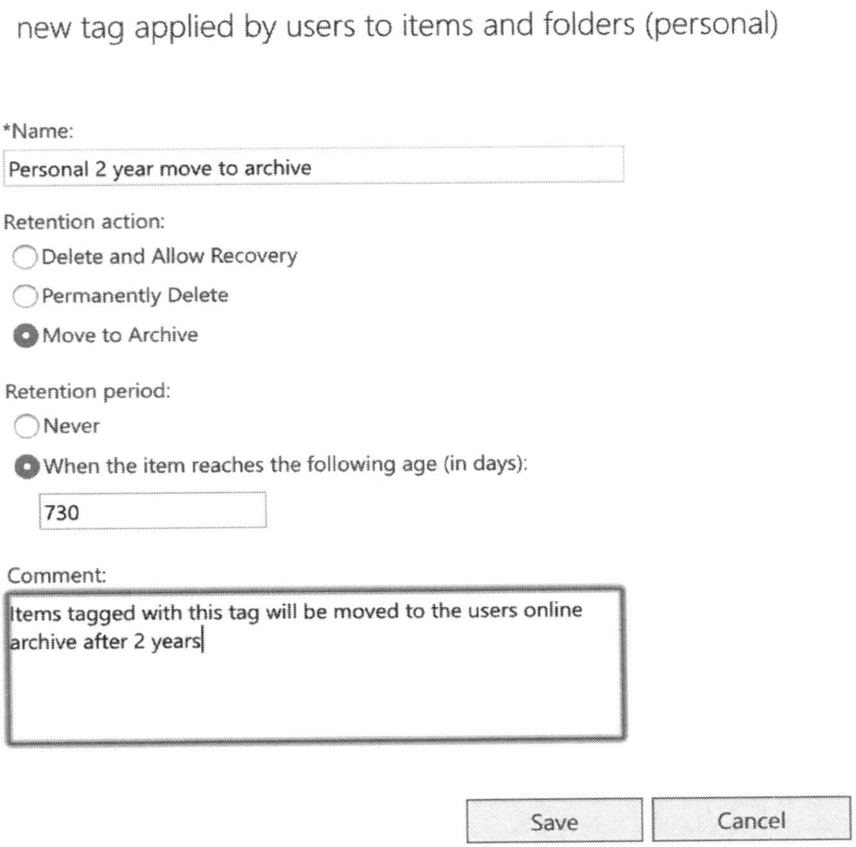

new tag applied by users to items and folders (personal)

*Name:
Personal 2 year move to archive

Retention action:
Delete and Allow Recovery
Permanently Delete
Move to Archive

Retention period:
Never
When the item reaches the following age (in days):
730

Comment:
Items tagged with this tag will be moved to the users online archive after 2 years

Save Cancel

Figure 17.10 – The new retention tag settings

3. Click **Save** to complete the setup of your retention tag.
4. It is also possible to complete the setup of the retention tag through Exchange Online PowerShell by running the following command:

```
New-RetentionPolicyTag -Name "Personal-2-year-move-
to-archive" -Type All -AgeLimitForRetention 730
-RetentionActionMoveToArchive
```

5. Now that we have created our retention tag, we can create a retention policy from the Exchange admin center at `https://outlook.office365.com/ecp` under **Compliance Management | Retention Policies**. Click on the + sign and you will see the retention policy options, as in the following screenshot:

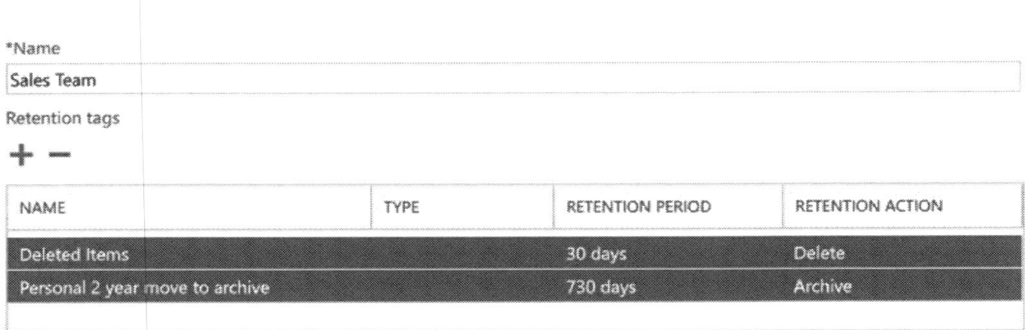

Figure 17.11 – A new retention policy

6. In this example, we will set the name of the policy as `Sales Team` and add two retention tags. One of the tags will be a default tag that will delete items in the **Deleted Items** folder after 30 days. The other tag will be a personal tag that will allow users to manually tag items to be moved to their online archive after 2 years (this is the tag we created in the previous step). Click **Save** to complete the setup of your policy.
7. It is also possible to complete the setup of the retention policy through Exchange Online PowerShell by running the following command:

```
New-RetentionPolicy "Sales-Team" -RetentionPolicyTagLinks"
Personal-2-year-move-to-archive","Deleted-Items"
```

Now that you have a retention policy with retention tags created, you can associate it with your chosen mailbox users from either the Exchange admin center or Exchange Online PowerShell. Details on how to complete this process can be found in the *References* section at the end of this chapter.

Creating a retention policy using the Security & Compliance Center

Creating a retention policy from the Security & Compliance Center allows you to apply retention principles to all of your Office 365 locations, not just Exchange Online. The principles of retention using this method are described in the *Understanding data governance and the retention requirements for your organization* section of this chapter.

To create retention policies using this method, you need to complete the following steps:

1. Log in to the Security & Compliance Center at `https://protection.office.com` and navigate to **Information governance** | **Retention**. You will then see the following page:

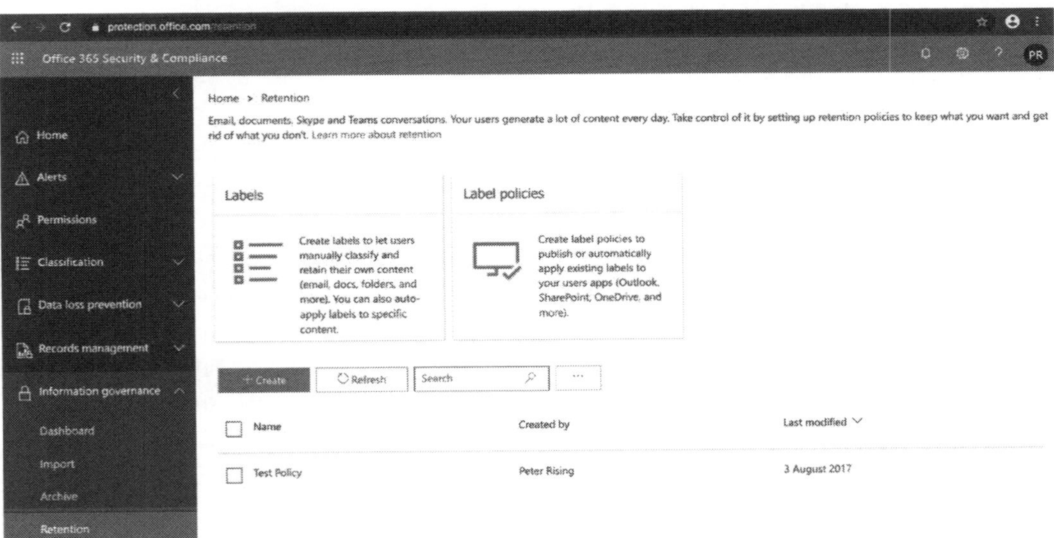

Figure 17.12 – Retention in the Security & Compliance Center

2. Click on **Create**. You will need to enter a name and description for your policy, as in the following screenshot:

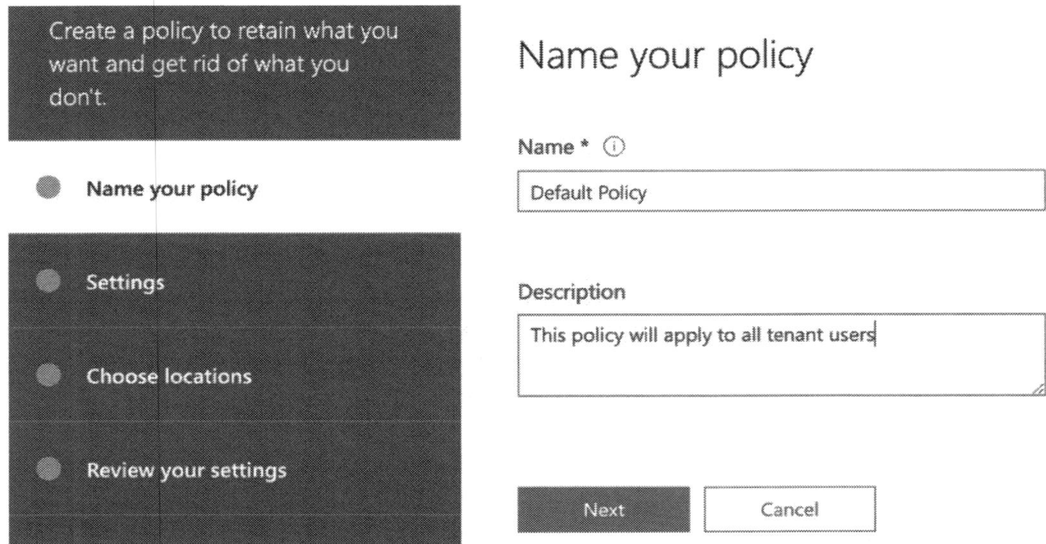

Figure 17.13 – Name your policy

3. Click **Next** and you can set your retention settings based on your requirements, such as how long you wish to retain content, whether the content to be deleted after the retention period, and whether or not to retain the content based on when it was created or when it was modified. These options are shown in the following screenshot:

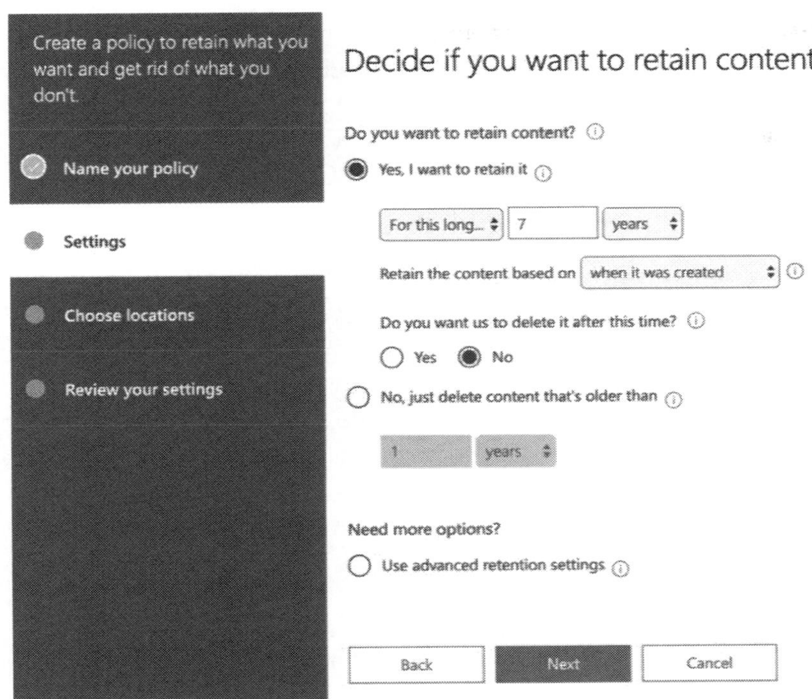

Figure 17.14 – The retention policy settings

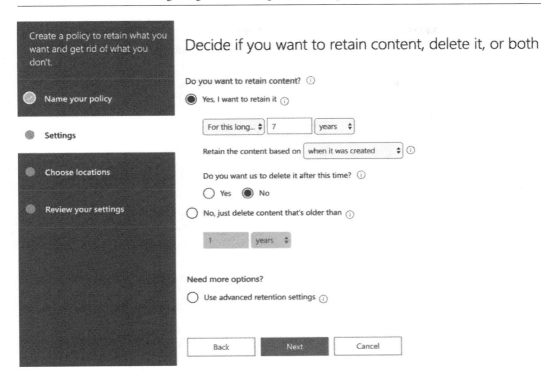

4. Click **Next** and you will now see the options to choose which Office 365 locations you can apply the policy to. These include **Exchange Online**, **SharePoint sites**, **OneDrive accounts**, **Office 365 groups**, and **Skype for Business**. You can filter the location selections to include or exclude accounts or sites as required. In addition, you can apply the policy to **Exchange Public Folders**, **Teams Channel messages**, and, finally, **Teams chats**. The following screenshot shows some of the options you will see here:

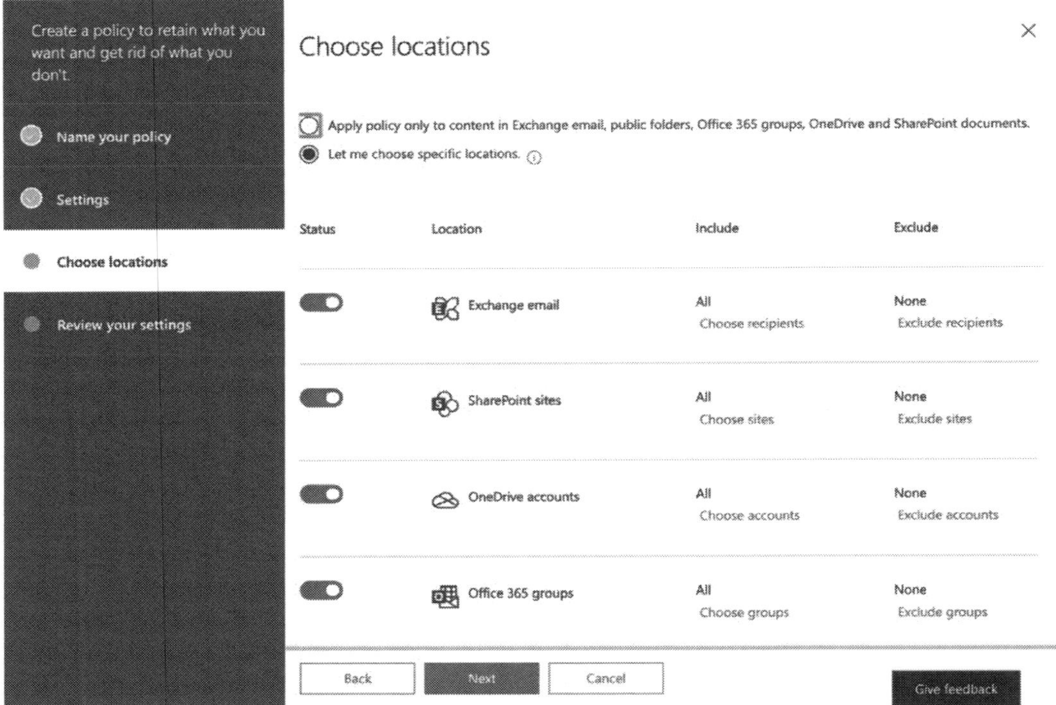

Figure 17.15 – Choosing locations

5. Click **Next** and you can review the settings for your retention policy. If you wish to make any final changes to the policy before creating it, you can click **Edit** next to each section of the policy, as shown:

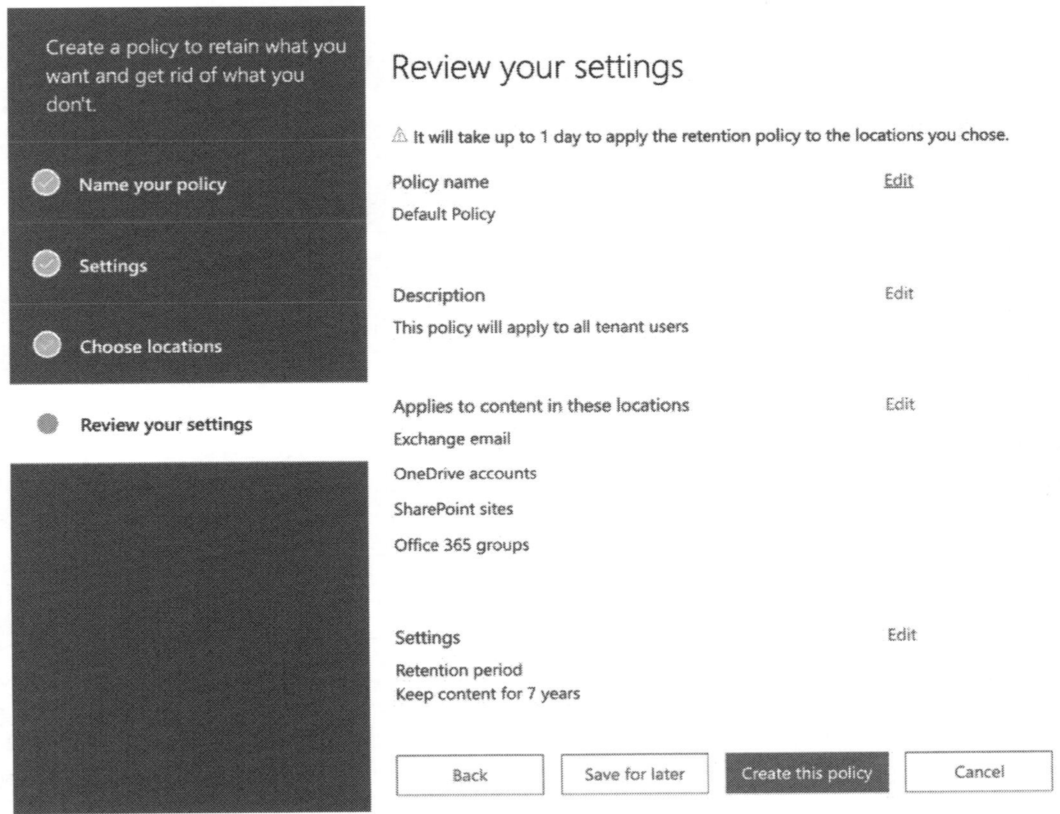

Figure 17.16 – Reviewing your settings

6. Click on **Create this policy** to complete the setup of your new retention policy.

   The preceding steps show you how to create a simple retention policy. In the **Settings** section of the preceding setup wizard, you can also choose **Advanced settings**, which gives you additional options, as in the following screenshot:

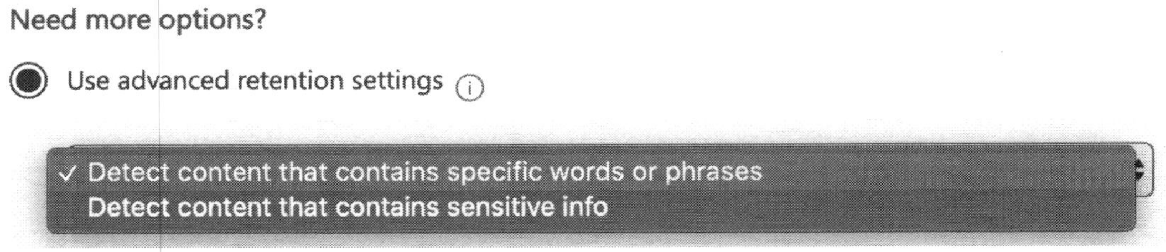

Figure 17.17 – Advanced retention settings

> **Important note**
>
> If you wish to set up a retention policy to apply to Teams channel messages and Teams chats, you need to set up a separate retention policy for Teams only. If you select the option to protect Teams content with a retention policy, you will see that the other Office 365 locations are automatically deselected.

Let's now learn how to create a supervision policy.

Creating a supervision policy

With **Supervision** in the Security & Compliance Center, you can define policies to record email and third-party communications so that they can be reviewed at a later time. In order to configure a supervision policy, we need to complete the following steps:

1. Log in to the Security & Compliance Center and click on **Supervision** from the left-hand menu. You can see the **Supervision** options in the following screenshot:

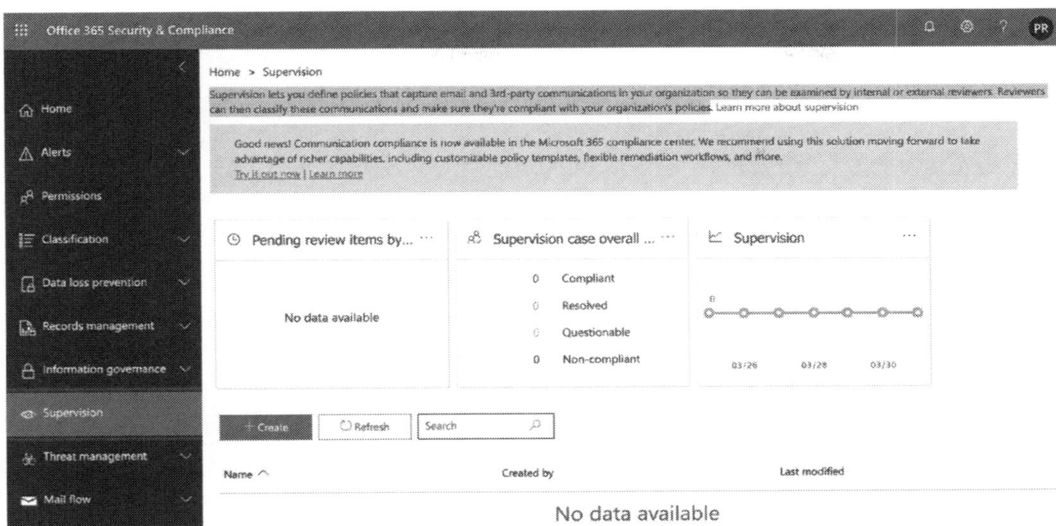

Figure 17.18 – Supervision in the Security & Compliance Center

2. Click on **Create**, which will launch the wizard to create a policy to capture and review communications. In the following example, we will set up a policy to monitor the communications of one of our tenant users, **Jane Bloggs**. Enter a name and description for your policy and then click **Next**, as in the following screenshot:

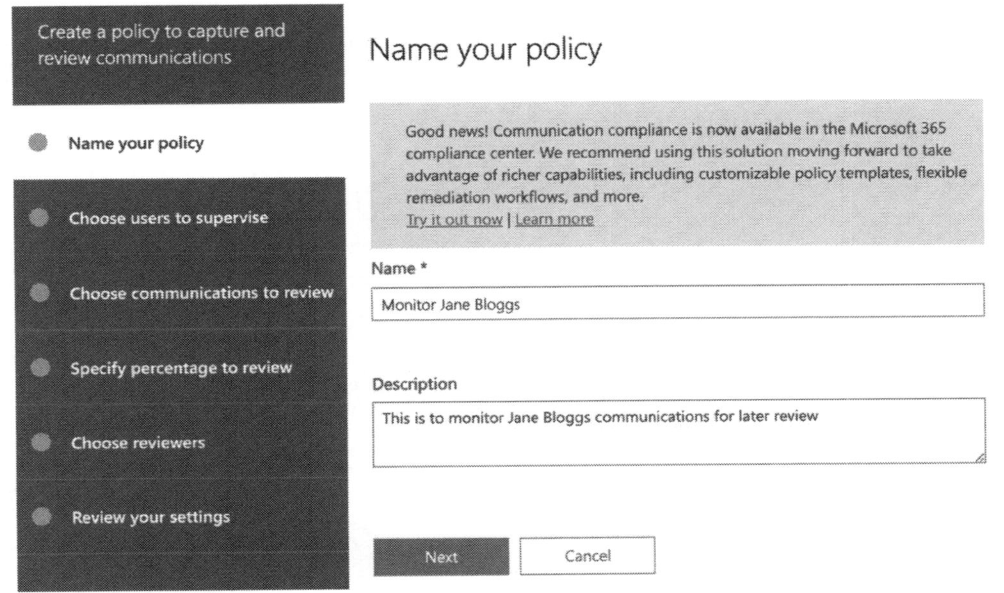

Figure 17.19 – Naming your policy

3. Now, you can choose users and groups to include or exclude from supervision. In this example, we will add a single user object (**Jane Bloggs**). If we added a group here instead of a user, we could also exclude any users from supervision by adding them to the **Non supervised users** section. These options are shown in the following screenshot:

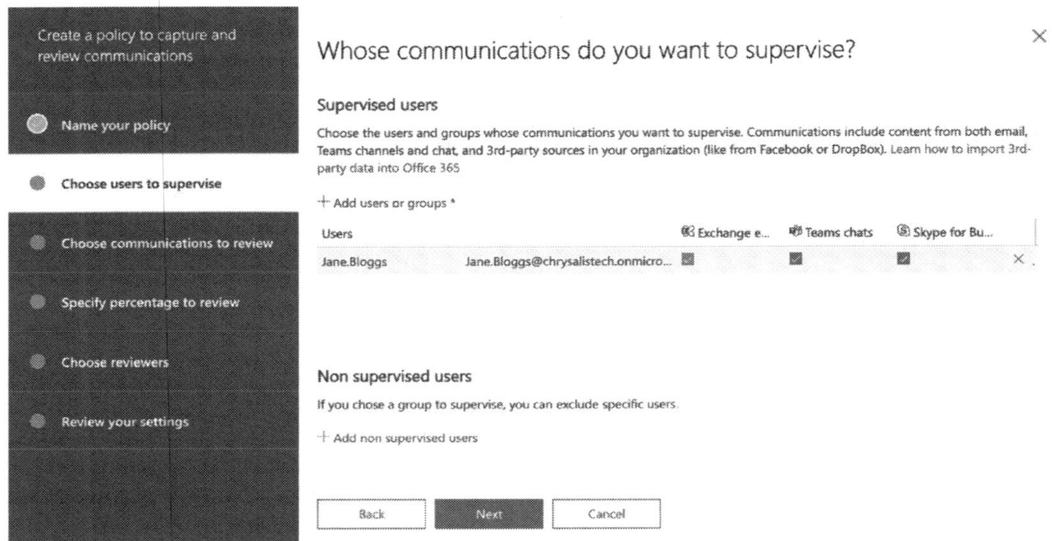

Figure 17.20 – Choose users or groups to supervise

4. Click **Next** and you now have the option to select which communications you wish to review, as in the following screenshot:

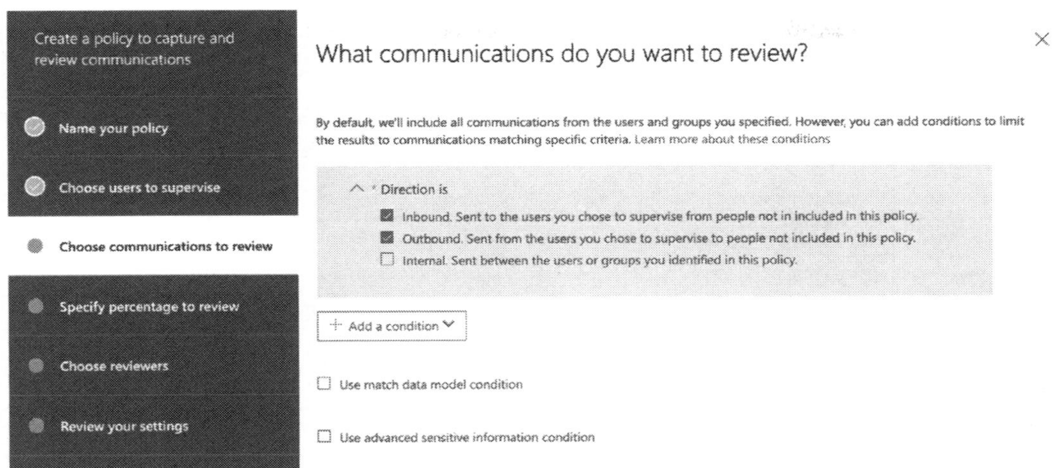

Figure 17.21 – Choosing communications to review

5. You can add conditions by clicking on **Add a condition**. You will see the following options:

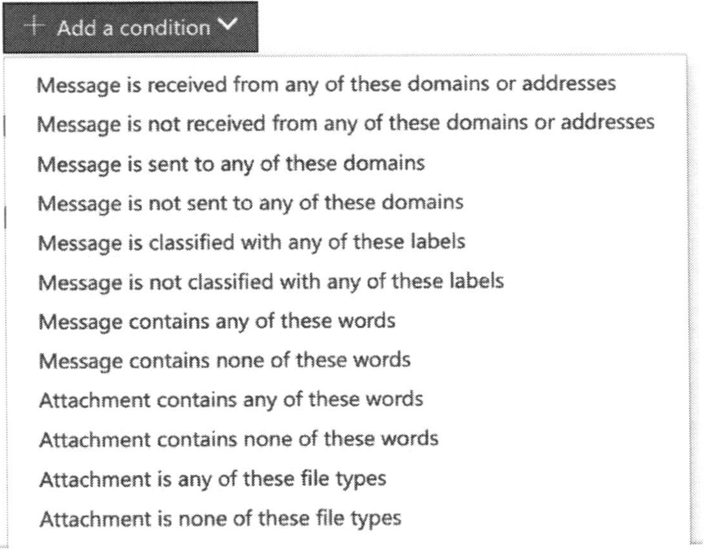

Figure 17.22 – Adding a condition

6. In this example, we will not set any additional conditions. Click **Next** and you can now choose the percentage of communications that you wish to review, as in the following screenshot. The default setting is **10%**:

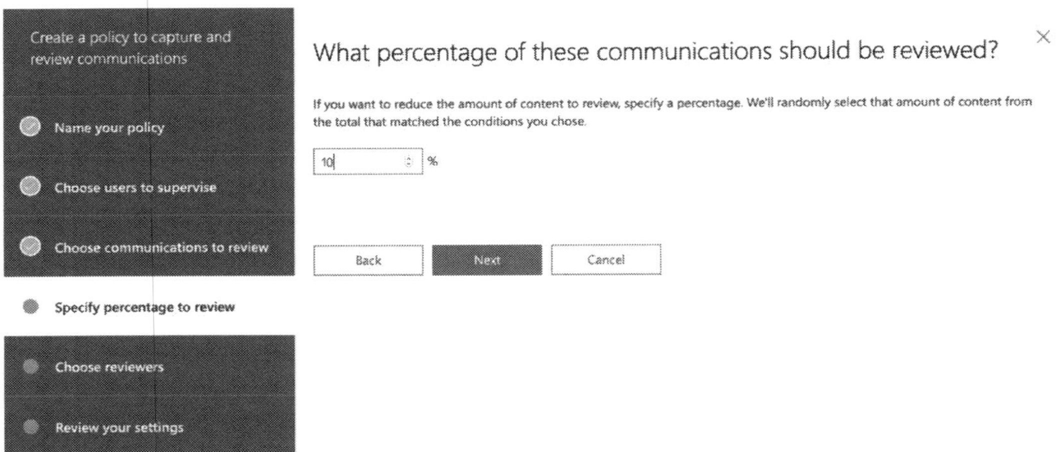

Figure 17.23 – Setting the monitor percentage

7. Click **Next** and you will now be able to choose the users who can review these communications. I have added the **Peter Rising** user, as shown:

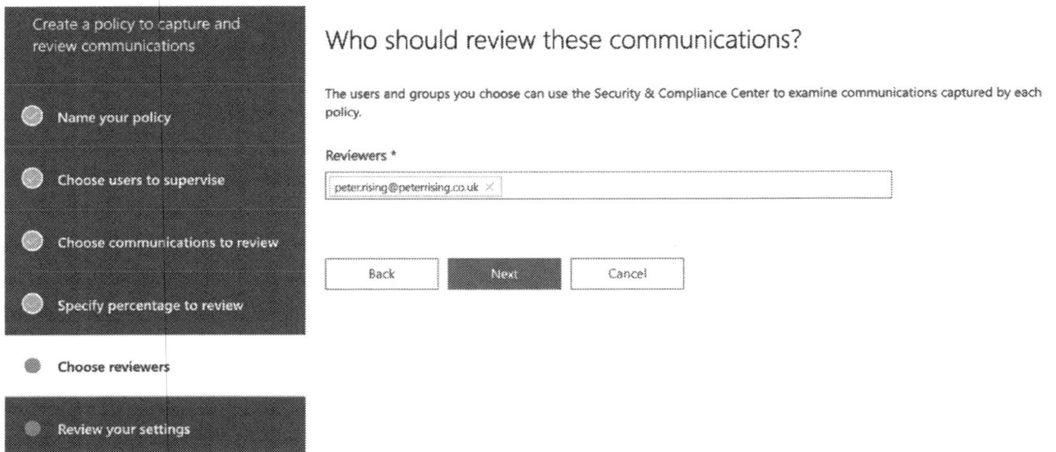

Figure 17.24 – Setting the reviewer

8. Click **Next**, which takes you to the **Review your settings** page. Make any final changes to each section of your policy by clicking on **Edit**, as the following screenshot illustrates:

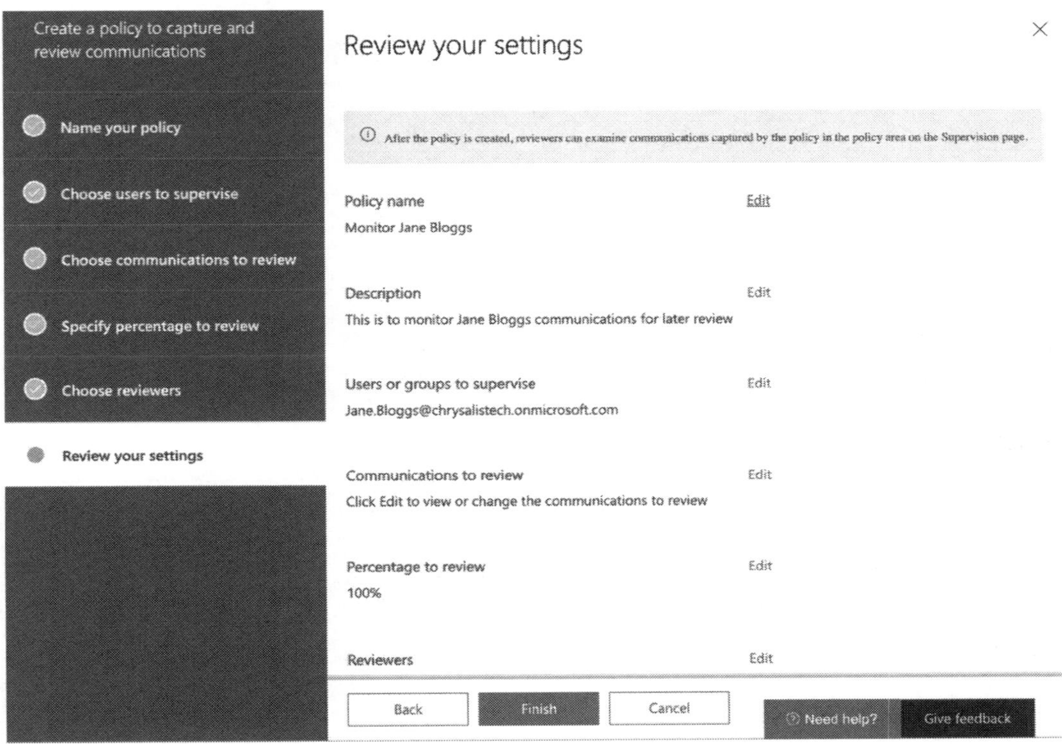

Figure 17.25 – Reviewing your settings

9. Click **Finish** to complete the setup of your supervision policy.
10. The reviewer that we set for the policy can now view the policy in the Security & Compliance Center by clicking on **Supervision** and clicking on the policy, as shown:

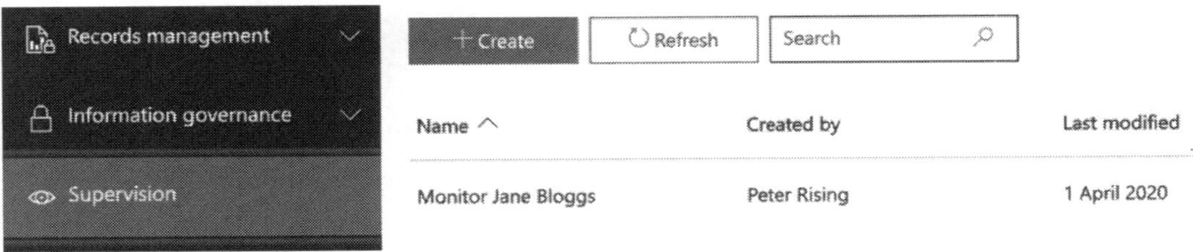

Figure 17.26 – Reviewer activity

11. Click on **Open**, as in the following screenshot:

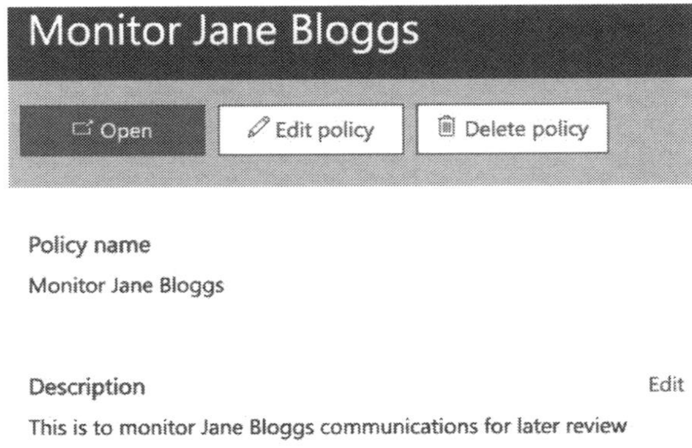

Figure 17.27 – Opening the review

12. You will now see the reviewer dashboard, as in the following screenshot:

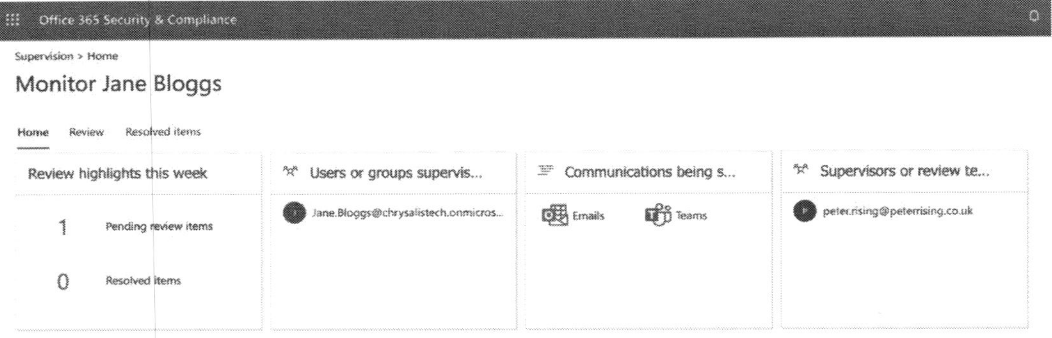

Figure 17.28 – Reviewer highlights

13. Click on the **Review** option at the top of the screen and you will be taken to the list of items in the supervision review, as in the following screenshot:

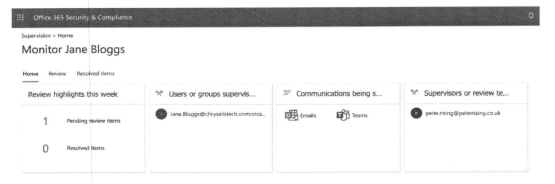

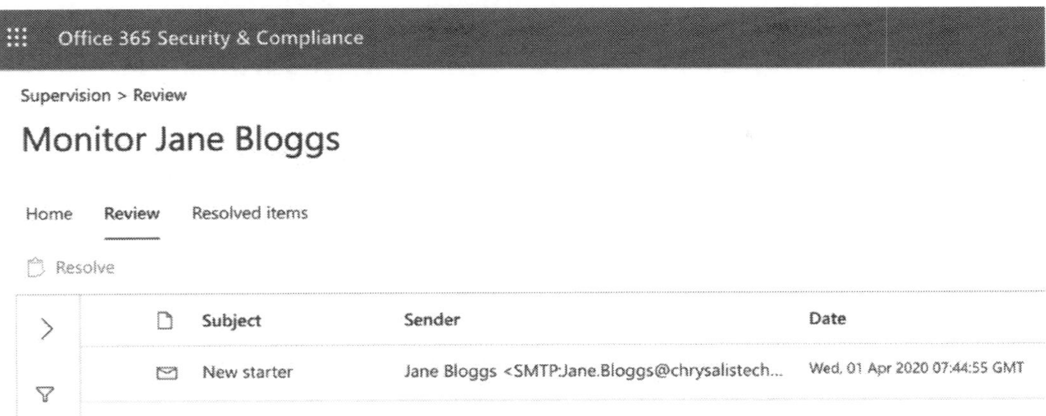

Figure 17.29 – Reviewing items

14. Highlight an item and you will see the content of the communication. You can take action to set the item to **Compliant**, **Non-compliant**, or **Questionable**, as well as adding any relevant comments. This is shown in the following screenshot:

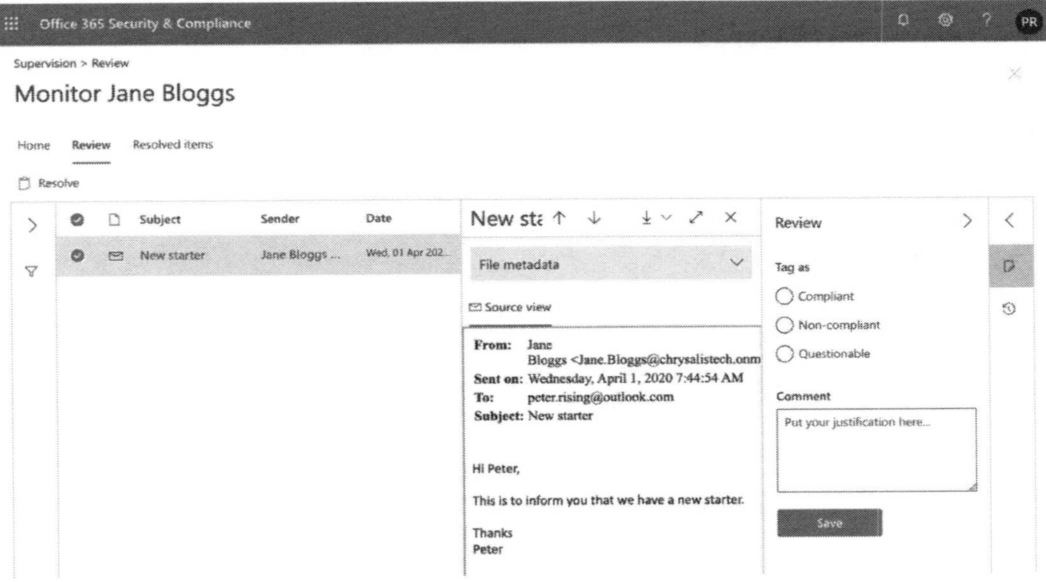

Figure 17.30 – Reviewing items

15. For this example, we will mark the item as **Compliant**. Click **Save**, then click on the < symbol and you will be able to see the completed review items in the three sections broken down, as in the following screenshot:

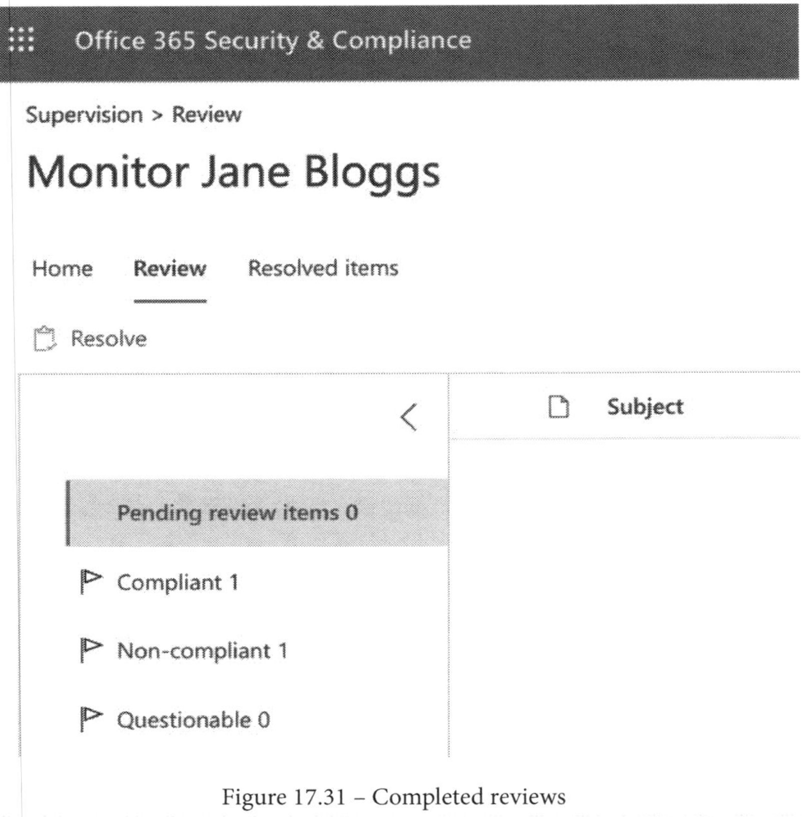

Figure 17.31 – Completed reviews

> **Important note**
> Any emails in policies will be processed in close to real time, while chats in Teams may take up to 24 hours to be visible to a reviewer.

In this section, we showed you how retention policies can be used to retain, or retain then delete, content across your Office 365 locations based on the criteria that you set in your policies.

You learned that email-specific retention policies can be configured in the Exchange admin center and set to use retention tags. We also showed you how you can use the Security & Compliance Center to set retention policies for the other Office 365 locations, including SharePoint Online, OneDrive, and Teams.

Finally, we showed you how reviewers can use supervision policies to monitor email and third-party communications in your organization.

Next, we will look at in-place holds and litigation holds and how these can be used to preserve or recover data.

Configuring litigation holds to preserve Office 365 data

The requirement to preserve electronically stored information is something that compliance administrators in any organization need to be prepared for. **In-Place Hold** and **Litigation Hold** are features that enable you to achieve the following:

- Place user mailboxes on hold
- Immutably preserve mailbox items
- Preserve mailbox content deleted by users

> **Important note**
> As of April 2020, the ability to create new in-place holds will be removed by Microsoft. From July 2020, the ability to manage existing in-place holds will also be removed. Therefore, in this section, we will only examine the process of configuring litigation holds

Litigation Hold

With **Litigation Hold**, you can preserve the content of your users' mailboxes. The preservation of content applies not only to the users' inbox and sent items but also to their deleted items and to the original versions of any items that may have been modified. Should the user have an archive mailbox, this will also be placed on hold.

In order to place a mailbox on **Litigation Hold**, you need to complete the following steps:

1. Log in to the Exchange admin center at `https://outlook.office365.com/ecp` and navigate to **recipients | mailboxes**, as in the following screenshot:

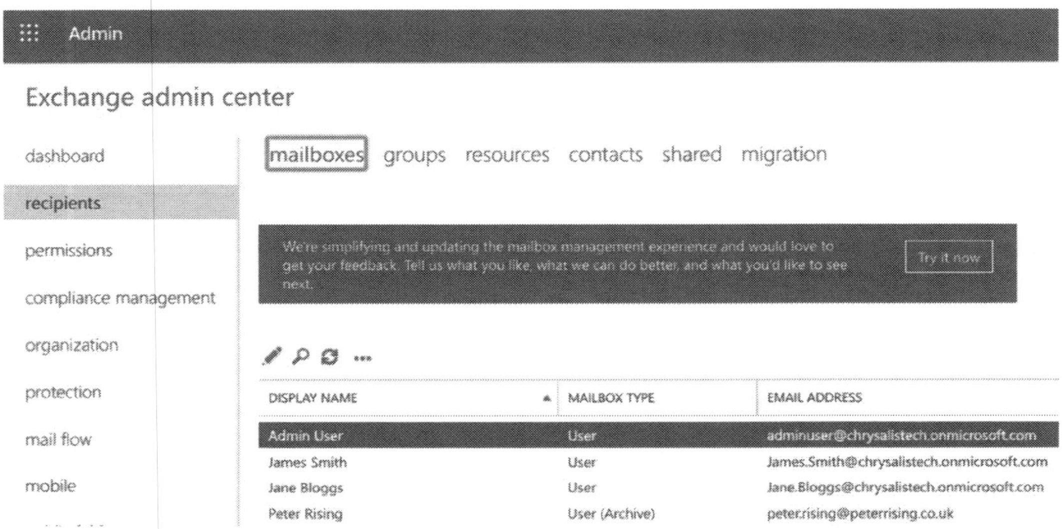

Figure 17.32 – Exchange admin center

2. Double-click to select the mailbox that you wish to place on hold and select **Mailbox Features**, as shown in the following example, where we will enable **Litigation Hold** for a user named **Jane Bloggs**:

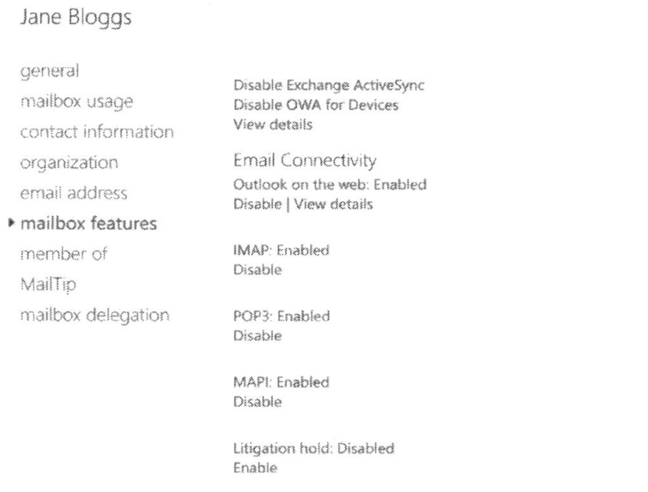

Figure 17.33 – Mailbox features

3. Under **Litigation hold: Disabled**, click the **Enable** option and you will see the options in the following screenshot:

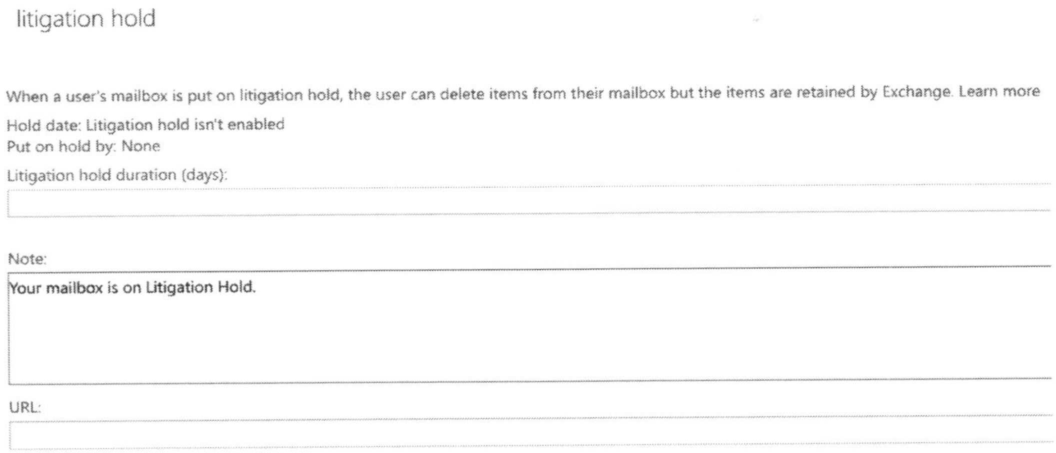

litigation hold

When a user's mailbox is put on litigation hold, the user can delete items from their mailbox but the items are retained by Exchange. Learn more

Hold date: Litigation hold isn't enabled
Put on hold by: None

Litigation hold duration (days):

Note:

Your mailbox is on Litigation Hold.

URL:

Figure 17.34 – The litigation hold options

4. Under **Litigation hold duration (days)**, enter the number of days that you wish to place the mailbox on hold for. If you leave this setting blank, the mailbox will be placed on hold indefinitely.
5. Under **Note**, you can enter a description for a reason for the hold, which will be visible to users of Outlook 2010 upward.
6. Finally, under **URL**, you can optionally add a link to provide the user with additional information relating to **Litigation Hold**.
7. Click on **Save**, then **Save** again, to complete the **Litigation Hold** enabling for the user.

You can also enable **Litigation Hold** on a user mailbox by using the Exchange Online PowerShell. To do this for our example user, **Jane Bloggs**, we need to run the following command:

```
Set-Mailbox jane.bloggs@chrysalistech.onmicrosoft.com
-LitigationHoldEnabled $true
```

As the preceding command does not specify a hold duration, the mailbox will be placed on indefinite hold. Should we wish to specify a hold duration, we would enter the command as follows:

```
Set-Mailbox jane.bloggs@chrysalistech.onmicrosoft.com
-LitigationHoldEnabled $true -LitigationHoldDuration1000
```

The preceding command places the mailbox on hold for 1,000 days. Should you wish to place all of your user mailboxes on hold, you could use the following command:

```
Get-Mailbox -ResultSize Unlimited -Filter "RecipientTypeDetails
-eq 'UserMailbox'" | Set-Mailbox -LitigationHoldEnabled $true
-LitigationHoldDuration2000
```

Once **Litigation Hold** is enabled on a mailbox, any items that are purged by the user are automatically preserved in accordance with the hold duration settings that were specified when the hold was enabled. Should no hold duration have been specified, then the item will be indefinitely preserved.

> **Important note**
> In order for a user mailbox to be successfully placed on litigation hold, the user must be assigned at least an Exchange Online (Plan 2) license.

In this section, we described the principles of **Litigation Hold** and how it can be used to preserve the content within users' mailboxes in Exchange Online, even if they were deleted and purged by the user. We showed you how to use the Exchange admin center and Exchange Online PowerShell to enable or disable the **Litigation Hold** feature for either single users or all Exchange Online users.

You also learned that hold durations can be applied in days and if no duration is specified, then the content is preserved indefinitely or until the hold is explicitly removed.

Next, we will show you how to import data into Office 365 using the Security & Compliance Center.

Importing data into Office 365 from the Security & Compliance Center

When you have all of your mailboxes migrated to Exchange Online, it is possible—and highly likely—that some users in your organization will have one or more `.pst` files stored on their local computers. This is due to the fact that archiving older mailbox content from Exchange on-premises mailboxes used to be a standard operating procedure for most organizations due to the limited storage capacity of Exchange Mailbox databases.

This creates an issue in that although your users' main mailbox has been migrated and now resides in Exchange Online, there could also be a significant amount of mailbox data scattered across various devices within your environment and, as such, this data is not protected by the compliance features available within Office 365.

In order to help IT administrators solve this problem, Microsoft has provided the **Import** feature, which can be found in the **Information governance** section of the Security & Compliance Center, as shown in the following screenshot:

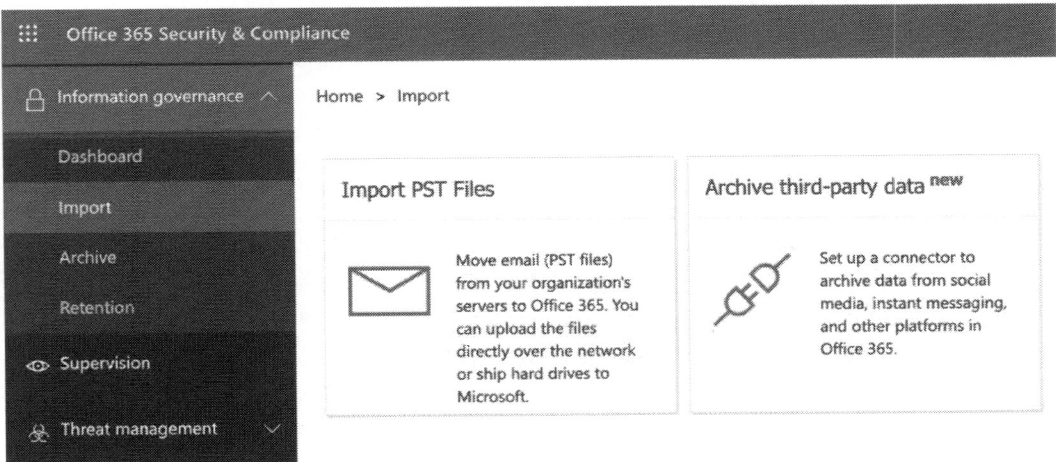

Figure 17.35 – The Import feature in the Security & Compliance Center

To use the **Import** feature, click on **Import PST Files** and you will then see the following options to import your PST files to Exchange Online:

- **Network upload**: This option allows you to upload `.pst` files yourself using Azure Storage to temporarily host the data. Once the files have been uploaded, you can import the `.pst` files to the relevant user mailboxes in Exchange Online.
- **Drive shipping**: This option requires you to copy all of the required `.pst` files to an encrypted hard drive. The drive will then be shipped to Microsoft, who uploads the data to Azure Storage on your behalf. Once uploaded, you can import the `.pst` files to the relevant user mailboxes in Exchange Online.

To run an import job from the Security & Compliance Center, you need to complete the following steps:

1. When you click on the **Import PST Files** option, you are taken to the **Import** wizard, as follows:

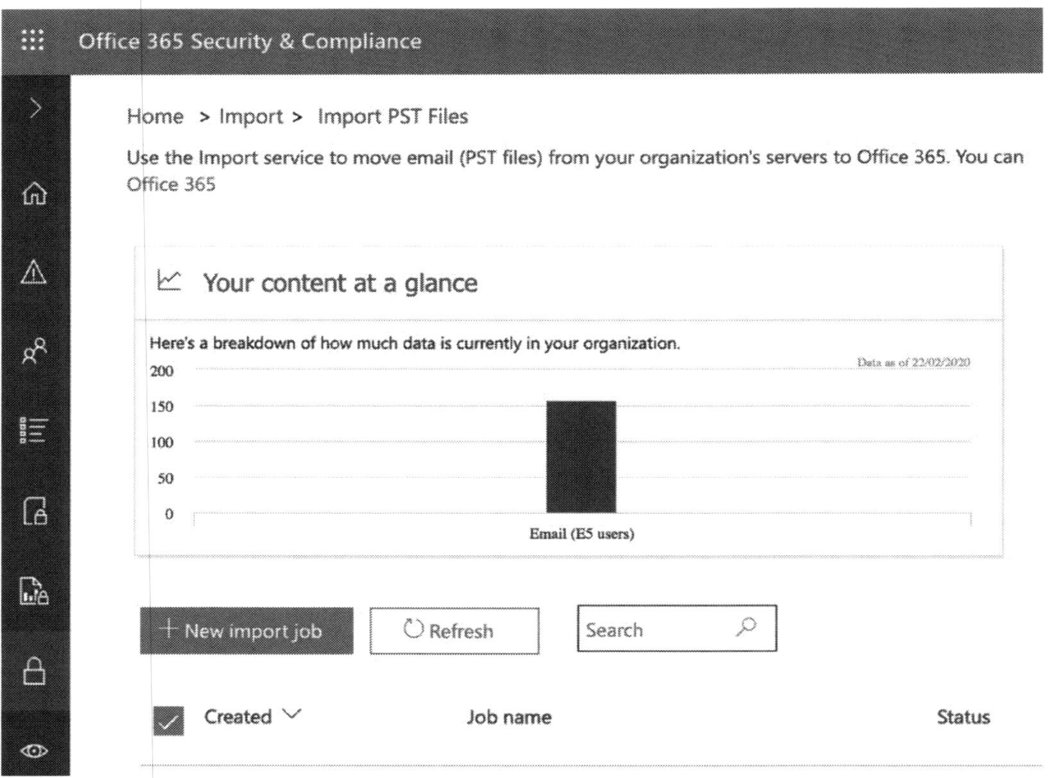

Figure 17.36 – Importing PST files

2. Click on the **New import job** option and you will see the options in the following screenshot:

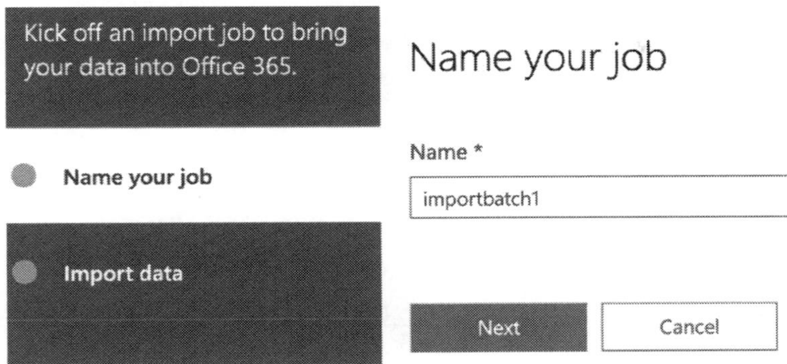

Figure 17.37 – Naming your import job

3. Enter a name for your import job and click on **Next**. You will see the options in the following screenshot:

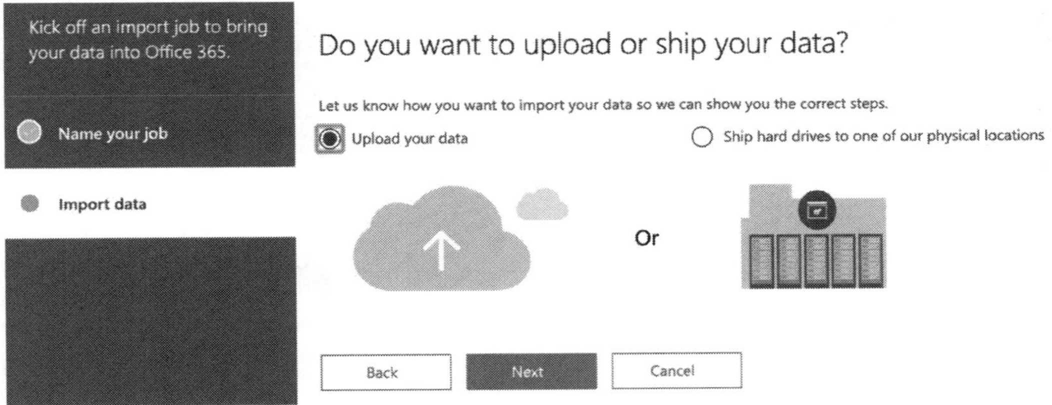

Figure 17.38 – The Import data options

4. For this example, we will choose the **Upload your data** option, as opposed to shipping hard drives to Microsoft. This shows you the options shown in the following screenshot:

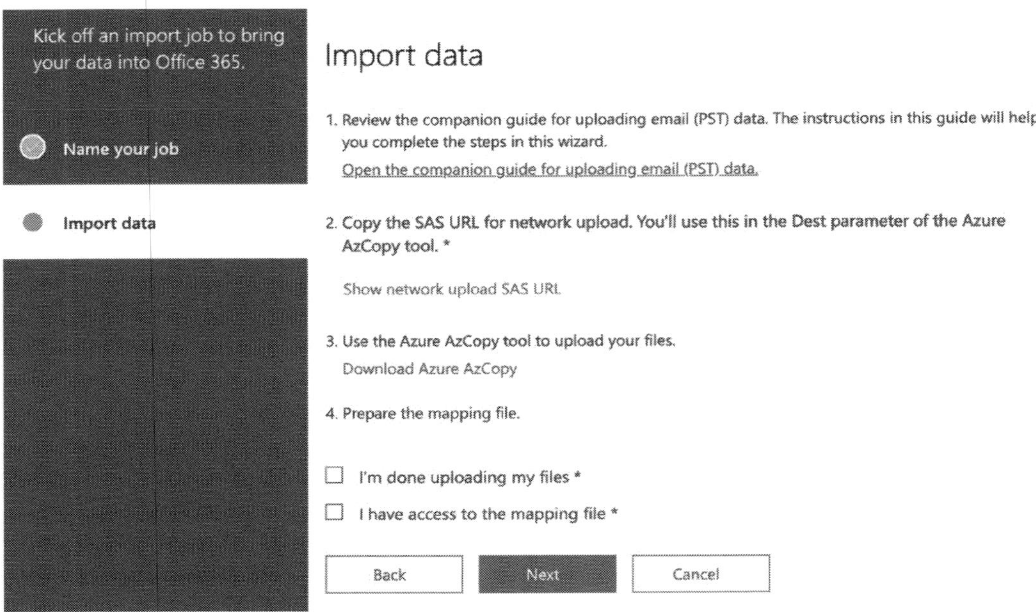

Figure 17.39 – The Import data options

5. Next, we need to choose **Show network upload SAS URL**, which shows you a unique link that you need to use when you upload your `.pst` files. This displays as shown in the following screenshot:

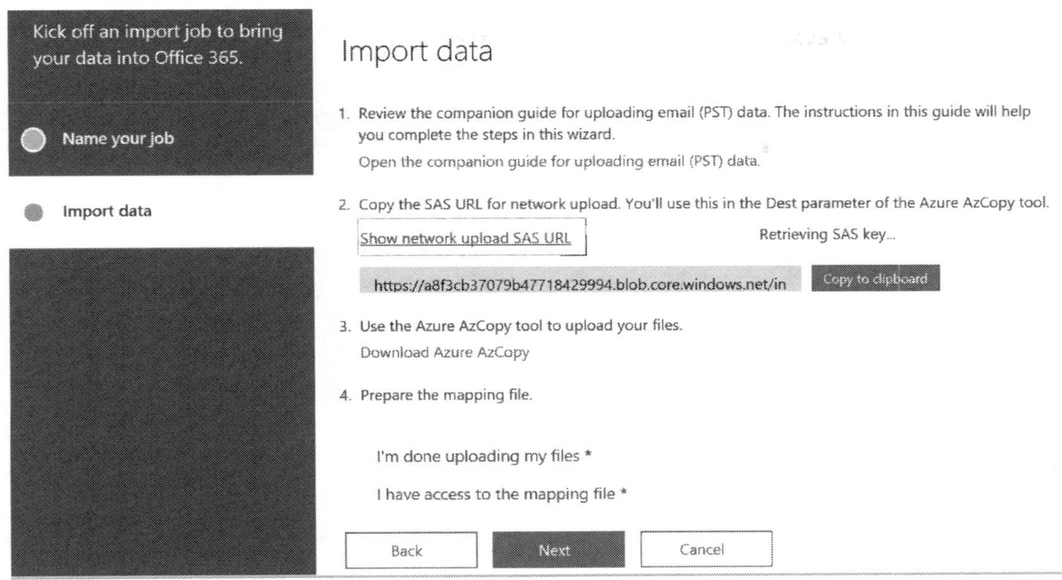

Figure 17.40 – The SAS URL

6. Click **Copy to clipboard**, then paste this value into a `.txt` file for when you need it later in the process.
7. Next, we need to click on **Download Azure AzCopy**. Once downloaded, you will need to install **AzCopy**, which is a short and simple install. Once installed, click on the **Start** button and search for **Microsoft Azure Storage AzCopy**. Double-click to open **AzCopy**, which will open a blue-colored command prompt.
8. Now that **AzCopy** is open, we need to run a command that will upload the `.pst` files into temporary Azure storage. The command you will need to run is in the following format:

```
AzCopy.exe /Source:<PST file folder> /Dest:<SAS URL>
/V:<Log file folder> /Y
```

An example of how this might look is as follows:

```
AzCopy.exe /Source:"\\Fileshare\archivepsts" /Dest:"h
ttps://3c3e5952a2764023ad14984.blob.core.windows.net/
ingestiondata?sv=2012-02-12&amp;se=9999-12-31T23%3A59%3A5
9Z&amp;sr=c&amp;si=IngestionSasForAzCopy20160112192049811
7&amp;sig=Vt5S4hVzlzMcBkuH8bH711atBffdrOS72TlV1mNdORg%3D"
/V:"c:\upload\upload.log" /Y
```

9. Once this command has been successfully executed, you will see that `AzCopy` has completed the upload task, as shown:

```
Finished 5 of total 5 file(s).
[2020/05/05 16:58:45] Transfer summary:
-----------------
Total files transferred: 5
Transfer successfully:   5
Transfer skipped:        0
Transfer failed:         0
Elapsed time:            00.00:22:38

C:\Program Files (x86)\Microsoft SDKs\Azure\AzCopy>_
```

Figure 17.41 – The successful AzCopy upload

10. Now that you have completed the upload, you will need to prepare a `.csv` file, which you will use to map `.pst` files that you imported using `AzCopy` to the target user mailboxes in Exchange Online. A sample `.csv` file can be downloaded from `https://go.microsoft.com/fwlink/p/?LinkId=544717`
11. Once your `.csv` file is prepared, you can return to the **Import Data** wizard, which we should still have open from *Step 6* of this process, and then click on **Next**. You will see the following:

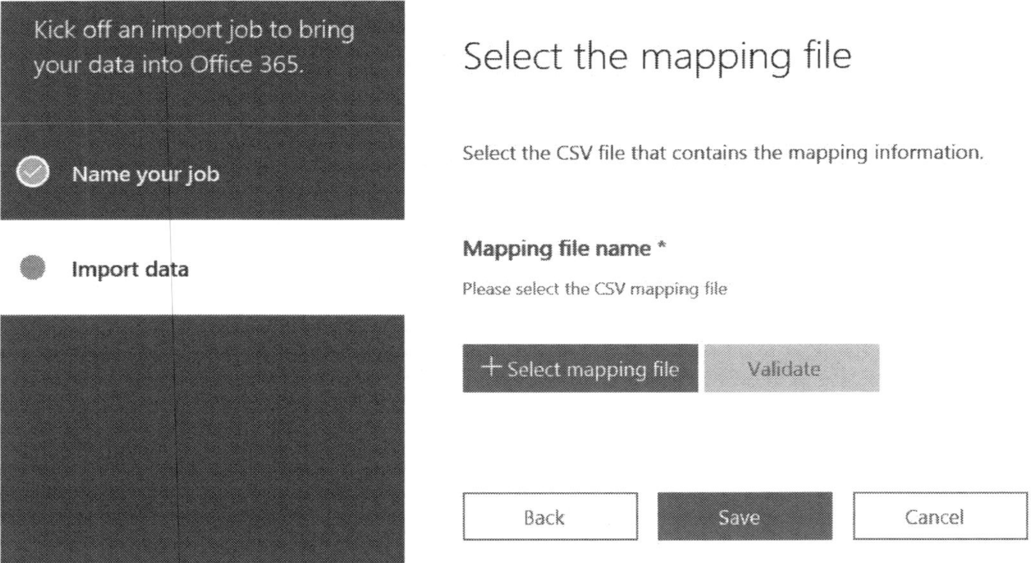

Figure 17.42 – Selecting the mapping file

12. Click on **Select mapping file**, then choose the `.csv` file that you prepared in *Step 11*. Click on **Validate** and you will see the following:

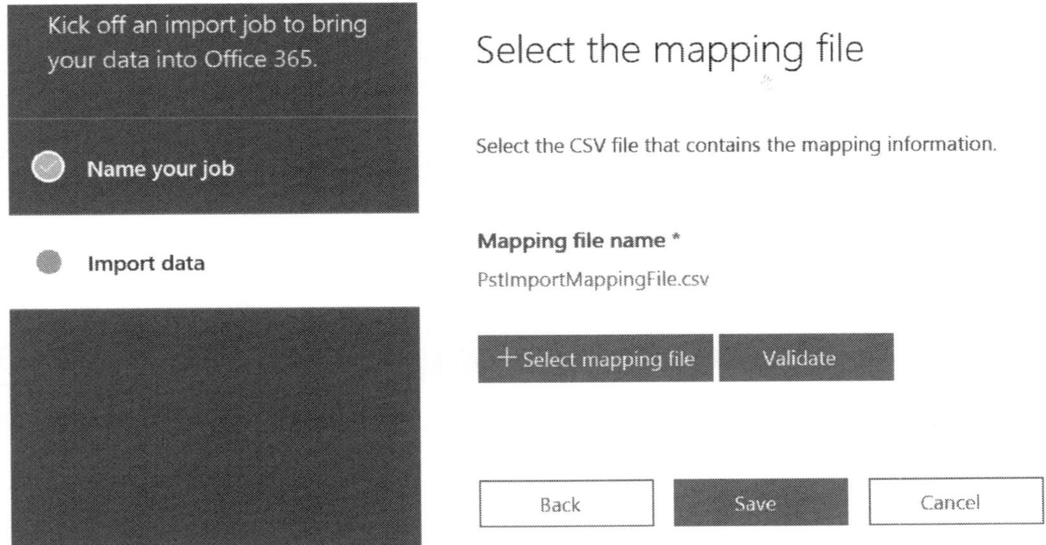

Figure 17.43 – Validating the mapping file

13. Click **Save**, then click **Close**, as shown:

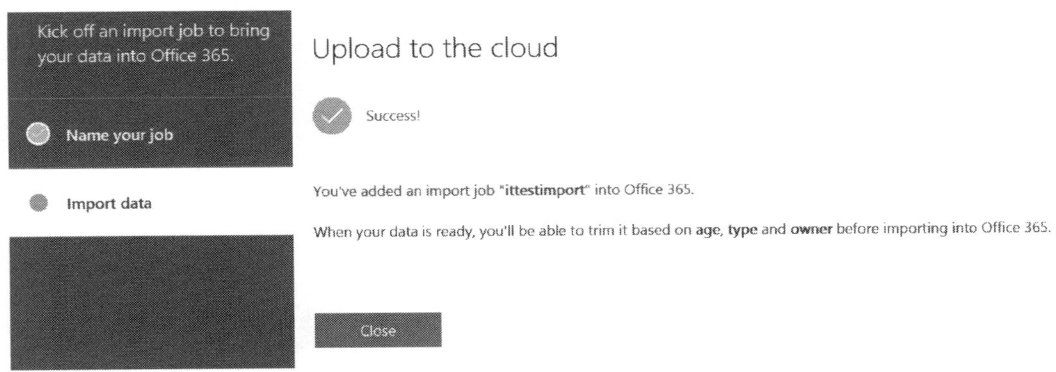

Figure 17.44 – The mapping file is successfully uploaded

The import job will now be shown as analyzed, as shown:

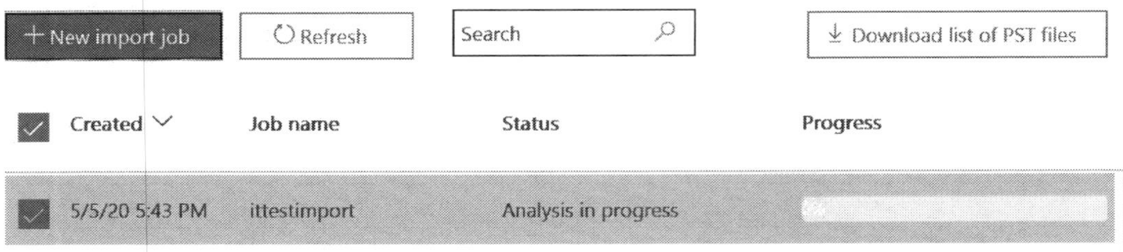

Figure 17.45 – The import job analysis

14. Once the analysis is complete, you can then click on **Ready to import to Office 365**, as shown:

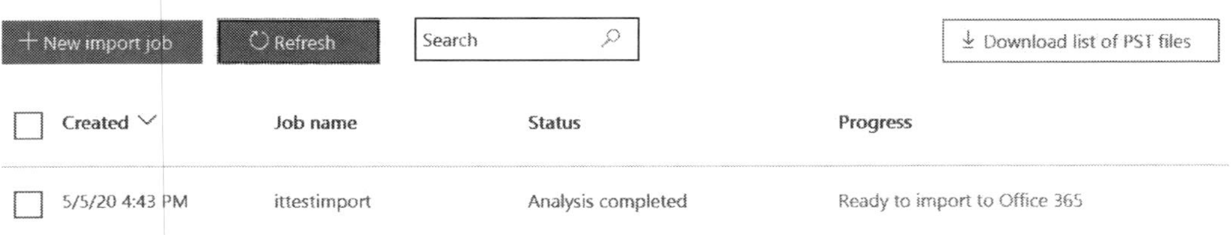

Figure 17.46 – The import job is ready to import to Office 365

15. The `.pst` files that were uploaded to Azure using `AzCopy`, and then imported using the `.csv` mapping file, are now copied into the user mailboxes that you entered in the `.csv` file.

The process of using `AzCopy` and the `.csv` mapping file is quite complex, and more detailed instructions for both of these upload options can be found in the *References* section at the end of this chapter.

> **Important note**
> In order to create import jobs from the Security & Compliance Center, you must use an administrative account that includes the **Mailbox Import/Export** permission

In this section, we described the available options to upload `.pst` files to temporary Azure storage, then imported these into the required user mailboxes in Exchange Online. You learned that there are two methods available to upload the `.pst` files to the Azure Storage location; these are network upload and drive shipping. Importing stray `.pst` files into Office 365 will ensure that the `.pst` files are subjected to your organization's compliance policies and settings.

In the final section of this chapter, we will examine the archiving options available within Microsoft 365.

Configuring archiving

The Microsoft 365 platform now also provides administrators with the means to import and archive third-party data. Much like the **Import** function of `.pst` files that we described in the previous section, this feature can be accessed from the Security & Compliance Center by navigating to **Information governance | Import**.

Choosing **Archive third-party data** will now direct you to the dedicated Microsoft 365 compliance center, which can be accessed at `https://compliance.microsoft.com`.

By choosing **Data connectors**, you will see the options in the following screenshot:

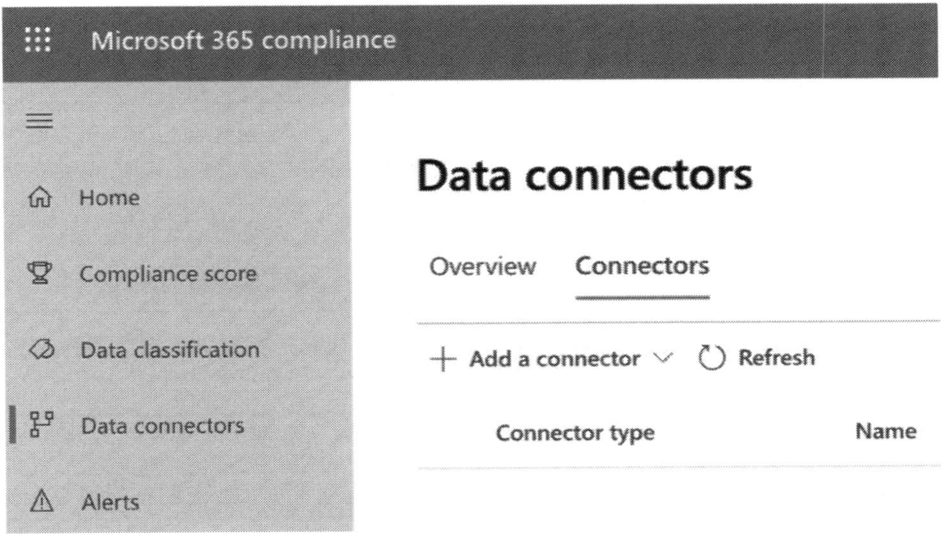

Figure 17.47 – Data connectors

By clicking on **Add a connector**, you will see the options displayed in the following screenshot:

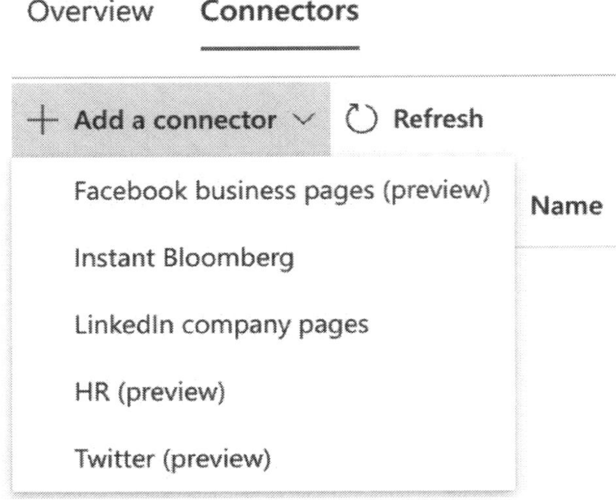

Figure 17.48 – Add a connector

When you import third-party data, it can be subject to Microsoft 365 compliance principles, such as **Litigation Hold** and In-Place Archiving. Further details on how to complete the import of third-party data into Microsoft 365 can be found in the *References* section at the end of this chapter.

In addition to the ability to archive third-party data, administrators can also enable the **In-Place Archive** feature for users. Also referred to as **Unlimited Archiving**, this provides users with additional storage that is separate from their main mailbox. When enabled, the online archive triggers a retention policy tag in the default retention policy that is set to move mailbox items that are over 2 years old to the **Archive** mailbox. The In-Place Archive feature can be enabled from the Security & Compliance Center by navigating to **Information governance | Archive**. This will show you the full list of all the mailbox users in your Office 365 tenant. By selecting a user, you can click to enable the online archive, as in the following screenshot:

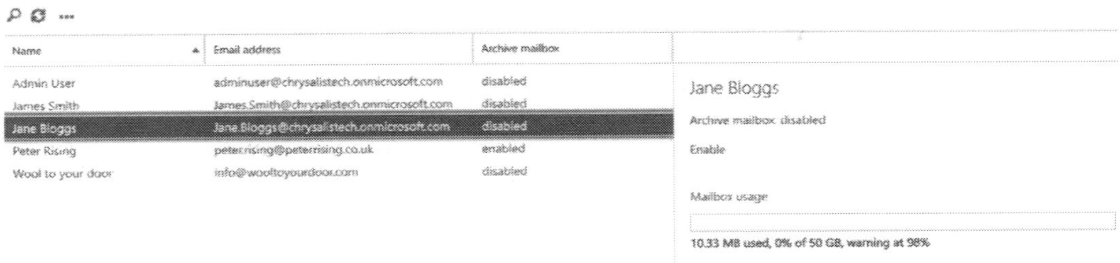
Home > Archive
Archive
Archive mailboxes provide additional email storage for the people in your organization. Using Outlook or Outlook Web App, people can view messages in their archive mailbox and move or copy messages between their primary and archive mailboxes. After an archive mailbox is enabled, messages older than two years are automatically moved to the archive mailbox by the default retention policy that's assigned to every mailbox in your organization. Learn more
Select one or more people to enable or disable their archive mailbox. If the person you're looking for isn't displayed in the list, try searching for them.
Name
Email address
Archive mailbox
Admin User
adminuser@chrysalistech.onmicrosoft.com
disabled
James Smith
James.Smith@chrysalistech.onmicrosoft.com
disabled
Jane Bloggs
Jane.Bloggs@chrysalistech.onmicrosoft.com
disabled
Peter Rising
peter.rising@peterrising.co.uk
enabled
Wool to your door
info@wooltoyourdoor.com
disabled
Jane Bloggs
Archive mailbox: disabled
Enable
Mailbox usage
10.33 MB used, 0% of 50 GB, warning at 98%

Figure 17.49 – Enabling the archive

Once the online archive is enabled for a user, they will see it appear in their email profile beneath their main mailbox in Microsoft Outlook. It is also accessible via Outlook on the web. As this is an online archive only, it is not possible to cache the contents of this mailbox; therefore, you must have an internet connection in order to view the contents of your online archive.

In this section, we explained how you now have the option to archive third-party data from the Security & Compliance Center so that content that is imported can be protected by the Microsoft 365 compliance features.

We also explained that the online (or in-place) archive can be enabled for your Exchange Online users to provide additional mailbox storage for your user mailboxes.

> **Important note**
>
> In order for a user to have an online archive enabled, they must be assigned either an Exchange Online (plan 2) license or an Exchange Online (plan 1) license with an Exchange Online Archiving license.

Summary

In this chapter, we introduced you to the principles of data governance and retention within a Microsoft 365 environment. We explained how to plan for the data governance and retention requirements for your organization by understanding your internal policies and industry obligations. We showed you how to navigate the Security & Compliance Center to view and interpret data governance reports and dashboards, and you also learned how retention policies can be applied from both the Exchange admin center and the Security & Compliance Center.

In addition, we explained how **Litigation Hold** can be used to preserve Office 365 data, even if a user has deleted it, how to import `.pst` files and third-party data into Office 365 via the information governance **Import** feature, and how the online archive can increase the capacity of Office 365 mailbox users with a separate archive mailbox.

In the next chapter, we will demonstrate the search and investigation tools available in Microsoft 365. You will learn how to use eDiscovery to carry out content searches, how to delegate eDiscovery permissions where appropriate, and how to manage eDiscovery cases.

Questions

1. Where in the Security & Compliance Center would you go to enable the Online Archive feature for users?

   a. **Information governance | Archive**

   b. **Records Management | Archive**

   c. **Permissions | Archive**

   d. **Mail flow | Archive**

2. True or false – **Litigation Hold** can be enabled for a mailbox user with only an Exchange Online (Plan 1) license?

   a. True

   b. False

3. Which of the following locations cannot be used to configure retention policies in Microsoft 365?

   a. The Exchange admin center

   b. The Security center

c. The Compliance center

d. The Security & Compliance Center

4. When enabling **Litigation Hold** for a user, what will happen if you do not specify a hold duration?

   a. The hold will not be enabled.

   b. The hold will be enabled with a hold duration of 365 days.

   c. The hold will preserve content indefinitely.

   d. The hold will be enabled, but will not apply.

5. True or false – an internet connection is required to view the contents of online archive folders.

   a. True

   b. False

6. Where can you set up data connectors to archive third-party application data into Microsoft 365?

   a. The Security & Compliance Center

   b. The Exchange admin center

   c. The Compliance center

   d. The Security center

7. What will happen if you try to include Teams channel messages and Teams chats in the same retention policy as other services, such as Exchange Online, SharePoint Online, and OneDrive?

   a. You will receive a warning that you should create separate retention policies, but you will be allowed to proceed.

   b. The retention policy will successfully be applied to all selected services.

   c. The other services will be automatically de-selected from the policy.

   d. The Teams selections will automatically be de-selected from the policy.

8. True or false – when creating a retention policy from the Security & Compliance Center, you can both delete and retain content based on the settings you configure?

   a. True

   b. False

9. How should **Litigation Hold** be applied to users?

   a. Globally

   b. At the user level

10. In order to create import jobs to import `.pst` files to Office 365, which of the following mailbox permissions must be assigned to your account?

    a. Records Management

    b. Mailbox Import/Export

    c. Discovery Management

    d. Recipient Management

References

Please refer to the following links for more information:

- Managing information governance: `https://docs.microsoft.com/en-us/microsoft-365/compliance/manage-information-governance?view=o365-worldwide`
- View the data governance reports: `https://docs.microsoft.com/en-gb/microsoft-365/compliance/view-the-data-governance-reports?view=o365-worldwide`
- An overview of retention policies: `https://docs.microsoft.com/en-us/microsoft-365/compliance/retention-policies?view=o365-worldwide`
- Creating a retention policy: `https://docs.microsoft.com/en-us/exchange/security-and-compliance/messaging-records-management/create-a-retention-policy`
- Applying retention policies to users: `https://docs.microsoft.com/en-us/exchange/security-and-compliance/messaging-records-management/apply-retention-policy`
- Creating supervision policies: `https://docs.microsoft.com/en-us/microsoft-365/compliance/configure-supervision-policies?view=o365-worldwide`
- In-place Hold and Litigation Hold: `https://docs.microsoft.com/en-us/exchange/security-and-compliance/in-place-and-litigation-holds`

- Using network upload to import `.pst` files to Office 365: `https://docs.microsoft.com/en-gb/microsoft-365/compliance/use-network-upload-to-import-pst-files?view=o365-worldwide`
- Using drive shipping to import `.pst` files to Office 365: `https://docs.microsoft.com/en-gb/microsoft-365/compliance/use-drive-shipping-to-import-pst-files-to-office-365?view=o365-worldwide`
- Archiving third-party data: `https://docs.microsoft.com/en-gb/microsoft-365/compliance/archiving-third-party-data?view=o365-worldwide`
- Enabling Online Archiving: `https://docs.microsoft.com/en-gb/microsoft-365/compliance/unlimited-archiving?view=o365-worldwide`

18 Search and Investigation

Compliance administrators in organizations may often be required to respond to legal investigations to locate and preserve information contained in your Office 365 locations. eDiscovery and content search tools within the Microsoft 365 Security and Compliance Center will provide you with these capabilities.

In this chapter, we will show you how these tools can be used to manage the search and investigation capabilities within your Microsoft 365 environment. You will learn how to implement content searches and eDiscovery to manage any required legal investigations. We will also demonstrate how to delegate eDiscovery roles to other users so they can also use eDiscovery tools with appropriate permissions. Finally, we will look at how to place content locations on hold, as well as export and analyze the results of content searches.

We shall cover these topics in the following order:

- Understanding eDiscovery and content search in Microsoft 365
- eDiscovery delegated role groups
- Creating eDiscovery cases, placing locations in hold, and performing content searches
- Exporting content search results

First, we will examine eDiscovery and content searches.

Understanding eDiscovery and content search in Microsoft 365

eDiscovery is a feature within Microsoft 365 that allows you to identify and provide information that pertains to any legal cases that may be in progress within your organization. Compliance administrators are able to set controls for who is able to create and manage eDiscovery cases in your environment in order to search for content within the following Office 365 locations:

- Exchange Online mailboxes
- Office 365 Groups
- SharePoint Online
- OneDrive
- Microsoft Teams
- Skype for Business conversations

There are three main components of eDiscovery available in the Security and Compliance Center, as follows:

- eDiscovery Cases
- Content Search
- Advanced eDiscovery

Let's look at each of these solutions in turn, starting with eDiscovery cases.

eDiscovery cases

eDiscovery cases allow you to control who is able to view and access an investigation. These cases are a collection of holds, searches, and exports, all contained within a single location. Cases can be created and executed from the Security and Compliance center by members of the eDiscovery Manager role group. Members of the Reviewer group can also view eDiscovery cases. Members of the eDiscovery Administrators role group have full access to all created eDiscovery cases. With eDiscovery cases, you can add sources, create holds and queries, export case results, and manage the life cycle of your case.

Content search

Content searches compliment eDiscovery cases and consist of searches and exports, but not holds. With content search, you are able to carry out powerful searches against your Office 365 services and locations, as well as associate your search with an existing eDiscovery case in order to identify specific information and preview, view, and export the results for analysis. This feature is particularly useful when you need to conduct large-scale searches across multiple Office 365 locations. In order to be able to perform searches, you must be a member of the **eDiscovery Manager** role group.

Advanced eDiscovery

Advanced eDiscovery is only available if you have **Office 365 E5**, **Microsoft 365 E5**, or **Office 365 E3** with the **Advanced Compliance** add-on, and provides enhanced analytical and communication capabilities that will enable you to more effectively analyze your search results.

With basic eDiscovery, it is possible to apply holds to Office 365 locations, carry out searches for items relevant to a case, and export any search and case results.

Advanced eDiscovery provides additional functionality that allows you to do the following:

- Add **Custodians** who will be specified as users who may own content relevant to the eDiscovery case.
- Manage **Communications** to automate notifications for a legal hold.
- Add the results of individual content searches to **Review Sets**, which can be monitored with advanced analytics tools including themes detection, email thread identification, and near-duplicate detection.
- View a list of **Jobs** showing all the jobs contained in an eDiscovery case, as well as their status and creation and completion dates.
- Use additional **Settings** features such as the **Case information** tab, which allows eDiscovery managers to easily modify basic case information. You can also use the **Access and Permissions** section to add or remove users responsible for the case.

In this section, we introduced you to the principles of Content search, eDiscovery, and Advanced eDiscovery in Microsoft 365. We explained that eDiscovery comes in two flavors, basic and advanced, and that content searches can be executed in conjunction with the eDiscovery cases that may be set up by eDiscovery managers.

We will explain these features in further detail as we progress through this chapter. Next, we will show you how to assign eDiscovery permissions in the Security and Compliance Center in order to control who has access to the powerful search and investigation features within your Microsoft 365 environment.

eDiscovery delegated role groups

Before you start using the eDiscovery cases and content hold features, it is important to assign the appropriate permissions to the users who need to have access to these tools. In this section, we will demonstrate how to do this from the Security and Compliance Center by adding users to the correct role group from the permissions page. The role that is used to control access is called **eDiscovery Manager**. This role also contains two subgroups, as follows:

- **eDiscovery Manager**: Can only view and edit cases that the user has access to
- **eDiscovery Administrator**: Can view and edit all cases, regardless of permissions

In order to assign eDiscovery permissions, you will need to be a member of the **Organization Management** role. To assign such permissions from the Security and Compliance Center, we need to take the following steps:

1. Log into the Security and Compliance Center at `https://protection.office.com` and navigate to **Permissions** in the left pane. You will see the options shown in the following screenshot:

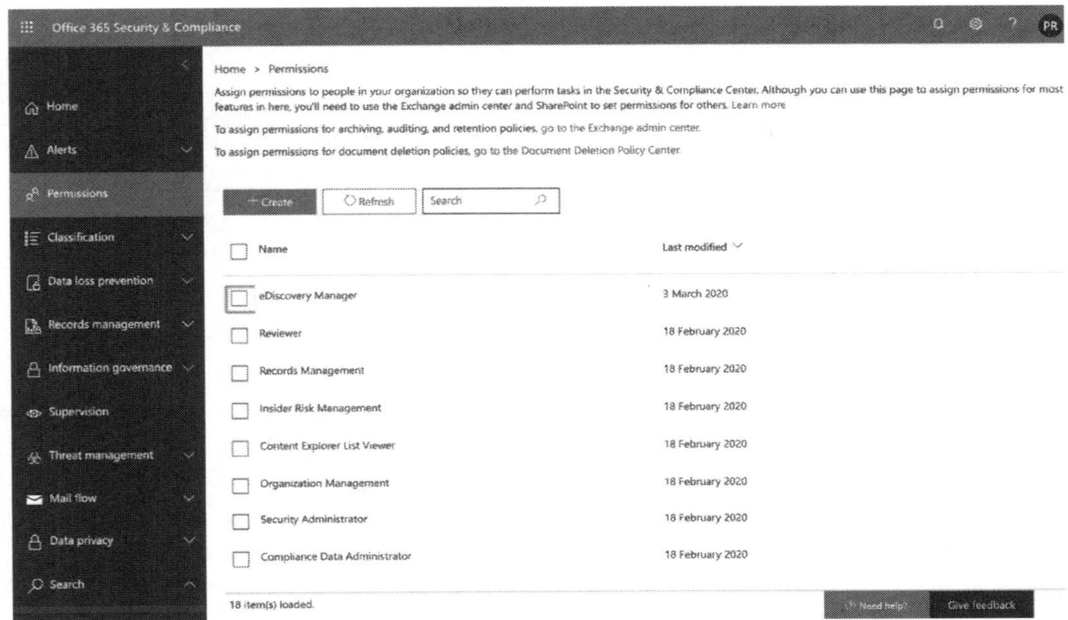

Figure 18.1 – Permissions in the Security and Compliance Center

2. Click on the checkbox next to the **eDiscovery Manager** role group. You will see the options shown in the following screenshot:

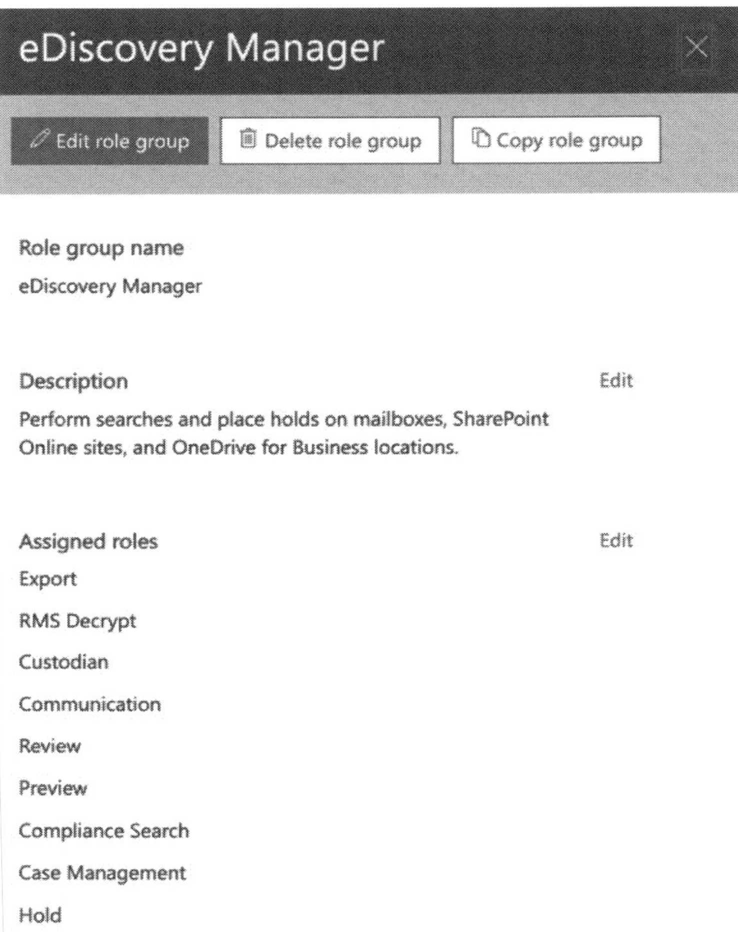

Figure 18.2 – eDiscovery Manager role group

3. The preceding screenshot shows the name and description for this role group, along with the roles that have been assigned to the group. Scroll down through the role group options to see the two role subgroups, which are called **eDiscovery Manager** and **eDiscovery Administrator**. These are shown in the following screenshot:

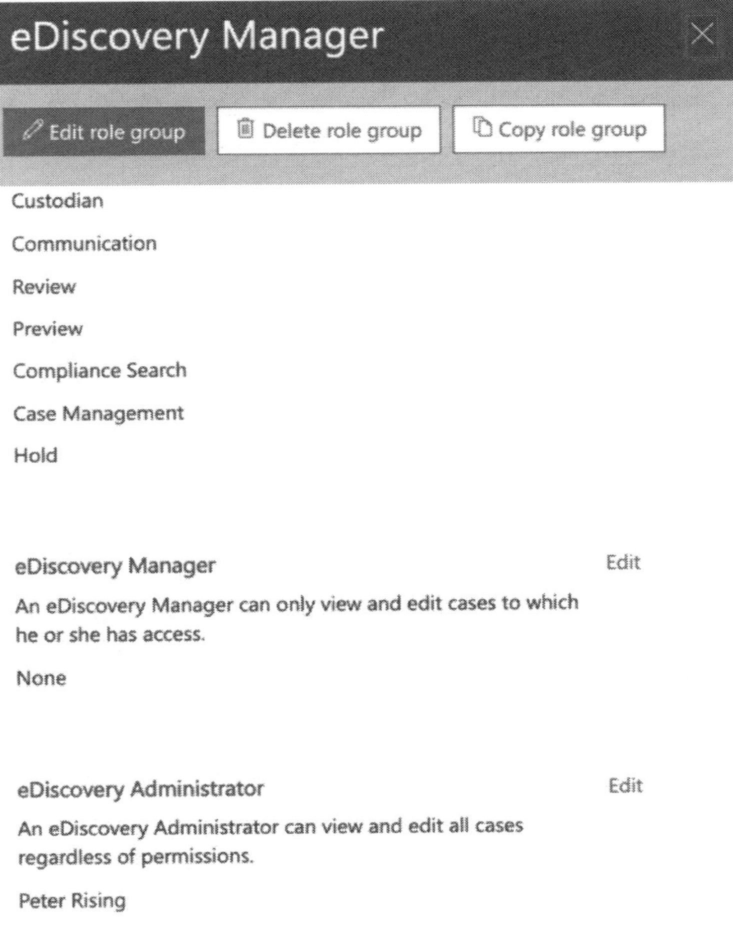

Figure 18.3 – Role subgroups

4. By clicking **Edit** next to either of the **eDiscovery Manager** or **eDiscovery Administrator** subgroups shown in the preceding screenshot, you can add the required users to these roles. This can be seen in the following screenshot, where we have edited the **eDiscovery Manager** role by clicking on **Choose eDiscovery Manager**:

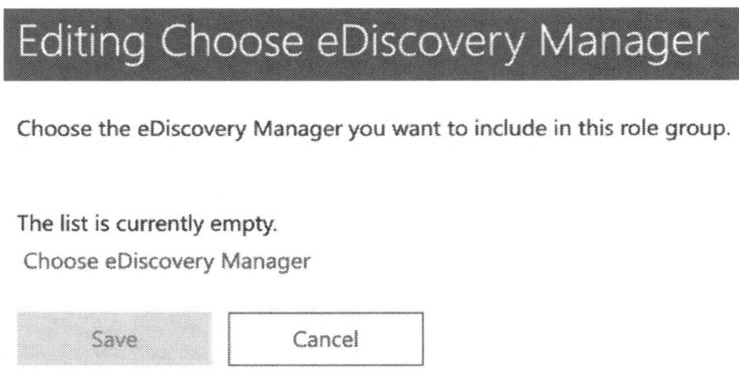

Figure 18.4 – Editing subgroup members

5. Choose **Add** and then select your chosen user, as per the example shown in the following screenshot, where we have selected a user called **Jane Bloggs** to be added to this role:

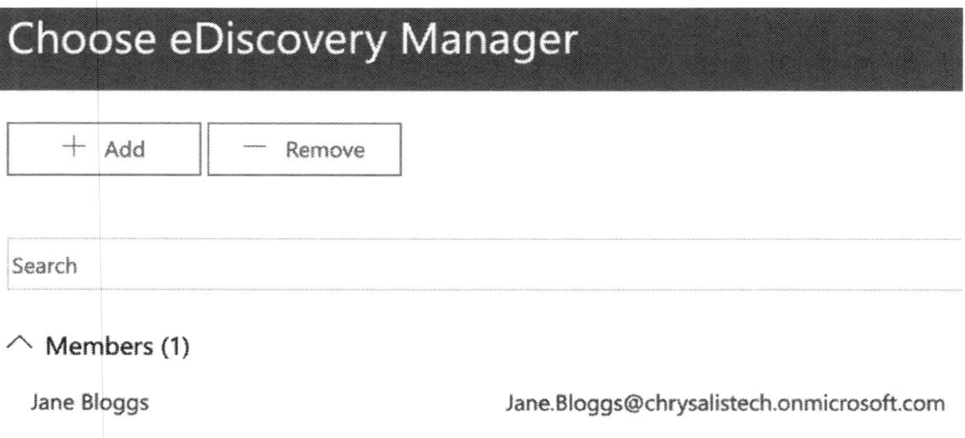

Figure 18.5 – Editing subgroup members

6. Click **Save** when you have added the required users, as shown in the following screenshot:

Figure 18.6 – Editing subgroup members

7. Finally, click **Close** to exit the role group settings.

It is also possible to assign users eDiscovery permissions by adding them to the following role groups:

- Compliance Administrator
- Organization Management
- Reviewer

> **Important note**
> More detailed information on all of the role groups that relate to eDiscovery can be found in the *References* section at the end of this chapter, under *Assigning eDiscovery permissions in the Security and Compliance Center.*

In addition to using the Security and Compliance Center to assign role groups to users, it is also possible to use the Security and Compliance Center PowerShell to set a mail-enabled security group. This group will be a member of the eDiscovery Managers subgroup within the main eDiscovery Manager role group.

However, the same ability does not apply to the eDiscovery Administrators subgroup, and there is a separate command called `Add-eDiscoveryCaseAdmin` that allows you to make a user an **eDiscovery Administrator**. This will only work if the user has already been assigned the Case Management role (which is a member of the Organization Management role).

An example of how to complete this task is shown in the following steps:

1. Log into the **Exchange admin center** and go to the **hybrid** section. Click on the option to **configure** under the **The Exchange PowerShell Module supports multi-factor authentication. Download the module to manage Exchange Online more securely** heading. This is shown in the following screenshot:

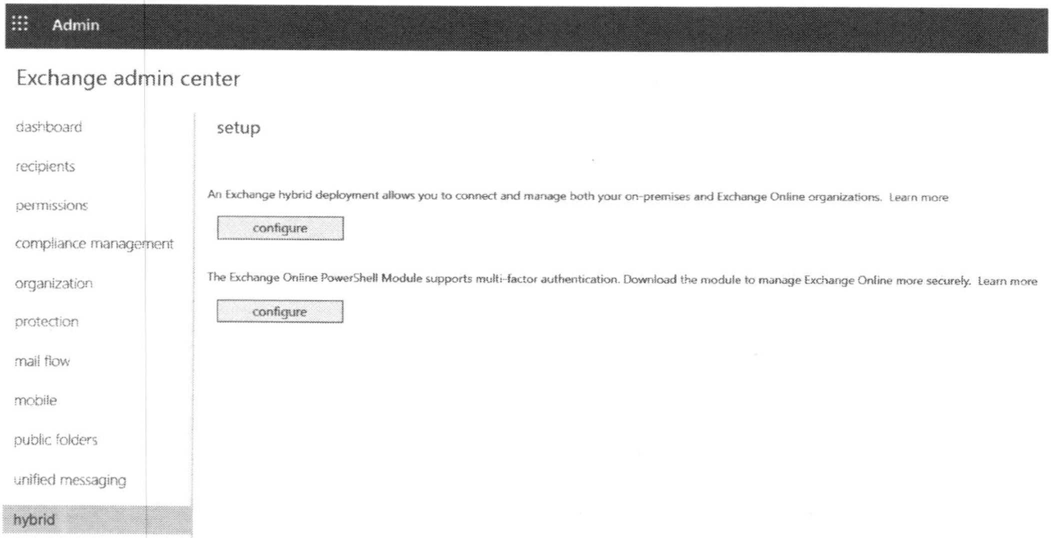

Figure 18.7 – Downloading the Exchange Online MFA compatible module

2. Complete the installation steps. After doing this, PowerShell will open. Next, you will need to use the `Connect-IPPSession` command to connect to the PowerShell session with administrative credentials. This is shown in the following example:

```
Connect-IPPSession -userprincipalname peter.rising@
peterrising.co.uk
```

3. Next, we will add the Discovery Case Admin role to a user called *James Smith* by running the following command:

```
Add-eDiscoveryCaseAdmin -User james.smith@chrysalistech.
onmicrosoft.com
```

4. The previous steps will appear in PowerShell, as shown in the following screenshot:

```
PS C:\Users\RisingP> Connect-IPPSSession -UserPrincipalName peter.rising@peterrising.co.uk
WARNING: Your connection has been redirected to the following URI:
"https://eur01b.ps.compliance.protection.outlook.com/PowerShell-LiveId?BasicAuthToOAuthConversion=true;PSVersion=5.1.18362.628 "
WARNING: The names of some imported commands from the module 'tmp_xufe5seq.fc3' include unapproved verbs that might make them less
discoverable. To find the commands with unapproved verbs, run the Import-Module command again with the Verbose parameter. For a list
of approved verbs, type Get-Verb.
PS C:\Users\RisingP> Add-eDiscoveryCaseAdmin -User james.smith@chrysalistech.onmicrosoft.com
PS C:\Users\RisingP>
```

Figure 18.8 – Security and Compliance PowerShell

> **Important note**
>
> More detailed information on using the Security and Compliance Center PowerShell can be found in the references section at the end of this chapter, under *Adding an eDiscovery Case Admin*.

In this section, we have explained how to assign users to eDiscovery-related role groups from the **Permissions** section of the Security and Compliance Center. You also learned that you can assign these roles using the Security and Compliance Center PowerShell. We showed you the four main role groups that are related to eDiscovery and the two subgroups that exist within the **eDiscovery Manager** role group.

Next, we will look at setting up eDiscovery cases, how to perform a content search, and how to place locations on hold.

Creating eDiscovery cases, placing locations on hold, and performing content searches

Now that you understand the principals and prerequisites for creating eDiscovery cases and content searches within Microsoft 365, let's go ahead and demonstrate the process of creating an eDiscovery case, placing locations on hold, and performing a content search. We will start with eDiscovery cases, which will also incorporate the step of placing some locations on hold.

Creating an eDiscovery case and placing locations on hold

To create an eDiscovery case from the Security and Compliance Center, we need to complete the following steps:

1. Go to `https://protection.office.com`, navigate to **eDiscovery | eDiscovery**, and click on **Create a case**. You will see the **New case** page, as shown in the following screenshot:

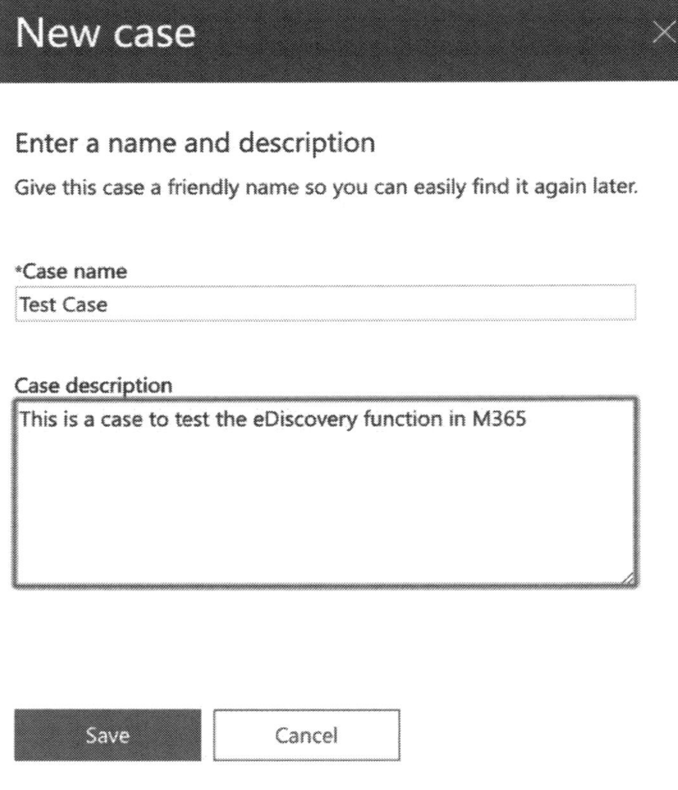

Figure 18.9 – New eDiscovery case

2. Enter a unique **Case name** and an optional **Case description**, and then click **Save**. Your new case will then appear in the case list, as shown in the following screenshot:

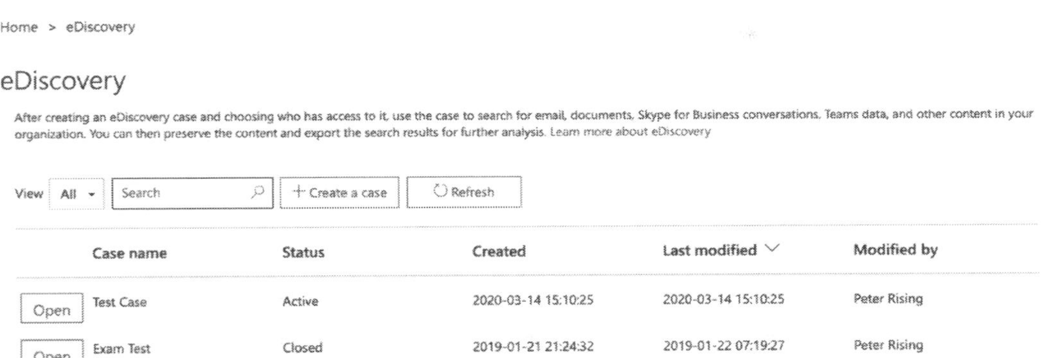

Figure 18.10 – List of eDiscovery cases

3. Now, we need to configure our **eDiscovery** case. To do this, click on **Open** next to the case name. You will see the options shown in the following screenshot:

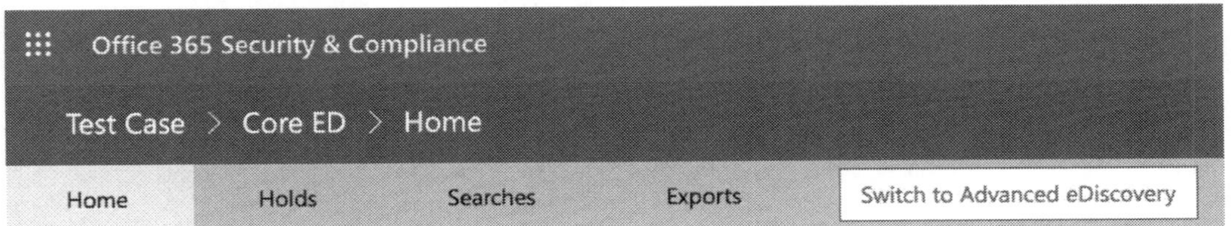

Figure 18.11 – eDiscovery case settings

4. The next thing we need to do is configure the **Holds** that will apply to our case. Click on **Holds** and enter a **Name** and an optional **Description**, as shown in the following screenshot:

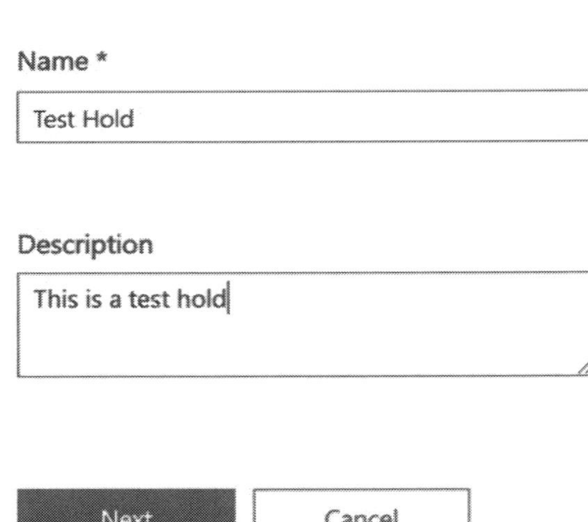

Figure 18.12 – Name your hold screen

5. Click **Next**. You now need to choose the locations that you wish to place on hold. For **Exchange email**, **Office 365 group email**, **Skype for Business**, **Teams messages**, and **To-Do**, you can filter your hold choices by **users**, **groups**, or **teams**.

   For **SharePoint sites**, **OneDrive accounts**, **Office 365 group sites**, and **Teams sites**, you can filter your choices by **Site**.

   Finally, if you wish to place a hold on **Exchange public folders**, you can move the toggle switch from **None** to **All**. These options are shown in the following screenshot:

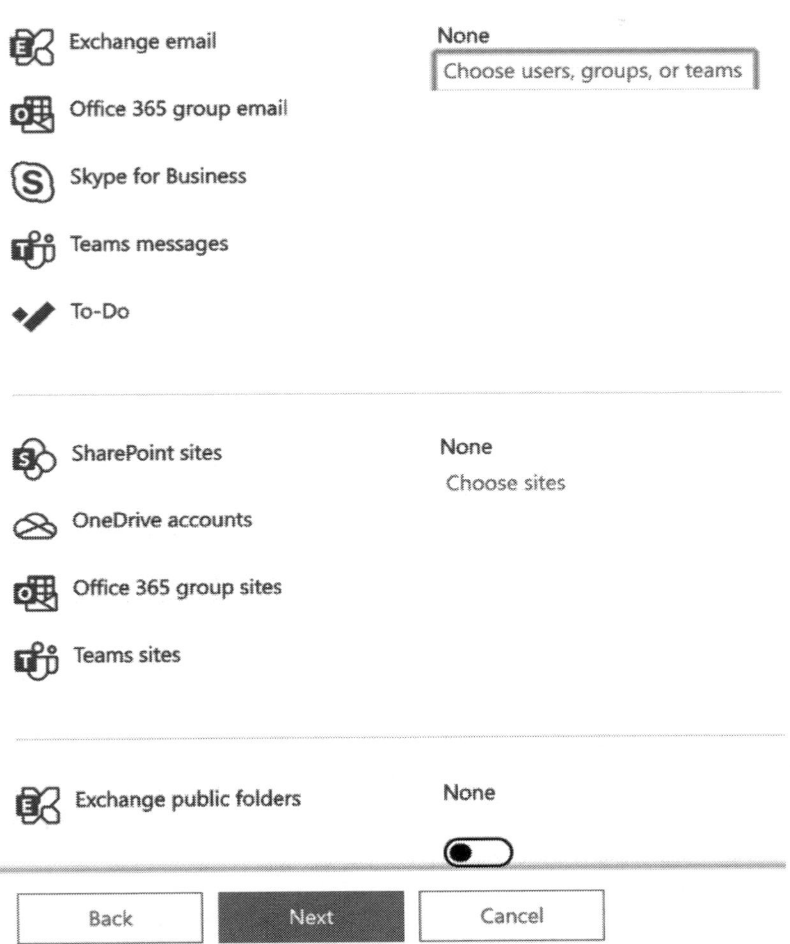

Figure 18.13 – Setting hold locations

6. When you have selected the settings for your hold, click **Next**. Once you've applied holds to locations, the content will be held until it's removed from that content location or the hold is completely deleted.

> **Important note**
>
> When a hold is applied, it will take up to 24 hours to take effect.

7. Next, you will see the option to add **Query conditions** to your hold. This is shown in the following screenshot:

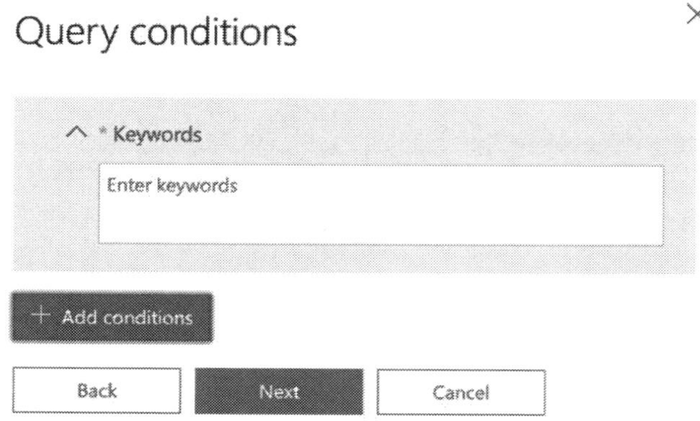

Figure 18.14 – Query conditions

8. This is an optional step where you can configure keywords that will be searched against. Only that content will be placed on hold. You can also click on **Add conditions**, which will enable you to select from 19 built-in conditions that will also filter your hold applications. The available conditions are shown in the following screenshot:

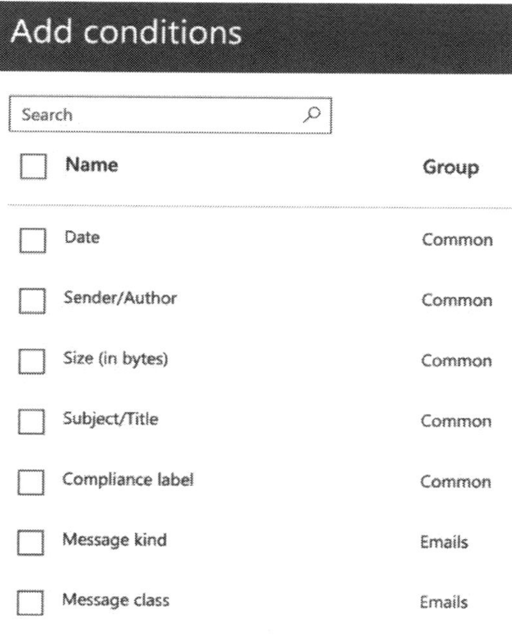

Figure 18.15 – Add conditions screen

9. Click **Next**. You will be taken to the **Review your settings** page, as shown in the following screenshot:

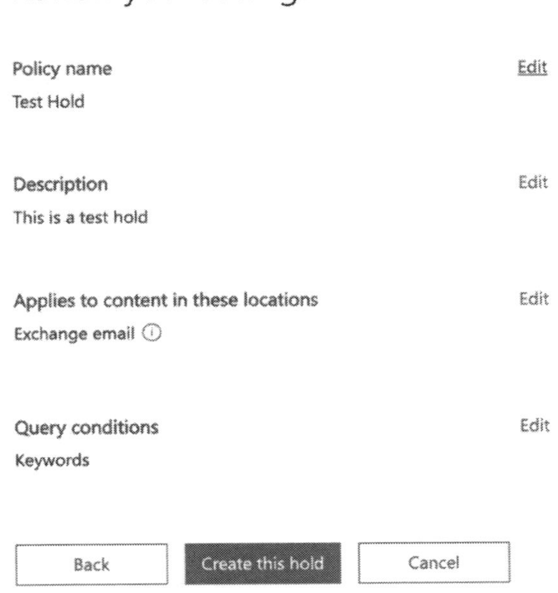

Figure 18.16 – Review our settings screen

10. By clicking **Create this hold**, your hold will appear on the main details page for your eDiscovery case.

Next, we will examine how to create a content search that will be associated with our eDiscovery case.

Performing a content search

Now that we have created our eDiscovery case and applied holds to locations, we can perform a content search. This will be associated with the case.

> **Important note**
>
> We discussed content searches earlier in this book in *Chapter 15, Security Analytics and Auditing Capabilities*. Content searches that are created and associated with eDiscovery cases will not appear in the **Search** page of the Security and Compliance Center – they will only be accessible from the **eDiscovery** page.

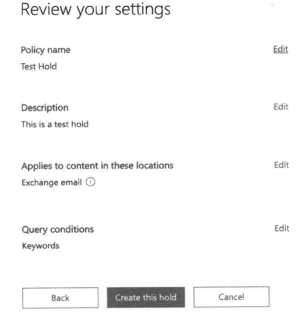

In order to configure a content search and associate it with our eDiscovery case, we need to complete the following steps:

1. To open the case that we created in the previous step, click on **Searches**, then **New search**. This will take you into the **Search query** options, as shown in the following screenshot:

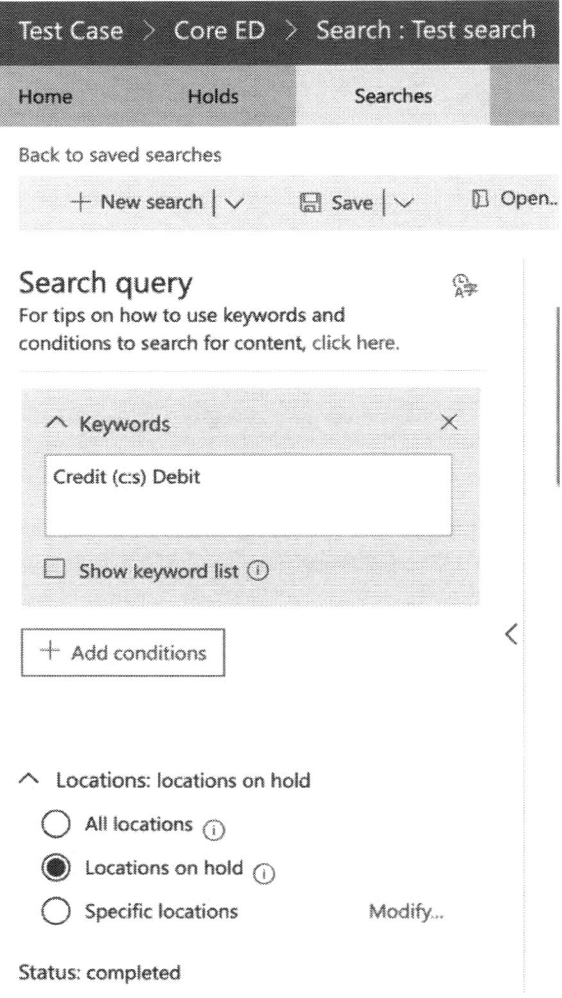

Figure 18.17 – New content search

2. Add any required **Keywords** and **Conditions** to your search query (in this example, we have added `Credit` and `Debit`). Then, under **Locations**, select **Locations on hold** and click on **Save**. Your search will now begin. The search results will be displayed in the details pane, as shown in the following screenshot:

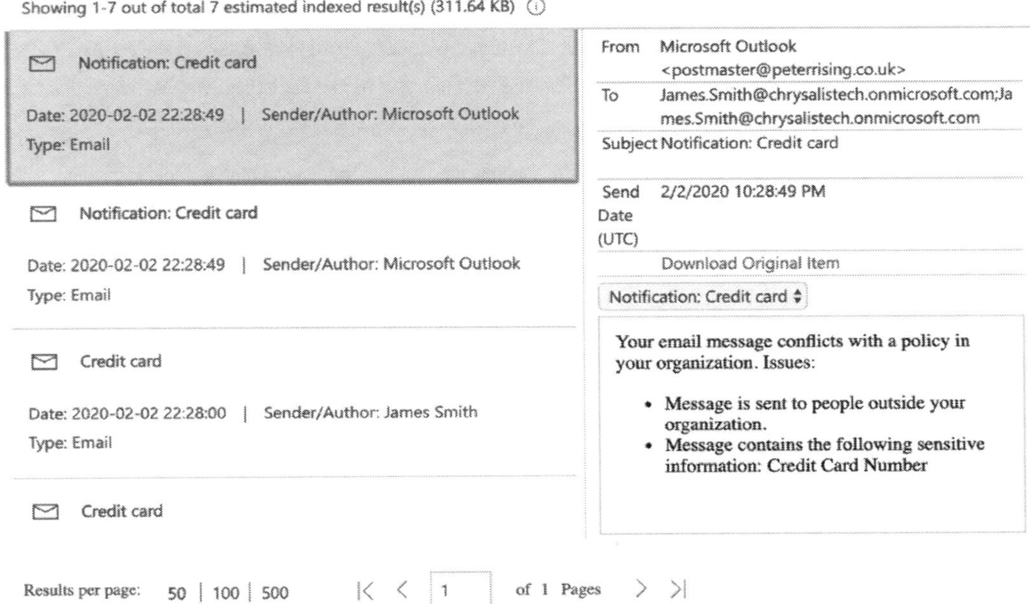

Figure 18.18 – Search results

In this section, you learned how to set up eDiscovery cases and place content on hold, as well as how to run a content search associated with your eDiscovery case hold settings and view the results.

In the final section of this chapter, we will show you how to export the results of your eDiscovery associated content searches.

Exporting content search results

Now that you have run your eDiscovery case with content search, you can export the search results using a Windows 7 or above computer, using Internet Explorer or the Microsoft Edge browser, and with Microsoft .NET Framework 4.7 installed. Should your device not meet these requirements, you will be unable to complete this process.

In order to successfully export your search results, you must also be assigned the **Export Management** role in the Security and Compliance Center. This role is part of the **eDiscovery Manager** role group, so if you are a member of this group, you will have the required permissions.

In order to complete the export process, you will need to carry out the following steps:

1. From the Security and Compliance Center, navigate to **eDiscovery | eDiscovery** and open the eDiscovery case that contains the content search that you wish to export. Click on **Export results**, as shown in the following screenshot:

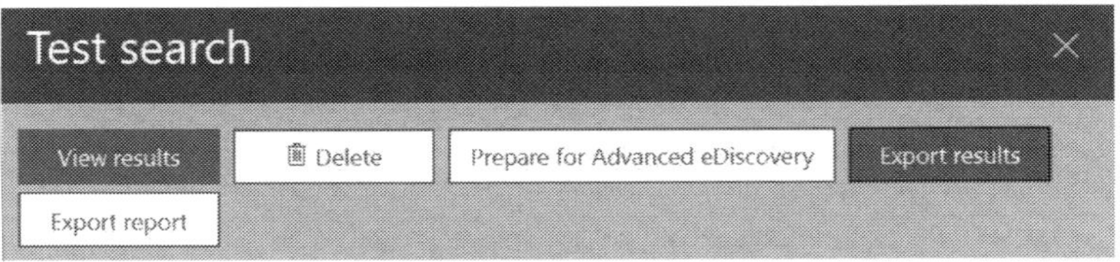

Figure 18.19 – Export results

2. Select your preferred **Output options** and click **Export**, as shown in the following screenshot:

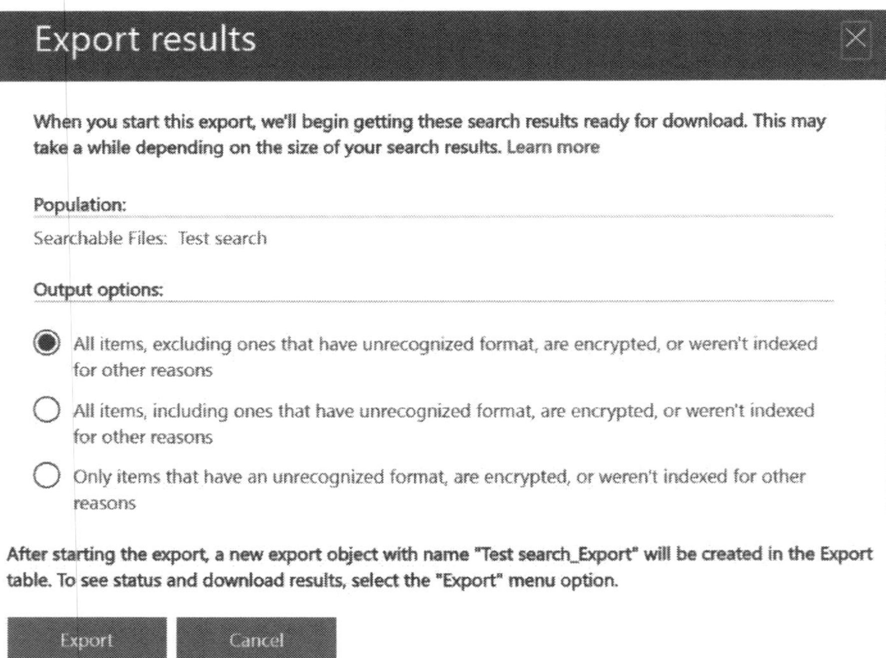

Figure 18.20 – Export results screen

3. Next, click on **Export report**, select your **Output options** once again, and click on **Generate report**, as shown in the following screenshot:

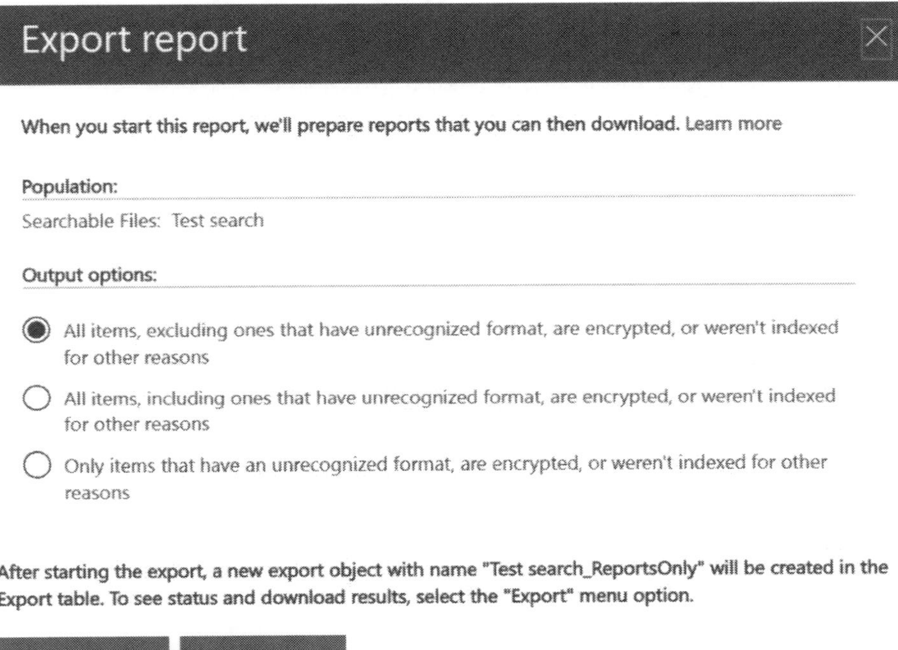

Figure 18.21 – Export report screen

4. Change to the **Exports** tab within your eDiscovery case and click the reports to open them once they are available to you, as shown in the following screenshot:

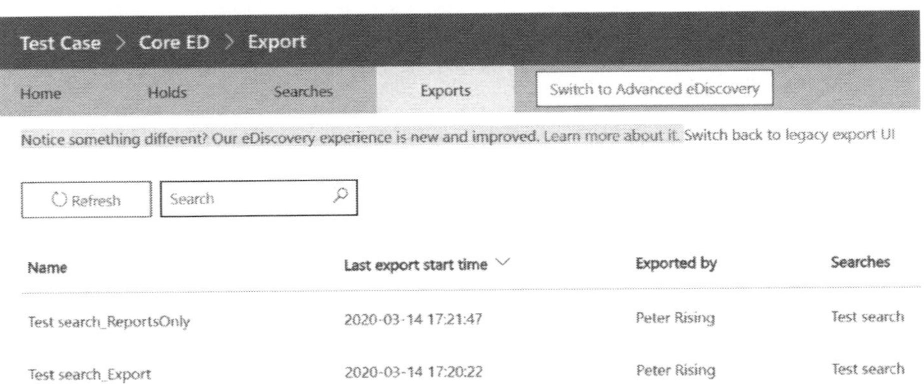

Figure 18.22 – Export tab in the Discovery case

5. Once you have opened the report, scroll down to the **Export key** section and click on **Copy to clipboard**, as shown in the following screenshot:

Figure 18.23 – Copying the export key to the clipboard

6. Next, click on **Download report**. The **eDiscovery Export Tool** will download and install onto your computer. Paste the export key that you copied earlier into the top field and browse to the location where you wish to save your exported content. Then, click on **Start**, as shown in the following screenshot:

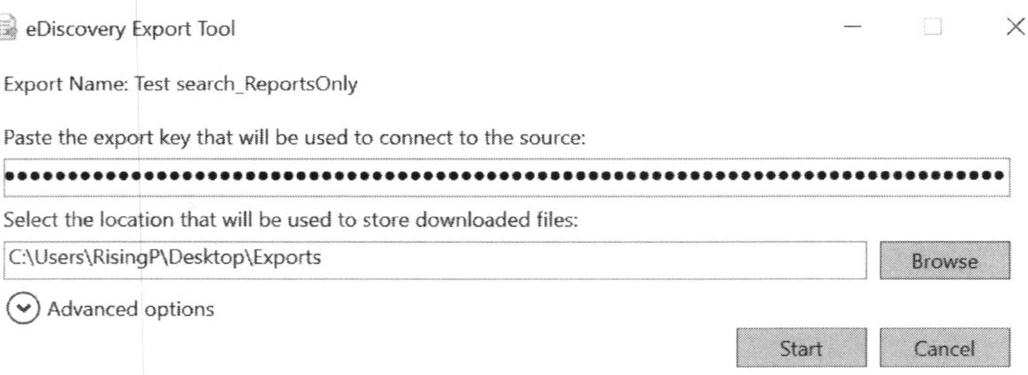

Figure 18.24 – eDiscovery Export Tool

7. Once the files have been downloaded, click on **Close**, as illustrated in the following screenshot:

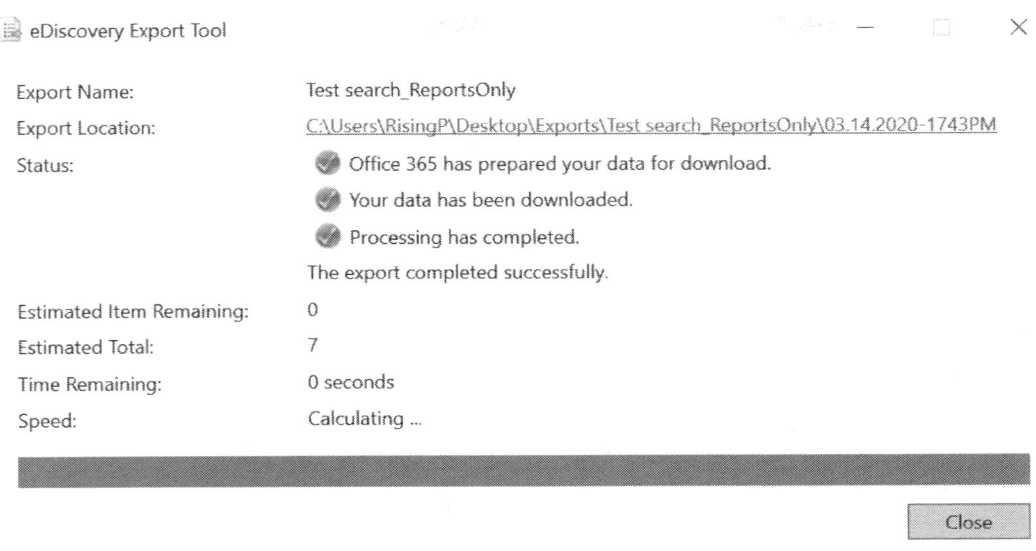

Figure 18.25 – eDiscovery export complete

8. Now, open the folder where you exported the reports. You will see the content shown in the following screenshot:

Name	Date modified	Type
Export Summary 03.14.2020-1745PM.csv	14/03/2020 17:45	Microsoft Excel Com...
manifest.xml	14/03/2020 17:45	XML Document
Results.csv	14/03/2020 17:45	Microsoft Excel Com...
trace.log	14/03/2020 17:45	Text Document

Figure 18.26 – Downloaded reports

You can view and analyze the reports that you have downloaded in Excel. The two main files you can review are called `Export Summary` and `Results`. These CSV files will contain the details that were requested in the search.

So, in this section, you learned that once you have created an eDiscovery case and associated a content search with your case, you are able to export the results by using a Windows Computer with either Internet Explorer or the Microsoft Edge browser. When generating the report, the eDiscovery Export Tool is installed and opened on your computer. You can download your reports to the chosen folder by copying and pasting the export key provided by the report generator.

Summary

In this chapter, we introduced you to the principles of search and investigation within your Microsoft 365 environment. You learned that you need to assign the eDiscovery Manager role to any users who you want to manage eDiscovery cases, and that you can then create eDiscovery cases from the Security and Compliance Center in order to place holds on your Office 365 locations.

Once an eDiscovery case had been created, we showed you how content searches can be associated with your eDiscovery case and applied to the held locations. These content searches can be set up with additional keywords and conditions in order to narrow down your search results.

Finally, we demonstrated that once a search was completed, we are able to preview the search results, as well as export reports to our local computer using the eDiscovery export tool, and then open and analyze the downloaded reports in Excel.

In the next chapter, we will discuss the steps required to plan for data privacy compliance in Microsoft 365. You will also learn how to access and interpret reports and dashboards that contain relevant GDPR data. Finally, we will show you how to conduct data subject requests from users who wish to review the personal information that the organization has stored for them.

Questions

1. Which of the following roles does not relate to eDiscovery?

   a. Compliance Administrator

   b. Security Administrator

   c. Organization Management

   d. eDiscovery Manager

   e. Reviewer

2. Which of the following licenses will allow you to use Advanced eDiscovery in your Microsoft 365 environment (choose two)?

   a. Office 365 E5

   b. Office 365 E1

   c. Office 365 E3

d. Office 365 E3 with Advanced Compliance add-on

e. Office 365 F1

f. Exchange Online (Plan 2)

3. The eDiscovery Manager role group includes two subgroups called eDiscovery Managers and eDiscovery Administrators.

   a. True

   b. False

4. Where in the Security and Compliance Center would you go to configure a content search that is to be associated with an eDiscovery case?

   a. **Search | Content Search**

   b. **eDiscovery | eDiscovery**

   c. **Search | Audit Log Search**

   d. **Permissions**

5. Users with the Reviewer role group permission can create eDiscovery cases.

   a. True

   b. False

6. Which of the following can't be used with the eDiscovery export tool?

   a. Internet Explorer

   b. Google Chrome

   c. Windows 7

   d. Windows 10

   e. Microsoft Edge

   f. Microsoft Excel

7. To export reports from eDiscovery cases, you must be assigned the Security Reader role.

   a. True

   b. False

8. After creating a hold in an eDiscovery case, how long will it take for the hold settings to take effect?

    a. 48 hours

    b. 12 hours

    c. 24 hours

    d. 96 hours

9. When a hold is applied to an item using an eDiscovery case, it will not be removed until either the case is modified to exclude the hold or the eDiscovery case is deleted.

    a. True

    b. False

10. When using a query with an eDiscovery case content search, which location option should be selected?

    a. Specific Locations

    b. All Locations

    c. Locations on Hold

References

Please refer to the following links for more information:

- eDiscovery in Office 365: `https://docs.microsoft.com/en-us/microsoft-365/compliance/ediscovery?view=o365-worldwide`
- Overview of Advanced eDiscovery: `https://docs.microsoft.com/en-gb/microsoft-365/compliance/overview-ediscovery-20?view=o365-worldwide`
- Assigning eDiscovery permissions in the Security and Compliance Center: `https://docs.microsoft.com/en-gb/microsoft-365/compliance/assign-ediscovery-permissions?view=o365-worldwide#rbac-roles-related-to-ediscovery`

- Adding an eDiscovery case admin: `https://docs.microsoft.com/en-us/powershell/module/exchange/policy-and-compliance-ediscovery/Add-eDiscoveryCaseAdmin?redirectedfrom=MSDN&view=exchange-ps`
- Keyword queries and search conditions for content search: `https://docs.microsoft.com/en-gb/microsoft-365/compliance/keyword-queries-and-search-conditions?view=o365-worldwide`
- Managing eDiscovery cases in the Security and Compliance Center: `https://docs.microsoft.com/en-us/microsoft-365/compliance/ediscovery-cases?view=o365-worldwide`

19 Data Privacy Compliance

All organizations need to have an understanding of their obligations to protect any personal data that they hold in line with **General Data Protection Regulation** (**GDPR**). A proactive approach when it comes to data protection is essential and will enable compliance administrators to ensure that their organization is meeting their regulatory responsibilities. Microsoft 365 provides you with some tools and dashboards that help you prepare for these requirements.

In this chapter, we will show you how to plan for regulatory compliance in Microsoft 365. You will also learn how to access and understand the available reports and dashboards that contain relevant GDPR data, including the Microsoft Compliance Score tool. Finally, we will show you how to conduct **Data Subject Requests** (**DSRs**) from users who wish to review the personal information that your organization has stored for them.

We will cover these topics in the following order:

- Planning for regulatory compliance in Microsoft 365
- Accessing the GDPR dashboards and reports
- Completing DSRs

Planning for regulatory compliance in Microsoft 365

In order to meet the requirements of GDPR when using a Microsoft 365 environment, Microsoft recommends that all organizations undertake a three-phase action plan to achieve the following outcomes.

Phase 1 – the first 30 days

In the first phase of your action plan, compliance administrators should focus on achieving the following:

- Gain an understanding of your GDPR requirements by using the Microsoft GDPR assessment tool, which can be accessed from `https://discover.microsoft.com/gdpr-readiness-assessment`.
- Begin a discovery exercise to identify the types of personal data stored within your Microsoft 365 environment.
- Assess risks by using the Microsoft Compliance Score tool, which can be found within Microsoft **Service Trust Portal** (**STP**) at `https://servicetrust.microsoft.com/`.

In order to gain the level of understanding that you require, you may wish to consider engaging a specialist GDPR consultancy; alternatively, you can review the vast quantity of GDPR-related material available on the Microsoft website, including the GDPR assessment tool mentioned previously. Links to these sorts of documents are included in the *References* section at the end of this chapter.

To start discovering the personal data used in your organization, you can use two of the tools included in the Security & Compliance Center. These tools are eDiscovery and **Content Search**. Further details on how to use these features can be found in *Chapter 17, Data Governance and Retention*.

Phase 2 – after 90 days

In Phase 2, you will need to start considering the following:

- Begin implementing the compliance settings in the Security & Compliance Center using data governance and compliance tools such as Microsoft Compliance Score and sensitivity labeling, along with eDiscovery cases and **Content search**.
- Protect administrator and user accounts using **Multi-Factor Authentication** (**MFA**) and Conditional Access.

- Monitor the audit log regularly for any suspicious or malicious behavior.
- Protect sensitive data by implementing **Data Loss Prevention** (**DLP**).
- Use Advanced Threat Protection tools, such as anti-phishing policies.

These methods are all features contained within Microsoft 365 that we have discussed in earlier chapters of this book and will be available to you depending on your subscriptions.

Phase 3 – ongoing

The first two phases represent discovery and implementation. Phase 3 needs to continue the practices that you have established and you need to develop them further, as required, by taking the following steps:

- Continue to monitor and refine all the settings that you configured in Phase 2.
- Consider implementing advanced data governance practices by updating your Azure AD subscriptions to include Identity Protection and automatic labeling based on sensitive information types.
- Ensure that retention policies are set to retain information for only as long as required by both the internal company policy and the relevant industry regulations.
- Use Microsoft Cloud App Security to monitor all cloud application usage and implement advanced alerting.
- Ensure that sensitive data is accessed only from compliant devices using Intune with Conditional Access.

Once again, these methods are all features contained within Microsoft 365 that we have discussed in earlier chapters of this book and will also be available to you depending on your subscriptions.

> **Important note**
>
> In order to deploy some or all of the previously mentioned features, it is crucial to understand what your Microsoft 365 tenant is licensed for. Some features, such as Advanced Threat Protection, may be activated at a tenant level with a single license. This does not mean, however, that you are properly licensed to use the feature for all of your Office 365 users.

In this section, we advised you how to plan and prepare for data privacy compliance in your Microsoft 365 environment with a three-phased approach consisting of discovery and analysis, implementation, and, finally, reinforcement and ongoing improvement. You will now have an understanding of how to implement your GDPR strategy within your organization.

Next, we will show you how to access and interpret the GDPR dashboards and reports.

Accessing the GDPR dashboards and reports

Microsoft 365 provides you with a number of ways to discover, address, and monitor your GDPR requirements within your organization. The three key tools available to compliance administrators to fulfill these requirements are as follows:

- Microsoft STP
- The Microsoft Compliance Score tool
- The GDPR dashboard and GDPR toolbox

In this section, we will examine each of these features in turn and explain their purpose, starting with STP.

Service Trust Portal

Microsoft STP consists of a website containing a variety of tools and resources to help you implement and maintain security, privacy, and compliance best practices. STP can be accessed via your web browser by going to `https://servicetrust.microsoft.com`. This is shown in the following screenshot:

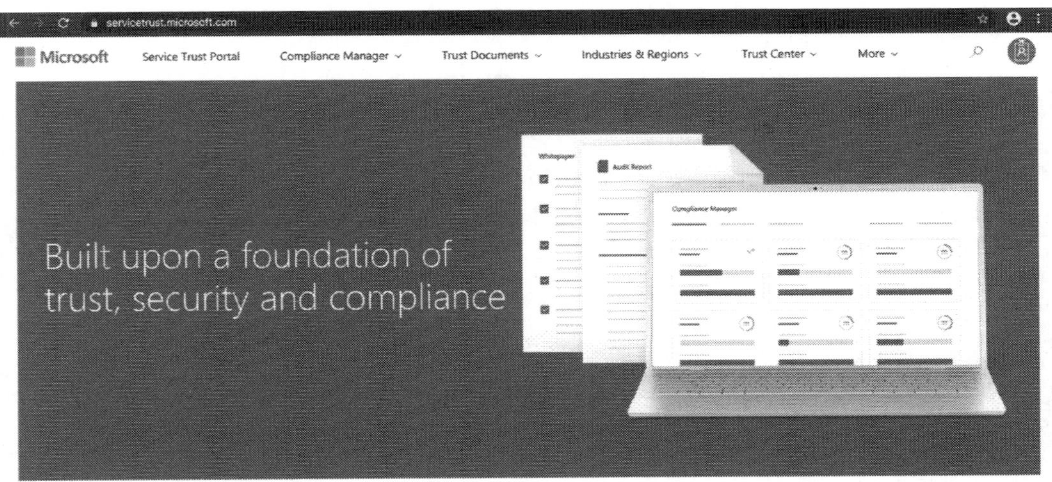
servicetrust.microsoft.com
Microsoft
Service Trust Portal
Compliance Manager
Trust Documents
Industries & Regions
Trust Center
More
Built upon a foundation of trust, security and compliance
Audit Reports
Review the available independent audit reports for Microsoft's Cloud services, which provide information about compliance with data protection standards and regulatory requirements, such as International Organization for Standardization (ISO), Service Organization Controls (SOC), National Institute of Standards and Technology (NIST), Federal Risk and Authorization Management Program (FedRAMP), and the General Data Protection

Figure 19.1 – STP

The STP dashboard shows some links at the top of the screen, which include the following:

- **Compliance Manager**: Provides an at-a-glance summary of the shared responsibility model for your organizations and Microsoft's data. It also includes a risk assessment workflow, management tools, and intelligent tracking.
- **Trust Documents**: This includes guides on audit reports, data protection, and security and compliance.
- **Industries & Regions**: Guides on industry and regional solutions.
- **Trust Center**: Contains information and links to principles of maintaining data integrity in the cloud.
- **Links to further resources**
- **A Library**: Where you may save reports and whitepapers relevant to your organization in one place

The STP is a one-stop-shop for information and guidance relating to the subject of data privacy compliance.

Next, let's look at Microsoft Compliance Score.

Microsoft Compliance Score

Although still currently in public preview at the time of writing this book, Microsoft Compliance Score consists of a dashboard, which can be accessed by going to the Microsoft 365 compliance center at `https://compliance.microsoft.com` and then clicking on **Compliance score**. This will look as in the following screenshot:

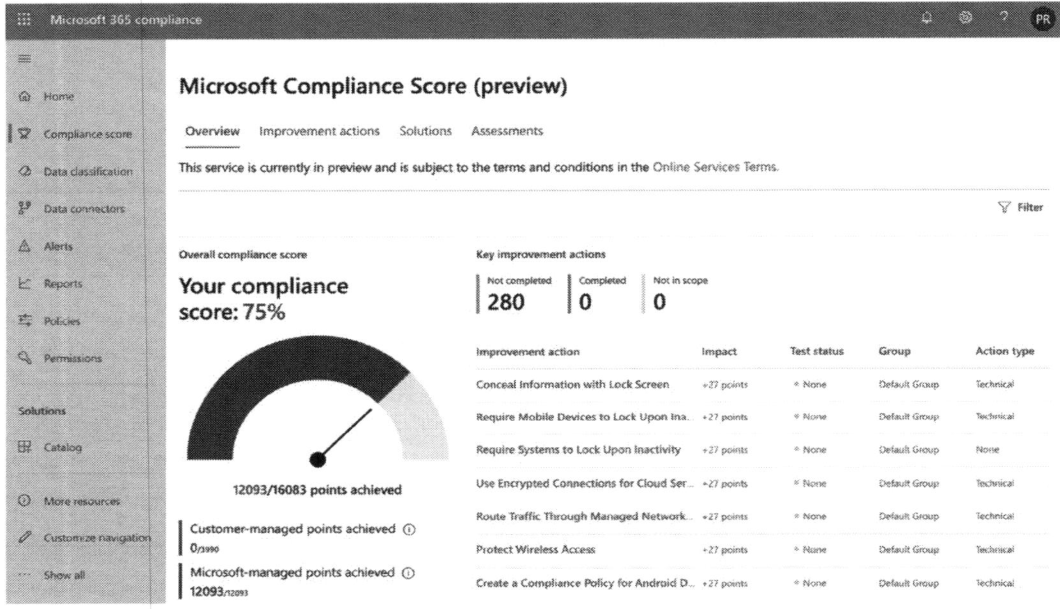

Figure 19.2 – The Compliance Score dashboard

The **Compliance Score** dashboard offers a simple and user-friendly experience to provide you with information relating to your organizational compliance. You will see a risk-based score, which measures your progress in addressing outstanding tasks that, when completed, will mitigate any risks that may exist relating to data protection and industry regulations.

Compliance Score is an evolution of the Compliance Manager feature that is currently available on STP, which we described previously in this chapter. Compliance Score uses the same backend as Compliance Manager, so any data present in **Compliance Manager** will also be available to you within Compliance Score.

As already stated, Compliance Score is in public preview at the time of writing this book. However, Microsoft recommends that the newer Compliance Score experience is used when you start to address your organizational compliance management activities.

The **Compliance Score** dashboard is broken down into four sections, as in the following screenshot:

Microsoft Compliance Score (preview)

Overview Improvement actions Solutions Assessments

Figure 19.3 – The Compliance Score sections

The **Overview** section shows you a quick view of your current score and key improvement actions. This is shown in the following screenshot:

Overview Improvement actions Solutions Assessments

This service is currently in preview and is subject to the terms and conditions in the Online Services Terms.

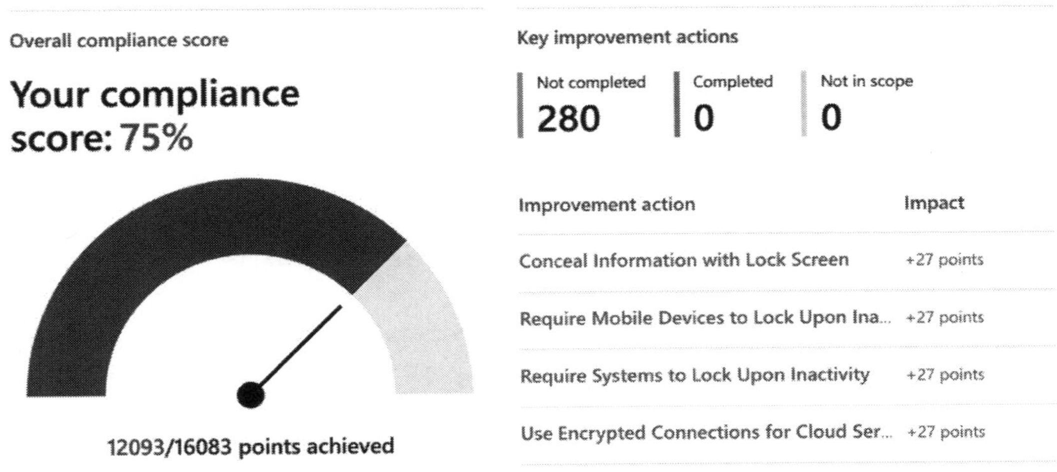

Figure 19.4 – Overview

The **Improvement actions** section shows you a list of all recommend actions that you can take to improve your overall compliance score. This list can be exported to a spreadsheet if required and when you click on each improvement, you will see further details on that particular recommendation, along with information on how to implement the improvement. This is shown in the following screenshot:

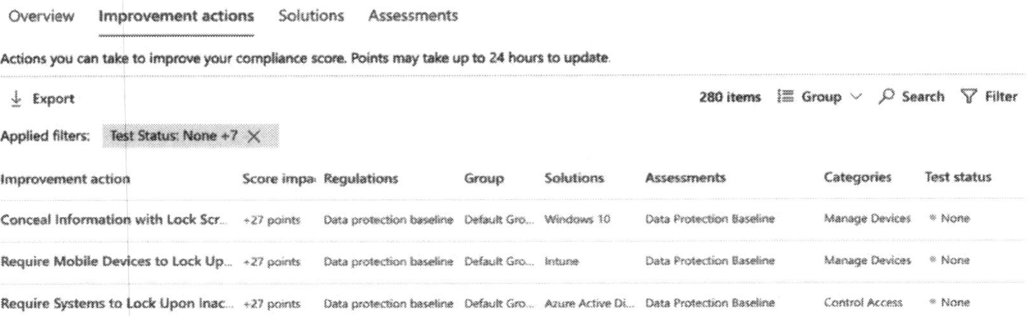

Figure 19.5 – Improvement actions

The **Solutions** section shows you how individual Microsoft 365 solutions contribute to your overall compliance score and how your score could potentially be improved per solution, as in the following screenshot:

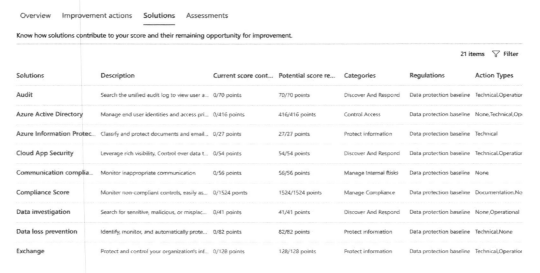

Microsoft Compliance Score (preview)

Overview Improvement actions **Solutions** Assessments

Know how solutions contribute to your score and their remaining opportunity for improvement.

21 items Filter

Solutions	Description	Current score cont...	Potential score re...	Categories	Regulations	Action Types
Audit	Search the unified audit log to view user a...	0/70 points	70/70 points	Discover And Respond	Data protection baseline	Technical,Operatior
Azure Active Directory	Manage end user identities and access pri...	0/416 points	416/416 points	Control Access	Data protection baseline	None,Technical,Op
Azure Information Protec...	Classify and protect documents and email...	0/27 points	27/27 points	Protect information	Data protection baseline	Technical
Cloud App Security	Leverage rich visibility, Control over data t...	0/54 points	54/54 points	Discover And Respond	Data protection baseline	Technical,Operatior
Communication complia...	Monitor inappropriate communication	0/56 points	56/56 points	Manage Internal Risks	Data protection baseline	None
Compliance Score	Monitor non-compliant controls, easily as...	0/1524 points	1524/1524 points	Manage Compliance	Data protection baseline	Documentation,No
Data investigation	Search for sensitive, malicious, or misplac...	0/41 points	41/41 points	Discover And Respond	Data protection baseline	None,Operational
Data loss prevention	Identify, monitor, and automatically prote...	0/82 points	82/82 points	Protect information	Data protection baseline	Technical,None
Exchange	Protect and control your organization's inf...	0/128 points	128/128 points	Protect information	Data protection baseline	Technical,Operatior

Figure 19.6 – Solutions

The **Assessments** section shows you an evaluation of the templates that contribute to your organization's score. **Assessments** groups together any actions that make up the requirements of an industry standard or regulation:

Microsoft Compliance Score (preview)

Overview Improvement actions Solutions Assessments

Assessments help you implement data protection controls specified by compliance, security, privacy, and data protection standards, regulations, and laws. Assessments include actions that have been taken by Microsoft to protect your data, and they're completed when you take action to implement the controls included in the assessment. Learn how to manage assessments in Compliance Manager

Manage assessments in Compliance Manager Microsoft actions in Compliance Manager 1 item Search Filter Group

Assessment	Status	Assessment progr...	Customer manage...	Microsoft manage...	Group	Product
Data Protection Baseline	InProgress	79%	0 of 280 completed	709 of 709 completed	Default Group	Microsoft 365

Figure 19.7 – Assessments

Assessments cannot currently be started from the **Compliance Score** dashboard; instead, you need to click on the **Manage assessments in Compliance Manager** option, which takes you to **Compliance Manager** within the STP. You can start an assessment by clicking on **Add Assessment**, as shown:

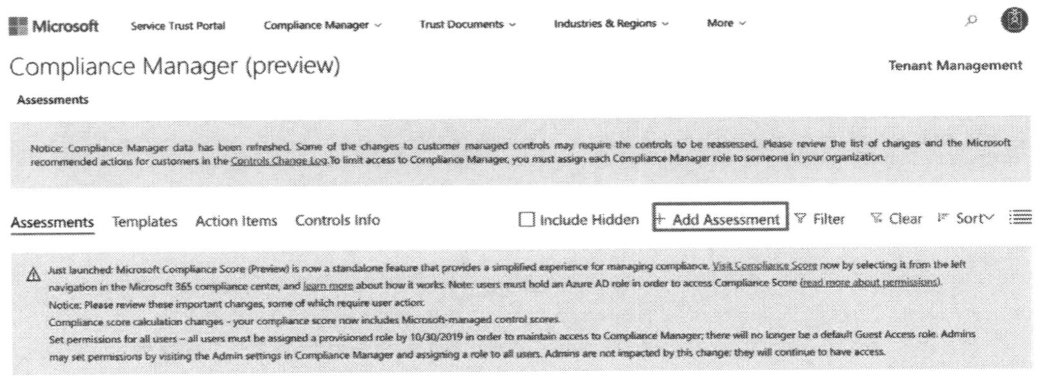

Figure 19.8 – The Add Assessment option from Compliance Manager

You can associate built-in Microsoft templates for your assessment from the **Assessment** wizard, shown in the following screenshot:

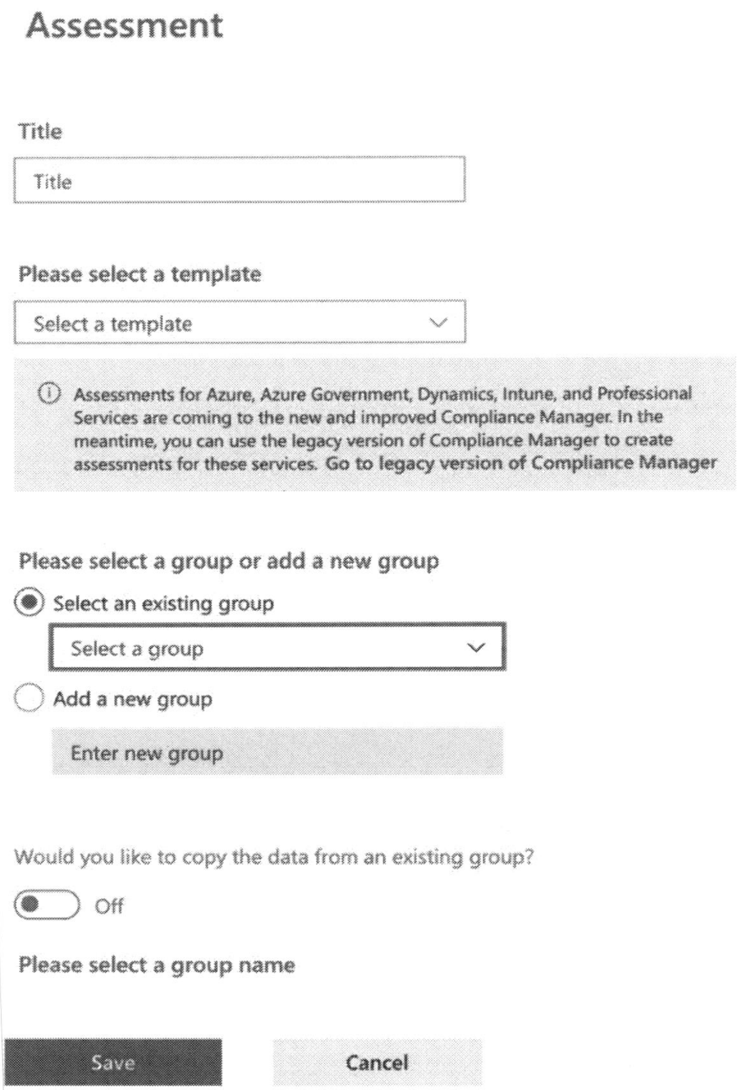

Figure 19.9 – The Assessment wizard

When you click on **Save**, your assessment will begin and you can immediately view its progress either from Compliance Manager or Compliance Score.

Next, let's look at the GDPR dashboard and the GDPR toolbox.

The GDPR dashboard and the GDPR toolbox

The GDPR dashboard can be accessed from the Microsoft 365 Security & Compliance Center by going to `https://protection.office.com` and navigating to **Data privacy | GDPR dashboard**.

The dashboard displays tiles that link to other content relating to GDPR, which include the following:

- The GDPR toolbox
- DSRs
- Data classification statistics
- Risks and threats

The GDPR dashboard is shown in the following screenshot:

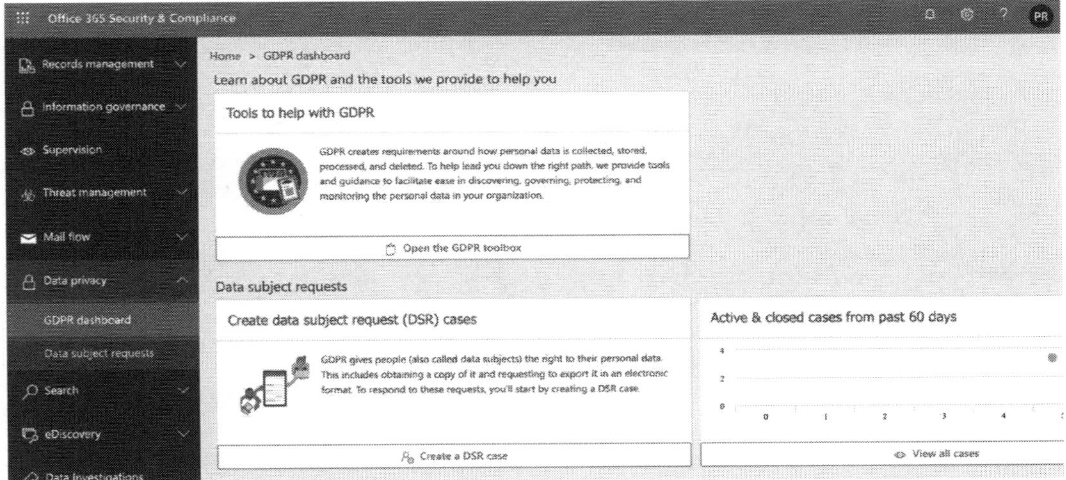

Figure 19.10 – The GDPR dashboard

The GDPR toolbox is the first tile visible on the GDPR dashboard. When you click on **Open the GDPR toolbox**, it pops out as a sub-menu, as shown:

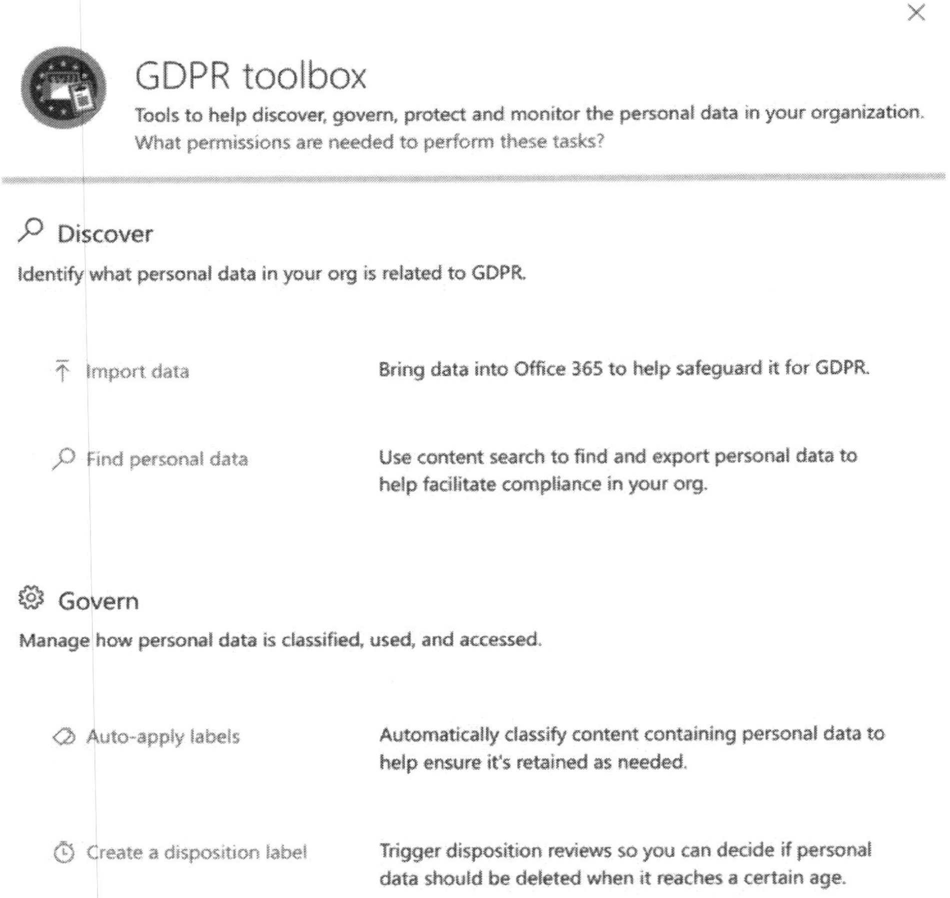

GDPR toolbox

Tools to help discover, govern, protect and monitor the personal data in your organization.
What permissions are needed to perform these tasks?

Discover

Identify what personal data in your org is related to GDPR.

Import data — Bring data into Office 365 to help safeguard it for GDPR.

Find personal data — Use content search to find and export personal data to help facilitate compliance in your org.

Govern

Manage how personal data is classified, used, and accessed.

Auto-apply labels — Automatically classify content containing personal data to help ensure it's retained as needed.

Create a disposition label — Trigger disposition reviews so you can decide if personal data should be deleted when it reaches a certain age.

Figure 19.11 – The GDPR toolbox

The toolbox consists of a collection of tools that can be used by compliance administrators to configure the GDPR-related settings, which are broken up into the following categories:

- **Discover**
- **Govern**
- **Protect**
- **Monitor & respond**

The **Discover** category allows you to identify personal data in your organization relating to GDPR, as shown:

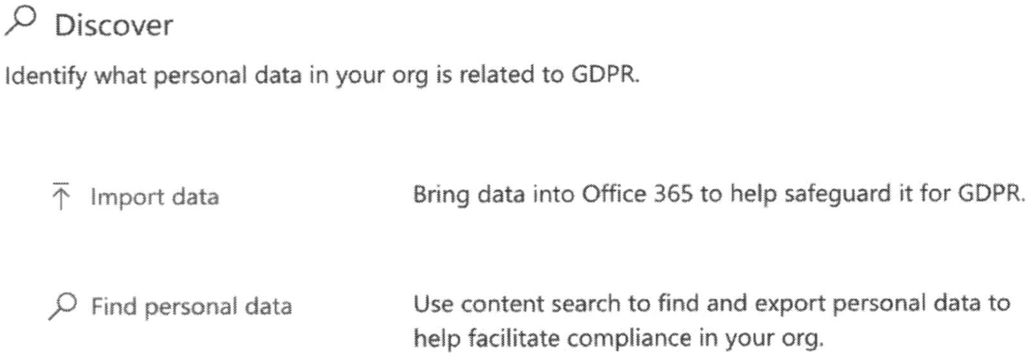

Discover

Identify what personal data in your org is related to GDPR.

Import data	Bring data into Office 365 to help safeguard it for GDPR.
Find personal data	Use content search to find and export personal data to help facilitate compliance in your org.

Figure 19.12 – The Discover category

The **Govern** category allows you to manage how personal data in your organization is classified and consumed, as the following screenshot shows:

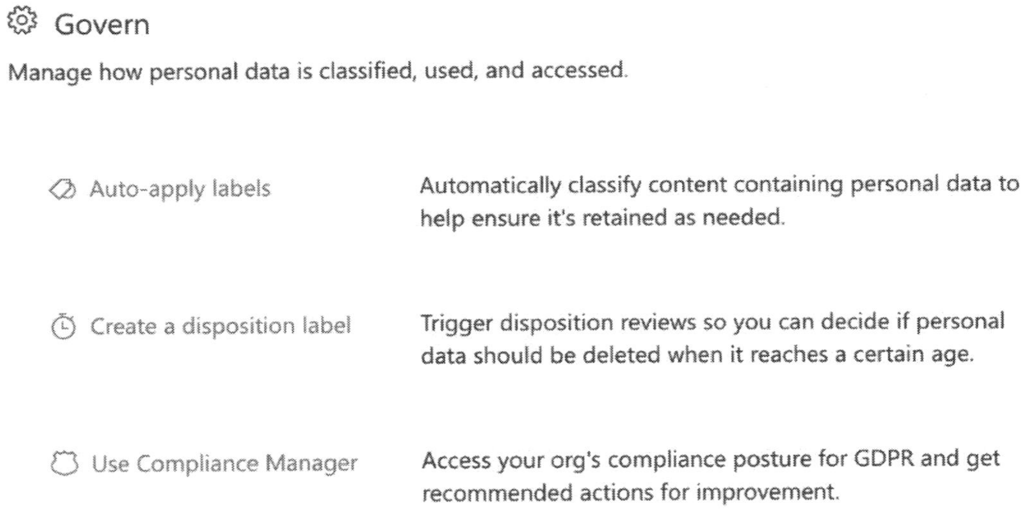

Govern

Manage how personal data is classified, used, and accessed.

Auto-apply labels	Automatically classify content containing personal data to help ensure it's retained as needed.
Create a disposition label	Trigger disposition reviews so you can decide if personal data should be deleted when it reaches a certain age.
Use Compliance Manager	Access your org's compliance posture for GDPR and get recommended actions for improvement.

Figure 19.13 – The Govern category

The **Protect** category allows you to set up security and cyberthreat policies, as shown:

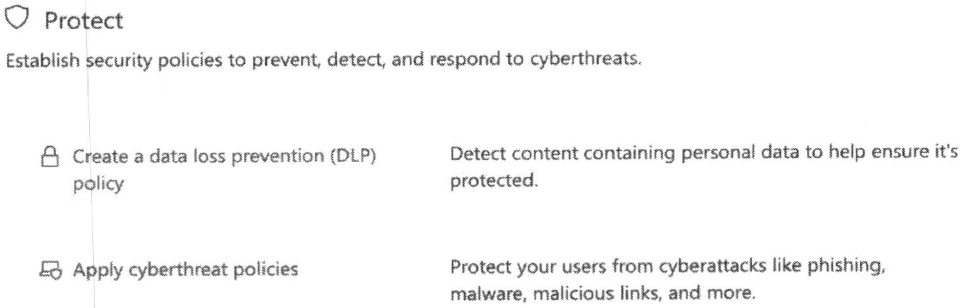

Protect

Establish security policies to prevent, detect, and respond to cyberthreats.

Create a data loss prevention (DLP) policy	Detect content containing personal data to help ensure it's protected.
Apply cyberthreat policies	Protect your users from cyberattacks like phishing, malware, malicious links, and more.

Figure 19.14 – The Protect category

The **Monitor & respond** category enables you to track label usage, respond to legal investigations, review and explore label usage, and much more, as shown:

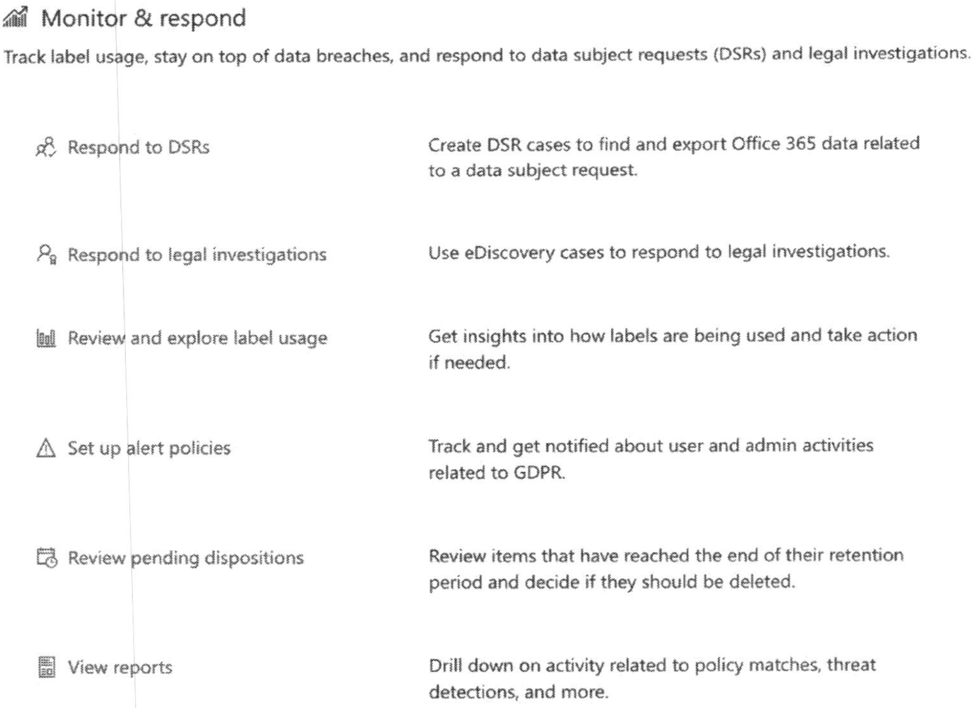

Monitor & respond

Track label usage, stay on top of data breaches, and respond to data subject requests (DSRs) and legal investigations.

Respond to DSRs	Create DSR cases to find and export Office 365 data related to a data subject request.
Respond to legal investigations	Use eDiscovery cases to respond to legal investigations.
Review and explore label usage	Get insights into how labels are being used and take action if needed.
Set up alert policies	Track and get notified about user and admin activities related to GDPR.
Review pending dispositions	Review items that have reached the end of their retention period and decide if they should be deleted.
View reports	Drill down on activity related to policy matches, threat detections, and more.

Figure 19.15 – The Monitor & respond category

All of the items listed in the previously mentioned categories in the GDPR toolbox will link you to other features or services within the Security & Compliance Center.

For example, if you select the **Find personal data** option under the **Discover** category, this takes you directly into the **Search | Content Search** feature, as shown:

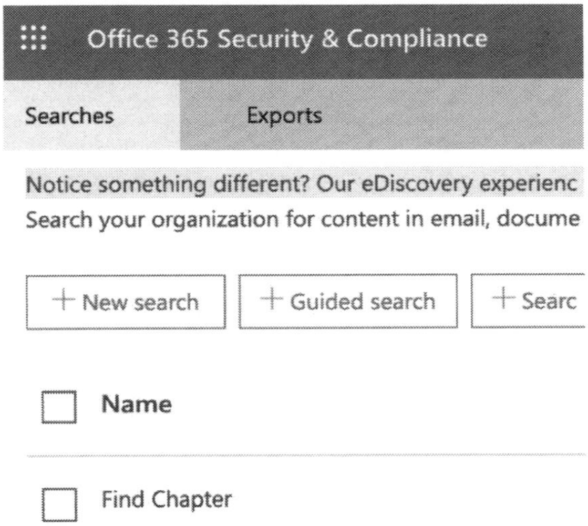

Figure 19.16 – The Content Search feature via the GDPR toolbox

So, essentially, the GDPR toolbox is a collection of handy shortcuts that guide you to the feature or service that you need to configure in relation to your organization's GDPR compliance.

All of the features that are linked from the GDPR toolbox have been discussed either in this chapter or another chapter of this book.

In this section, we demonstrated how to access the available GDPR-related dashboards and reports from the Security & Compliance Center. You learned that there are three main areas to focus on when managing your GDPR settings.

Microsoft STP is a website that collects together useful links to GDPR guidelines.

The Microsoft Compliance Score tool provides a user-friendly dashboard where you can view your organization's current compliance score and assess and implement improvements to increase your score.

Finally, the GDPR dashboard and GDPR toolbox contain links to other services and features within the Security & Compliance Center, where you can configure and apply settings related to GDPR by using the **Discover**, **Govern**, **Protect**, and **Monitor & respond** tabs.

In the final section of this chapter, we will show you how DSRs can be completed within Microsoft 365 when a user requests information relating to their personal data that is held in your organization.

Completing DSRs

GDPR refers to individuals within the European Union as data subjects. Under GDPR, data subjects have the right to access any of their personal data within Microsoft 365. Personal data is defined as "*any information relating to an identified or identifiable natural person.*"

When a data subject makes a request to take action relating to their personal information, the Microsoft 365 Security & Compliance Center can be used to create a DSR in order for the organization to be able to fulfill its obligations to its user (or data subject). DSRs can be configured to locate information stored in the following Microsoft 365 locations:

- User mailboxes
- Skype for Business conversations
- Microsoft Teams one-to-one chats
- Mailboxes associated with Office 365 groups
- SharePoint Online Sites
- OneDrive accounts
- Microsoft Teams sites
- Office 365 group sites
- Exchange Online public folders

In order to create a DSR case, we need to take the following steps:

1. Log in to the Security & Compliance Center at `https://protection.office.com` and navigate to **Data privacy | Data subject requests**. This is shown in the following screenshot:

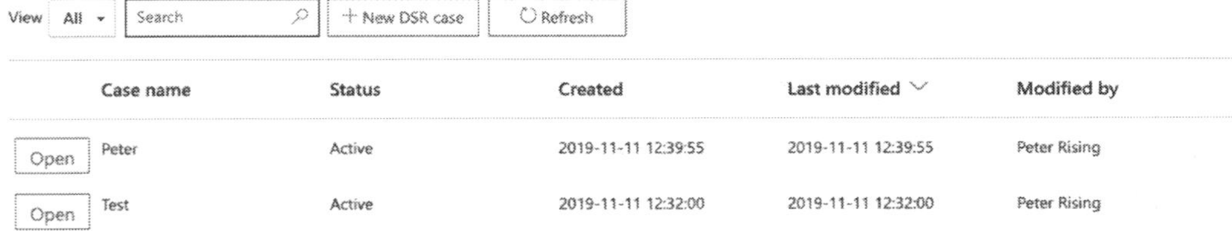

Figure 19.17 – Data subject requests

2. Click on **New DSR case** and then enter a name and an optional description for your case, as shown:

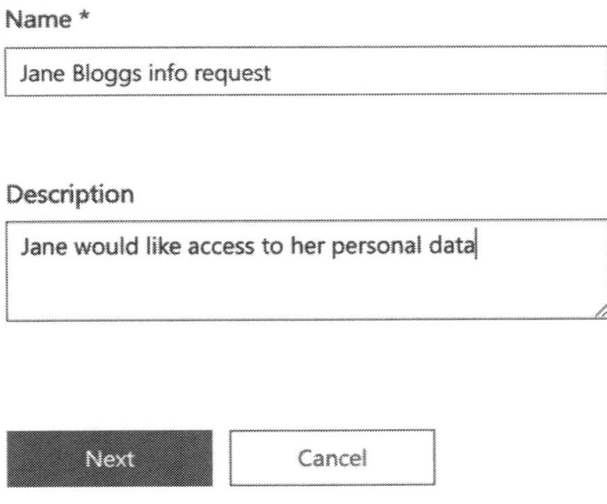

Figure 19.18 – A new DSR case

3. Click **Next**, then enter the name of your data subject by searching for the username of the person who made the request. This is shown in the following screenshot:

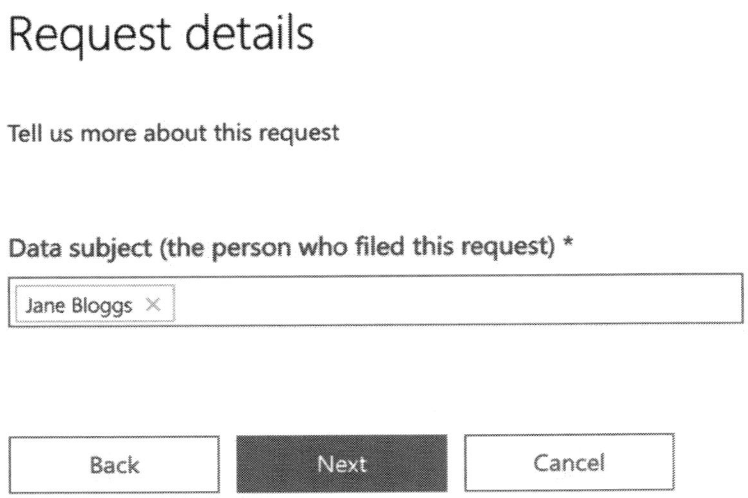

Request details

Tell us more about this request

Data subject (the person who filed this request) *

Jane Bloggs ×

Back Next Cancel

Figure 19.19 – Request details

4. Click **Next** and you will be able to **Confirm your case settings**, as shown:

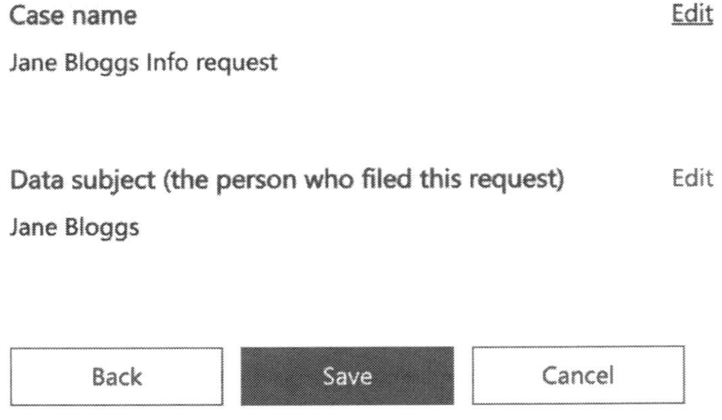

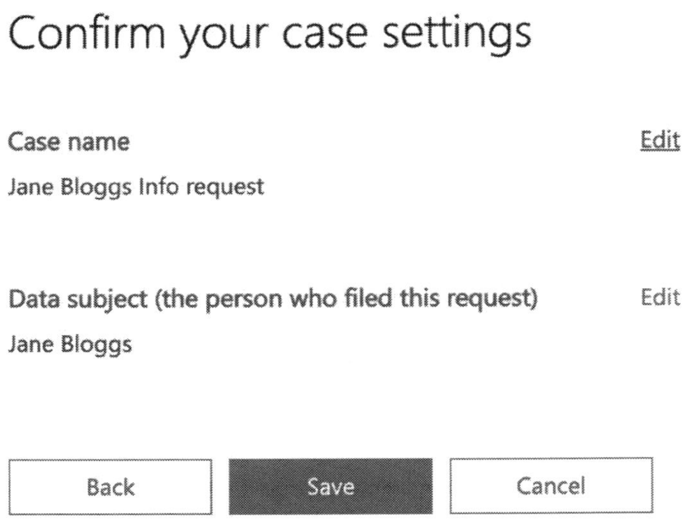

Figure 19.20 – Confirm your case settings

5. Click **Save**. That completes the setup of your DSR case. You will see the options shown in the following screenshot:

Successfully created new DSR case

If you run the search now, we'll look for data in Exchange email and public folders, Skype and Teams conversations, To-Do tasks, SharePoint and Teams sites, and OneDrive accounts.

Show me search results | Finish

Figure 19.21 – Successful creation of a DSR case

6. If you want to run the case search at a later time, you can click on **Finish**. However, in this example, we will run the case search immediately by clicking on **Show me search results**. This will take you directly to the content search, as shown:

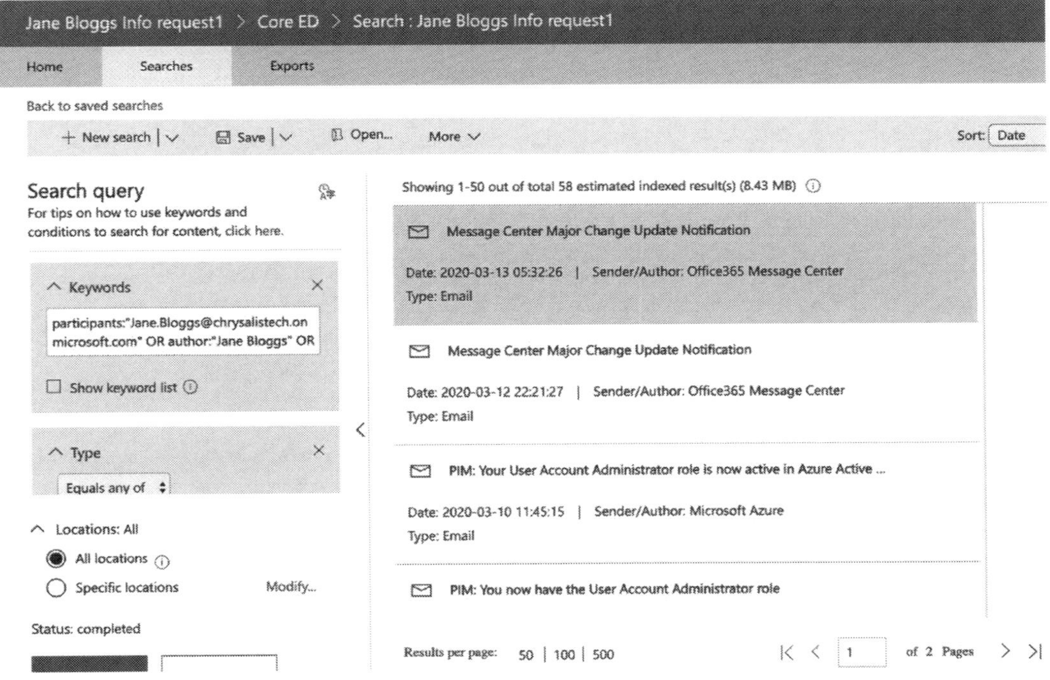

Figure 19.22 – A new content search

7. Once the content search is complete, you can click on **Back to saved searches**, and you will see the search in the search list, as shown:

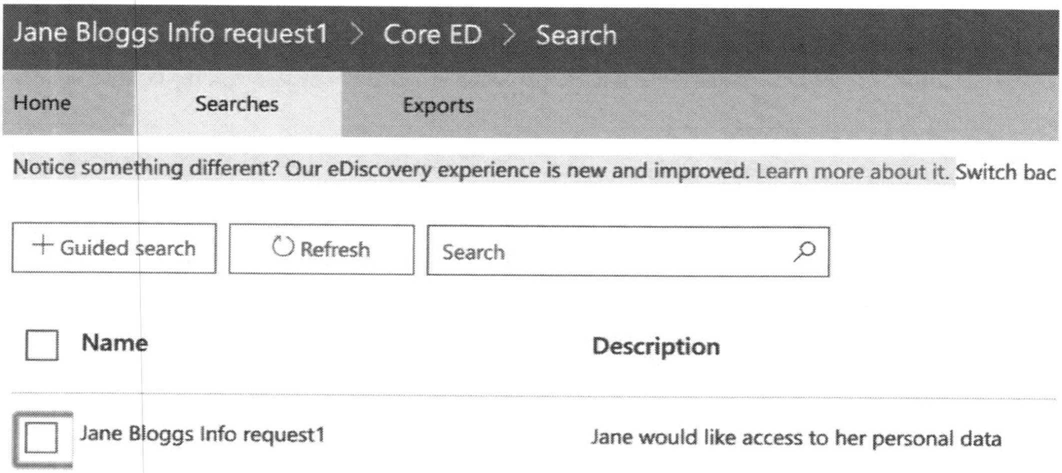

Figure 19.23 – The DSR case is saved as a content search

From this point, you can click on the search and re-run it or export the report and results in the same manner as you would in a normal content search. Content searches and exporting the results of content searches are covered in more detail in *Chapter 17, Data Governance and Retention*, and in *Chapter 16, Personal Data Protection in Microsoft 365*.

In this section, you learned that users (or data subjects) are entitled to request access to the personal information that is stored by your organization. We showed you how to use the Security & Compliance Center to run a DSR case, which in turn creates a content search that can be exported and provided to the requestor so that they can review the results.

Summary

In this chapter, we introduced you to the principles of planning to meet your regulatory compliance requirements under GDPR within your Microsoft 365 environment. You learned that planning to implement your GDPR strategy can be logically divided into three stages, consisting of discovery and analysis, implementation, and, finally, reinforcement and ongoing improvement.

We also demonstrated the various GDPR dashboards and reports that are available and can help you to investigate and maintain compliance principles. The tools available included STP, the Microsoft Compliance Score tool, and, finally the GDPR dashboard and GDPR toolbox.

Finally, we looked at how you are obliged to respond to requests from your Microsoft 365 users for access to personal information relating to them that is stored by your organization, and how you can do this by carrying out a DSR from the Security & Compliance Center. Compliance administrators can set up and manage DSR cases, which can then be saved and run as content searches and the results exported and provided to the requesting user.

This is the final chapter of this book. We have included a mock examination after this that closely reflects the actual test.

Questions

1. True or false – users who formally request access to their personal data within Microsoft 365 are referred to as data subjects.

   a. True

   b. False

2. Where in the Security & Compliance Center would you go to access the GDPR dashboard?

   a. **Search | GDPR dashboard**

   b. **Data privacy | GDPR dashboard**

   c. **Information Governance | GDPR dashboard**

   d. **eDiscovery | GDPR dashboard**

3. Which of the following tools or dashboards does not relate to GDPR?

   a. Microsoft Compliance Score

   b. STP

   c. The GDPR dashboard

   d. Message trace

   e. The GDPR toolbox

4. Which section of the GDPR toolbox would you go to find personal data?

   a. Govern

   b. Monitor & respond

   c. Protect

   d. Discover

5. True or false – the process of creating a DSR involves setting up a content search.

   a. True

   b. False

6. Where would you go to access the Microsoft Compliance Score dashboard?

   a. `https://compliance.microsoft.com`

   b. `https://protection.office.com`

   c. `https://portal.azure.com`

   d. `https://security.microsoft.com`

7. True or false – it is possible to re-run a DSR case content search after it has completed.

   a. True

   b. False

8. True or false – you can manage assessments directly from the Microsoft Compliance Score dashboard.

   a. True

   b. False

9. Which of the following is not one of the four section headers within the GDPR toolbox?

   a. Protect

   b. Investigate

   c. Discover

   d. Govern

   e. Monitor & respond

10. Where on the Microsoft Compliance Score dashboard can you view recommendations to enhance your score, along with implementation guidance?

   a. Assessments

   b. Overview

   c. Improvement actions

   d. Solutions

References

Please refer to the following links for more information:

- Preparing for GDPR: https://docs.microsoft.com/en-us/microsoft-365/compliance/gdpr-action-plan?wt.mc_id=4039827&view=o365-worldwide
- Industry certifications: https://docs.microsoft.com/en-us/office365/servicedescriptions/office-365-platform-service-description/compliance-servicedesc?wt.mc_id=4039827
- DSRs: https://docs.microsoft.com/en-us/microsoft-365/compliance/gdpr-dsr-office365?toc=%2Fmicrosoft-365%2Fenterprise%2Ftoc.json%3Fwt.mc_id%3D4039827&view=o365-worldwide
- Managing GDPR DSRs: https://docs.microsoft.com/en-gb/microsoft-365/compliance/manage-gdpr-data-subject-requests-with-the-dsr-case-tool?view=o365-worldwide
- Microsoft Compliance Score: https://docs.microsoft.com/en-gb/microsoft-365/compliance/compliance-score?view=o365-worldwide
- The GDPR-readiness assessment tool: https://discover.microsoft.com/gdpr-readiness-assessment/
- Microsoft STP: https://docs.microsoft.com/en-gb/microsoft-365/compliance/get-started-with-service-trust-portal?view=o365-worldwide
- Permissions in the Security & Compliance Center: https://docs.microsoft.com/en-us/microsoft-365/security/office-365-security/permissions-in-the-security-and-compliance-center?view=o365-worldwide

Section 5: Mock Exam and Assessment

This section contains a chapter on mock exams with the type of questions you may expect to encounter in the actual test. The answers and explanations follow in the next chapter, and finally, the answers to all of the practice questions from each chapter in the book. This part of the book comprises the following chapters:

20 Mock Exam

This chapter consists of 25 exam questions, which are designed to be as close as possible to the actual test. All of the questions are multiple choice, and there may be more than one correct answer for each question that you will need to select in order to get the question right. Some of the questions that follow will be in the form of a case study:

1. You are operating on a hybrid Microsoft 365 environment. All of your devices run Windows 10 and are managed using Microsoft Intune. You need to create a Conditional Access policy that will enforce **multi-factor authentication** (**MFA**) when users connect to Microsoft 365 services from outside of your office premises. What should you do first?

   A. From the Azure portal, under **Conditional Access | Named Locations**, click on **New Location**, and add the IP ranges for all of your organizations' premises.

   B. From the Azure portal, under **Conditional Access | Policies**, create a new policy to require MFA for all users, and set the policy to apply to all locations, excluding all trusted locations.

   C. From the Azure portal, under **Conditional Access | VPN Connectivity**, create a new certificate.

   D. From the Azure portal, under **Conditional Access | Policies**, set **Baseline Policy: End user Protection** to **Enabled**.

2. Your organization has Microsoft 365 E5 licenses for all users. You want to implement **Advanced Threat Protection** (**ATP**) safe attachments throughout the organization. Your users must be able to open attachments with the minimum amount of delay, but it is crucial that all attachments are scanned so that any that contain malware can be blocked. What actions should you take within ATP?

   A. Set the delivery action to **Monitor**.

   B. Set the delivery action to **Block**.

   C. Set the delivery action to **Replace**.

   D. Set the delivery action to **Dynamic Delivery**.

3. Your organization is running a traditional on-premises **Active Directory** (**AD**) environment using Exchange 2010 SP3 for email. You have been asked to plan the rollout and migration to Exchange Online on the Office 365 platform. You need to enable hybrid identity between AD and Azure AD by installing and configuring Azure AD Connect. It is vital that any users who are migrating to Exchange Online are authenticated via your on-premises AD environment when they connect to Office 365 services. Your solution must involve minimal effort in terms of time and additional infrastructure. Which identity method should you configure?

   A. Cloud only

   B. **Password hash-synchronization** (**PHS**)

   C. **Active Directory Federation Services** (**AD FS**)

   D. **Pass-through authentication** (**PTA**)

4. Your organization is operating a Microsoft 365 environment using hybrid identity with your on-premises AD. All 500 users have had their mailboxes migrated to Exchange Online, and all data has been migrated to OneDrive and SharePoint Online. Each user in the organization has been assigned an Office 365 E3 license. There are no other license subscriptions currently available in your tenant. You need to roll-out Azure Information Protection and enable unified labeling so that labels and label policies may be deployed from the Security and Compliance Center. The labels that you create need to be automatically applied to any user content that matches a number of sensitive information types built into Office 365. You purchase and assign Azure Information Protection (P1) licenses for all of your users.
   Does this achieve the goal?

   A. Yes

   B. No

5. You need to create a retention policy in the Security and Compliance Center that will retain content containing sensitive financial information. The content must be retained for 7 years, based on when it was created, and, at the end of the retention period, the content should be deleted. You create a retention policy as shown in the following screenshot:

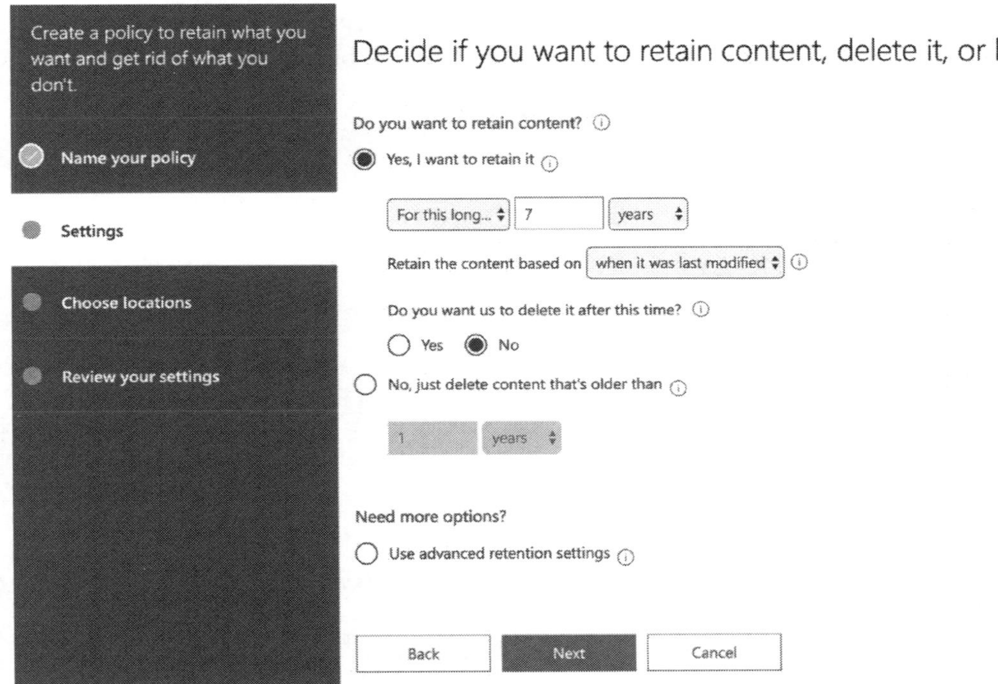

Figure 20.1 – Creating a retention policy

Does this achieve the goal?

A. Yes

B. No

6. You are operating a Microsoft 365 environment and use Microsoft Intune to manage your organization's Apple iOS devices. You need to ensure that any jailbroken devices are blocked and marked as non-compliant. What should you do in Microsoft Intune?

A. Create a **Device compliance** policy and configure the **Device Properties** settings.

B. Create a **Device compliance** policy and configure the **Device Health** settings.

C. Create a **Device configuration** profile and configure the **Device Restrictions** settings.

D. Create a **Device configuration** profile and configure the **Device Features** settings.

7. You are operating a Microsoft 365 environment in your organization that has 300 users, all of whom have Microsoft 365 E5 licenses assigned. You need to configure Azure AD Identity Protection to ensure that users will be required to change their password if a risk-level condition setting is matched. What must you do?

   A. Set up a **sign-in risk policy** in the Azure portal.

   B. Set up an **MFA registration policy** in the Azure portal.

   C. Set up a **user risk policy** in the Azure portal.

   D. Set up a **Conditional Access policy** in the Azure portal.

8. Your organization uses Exchange Online mailboxes for all user email communications. The HR department has informed you that a user is suspected of sending confidential information via email to external recipients. You need to ensure that you are able to review any such messages, including any that the user may have deleted. What should you do?

   A. Perform a **Content search** from the Security and Compliance Center.

   B. Use the Exchange admin center to place the suspected user's mailbox on **Litigation Hold**.

   C. Perform an **Audit log search** from the Security and Compliance Center.

   D. Perform a **Message Trace** from the **Mail flow** section of the Security and Compliance Center.

9. Your organization is using Microsoft Cloud App Security. You have been asked by the HR department to set up alerts whenever vast amounts of file downloads are completed by a user in a short period of time within your Microsoft 365 environment. You log in to the Cloud App Security portal at `https://portal.cloudappsecurity.com` and navigate to **Control | Templates** and click the + sign next to the template named **Mass download by a single user** to create an activity policy. Does this satisfy requirements?

   A. Yes

   B. No

10. Your organization is using Microsoft Cloud App Security. You have been asked by the HR department to search for activity by a user on a particular file that is hosted in SharePoint Online within your Microsoft 365 environment. Where would you go in the Cloud App Security portal to check this information?

    A. **Investigate** | **Files**

    B. **Investigate** | **Activity Log**

    C. **Investigate** | **Users and Account**

    D. **Investigate** | **Security Configuration**

Case Study

The following is a case study followed by five questions.

Overview

Chrysalis Technologies is a technology company with 2,000 users across multiple global locations. These include 1,000 users in the main office in London, 500 users in Toronto, and 500 users in Mumbai.

Internal network configuration

Chrysalis Technologies' internal network consists of a single domain forest. The functional levels for both the forest and domain are set to Windows Server 2012 R2. The IP address ranges are shown as follows:

Location	**IP address range**
London Internal network	192.168.0.0/20
London External network	212.109.83.0/28
Toronto Internal network	192.168.5.0/20
Toronto External network	215.107.83.0/28
Mumbai Internal network	192.168.8.0/20
Mumbai External network	212.129.83.0/28

These locations are connected via MPLS. Chrysalis Technologies uses the following operating systems:

- Windows Server 2016
- Windows Server 2012 R2
- Windows 10 Enterprise

Exchange 2010 SP3 is used for email services. The following servers are present within the AD infrastructure:

Location	Name	Role	OS
London	LONDC01	Domain Controller	Windows Server 2016
London	LONDC02	Domain Controller	Windows Server 2012 R2
London	LONEX01	Exchange 2010	Windows Server 2012 R2
London	LONEX02	Exchange 2010	Windows Server 2012 R2
Toronto	TORDC01	Domain Controller	Windows Server 2016
Toronto	TOREX01	Exchange 2010	Windows Server 2012 R2
Mumbai	MUMDC01	Domain Controller	Windows Server 2012 R2
Mumbai	MUMEX01	Exchange 2010	Windows Server 2012 R2

Cloud configuration

Chrysalis Technologies has a Microsoft 365 tenant and have purchased Microsoft 365 E5 licenses for all of their users. However only four users have been assigned licenses in the Office 365 tenant thus far.

Azure AD Connect has been configured to synchronize all on-premises user accounts to Azure AD using pass-through authentication. The **Password writeback** and **Exchange Hybrid** options were also selected when **Azure Active Directory Connect** (**AADC**) was configured.

Planned changes

Chrysalis Technologies plans to make the following changes:

- Migrate all email users in the Toronto Office to Exchange Online by setting up hybrid coexistence.
- Set up Azure AD Privileged Identity Management.
- Set up MFA for all privileged accounts using Conditional Access.

Security requirements

Chrysalis Technologies wishes to apply security settings as follows:

- Set up a group called MFA users to include all the Azure AD user accounts from the Toronto office. This group will be used to ensure that all users from the Toronto office are required to use MFA when accessing their Office 365 accounts outside of any of the business locations.
- Set up a group called AIP Pilot users to provide Azure Information Protection policies to a pilot group of users.
- Implement a permanent eligible user administrator role for a user named *James Smith* who is based at the London office.
- Ensure that a self-service password reset requires a minimum of two authentication methods for users to reset their own passwords.

General requirements

Chrysalis Technologies would like to minimize the deployment of any new servers to their Active Directory environment where possible:

11. (CASE STUDY QUESTION 1) Which of the following IP address ranges need to be added as named or trusted locations in order to meet the security requirements for MFA? (Choose all that apply)

    A. `192.168.8.0/20`

    B. `212.129.83.0/28`

    C. `192.168.0.0/20`

    D. `212.109.83.0/28`

    E. `215.107.83.0/28`

12. (CASE STUDY QUESTION 2) You connect to Azure AD Privileged Identity Management and configure a role's eligibility, as shown in the following screenshot:

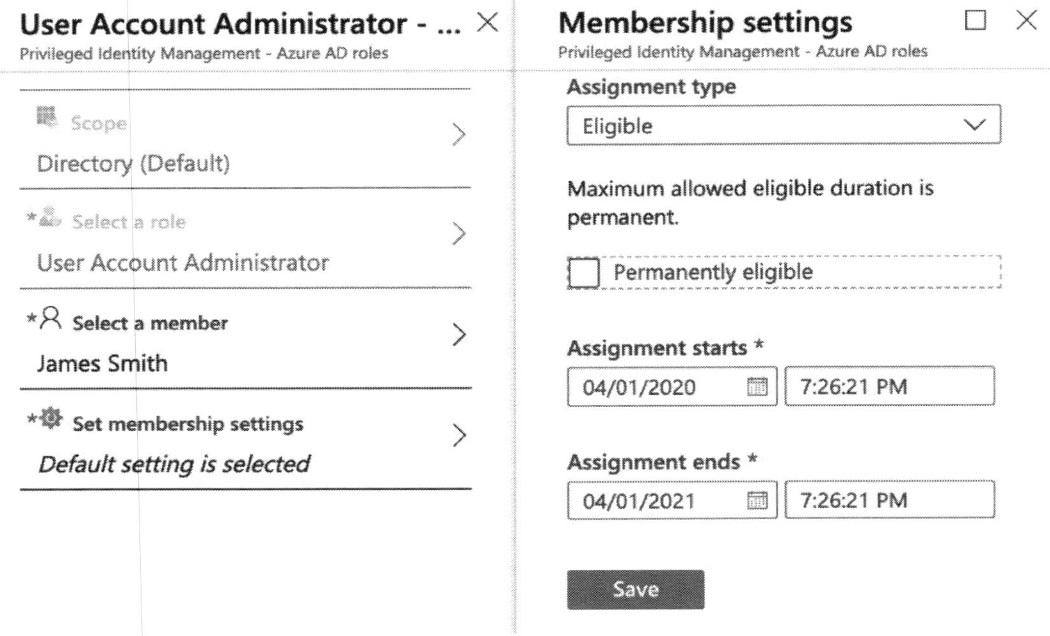

Figure 20.2 – Azure AD Privileged Identity Management

Does this meet the security requirements identified by Chrysalis Technologies?

A. Yes

B. No

13. (CASE STUDY QUESTION 3) You create an Azure AD Security Group called MFA Users and add all users from the London and Mumbai offices to the group. You then create a Conditional Access policy that enforces MFA for all users in the tenant but excludes all trusted locations. Does this meet the security requirements identified by Chrysalis Technologies?

A. Yes

B. No

14. (CASE STUDY QUESTION 4) You install a new Windows 2016 server and set up Exchange 2016 on this server in readiness to run the Hybrid Configuration Wizard, which will establish rich coexistence between the Exchange On-premises and Exchange Online accounts for Chrysalis Technologies. Given that one of the general requirements of this project is to minimize the installation of any new servers where possible, is this new server still necessary in order to meet the planned changes?

    A. Yes

    B. No

15. (CASE STUDY QUESTION 5) You configure the settings of **Self-service password reset** (**SSPR**) as shown in the following screenshot:

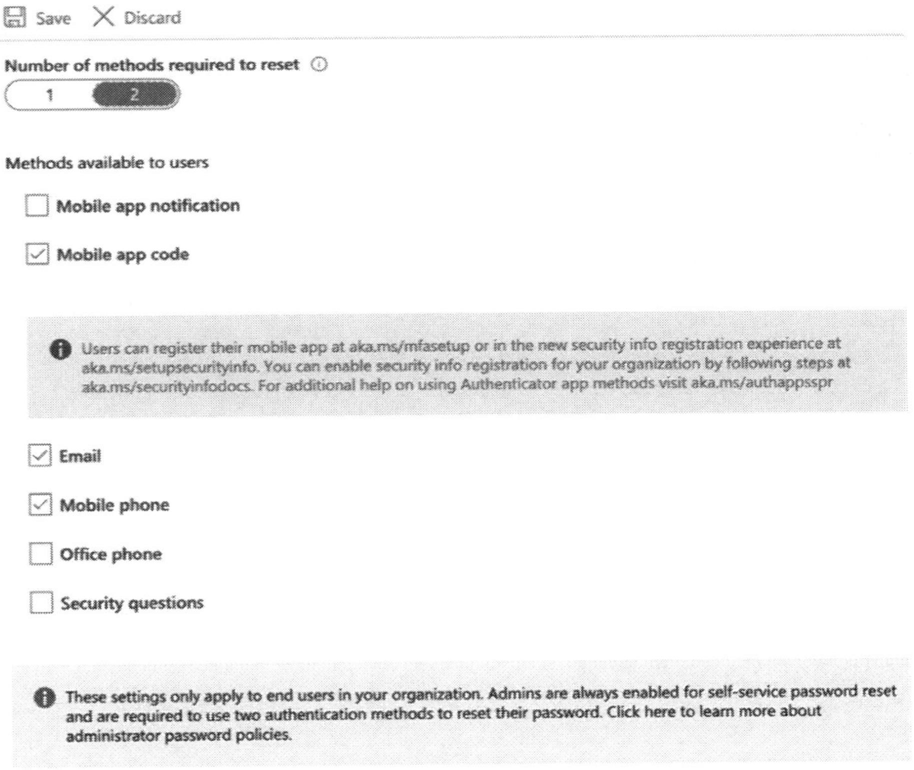

Save X Discard

Number of methods required to reset

1 2

Methods available to users

☐ Mobile app notification

☑ Mobile app code

Users can register their mobile app at aka.ms/mfasetup or in the new security info registration experience at aka.ms/setupsecurityinfo. You can enable security info registration for your organization by following steps at aka.ms/securityinfodocs. For additional help on using Authenticator app methods visit aka.ms/authappsspr

☑ Email

☑ Mobile phone

☐ Office phone

☐ Security questions

These settings only apply to end users in your organization. Admins are always enabled for self-service password reset and are required to use two authentication methods to reset their password. Click here to learn more about administrator password policies.

Figure 20.3 – Self-service password reset

Does this meet the security requirements defined by Chrysalis Technologies?

A. Yes

B. No

Questions 16–20 present you with a common scenario, followed by an objective, and configuration settings that may, or may not, fulfil the objective:

16. You have an Office 365 tenant. Users are assigned Microsoft 365 E5 licenses. Azure AD Connect has been set up to provide a hybrid identity methodology with the following settings:

    A. Password hash synchronization: Enabled

    B. Pass-through authentication: Disabled

    C. Password writeback: Disabled

    D. Exchange hybrid deployment: Enabled

    E. User writeback: Disabled

    F. Device writeback: Disabled

    G. Directory extension attribute sync: Disabled

    H. Hybrid Azure AD join: Disabled

    You need to ensure that the automatic joining of Windows 10 devices to Azure Active Directory is enabled. You enable pass-through authentication. Does this solution meet requirements?

    A. Yes

    B. No

17. You have an Office 365 tenant. Users are assigned Microsoft 365 E5 licenses. Azure AD Connect has been set up to provide a hybrid identity methodology with the following settings:

    A. Password hash synchronization: Enabled

    B. Password writeback: Disabled

    C. Exchange hybrid deployment: Enabled

    D. User writeback: Disabled

    E. Device writeback: Disabled

    F. Directory extension attribute sync: Disabled

You need to ensure that the automatic joining of Windows 10 devices to Azure Active Directory is enabled. You configure Hybrid Azure AD join. Does this solution meet requirements?

A. Yes

B. No

18. You have an Office 365 tenant. Users are assigned Microsoft 365 E5 licenses. Azure AD Connect has been set up to provide a hybrid identity methodology with the following settings:

    A. Password hash synchronization: Enabled

    B. Password writeback: Disabled

    C. Exchange hybrid deployment: Enabled

    D. User writeback: Disabled

    E. Device writeback: Disabled

    F. Directory extension attribute sync: Disabled

    You need to ensure that the automatic joining of Windows 10 devices to Azure Active Directory is enabled. You enable Device Writeback. Does this solution meet requirements?

    A. Yes

    B. No

19. You have an Office 365 tenant. Users are assigned Microsoft 365 E5 licenses. Azure AD Connect has been set up to provide a hybrid identity methodology with the following settings:

    A. Password hash synchronization: Enabled

    B. Password writeback: Disabled

    C. Exchange hybrid deployment: Enabled

    D. User writeback: Disabled

    E. Device writeback: Disabled

    F. Directory extension attribute sync: Disabled

You need to ensure that the automatic joining of Windows 10 devices to Azure Active Directory is enabled. You enable the Directory extension attribute sync feature. Does this solution meet requirements?

A. Yes

B. No

20. You have an Office 365 tenant. Users are assigned Microsoft 365 E5 licenses. Azure AD Connect has been set up to provide a hybrid identity methodology with the following settings:

A. Password hash synchronization: Enabled

B. Password writeback: Disabled

C. Exchange hybrid deployment: Enabled

D. User writeback: Disabled

E. Device writeback: Disabled

F. Directory extension attribute sync: Disabled

You need to ensure that the automatic joining of Windows 10 devices to Azure Active Directory is enabled. You disable password hash synchronization. Does this solution meet requirements?

A. Yes

B. No

21. You have a Microsoft 365 tenant with Office 365 E3 licenses assigned to all users. Users are already using Azure Rights Management features to protect content that they are sharing externally. You now need to configure Azure Information Protection with unified labeling within your Microsoft 365 environment. Automatic classification of content based on a match to the built-in sensitive information types must be a feature that is configured in your AIP labels and policies. Which of the following subscriptions will enable the use of automatic labeling? Choose all that apply.

A. Azure Information Protection P1

B. EM+S E3

C. EM+S E5

D. Microsoft 365 Business

E. Azure Information Protection P2

F. Microsoft 365 E5

G. Microsoft 365 E3

22. You have a tenant with Microsoft 365 E5 licenses assigned to all users. You are planning to use Windows Defender Advanced Threat Protection in your environment and, as part of this, you want to leverage the Microsoft Office 365 Attack Simulator to test the awareness of your users in relation to safely opening emails and attachments. Which of the following is a prerequisite for running the Attack Simulator tool?

    A. Enable **multi-factor authentication** (**MFA**)

    B. Implement Safe Attachments policies

    C. Implement Safe Links policies

    D. Configure Azure AD Identity Protection

23. You have a Microsoft 365 subscription. You have enabled auditing in the Security and Compliance Center. You now need to ensure that it is enabled for all your Exchange Online users. What steps do you need to take?

    A. From the Exchange admin center, create a new mail flow transport rule.

    B. Run the `Set-MailboxDatabase` command from the Exchange Online PowerShell.

    C. Run the `Set-Mailbox` command from the Exchange Online PowerShell.

    D. In the Security and Compliance Center, create a new audit retention policy from the audit log search feature.

24. You are a Microsoft 365 administrator for an organization based in Melbourne. You have been asked to create retention policies to protect the data within your organization. The retention policies must retain all Australian financial data for a period of 7 years. The content must be retained based on the date it was created. When the content reaches the end of the retention period, it must be automatically deleted. All Office 365 locations must be covered by a retention policy. What do you need to do in order to fulfill these requirements?

    A. Set up one retention policy in the Security and Compliance Center, and set it to apply to the default Office 365 locations.

    B. Set up one retention policy in the Security and Compliance Center, and set it to the option of **Let me choose specific locations**.

C. Set up two retention policies in the Security and Compliance Center, and set the option of **Let me choose specific locations** on each policy.

D. Set up one retention policy in the Exchange admin center.

25. You are a Microsoft 365 administrator. You have been asked to implement DLP policies within your organization. The first DLP policy you need to create must prevent the accidental sharing of sensitive UK medical data. The policy must be applied to all available Office 365 locations and be set to detect content that is shared outside of your organization. The policy needs to be tested first and should not be fully activated at this time, but should instead be set to test mode and to notify with policy tips. You open the Security and Compliance Center and create a new DLP policy with the settings shown in the following screenshot:

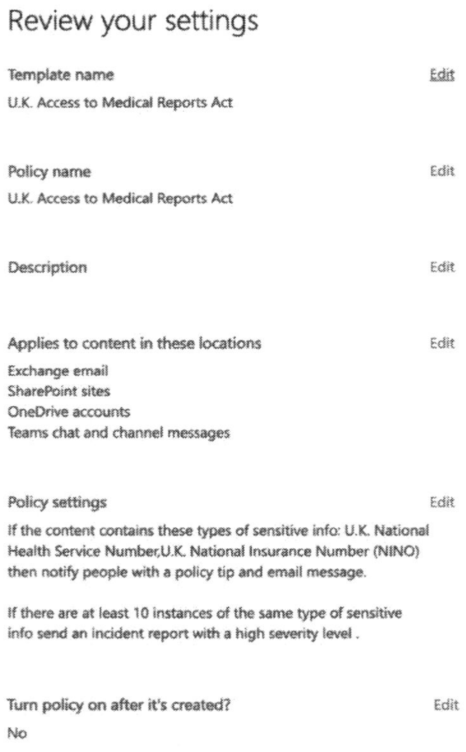

Review your settings

Template name — Edit
U.K. Access to Medical Reports Act

Policy name — Edit
U.K. Access to Medical Reports Act

Description — Edit

Applies to content in these locations — Edit
Exchange email
SharePoint sites
OneDrive accounts
Teams chat and channel messages

Policy settings — Edit
If the content contains these types of sensitive info: U.K. National Health Service Number,U.K. National Insurance Number (NINO) then notify people with a policy tip and email message.

If there are at least 10 instances of the same type of sensitive info send an incident report with a high severity level .

Turn policy on after it's created? — Edit
No

Figure 20.4 – Review your settings

Does this achieve the required results?

A. Yes

B. No

21
Mock Exam Answers

In this chapter, we will review the mock exam from the previous chapter and provide the answers to each question, as well as explanations for them.

Answers and explanations

1. A

   Explanation: You need to set up a New Location and add the IP ranges for all of your organization's premises. This will ensure that Azure AD has your named/trusted locations established before you set up any policies that may reference them as inclusions or exclusions.

   You should not create a new policy to require MFA for all users, but you should set the policy to apply to all locations and exclude all trusted locations. Doing so would not be effective until you have completed the required first step, which is adding the IP addresses that represent your named/trusted locations.

   You should not create a new certificate under **VPN Connectivity**. This task is completely irrelevant to the defined requirement.

   You should not set **Baseline Policy: End user Protection** to **Enabled**. Baseline policies are inflexible and can only be turned on or off. No granular settings can be modified. At the time of writing this book, baseline policies are scheduled to be deprecated by Microsoft.

2. D

   Explanation: You should set the delivery action to **Dynamic Delivery**. This will ensure that when the user clicks to access the attachment, it will detonate in Microsoft's sandbox and be checked for malware. If it's safe, it will be opened. This is the fastest way to safely open attachments.

   You should not set the delivery action to **Monitor**. This will immediately deliver the messages with the attachments and then monitor what happens with any detected malware. A malware scan must be completed before the user can open the attachment.

   You should not set the delivery action to **Block**. This will prevent any messages with detected malware from proceeding and send any such emails to quarantine. You should not set the delivery action to **Replace**. This will remove detected malware attachments and notify the users of this.

3. D

   Explanation: You should configure **Pass-through authentication**. This fulfills the requirement to set authentication for Office 365 via the on-premises AD environment, and also minimizes the effort and need for additional infrastructure. You should not configure **Cloud only**. This is the native identity methodology for Office 365 and will not fulfill the desired requirement, which is to synchronize with AD and provide a hybrid identity configuration.

   You should not configure **Password hash-synchronization**. This method establishes a same sign-on experience, but authentication of Office 365 logins will be carried out by Office 365, not the on-premises AD environment.

   You should not configure **Active Directory Federation Services**. While this method will fulfill the requirement to authenticate Office 365 logins via the on-premises infrastructure, it does not represent the requirement to use minimal effort and deploy additional infrastructure since AD FS requires significant planning and additional servers.

4. B

   Explanation: The requirement states that labels need to be automatically applied when a match to a Sensitive Information type is detected. An Azure Information Protection (P2) license will be required to achieve this goal. Only Azure Information Protection (P1) licenses have been purchased.

5. B

   Explanation: The settings in this screenshot do not meet requirements as they are set to retain content based on when it was last modified, not when it was created. In addition, the content needed to be deleted at the end of the retention period. The screenshot shows that the setting "**Do you want us to delete it after this time?**" is set to **No**.

6. B

   Explanation: You need to create a **device compliance policy** and configure the **Device Health** settings. The **Device Health** settings contain the option to block jailbroken devices and mark them as non-compliant.

   You should not create a **device compliance policy** and configure the **Device Properties** settings as this setting does not allow you to block jailbroken devices and mark them as non-compliant. You would use this setting to set the minimum and maximum OS versions for iOS devices.

   You should not create a **device configuration profile** and configure the **Device Restrictions** settings as this setting does not allow you to block jailbroken devices and mark them as non-compliant. This will instead allow you to create multiple restriction settings for your iOS devices, including password settings and App store settings.

   You should not create a **Device configuration profile** and configure the **Device Features** settings as this setting does not allow you to block jailbroken devices and mark them as non-compliant. This will instead allow you to create multiple feature settings for your iOS devices, including AirPrint, App Notifications, and Wallpaper.

7. C

   Explanation: You need to create a **user risk policy** in the Azure portal. This will allow you to force a user to change their password when the risk level condition is matched.

   You should not create a **sign-in risk policy** in the Azure portal. This will not allow you to enforce a password reset. Instead, this setting allows you to enforce MFA. You should not create an **MFA registration policy** in the Azure portal. This will not allow you to enforce a password reset. Instead, this setting allows you to require Azure MFA registration.

   You should not create a **Conditional Access Policy** in the Azure portal. While you can use risk-based conditional access to detect sign-in risk levels, you are unable to detect user risk, and also cannot force a password change.

8. B

   Explanation: You should use the Exchange Admin Center to place the suspected user's mailbox on **Litigation Hold**. This will ensure that even if the user deletes any messages, they can be accessed and reviewed by administrators.

   You should not perform a **Content search** from the Security and Compliance Center. With a Content search, you can search for user activity using search queries, but you are unable to place content on hold.

   You should not perform an **audit log search** from the Security and Compliance Center. With an audit search, you can search for admin and user activity, but you are unable to place content on hold.

   You should not perform a **Message Trace** from the **Mail Flow** section of the Security and Compliance Center. This will allow you to search for messages that have been sent and received in Exchange Online, but it will not enable you to place content on hold.

9. A

   Explanation: **The Mass download by a single user** policy template will fulfill all of the requirements.

10. A, B

    Explanation: You could go to **Investigate | Files** in the Cloud App Security portal. This will show you all recent file activity, where you can filter by queries, apps, owner and access level settings, file types, and policy matches.

    You could also go to **Investigate | Activity Log**. This will show you a wide range of activities, but these can also be filtered by file and folder activities.

    You should not use **Investigate | Users and Accounts**. This will show you information about all of your users and accounts, such as account settings, alerts, and governance.

    You should not use **Investigate | Security Configuration**. This area will allow you to carry out a security configuration assessment of your Azure environment.

11. (CASE STUDY ANSWER 1) B, D, E

    Explanation: You should add B, D, and E as these are external IP address ranges and will be needed to establish Named/Trusted locations.

    You should not add A or C as these are internal IP address ranges and irrelevant to Named/Trusted locations.

12. (CASE STUDY ANSWER 2) B

    Explanation: This does not meet security requirements as the **Permanently eligible** selection is unchecked.

13. (CASE STUDY ANSWER 3) B

    Explanation: This does not meet security requirements as the MFA Users group was supposed to contain users from only the Toronto office, and not the London or Mumbai offices.

14. (CASE STUDY ANSWER 4) A

    Explanation: When configuring an Exchange Hybrid, it is a Microsoft recommended and supported practice to retain at least one Exchange Server at the end of your migration as a management server.
    Exchange 2016 is recommended as the Hybrid server in order to make the latest features available. Additionally, Microsoft have announced that Exchange 2010 support will cease in October 2020. Therefore, installing Exchange 2016 in the environment overrides the business requirement to minimize additional servers.

15. (CASE STUDY ANSWER 5) A

    Explanation: This meets security requirements, which state that SSPR must require users to provide two authentication methods in order to reset their passwords.

16. B

    Explanation: This does not meet requirements as **Pass-through authentication** has no bearing on joining devices to Azure AD.

17. A

    Explanation: This meets requirements as configuring **Hybrid Azure AD join** will automatically join on-premises, domain- joined devices to Azure AD.

18. B

    Explanation: This does not meet requirements as **Device Writeback** has no bearing on joining devices to Azure AD.

19. B

    Explanation: This does not meet requirements as **Directory extension attribute sync** has no bearing on joining devices to Azure AD.

20. B

    Explanation: This does not meet requirements as **Password hash synchronization** has no bearing on joining devices to Azure AD.

21. C, E, and F

    Explanation: EM+S E5, Azure Information Protection P2, and Microsoft 365 E5 all support automatic labeling.

    Azure Information Protection P1, EM+S E3, Microsoft 365 Business, and Microsoft 365 E3 only support manual classification of content using sensitivity labels.

22. A

    Explanation: **Multi-Factor Authentication** must be enabled in your tenant in order to use **Attack Simulator**.

    Safe Attachments and **Safe Links** policies, as well as **Azure AD Identity protection**, have no bearing on the ability to run Attack Simulator.

23. C

    Explanation: The `Set-Mailbox` command must be used from the Exchange Online PowerShell, as per the following example:

    ```
    Set-Mailbox -Identity "Jane Bloggs" -AuditEnabled $true
    ```

    You would not use the `Set-MailboxDatabase` command as this would apply only to databases that are relevant to Exchange on-premises.

    You would not create a new mail flow transport rule from the Exchange Admin Center. Transport rules have no bearing on Exchange Online auditing.

    You would not create a new audit retention policy in the Security and Compliance Center. Audit retention policies are used to determine how long to retain audit logs in your organization.

24. C

    Explanation: You need to create two separate retention policies in the Security and Compliance Center and set each one to choose specific locations. The first policy should be set to target Exchange email, SharePoint sites, OneDrive accounts, Office 365 groups, Skype for Business, and Exchange public folders. The second policy should be set to target only Teams channel messages and Teams chats. This is because Teams-related retention policies cannot be configured in the same policy as other Office 365 locations – they require a dedicated policy.

You should not create a single retention policy in the Security and Compliance Center and apply it to the default Office 365 locations. This does not include Teams. The requirements are that all Office 365 locations must be targeted for retention.

You should not create a single retention policy in the Security and Compliance Center, but you should select the option to **Let me choose specific locations**. You must target all Office 365 locations for retention. A single policy will not allow you to protect Teams and other Office 365 locations.

You should not create a single retention policy in the Exchange Admin Center. The Exchange Admin center can only be used to create retention policies that apply to Exchange Online. The requirement was that retention must be applied to all Office 365 locations.

25. B

    Explanation: The policy does not meet the required conditions as it is not set to **Test** mode with notifications, and is instead turned off completely.

22 Assessments

In the following pages, we will review all practice questions from each of the chapters in this book, and provide the correct answers (and explanations, where applicable).

Chapter 1 – Planning for Hybrid Identity

1. c. **Multi-Factor Authentication** (**MFA**).

   Explanation: MFA is a secure authentication method as opposed to an identity method.

2. b. The IdFix tool.

   Explanation: IdFix is a tool that scans **Active Directory** (**AD**) and identifies any objects with attributes that are incompatible with Office 365 or that would result in a conflict or duplicate object.

3. b. False

   Explanation: Password hash synchronization provides the same sign-on experience, where users are authenticated directly to Office 365/Azure AD.

4. d. Azure AD Premium P1

   Explanation: Azure AD Premium P1 is the minimum subscription requirement for **Self-Service Password Reset** (**SSPR**). It is also available with Azure AD Premium P2. Intune and Azure Information Protection P1 licenses bear no relevance to SSPR.

5. a. `Start-ADSyncSyncCycle -PolicyType Initial`

   Explanation: The `Start-ADSyncSyncCycle -PolicyType Initial` command will run a full synchronization. The `Start-ADSyncSyncCycle -PolicyType Delta` command will run only a delta/incremental synchronization. The remaining options in this question are not valid commands.

6. a. True

   Explanation: Conditional Access is as described in the statement in this question.

7. d. 40

   Explanation: 40 is the maximum number of agents permitted.

8. c. Every 30 minutes

   Explanation: Azure AD Connect will automatically perform a synchronization to Azure AD every 30 minutes. Manual synchronizations may also be performed on demand.

9. a. Code with the Microsoft Authenticator app, and b. SMS message to mobile device.

   Explanation: Security questions and email addresses are not valid methods.

10. b. 2

    Explanation: Two Web Application Proxy servers is the minimum recommended requirement as per Microsoft best practice guidelines.

Chapter 2 – Authentication and Security

1. a. True

   Explanation: N/A

2. b. OAuth token

   Explanation: OAuth tokens can be used with MFA, not SSPR.

3. c. Global Administrator

   Explanation: The other roles do not have the required privileges

4. c. Five

   Explanation: N/A

5. a. True

   Explanation: Users may not create access reviews but may be configured as reviewers by administrators.

6. a. `New-AzureADMSGroup`

   Explanation: `New-AzureADGroup` will create a new Azure AD group to which members must be statically added. `New-UnifiedGroup` will create a new Office 365 group. `Set-UnifiedGroup` will allow changes to be made to existing Office 365 groups.

7. a. True

   Explanation: N/A

8. c. After 14 days

   Explanation: N/A

9. b and d. SSPR with password writeback is a feature of both Azure AD Premium P1 and P2.

   Explanation: N/A

10. a. True

    Explanation: N/A

Chapter 3 – Implementing Conditional Access Policies

1. a. Require Azure Advanced Threat Protection

   Explanation: Require Azure Advanced Threat Protection is not a condition that exists or that can be applied to any Microsoft 365 location or service.

2. a. True

   Explanation: N/A

3. d. Block modern authentication

   Explanation: No such baseline policy exists.

4. a. Setting named locations in Azure AD, and c. Setting up MFA trusted IPs

   Explanation: The other options do not relate to Conditional Access.

5. a. True

   Explanation: N/A

6. d. The Azure portal under **Azure Active Directory | Monitoring | Sign-ins**

   Explanation: The other options do not provide the ability to monitor Conditional Access events.

7. a. Sign-in risk, b. Locations, and e. Device platforms

   Explanation: The three correct answers are available under the **Assignments | Conditions** section of a Conditional Access policy. Directory Roles is available under **Assignments | Users and Groups**, while MFA is available under **Access Controls | Grant**.

8. a. True

   Explanation: N/A

9. d. Linux

   Explanation: N/A

10. a. True

    Explanation: N/A

Chapter 4 – Role Assignment and Privileged Identities in Microsoft 365

1. b. Security Reader

   Explanation: Security Reader is an actual role, not a role component.

2. b. False

   Explanation: Azure AD Premium P2 is the requirement for **Privileged Identity Management** (**PIM**).

3. a. In the **Access Control (IAM)** option within the **Resource** blade

   Explanation: N/A

4. a. Privileged Role Administrator, and c. Security Administrator

   Explanation: N/A

5. a. True

   Explanation: N/A

6. a. Wait for an email notification that contains the PIM approver's response to the request, and c. Log in to the Azure portal, navigate to **Privileged Identity Management**, and select **My requests**.

   Explanation: N/A

7. c. Azure AD Basic

   Explanation: N/A

8. a. True

   Explanation: N/A

9. d. The approval will automatically be sent to the PIM administrator.

   Explanation: N/A

10. a. True

    Explanation: N/A

Chapter 5 – Azure AD Identity Protection

1. b. Flagged Users

   Explanation: N/A

2. a. True

   Explanation: An MFA registration policy may be configured from the Azure AD Identity Protection portal under the **Protect** section.

3. b. MFA authentication

   Explanation: MFA in fact helps to mitigate sign-in risk.

4. b. Azure AD Premium P2

   Explanation: Identity Protection is not available with the other subscriptions.

5. a. True

   Explanation: This can be achieved by using **User risk** and **Sign in risk** policies from Azure AD Identity Protection.

6. b. 14 days

   Explanation: N/A

7. c. Ensure your break-glass account is excluded from the user risk policy and the sign-in risk policy.

   Explanation: The other options are not relevant to the goal.

8. b. False

   Explanation: With a user risk policy, you may enforce a password reset. To enforce MFA, you would use a sign-in risk policy.

9. c. Moderate

   Explanation: No such level exists.

10. a. True

    Explanation: Administrators may apply these settings in Azure AD Identity Protection by navigating to **Report | Risky Users**, highlighting the user, and then selecting the option to **Confirm user compromised**.

Chapter 6 – Configuring an Advanced Threat Protection Solution

1. b. Windows 10 workstation

   Explanation: N/A

2. d. Monthly

   Explanation: N/A

3. a. True

   Explanation: EM+S E5 or a standalone Azure ATP license is the minimum requirement.

4. a. Azure ATP portal, b. Azure ATP sensor, and d. Azure ATP cloud service.

   Explanation: Neither Azure ATP Configuration Manager nor Azure ATP Cloud App Security exist.

5. a. True

   Explanation: N/A

6. b. Pending, and d. Deferred

   Explanation: N/A

7. b. Directory services report

   Explanation: No such report exists

8. a. True

   Explanation: This can be achieved by accessing the Azure ATP portal, navigating to **Configuration | Windows Defender ATP**, and setting the option for **Integration with Windows Defender ATP** to **On**.

9. a. Excel (`xlsx`)

   Explanation: N/A

10. a. True

    Explanation: Azure **Advanced Threat Protection** (**ATP**) creates three Azure AD groups – Administrators, Viewers, and Users.

Chapter 7 – Configuring Microsoft Defender ATP to Protect Devices

1. a. Microsoft 365 E5, and c. Windows 10 Enterprise E5

   Explanation: The remaining answers will not enable the use of Microsoft Defender ATP.

2. a. True

   Explanation: This can be achieved by configuring an Endpoint Protection **Device configuration profile**.

3. a. `securitycenter.windows.com`, and b. `securitycenter.microsoft.com`

   Explanation: The other URLs are not valid.

4. b. Endpoint Protection

   Explanation: The remaining choices would not enable the required configuration.

5. a. **Control Panel | Windows Features**

   Explanation: The remaining choices would not enable the required configuration.

6. a. True

   Explanation: **Windows Defender Application Guard** (**WDAG**) may be configured and deployed using either **System Center Configuration Manager** (**SCCM**) or Intune.

7. b. **Settings**

   Explanation: The remaining choices would not enable the required configuration.

8. a. 30 days

   Explanation: N/A

9. a. True

   Explanation: This can be done when configuring Microsoft Defender ATP for the first time during step 3 of the setup.

10. a. **Current Status**, and c. **Status History**

    Explanation: The remaining choices are not available options.

Chapter 8 – Message Protection in Office 365

1. c. Office 365 Enterprise E3

   Explanation: ATP is not included with Office 365 E3.

2. a. True

   Explanation: You can use `Get-SafeAttachmentPolicy`, `Get-SafeAttachmentPolicy`, `New-SafeAttachmentPolicy`, or `Remove-SafeAttachmentPolicy`.

3. b. `New-SafeLinksRule`

   Explanation: `New-SafeLinksRule` will allow you to create a custom safe links rule. `Get-SafeLinksRule` allows you to view the safe links rule settings. `Set-SafeLinksRule` lets you edit existing safe links rule settings. `Start-SafeLinksRule` is not a valid command.

4. c. 7

   Explanation: N/A

5. a. True

   Explanation: N/A

6. d. **Threat management | Policy**

   Explanation: N/A

7. d. Move message to the deleted items folder.

   Explanation: N/A

8. a. True

   Explanation: N/A

9. a. Block, b. Dynamic Delivery, and d. Monitor

   Explanation: Edit and Scan are not valid actions.

10. b. False

    Explanation: **Sender Policy Framework** (**SPF**) does not prevent users from sending external emails. It is used to ensure that external mails can be verified as originating from authorized sources to prevent spoofing.

Chapter 9 – Threat Intelligence and Tracking

1. b. Service Administrator

   Explanation: The Service Administrator may only open and manage service requests, and view and share message center posts.

2. a. True

   Explanation: N/A

3. c. 30 days

   Explanation: N/A

4. a. **Threat management | Review**

   Explanation: The quarantine is not accessible from the other sections.

5. b. False

   Explanation: The maximum setting is 30 days.

6. d. Whale phishing

   Explanation: N/A

7. b. False

   Explanation: N/A

8. b. Open Message

   Explanation: N/A

9. a. True

   Explanation: N/A

10. b. The **Security trends** widget

    Explanation: N/A

Chapter 10 – Using Azure Sentinel to Monitor Microsoft 365 Security

1. a. True

   Explanation: Azure Sentinel is capable of connecting to both Microsoft native, and third-party data sources

2. c. **Configuration | Playbooks**

   Explanation: Playbooks are configured in the Azure portal from the **Configuration | Playbooks** section

3. d. Connect to a workspace

   Explanation: Connecting to a workspace is the first task to complete. This must be done before you can setup a data connector, or create and connect to a playbook

4. b. Contributor

   Explanation: Contributor permissions are required to enable Azure Sentinel

5. a. True

   Explanation: N/A

6. b. `https://portal.azure.com`

   Explanation: Azure Sentinel must be setup from the Azure portal. There is no option to set up Azure Sentinel from the other listed portals

7. b. False

   Explanation: Azure Sentinel is a SIEM tool

Chapter 11 – Controlling Secure Access to Information Stored in Office 365

1. a. True

   Explanation: **Privileged Access Management** (**PAM**) currently only supports Exchange Online, and no other Office 365 locations.

2. b. 5

   Explanation: N/A

3. c. 4 hours

   Explanation: N/A

4. d. Task group

   Explanation: A task group is not a policy type.

5. b. Unmanaged users

   Explanation: N/A

6. c. **Settings | Security & privacy**

   Explanation: N/A

7. a. Invite user, c. Create user

   Explanation: N/A

8. b. False

   Explanation: SharePoint Online external sharing settings are set from the SharePoint Admin Center.

9. a. Microsoft 365 E5, and D. Office 365 E5

   Explanation: The customer lockbox is only available in E5 subscriptions.

10. a. True

    Explanation: This can be set up by using a Conditional Access Policy.

Chapter 12 – Azure Information Protection

1. b. EM+S E3

   Explanation: N/A

2. a. True

   Explanation: This can be done with the `Enable-AIPService` command.

3. b. AADRM

   Explanation: N/A

4. b. Highlight

   Explanation: N/A

5. a. True

   Explanation: Unified labeling enables sensitivity labels to be used on other platforms, such as macOS.

6. b. `Install-AIPScanner`

   Explanation: The other commands listed are invalid.

7. d. The Azure Information Protection viewer, and e. The track and revoke option within Microsoft Office applications.

   Explanation: N/A

8. b. False

   Explanation: The Azure Information Protection scanner requires a server.

9. a. `Add-AIPServiceRoleBasedAdministrator`

   Explanation: N/A

10. a. User Administrator

    Explanation: N/A

Chapter 13 – Data Loss Prevention

1. a. True

   Explanation: N/A

2. b. PowerApps, and e. Yammer groups

   Explanation: N/A

3. c. **Reports | Dashboard**

   Explanation: N/A

4. c. Dictionary (regular expression)

   Explanation: There is no such setting.

5. a. True

   Explanation: Conditions are set within **Data loss prevention** (**DLP**) policy rules, and the actions will be applied if the policy is triggered.

6. b. Exchange Admin Center

   Explanation: The only other location you can configure DLP policies is from the Exchange Admin Center.

7. b. False

   Explanation: When DLP policies are set to test with policy tips, users will receive policy tips and administrators will receive alerts relating to the DLP policy.

8. b. Teams Chat, and c. Channel Messages

   Explanation: Only Teams Chat and Channel Messages may be protected.

9. b. Distribution Groups

   Explanation: Distribution Groups are used to target or exclude Exchange email content from DLP policies.

10. b. False

    Explanation: Policy tips are not available within Office for Mac.

Chapter 14 – Cloud App Discovery and Security

1. b. Advanced Cloud App Security

   Explanation: Advanced Cloud App Security is not the name of a product.

2. b. False

   Explanation: Cloud App Security may be used with Office 365 Enterprise E5, EM+S E5, and Microsoft 365 E5.

3. b. Administrator overview

   Explanation: There is no such report as Administrator overview.

4. a. True

   Explanation: Session Based Conditional Access policies may be set up within the Azure portal and then integrated with Cloud App Security.

5. d. **Discover | Cloud app catalog**

   Explanation: N/A

6. a. Send alert as email, c. Send alert as text message, and e. Send alerts to Power Automate

   Explanation: Microsoft Flow and RSS feeds are not available as alerts.

7. a. Security Administrator, and c. Global Administrator

   Explanation: Only the Security Administrator and Global Administrator roles have permission to configure Cloud App Security.

8. a. True

   Explanation: This may be configured from the **Discover | Create snapshot report** option.

9. d. `https://portal.cloudappsecurity.com`

   Explanation: The other options are not valid URLs.

10. c. **Investigate | Files**

    Explanation: **Investigate | Files** will show you activity on files. You could also use **Investigate | Activity log**. The other option in this question would not provide you with information on files.

Chapter 15 – Security Analytics and Auditing Capabilities

1. b. From the Excel telemetry dashboard workbook

   Explanation: Telemetry data may only be viewed by using the telemetry Excel workbook.

2. b. False

   Explanation: Audit logging may be turned on from the Security and Compliance Center. However, PowerShell must be used if you want to turn it off.

3. b. `https://devicemanagement.portal.azure.com`

   Explanation: The other URLs link to other Microsoft 365 dashboards.

4. d. `Set-AdminAuditLogConfig -UnifiedAuditLogIngestionEnabled $true`

   Explanation: The other commands are not valid.

5. a. True

   Explanation: The telemetry agent collects telemetry data and sends it to the shared folder. The telemetry processor then collects the data from the shared folder and sends it to the telemetry database. Finally, the data placed in the database is presented in the telemetry dashboard.

6. a. **Alerts | Alert Policies**

   Explanation: **Alerts | Alert policies** will allow you to set up a policy for audit alerts.

7. c. EM+S E3

   Explanation: EM+S E3 does not have rights to configure Desktop Analytics. You would need one of the other licenses listed in the options.

8. c. 90

   Explanation: 90 days is the maximum number of days that the audit log can provide information. However, it is possible to set up an audit log retention policy.

9. c. Office Deployment Tool

   Explanation: The Office Deployment Tool will deploy Microsoft Office, not Windows diagnostics.

10. a. True

    Explanation: Several default polices for alerts are available.

Chapter 16 – Personal Data Protection in Microsoft 365

1. a. True

   Explanation: Content searches may be applied to all Office 365 locations, or to specific locations by clicking on **Modify** within the search. This will enable you to select individual services such as Exchange email, Teams messages, SharePoint sites, and OneDrive accounts.

2. c. **Classification | Retention labels**

   Explanation: **Retention labels** cannot be configured from the other options.

3. a. True

   Explanation: The eDiscovery export tool may be used to export content search results and reports.

4. d. Threat detection reports

   Explanation: Threat detection reports relate to security as opposed to compliance.

5. b. **Guided search**

   Explanation: As well as **New search,** you may conduct a **Guided search**, which will initiate a wizard to take you through the process of setting up a content search.

6. a. File plan descriptors

   Explanation: File plan descriptors will automatically apply labels to content based on conditions that are set within file plan descriptors.

7. b. False

   Explanation: If you have file plan descriptors enabled in your retention label, then it is not possible to choose settings to manually apply the retention labels.

8. c. **Search | Content search**

   Explanation: You would typically start the content search from **Search | Content search**. It is also possible to start a content search from within an eDiscovery case. Therefore, **eDiscovery | Advanced eDiscovery**, and **eDiscovery | eDiscovery** are both possible answers.

9. a. **Control | Templates**

   Explanation: From the **Control | Templates** option, you may highlight a template and choose the option to **Create Policy**. You may also create policies from the **Control | Policies** option, however, you may not base policies on a template from here.

10. a. True

    Explanation: This can be done from the **Outlook Web App** (**OWA**) by right-clicking on a message and selecting **Assign policy**.

Chapter 17 – Data Governance and Retention

1. a. **Information governance | Archive**

   Explanation: The other options will not allow you to enable the online archives. It is, however, also possible to enable online archives for users in the Exchange admin center.

2. b. False

   Explanation: Exchange Online Plan 2 is the minimum requirement to set Litigation Hold for a user mailbox.

3. b. The Security Center

   Explanation: Retention policies are a compliance feature, not a security feature.

4. c. The hold will preserve content indefinitely.

   Explanation: Unless a hold duration is specified, the hold will have no end date and will continue indefinitely or until the hold is removed.

5. a. True

   Explanation: One of the main reasons for an Online Archive is to minimize the space that **Offline Outlook Data** (**OST**) files take up on a user's computer. Therefore, Online Archives (as the name suggests) may only be accessed when connected to the internet.

6. c: The compliance center

   Explanation: This may only be done from the Microsoft 365 compliance center.

7. c. The other services will be automatically deselected from the policy.

   Explanation: **Teams Channel Messages** and **Teams Chats** may not exist in the same retention policy as other Office 365 services.

8. a. True

   Explanation: A retention policy is flexible and includes settings that will allow you to delete or retain content depending upon your requirements.

9. b. At the user level

   Explanation: Litigation Hold must be applied at the user level.

10. b. Mailbox Import/Export

    Explanation: The other roles will not allow `pst` import.

Chapter 18 – Search and Investigation

1. b. Security Administrator

   Explanation: eDiscovery is a compliance feature, not a security feature.

2. a. Office 365 E5, and d. Office 365 E3 with the Advanced Compliance add-on

   Explanation: None of the other licenses listed will allow Advanced eDiscovery.

3. a. True

   Explanation: N/A

4. b. **eDiscovery | eDiscovery**

   Explanation: This function may not be completed within a standard content search.

5. b. False

   Explanation: A reviewer may view, but not create or edit.

6. b. Google Chrome

   Explanation: Internet Explorer and Edge are the only eDiscovery-compatible browsers when exporting eDiscovery reports and results.

7. b. False

   Explanation: The Security Reader does not have these rights.

8. c. 24 hours

   Explanation: N/A

9. a. True

   Explanation: N/A

10. c. Locations on Hold

    Explanation: The other selections would negate the settings already defined in the eDiscovery case.

Chapter 19 – Data Privacy Compliance

1. a. True

   Explanation: N/A

2. b. **Data privacy | GDPR dashboard**

   Explanation: The other options are not valid.

3. d. Message trace

   Explanation: Message Trace is a mail flow interrogation tool.

4. d. **Discover**

   Explanation: The other options do not enable you to carry out the required function.

5. a. True

   Explanation: A **Data Subject Request** (**DSR**) will trigger the content search as part of the process.

6. a. `https://compliance.microsoft.com`

   Explanation: This feature may only be accessed via the Microsoft 365 compliance center.

7. a. True

   Explanation: N/A

8. b. False

   Explanation: The ability to manage assessments directly from the **Microsoft Compliance Score dashboard** feature is not yet available from this dashboard. You can do so by accessing the **Microsoft Compliance Manager** tool.

9. b. Investigate

   Explanation: N/A

10. c. Improvement actions

    Explanation: You will find these recommendations in the **Improvement actions** section.

Other Books You May Enjoy

If you enjoyed this book, you may be interested in these other books by Packt:

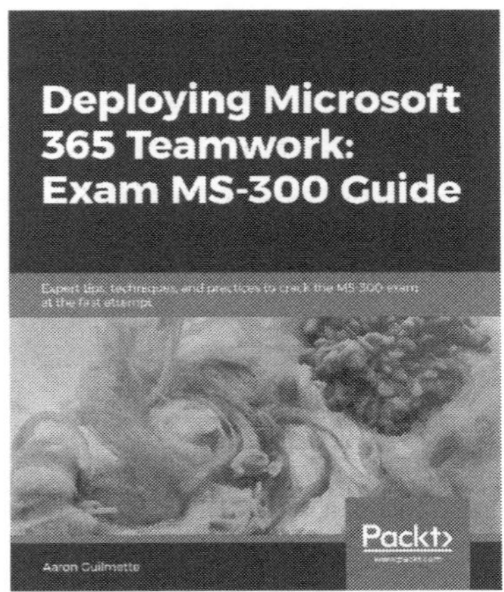

Deploying Microsoft 365 Teamwork: Exam MS-300 Guide

Aaron Guilmette

ISBN: 978-1-83898-773-2

- Discover the different Microsoft services and features that make up Office 365
- Configure cloud services for your environment and extend your infrastructure's capabilities
- Understand site architecture, site settings, and hub settings in SharePoint Online
- Explore business connectivity services for view and access options in SharePoint Online
- Configure Yammer to integrate with Office 365 groups, SharePoint, and Teams
- Deploy SharePoint Online, OneDrive for Business, and Microsoft Teams successfully, including bots and connectors

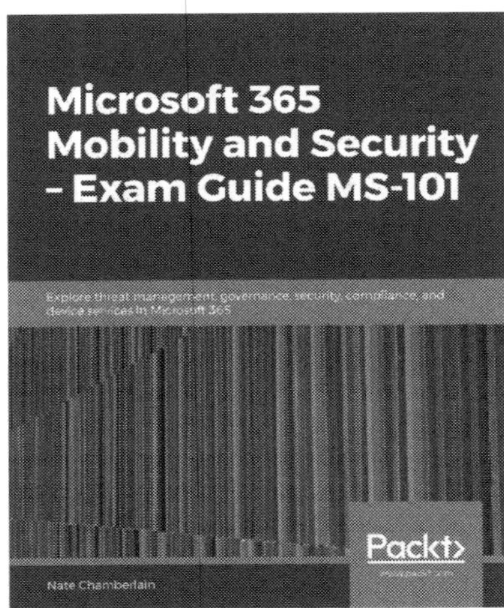

Microsoft 365 Mobility and Security – Exam Guide MS-101

Nate Chamberlain

ISBN: 978-1-83898-465-6

- Implement modern device services
- Discover tools for configuring audit logs and policies
- Plan, deploy, and manage Microsoft 365 services such as MDM and DLP
- Get up to speed with configuring eDiscovery settings and features to enhance your organization's ability to mitigate and respond to issues
- Implement Microsoft 365 security and threat management
- Explore best practices for effectively configuring settings

Leave a review - let other readers know what you think

Please share your thoughts on this book with others by leaving a review on the site that you bought it from. If you purchased the book from Amazon, please leave us an honest review on this book's Amazon page. This is vital so that other potential readers can see and use your unbiased opinion to make purchasing decisions, we can understand what our customers think about our products, and our authors can see your feedback on the title that they have worked with Packt to create. It will only take a few minutes of your time, but is valuable to other potential customers, our authors, and Packt. Thank you!

Index

Symbols

A

B

C

D

M

O

P

Q

R

S

T

U

W

Made in the USA
Monee, IL
25 August 2021

76402764R00369